SOCIAL STATISTICS FOR A DIVERSE SOCIETY

Seventh Edition

SOCIAL STATISTICS FOR A DIVERSE SOCIETY

Seventh Edition

Chava Frankfort-Nachmias
University of Wisconsin

Anna Leon-Guerrero
Pacific Lutheran University

Los Angeles | London | New Delhi
Singapore | Washington DC

Los Angeles | London | New Delhi
Singapore | Washington DC

FOR INFORMATION:

SAGE Publications, Inc.

2455 Teller Road

Thousand Oaks, California 91320

E-mail: order@sagepub.com

SAGE Publications Ltd.

1 Oliver's Yard

55 City Road

London EC1Y 1SP

United Kingdom

SAGE Publications India Pvt. Ltd.

B 1/I 1 Mohan Cooperative Industrial Area

Mathura Road, New Delhi 110 044

India

SAGE Publications Asia-Pacific Pte. Ltd.

3 Church Street

#10-04 Samsung Hub

Singapore 049483

Acquisitions Editor: Jerry Westby

Publishing Associate: MaryAnn Vail

Associate Digital Editor: Rachael Leblond

Production Editor: Laura Barrett

Copy Editor: Amy Rosenstein

Typesetter: C&M Digitals (P) Ltd.

Proofreader: Jennifer Grubba

Indexer: Will Ragsdale

Cover Designer: Candice Harman

Marketing Manager: Erica DeLuca

Printed in the United States of America

Library of Congress Cataloging-in-Publication Data

Frankfort-Nachmias, Chava.

Social statistics for a diverse society / Chava Frankfort-Nachmias, University of Wisconsin, Anna Leon-Guerrero, Pacific Lutheran University. — Seventh edition.

pages cm
Includes bibliographical references and index.

ISBN 978-1-4833-3354-0 (pbk. : alk. paper)

1. Social sciences—Statistical methods.
2. Statistics. I. Leon-Guerrero, Anna. II. Title.

HA29.N25 2015
519.5—dc23   2013032390

This book is printed on acid-free paper.

14 15 16 17 10 9 8 7 6 5 4 3 2

Brief Contents

DETAILED CONTENTS

PREFACE

Statistics is not just a part of our lives in the form of news bits or information. And it isn't just numbers either. Throughout this book, we encourage you to move beyond being just a consumer of statistics and begin to recognize and use the many ways that statistics can increase our understanding of our world.

Recently data has been characterized as "big,"[1] referring not only to the amount of available data, but also to the application of such information. Data are used to predict public opinion, health and illness, consumer spending, and even a presidential election. Throughout our text, we emphasize the relevance of statistics in our daily and professional lives. How Americans feel about a variety of political and social topics—the economy, same-sex marriage, gun control, immigration, health care reform, or our president—are measured by surveys and polls and reported daily by the news media. The latest from a health care study on women was just reported on a morning talk show. And that outfit you just purchased—it didn't go unnoticed. The study of consumer trends, specifically focusing on teens and young adults, helps determine commercial programming, product advertising and placement, and, ultimately, consumer spending. President Obama's 2012 re-election campaign victory was attributed in part to a team of data experts who analyzed voter files to predict likely voters.

As social scientists, we have always known that statistics can be a valuable set of tools to help us analyze and understand the differences in our American society and the world. We use statistics to track demographic trends, to assess differences among groups in society, and to make an impact on social policy and social change. Statistics can help us gain insight into real-life problems that affect our lives.

▣ TEACHING AND LEARNING GOALS

The following three teaching and learning goals continue to be the guiding principles of our book, as they were in the sixth edition.

The first goal is to introduce you to social statistics and demonstrate its value. Although most of you will not use statistics in your own student research, you will be expected to read and interpret statistical information presented by others in professional and scholarly publications, in the workplace, and in the popular media. This book will help you understand the concepts behind the statistics so that you will be able to assess the circumstances in which certain statistics should and should not be used.

Our second goal is to demonstrate that substance and statistical techniques are truly related in social science research. A special quality of this book is its integration of statistical techniques with

---

[1] Big data is described by Viktor Mayer-Schönberger and Kenneth Cukier in *Big Data: A Revolution That Will Transform How We Live, Work, and Think* (2013).

substantive issues of particular relevance in the social sciences. Your learning will not be limited to statistical calculations and formulas. Rather, you will become proficient in statistical techniques while learning about social differences and inequality through numerous substantive examples and real-world data applications. Because the world we live in is characterized by a growing diversity—where personal and social realities are increasingly shaped by race, class, gender, and other categories of experience—this book teaches you basic statistics while incorporating social science research related to the dynamic interplay of social variables.

Many of you may lack substantial math background, and some of you may suffer from the "math anxiety syndrome." This anxiety often leads to a less-than-optimal learning environment, with students trying to memorize every detail of a statistical procedure rather than attempting to understand the general concept involved. Hence, our third goal is to address math anxiety by using straightforward prose to explain statistical concepts and by emphasizing intuition, logic, and common sense over rote memorization and derivation of formulas.

▣ DISTINCTIVE AND UPDATED FEATURES OF OUR BOOK

The three learning goals we emphasize are accomplished through a variety of specific and distinctive features throughout this book.

A Close Link Between the Practice of Statistics, Important Social Issues, and Real-World Examples. A special quality of this book is its integration of statistical technique with pressing social issues of particular concern to society and social science. We emphasize how the conduct of social science is the constant interplay between social concerns and methods of inquiry. In addition, the examples throughout the book—mostly taken from news stories, government reports, public opinion polls, scholarly research, and the National Opinion Research Center's General Social Survey—are formulated to emphasize to students like you that we live in a world in which statistical arguments are common. Statistical concepts and procedures are illustrated with real data and research, providing a clear sense of how questions about important social issues can be studied with various statistical techniques.

A Focus on Diversity: U.S. and International. A strong emphasis on race, class, and gender as central substantive concepts is mindful of a trend in the social sciences toward integrating issues of diversity in the curriculum. This focus on the richness of social differences within our society and our global neighbors is manifested in the application of statistical tools to examine how race, class, gender, and other categories of experience shape our social world and explain social behavior. There is a special focus on the interplay between local and global concern. Throughout the text, we rely on data from the International Social Survey Programme, and we created a special global data set for this edition to help expand our statistical focus beyond the United States.

Reading the Research Literature. In your student career and in the workplace, you may be expected to read and interpret statistical information presented by others in professional and scholarly publications. The statistical analyses presented in these publications are a good deal more complex than most class and textbook presentations. To guide you in reading and interpreting research reports written by social scientists, most chapters include a section presenting excerpts of published research reports using the statistical concepts under discussion. Additionally, we include A Closer

Look section in several chapters, advising students about the common errors and limitations in data collection and analysis.

Tools to Promote Effective Study. Each chapter concludes with a list of main points and key terms discussed in that chapter. Boxed definitions of the key terms also appear in the body of the chapter, as do learning checks keyed to the most important points. Key terms are also clearly defined and explained in the glossary, another special feature in our book. Answers to all the odd-numbered exercises and Learning Checks in the text are included at the end of the book, as well as on the study site at **edge.sagepub.com/frankfort7e**. Complete step-by-step solutions are in the manual for instructors, available from the publisher on adoption of the text.

Emphasis on Computing. SPSS for Windows is used throughout the book, although the use of computers is not required to learn from the text. Real data are used to motivate and make concrete the coverage of statistical topics. These data, from the General Social Survey (GSS), Health Information National Trends Survey (HINTS), Monitoring the Future (MTF) survey, and the global data set constructed for this edition, are available on the study site at **edge.sagepub.com/frankfort7e**. At the end of each chapter, we feature a demonstration of a related SPSS procedure along with a set of exercises.

▣ HIGHLIGHTS OF THE SEVENTH EDITION

We have made a number of important changes to this book in response to the valuable comments that we have received from the many instructors adopting the sixth edition and from other interested instructors (and their students).

- *Chapter reorganization:* In this edition, we've merged the discussions on measures of association for nominal and ordinal data (including lambda and gamma) with chi-square in one chapter. The text concludes with chapters on analysis of variance and regression and correlation.
- *Real-world examples and exercises:* A hallmark of our first six editions was the extensive use of real data from a variety of sources for chapter illustrations and exercises. Throughout this edition, we have updated the majority of exercises and examples based on GSS, MTF, and HINTS surveys, our global data set, or U.S. Census data.
- *GSS 2010, HINTS 2012, MTF 2011, and Global 2013:* As a companion to the seventh edition's SPSS demonstrations and exercises, we have created four data sets. The GSS10SSDS. SAV contains an expanded selection of variables and cases from the 2010 GSS. The HINTS12SSDS.SAV contains 50 variables from the 2012 Health Information National Trends Survey, administered by the National Cancer Institute. HINTS, a nationally representative survey collected in both English and Spanish, aims to monitor changes in the rapidly evolving field of health communication. The MTF11SSDS.SAV contains a selection of variables and cases from the Monitoring the Future 2011 survey conducted by the University of Michigan Survey Research Center. MTF is a survey of 12th-grade students, and it explores drug use and criminal behavior. GLOBAL13SSDS.SAV includes data measuring the social, economic, and political conditions of 70 countries. SPSS exercises at the end of each chapter use certain variables from all data modules. There is ample opportunity for instructors to develop their own SPSS exercises using these data.

- *Supplemental tools on important topics:* The seventh edition's discussion of inferential statistics remains focused on *t*, *Z*, chi-square, and regression and correlation. For selected chapters, we have added a new section, Focus on Interpretation. In these sections, we highlight the interpretation of data or specific statistical calculations (some calculated via SPSS). Being statistically literate involves more than just completing a calculation; it also includes learning how to apply and interpret statistical information and being able to say what it means.

⑤SAGE edge™

edge.sagepub.com/frankfort7e

SAGE edge offers a robust online environment featuring an impressive array of tools and resources for review, study, and further exploration, keeping both instructors and students on the cutting edge of teaching and learning. SAGE edge content is open access and available on demand. Learning and teaching has never been easier!

SAGE edge for students provides a personalized approach to help students accomplish their coursework goals in an easy-to-use learning environment.

- Mobile-friendly **eFlashcards** strengthen understanding of key terms and concepts.
- Mobile-friendly practice **quizzes** allow for independent assessment by students of their mastery of course material.
- A customized online **action plan** includes tips and feedback on progress through the course and materials, which allows students to individualize their learning experience.
- **Web exercises** and meaningful web links facilitate student use of internet resources, further exploration of topics, and responses to critical thinking questions.
- EXCLUSIVE! Access to full-text **SAGE journal articles** that have been carefully selected to support and expand on the concepts presented in each chapter.
- Access to four new **data sets** including GSS 2010, HINTS 2012, MTF2011 and Global 2013.

SAGE edge for instructors supports teaching by making it easy to integrate quality content and create a rich learning environment for students.

- **Test banks** provide a diverse range of pre-written options as well as the opportunity to edit any question and/or insert personalized questions to effectively assess students' progress and understanding.
- **Sample course syllabi** for semester and quarter courses provide suggested models for structuring one's course.
- Editable, chapter-specific **PowerPoint®** slides offer complete flexibility for creating a multimedia presentation for the course.
- EXCLUSIVE! Access to full-text **SAGE journal articles** have been carefully selected to support and expand on the concepts presented in each chapter to encourage students to think critically.
- **Multimedia content** includes web resources and web exercises that appeal to students with different learning styles.

- **Lecture notes** summarize key concepts by chapter to ease preparation for lectures and class discussions.
- Lively and stimulating **ideas for class activities** that can be used in class to reinforce active learning.
- **Chapter-specific discussion questions** help launch classroom interaction by prompting students to engage with the material and by reinforcing important content.
- A **Course cartridge** provides easy LMS integration.

▣ ACKNOWLEDGMENTS

We are both grateful to Jerry Westby, Series Editor for SAGE Publications, for his commitment to our book and for his invaluable assistance through the production process.

Many manuscript reviewers recruited by SAGE provided invaluable feedback. For their comments to the seventh edition, we thank:

Walter F. Carroll, Bridgewater State University

Andrew S. Fullerton, Oklahoma State University

David A. Gay, University of Central Florida

Judith G. Gonyea, Boston University

Megan Henly, University of New Hampshire

Patricia A. Jaramillo, The University of Texas at San Antonio

Brett Lehman, Louisiana State University

James W. Love, California State University, Fullerton

Kay Kei-Ho Pih, California State University, Northridge

For their comments to the sixth edition, we thank

Diane Balduzy, Massachusetts College of Liberal Arts

Ellen Berg, California State University–Sacramento

Robert Carini, University of Louisville

Melissa Evans-Andris, University of Louisville

Meredith Greif, Georgia State University

Kristen Kenneavy, Ramapo College

Dave Rausch, West Texas A&M University

Billy Wagner, California State University–Channel Islands

Kevin Yoder, University of North Texas

For their comments to the fifth edition, we thank

Anna A. Amirkhanyan, The American University

Robert Carini, University of Louisville

Patricia Case, University of Toledo

Stanley DeViney, University of Maryland Eastern Shore

David Gay, University of Central Florida

Dusten R. Hollist, University of Montana

Ross Koppel, University of Pennsylvania

Benny Marcus, Temple University

Matt G. Mutchler, California State University Dominguez Hills

Mahasin C. Owens-Sabir, Jackson State University

Dave Rausch, West Texas A&M University

Kevin Yoder, University of North Texas

We are grateful to MaryAnn Vail and Laura Barrett for guiding the book through the production process. We would also like to acknowledge Theresa Accomazzo, Rachael Leblond, and the rest of the SAGE staff for their assistance and support throughout this project.

Both of us extend our deepest appreciation to Michael Clark for creating the student data sets that accompany the seventh edition. Additionally, we are grateful to Ben Gilbertsen and Kaitlyn Elms for their work on our individual chapters.

Chava Frankfort-Nachmias would like to thank and acknowledge her friends and colleagues for their unending support; she also would like to thank her students: I am grateful to my students at the University of Wisconsin–Milwaukee, who taught me that even the most complex statistical ideas can be simplified. The ideas presented in this book are the products of many years of classroom testing. I thank my students for their patience and contributions.

Finally, I thank my partner, Marlene Stern, for her love and support.

Anna Leon-Guerrero expresses her thanks to the following: I wish to thank my PLU statistics students. My passion for and understanding of teaching statistics grow with each semester and class experience. I am grateful for the teaching and learning opportunities that we have shared.

I would like to express my gratitude to friends and colleagues for their encouragement and support throughout this project. My love and thanks to my husband, Brian Sullivan.

Chava Frankfort-Nachmias
University of Wisconsin–Milwaukee

Anna Leon-Guerrero
Pacific Lutheran University

ABOUT THE AUTHORS

Chava Frankfort-Nachmias is an Emeritus Professor of Sociology at the University of Wisconsin–Milwaukee. She is the coauthor of *Research Methods in the Social Sciences* (with David Nachmias), coeditor of *Sappho in the Holy Land* (with Erella Shadmi) and numerous publications on ethnicity and development, urban revitalization, science and gender, and women in Israel. She was the recipient of the University of Wisconsin System teaching improvement grant on integrating race, ethnicity, and gender into the social statistics and research methods curriculum. She is also the coauthor (with Anna Leon-Guerrero) of *Essentials of Social Statistics*.

Anna Leon-Guerrero is Professor of Sociology at Pacific Lutheran University in Washington. She received her Ph.D. in sociology from the University of California–Los Angeles. She teaches courses in statistics, social theory, and social problems. Her areas of research and publications include family business, social welfare policy, and social service program evaluation. She is also the author of *Social Problems: Community, Policy, and Social Action.*

Chapter 1

The What and the Why of Statistics

Are you taking statistics because it is required in your major—not because you find it interesting? If so, you may be feeling intimidated because you know that statistics involves numbers and math. Perhaps you feel intimidated not only because you're uncomfortable with math but also because you suspect that numbers and math don't leave room for human judgment or have any relevance to your own personal experience. In fact, you may even question the relevance of statistics to understanding people, social behavior, or society.

In this book, we will show you that statistics can be a lot more interesting and easy to understand than you may have been led to believe. In fact, as we draw on your previous knowledge and experience and relate materials to interesting and important social issues, you'll begin to see that statistics is not just a course you have to take but a useful tool as well.

There are two reasons why learning statistics may be of value to you. First, you are constantly exposed to statistics every day of your life. Marketing surveys, voting polls, and the social research findings appear daily in newspapers and popular magazines. By learning statistics, you will become a sharper consumer of statistical material. Second, as a major in the social sciences, you may be expected to read and interpret statistical information presented to you in the workplace. Even if conducting research is not a part of your job, you may still be expected to understand and learn from other people's research or to be able to write reports based on statistical analyses.

Just what *is* statistics anyway? You may associate the word with numbers that indicate birthrates, conviction rates, per capita income, marriage and divorce rates, and so on. But the word statistics also refers to a set of procedures used by social scientists. They use these procedures to organize, summarize, and communicate information. Only information represented by numbers can be the subject of statistical analysis. Such information is called **data**; researchers use statistical procedures to analyze data to answer research questions and test theories. It is the latter usage—answering research questions and testing theories—that this textbook explores.

Statistics   A set of procedures used by social scientists to organize, summarize, and communicate information.

Data   Information represented by numbers, which can be the subject of statistical analysis.

▣ THE RESEARCH PROCESS

To give you a better idea of the role of statistics in social research, let's start by looking at the **research process**. We can think of the research process as a set of activities in which social scientists engage so that they can answer questions, examine ideas, or test theories.

As illustrated in Figure 1.1, the research process consists of five stages:

1. Asking the research question

2. Formulating the hypotheses

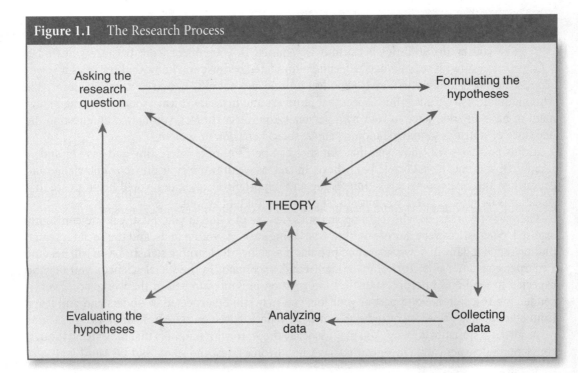

Figure 1.1   The Research Process

3. Collecting data

4. Analyzing data

5. Evaluating the hypotheses

Each stage affects the *theory* and is affected by it as well. Statistics is most closely tied to the data analysis stage of the research process. As we will see in later chapters, statistical analysis of the data helps researchers test the validity and accuracy of their hypotheses.

Research process A set of activities in which social scientists engage to answer questions, examine ideas, or test theories.

回 ASKING RESEARCH QUESTIONS

The starting point for most research is asking a *research question*. Consider the following research questions taken from a number of social science journals:

How will the Affordable Care Act influence the quality of health care?

Has support for gay marriage increased during the past decade?

Does race or ethnicity predict voting behavior?

What factors affect the economic mobility of female workers?

These are all questions that can be answered by conducting **empirical research**—research based on information that can be verified by using our direct experience. To answer research questions, we cannot rely on reasoning, speculation, moral judgment, or subjective preference. For example, the questions "Is racial equality good for society?" and "Is an urban lifestyle better than a rural lifestyle?" cannot be answered empirically because the terms *good* and *better* are concerned with values, beliefs, or subjective preference and, therefore, cannot be independently verified. One way to study these questions is by defining *good* and *better* in terms that can be verified empirically. For example, we can define *good* in terms of economic growth and *better* in terms of psychological well-being. These questions could then be answered by conducting empirical research.

Empirical research Research based on evidence that can be verified by using our direct experience.

You may wonder how to come up with a research question. The first step is to pick a question that interests you. If you are not sure, look around! Ideas for research problems are all around you, from media sources to personal experience or your own intuition. Talk to other people, write down your own observations and ideas, or learn what other social scientists have written about.

Take, for instance, the issue of gender and work. As a college student about to enter the labor force, you may wonder about the similarities and differences between women's and men's work experiences and about job opportunities when you graduate. Here are some facts and observations based on research reports: In 2012, women who were employed full time earned about $691 per week on average; men who were employed full time earned $854 per week on average.[1] Women's and men's work are also very different. Women continue to be the minority in many of the higher ranking and higher salaried positions in professional and managerial occupations. For example, in 2010 women made up 9.7% of civil engineers, 32.3% of physicians, 25.5% of dentists, and 1.5% of electricians. In comparison, among all those employed as preschool and kindergarten teachers, 97% were women. Among all receptionists and information clerks in 2010, 92.7% were women.[2] Another noteworthy development in the history of labor in the United States took place in January 2010: Women outnumbered men for the first time by holding 50.3% of the nonfarm payroll jobs.[3] These observations may prompt us to ask research questions such as the following: How much change has there been in women's work over time? Are women paid, on average, less than men for the same type of work?

✓ *Learning Check*

Identify one or two social science questions amenable to empirical research. You can almost bet that you will be required to do a research project sometime in your college career. Get a head start and start thinking about a good research question now.

▣ THE ROLE OF THEORY

You may have noticed that each preceding research question was expressed in terms of a *relationship*. This relationship may be between two or more attributes of individuals or groups, such as gender and income or gender segregation in the workplace and income disparity. The relationship between attributes or characteristics of individuals and groups lies at the heart of social scientific inquiry.

Most of us use the term *theory* quite casually to explain events and experiences in our daily life. We may have a "theory" about why our boss has been so nice to us lately or why we didn't do so well on our last history test. In a somewhat similar manner, social scientists attempt to explain the nature of social reality. Whereas our theories about events in our lives are commonsense explanations based on educated guesses and personal experience, to the social scientist, a theory is a more precise explanation that is frequently tested by conducting research.

A **theory** is an explanation of the relationship between two or more observable attributes *of* individuals or groups. The theory attempts to establish a link between what we observe (the data) and our conceptual understanding of why certain phenomena are related to each other in a particular way. For instance, suppose we wanted to understand the reasons for the income disparity between men and women; we may wonder whether the types of jobs men and women have and the organizations in which they work have something to do with their wages.

Theory   An elaborate explanation of the relationship between two or more observable attributes of individuals or groups.

One explanation for gender inequality in wages is *gender segregation in the workplace*—the fact that American men and women are concentrated in different kinds of jobs and occupations. What is the significance of gender segregation in the workplace? In our society, people's occupations and jobs are closely associated with their level of prestige, authority, and income. The jobs in which women and men are segregated are not only different but also unequal. Although the proportion of women in the labor force has markedly increased, women are still concentrated in occupations with low pay, low prestige, and few opportunities for promotion. Thus, gender segregation in the workplace is associated with unequal earnings, authority, and status. In particular, women's segregation into different jobs and occupations from those of men is the most immediate cause of the pay gap. Women receive lower pay than men do even when they have the same level of education, skills, and experience as men in comparable occupations.

回 FORMULATING THE HYPOTHESES

So far, we have come up with a number of research questions about the income disparity between men and women in the workplace. We have also discussed a possible explanation—a theory—that helps us make sense of gender inequality in wages. Is that enough? Where do we go from here?

Our next step is to test some of the ideas suggested by the gender segregation theory. But this theory, even if it sounds reasonable and logical to us, is too general and does not contain enough specific information to be tested. Instead, theories suggest specific concrete predictions about the way that observable attributes of people or groups are interrelated in real life. These predictions, called **hypotheses**, are tentative answers to research problems. Hypotheses are tentative because they can be verified only after they have been tested empirically.[4] For example, one hypothesis we can derive from the gender segregation theory is that wages in occupations in which the majority of workers are female are lower than the wages in occupations in which the majority of workers are male.

Hypothesis   A tentative answer to a research problem.

Not all hypotheses are derived directly from theories. We can generate hypotheses in many ways—from theories, directly from observations, or from intuition. Probably, the greatest source of hypotheses is the professional literature. A critical review of the professional literature will familiarize you with the current state of knowledge and with hypotheses that others have studied.

Let's restate our hypothesis:

Wages in occupations in which the majority of workers are female are lower than the wages in occupations in which the majority of workers are male.

Note that this hypothesis is a statement of a relationship between two characteristics that vary: *wages* and *gender composition* of occupations. Such characteristics are called variables. A **variable** is a property of people or objects that takes on two or more values. For example, people can be classified into a number of *social class* categories, such as upper class, middle class, or working class. Similarly, people have different levels of education; therefore, *education* is a variable. *Family income* is a variable; it can take on values from zero to hundreds of thousands of dollars or more. *Wages* is a variable, with values from zero to thousands of dollars or more. Similarly, *gender composition* is a variable. The percentage of females (or males) in an occupation can vary from 0 to 100. (See Figure 1.2 for examples of some variables and their possible values.)

Variable   A property of people or objects that takes on two or more values.

Each variable must include categories that are both *exhaustive* and *mutually exclusive*. Exhaustiveness means that there should be enough categories composing the variables to classify every observation. For example, the common classification of the variable *marital status* into the categories "married," "single," "divorced," and "widowed" violates the requirement of exhaustiveness. As defined, it does not allow us to classify same-sex couples or heterosexual couples who are not legally married. (We can make every variable exhaustive by adding the category "other" to the list of categories. However, this practice is not recommended if it leads to the exclusion of categories that have theoretical significance or a substantial number of observations.)

Figure 1.2   Variables and Value Categories

Variable	Categories
Social class	Upper class Middle class Working class
Religion	Christian Jewish Muslim
Monthly income	$1,000 $2,500 $10,000 $15,000
Gender	Male Female

Mutual exclusiveness means that there is only one category suitable for each observation. For example, we need to define *religion* in such a way that no one would be classified into more than one category. For instance, the categories "Protestant" and "Methodist" are not mutually exclusive because Methodists are also considered Protestant and, therefore, could be classified into both categories.

✓ *Learning*
Check

Review the definitions of exhaustive *and* mutually exclusive. *Now look at Figure 1.2. What other categories could be added to the variable* religion *to be exhaustive and mutually exclusive? What other categories could be added to* social class? *To income?*

Social scientists can choose which level of social life to focus their research on. They can focus on individuals or on groups of people such as families, organizations, and nations. These distinctions are referred to as **units of analysis**. A variable is a property of whatever the unit of analysis is for the study. Variables can be properties of individuals, of groups (e.g., the family or a social group), of organizations (e.g., a hospital or university), or of societies (e.g., a country or a nation). For example, in a study that looks at the relationship between individuals' level of education and their income, the variable *income* refers to the income level of an individual. On the other hand, a study that compares how differences in corporations' revenues relate to differences in the fringe benefits they provide to their employees uses the variable *revenue* as a characteristic of an organization (the corporation). The variables *wages* and *gender composition* in our example are characteristics of occupations. Figure 1.3 illustrates different units of analysis frequently employed by social scientists.

Unit of analysis   The level of social life on which social scientists focus. Examples of different levels are individuals and groups.

✓ *Learning*
Check

Remember that research question you came up with? Can you formulate a hypothesis you could test? Remember that the variables must take on two or more values and you must determine the unit of analysis.

Independent and Dependent Variables: Causality

Hypotheses are usually stated in terms of a relationship between an *independent* and a *dependent variable*. The distinction between an independent and a dependent variable is important in the language of research. Social theories often intend to provide an explanation for social patterns or causal relations between variables. For example, according to the gender segregation theory,

Figure 1.3   Examples of Units of Analysis

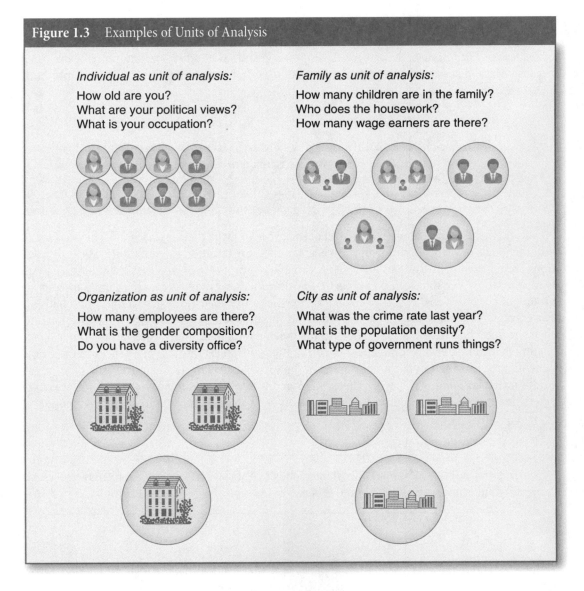

In the language of research, the variable the researcher wants to explain (the "effect") is called

gender segregation in the workplace is the primary explanation (although certainly not the only one) of the male-female earning gap. Why should jobs where the majority of workers are women pay less than jobs that employ mostly men? One explanation is that

> societies undervalue the work women do, regardless of what those tasks are, because women do them. . . . For example, our culture tends to devalue caring or nurturant work at least partly because it is done by women. This tendency accounts for child care workers' low rank in the pay hierarchy.[5]

In the language of research, the variable the researcher wants to explain (the "effect") is called the **dependent variable**. The variable that is expected to "cause" or account for the dependent variable is called the **independent variable**. Therefore, in our example, *gender composition of occupations* is the independent variable, and *wages* is the dependent variable.

Dependent variable   The variable to be explained (the "effect").

Independent variable   The variable expected to account for (the "cause" of) the dependent variable.

Cause-and-effect relationships between variables are *not* easy to infer in the social sciences. To establish that two variables are causally related, you need to meet three conditions: (1) The cause has to precede the effect in time, (2) there has to be an empirical relationship between the cause and the effect, and (3) this relationship cannot be explained by other factors.

Let's consider the decades-old debate about controlling crime through the use of prevention versus punishment. Some people argue that special counseling for youths at the first sign of trouble and strict controls on access to firearms would help reduce crime. Others argue that over-hauling federal and state sentencing laws to stop early prison releases is the solution. In the early 1990s, Washington and California adopted "three strikes and you're out" legislation, imposing life prison terms on three-time felony offenders. Such laws are also referred to as habitual or persistent offender laws. Twenty six other states and the federal government adopted similar measures, all advocating a "get tough" policy on crime; the most recent legislation was in 2012 in the state of Massachusetts. Let's suppose that years after the measure was introduced, the crime rate declined in some of these states; in fact, advocates of the measure have identified declining crime rates as evidence of its success. Does the observation that the incidence of crime declined mean that the new measure caused this reduction? Not necessarily! Perhaps the rate of crime had been going down for other reasons, such as improvement in the economy, and the new measure had nothing to do with it. To demonstrate a cause-and-effect relationship, we would need to show three things: (1) The enactment of the "three strikes and you're out" measure was empirically associated with a decrease in crime, (2) the reduction of crime actually occurred *after* the enactment of this measure, and (3) the relationship between the reduction in crime and the "three strikes and you're out" policy is not due to the influence of another variable (e.g., the improvement of overall economic conditions).

Independent and Dependent Variables: Guidelines

Because of the limitations in inferring cause-and-effect relationships in the social sciences, be cautious about using the terms *cause* and *effect* when examining relationships between variables. However, using the terms *independent variable* and *dependent variable* is still appropriate even when this relationship is not articulated in terms of direct cause and effect. Here are a few guidelines that may help you identify the independent and dependent variables:

1. The dependent variable is always the property that you are trying to explain; it is always the object of the research.

2. The independent variable usually occurs earlier in time than the dependent variable.

3. The independent variable is often seen as influencing, directly or indirectly, the dependent variable.

The purpose of the research should help determine which is the independent variable and which is the dependent variable. In the real world, variables are neither dependent nor independent; they can be switched around depending on the research problem. A variable defined as independent in one research investigation may be a dependent variable in another.[6] For instance, *educational attainment* may be an independent variable in a study attempting to explain how education influences political attitudes. However, in an investigation of whether a person's level of education is influenced by the social status of his or her family of origin, *educational attainment* is the dependent variable. Some variables, such as race, age, and ethnicity, because they are primordial characteristics that cannot be explained by social scientists, are never considered dependent variables in a social science analysis.

✓ *Learning Check*

> *Identify the independent and dependent variables in the following hypotheses:*
>
> - *Younger Americans are more likely to support stricter gun control laws than older Americans.*
> - *People who attend church regularly are more likely to oppose abortion than people who do not attend church regularly.*
> - *Elderly women are more likely to live alone than elderly men.*
> - *Individuals with postgraduate education are likely to have fewer children than those with less education.*
>
> *What are the independent and dependent variables in your hypothesis?*

▣ COLLECTING DATA

Once we have decided on the research question, the hypothesis, and the variables to be included in the study, we proceed to the next stage in the research cycle. This step includes measuring our variables and collecting the data. As researchers, we must decide how to measure the variables of interest to us, how to select the cases for our research, and what kind of data collection techniques we will be using. A wide variety of data collection techniques are available to us, from direct observations to survey research, experiments, or secondary sources. Similarly, we can construct numerous measuring instruments. These instruments can be as simple as a single question included in a questionnaire or as complex as a composite measure constructed through the combination of two or more questionnaire items. The choice of a particular data collection method or instrument to measure our variables depends on the study objective. For instance, suppose we decide to study how social class position is related to attitudes about abortion. Since attitudes about abortion are not directly observable, we need to collect data by asking a group of people questions about their attitudes and opinions. A suitable method of data collection for this project would be a *survey* that uses some kind of questionnaire or interview guide to elicit verbal reports from respondents. The questionnaire could include numerous questions designed to measure attitudes toward abortion, social class, and other variables relevant to the study.

How would we go about collecting data to test the hypothesis relating the gender composition of occupations to wages? We want to gather information on the proportion of men and women in different occupations and the average earnings for these occupations. This kind of information is routinely collected by the government and published in sources such as bulletins distributed by the U.S. Department of Labor's Bureau of Labor Statistics and the U.S. Census Bureau's *Statistical Abstract of the United States*. The data obtained from these sources could then be analyzed and used to test our hypothesis.

Levels of Measurement

The statistical analysis of data involves many mathematical operations, from simple counting to addition and multiplication. However, not every operation can be used with every variable. The type of statistical operations we employ depends on how our variables are measured. For example, for the variable *gender,* we can use the number 1 to represent females and the number 2 to represent males. Similarly, 1 can also be used as a numerical code for the category "one child" in the variable *number of children*. Clearly, in the first example, the number is an arbitrary symbol that does not correspond to the property "female," whereas in the second example the number 1 has a distinct numerical meaning that does correspond to the property "one child." The correspondence between the properties we measure and the numbers representing these properties determines the type of statistical operations we can use. The degree of correspondence also leads to different ways of measuring—that is, to distinct *levels of measurement*. In this section, we will discuss three levels of measurement: *nominal*, *ordinal*, and *interval ratio*.

Nominal Level of Measurement

At the nominal level of measurement, numbers or other symbols are assigned a set of categories for the purpose of naming, labeling, or classifying the observations. *Gender* is an example of a nominal-level variable. Using the numbers 1 and 2, for instance, we can classify our observations into the categories "females" and "males," with 1 representing females and 2 representing males. We could use any of a variety of symbols to represent the different categories of a nominal variable; however, when numbers are used to represent the different categories, we do not imply anything about the magnitude or quantitative difference between the categories. Because the different categories (e.g., males vs. females) vary in the quality inherent in each but not in quantity, nominal variables are often called *qualitative*. Other examples of nominal-level variables are political party, religion, and race.

Nominal measurement　　Numbers or other symbols are assigned to a set of categories for the purpose of naming, labeling, or classifying the observations.

Ordinal Level of Measurement

Whenever we assign numbers to rank-ordered categories ranging from low to high, we have an **ordinal** level of measurement. *Social class* is an example of an ordinal variable. We might classify individuals with respect to their social class status as "upper class," "middle class," or "working class." We can say that a person in the category "upper class" has a higher class position than a person in a "middle-class" category (or that a "middle-class" position is higher than a "working-class" position), but we do not know the magnitude of the differences between the categories—that is, we don't know how much higher "upper class" is compared with the "middle class."

Many attitudes that we measure in the social sciences are ordinal-level variables. Take, for instance, the following statement used to measure attitudes toward gun control: "There should be background checks for private and gun show sales." Respondents are asked to mark the number representing their degree of agreement or disagreement with this statement. One form in which a number might be made to correspond with the answers can be seen in Table 1.1. Although the differences between these numbers represent higher or lower degrees of agreement with same-sex marriage, the distance between any two of those numbers does not have a precise numerical meaning.

Ordinal measurement   Numbers are assigned to rank-ordered categories ranging from low to high.

Interval-Ratio Level of Measurement

If the categories (or values) of a variable can be rank-ordered, and if the measurements for all the cases are expressed in the same units, then an **interval-ratio** level of measurement has been achieved. Examples of variables measured at the interval-ratio level are *age*, *income*, and *SAT scores*. With all these variables, we can compare values not only in terms of which is larger or smaller but also in terms of *how much* larger or smaller one is compared with another. In some discussions of levels of measurement, you will see a distinction made between interval-ratio variables that have a natural zero point (where zero means the absence of the property) and those variables that have zero as an arbitrary point. For example, weight and length have a natural zero point, whereas temperature has an arbitrary zero point. Variables with a natural zero point are also called *ratio*

Table 1.1   Ordinal Ranking Scale

Rank	Value
1	Strongly agree
2	Agree
3	Neither agree nor disagree
4	Disagree
5	Strongly disagree

variables. In statistical practice, however, ratio variables are subjected to operations that treat them as interval and ignore their ratio properties. Therefore, no distinction between these two types is made in this text.

Interval-ratio measurement   Measurements for all cases are expressed in the same units.

Cumulative Property of Levels of Measurement

Variables that can be measured at the interval-ratio level of measurement can also be measured at the ordinal and nominal levels. As a rule, properties that can be measured at a higher level (interval-ratio is the highest) can also be measured at lower levels, but not vice versa. Let's take, for example, *gender composition of occupations*, the independent variable in our research example. Table 1.2 shows the percentage of women in five major occupational groups as reported in the *Statistical Abstract of the United States: 2012.*

The variable *gender composition* (measured as the percentage of women in the occupational group) is an interval-ratio variable and, therefore, has the properties of nominal, ordinal, and interval-ratio measures. For example, we can say that the management group differs from the natural resources group (a nominal comparison), that service occupations have more women than the other occupational categories (an ordinal comparison), and that service occupations have 35.6 percentage points more women (56.8 − 21.2) than production occupations (an interval-ratio comparison).

The types of comparisons possible at each level of measurement are summarized in Table 1.3 and Figure 1.4. Note that differences can be established at each of the three levels, but only at the interval-ratio level can we establish the magnitude of the difference.

Levels of Measurement of Dichotomous Variables

A variable that has only two values is called a **dichotomous variable**. Several key social factors, such as gender, employment status, and marital status, are dichotomies—that is, you are

Table 1.2   Gender Composition of Five Major Occupational Groups

Occupational Group	Women in Occupation (%)
Management, professional, and related occupations	51.5
Service occupations	56.8
Production, transportation, and materials occupations	21.2
Sales and office occupations	62.9
Natural resources, construction, and maintenance occupations	4.6

Source: U.S. Census Bureau, *Statistical Abstract of the United States: 2012,* Table 616.

✓ *Learning*
Check

Make sure you understand these levels of measurement. As the course progresses, your instructor is likely to ask you what statistical procedure you would use to describe or analyze a set of data. To make the proper choice, you must know the level of measurement of the data.

Table 1.3   Levels of Measurement and Possible Comparisons

Level	*Different or Equivalent*	*Higher or Lower*	*How Much Higher*
Nominal	Yes	No	No
Ordinal	Yes	Yes	No
Interval-ratio	Yes	Yes	Yes

Figure 1.4   Levels of Measurement and Possible Comparisons: Education Measured on Nominal, Ordinal, and Interval-Ratio Levels

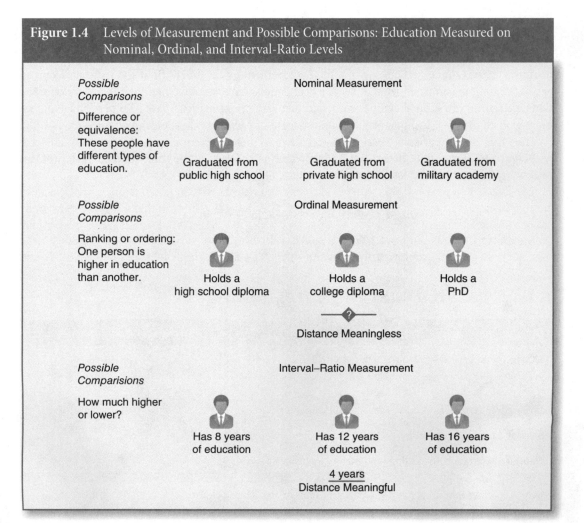

Possible Comparisons

Nominal Measurement

Difference or equivalence: These people have different types of education.

Graduated from public high school   Graduated from private high school   Graduated from military academy

Possible Comparisons

Ordinal Measurement

Ranking or ordering: One person is higher in education than another.

Holds a high school diploma   Holds a college diploma   Holds a PhD

Distance Meaningless

Possible Comparisions

Interval–Ratio Measurement

How much higher or lower?

Has 8 years of education   Has 12 years of education   Has 16 years of education

4 years
Distance Meaningful

male or female, employed or unemployed, married or not married. Such variables may seem to be measured at the nominal level: You fit in either one category or the other. No category is naturally higher or lower than the other, so they can't be ordered.

Dichotomous variable   A variable that has only two values.

However, because there are only two possible values for a dichotomy, we can measure it at the ordinal or the interval-ratio level. For example, we can think of "femaleness" as the ordering principle for gender, so that "female" is higher and "male" is lower. Using "maleness" as the ordering principle, "female" is lower and "male" is higher. In either case, with only two classes, there is no way to get them out of order; therefore, gender could be considered at the ordinal level.

Dichotomous variables can also be considered to be interval-ratio level. Why is this? In measuring interval-ratio data, the size of the interval between the categories is *meaningful*: The distance between 4 and 7, for example, is the same as the distance between 11 and 14. But with a dichotomy, there is only one interval. Therefore, there is really no other distance to which we can compare it.

Mathematically, this gives the dichotomy more power than other nominal-level variables (as you will notice later in the text).

For this reason, researchers often dichotomize some of their variables, turning a multicategory nominal variable into a dichotomy. For example, you may see race (originally divided into many categories) dichotomized into "white" and "nonwhite." Though this is substantively suspect, it may be the most logical statistical step to take.

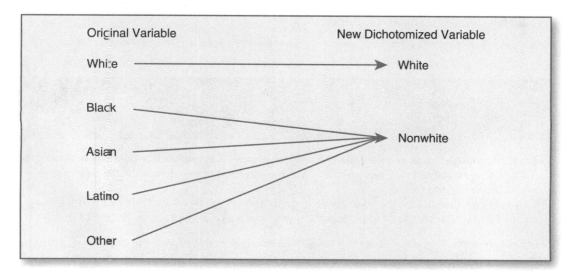

When you dichotomize a variable, be sure that the two categories capture a distinction that is important to your research question (e.g., a comparison of the number of white vs. nonwhite U.S. senators).

Discrete and Continuous Variables

The statistical operations we can perform are also determined by whether the variables are continuous or discrete. *Discrete* variables have a minimum-sized unit of measurement, which cannot be subdivided. The number of children per family is an example of a discrete variable because the minimum unit is one child. A family may have two or three children, but not 2.5 children. The variable *wages* in our research example is a discrete variable because currency has a minimum unit (1 cent), which cannot be subdivided. One can have $101.21 or $101.22 but not $101.21843. Wages cannot differ by less than 1 cent—the minimum-sized unit.

Unlike discrete variables, continuous variables do not have a minimum-sized unit of measurement; their range of values can be subdivided into increasingly smaller fractional values. *Length* is an example of a continuous variable because there is no minimum unit of length. A particular object may be 12 in. long, it may be 12.5 in. long, or it may be 12.532011 in. long. Although we cannot always measure all possible length values with absolute accuracy, it is possible for objects to exist at an infinite number of lengths.[7] In principle, we can speak of a tenth of an inch, a ten thousandth of an inch, or a ten trillionth of an inch. The variable *gender composition of occupations* is a continuous variable because it is measured in proportions or percentages (e.g., the percentage of women in medicine), which can be subdivided into smaller and smaller fractions.

This attribute of variables—whether they are continuous or discrete—affects subsequent research operations, particularly measurement procedures, data analysis, and methods of inference and generalization. However, keep in mind that, in practice, some discrete variables can be treated as if they were continuous, and vice versa.

✓ *Learning*
Check

> *Name three continuous and three discrete variables. Determine whether each of the variables in your hypothesis is continuous or discrete.*

▣ A Closer Look 1.1
    A Cautionary Note: Measurement Error

Social scientists attempt to ensure that the research process is as error free as possible, beginning with how we construct our measurements. We pay attention to two characteristics of measurement: reliability and validity.

Reliability means that the measurement yields consistent results each time it is used. For example, asking a sample of individuals "Do you approve or disapprove of President Obama's job performance?" is more reliable than asking "What do you think of President Obama's job performance?" While responses to the second question are meaningful, the answers might be vague and could be subject to different interpretation. Researchers look for the consistency of measurement over time, in relationship with other related measures, or in measurements or observations made by two or more researchers. Reliability is a prerequisite for validity: We cannot measure a phenomenon if the measure we are using gives us inconsistent results.

Validity refers to the extent to which measures indicate what they are intended to measure. While standardized IQ tests are reliable, it is still debated whether such tests measure intelligence or one's test-taking ability. A measure may not be valid due to individual error (individuals may want to provide socially desirable responses) or method error (questions may be unclear or poorly written).

Specific techniques and practices for determining and improving measurement reliability and validity are the subject of research methods courses.

ANALYZING DATA AND EVALUATING THE HYPOTHESES

Following the data collection stage, researchers analyze their data and evaluate the hypotheses of the study. The data consist of codes and numbers used to represent our observations. In our example, each occupational group would be represented by two scores: (1) the percentage of women and (2) the average wage. If we had collected information on 100 occupations, we would end up with 200 scores, 2 per occupational group. However, the typical research project includes more variables; therefore, the amount of data the researcher confronts is considerably larger. We now must find a systematic way to organize these data, analyze them, and use some set of procedures to decide what they mean. These last steps make up the *statistical analysis* stage, which is the main topic of this textbook. It is also at this point in the research cycle that statistical procedures will help us *evaluate* our research hypothesis and assess the theory from which the hypothesis was derived.

Descriptive and Inferential Statistics

Statistical procedures can be divided into two major categories: *descriptive statistics* and *inferential statistics*. Before we can discuss the difference between these two types of statistics, we need to understand the terms *population* and *sample*. A **population** is the total set of individuals, objects, groups, or events in which the researcher is interested. For example, if we were interested in looking at voting behavior in the last presidential election, we would probably define our population as all citizens who voted in the election. If we wanted to understand the employment patterns of Latinas in our state, we would include in our population all Latinas in our state who are in the labor force.

Population   The total set of individuals, objects, groups, or events in which the researcher is interested.

Although we are usually interested in a population, quite often, because of limited time and resources, it is impossible to study the entire population. Imagine interviewing all the citizens of the United States who voted in the last election or even all the Latinas who are in the labor force in our state. Not only would that be very expensive and time-consuming, but we would also probably have a very hard time locating everyone! Fortunately, we can learn a lot about a population if we carefully select a subset from that population. A subset selected from a population is called a **sample**. Researchers usually collect their data from a sample and then generalize their observations to the larger population.

Sample   A relatively small subset selected from a population.

Descriptive statistics includes procedures that help us organize and describe data collected from either a sample or a population. Occasionally data are collected on an entire population, as in a census. **Inferential statistics**, on the other hand, is concerned with making predictions or inferences about a population from observations and analyses of a sample. For instance, the General Social Survey (GSS), from which numerous examples presented in this book are drawn, is conducted every other year by the National Opinion Research Center (NORC) on a representative sample of several thousands of respondents (e.g., a total of 4,901 cases were included in the GSS 2010: 2,044 new cases and re-interviews with 2,857 respondents from the 2006 and 2008 GSS). The survey, which includes several hundred questions, is designed to provide social science researchers with a readily accessible database of socially relevant attitudes, behaviors, and attributes of a cross section of the U.S. adult population. NORC has verified that the composition of the GSS samples closely resembles census data. But because the data are based on a sample rather than on the entire population, the average of the sample does not equal the average of the population as a whole. For example, in the 2010 GSS, men and women were asked to report their total years of education. GSS researchers found the average to be 13.47 years, a little more than a year beyond a high school degree. This average probably differs from the average of the population from which the GSS sample was drawn. The tools of statistical inference help determine the accuracy of the sample average obtained by the researchers.

Descriptive statistics   Procedures that help us organize and describe data collected from either a sample or a population.

Inferential statistics   The logic and procedures concerned with making predictions or inferences about a population from observations and analyses of a sample.

Evaluating the Hypotheses

At the completion of these descriptive and inferential procedures, we can move to the next stage of the research process: the assessment and evaluation of our hypotheses and theories in light of the analyzed data. At this next stage, new questions might be raised about unexpected trends in the data and about other variables that may have to be considered in addition to our original variables. For example, we may have found that the relationship between gender composition of occupations and earnings can be observed with respect to some groups of occupations but not others. Similarly, the relationship between these variables may apply for some racial/ethnic groups but not for others.

These findings provide evidence to help us decide how our data relate to the theoretical framework that guided our research. We may decide to revise our theory and hypothesis to take account of these later findings. Recent studies are modifying what we know about gender segregation in the workplace. These studies suggest that race as well as gender shapes the occupational structure in the United States and helps explain disparities in income. This reformulation of the theory calls for a modified hypothesis and new research, which starts the circular process of research all over again.

Statistics provides an important link between theory and research. As our example on gender segregation demonstrates, the application of statistical techniques is an indispensable part of the research process. The results of statistical analyses help us evaluate our hypotheses and theories, discover unanticipated patterns and trends, and provide the impetus for shaping and reformulating our theories. Nevertheless, the importance of statistics should not diminish the significance of the preceding phases of the research process. Nor does the use of statistics lessen the importance of our own judgment in the entire process. Statistical analysis is a relatively small part of the research process, and even the most rigorous statistical procedures cannot speak for themselves. If our research questions are poorly conceived or our data are flawed due to errors in our design and measurement procedures, our results will be useless.

▣ LOOKING AT SOCIAL DIFFERENCES

By the middle of this century, if current trends continue unchanged, the United States will no longer be a predominantly European society. Due mostly to renewed immigration and higher birthrates, the United States is being transformed into a "global society" in which nearly half the population will be of African, Asian, Latino, or Native American ancestry. Is the increasing diversity of American society relevant to social scientists? What impact will such diversity have on the research methodologies we employ?

In a diverse society stratified by race, ethnicity, class, and gender, less partial and distorted explanations of social relations tend to result when researchers, research participants, and the research process itself reflect that diversity. Such diversity shapes the research questions we ask, how we observe and interpret our findings, and the conclusions we draw.

How does a consciousness of social differences inform social statistics? How can issues of race, class, gender, and other demographic categories shape the way we approach statistics? A statistical approach that focuses on social differences uses statistical tools to examine how variables such as race, class, and gender as well as other demographic categories such as age, religion, and sexual orientation shape our social world and explain our social behavior. Numerous statistical procedures can be applied to describe these processes, and we will begin to look at some of those options in the next chapter. For now, let's preview briefly some of the procedures that can be employed to analyze social differences.

In Chapter 2, we will learn how to organize information using descriptive techniques, such as frequency distributions, percentage distributions, ratios, and rates. These statistical tools can also be employed to learn about the characteristics and experiences of groups in our society that have not been as visible as other groups. For example, in a series of special reports published by the U.S. Census Bureau over the past few years, these descriptive statistical techniques have been used to describe the characteristics and experiences of those who are foreign born and ethnic minorities in America.

In Chapter 3, we illustrate how graphic devices can highlight diversity. In particular, graphs help us explore the differences and similarities among the many social groups coexisting within the American society and emphasize the rapidly changing composition of the U.S. population. Using data published by the U.S. Census Bureau, we discuss various graphic devices that can be used to display differences and similarities among elderly Americans.

Whereas the similarities and commonalities in social experiences can be depicted using measures of central tendency (Chapter 4), the differences and diversity within social groups can be described using statistical measures of variation. For instance, we may want to analyze the changing age composition in the United States or compare the degree of racial/ethnic or religious diversity in the 50 states. Measures such as the standard deviation and the index of qualitative variation (IQV) are calculated for these purposes. For example, using IQV, we demonstrate that Maine is the least diverse state and Hawaii is the most diverse (Chapter 5).

We will learn about inferential statistics and bivariate analyses in Chapters 6 through 13. First, we begin with a review of the bases of inferential statistics—the normal distribution, sampling and probability, and estimation—in Chapters 6 to 8. In Chapters 9 to 13, working with sample data, we examine the relationship among class, sex, or ethnicity and several social behaviors and attitudes. Inferential statistics, such as the t test, chi-square, and F statistic, help us determine the error involved in using our samples to answer questions about the population from which they are drawn. In addition, we review several methods of bivariate analysis, which are especially suited for examining the association between different social behaviors and variables such as race, class, ethnicity, gender, and religion. We use these methods of analysis to show not only how each of these variables operates independently in shaping behavior but also how they interlock in shaping our experience as individuals in society.[8]

▣ A Closer Look 1.2
A Tale of Simple Arithmetic:
How Culture May Influence How We Count

A second-grade schoolteacher posed this problem to the class: "There are four blackbirds sitting in a tree. You take a slingshot and shoot one of them. How many are left?"

"Three," answered the seven-year-old European with certainty. "One subtracted from four leaves three."

"Zero," answered the seven-year-old African with equal certainty. "If you shoot one bird, the others will fly away."*

---

*Working Woman, January 1991, p. 45.

Whichever model of social research you use—whether you follow a traditional one or integrate your analysis with qualitative data, whether you focus on social differences or any other aspect of social behavior—remember that any application of statistical procedures requires a basic understanding of the statistical concepts and techniques. This introductory text is intended to familiarize you with the range of descriptive and inferential statistics widely applied in the social sciences. Our emphasis on statistical techniques should not diminish the importance of human judgment and your awareness of the person-made quality of statistics. Only with this awareness can statistics become a useful tool for viewing social life.

▣ A Closer Look 1.3
Are You Anxious About Statistics?

Some of you are probably taking this introductory course in statistics with a great deal of suspicion and very little enthusiasm. The word statistics may make you anxious because you associate statistics with numbers, formulas, and abstract notations that seem inaccessible and complicated. It appears that statistics is not as integrated into the rest of your life as are other parts of the college curriculum.

Statistics is perhaps the most anxiety-provoking course in any social science curriculum. This anxiety often leads to a less than optimum learning environment, with students often trying to memorize every detail of a statistical procedure rather than trying to understand the general concept involved.

After many years of teaching statistics, we have learned that what underlies many of the difficulties students have in learning statistics is the belief that it involves mainly memorization of meaningless formulas.

There is no denying that statistics involves many strange symbols and unfamiliar terms. It is also true that you need to know some math to do statistics. But although the subject involves some mathematical computations, you will not be asked to know more than four basic operations: addition, subtraction, multiplication, and division. The language of statistics may appear difficult because these operations (and how they are combined) are written in a code that is unfamiliar to you. Those abstract notations are simply part of the language of statistics; much like learning any foreign language, you need to learn the alphabet before you can "speak the language." Once you understand the vocabulary and are able to translate the symbols and codes into terms that are familiar to you, you will feel more relaxed and begin to see how statistical techniques are just one more source of information.

The key to enjoying and feeling competent in statistics is to frame anything you do in a familiar language and in a context that is relevant and interesting. Therefore, you will find that this book emphasizes intuition, logic, and common sense over rote memorization and derivation of formulas. We have found that this approach reduces statistics anxiety for most students and improves learning.

Another strategy that will help you develop confidence in your ability to do statistics is working with other people. This book encourages collaboration in learning statistics as a strategy designed to help you overcome statistics anxiety. Over the years, we have learned that students who are intimidated by statistics do not like to admit it or talk about it. This avoidance

(Continued)

(Continued)

mechanism may be an obstacle to overcoming statistics anxiety. Talking about your feelings with other students will help you realize that you are not the only one who suffers from fears of inadequacy about statistics. This sharing process is at the heart of the treatment of statistics anxiety, not because it will help you realize that you are not the "dumbest" one in the class after all, but because talking to others in a "safe" group setting will help you take risks and trust your own intuition and judgment. Ultimately, your judgment and intuition lie at the heart of your ability to translate statistical symbols and concepts into a language that makes sense and to interpret data using newly acquired statistical tools.*

*This discussion is based on Sheila Tobias's pioneering work on mathematics anxiety. See especially Sheila Tobias, *Overcoming Math Anxiety* (New York: Norton, 1995), Chapters 2 and 8.

MAIN POINTS

- Statistics are procedures used by social scientists to organize, summarize, and communicate information. Only information represented by numbers can be the subject of statistical analysis.

- The research process is a set of activities in which social scientists engage to answer questions, examine ideas, or test theories. It consists of the following stages: asking the research question, formulating the hypotheses, collecting data, analyzing data, and evaluating the hypotheses.

- A theory is an elaborate explanation of the relationship between two or more observable attributes of individuals or groups.

- Theories offer specific concrete predictions about the way observable attributes of people or groups would be interrelated in real life. These predictions, called hypotheses, are tentative answers to research problems.

- A variable is a property of people or objects that takes on two or more values. The variable that the researcher wants to explain (the "effect") is called the dependent variable. The variable that is expected to "cause" or account for the dependent variable is called the independent variable.

- Three conditions are required to establish causal relations: (1) The cause has to precede the effect in time, (2) there has to be an empirical relationship between the cause and the effect, and (3) this relationship cannot be explained by other factors.

- At the nominal level of measurement, numbers or other symbols are assigned to a set of categories to name, label, or classify the observations. At the ordinal level of measurement, categories can be rank ordered from low to high (or vice versa). At the interval-ratio level of measurement, measurements for all cases are expressed in the same unit.

- A population is the total set of individuals, objects, groups, or events in which the researcher is interested. A sample is a relatively small subset selected from a population.

- Descriptive statistics includes procedures that help us organize and describe data collected from either a sample or a population. Inferential statistics is concerned with making predictions or inferences about a population from observations and analyses of a sample.

KEY TERMS

data
dependent variable
descriptive statistics
dichotomous variable
empirical research
hypothesis
independent variable

inferential statistics
interval-ratio
  measurement
nominal measurement
ordinal measurement
population
research process

sample
statistics
theory
unit of analysis
variable

$SAGE edge™

Sharpen your skills with SAGE edge at **edge.sagepub.com/frankfort7e**. **SAGE edge for students** provides a personalized approach to help you accomplish your coursework goals in an easy-to-use learning environment.

SPSS DEMONSTRATION

Introduction to Data Sets and Variables

We'll be using a set of computer data and exercises at the end of each chapter. All computer exercises are based on the program IBM SPSS version 21.0.

Throughout this textbook, you'll be working with four data sets. The GSS10SSDS.SAV contains a selection of variables and cases from the 2010 GSS. The GSS has been conducted biennially since 1972. Conducted for the National Data Program for the Social Sciences at the NORC at the University of Chicago, the GSS was designed to provide social science researchers with a readily accessible database of socially relevant attitudes, behaviors, and attributes of a cross section of the U.S. population. Next to the U.S. Census data, the GSS is the most frequently analyzed source of social science information by educators, legislators, and media outlets.

GLOBAL13SSDS.SAV is a data set exclusive to this text. Data are drawn from several publicly available data sets, including the Central Intelligence Agency World Factbook, the World Bank, and the United Nations Office on Drugs and Crime. We've selected data for 70 countries measuring economic, political, and social conditions of each. Several variables were selected based on timely debates both on national and international levels.

The MTF11SSDS.SAV contains variables and cases from the Monitoring the Future (MTF) survey, collected by the University of Michigan Survey Research Center. MTF is a survey of 12th-grade students, part of a series of surveys that began in 1975 to explore changes in youth values, behaviors, and lifestyle. For 2011, the MTF includes questions on the use of licit and illicit drugs.

HINTS12SSDS.SAV contains variables from the 2012 Health Information National Trends Survey (HINTS), administered by the National Cancer Institute. HINTS, a nationally representative survey collected in both English and Spanish, aims to monitor changes in the rapidly evolving field of health communication. The entire 2012 HINTS data set contains data collected from a total of 3,959 respondents.

The GSS, MTF, and HINTS data sets each include a random sample of 1,500 respondents.

The SPSS appendix found on this text's study site explains the basic operation and procedures for SPSS for Windows Student Version. We strongly recommend that you refer to this appendix before beginning the SPSS exercises.

Exercises

When you begin using a data set, you should take the time to review your variables. What are the variables called? What do they measure? What do they mean? There are several ways to do this.

To review your data, you must first open the data file. Files are opened in SPSS by clicking on *File*, then *Open*, and then *Data*. After switching directories and drives to the appropriate location of the files (which may be on a hard disk or on a ZIP drive), you select one data file and click on *Open*. This routine is the same each time you open a data file. SPSS automatically opens each data file in the SPSS Data Editor window labeled Data View. We'll use GSS10SSDS.SAV for this demonstration.

One way to review the complete list of variables in a file is to click on the *Utilities* choice from the main menu, then on *Variables* in the list of submenu choices. A dialog box should open (as depicted in Figure 1.5). The SPSS variable names, which are limited to eight characters or less, are listed in the scroll box (*left* column). When a variable name is highlighted, the descriptive label for that variable is listed, along with any missing values and, if available, the value labels for each variable category. (As you use this feature, please note that sometimes SPSS mislabels the variable's measurement level. Always confirm that the reported SPSS measurement level is correct.) SPSS allows you to display data in alphabetical order (based upon the variable name) or in the order presented in the file (which may not be alphabetical).

A second way to review all variables is through the Variable View window. Notice on the bottom of your screen that there are two tabs, one for *Data View* and the other for *Variable View*. Click on *Variable View*, and you'll see all the variables listed in the order in which they appear in the Data View window (as depicted in Figure 1.6). Each column provides specific information about the variables. The columns labeled "Label" and "Values" provide the variable label (a brief label of what it's measuring) and value labels (for each variable category).

Figure 1.5   Utilities-Variables Dialog Box

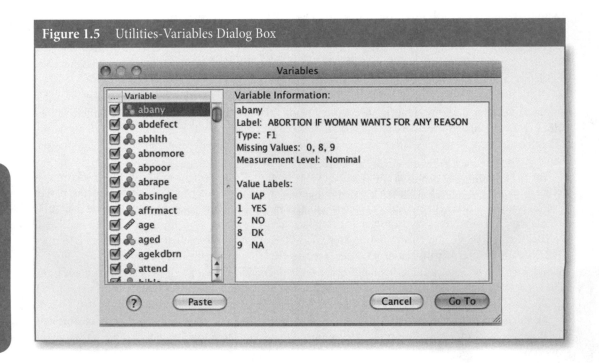

Figure 1.6   Variable View Window for GSS2010

	Name	Type	Width	Decimals	Label	Values	Missing	Columns	Align	Measure	Role
1	abany	Numeric	1	0	ABORTION IF...	{0, IAP}...	0, 8, 9	8	Right	Nominal	Input
2	abdefect	Numeric	1	0	STRONG CHAN...	{0, IAP}...	0, 8, 9	8	Right	Nominal	Input
3	abhlth	Numeric	1	0	WOMANS HEAL...	{0, IAP}...	0, 8, 9	8	Right	Nominal	Input
4	abnomore	Numeric	1	0	MARRIED--WA...	{0, IAP}...	0, 8, 9	8	Right	Nominal	Input

SPSS PROBLEM

Based on the *Utilities-Variables* option, review the variables from the GSS10SSDS. Can you identify three nominal variables, three ordinal variables, and at least one interval-ratio variable? Based on the information in the dialog box or Variable View window, you should be able to identify the variable name, variable label, and category values. You can do the same for the other data sets: MTF11SSDS, HINTS12SSDS, and GLOBAL13SSDS.

CHAPTER EXERCISES

1. In your own words, explain the relationship of data (collecting and analyzing) to the research process. (Refer to Figure 1.1.)

2. Construct potential hypotheses or research questions to relate the variables in each of the following examples. Also, write a brief statement explaining why you believe there is a relationship between the variables as specified in your hypotheses.
   a. Gender and educational level
   b. Income and race
   c. The crime rate and the number of police in a city
   d. Life satisfaction and marital status
   e. A nation's military expenditures as a percentage of its gross domestic product and that nation's overall level of security
   f. Care of elderly parents and ethnicity

3. Determine the level of measurement for each of the following variables:
   a. The number of people in your family
   b. Place of residence classified as urban, suburban, or rural
   c. The percentage of university students who attended public high school
   d. The rating of the overall quality of a textbook, on a scale from "Excellent" to "Poor"
   e. The type of transportation a person takes to work (e.g., bus, walk, car)
   f. Your annual income
   g. The U.S. unemployment rate
   h. The presidential candidate that the respondent voted for in 2012

4. For each of the variables in Exercise 3 that you classified as interval ratio, identify whether it is discrete or continuous.

Exercises

5. Why do you think men and women, on average, do not earn the same amount of money? Develop your own theory to explain the difference. Use three independent variables in your theory, with annual income as your dependent variable. Construct hypotheses to link each independent variable with your dependent variable.

6. For each of the following examples, indicate whether it involves the use of descriptive or inferential statistics. Justify your answer.
    a. The number of unemployed people in the United States
    b. Determining students' opinion about the quality of food at the cafeteria based on a sample of 100 students
    c. The national incidence of breast cancer among Asian women
    d. Conducting a study to determine the rating of the quality of a new smartphone, gathered from 1,000 new buyers
    e. The average GPA of various majors (e.g., sociology, psychology, English) at your university
    f. The change in the number of immigrants coming to the United States from Southeast Asian countries between 2005 and 2010

7. Identify three social problems or issues that can be investigated with statistics. (One example of a social problem is criminal acts, such as murder.) Which one of the three issues would be the most difficult to study? Which would be the easiest? Why?

8. Construct measures of political participation at the nominal, ordinal, and interval-ratio levels. (*Hint:* You can use behaviors such as voting frequency or political party membership.) Discuss the advantages and disadvantages of each.

9. Variables can be measured according to more than one level of measurement. For the following variables, identify at least two levels of measurement. Is one level of measurement better than another? Explain.
    a. Individual age
    b. Annual income
    c. Religiosity
    d. Student performance
    e. Social class
    f. Attitude toward gun control

Chapter 2

Organization of Information

Frequency Distributions

A s social researchers, we often have to deal with very large amounts of data. For example, in a typical survey, by the completion of your data collection phase you will have accumulated thousands of individual responses represented by a jumble of numbers. To make sense out of these data, you will have to organize and summarize them in some systematic fashion. The most basic method for organizing data is to classify the observations into a frequency distribution. A **frequency distribution** is a table that reports the number of observations that fall into each category of the variable we are analyzing. Constructing a frequency distribution is usually the first step in the statistical analysis of data.

Frequency distribution   A table reporting the number of observations falling into each category of the variable.

▣ FREQUENCY DISTRIBUTIONS

Immigration has been described as "remaking America with political, economic, and cultural ramifications".[1] Globalization has fueled migration, particularly since the beginning of the 21st century. Workers migrate because of the promise of employment and higher standards of living than their home countries. Data reveal that the United States is the destination for many migrants.[2] The U.S. Census Bureau uses the term *foreign born* to refer to those who are not U.S. citizens at birth. The U.S. Census estimates that nearly 12.9% of the U.S. population or approximately 40 million people are foreign born.[3] Immigrants are not one homogeneous group but are many diverse groups. Table 2.1 shows the frequency distribution of the world region of birth for the foreign-born population.

Table 2.1   Frequency Distribution for Categories of World Region of Birth for Foreign-Born Population, 2010

World Region of Birth	Frequency (f)
Africa	1,607,000
Asia	11,284,000
Europe	4,817,000
Latin America and the Caribbean	21,224,000
Northern America	807,000
Oceania	217,000
Total (N)	39,956,000

Source: Elizabeth Grieco, Yesenia Acosta, C. Patricia de la Cruz, Christine Gambino, Thomas Gryn, Luke Larsen, Edward Trevelyan, and Nathan Walters. *The Foreign-Born Population in the United States: 2010* (ACS-19; Washington, DC: U.S. Census Bureau), 2012.

Note that the frequency distribution is organized in a table, which has a number (2.1) and a descriptive title. The title indicates the kind of data presented: "Categories of World Region of Birth for Foreign-Born Population". The table consists of two columns. The first column identifies the variable (world region of birth) and its categories. The second column, headed "Frequency (f)," tells the number of cases in each category as well as the total number of cases (N = 39,956,000). Note also that the source of the table is clearly identified in a source note. It tells us that the data are from a 2012 U.S. Census report (though the information is based on 2010 data). In general, the source of data for a table should appear as a source note unless it is clear from the general discussion of the data.

What can you learn from the information presented in Table 2.1? The table shows that as of 2010, approximately 40 million people were classified as foreign born. Out of this group, the majority, about 21.2 million people, were from Latin America, 11.3 million were from Asia, followed by 4.8 million from Europe.

回 PROPORTIONS AND PERCENTAGES

Frequency distributions are helpful in presenting information in a compact form. However, when the number of cases is large, the frequencies may be difficult to grasp. To standardize these raw frequencies, we can translate them into relative frequencies—that is, proportions or percentages.

A **proportion** is a relative frequency obtained by dividing the frequency in each category by the total number of cases. To find a proportion (p), divide the frequency (f) in each category by the total number of cases (N):

$$p = \frac{f}{N} \qquad (2.1)$$

where

f = frequency

N = total number of cases

We've calculated the proportion for the three largest groups of foreign born. First, the proportion of foreign born originally from Latin America is

$$\frac{21,224,000}{39,956,000} = .53$$

The proportion of foreign born who were originally from Asia is

$$\frac{11,284,000}{39,956,000} = .28$$

The proportion of foreign born who were originally from Europe is

$$\frac{4,817,000}{39,956,000} = .12$$

The proportion of foreign born who were originally from other reported areas is

$$\frac{2,631,000}{39,956,000} = .07$$

We rounded this last proportion from .065 to .07. Confirm this calculation on your own. You can also calculate the proportion individually for Africa, Northern America, and Oceania.

Proportions should always sum to 1.00 (allowing for some rounding errors). Thus, in our example the sum of the six proportions is

$$.53 + .28 + .12 + .07 = 1.0$$

To determine a frequency from a proportion, we simply multiply the proportion by the total N:

$$f = p(N) \qquad (2.2)$$

Thus, the frequency of foreign born from Asia can be calculated as

$$0.28(39,956,000) = 11,187,680$$

Note that the obtained frequency differs somewhat from the actual frequency of 11,284,000. This difference is due to rounding off of the proportion. If we use the actual proportion instead of the rounded proportion, we obtain the correct frequency:

$$0.282410651(39,956,000) = 11,284,000$$

Proportion   A relative frequency obtained by dividing the frequency in each category by the total number of cases.

✓ *Learning*
Check

Compare Group A with Group B in Figure 2.1 and answer the following questions: Which group has the greater number of women? Which group has the larger proportion of women?

Figure 2.1   Numbers and Proportions

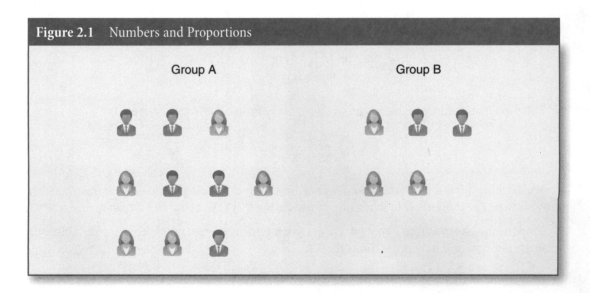

We can also express frequencies as percentages. A **percentage** is a relative frequency obtained by dividing the frequency in each category by the total number of cases and multiplying by 100. In most statistical reports, frequencies are presented as percentages rather than proportions. Percentages express the size of the frequencies as if there were a total of 100 cases.

To calculate a percentage, simply multiply the proportion by 100:

$$\text{Percentage}(\%) = \frac{f}{N}(100) \tag{2.3}$$

or

$$\text{Percentage }(\%) = p(100) \tag{2.4}$$

Thus, the percentage of respondents who were originally from Asia is

$$0.28(100) = 28\%$$

The percentage of respondents who were originally from Latin America is

$$0.53(100) = 53\%$$

Percentage   A relative frequency obtained by dividing the frequency in each category by the total number of cases and multiplying by 100.

Calculate the proportion of males and females in your statistics class. What proportion is female?

✓ *Learning Check*

▣ PERCENTAGE DISTRIBUTIONS

Percentages are usually displayed as percentage distributions. A **percentage distribution** is a table showing the percentage of observations falling into each category of the variable. For example, Table 2.2 presents the frequency distribution of categories of places of origin (Table 2.1) along with the corresponding percentage distribution. Percentage distributions (or proportions) should always show the base (*N*) on which they were computed. Thus, in Table 2.2 the base on which the percentages were computed is $N = 39,956,000$. While in most cases the total percentages should equal 100%, in Table 2.2, the total is 99.9%.

Percentage distribution   A table showing the percentage of observations falling into each category of the variable.

Table 2.2   Frequency and Percentage Distributions for Categories of World Region of Birth for Foreign Born, 2010

World Region of Birth	Frequency (f)	Percentage (%)
Africa	1,607,000	4.0
Asia	11,284,000	28.2
Europe	4,817,000	12.1
Latin America and the Caribbean	21,224,000	53.1
Northern America	807,000	2.0
Oceania	217,000	.5
Total (*N*)	39,956,000	99.9%

Source: Elizabeth Grieco, Yesenia Acosta, C. Patricia de la Cruz, Christine Gambino, Thomas Gryn, Luke Larsen, Edward Trevelyan, and Nathan Walters. *The Foreign-Born Population in the United States: 2010* (ACS-19; Washington, DC: U.S. Census Bureau), 2012.

▣ COMPARISONS

In Table 2.2, we illustrated that there are six primary places of origin for foreign born in the United States. These distinctions help us understand the specific characteristics and backgrounds of each group. We can resist the temptation to group all foreign born in one category and ask, for instance, is one group more educated than another? Is one group younger than the other groups? As students, as social scientists, and even as consumers, we are frequently faced with problems that call for some way to make clear and valid comparisons.

The decision to consider these groups separately or to pool them depends to a large extent on our research question. For instance, we know that in 2010, 19% of the foreign-born population were living in poverty.[4] Among the foreign born, poverty rates were highest among those from Latin America (24%) and lowest among those from Northern America (9.1%). What do these figures tell us about the demographic characteristics of foreign borns? Of Latin American foreign borns? Of Northern America foreign borns? To answer these questions and determine whether the two categories of region of birth have markedly different social characteristics, we need to *compare* them.

Several types of comparisons are quite common in the social sciences. One type is the comparison between groups that have different characteristics—for example, comparisons between older and younger Americans, white and Asian Pacific Islander, or as in our chapter example, between different categories of foreign-born individuals. Sometimes, we may be interested in looking at regional differences among groups or in comparing groups from different segments of society. You may have read news stories about contrasts in voting patterns between gun owners and non-gun owners or between liberals and conservatives. Also, we may be interested in comparing changes in the same group over time, such as the percentage change in foreign-born residents in the United States over the past decade or how the population has shifted from the cities toward the suburbs.

▣ STATISTICS IN PRACTICE: LABOR FORCE PARTICIPATION AMONG FOREIGN BORN

Very often, we are interested in comparing two or more groups that differ in size. Percentages are especially useful for making such comparisons. For example, we know that differences in socioeconomic status mark divisions between populations, indicating differential access to economic opportunities. Labor participation (either employed or seeking employment) is an important indicator of access to economic opportunities and is strongly associated with socioeconomic status. Table 2.3 shows the raw frequency distributions for the variable *labor force participation* for foreign-born individuals by race and Hispanic ethnicity. Notice that the title of the table includes the notation "(numbers in thousands)". The U.S. Census Bureau frequently presents figures this way, eliminating the set of three 0's at the end. The numbers can be converted to millions, by multiplying each by 1,000 (e.g. $4,138 \times 1,000 = 4,138,000$).

Which group has the highest relative number of persons who are not in the labor force? Because of the differences in the population sizes of the four groups, this is a difficult question to answer based on only the raw frequencies. To make a valid comparison, we have to compare the percentage distributions for all the three groups. These are presented in Table 2.4. Note that the percentage distributions make it easier to identify differences between the groups. The base N's are reported

Table 2.3   Employment Status of the Foreign-Born Population, by Race and Hispanic Ethnicity, 2010 (numbers in thousands)

Employment Status	White Non-Hispanic	Black Non-Hispanic	Asian Non-Hispanic	Hispanic
Employed	4,138	1,893	4,928	10,776
Unemployed	332	269	386	1,376
Not in labor force	2,893	736	2,758	5,010
Total (N)	7,363	2,898	8,072	17,162

Source: U.S. Census Bureau, *Statistical Abstract of the United States: 2012*, Table 589.

for each racial/ethnic group. Compared with the other groups, black non-Hispanic foreign-born individuals have the highest percentage employed in the labor force (1893/2898 = 65.3%). This group also has the highest percentage of unemployed (269/2898= 9.3%), followed by Hispanics (1376/17162 = 8.0%).

✓ *Learning*
Check

Examine Table 2.4 and answer the following questions: What is the percentage of white non-Hispanics who are employed? What is the base (N) for this percentage? What is the percentage of Hispanics who are not in the labor force? What is the base (N) for this percentage?

Table 2.4   Employment Status of the Foreign-Born Population by Race and Hispanic Ethnicity, 2010 (percentages)

Employment Status	White Non-Hispanic N = 7,363	Black Non-Hispanic N = 2,898	Asian Non-Hispanic N = 8,072	Hispanic N = 17,162
Employed	56.2%	65.3%	61.1%	62.8%
Unemployed	4.5	9.3	4.8	8.0
Not in labor force	39.3	25.4	34.2	29.2
Total	100%	100%	100.1%	100%

Source: U.S. Census Bureau, *Statistical Abstract of the United States: 2012*, Table 589.

Whenever one group is compared with another, the most meaningful conclusions can usually be drawn based on comparison of the relative frequency distributions. In fact, we are seldom interested in a single distribution. Most interesting questions in the social sciences are about differences between two or more groups.[5] The finding that the foreign-born population labor force participation patterns vary among different race and ethnic groups raises doubt about whether foreign borns can be legitimately regarded as a single, relatively homogeneous group. Further analyses could examine *why* these differences exist. Other variables that explain these differences could be identified (such as educational attainment, age, or previous work experience). These kinds of questions can be answered using more complex multivariate statistical techniques that involve more than two variables. The comparison of percentage distributions is an important foundation for these more complex techniques.

Before we continue, keep in mind that although we encourage you to begin thinking analytically about complex data, the basic procedures that we'll review in the first 5 chapters only allow you to draw some tentative conclusions about differences between groups. To make valid comparisons, you will need to consider the more complex techniques of sampling and statistical inference, which are discussed in Chapters 6 through 13. As you proceed through this book and master all the statistical concepts necessary for valid inference, you will be able to provide more complex interpretations.

▣ THE CONSTRUCTION OF FREQUENCY DISTRIBUTIONS

Up to now, you have been introduced to the general concept of a frequency distribution. We saw that data can be expressed as raw frequencies, proportions, or percentages. We also saw how to use percentages to compare distributions in different groups.

In this section, you will learn how to construct frequency distributions. Most often, this can be done by your computer, but it is important to go through the process to understand how frequency distributions are actually put together.

For nominal and ordinal variables, constructing a frequency distribution is quite simple. Count and report the number of cases that fall into each category of the variable along with the total number of cases (*N*). For the purpose of illustration, let's take a small random sample of 40 cases from a General Social Survey (GSS) sample and record their scores on the following variables: gender, a nominal-level variable; degree, an ordinal measurement of education; and age and number of children, both interval-ratio variables. The use of "male" and "female" in parts of this book is in keeping with the GSS categories for the variable "sex" (respondent's sex).

The gender of the respondents was recorded by the interviewer at the beginning of the interview. To measure degree, respondents were asked to indicate the highest degree completed: less than high school, high school, some college, bachelor's degree, and graduate degree. The first category represented the lowest level of education. Respondent age was calculated based on the respondent's birth year. The number of children was determined by the question, "How many children have you ever had?" The answers given by our subsample of 40 respondents are displayed in Table 2.5. Note that each row in the table represents a respondent, whereas each column represents a variable. This format is conventional in the social sciences.

You can see that it is going to be difficult to make sense of these data just by eyeballing Table 2.5. How many of these 40 respondents are males? How many said that they had a graduate degree? How

Table 2.5   A GSS Subsample of 40 Respondents

Gender of Respondent	Degree	Number of Children	Age
M	Bachelor	1	43
F	High school	2	71
F	High school	0	71
M	High school	0	37
M	High school	0	28
F	High school	6	34
F	High school	4	69

(Continued)

Table 2.5   (Continued)

Gender of Respondent	Degree	Number of Children	Age
F	Graduate	0	51
F	Bachelor	0	76
M	Graduate	2	48
M	Graduate	0	49
M	Less than high school	3	62
F	Less than high school	8	71
F	High school	1	32
F	High school	1	59
F	High school	1	71
M	High school	0	34
M	Bachelor	0	39
F	Bachelor	2	50
M	High school	3	82
F	High school	1	45
M	High school	0	22
M	High school	2	40
F	High school	2	46
M	High school	0	29
F	High school	1	75
F	High school	0	23
M	Bachelor	2	35
M	Bachelor	3	44
F	High school	3	47
M	High school	1	84
F	Graduate	1	45
F	Less than high school	3	24
F	Graduate	0	47
F	Less than high school	5	67
F	High school	1	21
F	High school	0	24
F	High school	3	49
F	High school	3	45
F	Graduate	3	37

Note: M, male; F, female.

many were older than 50 years of age? To answer these questions, we construct the frequency distributions for all four variables.

Frequency Distributions for Nominal Variables

Let's begin with the nominal variable, *gender*. First, we tally the number of males, then the number of females (the column of tallies has been included in Table 2.6 for the purpose of illustration). The tally results are then used to construct the frequency distribution presented in Table 2.6. The table has a title describing its content ("Frequency Distribution of the Variable Gender: GSS Subsample"). Its categories (male and female) and their associated frequencies are clearly listed; in addition, the total number of cases (*N*) is also reported. The Percentage column is the percentage distribution for this variable. To convert the Frequency column to percentages, simply divide each frequency by the total number of cases and multiply by 100. Percentage distributions are routinely added to almost any frequency table and are especially important if comparisons with other groups are to be considered. Immediately, we can see that it is easier to read the information. There are 25 females and 15 males in this sample. Based on this frequency distribution, we can also conclude that the majority of sample respondents are female.

> *Construct a frequency and percentage distribution for males and females in your statistics class.*

✓ *Learning Check*

Table 2.6   Frequency Distribution of the Variable Gender: GSS Subsample

Gender	Tallies	Frequency (f)	° Percentage
Male	ⅢⅢⅢ	15	37.5
Female	ⅢⅢⅢⅢⅢ	25	62.5
Total (*N*)		40	100.0

Frequency Distributions for Ordinal Variables

To construct a frequency distribution for ordinal-level variables, follow the same procedures outlined for nominal-level variables. Table 2.7 presents the frequency distribution for the variable degree. The table shows that 60.0%, a majority, indicated that their highest degree was a high school degree.

The major difference between frequency distributions for nominal and ordinal variables is the order in which the categories are listed. The categories for nominal-level variables do not have to be listed in any particular order. For example, we could list females first and males second without changing the nature of the distribution. Because the categories or values of ordinal variables are rank ordered, however, they must be listed in a way that reflects their rank—from the lowest to the

Table 2.7   Frequency Distribution of the Variable Degree: GSS Subsample

Degree	Tallies	Frequency (f)	Percentage
Less than high school	IIII	4	10.0
High school	IIII IIII IIII IIII IIII	24	60.0
Bachelor	IIII I	6	15.0
Graduate	IIII I	6	15.0
Total (N)		40	100.0

highest or from the highest to the lowest. Thus, the data on degree in Table 2.7 are presented in declining order from "less than high school" (the lowest educational category) to "graduate" (the highest educational category).

✓ *Learning*
Check

Figures 2.2, 2.3, and 2.4 illustrate the gender and degree data in stages as presented in Tables 2.5, 2.6, and 2.7. To convince yourself that classifying the respondents by gender (Figure 2.3) and by degree (Figure 2.4) makes the job of counting much easier, turn to Figure 2.2 and answer these questions: How many men are in the group? How many women? How many said that they completed a bachelor's degree? Now turn to Figure 2.3: How many men are in the group? How many women? Finally, examine Figure 2.4: How many said that they completed a bachelor's degree?

Frequency Distributions for Interval-Ratio Variables

We hope that you agree by now that constructing frequency distributions for nominal- and ordinal-level variables is rather straightforward. Simply list the categories and count the number of observations that fall into each category. Building a frequency distribution for interval-ratio variables with relatively few values is also easy. For example, when constructing a frequency distribution for number of children, simply list the number of children and report the corresponding frequency, as shown in Table 2.8.

Very often interval-ratio variables have a wide range of values, which makes simple frequency distributions very difficult to read. For example, take a look at the frequency distribution for the variable *age* in Table 2.9. The distribution contains age values ranging from 21 to 84 years. For a more concise picture, the large number of different scores could be reduced into a smaller number of groups, each containing a range of scores. Table 2.10 displays such a grouped frequency distribution of the data in Table 2.9. Each group, known as a *class interval*, now contains 10 possible scores instead of 1. Thus, the ages of 21, 22, 23, 24, 28, and 29 all fall into a single class interval of 20–29.

Figure 2.2 Forty Respondents From the GSS Subsample, Their Gender, and Their Level of Degree (see Table 2.5)

Figure 2.3   Forty Respondents From the GSS Subsample, Classified by Gender (see Table 2.6)

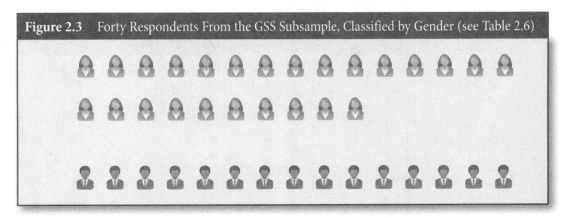

Figure 2.4   Forty Respondents From the GSS Subsample, Classified by Gender and Degree

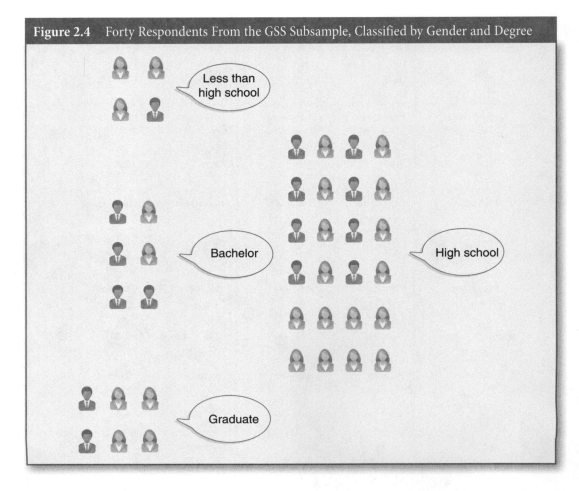

The second column of Table 2.10, Frequency, tells us the number of respondents who fall into each of the intervals—for example, that seven respondents fall into the class interval of 20–29. Having

Table 2.8   Frequency Distribution of Variable Number of
Children: GSS Subsample

Number of Children	Frequency (f)	Percentage
0	13	32.5
1	9	22.5
2	6	15.0
3	8	20.0
4	1	2.5
5	1	2.5
6	1	2.5
7+	1	2.5
Total (*N*)	40	100.0

Table 2.9   Frequency Distribution of the Variable Age: GSS Subsample

Age of Respondent	Frequency (f)	Age of Respondent	Frequency (f)
21	1	59	1
22	1	62	1
23	1	67	1
24	2	69	1
28	1	71	4
29	1	75	1
32	1	76	1
34	2	82	1
35	1	84	1
37	2		
39	1		
40	1		
43	1		
44	1		
45	3		
46	1		
47	2		
48	1		
49	2		
50	1		
51	1		

grouped the scores, we can clearly see that the biggest single age group is between 40 and 49 years (12 out of 40, or 30% of sample). The percentage distribution that we have added to Table 2.10 displays the relative frequency of each interval and emphasizes this pattern as well.

✓ *Learning Check*

Can you verify that Table 2.10 was constructed correctly? Use Table 2.9 to determine the frequency of cases that fall into the categories of Table 2.10.

Table 2.10   Grouped Frequency Distribution of the Variable Age: GSS Subsample

Age Category	Frequency (f)	Percentage
20–29	7	17.5
30–39	7	17.5
40–49	12	30.0
50–59	3	7.5
60–69	3	7.5
70–79	6	15.0
80–89	2	5.0
Total (N)	40	100.0

The decision as to how many groups to use and, therefore, how wide the intervals should be is usually up to the researcher and depends on what makes sense in terms of the purpose of the research. The rule of thumb is that an interval width should be large enough to avoid too many categories but not so large that significant differences between observations are concealed.[6] Obviously, the number of intervals depends on the width of each. For instance, if you are working with scores ranging from 10 to 60 and you establish an interval width of 10, you will have five intervals.

✓ *Learning Check*

If you are having trouble distinguishing between nominal, ordinal, and interval-ratio variables, go back to Chapter 1 and review the section on levels of measurement. The distinction between these three levels of measurement is important throughout the book.

▣ CUMULATIVE DISTRIBUTIONS

Sometimes, we may be interested in locating the relative position of a given score in a distribution. For example, we may be interested in finding out how many or what percentage of our sample was younger than 40 or older than 60. Frequency distributions can be presented in a cumulative fashion to answer such questions. A **cumulative frequency distribution** shows the frequencies at or below each category of the variable.

Cumulative frequency distribution   A distribution showing the frequency at or below each category (class interval or score) of the variable.

Cumulative frequencies are appropriate only for variables that are measured at an ordinal level or higher. They are obtained by adding to the frequency in each category the frequencies of all the categories below it.

Let's look at Table 2.11. It shows the cumulative frequencies based on the frequency distribution from Table 2.10. The cumulative frequency column, denoted by *Cf*, shows the number of persons at or below each interval. For example, you can see that 14 of the 40 respondents were 39 years old or younger, and 29 respondents were 59 years old or younger.

To construct a cumulative frequency distribution, start with the frequency in the lowest class interval (or with the lowest score, if the data are ungrouped), and add to it the frequencies in the next highest class interval. Continue adding the frequencies until you reach the last class interval.

Table 2.11   Grouped Frequency Distribution and Cumulative
Frequency for the Variable Age: GSS Subsample

Age Category	Frequency (f)	Cf
20–29	7	7
30–39	7	14
40–49	12	26
50–59	3	29
60–69	3	32
70–79	6	38
80–89	2	40
Total (*N*)	40	

The cumulative frequency in the last class interval will be equal to the total number of cases (*N*). In Table 2.11, the frequency associated with the first class interval (20–29) is 7. The cumulative frequency associated with this interval is also 7, since there are no cases below this class interval. The frequency for the second class interval is 7. The cumulative frequency for this interval is 7 + 7 = 14. To obtain the cumulative frequency of 26 for the third interval, we add its frequency (12) to the cumulative frequency associated with the second class interval (14). Continue this process until you reach the last class interval. Therefore, the cumulative frequency for the last interval is equal to 40, the total number of cases (*N*).

We can also construct a cumulative percentage distribution (*C%*), which has wider applications than the cumulative frequency distribution (*Cf*). A **cumulative percentage distribution** shows the percentage at or below each category (class interval or score) of the variable. A cumulative percentage distribution is constructed using the same procedure as for a cumulative frequency distribution except that the percentages—rather than the raw frequencies—for each category are added to the total percentages for all the previous categories.

Cumulative percentage distribution   A distribution showing the percentage at or below each category (class interval or score) of the variable.

▣ A Closer Look 2.1
Real Limits, Stated Limits, and Midpoints of Class Intervals

The intervals presented in Table 2.10 constitute the categories of the variable age that we used to classify the survey's respondents. In Chapter 1, we noted that our variables need to be both exhaustive and mutually exclusive. These principles apply to the intervals here as well. This means that each of the 40 respondents can be classified into one and only one category. In addition, we should be able to classify all the possible scores.

In our example, these requirements are met: Each observation score fits into only one interval, and there is an appropriate category to classify each individual score as recorded in Table 2.10. However, if you looked closely at Table 2.10, you may have noticed that there is actually a gap of 1 year between adjacent intervals. A gap could create a problem with scores that have fractional values. Though age is conventionally rounded down, let's suppose for a moment that respondent's age had been reported with more precision. Where would you classify a woman who was 49.25 years old? Notice that her age would actually fall between the intervals 40–49 and 50–59! To avoid this potential problem, use the real limits shown in the following table rather than the stated limits listed in Table 2.10.

Real limits extend the upper and lower limits of the intervals by .5. For instance, the real limits for the interval 40–49 are 39.5–49.5; the real limits for the interval 50–59 are 49.5–59.5; and so on. (Scores that fall exactly at the upper real limit or the lower real limit of the interval [e.g., 59.5 or 49.5] are usually rounded to the closest even number. The number 59.5 would be rounded to 60 and would thus be included in the interval 59.5–69.5.) In the following table, we include both the stated limits and real limits for the grouped frequency distribution of respondent's age. So where would you classify a respondent who was 49.25 years old? (Answer: In the interval 39.5–49.5.) How about 19.9? (In the interval 19.5–29.5.)

The midpoint is a single number that represents the entire interval. A midpoint is calculated by adding the lower and upper real limits of the interval and dividing by 2. The midpoint of the interval 19.5–29.5, for instance, is $(19.5 + 29.5) \div 2 = 24.5$. The midpoint for all the intervals of the table are displayed in the third column.

Even though grouped frequency distributions are very helpful in summarizing information, remember that they are only a summary and therefore involve a considerable loss of detail. Since most researchers and students have access to computers, grouped frequencies are used only when the raw data are not available. Most of the statistical procedures described in later chapters are based on the raw scores.

	Respondent's Age		
Stated Limits	**Real Limits**	**Midpoint**	**Frequency (f)**
20–29	19.5–29.5	24.5	7
30–39	29.5–39.5	34.5	7
40–49	39.5–49.5	44.5	12
50–59	49.5–59.5	54.5	3
60–69	59.5–69.5	64.5	3
70–79	69.5–79.5	74.5	6
80–89	79.5–89.5	84.5	2
Total (*N*)			40

In Table 2.12, we have added the cumulative percentage distribution to the frequency and percentage distributions shown in Table 2.10. The cumulative percentage distribution shows, for example, that 35% of the sample was younger than 40 years of age—that is, 39 years or younger.

Like the percentage distributions described earlier, cumulative percentage distributions are especially useful when you want to compare differences between groups. For an example of how cumulative percentages are used in a comparison, we used the 2010 GSS data to contrast the opinions of whites and blacks about whether they believe immigrants take jobs away from native-born Americans. Respondents were asked the following: "How much do you agree or disagree with the following statement? Immigrants take jobs away from people who were born in America."

The percentage distribution and the cumulative percentage distribution for whites and blacks are shown in Table 2.13. The cumulative percentage distributions suggest that a higher percentage of blacks agree to the statement that immigrants take away jobs. The two groups are separated by 9.9 percentage points—51.3% of black respondents indicated that they either strongly agreed or agreed to the statement, while 41.4% of white respondents said the same. (Note that a

Table 2.12 Grouped Frequency Distribution and Cumulative
Percentages for the Variable Age: GSS Subsample

Age Category	Frequency (f)	Percentage	C%
20–29	7	17.5	17.5
30–39	7	17.5	35.0
40–49	12	30.0	65.0
50–59	3	7.5	72.5
60–69	3	7.5	80.0
70–79	6	15.0	95.0
80–89	2	5.0	100.0
Total (N)	40	100.0	

higher percentage of whites disagree with the statement than blacks.) What might explain these differences? These data prompt many other questions about the role that race or other variables may play in attitudes about legal and unauthorized immigration. For instance, what would the differences be if we compared men with women? Whites with Latinos?

Table 2.13 Immigrants Take Jobs Away: White Versus Black
Respondents

	Whites		Blacks	
	%	C%	%	C%
Strongly agree	8.9	8.9	13.5	13.5
Agree	32.5	41.4	37.8	51.3
Neither	22.2	63.6	17.6	68.5
Disagree	28.5	92.1	24.3	93.2
Strongly disagree	7.9	100	6.8	100.0
Total	100.0		100.0	
(N)	369		74	

Source: Author created based on data from GSS, 2010.

回 RATES

Terms such as *birthrate*, *unemployment rate*, and *marriage rate* are often used by social scientists and demographers and then quoted in the popular media to describe population trends. But what exactly are rates, and how are they constructed? A **rate** is a number obtained by dividing the number of actual occurrences in a given time period by the number of possible occurrences. For example, to determine the poverty rate for 2011, the U.S. Census Bureau took the number of men and women in poverty in 2011 (actual occurrences) and divided it by the total population in 2011 (possible occurrences). The rate for 2011 can be expressed as

Poverty rate, 2011 = Number of people in poverty in 2011/Total population in 2011

Since 46,247,000 people were poor in 2011 and the number for the total population was 308,456,000, the poverty rate for 2011 can be expressed as

Poverty rate, 2011 = 46,247,000/308,456,00 = .15

The poverty rate in 2011 as reported by the U.S. Census Bureau was 15% (0.15 × 100). This means that for every 1,000 people, 150 were poor according to the U.S. Census Bureau definition. Rates are often expressed as rates per thousand or hundred thousand to eliminate decimal points and make the number easier to interpret.

The preceding poverty rate can be referred to as a *crude rate* because it is based on the total population. Rates can be calculated on the general population or on a more narrowly defined select group. For instance, poverty rates are often given for the number of people who are under 18 years—highlighting how our young are vulnerable to poverty. The poverty rate for those under 18 years is as follows:

Poverty rate for those 18 years or younger, 2011 = 16,134,000/73,737,000 = .22

We could even take a look at the poverty rate for older Americans:

Poverty rate for those 65 years of age or older, 2011 = 3,620,000/41,507,000 = .09

Rate   A number obtained by dividing the number of actual occurrences in a given time period by the number of possible occurrences.

Law enforcement agencies routinely record crime rates (the number of crimes committed relative to the size of a population), arrest rates (the number of arrests made relative to the number of crimes reported), and conviction rates (the number of convictions relative to the number of cases tried). Can you think of some other variables that could be expressed as rates?

✓ *Learning Check*

▣ STATISTICS IN PRACTICE: CIVILIAN LABOR FORCE PARTICIPATION RATES OVER TIME

Like percentages, rates are useful in making comparisons between different groups and over time. The overall participation rate of 64.7 for 2010 might be difficult to interpret by itself and will not answer our question of whether labor force participation rates have changed or how it has changed for specific groups. To illustrate how rates have changed over time, let's look at Table 2.14, which reports labor force participation rates since 1980. For all groups, the labor force participation rates are above 60%. The table shows that participation rates peaked in 2000 but have declined since then, likely due to the 2007–2009 recession. The projected rates for 2018 are still below the high set in 2000.

Table 2.14   Labor Force Participation Rate for Selected Racial Groups, 1980–2018 (Projected)

Year	Overall	White	Black	Asian
1980	63.8	64.1	61.0	NA
1990	66.5	66.9	64.0	NA
2000	67.1	67.3	65.8	67.2
2005	66.0	66.3	64.2	66.1
2010	64.7	65.1	62.2	64.7
2018 projected	64.5	64.5	63.3	65.0

Source: U.S. Census Bureau, *Statistical Abstract of the United States: 2012,* Table 587.

NA, not available.

✓ Learning Check

Make sure that you understand how to read tables. Can you explain how we reached the preceding conclusions based on the information in Table 2.14?

▣ READING THE RESEARCH LITERATURE: STATISTICAL TABLES[7]

Statistical tables that display frequency distributions or other kinds of statistical information are found in virtually every book, article, or newspaper report that makes any use of statistics. However, the inclusion of statistical tables in a report or an article doesn't necessarily mean that the research is more scientific or convincing. You will always have to ask what the tables are saying and judge whether the information is relevant or accurately presented and analyzed. Most statistical tables presented in the social science literature are a good deal more complex than those we describe in this chapter. The same information can sometimes be organized in many different ways, and because of space limitations the researcher may present the information with minimum detail.

In this section, we present some guidelines for how to read and interpret statistical tables displaying frequency distributions. The purpose is to help you see that some of the techniques described in this chapter are actually used in a meaningful way. Remember that it takes time and practice to develop the skill of reading tables. Even experienced researchers sometimes make mistakes when interpreting tables. So take the time to study the tables presented here, do the chapter exercises, and you will find that reading, interpreting, and understanding tables will become easier in time.

Basic Principles

The first step in reading any statistical table is to understand what the researcher is trying to tell you. There must be a reason for including the information, and usually the researcher tells you what it is. Begin your inspection of the table by reading its title. It usually describes the central contents of the table. Check for any source notes to the table. These tell the source of the data or the table and any additional information that the author considers important. Next, examine the column and row headings and subheadings. These identify the variables, their categories, and the kind of statistics presented, such as raw frequencies or percentages. The main body of the table includes the appropriate statistics (frequencies, percentages, rates, etc.) for each variable or group as defined by each heading and subheading.

Table 2.15 was taken from an article written by Yolanda Padilla and her colleagues (2006) about the disadvantages faced by the young children of Mexican immigrants in unmarried families. For their analysis, the researchers relied on data from the Fragile Families and Child Wellbeing Study,

Table 2.15   Percentage Distribution of Access to Public Benefits Among Mexican Immigrant and U.S.-Born Unmarried Mothers

Variables	*Mexican Immigrant*	*Mexican American*	*Black Non-Hispanic*	*White Non-Hispanic*	*Total U.S.-Born Population*
		U.S. Born			
Prenatal care in first 3 months of pregnancy	79	72.9	8.4	81.8	78.1
Health insurance					
Medicaid	77	79	7.2	70	69.1
Private	16.3	16.2	22.9	23.8	24.8
Other	6.7	4.8	6.9	5.2	6.1

(Continued)

Table 2.15   (Continued)

| Variables | Mexican Immigrant | U.S. Born | | | |
		Mexican American	Black Non-Hispanic	White Non-Hispanic	Total U.S.-Born Population
TANF receipt*	12.2	20.4	38.9	14.8	29.6
Food stamp receipt	21.3	40.3	53.5	30.4	45.8
Rent assistance	7.2	22.3	24.4	99	21.0
Head Start	5.2	5.4	3.5	3.8	4.0
WIC receipt**	84.6	88.1	86.7	76	84.6

*TANF, Temporary Assistance for Needy Families

**WIC, Women, Infants and Children Program.

Source: Adapted from Veronica Terriquez, Melissa Dalton Radey, Robert Hummer, and Eunjeong Kim, "The Living Conditions of U.S.-Born Children of Mexican Immigrants in Unmarried Families," *Hispanic Journal of Behavioral Sciences* 28, no. 3 (2006), p. 343.

a nationally representative, longitudinal survey that follows a cohort of new parents and their children for five years. They compared parental demographic and socioeconomic characteristics, formal and informal support, and child well-being indicators for Mexican immigrant and U.S.-born unmarried mothers. Table 2.15 summarizes the utilization of public benefits and programs by immigrant and U.S.-born groups. Note that the columns or rows do not add up to 100%.

Note that the frequency (*f*) for each category is not reported in Table 2.15. Although the table is quite simple, it is important to examine it carefully, including its title and headings, to make sure that you understand what the information means.

✓ *Learning Check*

Inspect Table 2.15 and answer the following questions:

- *What is the source of this table?*
- *How many variables are presented? What are their names?*
- *What is represented by the numbers presented in the second column? In the last row of the table?*

What do the authors tell us about the table?

Among unmarried mothers, there is no significant difference in access to prenatal care or infant health care (well-child visits) based on immigrant status. Differences in access to health insurance are evident only between Mexican immigrant mothers and non-Hispanic White mothers, who tend to have lower rates of Medicaid and higher rates of private insurance.

Immigrant mothers are significantly less likely to receive welfare assistance in the form of Temporary Assistance for Needy Families (TANF) than are U.S.-born mothers. Only about 12.2% of Mexican immigrant mothers receive TANF compared with 20.4% of U.S.-born Mexican mothers and 38.9% of non-Hispanic black mothers. Unmarried Mexican immigrant mothers do not differ significantly from non-Hispanic white mothers in this measure. The same pattern is observed for food stamps and rent assistance. Only 21.3% of unmarried Mexican immigrant mothers receive food stamps, and only 7.2% receive rent assistance. In terms of assistance from Head Start/Early Head Start, we found no significant difference between Mexican immigrants and natives. Finally, rates of receipt of Women, Infants and Children (WIC) Program benefits are similar across all groups, although Mexican immigrant mothers are slightly more likely to receive WIC benefits than are non-Hispanic White mothers.[8]

They conclude that in spite of having fewer resources, immigrant mothers are less likely than U.S.-born mothers to receive formal support (which includes access to public assistance and private health insurance).

For a more detailed analysis of the relationships between these variables, you need to consider some of the more complex techniques of bivariate (two variable) analysis and statistical inference. We consider these more advanced techniques beginning with Chapter 9.

Tables With a Different Format

Tables can sometimes present data for only a subset of the sample. For example, based on 2009 census data for U.S. white only adults, Table 2.16 shows percentages for selected demographic characteristics. However, only partial information on each of the variables is included, and therefore, the percentages do not add up to 100%.

Although the data displayed in Table 2.16 provide useful information, we are usually interested in answering questions that go beyond a simple description of how the variables are distributed. Most research usually goes on to make comparisons between groups or to compare one group at different times. For instance, to put the information on white adults presented in Table 2.16 into a more meaningful context, we may want to compare it with other racial groups. Such a comparison

Table 2.16   Selected Economic and Social Indicators for Whites, 2009

Indicators	*Percentage*
Family income of $200,000 or higher (in the last 12 months)	5.7
Bachelor's degree or higher	29.3
Below the poverty level (individuals)	11.7
Own a home	71

Source: U.S. Census Bureau, *Statistical Abstract of the United States: 2012*, Table 36.

allows us to answer questions such as how high is the percentage with a bachelor's degree or more, and is the 71% owning a home high or low?

Take a look at Table 2.17. It includes the information from Table 2.16, plus corresponding information on Asian Americans. Note the difference in all indicators reported in the table; for example, a higher percentage of Asians have a bachelor's degree or higher (49.7–29.3).

Table 2.17   Selected Economic and Social Indicators for White Only and Asian Only Adults, 2009

Indicators	Percentage of White Only	Percentage of Asian Only
Family income of $200,000 or higher (in the last 12 months)	5.7	8.9
Bachelor's degree or higher	29.3	49.7
Below the poverty level (individuals)	11.7	11.4
Own a home	71	59.4

Source: U.S. Census Bureau, Statistical Abstract of the United States: 2012, Table 36.

▣ CONCLUSION

In the introduction to this chapter, we told you that constructing a frequency distribution is usually the first step in the statistical analysis of data; we hope that by now you agree that constructing a basic frequency or percentage distribution is a fairly straightforward task. As you have seen in the examples in this chapter, distribution tables help researchers organize, summarize, display, and describe data. Trends within groups and differences or similarities between groups can be identified using a simple distribution table.

In the chapters that follow, you will find that frequency distribution tables provide the basic information for graphically displaying data and calculating measures of central tendency and variability. In other words, you will see frequency and percentage distributions again and again, so make sure that you have confidence in your ability to construct and read distribution tables before you proceed to the next chapters.

MAIN POINTS

• The most basic method for organizing data is to classify the observations into a frequency distribution—a table that reports the number of observations that fall into each category of the variable being analyzed.

• Constructing a frequency distribution is usually the first step in the statistical analysis of data.

• To obtain a frequency distribution for nominal and ordinal variables, count and report the number of cases that fall into each category of the variable along with the total number of cases (N).

• To construct a frequency distribution for interval-ratio variables that have a wide range of values, first combine the scores into a smaller number of groups—known as class intervals—each containing a number of scores.

• Proportions and percentages are relative frequencies. To construct a proportion, divide the frequency (*f*) in each category by the total number of cases (*N*). To obtain a percentage, divide the frequency (*f*) in each category by the total number of cases (*N*) and multiply by 100.

• Percentage distributions are tables that show the percentage of observations that fall into each category of the variable. Percentage distributions are routinely added to almost any frequency table and are especially important if comparisons between groups are to be considered.

• Cumulative frequency distributions allow us to locate the relative position of a given score in a distribution. They are obtained by adding to the frequency in each category the frequencies of all the categories below it.

• Cumulative percentage distributions have wider applications than cumulative frequency distributions. A cumulative percentage distribution is constructed by adding to the percentages in each category the percentages of all the categories below it.

• One other method of expressing raw frequencies in relative terms is known as a rate. Rates are defined as the number of actual occurrences in a given time period divided by the number of possible occurrences. Rates are often multiplied by some power of 10 to eliminate decimal points and make the number easier to interpret.

KEY TERMS

cumulative frequency distribution
cumulative percentage distribution

frequency distribution
percentage
percentage distribution

proportion
rate

⑤SAGE edge™

Sharpen your skills with SAGE edge at **edge.sagepub.com/frankfort7e**. **SAGE edge for students** provides a personalized approach to help you accomplish your coursework goals in an easy-to-use learning environment.

SPSS DEMONSTRATIONS

[GSS10SSDS]

Demonstration 1: Producing Frequency Distributions

In SPSS, you can review the frequency distribution for a single variable or for several variables at once. The frequency procedure is found in the *Descriptive Statistics* menu under *Analyze*. For this chapter, we will use the General Social Survey data set.

In the Frequencies dialog box (Figure 2.5), click on the variable name(s) in the left column and transfer the name(s) to the Variable(s) box. (In Figure 2.5, variables are listed according to their order in the data set, but the variables can also be listed alphabetically.) Remember, more than one variable can be selected at one time.

Figure 2.5 Frequencies Dialog Box

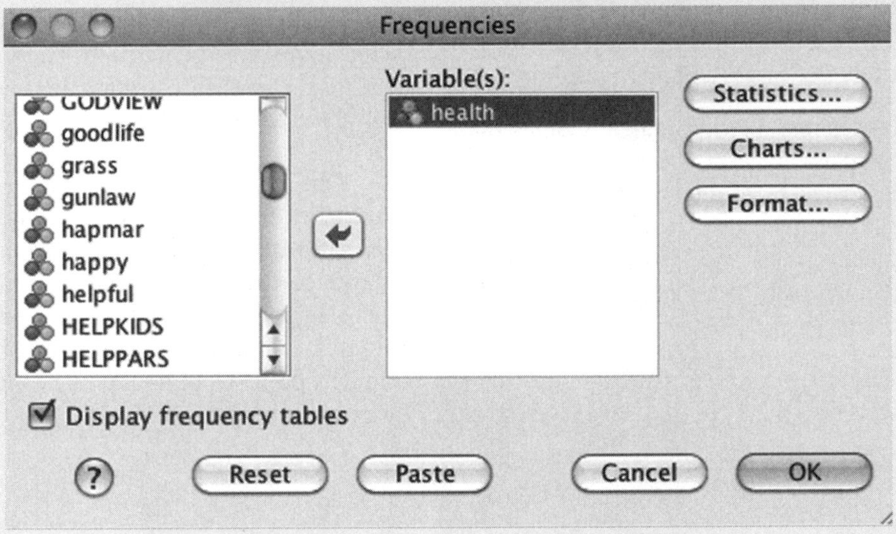

For our demonstration, let's select the variable HEALTH (respondent's condition of health). Click on *OK* to process the frequency. Respondents were asked to answer the question by indicating 1 – excellent, 2 – good, 3 – fair, and 4 – poor.

SPSS will produce two tables in a separate Output window, a statistics table (not presented here), and a frequency table. Use the Window scroll keys to move up and down the window to find the statistics and frequency tables for HEALTH. What level of measurement is this variable? (Refer to Chapter 1 to review definitions.)

In the first table, Statistics, SPSS identifies all the valid and missing responses to this question. Responses are coded missing if no answer was given.

In the frequency table (see Figure 2.6), the variable label is listed. The first column lists the value and value label for each category of HEALTH. What is the value for "excellent"? What is the label for "3"?

The next four columns contain important frequency information about the variable. The Frequency column shows the number of respondents who gave a particular response. Thus, we can see that 1,500 respondents are included in the data set, but only 977 provided a valid response, with 523 responses missing.

The Percent column calculates what percentage of the whole sample (1,500 cases) each of the responses represents. Thus, 16.7% of the total sample reported excellent health. In most instances, percentages reported in the third column, Valid Percent, is more useful. This column removes all the cases defined as missing and recalculates percentages based only on the valid responses. Recalculated based only on valid cases (977), the percentage of those who answered excellent is 25.6. The last column, Cumulative Percent, calculates cumulative percentages beginning with the first response. We know that 70.6% of the valid sample reported that their health was good or better (excellent).

Figure 2.6   Frequency Table for HEALTH

health CONDITION OF HEALTH

		Frequency	Percent	Valid Percent	Cumulative Percent
Valid	1 EXCELLENT	250	16.7	25.6	25.6
	2 GOOD	440	29.3	45.0	70.6
	3 FAIR	228	15.2	23.3	94.0
	4 POOR	59	3.9	6.0	100.0
	Total	977	65.1	100.0	
Missing	0 IAP	521	34.7		
	8 DK	1	.1		
	9 NA	1	.1		
	Total	523	34.9		
Total		1500	100.0		

Demonstration 2: Recoding Variables

Some variables may need to be recoded or reduced into a smaller number of categories or intervals in order to better present and understand the data. We could, for example, collapse HEALTH into a variable with three categories: excellent, good, and fair/poor. We would leave categories 1 and 2 alone, but combine categories 3 and 4. To accomplish this, we could use the SPSS commands *Transform–Recode Into Different Variables*.

For more detailed instruction on recoding variables, please refer to the section on Recoding Variables in the SPSS Appendix on the text's study site, which explains how to recode the variable EDUC (respondent's years of education).

After reviewing the SPSS Appendix, recode HEALTH into a new variable called RHEALTH. Frequencies for RHEALTH should look like Figure 2.7.

Figure 2.7   Frequency Table for RHEALTH

rhealth recoded health

		Frequency	Percent	Valid Percent	Cumulative Percent
Valid	1.00 excellent	250	16.7	25.6	25.6
	2.00 good	440	29.3	45.0	70.6
	3.00 fair/poor	287	19.1	29.4	100.0
	Total	977	65.1	100.0	
Missing	System	523	34.9		
Total		1500	100.0		

Exercises

SPSS PROBLEMS

[GSS10SSDS and GLOBAL13SSDS]

1. Use the SPSS Frequencies command to produce a frequency table for the variable MARITAL as measured in the GSS10SSDS. How would you describe where most students in the sample were raised?
   a. What percentage of the sample is divorced?
   b. What percentage of the sample is married?
   c. What percentage of the sample would you describe as being currently single? (Include all relevant categories.)

2. The GSS2010 SSDS included a series of questions on respondent's attitudes about immigrants. In the chapter, we examined the relationship between race and attitudes about immigrants and jobs (IMMJOBS). The other two GSS variables include IMMCRIME and IMMAMECO.
   a. Run frequencies for all the three variables (including IMMJOBS).
   b. Prepare a general statement summarizing your results from the three frequency tables. Identify the level of measurement for each variable. How would you describe respondents' attitudes about immigrants?

3. Based on GSS10SSDS, produce the frequency table for the RACIDIMP, the importance of one's racial identity.
   a. What is the level of measurement for this variable?
   b. Identify two independent variables (included in the GSS10SSDS data set) that may be related to RACIDIMP. Explain the relationship between these variables and RACINIMP.

4. The GSS2010 SSDS asked respondents to report in their highest year of school (EDUC). Run the frequency table for this variable. Collapse this interval ratio variable into an ordinal measure (omitting those who did not respond to the question). How many categories do you have? Prepare a frequency and cumulative percentage table of your recoded EDUC variable.

5. Collapse the variables LABORRATEFEMALE and LABORRATEMALE (included in GLOBAL13SSDS) into ordinal measures. How many categories do you have? Prepare a frequency and cumulative percentage table of your recoded variables. What can you conclude about the difference in labor force participation between males and females?

CHAPTER EXERCISES

1. Suppose you have surveyed 30 people and asked them whether they are white (W) or nonwhite (N), and how many traumas (serious accidents, rapes, or crimes) they have experienced in the past year. You also asked them to tell you whether they perceive themselves as being in the upper, middle, working, or lower class. Your survey resulted in the raw data presented in the table below:
   a. What level of measurement is the variable race? Class?
   b. Construct raw frequency tables for race and for class.
   c. What proportion of the 30 individuals is nonwhite? What percentage is white?
   d. What proportion of the 30 individuals identified themselves as middle class?

Race	Class	Trauma	Race	Class	Trauma
W	L	1	W	W	0
W	M	0	W	M	2
W	M	1	W	W	1
N	M	1	W	W	1
N	L	2	N	W	0
W	W	0	N	M	2
N	W	0	W	M	1
W	M	0	W	M	0
W	M	1	N	W	1
N	W	1	W	W	0
N	W	2	W	W	0
N	M	0	N	M	0
N	L	0	N	W	0
W	U	0	N	W	1
W	W	1	W	W	0

Source: Data based on GSS files for 1987 to 1991.

Notes: Race: W, white; N, nonwhite; Class: L, lower class; M, middle class; U, upper class; W, working class.

2. Using the data and your raw frequency tables from Exercise 1, construct a frequency distribution for class.
   a. Which is the smallest perceived class?
   b. Which two classes include the largest percentages of people?

3. Using the data from Exercise 1, construct a frequency distribution for trauma.
   a. What level of measurement is used for the trauma variable?
   b. Are people more likely to have experienced no traumas or only one trauma in the past year?
   c. What proportion has experienced one or more traumas in the past year?

Exercises

4. Suppose you are using a sample from the 2010 GSS data for a research project on education in the United States. The GSS includes a question that asks for the number of years of education. Based on 775 individuals, the GSS reports the following frequency distribution for years of education:

Years of Education	Frequency
0	2
2	2
3	1
4	4
5	2
6	8
7	7
8	15
9	23
10	33
11	38
12	207
13	58
14	102
15	33
16	127
17	30
18	36
19	17
20	30

a. What is the level of measurement of years of education?
b. Construct a frequency table, with cumulative percentages, for years of education.
c. How many respondents have 8 or fewer years of education? What percentage of the sample does this value represent?
d. Suppose that you are really more interested in the general level of education than in the raw number of years of education, so you would like to group the data into four categories that better reflect your interests. Assume that anyone with 12 years of education is a high school graduate, and that anyone with 16 years of education is a college graduate. Construct a cumulative frequency table for education in four categories based on these assumptions. What percentage of the sample has graduated from college? What percentage of the sample has not graduated from high school?

5. A question on whether immigrants were good for America was included in the GSS 2010. Results are provided in the table below, noting the percentage who agree or strongly agree by political party (not all responses are reported here so totals will not add up to 100%). Do these data support the statement that people's views on immigration are related to their political party affiliation? Why or why not?

	Strong Democrat %	Independent %	Strong Republican %
Agree Strongly	9.1	7.7	2.1
Agree	47.7	34.6	47.9

6. How many hours per week do you spend on e-mail? In 2010, the GSS included a question on number of hours spent on e-mail. Data are presented here for a sample of 99 men and women.

E-mail hours per week	Frequency
0	19
1	20
2	13
3	5
4	2
5	6
6	5
7	2
8	3
9	1
10 or more	23

 a. Compute the cumulative frequency and cumulative percentage distribution for the data.
 b. What proportion of the sample spent 3 hours or less per week on e-mail?
 c. What proportion of the sample spent 6 or more hours per week on e-mail?

7. The tables below present the frequency distributions for education by gender and race based on the GSS 2010. Use them to answer the following questions.

	Race	
Education	White (f)	Black (f)
Less than high school	72	26
High school graduate	272	59
Junior college	46	10
Bachelor	118	16
Graduate	77	7

	Sex	
Education	Male (f)	Female (f)
Less than high school	46	67
High school graduate	151	214
Junior college	24	37
Bachelor	65	81
Graduate	43	49

a. Construct tables based on percentages and cumulative percentages of educational attainment for race and gender.

b. What percentage of males has continued their education beyond high school? What is the comparable percentage for females?

c. What percentage of whites has completed high school or less? What is the comparable percentage for blacks?

d. Are the cumulative percentages more similar for men and women or for the racial and ethnic groups? (In other words, where is there more inequality?) Explain.

8. The Centers for Disease Control and Prevention (2012) estimated the rate of new HIV infections for 2010. The rates are infections per 100,000 individuals and are reported separately for men and women by racial/ethnic group.

	Men	Women
	Rates per 100,000 Individuals	Rates per 100,000 Individuals
Black	103.6	38.1
Hispanic	45.5	8.0
White	15.8	1.9

Source: Centers for Disease Control and Prevention, "New HIV Infections in the United States," (2012). Retrieved from http://www.cdc.gov/nchhstp/newsroom/docs/2012/HIV-Infections-2007-2010.pdf.

Write a brief statement summarizing the difference in rates between men and women.

9. From the GSS2010, we report the number of children reported by subsample of male and female respondents.

	Males (f)	Females (f)
0	94	92
1	52	72
2	71	127
3	47	91
4	30	38
5 or more	33	27
Total (N)	327	447

a. What is the level of measurement for number of children?
b. What percentage of males and females had 3 children or more? Calculate the percentages for males and females separately.
c. Calculate the cumulative percentages for each. What do the cumulative percentages reveal about the difference in the number of children between males and females?

10. The U.S. Bureau of Justice reports the estimated percent of sentenced prisoners under state and federal jurisdiction by sex and age, as of December 31, 2011. Percentages are presented in the table below. Due to rounding the totals may not equal 100%.

	All Males (%)	All Females (%)
18–19	1.5	.9
20–24	12.4	11.2
25–29	16.3	17.4
30–34	16.5	17.5
35–39	13.7	14.8
40–44	12.5	14.1
45–49	11.0	11.8
50–54	7.7	7.0
55–59	4.2	3.2
60–64	2.2	1.4
65+	1.8	.9

Source: Carson, E., Ann Sabol, and William Sabol, "Prisoners in 2011" (2012). Retrieved from http://bjs.gov/content/pub/pdf/p11.pdf.

Exercises

a. Calculate a cumulative percentage distribution for males.
b. Calculate a cumulative percentage distribution for females.

11. In this exercise, we examine the rate of sexual violence against females reported by Michael Planty and his colleagues (2013). The table includes the rate of victimization per 1,000 females age 12 or older for three time periods.

	1994–1998	1999–2004	2005–2010
12–17	11.3	7.6	4.1
18–34	7.0	5.3	3.7
35–64	2.0	1.8	1.5
65 or older	0.1*	0.2*	0.2*

*Interpret with caution; estimate based on 10 or fewer sample cases, or coefficient of variation is greater than 50%.

Source: Planty, Michael, Lynn Langton, Christopher Krebs, Marcus Berzofsky, and Hope Smiley-McDonald, "Female Victims of Sexual Violence, 1994–2010" (2013). Retrieved from http://bjs.gov/content/pub/pdf/fvsv9410.pdf.

a. The rates are highest for which age group over the three time periods?
b. How would you characterize the relationship between victim age and rate of victimization? Explain the reason for your answer.

12. In 2011 the Gallup Organization reported that for the first time a majority of Americans believe same-sex marriage should be legally recognized. In its report, data for different demographic groups and changes in their level of support were reported for 2010 and 2011. Review each demographic variable and summarize the percent change between years.

	% should be legal, 2010	% should be legal, 2011
Sex and Age		
Men, 18 to 49	48	61
Men, 50+	32	35
Women, 18 to 49	58	65
Women, 50+	37	45
Age		
18–34 years	54	70

	% should be legal, 2010	% should be legal, 2011
35–54 years	50	53
55+ years	33	39
Political affiliation		
Democrats	56	69
Independent	49	59
Republicans	28	28
Political Views		
Liberals	70	78
Moderates	56	65
Conservatives	25	28

Source: Frank Newport, "For First Time, Majority of Americans Favor Legal Gay Marriage," May 20, 2011. Retrieved from http://www.gallup.com/poll/147662/First-Time-Majority-Americans-Favor-Legal-Gay-Marriage.aspx. Copyright © (2011) Gallup, Inc. All rights reserved. The content is used with permission; however, Gallup retains all rights of republication.

13. In the following table, we present selected items from a demographic portrait of likely voting Americans days before the 2012 Presidential Election. (Either due to rounding or the omission of no response categories, not all row totals will equal 100%.)

	Barack Obama and Joe Biden (%)	Mitt Romney and Paul Ryan (%)
Sex		
Men	43	53
Women	52	44
Race		
Non-Hispanic white	39	57
Total nonwhite	78	19
Non-Hispanic black	92	6
Age		
18–29 years	57	38
30–49 years	49	48
50–64 years	46	50

(Continued)

(Continued)

	Barack Obama and Joe Biden (%)	Mitt Romney and Paul Ryan (%)
65 years and older	42	55
Education		
High school or less	48	47
Some college	46	50
College graduate	43	55
Postgraduate	57	39
Income level		
Less than $36,000	59	36
$36,000–$89,999	47	50
$90,000 or more	41	57
Religious affiliation		
Protestant/Christian	41	56
Catholic	52	45
No religion	67	26

Source: Gallup Organization, "Romney 49%, Obama 48% in Gallup's Final Election Survey," November 5, 2012. Retrieved from http://www.gallup.com/poll/158519/romney-obama-gallup-final-election-survey.aspx. Copyright © (2012) Gallup, Inc. All rights reserved. The content is used with permission; however, Gallup retains all rights of republication.

a. For each of the variables, identify the level of measurement.
b. How would you characterize the pattern of support for Barack Obama and Joe Biden? For Mitt Romney and Paul Ryan?

14. We compare educational attainment between native born and foreign born in 2010. Native born refers to anyone born in the United States. The comparative table identifies four categories of education. Write a statement summarizing the difference between the two groups.

	Less Than High School Graduate	High School Graduate or Equivalency	Some College or Associate's Degree	Bachelor's Degree or Higher
Native	11.0	29.7	30.9	28.4
Foreign born	31.7	22.5	18.8	27.0

Source: Grieco et al., 2012.

Chapter 3

Graphic Presentation

Chapter Learning Objectives

❖ Constructing and interpreting a pie chart, bar graph, histogram, line graph, and time-series chart

❖ Analyzing and interpreting charts and graphs in the literature

Y ou have probably heard that "a picture is worth a thousand words." The same can be said about statistical graphs because they summarize hundreds or thousands of numbers. Graphs tell a story in pictures rather than in words or numbers and are utilized in news stories, research reports, or government documents. Many are intimidated by statistical information presented in frequency distributions or in other tabular forms, but find the same information to be readable and understandable when presented graphically.

In this chapter, you will learn about some of the most commonly used graphical techniques. We concentrate less on the technical details of how to create graphs and more on how to choose the appropriate graphs to make statistical information coherent. We also focus on how to interpret information presented graphically.

As we introduce the various graphical techniques, we also show you how to use graphs to tell a story. The particular story we tell in this chapter is that of the elderly in the United States. Demographers predict that over the next several decades, our nation's overall population growth will be among middle-aged and older Americans, what has been referred to as the graying of America. "Population aging is a long-range trend that will characterize our society as we continue into the 21st century. It is a force we all will cope with for the rest of our lives," warns gerontologist Harry Moody.[1]

The different types of graphs introduced in this chapter demonstrate the many facets and challenges of our aging society. People have tended to talk about seniors as if they were a homogeneous group, but the different graphical techniques we illustrate here dramatize the wide variations in economic characteristics, living arrangements, and family status among people aged 65 and older. Most of the statistical information presented in this chapter is based on reports prepared by statisticians from the U.S. Census Bureau and other government agencies that gather information about the elderly in the United States and internationally.

Numerous graphing techniques are available to you, but here we focus on just a few of the most widely used ones in the social sciences. The first two, the pie chart and bar graph, are appropriate for nominal and ordinal variables. The next two, histograms and line graphs, are used with interval-ratio variables. We also discuss statistical maps and time-series charts. The statistical map is most often used with interval-ratio data. Finally, time-series charts are used to show how some variables change over time.

THE PIE CHART: RACE AND ETHNICITY OF THE ELDERLY

The elderly population of the United States is racially heterogeneous. As the data in Table 3.1 show, of the total 40,489,000 elderly (defined as persons 65 years and older) in 2009–2011, the two largest racial groups were whites (34.4 million)[2] and blacks (3.4 million).

A **pie chart** shows the differences in frequencies or percentages among the categories of a nominal or an ordinal variable. The categories are displayed as segments of a circle whose pieces add up to 100% of the total frequencies. The pie chart shown in Figure 3.1 displays the same information that Table 3.1 presents. Although you can inspect these data in Table 3.1, you can interpret the information more easily by seeing it presented in the pie chart in Figure 3.1. It shows that the elderly population is predominantly white (85%), followed by black (8.5%) Americans.

✓ *Learning*
Check

> *Notice that the pie chart contains all the information presented in the frequency distribution. Like the frequency distribution, charts have an identifying number, a title that describes the content of the figure, and a reference to a source. The frequency or percentage is represented both visually and in numbers.*

Pie chart   A graph showing the differences in frequencies or percentages among the categories of a nominal or an ordinal variable. The categories are displayed as segments of a circle whose pieces add up to 100% of the total frequencies.

Note that the percentages for several of the racial groups are about 3.5% or less. It might be better to combine categories—American Indian, Asian, Native Hawaiian—into an "other races" category. This will leave us with three distinct categories: White, Black, and Other and Two or More Races. The revised pie chart is presented in Figure 3.2. Confirm for yourself how the percentages are derived from Table 3.1. We can highlight the diversity of the elderly population by "exploding"

Table 3.1 Three-Year Estimates of the U.S. Population 65 Years and Over by Race, 2009–2011

Race	Frequency (f)	Percentage (%)
White alone	34,415,650	85.0
Black alone	3,441,565	8.5
American Indian alone	202,445	0.5
Asian alone	1,417,115	3.5
Native Hawaiian or Pacific Islander alone	40,489	0.1
Some other race alone	607,335	1.5
Two or more races combined	364,401	0.9
Total	40,489,000	100.0

Source: U.S. Census Bureau, *American Fact Finder*, 2011, Table S0103.

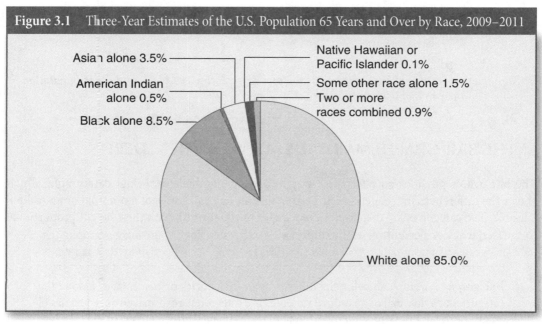

Figure 3.1 Three-Year Estimates of the U.S. Population 65 Years and Over by Race, 2009–2011

Source: U.S. Census Bureau, *American Fact Finder*, 2011, Table S01013.

the pie chart, moving the segments representing these groups slightly outward to draw them to the viewer's attention.

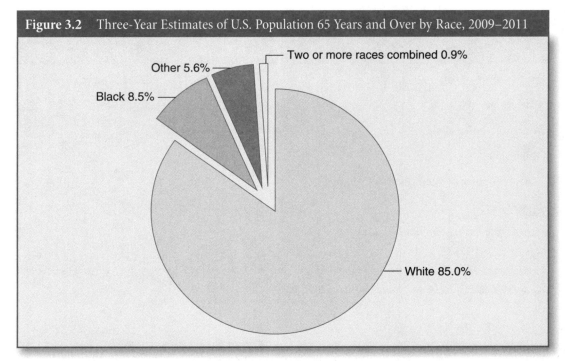

Figure 3.2   Three-Year Estimates of U.S. Population 65 Years and Over by Race, 2009–2011

Source: U.S. Census Bureau, *American Fact Finder*, 2011, Table S01013.

✓ *Learning*
Check

Note that we "exploded" the segment of the pies representing the black and other population groups in order to highlight the proportion of whites.

▣ THE BAR GRAPH: MARITAL STATUS OF THE ELDERLY

The **bar graph** provides an alternative way to present nominal or ordinal data graphically. It shows the differences in frequencies or percentages among categories of a nominal or an ordinal variable. The categories are displayed as rectangles of equal width with their height proportional to the frequency or percentage of the category.

Bar graph   A graph showing the differences in frequencies or percentages among the categories of a nominal or an ordinal variable. The categories are displayed as rectangles of equal width with their height proportional to the frequency or percentage of the category.

Let's illustrate the bar graph with an overview of the marital status of the elderly. Figure 3.3 is a bar graph displaying the percentage distribution of persons 65 years old and over by marital status in 2010. This chart is interpreted similar to a pie chart except that the categories of the variable are

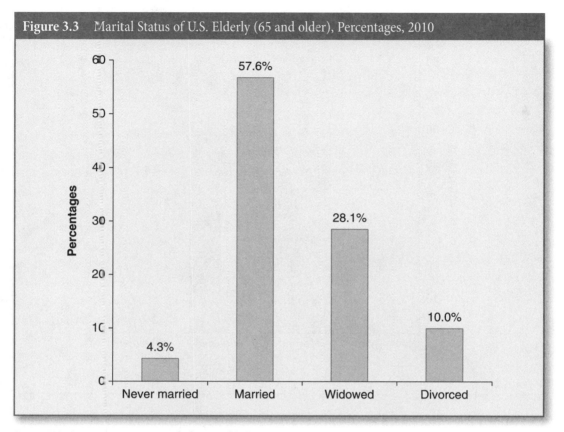

Figure 3.3 Marital Status of U.S. Elderly (65 and older), Percentages, 2010

Source: U.S. Census Bureau, *Statistical Abstract of the United States: 2012*, Table 34.

arrayed along the horizontal axis (sometimes referred to as the *X*-axis) and the percentages along the vertical axis (sometimes referred to as the *Y*-axis). This bar graph is easily interpreted: It shows that in 2010, 57.6% were married, 28.1% were widowed, 10% divorced, and 4.3% never married.

Construct a bar graph by first labeling the categories of the variables along the horizontal axis. For these categories, construct rectangles of equal width, with the height of each proportional to the frequency or percentage of the category. Note that a space separates each of the categories to make clear that they are nominal categories.

Bar graphs are often used to compare one or more categories of a variable among different groups. For example, the longevity of women is the major factor in the gender differences in marital and living arrangements.[3] In addition, elderly widowed men are more likely to remarry than elderly widowed women.

Suppose we want to show how the patterns in marital status differ between men and women. Figure 3.4 compares the marital status for women and men 65 years and older in 2010. We can also construct bar graphs horizontally, with the categories of the variable arrayed along the vertical axis and the percentages or frequencies displayed on the horizontal axis, as displayed in Figure 3.4. It clearly shows that elderly women are more likely than elderly men to be widowed and elderly men are more likely to be married than elderly women.

Figure 3.4   Marital Status of U.S. Elderly (65 and older) by Gender (Percentages), 2010

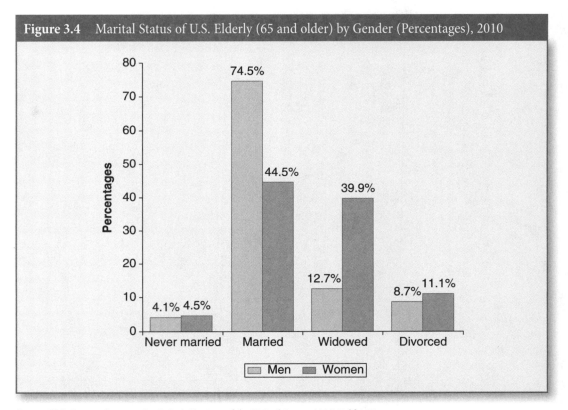

Source: U.S. Census Bureau, *Statistical Abstract of the United States: 2012*, Table 34.

▣ THE STATISTICAL MAP: THE GEOGRAPHIC DISTRIBUTION OF THE ELDERLY

Since the 1960s, the elderly have been relocating to the South and the West of the United States. It is projected that by 2020 these regions will increase their elderly population by as much as 80% (though recent census data reveal that the recession that began in 2008 has halted this dominant immigration trend). We can display these dramatic geographical changes in American society by using a statistical map. Maps are especially useful for describing geographical variations in variables, such as population distribution, voting patterns, crime rates, or labor force composition.

Let's look at Figure 3.5. It presents a statistical map, by state, of the percentage of the population 65 years and over for 2009–2011. The variable *percentage of the population* has four categories: less than 10%, 10% to 11.9%, 12% to 13.9%, and 14% or more. Each category is represented by a different shading (or color code), and the states are shaded depending on their classification into the different categories. To make it easier to read a map that you construct and to identify its patterns, keep the number of categories relatively small—say, not more than five.

Maps can also display geographical variations on the level of cities, counties, city blocks, census tracts, and other units. Your choice of whether to display variations on the state level or for smaller units will depend on the research question you wish to explore.

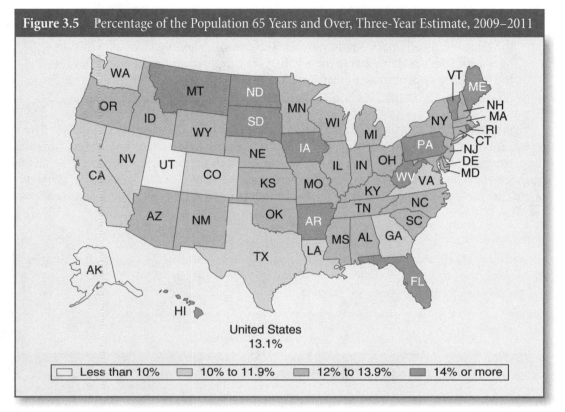

Figure 3.5   Percentage of the Population 65 Years and Over, Three-Year Estimate, 2009–2011

United States
13.1%

☐ Less than 10%   ☐ 10% to 11.9%   ☐ 12% to 13.9%   ☐ 14% or more

Source: U.S. Census Bureau, *American Fact Finder*, 2012, Table GCT0103.

✓ *Learning Check*

Can you think of a few other examples of data that could be described using a statistical map? What type of data are organized at the state level?

▣ THE HISTOGRAM

The **histogram** is used to show the differences in frequencies or percentages among categories of an interval-ratio variable. The categories are displayed as contiguous bars, with width proportional to the width of the category and height proportional to the frequency or percentage of that category. A histogram looks very similar to a bar chart except that the bars are contiguous to each other (touching) and may not be of equal width. In a bar chart, the spaces between the bars visually indicate that the categories are separate. Examples of variables with separate categories are *marital status* (married, single), *gender* (male, female), and *employment status* (employed, unemployed). In a histogram, the touching bars indicate that the categories or intervals are ordered from low to high in a meaningful way. For example, the categories of the variables *hours spent studying, age,* and *years of school completed* are contiguous, ordered intervals.

Histogram   A graph showing the differences in frequencies or percentages among the categories of an interval-ratio variable. The categories are displayed as contiguous bars, with width proportional to the width of the category and height proportional to the frequency or percentage of that category.

Figure 3.6 is a histogram displaying the percentage distribution of the population 55 years and over by age. To construct the histogram of Figure 3.6, arrange the age intervals along the horizontal axis and the percentages (or frequencies) along the vertical axis. For each age category, construct a bar with the height corresponding to the percentage of the elderly in the population in that age category. The width of each bar corresponds to the number of years that the age interval represents. The area that each bar

✓ *Learning*
 Check

When bar charts or histograms are used to display the frequencies of the categories of a single variable, the categories are shown on the X-axis and the frequencies on the Y-axis. In a horizontal bar chart or histogram, this is reversed.

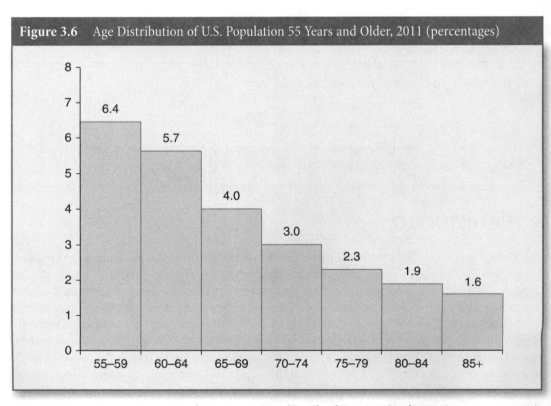

Figure 3.6   Age Distribution of U.S. Population 55 Years and Older, 2011 (percentages)

Source: U.S. Census Bureau, Current Population Survey, Annual Social and Economic Supplement, 2011.

occupies tells us the proportion of the population that falls into a given age interval. The histogram is drawn with the bars touching each other to indicate that the categories are contiguous. The percentages will not equal 100, as the total percent under 55 years of age (75.1%) is not represented in Figure 3.6.

▣ STATISTICS IN PRACTICE: GENDER AND AGE

We can also use the histogram to depict more complex trends. Let's consider for a moment some of these trends as described by Moody (2010):

Life expectancy at birth was 47 in 1900, but is now nearly 77. A hundred years ago, only 4% of the population was over the age of 65; today, that figure has jumped to 13%. The pace of growth has continued in the first decade of the 21st century, and soon the baby boom generation—those born between 1946 and 1964—will be moving into the ranks of senior citizens.[4]

The histogram can give us a visual impression of these demographic trends. For an illustration, let's look at Figures 3.7 and 3.8. Both are applications of the histogram. They examine, by gender, age distribution patterns in the U.S. population for 1955 and 2010 (projected). Note that in both figures, age groups are arranged along the vertical axis, whereas the frequencies (in millions of people) are along the horizontal axis. Each age group is classified by males on the left and females on the right. Because this type of histogram reflects age distribution by gender, it is also called an age-sex pyramid.

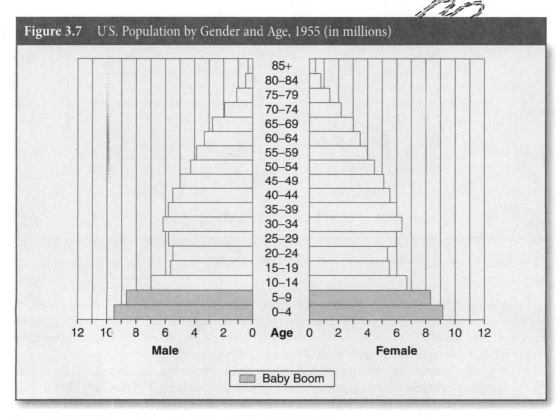

Figure 3.7 US. Population by Gender and Age, 1955 (in millions)

Source: U.S. Census Bureau, Current Population Reports, P23–178, 1992.

Visually compare the different pieces of data presented in these graphs. By observing where age groups are concentrated, you can discern major patterns in age distribution over time. Note the different shapes of Figures 3.7 and 3.8. Whereas in 1955 the largest group in the population was 0 to 9 years old, in 2010 the largest age group was 45 to 54 years old. These dramatic changes reflect the "graying" of the baby boom (born 1946–1965) generation. Almost 84 million babies were born in the United States from 1946 to 1965, which is 60% more than were born during the preceding two decades. In 2010, as the baby boom generation reached 45 to 64, the number of middle-aged and elderly Americans increased dramatically.

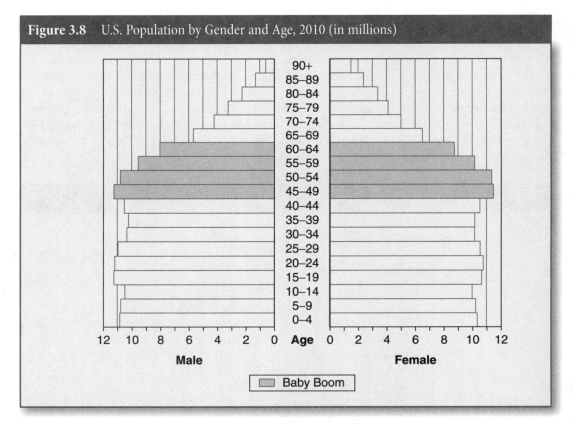

Figure 3.8   U.S. Population by Gender and Age, 2010 (in millions)

Source: U.S. Census Bureau, *Statistical Abstract of the United States: 2010*, Table 8.

Observe the differences in the number of men and women as age increases. These differences are especially noticeable in Figure 3.8. For example, between ages 70 and 74, women outnumber men 5:4.2; for those 85 years and over, women outnumber men almost 2:1. These differences reflect the fact that at every age male mortality exceeds female mortality.

Although the "graying" of America is a fact today, the age projections for the near future reveal that the younger generations, and particularly the so-called Generation Y (born 1980–1995), will have outnumbered the baby boom generation as early as by 2015. The population projections for

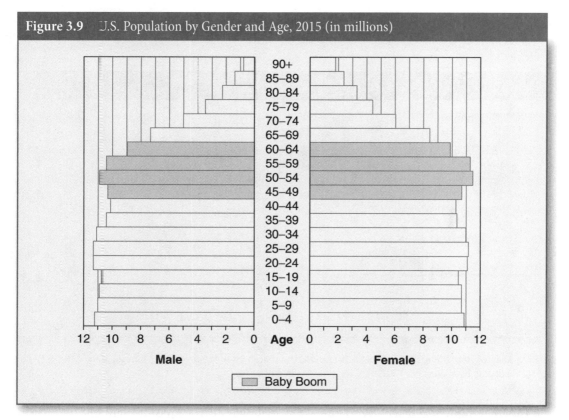

Figure 3.9   U.S. Population by Gender and Age, 2015 (in millions)

Source: U.S. Census Bureau, *Statistical Abstract of the United States: 2010,* Table 8.

2015 are presented in Figure 3.9. A major reason behind this phenomenon is "the large waves of migrants—legal and illegal—arriving [in the United States] since 1975," whose children have joined Generation Y and contribute to the younger population's challenge to the graying baby boomers.[5]

✓ *Learning Check*

Note that when we want to use the histogram to compare groups, we must show a histogram for each group (see Figures 3.7, 3.8, and 3.9). When we compare groups on the bar chart, we are able to compare two or more groups on the same bar chart (see Figure 3.4).

▣ THE LINE GRAPH

Numerical growth of the elderly population is taking place worldwide, occurring in both developed and developing countries. In 1994, 30 nations had elderly populations of at least 2 million; demographic projections indicate that there will be 55 such nations by 2020. Japan is one of the nations experiencing dramatic growth of its elderly population. Figure 3.10 is a line graph displaying the elderly population of Japan by age.

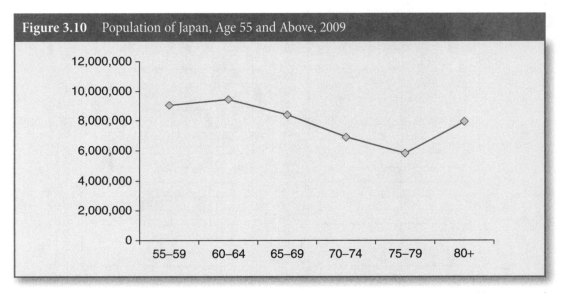

Figure 3.10   Population of Japan, Age 55 and Above, 2009

Source: Adapted from Ministry of Internal Affairs and Communications of Japan, Statistics Bureau, *Monthly Report April 2010*, Population Estimates.

The **line graph** is another way to display interval-ratio distributions; it shows the differences in frequencies or percentages among categories of an interval-ratio variable. Points representing the frequencies of each category are placed above the midpoint of the category and are joined by a straight line. Notice that in Figure 3.10 the age intervals are arranged on the horizontal axis and the frequencies along the vertical axis. Instead of using bars to represent the frequencies, however, points representing the frequencies of each interval are placed above the midpoint of the intervals. Adjacent points are then joined by straight lines.

Line graph   A graph showing the differences in frequencies or percentages among categories of an interval-ratio variable. Points representing the frequencies of each category are placed above the midpoint of the category and are joined by a straight line.

Both the histogram and the line graph can be used to depict distributions and trends of interval-ratio variables. How do you choose which one to use? To some extent, the choice is a matter of individual preference, but in general, line graphs are better suited for comparing how a variable is distributed across two or more groups or across two or more time periods. For example, Figure 3.11 compares the elderly population in Japan for 2000 with the projected elderly population for the years 2010 and 2020.

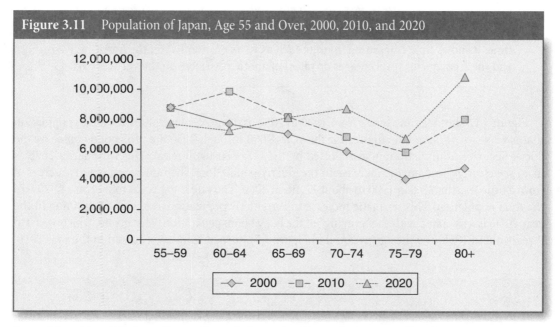

Figure 3.11 Population of Japan, Age 55 and Over, 2000, 2010, and 2020

Source: Adapted from U.S. Census Bureau, Center for International Research, International Database, 2007.

Let's examine this line graph. It shows that Japan's population of age 65 and over is expected to grow dramatically in the coming decades. According to projections, Japan's oldest-old population, those 80 years or older, is also projected to grow rapidly, from about 4.8 million (less than 4% of the total population) to 10.8 million (8.9%) by 2020. This projected rise has already led to a reduction in retirement benefits and other adjustments to prepare for the economic and social impact of a rapidly aging society.[6]

✓ *Learning Check*

Look closely at the line graph shown in Figure 3.11, comparing 2010 and 2020 data. How would you characterize the population increase among the Japanese elderly?

▣ TIME-SERIES CHARTS

We are often interested in examining how some variables change over time. For example, we may be interested in showing changes in the labor force participation of Latinas over the past decade, changes in the public's attitude toward abortion rights, or changes in divorce and marriage rates. A **time-series chart** displays changes in a variable at different points in time. It involves two variables: (1) *time*, which is labeled across the horizontal axis, and (2) another variable of interest whose values (frequencies, percentages, or rates) are labeled along the vertical axis. To construct a time-series chart, use a series of dots to mark the value of the variable at each time interval, and then join the dots by a series of straight lines.

Time-series chart   A graph displaying changes in a variable at different points in time. It shows time (measured in units such as years or months) on the horizontal axis and the frequencies (percentages or rates) of another variable on the vertical axis.

Figure 3.12 shows a time series from 1900 to 2050 of the percentage of the total U.S. population that is 65 years or older (the figures for the years 2000 through 2050 are projections made by the Social Security Administration, as reported by the U.S. Census Bureau). This time series enables us to see clearly the dramatic increase in the elderly population. The number of elderly increased from a little less than 5% in 1900 to about 12.4% in 2000. The rate is expected to increase to 20% of the total population. This dramatic increase in the elderly population, especially beginning in the year 2010, is associated with the "graying" of the baby boom generation. This group, which was 0 to 9 years old in 1955 (see the age pyramid in Figure 3.7), turned 55 to 64 years old in the year 2010.

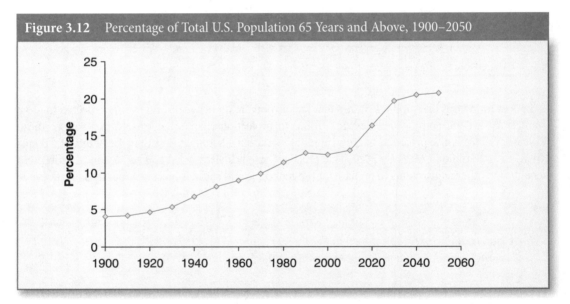

Figure 3.12   Percentage of Total U.S. Population 65 Years and Above, 1900–2050

Source: Federal Interagency Forum on Aging Related Statistics, *Older Americans 2004: Key Indicators of Well Being,* 2004.

The implications of these demographic changes are enormous. To cite just a few, there will be more pressure on the health care system and on private and public pension systems. In addition, because the voting patterns of the elderly differ from those of younger people, the "graying" of America will have major political effects.

Often, we are interested in comparing changes over time for two or more groups. Let's examine Figure 3.13, which charts the trends in the percentage of divorced elderly from 1960 to 2050 for men and women. This time-series graph shows that the percentage of divorced elderly men and elderly women was about the same until 2000. For both groups, the percentage increased from less than 2% in 1960 to about 5% in 1990.[7] According to projections, however, there will be significant increases in the percentage of men and especially women who are divorced: from 5% of all the elderly in 1990 to 8.4% of all elderly men and 13.6% of all elderly women by the year 2050. This sharp upturn and the gender divergence are clearly emphasized in Figure 3.13.

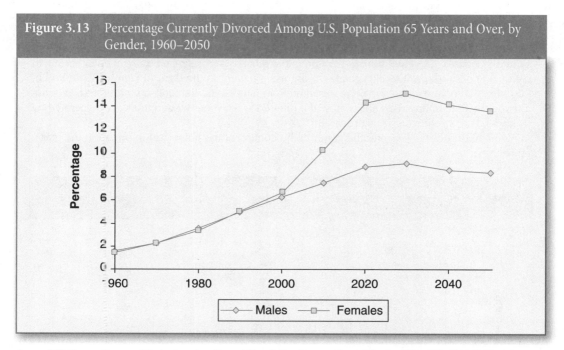

Figure 3.13   Percentage Currently Divorced Among U.S. Population 65 Years and Over, by Gender, 1960–2050

Source: U.S. Census Bureau, *65+ in America, Current Population Reports, Special Studies,* P23–190, 1996, Table 6-1.

✓ *Learning Check*

How does the time-series chart differ from a line graph? The difference is that line graphs display frequency distributions of a single variable, whereas time-series charts display two variables. In addition, time is always one of the variables displayed in a time-series chart.

🔲 **A Closer Look 3.1**
   A Cautionary Note: Distortions in Graphs

In this chapter, we have seen that statistical graphs can give us a quick sense of the main patterns in the data. However, graphs can not only quickly inform us, they can also quickly deceive us. Because we are often more interested in general impressions than in detailed analyses of the

(Continued)

(Continued)

numbers, we are more vulnerable to being swayed by distorted graphs. Edward Tufte in his 1983 book *The Visual Display of Quantitative Information* not only demonstrates the advantages of working with graphs but also offers a detailed discussion of some of the pitfalls in the application and interpretation of graphics.

Probably the most common distortions in graphical representations occur when the distance along the vertical or horizontal axis is altered either by not using 0 as the baseline (as demonstrated in Figures 3.14a and b) or in relation to the other axis. Axes may be stretched or shrunk to create any desired result to exaggerate or disguise a pattern in the data. In Figures 3.14a and b, 2009 international data on female representation in national parliaments are presented. Without altering the data in any way, notice how the difference between the countries is exaggerated by using 30 as a baseline (as in Figure 3.14b).

Remember: Always interpret the graph in the context of the numerical information the graph represents.

Figure 3.14   Female Representation in National Parliaments, 2009: (a) Using 0 as the Baseline and (b) Using 30 as the Baseline

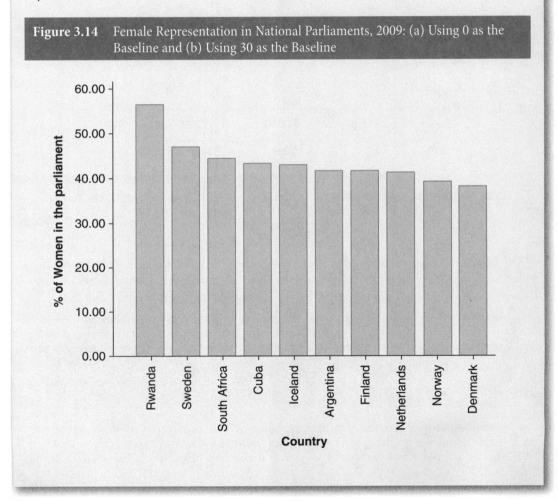

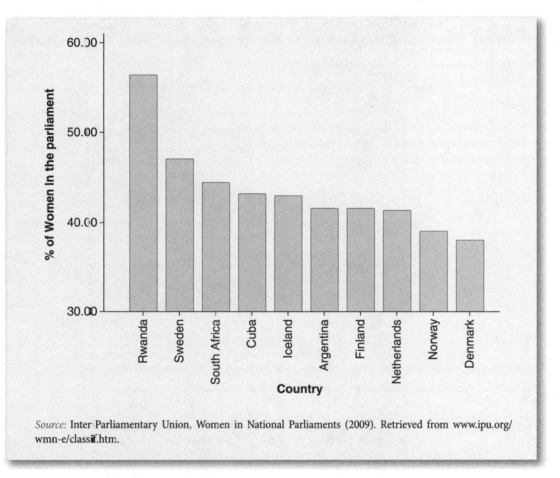

Source: Inter-Parliamentary Union, Women in National Parliaments (2009). Retrieved from www.ipu.org/wmn-e/classif.htm.

▣ STATISTICS IN PRACTICE: THE GRAPHIC PRESENTATION OF EDUCATION

We now illustrate some additional ways in which graphics can be used to highlight diversity visually. In particular, we show how graphs can help us (a) explore the differences and similarities among the many social groups coexisting within American society and (b) emphasize the rapidly changing composition of the U.S. population. Indeed, because of the heterogeneity of American society, the most basic question to ask when you look at data is "compared with what?" This question is not only at the heart of quantitative thinking[8] but underlies inclusive thinking as well.

Three types of graphs—the bar chart, the line graph, and the time-series chart—are particularly suitable for making comparisons among groups. In this section, we will take a closer look at educational attainment. Let's begin with the bar chart displayed in Figure 3.15. It compares the percentage of those with a college degree by race/ethnicity and gender. Overall, the group with the highest percentage of college graduates is Asian and Pacific Islanders. The group with

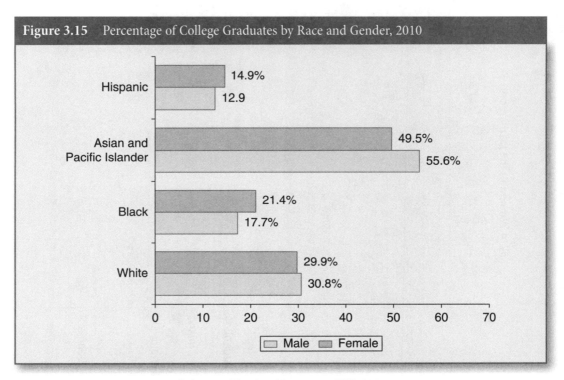

Figure 3.15   Percentage of College Graduates by Race and Gender, 2010

Source: U.S. Census Bureau, *Statistical Abstract of the United States: 2012*, Table 230.

the lowest is Hispanic. A higher percentage of white and Asian and Pacific Islander males had a college degree in comparison with white and Asian and Pacific Islander females. In contrast, a higher percentage of black and Hispanic females had a college degree compared with black and Hispanic males.

The line graph provides another way of looking at differences based on gender, race/ethnicity, or other attributes such as class, age, or sexual orientation. Figure 3.16 compares the educational attainment of three age cohorts, reflecting the development of mass education in the United States during the past 50 years.

The data illustrate that the percentage of Americans who completed 5 to 8 years of education has declined by age cohort, from 5% among Americans 55 years and older to 2.6% for those 25 to 34 years old. The corresponding trend illustrated in Figure 3.16 is the increase in the percentage of Americans who have completed 13 to 15 years or 16 years or more. The percent is highest at 34% among those 25 to 34 years of age and lowest (27.6%) for Americans 55 years or older.

Finally, Figure 3.17 is a time-series chart showing changes over time in college graduate rates among whites, blacks, Asian Pacific Islanders, and Hispanics.

To conclude, the three examples of graphs in this section as well as other examples throughout this chapter have illustrated how graphical techniques can portray the complexities of the social world by emphasizing the distinct characteristics of age, gender, and ethnic groups. By depicting similarities and differences, graphs help us better grasp the richness and complexities of the social world.

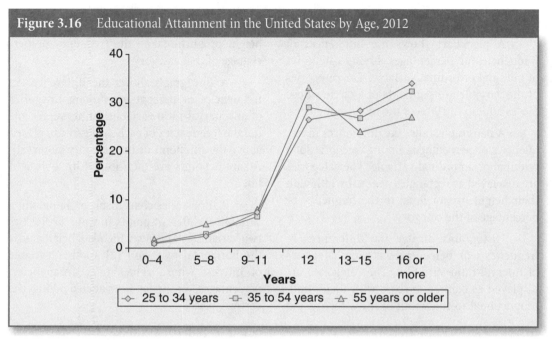

Figure 3.16 Educational Attainment in the United States by Age, 2012

Source: U.S. Census Bureau, *Educational Attainment,* CPS Historical Time Series Tables, 2012, Table A-1.

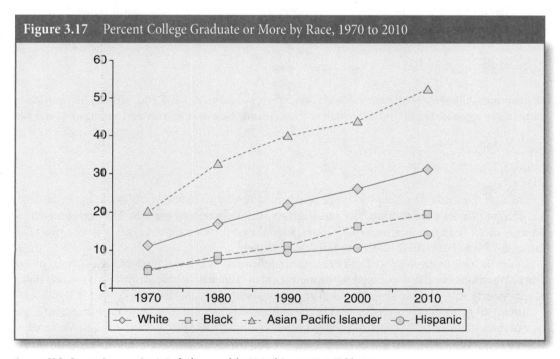

Figure 3.17 Percent College Graduate or More by Race, 1970 to 2010

Source: U.S. Census Bureau, *Statistical Abstract of the United States: 2012,* Table 229.

Note: Persons of Hispanic origin may be any race.

MAIN POINTS

- A pie chart shows the differences in frequencies or percentages among categories of nominal or ordinal variable. The categories of the variable are segments of a circle whose pieces add up to 100% of the total frequencies.

- A bar graph shows the differences in frequencies or percentages among categories of a nominal or an ordinal variable. The categories are displayed as rectangles of equal width with their height proportional to the frequency or percentage of the category.

- Histograms display the differences in frequencies or percentages among categories of interval-ratio variables. The categories are displayed as contiguous bars with their width proportional to the width of the category and height proportional to the frequency or percentage of that category.

- A line graph shows the differences in frequencies or percentages among categories of an interval-ratio variable. Points representing the frequencies of each category are placed above the midpoint of the category (interval). Adjacent points are then joined by a straight line.

- A time-series chart displays changes in a variable at different points in time. It displays two variables: (1) time, which is labeled across the horizontal axis, and (2) another variable of interest whose values (e.g., frequencies, percentages, or rates) are labeled along the vertical axis.

KEY TERMS

bar graph	line graph	time-series chart
histogram	pie chart	

⑤SAGE edge™

Sharpen your skills with SAGE edge at **edge.sagepub.com/frankfort7e**. **SAGE edge for students** provides a personalized approach to help you accomplish your coursework goals in an easy-to-use learning environment.

SPSS DEMONSTRATIONS

[HINTS12SSDS]

Demonstration 1: Producing a Bar Chart

SPSS for Windows greatly simplifies and improves the production of graphics. The program offers a separate choice from the main menu bar, *Graphs*, which lists more than a dozen types of graphs that SPSS can create. We will use HINTS12SSDS for this demonstration.

Under the *Graphs* menu select *Legacy Dialogs*, and then *Bar*, which will produce various types of bar charts. We will use bar charts to display the distribution of the nominal variable MaritalStatus (marital status of respondent). After clicking on *Bar*, you will be presented with the initial dialog box shown in Figure 3.18.

Almost all graphics procedures in SPSS begin with a dialog box that allows you to choose exactly the type of chart you want to construct. Many graph types can display more than one variable (the Clustered or Stacked choices). We will keep things simple here, so click on *Simple*, then on *Define*. When you do so, the main dialog box for simple bar charts opens (Figure 3.19).

The variable MaritalStatus should be placed in the box labeled "Category Axis." In the "Bars Represent" box, click on the "% of cases" radio button. This choice changes the default statistic from the number of

Figure 3.18 Bar Charts Dialog Box

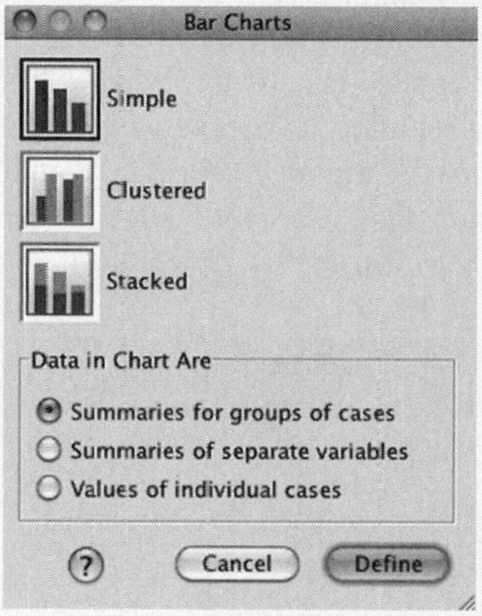

Figure 3.19 Simple Bar Charts Dialog Box

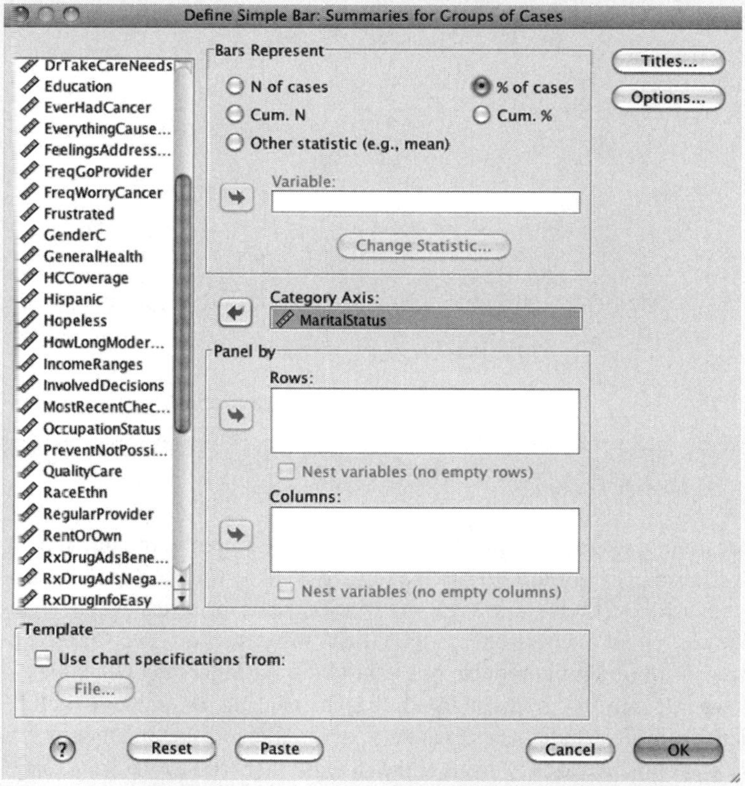

cases to percentages, which are normally more useful for comparison purposes. Click on *OK* to submit your request. (You should note that SPSS automatically excludes missing values. You can change this by clicking on *Options*. Click in the box labeled "Display groups defined by missing values" to turn on this choice. Then click on *Continue*, then on *OK* to submit your request to SPSS.)

The bar chart for MaritalStatus is presented in an output window labeled SPSS Viewer. You can see in Figure 3.20 that the bar chart for MaritalStatus has six bars because the only valid responses to this question are "married," "living as married," "divorced," "widowed," "separated," and "single, never been married."

SPSS graphs can be edited by selecting *Edit*, then *Edit Content*, *In Separate Window*, which moves the graph to its own window (*Chart Editor*) and displays various editing tools and choices.

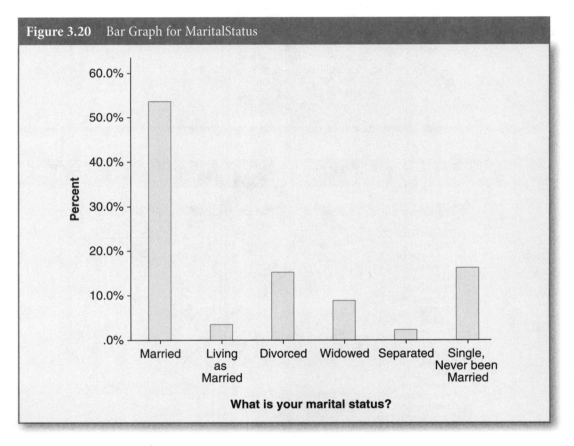

Figure 3.20 Bar Graph for MaritalStatus

Demonstration 2: Producing a Histogram

Histograms are used to display interval or ratio variables. We'll use the variable WhenDiagnosedCancer (age diagnosed with cancer) from the 2012 HINTS file. Under the *Graphs–Legacy Dialogs* menu in SPSS, select the *Histogram*. Click on these choices and you will see the dialog box shown in Figure 3.21.

Histograms are created for one variable at a time (that's why there was no opening dialog box as for bar charts). You simply insert (drag) the variable you want to display in the first empty box. You don't need to worry about missing values in histograms; unlike the bar chart default, SPSS automatically deletes them from the display. Notice that SPSS includes icons to indicate the level of measurement for each variable. Interval-ratio variables (or scale variables as SPSS refers to them) is matched with a ruler icon. Click on the *OK* button (on the bottom left-hand corner) to process this request. The resulting histogram is shown in Figure 3.22.

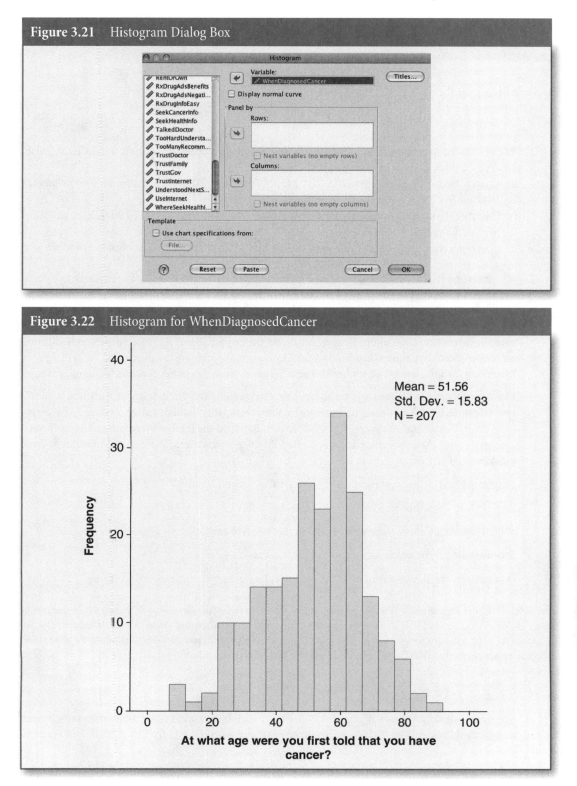

Figure 3.21 Histogram Dialog Box

Figure 3.22 Histogram for WhenDiagnosedCancer

Mean = 51.56
Std. Dev. = 15.83
N = 207

At what age were you first told that you have cancer?

SPSS automatically decided the appropriate width for each interval based on the range of the variable and the optimal number of bars to be displayed on a screen. The histogram also includes the calculation for mean and standard deviation, which will be discussed in Chapters 4 and 5.

SPSS PROBLEMS

[HINTS12SSDS]

1. You've decided to examine the differences in the age of male and female subjects in HINTS2012 data set. You examine AGEGRPA (age group of respondent).
   a. Construct a bar graph for AGEGRPA (*Hint:* From the SPSS menu, choose *Graphs–Legacy Dialogs–Bar.*).
   b. Construct bar graphs separately for men and women (insert the variable GENDERC in the Panel by/Columns box).
   c. Briefly describe overall age distribution and the difference in age groups between men and women.

2. Are individuals with higher educational attainment more likely to look for information about health or medical topics from any source? Construct separate pie charts for SeekHealthInfo (does respondent look for information about health or medical topics?). You will need to select *Pie* under *Graphs–Legacy Dialogs*. In the first dialog box, select "Summaries for groups of cases." Then, make sure you select *% of cases* under *Slices Represent.* In the box for *Define slices by,* insert SeekHealthInfo and in the *Panel by/Columns* box insert Education (degree). Compare the pie charts. What difference in seeking for information about health exists between the different educational (degree) groups?

3. Examine if there is a difference in responses between men and women in terms of their health condition (GeneralHealth) and their occupational status (OccupationStatus) and whether they have ever been diagnosed as having cancer (EverHadCancer). Based on the level of measurement for each variable, determine the appropriate graphic display. Produce separate graphs for men and women. What differences, if any, are evident in the data?

4. Determine how best to represent the following variables graphically:

   RentOrOwn—whether respondent rents or owns her/his house

   WhenDiagnosedCancer—age when first told that you had cancer

   IncomeRanges—annual family income of respondent

   QualityCare—how respondent rates the quality of health care she/he received in the last 12 months

Note: Before constructing the histogram or pie chart, you may want to review the variable by first using the *Frequencies* or *Utilities–Variables* command. The levels of measurement for several variables are mislabeled in SPSS. If you are using the *Utilities–Variables* option to review each variable and its level of measurement, you should confirm the level of measurement by reviewing the variable's frequency table (*Analyze–Descriptive–Frequencies*).

CHAPTER EXERCISES

1. The time-series chart shown in Figure 3.23 displays trends for presidential election voting rates by race and Hispanic origin 1996–2012. Analysts noted how for the first time in the 2012 Presidential election,

black voting rates exceeded the rates for non-Hispanic whites. Overall votes cast were higher in 2012 than 2008 (131,948,000 vs. 131,144,000—data not reported in the figure), an increase attributed to minority voters. Describe the variation in voting rates for the four racial and Hispanic origin groups.

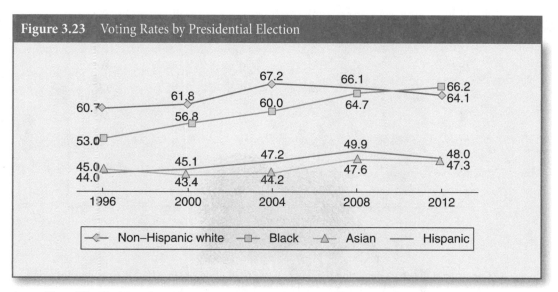

Figure 3.23 Voting Rates by Presidential Election

Source: Thom File, *The Diversifying Electorate—Voting Rates by Race and Hispanic Origin in 2012 (and other recent elections),* Current Population Survey (P20-568), 2013, Figure 1.

2. We selected a sample of people from the International Social Survey Program (ISSP) 2000. Raw data are presented for their sex (SEX), social class (CLASS), and number of household members (HOMPOP). CLASS is a subjective measure, with respondents indicating L = *lower*, W = *working*, M = *middle*, and U = *upper*.

Sex	Hompop	Class	Sex	Hompop	Class
F	1	L	F	2	U
F	3	W	M	2	M
F	1	M	F	4	W
M	2	M	M	2	U
F	3	M	M	4	M
M	2	U	M	4	W
F	7	L	M	2	M

(Continued)

(Continued)

Sex	Hompop	Class	Sex	Hompop	Class
M	3	M	F	1	W
M	4	M	M	2	U
F	1	M	M	4	W
F	2	M	F	7	M
M	5	L	M	3	M
M	4	M	M	4	M
M	4	L	F	4	M
M	3	W	F	5	L

a. Construct a pie chart depicting the percentage distribution of sex. (*Hint:* Remember to include a title, percentages, and appropriate labels.)

b. Construct a pie chart showing the percentage distribution of social class.

c. Construct a graph with two pie charts comparing the percentage distribution of social class membership by sex.

3. We continue our analysis of the U.S. elderly population, examining household income for 2010. A histogram is presented in Figure 3.24. Write a brief statement describing the data.

4. Using the data from Exercise 2, construct bar graphs showing percentage distributions for sex and class. Remember to include appropriate titles, percentages, and labels.

5. Suppose you want to compare the number of household members for women and men (based on the ISSP data in Exercise 2).

a. Construct a grouped bar graph (similar to Figure 3.4) to show the percentage distribution of the number of household members by sex.

b. Which group reported the largest family size?

c. Why shouldn't you construct a grouped bar chart showing the frequencies rather than the percentages?

6. Policy analysts have noted that the number of those without health insurance is increasing in the United States. Access to health insurance has been identified as an important social issue. Data from the National Center for Health Statistics (2013) are presented below (see Table 3.2), measuring the percent of persons with no health insurance for at least part of 2011 by selected characteristics. Note: Characteristic totals will not equal 100%.

a. What can be said about who did not have health insurance in 2011? How does the percentage of those without health insurance vary by each demographic characteristic?

b. For each variable, what would be the best way to graphically present the data?

Exercises

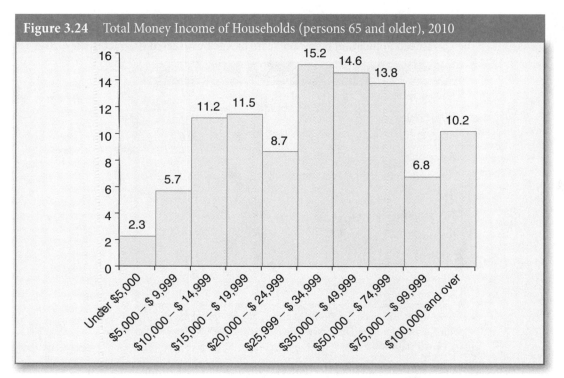

Figure 3.24　Total Money Income of Households (persons 65 and older), 2010

Source: U.S. Census Bureau, Current Population Survey, Annual Social and Economic Supplement, 2011.

Table 3.2　The Uninsured Population below 65 Years of Age by Selected Characteristics, 2011

Characteristic	Percentage
Age	
Below 18 years	7.0
18–44 years	25.4
45–64 years	15.4
Percent of the poverty level	
Below 100%	28.4
100–199%	30.0
200–399%	16.5
400% or more	5.2

(Continued)

Exercises

(Continued)

Table 3.2   The Uninsured Population below 65 Years of Age by Selected Characteristics, 2011

Characteristic	Percentage
Race origin	
White only	16.7
Black only	20.6
Asian only	16.5
American Indian or Alaska Native only	34.2
Two or more races	16.0
Geographic region	
Northeast	11.8
Midwest	13.4
South	20.4
West	20.0

Source: National Center for Health Statistics, *Health, United States, 2012: With Special Feature on Emergency Care* (Hyattsville, MD: National Center for Health Statistics, 2013).

7. Is racism in the past? This question was posed to 2010 General Social Survey respondents. Responses for 171 whites and 40 blacks are presented below. Construct a chart or graph that best displays this information. (Data could be presently separately by racial groups.)

Racism Is in the Past	White (f)	Black (f)
Strongly agree	28	6
Agree	64	6
Somewhat disagree	53	15
Strongly disagree	26	13
Total (N)	171	40

8. Data on educational attainment (percent of population by degree) for 2010 are presented separately for males and females.

	Not a High School Graduate	High School Graduate	Some College, but No Degree	Associate's Degree	Bachelor's Degree	Advanced Degree
Male	13.4	31.9	16.5	8.0	19.4	10.9
Female	12.4	30.7	17.1	10.2	19.4	10.2

Source: U.S. Census Bureau, *Statistical Abstract of the United States: 2012*, Table 231.

a. Construct a graph or chart that best displays this information.

b. Explain why the graph you selected is appropriate.

9. Use the data on educational level in Chapter 2, Exercise 4, for this problem.

   a. What level of measurement is "years of education"? Why can you use a histogram to graph the distribution of education, in addition to a bar chart?

   b. Construct a histogram for years of education, using equal-spaced intervals of 4 years. Don't use percentages in this chart.

10. The 2010 General Social Survey (GSS) data on educational level can be further broken down by race as follows:

   a. Construct two histograms for education, using percentages for whites ($N = 584$) and one for blacks ($N = 118$).

   b. Describe the differences in educational attainment by race.

Years of Education	Whites	Blacks
0	2	0
1	0	0
2	1	1
3	0	0
4	2	1
5	2	0
6	7	1
7	4	2
8	11	3
9	15	2
10	21	11
11	21	10
12	168	27
13	42	8
14	71	23
15	21	7
16	106	11
17	21	3
18	32	3
19	14	3
20	23	2

11. In Chapter 2, Exercise 6, we examined the amount of hours per week spent on e-mail among a subsample of GSS 2010 respondents. What would be the most appropriate graphic presentation for the data? Explain the reason for your answer.

E-mail Hours Per Week	Frequency
0	19
1	20
2	13
3	5
4	2
5	6
6	5
7	2
8	3
9	1
10 or more	23

12. Examine the bar chart representing the percentage of people speaking a language other than English at home as shown in Figure 3.25.
    a. Overall, which age group had the lowest percentage speaking a language other than English at home? Which age group had the highest?
    b. Describe the differences between the 2002 and 2008 percentages.

Figure 3.25 Percentage of People Speaking a Language Other Than English at Home Among the Population Aged 5 and Over, by Age, 2002 and 2008

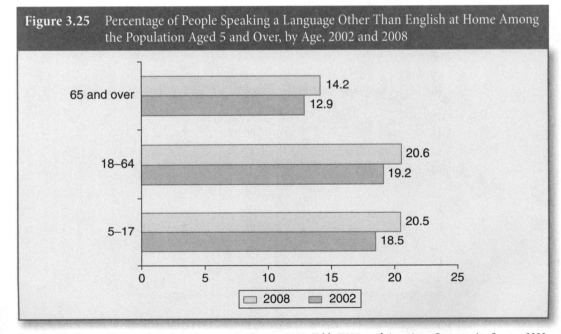

Source: U.S. Census Bureau, American Community Survey, 2002, Table P035, and American Community Survey, 2008, Table C16007.

13. Decide how to graphically present the GSS data on the number of children (by gender of respondent) from Chapter 2, Exercise 9.

   a. Would you choose to use bar charts or pie charts? Explain the reason for your answer.

   b. Construct your graph to represent all the data, including appropriate titles and labels.

14. The National Center for Education Statistics summarized the 2010 median annual earnings of full-time, full-year wage and salary workers ages 25–34 (refer to Figure 3.26). Write a brief summary of the difference in earnings between educational attainment categories and by sex of the worker. Which group has an earnings advantage?

Figure 3.26 Median Annual Earnings of Full-Time, Full-Year Wage and Salary Workers Ages 25–34, by Educational Attainment and Sex, 2010

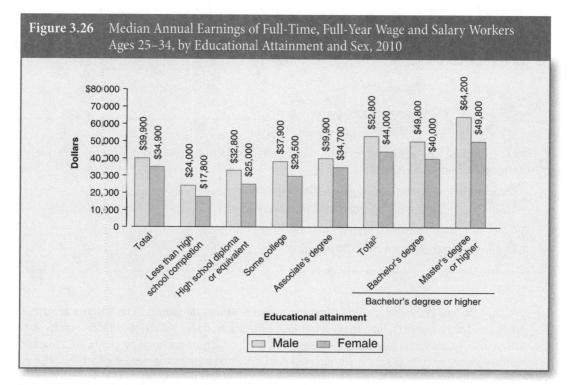

Source: National Center for Education Statistics, *The Condition of Education, 2012,* Figure 49-2.

Chapter 4

Measures of Central Tendency

Chapter Learning Objectives

❖ Defining all measures of central tendency, explaining their differences, relative strengths and weaknesses
❖ Determining the mode in a given distribution
❖ Finding or calculating the median and percentiles
❖ Calculating the mean
❖ Determining the shape of a distribution

In Chapters 2 and 3, we learned that frequency distributions and graphical techniques are useful tools for describing data. The main advantage of using frequency distributions or graphs is to summarize quantitative information in ways that can be easily understood even by a lay audience. Often, however, we need to describe a large set of data involving many variables for which graphs and tables may not be the most efficient tools. For instance, let's say that we want to present information on the income, education, and political party affiliation of both men and women. Presenting this information might require up to six frequency distributions or graphs. The more variables we add, the more complex the presentation becomes.

Another way of describing a distribution is by selecting a single number that describes or summarizes the distribution more concisely. Such numbers describe what is typical about the distribution, for example, the average income among Latinos who are college graduates or the most common party identification among the rural poor. Numbers that describe what is average or typical of the distribution are called measures of central tendency.

Measures of central tendency   Categories or scores that describe what is average or typical of the distribution.

In this chapter, we will learn about three measures of central tendency: the mode, the median, and the mean. You are probably somewhat familiar with these measures. The terms median income and average income, for example, are used quite a bit even in the popular media. Each describes what is most typical, central, or representative of the distribution. In this chapter, we will also learn about how these measures differ from one another. We will see that the choice of an appropriate measure of central tendency for representing a distribution depends on three factors: (1) the way the variables are measured (their level of measurement), (2) the shape of the distribution, and (3) the purpose of the research.

▣ THE MODE

The mode is the category or score with the largest frequency or percentage in the distribution. Of all the averages discussed in this chapter, the mode is the easiest one to identify. Simply locate the category represented by the highest frequency in the distribution.

Mode   The category or score with the highest frequency (or percentage) in the distribution.

We can use the mode to determine, for example, the most common foreign language spoken in the United States today. English is clearly the language of choice in public communication in the United States, but you may be surprised by the U.S. Census Bureau's finding that 1 out of every 5 people living in the United States speaks 1 of 155 different languages other than English at home. Record immigration from many countries since 1980 has contributed to a sharp increase in the number of people who speak a foreign language.[1]

What is the most common foreign language spoken in the United States today? To answer this question, look at Table 4.1, which lists the 10 most commonly spoken foreign languages in the United States and the number of people who speak each language. The table shows that Spanish is the most common; more than 35 million people speak Spanish. In this example, we refer to "Spanish" as the mode—the category with the largest frequency in the distribution.

Table 4.1   Ten Most Common Foreign Languages
Spoken in the United States, 2009

Language	Number of Speakers
Spanish	35,468,501
Chinese	2,600,150
Tagalog	1,513,734
French	1,305,503
Vietnamese	1,251,468
German	1,109,216
Korean	1,039,021
Russian	881,723
Arabic	845,396
Italian	753,992

Source: U.S. Census Bureau, *Statistical Abstract of the United States: 2012*,
Table 53.

The mode is always a category or score, *not* a frequency. Do not confuse the two. That is, the mode in the previous example is "Spanish," not its frequency of 35,468,501.

The mode is not necessarily the category with the majority (i.e., more than 50%) of cases, as it is in Table 4.1; it is simply the category in which the largest number (or proportion) of cases fall. For example, Figure 4.1 is a pie chart showing the answers of 2010 General Social Survey (GSS) respondents to the following question: "Would you say your own health, in general, is excellent, good, fair, or poor?" Note that the highest percentage (45.04) of respondents is associated with the answer "good." The answer "good" is therefore the mode.

The mode is used to describe nominal variables. Recall that with nominal variables—such as foreign languages spoken in the United States, race/ethnicity, or religious affiliation—we are only able to classify respondents based on a qualitative and not a quantitative property. By describing the most commonly occurring category of a nominal variable (such as Spanish in our example), the mode thus reflects the most important element of the distribution of a variable measured at the nominal level. The mode is the only measure of central tendency that can be used with nominal-level variables. It can also be used to describe the most commonly occurring category in any distribution. For example, the variable *health* presented in Figure 4.1 is an ordinal variable.

In some distributions, there are two scores or categories with the highest frequency. Such distributions have two modes and are said to be *bimodal*. For instance, Figure 4.2 is a bar graph showing the response of 2010 GSS respondents to the following question: "If you were asked to use one of four names for your social class, which would you say you belong to: the lower class, the working class, the middle class, or the upper class?" The same percentage of respondents (approximately 44%) identified themselves as "working class" or "middle class." Both response categories have the highest frequency, and therefore, both are the modes. We can describe this distribution as bimodal.

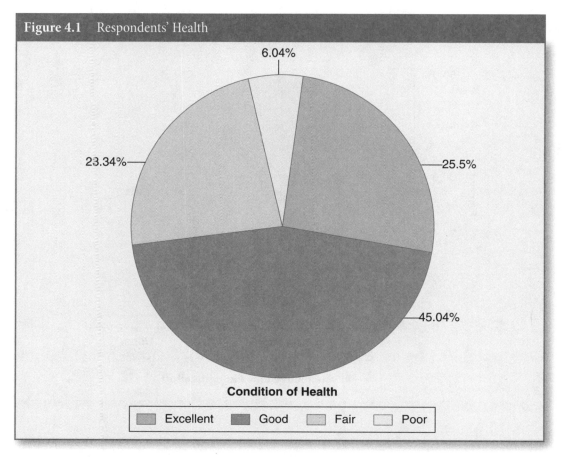

Figure 4.1 Respondents' Health

Source: Douglas S. Massey. "The Social and Economic Origins of Immigration," Annals, AAPSS (July 1990): 510.

When two scores or categories with the highest frequencies are quite close (but not identical) in frequency, the distribution is still "essentially" bimodal. In these situations, you should not rely on merely reporting the (true) mode, but instead report the two highest frequency categories.

✓ *Learning Check*

Listed below are the political party affiliations of 15 individuals. Find the mode.

Democrat	Republican	Democrat	Republican	Republican
Independent	Democrat	Democrat	Democrat	Republican
Independent	Democrat	Independent	Republican	Democrat

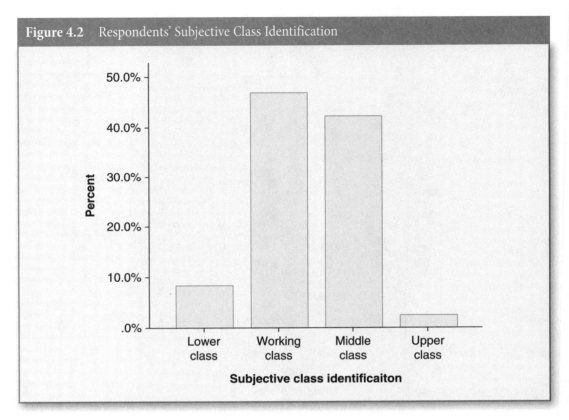

Figure 4.2 Respondents' Subjective Class Identification

◉ THE MEDIAN

The **median** is a measure of central tendency that can be calculated for variables that are at least at an ordinal level of measurement. The median represents the exact middle of a distribution; it is the score that divides the distribution into two equal parts so that half the cases are above it and half below it. For example, according to the U.S. Bureau of Labor Statistics, the median weekly earnings of full-time wage and salary workers in 2012 was $768.[2] This means that half the workers in the United States earned more than $768 a week and half earned less than $768. Since many variables used in social research are ordinal, the median is an important measure of central tendency.

Median   The score that divides the distribution into two equal parts so that half the cases are above it and half below it.

For instance, what are the opinions of Americans about their children's future? How can we describe their levels of confidence in their children's future? To answer this question, the 2010 GSS asked respondents what they thought their children's standard of living would be like when they reach their parent's current age. Respondents selected from the response options of "much better," "somewhat better," "about the same," "somewhat worse," or "much worse" (respondents without children were allowed to report "no children"). Ratings of parents' anticipated standard of living for their children is an ordered (ordinal) variable. Thus, to estimate the average rating, we need to use a measure of central tendency appropriate for ordinal variables. The median is a suitable measure for those variables whose categories or scores can be arranged in order of magnitude from the lowest to the highest. Therefore, the median can be used with ordinal or interval ratio variables, for which scores can be at least rank ordered, but cannot be calculated for variables measured at the nominal level.

Finding the Median in Sorted Data

It is very easy to find the median. In most cases, it can be done by a simple inspection of the sorted data. The location of the median score differs somewhat, depending on whether the number of observations is odd or even. Let's first consider two examples with an odd number of cases.

An Odd Number of Cases

Suppose we are looking at the responses of five people to the question, "Thinking about the economy, how would you rate economic conditions in this country today?" Following are the responses of these five hypothetical persons:

Poor
Good
Only fair
Poor
Excellent
Total (N) = 5

To locate the median, first arrange the responses in order from the lowest to the highest (or the highest to the lowest):

Poor
Poor
Only fair
Good
Excellent
Total (N) = 5

The median is the response associated with the middle case. Find the middle case when N is odd by adding 1 to N and dividing by 2: $(N + 1)/2$. Since N is 5, you calculate $(5 + 1)/2 = 3$. The middle case is thus the third case, and the median is "only fair," the response associated with the third case. Notice that the median divides the distribution exactly in half so that there are two respondents who are more satisfied and two respondents who are less satisfied.

Now let's look at another example. The following is a list of the number of hate crimes reported in the nine most populous U.S. states in the year 2011.[3]

Number
1,204
189
566
139
89
60
277
417
21
Total (N) = 9

To locate the median, first arrange the number of hate crimes in order from the lowest to the highest: The middle case is $(9 + 1)/2 = 5$, the fifth state, Texas. The median is 189, the number of hate crimes associated with Texas. It divides the distribution exactly in half so that there are four states with fewer hate crimes and four with more (this is illustrated in Figure 4.3a).

Number
21
60
89
139
189
277
417
566
1,204
Total (N) = 9[a]

a. The states associated with the number of hate crimes listed above (in the same order of the listing) are Georgia, Pennsylvania, Illinois, Florida, Texas, Ohio, Michigan, New York, and California.

Figure 4.3 Finding the Median Number of Hate Crimes for (a) Nine States and (b) Eight States

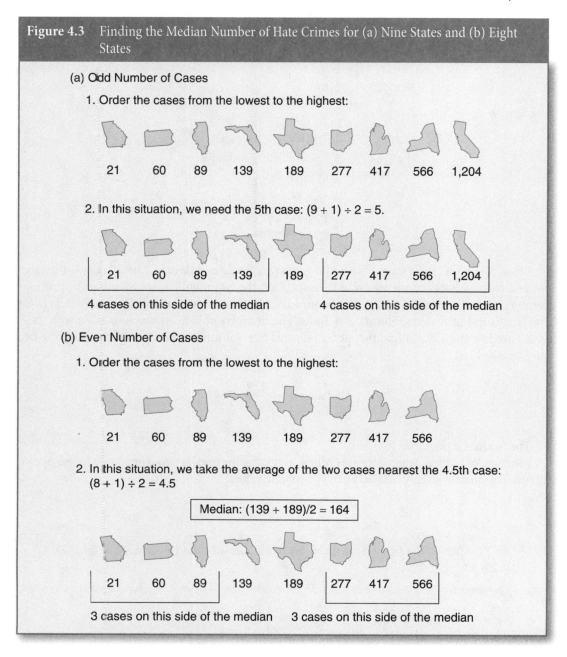

(a) Odd Number of Cases

    1. Order the cases from the lowest to the highest:

| 21 | 60 | 89 | 139 | 189 | 277 | 417 | 566 | 1,204 |

    2. In this situation, we need the 5th case: $(9 + 1) \div 2 = 5$.

| 21 | 60 | 89 | 139 | 189 | 277 | 417 | 566 | 1,204 |

    4 cases on this side of the median   4 cases on this side of the median

(b) Even Number of Cases

    1. Order the cases from the lowest to the highest:

| 21 | 60 | 89 | 139 | 189 | 277 | 417 | 566 |

    2. In this situation, we take the average of the two cases nearest the 4.5th case: $(8 + 1) \div 2 = 4.5$

Median: $(139 + 189)/2 = 164$

| 21 | 60 | 89 | 139 | 189 | 277 | 417 | 566 |

    3 cases on this side of the median   3 cases on this side of the median

An Even Number of Cases

Now let's delete the last score to make the number of states even (Figure 4.3b). The scores have already been arranged in ascending order.

Again, to locate the median, first arrange the number of hate crimes in order from the lowest to the highest:

Number
21
60
89
139
189
277
417
566
Total (N) = 8

When N is even (eight states), we no longer have a single middle case. The median is therefore located halfway between the two middle cases. Find the two middle cases by using the previous formula: $(N + 1)/2$, or $(8 + 1)/2 = 4.5$. In our example, this means that you average the scores for the fourth and fifth states, Florida and Texas. The numbers of hate crimes associated with these states are 139 and 189. To find the median for this interval-ratio variable, simply average the two middle numbers:

$$\text{Median} = \frac{139 + 189}{2} = 164$$

The median is therefore 164.

As a note of caution, when data are ordinal, averaging the middle two scores is no longer appropriate. The median simply falls between two middle values.

✓ *Learning*
Check

Find the median of the following distribution of an interval-ratio variable: 22, 15, 18, 33, 17, 5, 11, 28, 40, 19, 8, 20.

Finding the Median in Frequency Distributions

Often our data are arranged in frequency distributions. Take, for instance, the frequency distribution displayed in Table 4.2. It shows the political views of GSS respondents in 2010.

To find the median, we need to identify the category associated with the observation located at the middle of the distribution. We begin by specifying N, the total number of respondents. In this particular example, $N = 1,457$. We then use the formula $(N + 1)/2$, or $(1,457 + 1)/2 = 729$. The median is the value of the category associated with the 729th case. The cumulative frequency (Cf)

Table 4.2   Political Views of GSS Respondents, 2010

Political View	Frequency (f)	Cf	Percentage	C%
Extremely liberal	57	57	3.9	3.9
Liberal	168	225	11.5	15.4
Slightly liberal	187	412	12.8	28.3
Moderate	535	947	36.7	65.0
Slightly conservative	213	1,160	14.6	79.6
Conservative	239	1,399	16.4	96.0
Extremely conservative	58	1,457	4.0	100.0
Total (N)	1,457		100.0	

of the 729th case falls in the category "moderate"; thus, the median is "moderate." This may seem odd; however, the median is always the value of the response category, not the frequency.

A second approach to locating the median in a frequency distribution is to use the cumulative percentages column, as shown in the last column of Table 4.2. In this example, the percentages are cumulated from "extremely liberal" to "extremely conservative." We could also cumulate the other way, from "extremely conservative" to "extremely liberal." To find the median, we identify the response category that contains a cumulative percentage value equal to 50%. The median is the value of the category associated with this observation.[4] Looking at Table 4.2, the percentage value equal to 50% falls within the category "moderate." The median for this distribution is therefore "moderate." If you are not sure why the middle of the distribution—the 50% point—is associated with the category "moderate," look again at the cumulative percentage column (C%). Notice that 28.3% of the observations are accumulated below the category "moderate" and that 65.0% are accumulated up to and including the category "moderate." We know, then, that the percentage value equal to 50% is located somewhere within the "moderate" category.

For a review of cumulative distributions, refer to Chapter 2.

✓ *Learning Check*

▣ STATISTICS IN PRACTICE: GENDERED INCOME INEQUALITY

We can use the median to compare groups. Consider the significant changes that have taken place during the past few decades in the income levels of men and women in the United States. Income levels profoundly influence our lives both socially and economically. Higher income is associated with increased education and work experience for both men and women.

Figure 4.4 compares the median incomes for men and women in 1973 and in 2011. Because the median is a single number summarizing central tendency in the distribution, we can use it to note differences between subgroups of the population or changes over time. In this example, the

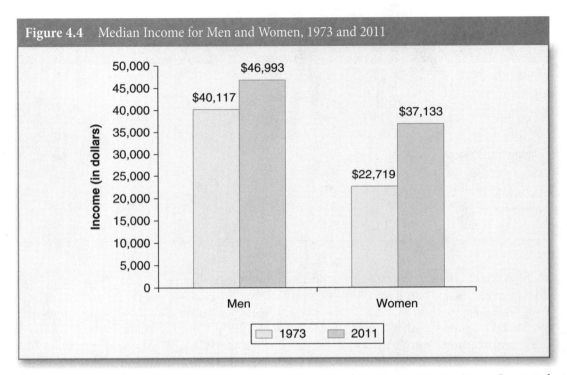

Figure 4.4 Median Income for Men and Women, 1973 and 2011

Sources: Data for 1973 obtained from the U.S. Census Bureau, Current Population Reports P60–226, *Income, Poverty and Health Insurance Coverage in the United States: 2003*. Data for 2011 obtained from the U.S. Census Bureau, American Community Survey, 2011.

increase in median income from 1973 to 2011 clearly shows a significant income gain for women. However, that said, in 2011 women still made, on average, about $10,000 less than men ($37,133 vs. $46,993, respectively).

✓ *Learning Check*

Examine Figure 4.4 and contrast the median incomes of women and men over the three decades. What can you learn about gender and income?

Locating Percentiles in a Frequency Distribution

The median is a special case of a more general set of measures of location called *percentiles*. A **percentile** is a score at or below which a specific percentage of the distribution falls. The *n*th percentile is a score below which *n*% of the distribution falls. For example, the 75th percentile is a score that divides the distribution so that 75% of the cases are below it. The median is the

50th percentile. It is a score that divides the distribution so that 50% of the cases fall below it. Like the median, percentiles require that data be ordinal or higher in level of measurement. Percentiles are easy to identify when the data are arranged in frequency distributions.

Percentile   A score below which a specific percentage of the distribution falls.

To help illustrate how to locate percentiles in a frequency distribution, we display in Table 4.3 the frequency distribution, the percentage distribution, and the cumulative percentage distribution of opinion about police job performance of respondents for the 2008 Monitoring the Future (MTF) survey.

The 50th percentile (the median) is "Fair," meaning that 50% of the respondents view police job performance above "Fair" and 50% of the respondents view police job performance as "Fair" or below "Fair" (as you can see from the cumulative percentage column, 50% falls somewhere in the third category, associated with the category "Fair"). Similarly, the 20th percentile is "Poor" because 20% of the respondents view police job performance as "Poor" or below "Poor."

Percentiles are widely used to evaluate relative performance on standardized achievement tests, such as the SAT or ACT. Let's suppose that your ACT score was 29. To evaluate your performance for the college admissions officer, the testing service translated your score into a percentile rank. Your percentile rank was determined by comparing your score with the scores of all other students who took the test at the same time. Suppose for a moment that 90% of all students received a lower ACT score than you (and 10% scored above you). Your percentile rank would have been 90. If, however, there were more students who scored better than you—let's say that 15% scored above you and 85% scored lower than you—your percentile rank would have been 85.

Another widely used measure of location is the *quartile*. The lower quartile is equal to the 25th percentile and the upper quartile is equal to the 75th percentile. (Can you locate the upper quartile in Table 4.3?) A college admissions office interested in accepting the top 25% of its applicants based on their SAT scores could calculate the upper quartile (the 75th percentile) and accept everyone whose score is equivalent to the 75th percentile or higher. (Note that they would be calculating percentiles based on the scores of their applicants, not of all students in the nation who took the SAT.)

Table 4.3   Frequency Distribution for Police Job Performance: 2008 MTF Respondents

Police Job Performance	Frequency (f)	Percentage	C%
Very poor	125	9.9	9.9
Poor	201	15.9	25.8
Fair	452	35.7	61.5
Good	380	30.0	91.5
Very good	108	8.5	100.0
Total (N)	1,266	100.0	

▣ THE MEAN

The arithmetic **mean** is by far the best known and most widely used measure of central tendency. The mean is what most people call the "average." The mean is typically used to describe central tendency in interval-ratio variables such as income, age, and education. You are probably already familiar with how to calculate the mean. Simply add up all the scores and divide by the total number of scores.

Mean   A measure of central tendency that is obtained by adding up all the scores and dividing by the total number of scores. It is the arithmetic average.

Firearm statistics, for example, can be analyzed using the mean. Table 4.4 shows the 2011 gun ownership rates (per 100 population) for 15 of the most populous countries in the world. We want to summarize the information presented in this table by calculating some measure of central tendency. Because the variable "gun ownership rate" is an interval-ratio variable, we will select the arithmetic mean as our measure of central tendency.

To find the mean gun ownership rate (number of guns per 100 people) for the data presented in Table 4.4, add up the gun ownership rates for all the countries and divide the sum by the number of countries:

$$\text{Mean} = \frac{\begin{matrix}(4.9+4.2+88.8+0.5+8.0+11.6+1.5+\\8.9+0.6+15.0+1.7+3.5+30.3+12.5+7.3)\end{matrix}}{15} = \frac{199}{15} = 13.3$$

The mean gun ownership rate for 15 of the most populous countries in the world is 13.3.[5] That means in these 15 countries, the average number of guns per 100 people is 13.3.

Table 4.4   2011 Gun Ownership Rates per 100 People for 15 of the Most Populous Countries

Country	Gun Ownership Rate per 100 Population
China	4.9
India	4.2
United States	88.8
Indonesia	0.5
Brazil	8.0
Pakistan	11.6

Country	Gun Ownership Rate per 100 Population
Nigeria	1.5
Russia	8.9
Japan	0.6
Mexico	15.0
Vietnam	1.7
Egypt	3.5
Germany	30.3
Turkey	12.5
Iran	7.3

Source: United Nations Office on Drugs and Crime, *2011 Annual Report.*

Calculating the Mean

Another way to calculate the arithmetic mean is to use a formula. Beginning with this section, we introduce a number of formulas that will help you calculate some of the statistical concepts that we are going to present. A formula is a shorthand way to explain what operations we need to follow to obtain a certain result. So instead of saying "add all the scores together and then divide by the number of scores," we can define the mean by the following formula:

$$\bar{Y} = \frac{\Sigma Y}{N} \tag{4.1}$$

Let's take a moment to consider these new symbols because we continue to use them in later chapters. We use Y to represent the raw scores in the distribution of the variable of interest; $\bar{Y}$ is pronounced "Y-bar" and is the mean of the variable of interest. The symbol represented by the Greek letter Σ is pronounced "sigma," and it is used often from now on. It is a summation sign (just like the + sign) and directs us to sum whatever comes after it. Therefore, ΣY means "add up all the raw Y scores." Finally, the letter N, as you know by now, represents the number of cases (or observations) in the distribution.

Let's summarize the symbols as follows:

Y = the raw scores of the variable Y

$\bar{Y}$ = the mean of Y

ΣY = the sum of all the Y scores

N = the number of observations or cases

Now that we know what the symbols mean, let's work through another example. The following are the ages of the 10 students in a graduate research methods class:

21, 32, 23, 41, 20, 30, 36, 22, 25, 27

What is the mean age of the students?

For these data, the ages included in this group are represented by Y; $N = 10$, the number of students in the class; and ΣY is the sum of all the ages:

$$\Sigma Y = 21 + 32 + 23 + 41 + 20 + 30 + 36 + 22 + 25 + 27 = 277$$

Thus, the mean age is

$$\bar{Y} = \frac{\Sigma Y}{N} = \frac{277}{10} = 27.7$$

The mean can also be calculated when the data are arranged in a frequency distribution. We have presented an example involving a frequency distribution in A Closer Look 4.1.

▣ A Closer Look 4.1
Finding the Mean in a Frequency Distribution

When data are arranged in a frequency distribution, we must give each score its proper weight by multiplying it by its frequency. We can use the following modified formula to calculate the mean:

$$\bar{Y} = \frac{\Sigma f Y}{N}$$

where

Y = the raw scores of the variable Y

$\bar{Y}$ = the mean of Y

$\Sigma f Y$ = the sum of all the fYs

N = the number of observations or cases

We now illustrate how to calculate the mean from a frequency distribution using the preceding formula. In the 2010 GSS, respondents were asked about what they think is the ideal number of children for a family. Their responses are presented in the following table.

Ideal Number of Children: GSS 2010

Number of Children (Y)	Frequency (f)	Frequency × Y (f Y)
0	8	0
1	29	29
2	477	954
3	238	714
4	83	332
5	18	90
6	9	54
Total	$N = 862$	$\Sigma fY = 2{,}173$

Notice that to calculate the value of ΣfY (Column 3), each score (Column 1) is multiplied by its frequency (Column 2), and the products are then added together. When we apply the formula

$$\bar{Y} = \frac{\Sigma f Y}{N} = \frac{2{,}173}{862} = 2.52$$

we find that the mean for the ideal number of children is 2.52.

If you are having difficulty understanding how to find the mean in a frequency distribution, examine this table. It explains the process without using any notation.

✓ *Learning Check*

Finding the Mean in a Frequency Distribution

	Number of people per house	Number of houses like this	Number of people such houses contribute
	1	3	3
	2	5	10
	3	1	3
	4	1	4

Total number of peple: 20
Total number of houses: 10
Mean number of people per house: 20/10 = 2

(Continued)

(Continued)

Here is another example. The following tables are frequency distributions of years of education for American Indians or Alaska Natives and Hispanic American GSS 2010 respondents. Calculate the mean level of education for each of the two groups by applying the formula for calculating the mean in a frequency distribution.

Years of Education for American Indians or Alaska Natives: GSS 2010

Education (Y)	Frequency (f)	Frequency × Y (fY)
4	1	4
8	1	8
11	3	33
12	3	36
13	2	26
14	2	28
16	1	16
Total	$N = 13$	$\Sigma fY = 151$
	$\overline{Y} = 11.62$	

Years of Education for Hispanic Respondents: GSS 2010

Education (Y)	Frequency (f)	Frequency × Y (fY)
4	2	8
6	3	18
7	1	7
8	2	16
9	4	36
11	7	77
12	13	156
13	6	78
14	5	70
15	2	30
16	5	80
17	1	17
Total	$N = 51$	$\Sigma fY = 593$
	$\overline{Y} = 11.63$	

Examine the tables showing years of education for American Indians or Alaska Natives and Hispanic respondents. Note the similarities and differences between the two groups. Education is a major component of social class. You may want to take your analysis one step further. SPSS Problem 3 at the end of this chapter provides specific instructions that will help you explore the relationship between social class and the number of children that couples decided to have.

✓ *Learning*
Check

The following distribution is the same as the one you used to calculate the median in an earlier Learning Check: 22, 15, 18, 33, 17, 5, 11, 28, 40, 19, 8, 20. Calculate the mean. Is it the same as the median, or is it different?

Understanding Some Important Properties of the Arithmetic Mean

The following three mathematical properties make the mean the most important measure of central tendency. It is, in fact, a concept that is basic to numerous and more complex statistical operations.

Interval-Ratio Level of Measurement

Because it requires the mathematical operations of addition and division, the mean can be calculated only for variables measured at the interval-ratio level. This is the only level of measurement that provides numbers that can be added and divided.

Center of Gravity

Because the mean (unlike the mode and the median) incorporates all the scores in the distribution, we can think of it as the center of gravity of the distribution. That is, the mean is the point that perfectly balances all the scores in the distribution. If we subtract the mean from each score and add up all the differences, the sum will always be zero!

✓ *Learning*
Check

Why is the mean considered the center of gravity of the distribution? Think of the last time you were in a park on a seesaw (it may have been a long time ago) with a friend who was much heavier than you. You were left hanging in the air until your friend moved closer to the center. In short, to balance the seesaw a light person far away from the center (the mean) can balance a heavier person who is closer to the center. Can you illustrate this principle with a simple income distribution?

Sensitivity to Extremes

The examples we have used to show how to compute the mean demonstrate that, unlike with the mode or the median, every score enters into the calculation of the mean. This property makes the mean sensitive to extreme scores in the distribution. The mean is pulled in the direction of either very high or very low values. A glance at Figure 4.5 should convince you of that. Figures 4.5a and b show the incomes of 10 individuals. In Figure 4.5b, the income of one individual has shifted from $5,000 to $35,000. Notice the effect it has on the mean; it shifts from $3,000 to $6,000! The mean is disproportionately affected by the relatively high income of $35,000 and is misleading as a measure of central tendency for this distribution. Notice that the median's value is not affected by this extreme score; it remains at $3,000. Thus, the median gives us better information on the typical income for this group.

Illustrating the Seesaw Principle

a. Three people, weights 60, 120, and 180, all stand on a seesaw. The fulcrum is placed at 120. The mean is (60 + 120 + 180)/3. The seesaw balances.

060 070 080 090 100 110 120 130 140 150 160 170 180 190 200 210 220 230 240

b. The 180-pound person is replaced by a 240-pound person, but we do not move the fulcrum. The seesaw slowly falls to the right.

060 070 080 090 100 110 120 130 140 150 160 170 180 190 200 210 220 230 240

c. We move the fulcrum to 140. The new mean is (60 + 120 + 240)/3. The seesaw balances again.

060 070 080 090 100 110 120 130 140 150 160 170 180 190 200 210 220 230 240

In the next section, we will see that because of the sensitivity of the mean, it is not suitable as a measure of central tendency in distributions that have a few very extreme values on one side of the distribution. (A few extreme values are no problem if they are not mostly on one side of the distribution.)

✓ *Learning*
Check

When asked to choose the appropriate measure of central tendency for a distribution, remember that the level of measurement is not the only consideration. When variables are measured at the interval-ratio level, the mean is usually the measure of choice, but remember that extreme scores in one direction make the mean unrepresentative and the median or mode may be the better choice.

Figure 4.5 The Value of the Mean Is Affected by Extreme Scores: (a) No Extreme Scores and (b) One Extreme Score

(a) No extreme scores: The mean is $3,000

Income (Y)	Frequency (f)	fY
1,000	1	1,000
2,000	2	4,000
3,000	4	12,000
4,000	2	8,000
5,000	1	5,000
	$N = 10$	$\Sigma fY = 30,000$

$$\text{Mean} = \frac{\Sigma fY}{N} = \frac{30,000}{10} = \$3,000$$

Median = $3,000

(b) One extreme score: The mean is $6,000

Income (Y)	Frequency (f)	fY
1,000	1	1,000
2,000	2	4,000
3,000	4	12,000
4,000	2	8,000
35,000	1	35,000
	$N = 10$	$\Sigma fY = 60,000$

$$\text{Mean} = \frac{\Sigma fY}{N} = \frac{60,000}{10} = \$6,000$$

Median = $3,000

▣ THE SHAPE OF THE DISTRIBUTION: TELEVISION, EDUCATION, AND SIBLINGS

In this chapter, we have looked at the way in which the mode, median, and mean reflect central tendencies in the distribution. Distributions (this discussion is limited to distributions of interval-ratio variables) can also be described by their general shape, which can be easily represented visually. A distribution can be either symmetrical or skewed, depending on whether there are a few extreme values at one end of the distribution.

A distribution is **symmetrical** (Figure 4.6a) if the frequencies at the right and left tails of the distribution are identical, so that if it is divided into two halves, each will be the mirror image of the other. In a unimodal, symmetrical distribution, the mean, median, and mode are identical.

Symmetrical distribution   The frequencies at the right and left tails of the distribution are identical; each half of the distribution is the mirror image of the other.

We can illustrate the differences among the three types of distributions by examining three variables in the 2010 GSS.[6] The frequency distributions for these three variables are presented in Tables 4.5 through 4.7, and the corresponding graphs are depicted in Figures 4.7 through 4.9.

The Symmetrical Distribution

First, let's examine Table 4.5 and Figure 4.7, displaying the distribution of the number of hours per day spent watching television. Notice that the largest number (247) watch television 2 hours/day (mode = 2.0), and about a fairly similar number (204 and 188, respectively) reported either 1 or 3 hours of watching television per day. As shown in Figure 4.7, the mode, the median, and the mean are almost identical, and they coincide at about the middle of the distribution.

The distribution of number of hours spent per week watching television in Table 4.5 and Figure 4.7 is a nearly symmetrical distribution with the mean, the median, and the mode being almost identical.

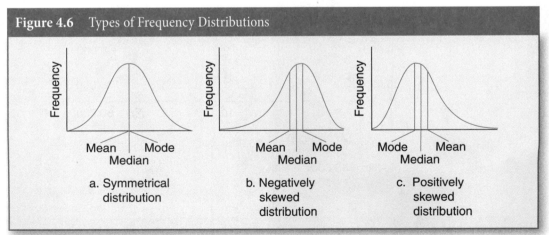

Figure 4.6   Types of Frequency Distributions

Table 4.5   Hours Spent per Day Watching Television

Hours Spent per Day Watching TV	Frequency (f)	fY	Percentage	C%
1	204	204	31.9	31.9
2	247	494	38.7	70.6
3	188	564	29.4	100.0
Total	639	$\sum fy = 1{,}262$	100.0	

$$\bar{Y} = \frac{\sum fy}{N} = \frac{1{,}262}{639} = 1.97$$

Median = 2.0
Mode = 2.0

Figure 4.7   Hours Spent per Day Watching Television

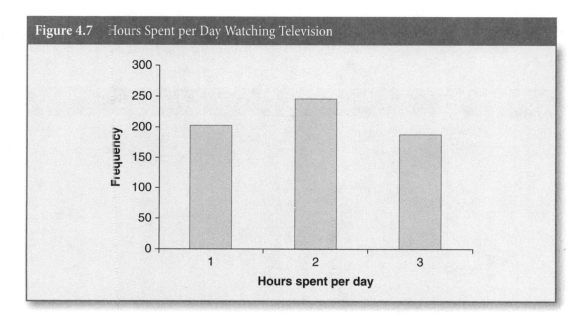

The Positively Skewed Distribution

Now let's examine Table 4.6 and Figure 4.8, displaying the distribution of the number of siblings of a respondent.

Note that the largest number of respondents (312) has two brothers and/or sisters. Also note that few people report having six or more siblings. Notice also that in this distribution, the mean, the median, and the mode have different values, with the mode having the lowest value (mode = 2.00),

Table 4.6   Number of Brothers and Sisters

Number of Siblings	Frequency (f)	fY	Percentage	C%
0	55	0	4.0	4.0
1	292	292	21.1	25.1
2	312	624	22.5	47.6
3	229	687	16.5	64.1
4	186	744	13.4	77.5
5	122	610	8.8	86.4
6	71	426	5.1	91.5
7	72	504	5.2	96.7
8	46	368	3.3	100.0
Total	1,385	4,255	100.0	

$$\bar{Y} = \frac{\sum fy}{N} = \frac{4,255}{1,385} = 3.07$$

Median = 3.0
Mode = 2.0

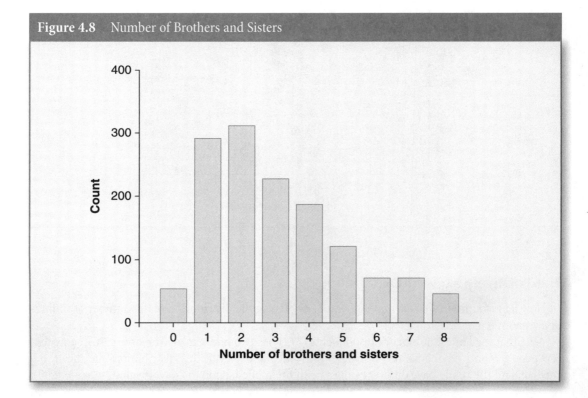

Figure 4.8   Number of Brothers and Sisters

the median having the second lowest value (median = 3.0), and the mean having the highest value (mean = 3.07)

The distribution as depicted in Table 4.6 and Figure 4.8 is positively skewed. As a general rule, for skewed distributions the mean, the median, and the mode do not coincide. The mean, which is always pulled in the direction of extreme scores, falls closest to the tail of the distribution where a small number of extreme scores are located.

The Negatively Skewed Distribution

Now examine Table 4.7 and Figure 4.9 for the number of years spent in school among those respondents who did not finish high school. Here you can see the opposite pattern. The distribution of the number of years spent in school for those without a high school diploma is a negatively skewed distribution. First, note that the largest number of years spent in school are

---

Positively skewed distribution   A distribution with a few extremely high values.

Skewed distribution   A distribution with a few extreme values on one side of the distribution.

Negatively skewed distribution   A distribution with a few extremely low values.

Table 4.7   Years of School Among Respondents Without a High School Degree

Years of School	Frequency (f)	fY	Percentage	C%
0	5	0	2.0	2.0
2	2	4	0.8	2.8
3	1	3	0.4	3.2
4	6	24	2.4	5.6
5	4	20	1.6	7.2
6	24	144	9.6	16.8
7	10	70	4.0	20.8
8	26	208	10.4	31.2
9	38	342	15.2	46.4
10	66	660	26.4	72.8
11	68	748	27.2	100.0
Total	250	2,223	100.0	

$$\overline{Y} = \frac{\sum fy}{N} = \frac{2,223}{250} = 8.89$$

Median = 10.0
Mode = 11.0

Figure 4.9 Years of School Among Respondents Without a High School Degree

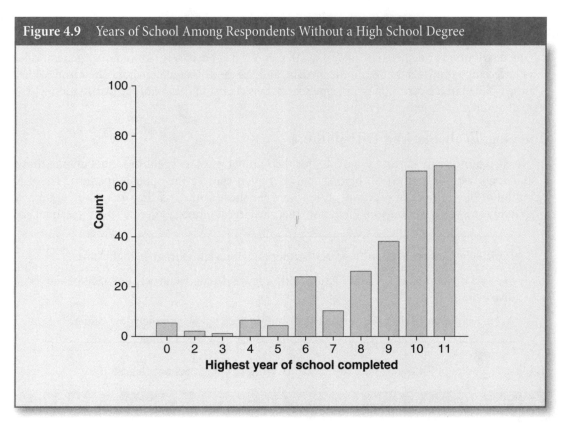

concentrated at the high end of the scale (11 years) and that there are fewer respondents at the low end. The mean, the median, and the mode also differ in values as they did in the previous example. However, here the mode has the highest value (mode = 11.0), the median has the second highest value (median = 10.0), and the mean has the lowest value (mean = 8.89).

Guidelines for Identifying the Shape of a Distribution

Following are some useful guidelines for identifying the shape of a distribution.

1. In unimodal distributions, when the mode, the median, and the mean coincide or are almost identical, the distribution is symmetrical.

2. When the mean is higher than the median (or is positioned to the right of the median), the distribution is positively skewed.

3. When the mean is lower than the median (or is positioned to the left of the median), the distribution is negatively skewed.

✓ *Learning*
Check

> *To identify positively and negatively skewed distributions, look at the tail on the chart. If the tail points to the right (the positive end of the X-axis), the distribution is positively skewed. If the tail points to the left (the negative, or potentially negative, end of the X-axis), the distribution is negatively skewed.*

▣ CONSIDERATIONS FOR CHOOSING A MEASURE OF CENTRAL TENDENCY

So far, we have considered three basic kinds of averages: the mode, the median, and the mean. Each can represent the central tendency of a distribution. But which one should we use? The mode? The median? The mean? Or, perhaps, all of them? There is no simple answer to this question. However, in general, we tend to use only one of the three measures of central tendency, and the choice of the appropriate one involves a number of considerations. These considerations and how they affect our choice of the appropriate measure are presented in the form of a decision tree in Figure 4.10.

Level of Measurement

One of the most basic considerations in choosing a measure of central tendency is the variable's level of measurement. The valid use of any of the three measures requires that the data be measured at the level appropriate for that measure or higher. Thus, as shown in Figure 4.10, with nominal variables our choice is restricted to the mode as a measure of central tendency.

However, with ordinal data, we have two choices: the mode or the median (or sometimes both). Our choice depends on what we want to know about the distribution. If we are interested in showing what is the most common or typical value in the distribution, then our choice is the mode. If, however, we want to show which value is located exactly in the middle of the distribution, then the median is our measure of choice.

When the data are measured on an interval-ratio level, the choice between the appropriate measures is a bit more complex and is restricted by the shape of the distribution.

Skewed Distribution

When the distribution is skewed, the mean may give misleading information on the central tendency because its value is affected by extreme scores in the distribution. The median (see, e.g., A Closer Look 4.2) or the mode can be chosen as the preferred measure of central tendency because neither is influenced by extreme scores. For instance, when examining the number of years that GSS respondents without a high school diploma completed (Table 4.7, Figure 4.9), the mean does not provide as accurate a representation of the "typical" number of years that an individual without a high school degree has spent in school as the median and the mode. Thus, either one could be used as an "average," depending on the research objective.

Figure 4.10 How to Choose a Measure of Central Tendency

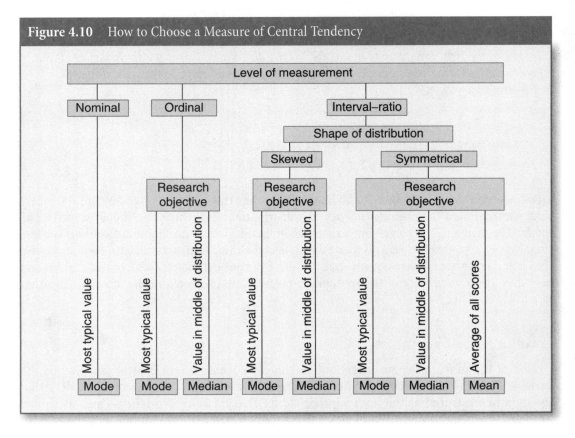

Symmetrical Distribution

When the distribution we want to analyze is symmetrical, we can use any of the three averages. Again, our choice depends on the research objective and what we want to know about the distribution. In general, however, the mean is our best choice because it contains the greatest amount of information and is easier to use in more advanced statistical analyses.

🔲 A Closer Look 4.2
A Cautionary Note: Representing Income

Personal income is frequently positively skewed because there are a few people with very high incomes; therefore, the mean may not be the most appropriate measure to represent "average" income. For example, the 2011 American Community Survey—an ongoing survey of economic and income statistics—reported the 2011 mean and median annual earnings of white, black, and Latino households in the United States. In the figure below, we compare the mean and median income for each group.

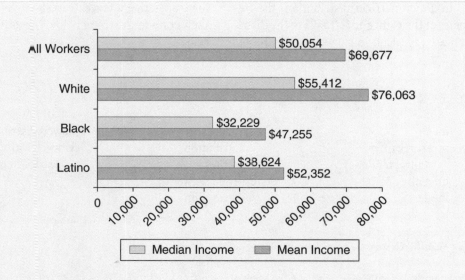

Source: U.S. Census Bureau, American Community Survey, 2011.

As shown, for all groups, the reported mean is higher than the median. This discrepancy indicates that household income in the United States is highly skewed, with the mean overrepresenting those households in the upper-income bracket and misrepresenting the income of the average household. A preferable alternative (also shown) is to use the median annual earnings of these groups.

Since the earnings of whites are the highest in comparison with all other groups, it is useful to look at each group's median earnings relative to the earnings of whites. For example, blacks were paid just 58 cents ($32,229/$55,412) and Latinos were paid 70 cents ($38,624/$55,412) for every $1 paid to whites.

MAIN POINTS

• The mode, the median, and the mean are measures of central tendency—numbers that describe what is average or typical about the distribution.

• The mode is the category or score with the largest frequency (or percentage) in the distribution. It is often used to describe the most commonly occurring category of a nominal level variable.

• The median is a measure of central tendency that represents the exact middle of the distribution. It is calculated for variables measured on at least an ordinal level of measurement.

• The mean is typically used to describe central tendency in interval-ratio variables, such as income, age, or education. We obtain the mean by summing all the scores and dividing by the total (N) number of scores.

- In a symmetrical distribution, the frequencies at the right and left tails of the distribution are identical. In skewed distributions, there are either a few extremely high (positive skew) or a few extremely low (negative skew) values.

KEY TERMS

mean

measures of
central tendency

median

mode

negatively skewed
distribution

percentile

positively skewed
distribution

skewed distribution

symmetrical
distribution

$SAGE edge™

Sharpen your skills with SAGE edge at **edge.sagepub.com/frankfort7e. SAGE edge for students** provides a personalized approach to help you accomplish your coursework goals in an easy-to-use learning environment.

SPSS DEMONSTRATIONS

[GLOBAL13SSDS]

*Demonstration 1: Producing Measures
of Central Tendency With Frequencies*

The Frequencies command, which we demonstrated in Chapter 2, also has the ability to produce the three measures of central tendency discussed in this chapter. We will use Frequencies to calculate measures of central tendency for SUICIDEFCAT (categorical percentages of international female suicide rates) and WOMENPARCAT (categorical percentages of women holding office at the national level in their respective countries).

Click on *Analyze, Descriptive Statistics*, then *Frequencies*. Place SUICIDEFCAT and WOMENPARCAT in the Variable(s) box. Then click on the *Statistics* button. You will see that the Central Tendency box (Figure 4.11) lists four choices, but we will click on only the first three. Then click on *Continue*, then on *OK* to process this request.

The statistics box for WOMENPARCAT and SUICIDEFCAT is displayed here. We have also displayed the frequency distribution for SUICIDEFCAT (Figure 4.12). SUICIDEFCAT is an ordinal variable, which means that the mode and median are appropriate measures of central tendency. SPSS has no idea that these variables are measured on an ordinal scale. In other words, SPSS produces exactly the output we asked for, without regard for whether the output is correct for this type of variable. It's up to you to select the proper measure of central tendency.

The median for the variable SUICIDEFCAT is 3.00, which is close to the mean value. Since we know the value of the median, we can say that roughly half of the countries in our sample have a female suicide rate higher than 3.00 and half have a female suicide rate lower than 3.00. In addition, SUICIDEFCAT is trimodal,

Figure 4.11   Statistics Dialog Box

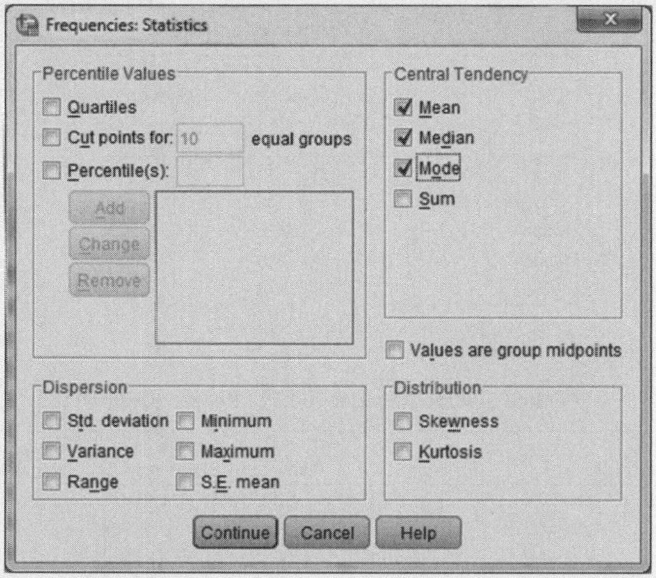

which means that there are three modes with the same highest frequency. If two or more categories have exactly the same frequency, SPSS reports the smallest modal value, but it also reports as a footnote that multiple modes exist. By examining the frequency distribution included in Figure 4.12, we can see that female suicide rates were the same for the categories "0.00–2.00," "4.01–6.00," and "6.01 or Higher," thus producing three modes.

Figure 4.12 also displays the measures of central tendency for WOMENPARCAT. Since WOMENPARCAT is an ordinal variable, we can use the median and mode to summarize its distribution. The median is 2.0, which corresponds to the response "10.1–30.0%." We can confirm from the cumulative percentages (not shown) that about 60% of the countries in our sample have between 10% and 30% of women in office at the national level; the remaining 40% (which is not shown here) either have less than 10.0% or more than 30.1% of women in office at the national level. The mode was also "10–30%," meaning that the majority of countries in our sample had between 10% and 30% of women comprise their national-level office populations.

[GSS10SSDS]

Demonstration 2: Producing
Measures of Central Tendency With Descriptives

We begin this exercise by telling the computer that we want our results split by sex. That is, we want separate results for males and females. Select *Data, Split File, Organize Output by Groups.* Insert the variable *sex* into the box labeled "Groups Based on." Click *OK.* Now SPSS will filter our results by SEX.

Figure 4.12 Selected Output for WOMENPARCAT and SUICIDEFCAT

Statistics

		Percentage of Women Holding a National Office (Ordinal)	Female Suicide Rate per 100,000 people (Ordinal)
N	Valid	70	36
	Missing	0	34
Mean		2.000	2.5566
Median		2.000	3.0000
Mode		2.0	1.00ª

a. Multiple modes exist. The smallest value is shown

Female Suicide Rate per 100,000 People (Ordinal)

		Frequency	Percent	Valid Percent	Cumulative Percent
Valid	0.00-2.00	10	14.3	27.8	27.8
	2.01-4.00	6	8.6	16.7	44.4
	4.01-6.00	10	14.3	27.8	72.2
	6.01 or Higher	10	14.3	27.8	100.0
	Total	36	51.4	100.0	
Missing	System	34	48.6		
Total		70	100.0		

When you want to calculate the mean of interval-ratio variables but you don't need to view the actual frequency table listing the responses in each category, the Descriptives procedure is often the best choice. Descriptives can be found by clicking on *Analyze, Descriptive Statistics,* and then *Descriptives.*

Figure 4.13 Descriptives Dialog Box

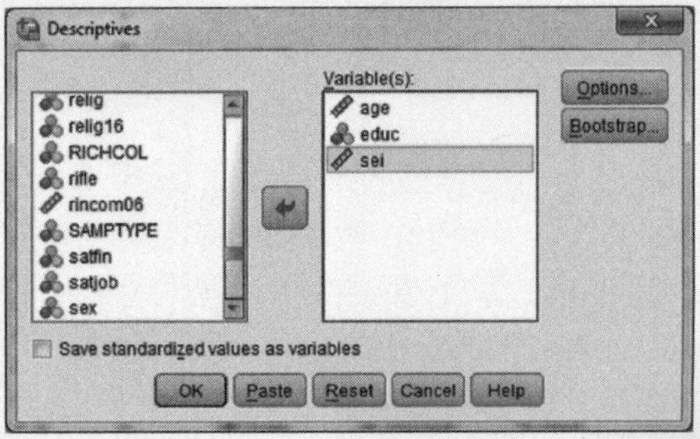

Figure 4.14 Descriptive Statistics[a]

Descriptive Statistics[a]

	N	Minimum	Maximum	Mean	Std. Deviation
AGE OF RESPONDENT	842	18	89	49.16	17.824
HIGHEST YEAR OF SCHOOL COMPLETED	851	0	20	13.31	3.005
RESPONDENT SOCIOECONOMIC INDEX	791	17.1	97.2	48.630	18.4985
Valid N (listwise)	782				

a. RESPONDENTS SEX = FEMALE

The Descriptives dialog box (Figure 4.13) is uncomplicated and requires only that you place the variables of interest (AGE, EDUC, SEI) in the Variable(s) box. By default, Descriptives will calculate the mean, standard deviation (to be discussed in Chapter 5), minimum, maximum, and the number of cases with a valid response.

You will need to scroll through your SPSS output to locate the descriptive statistics for female respondents. Figure 4.14 displays these descriptive statistics for AGE, EDUC (years of education), and SEI (socioeconomic index) for female GSS respondents in 2010.

The output from Descriptives automatically lists the variables in the order that we specified in the dialog box. Based on the output, we can determine that on average, female respondents were 49.16 years old, had approximately 13.31 years of education, and had a socioeconomic index score of 48.63.

SPSS PROBLEMS

[GSS10SSDS]

1. Create a frequency distribution, including any appropriate measures of central tendency, for HOMOSEX.
    a. Which measure of central tendency, mean or median, is most appropriate to summarize the distribution of HOMOSEX? Explain why.
    b. Suppose we are interested in whether or not males and females have the same attitudes about homosexual relations. Create a frequency distribution, including any appropriate measures of central tendency, for HOMOSEX, this time separating results for men and women. (Use the *Data–Split File* command by clicking on *Data, Split File, Organize Output by Groups*, insert the variable SEX into the box labeled "Groups Based on" and click *OK*. Are there any differences in their measures of central tendency? Explain. (Remember, once you have completed this exercise, reset the Split File command to include all cases by clicking on *Data, Split File, Analyze All Cases, Do Not Create Groups.*)
    c. Repeat b), this time using PREMARSX (acceptance of premarital sex) as your variable.

2. We are interested in investigating whether males and females have equal levels of education. Use the variable EDUC with the Frequencies procedure to produce frequency tables and the mean, the median, and the mode separately for males and females (as described in 1b).

   a. On average, do men and women have equal levels of education? Use all the available information to answer this question.

   b. When we use statistics to describe the social world, we should always go beyond merely using statistics to describe the condition of various social groups. Just as important is our interpretation of the statistics and some judgment as to whether any differences that we find between groups seem to be of practical importance; that is, do they make a practical difference in the world? Do you think any differences you discovered between male and female educational levels are important enough to have an effect on such things as the ability to get a job or the salary that someone makes? Explain the reason for your answer.

3. Some people believe that social class influences the number of children that couples decide to have. Use SPSS to investigate this question with the GSS data file. (The variable CHILDS measures the respondent's number of children.) To get the necessary information, have SPSS split the file by CLASS and then run Frequencies for CHILDS.

   a. What is the best measure of central tendency to represent the number of children in a household? Why?

   b. Which social class has more children per respondent?

   c. Rerun your analysis, this time with the variable CHLDIDEL (ideal number of children). Is there a difference among the social class categories? Explain.

4. Picking an appropriate statistic to describe the central tendency of a distribution is a critical skill. Based on the GSS10SSDS, determine the appropriate measure(s) of central tendency for the following variables:

   a. How often do respondents watch television? [TVHOURS]

   b. Respondents' political views. [POLVIEWS]

   c. Number of hours a respondent worked last week. [HRS1]

   d. Whether respondents have a gun in their home. [OWNGUN]

   e. Number of brothers and sisters of those sampled. [SIBS]

   f. Does respondent support legalization of marijuana? [GRASS]

5. The educational attainment of American Indians, Alaska Natives, and Hispanic American respondents was compared in A Closer Look 4.1. You can use SPSS to do similar comparisons with other variables. For example, it may be interesting to look at levels of marital satisfaction and compare the number of hours that men and women spend watching TV per day. There is more than one method to get the frequency distributions of hours per day watching TV for these groups, but the easiest thing might be to use the *Split File* command (as described in 1b). Use the GSS10SSDS for this exercise. Click on *Data, Split File, Organize Output by Groups*, place the variables HAPMAR and SEX (in that order) in the "Groups Based on" box, and then click *OK*. HAPMAR has three categories of interest: 1 = *very happy*, 2 = *pretty happy*, 3 = *not too happy*. SEX has two valid values 1 = *male* and 2 = *female*. Essentially, you have told SPSS to create a separate set of output for each group defined by the combination of the values of HAPMAR and SEX.

   a. Create a frequency distribution by clicking on *Analyze, Descriptive Statistics, Frequencies*. Select the variable TVHOURS, as well as all appropriate measures of central tendency under the *Statistics* opticn. Click *OK*. SPSS will create a great deal of output; all you need to do is find the appropriate frequency tables and measures of central tendency. For example, to find and report the frequency table for males who are pretty happy, look for the section with values of Happiness of Marriage = Pretty Happy and Respondent's Sex = Male.

b. Do you notice any gaps in hours spent watching TV between men and women at different levels of marital satisfaction?

CHAPTER EXERCISES

1. The following frequency distribution contains information about people's self-evaluations of their lives.

Respondent Assessment of Life	*Frequency*	*Percentage*	*Cumulative Percentage*
Exciting	470	48.3	48.3
Routine	444	45.6	93.9
Dull	60	6.1	100.0
Total	974	100.0	

Source: GSS, 2010

a. Find the mode.
b. Find the median.
c. Interpret the mode and the median.
d. Why would you not want to report the mean for this variable?

2. Same-sex unions have increasingly become a heated political issue. The 2010 GSS asked respondents' opinions on homosexual relations. Four response categories ranged from "Always Wrong" to "Not Wrong at All." See the following frequency distribution:

Homosexual Relations	*Frequency*	*Percentage*	*Cumulative Percentage*
Always wrong	467	50.2	50.2
Almost always wrong	41	4.4	54.6
Sometimes wrong	76	8.2	62.8
Not wrong at all	346	37.2	100.0
Total	930	100.0	

a. At what level is this variable measured? What is the mode for this variable?

b. Calculate the median for this variable. In general, how would you characterize the public's attitude about homosexual relations?

3. The following frequency distribution contains information on the number of hours worked last week for a sample of 32 Latino adults.

Hours Worked Last Week	Frequency	Percentage	Cumulative Percentage
20	3	9.4	9.4
25	2	6.3	15.6
28	1	3.1	18.8
29	1	3.1	21.9
30	3	9.4	31.3
32	1	3.1	34.4
40	14	43.8	78.1
50	2	6.3	84.4
52	1	3.1	87.5
55	1	3.1	90.6
60	1	3.1	93.8
64	1	3.1	96.9
70	1	3.1	100.0
Total	32	100.0	

Source: GSS, 2010.

a. What is the level of measurement, mode, and median for "hours worked last week"?

b. Construct quartiles for weeks worked last year. What is the 25th percentile? The 50th percentile? The 75th percentile? Why don't you need to calculate the 50th percentile to answer this question?

4. Using data from the 2010 GSS, the following is the frequency distribution for respondent opinion of whether racism is no longer present in the United States:

Racism in the Past	Frequency
Strongly Agree	94
Somewhat Agree	142
Somewhat Disagree	160
Strongly Disagree	84

   a. Calculate the median category for this variable.

   b. Also, report which category contains the 20th and 80th percentiles.

5. Does health status vary with age? The following table, taken from the 2010 GSS, depicts the health status across various age groups (not all ages are displayed).

Health Status	Age Group			
	18–29	30–39	40–49	50–59
Excellent	56	55	41	38
Good	71	77	87	74
Fair	34	34	34	44
Poor	3	3	6	17

   a. Calculate the median and mode for each age group.

   b. Use this information to characterize whether health status varies by age. Does the median or mode provide a better description of the data? Do the statistics support the idea that some age groups are healthier than others?

6. The number of Americans on Medicare is increasing as expected with the aging baby boomer population. The following table shows the number of Americans on Medicare in 2005 and 2009 for eight U.S. states. *Note:* The numbers listed are in thousands.

State	2005	2009
Alabama	740	828
Delaware	125	145
Florida	3,008	3,289

(Continued)

(Continued)

State	2005	2009
Illinois	1,674	1,806
Minnesota	691	767
New Hampshire	185	217
New York	2,758	2,937
Washington	807	938

Source: U.S. Census Bureau, *The 2012 Statistical Abstract*, Table 147.

a. Calculate the mean number of Americans on Medicare in these eight states for both 2005 and 2009. How would you characterize the difference in the number of Americans on Medicare between 2005 and 2009? Does the mean adequately represent the central tendency of the distribution of Americans on Medicare in each year for these eight states? Why or why not?

b. Recalculate the mean for each year after removing Florida, Illinois, and New York from the table. Is the mean now a better representation of central tendency for the remaining five states? Explain.

7. U.S. households have become smaller over the years. The following table from the 2010 GSS contains information on the number of people currently aged 18 years or older living in a respondent's household. Calculate the mean number of people living in a U.S. household in 2010.

Household Size	Frequency
1	381
2	526
3	227
4	200
5	96
6	42
7	19
8	5
9	2
10	2
Total	1,500

8. In Exercise 6, you calculated the mean number of Americans on Medicare. We now want to test whether the distribution of Americans on Medicare is symmetrical or skewed.

a. Calculate the median and mode for each year, using all eight states. Based on these results and the means, how would you characterize the distribution of Americans on Medicare for each year?

b. Does the mean or median best represent the central tendency of each distribution? Why?

c. If you found the distributions to be skewed, what might be the statistical cause?

9. In Exercise 7, you examined U.S. household size in 2010. Using these data, construct a histogram to represent the distribution of household size.

a. From the appearance of the histogram, would you say the distribution is positively or negatively skewed? Why?

b. Now calculate the median for the distribution and compare this value with the value of the mean from Exercise 7. Do these numbers provide further evidence to support your decision about how the distribution is skewed? Why do you think the distribution of household size is asymmetrical?

10. Exercise 3 used GSS data on the number of hours worked per week for a sample of 32 Latino adults.

a. Calculate the mean number of hours worked per week.

b. Compare the value of the mean with those you have already calculated for the median. Without constructing a histogram, describe whether and how the distribution of weeks worked per year is skewed.

11. You listen to a debate between two politicians discussing the economic health of the United States. One politician says that the average income of all workers in the United States is $72,235; the other says that American workers make, on average, only $52,029, so Americans are not as well off as the first politician claims. Is it possible for both these politicians to be correct? If so, explain how.

12. Discuss the advantages and disadvantages of all three measures of central tendency. Are you confident that one of these three is the best measure of central tendency? If so, why?

13. Do male murder rates vary with country population? Investigate this question using the following data for selected countries grouped by population size, the top 10 countries and the bottom 10. Calculate the mean and median for each group of countries. Where is the murder rate for males the highest? Do the mean and median have the same pattern for the two groups?

2008–2010 Male Murder Rate per 100,000			
Top 10 by Population	*Murder Rate*	*Bottom 10 by Population*	*Murder Rate*
China	2.2	Vietnam	2.6
India	3.9	Egypt	2.2
United States	6.6	Germany	0.9
Indonesia	13.9	Turkey	8.6
Brazil	54.7	Iran	2.3
Pakistan	4.3	Democratic Republic of the Congo	35.8
Nigeria	18.2	France	1.9
Russia	29.1	United Kingdom	1.7
Japan	0.4	Italy	1.6
Mexico	23.0	South Korea	2.2

Source: United Nations Office on Drugs and Crime, *2011 Annual Report.*

Exercises

14. Many policymakers are interested in different measures of participation in the labor force. Use the information from the 2010 GSS to explore how labor force participation varies by sex (not all categories shown; some collapsed).

Participation in Labor Force	Males	Females
Working	390	441
Not Working/Unemployed	66	42
Keeping House	18	163
Total	474	646

Calculate the appropriate measures of central tendency for males and females. How would you describe their labor force participation rates? Are they similar or different and why? Use the appropriate measures of central tendency that you calculated to support your answer.

15. Infant mortality rates are a key indicator of the quality of health care a country can provide for its citizens. The following table shows infant mortality rates for selected countries based on estimates reported by the Central Intelligence Agency World Factbook 2010.

Country	Infant Mortality Rates
Afghanistan	121.63
Canada	4.85
Colombia	15.92
Finland	3.40
Luxembourg	4.39
Panama	11.32
Rwanda	62.51
Syria	15.12
Turkey	23.07
United States	6.00
Zimbabwe	28.23

a. Calculate the mean and median infant mortalities reported for the 11 countries presented above.
b. Is this distribution skewed? If yes, how do you know?
c. Provide two possible explanations that might explain why countries have very low infant mortality rates while others have very high infant mortality rates.

Chapter 5

Measures of Variability

Chapter Learning Objectives

- ❖ Understanding the importance of measuring variability
- ❖ Learning how to calculate and interpret the index of qualitative variation (IQV), range, interquartile range, the variance, and the standard deviation
- ❖ Understanding the criteria for choosing a measure of variation

I n the previous chapter, we looked at measures of central tendency: the mean, the median, and the mode. With these measures, we can use a single number to describe what is average for or typical of a distribution. Although measures of central tendency can be very helpful, they tell only part of the story. In fact, when used alone, they may mislead rather than inform. Another way of summarizing a distribution of data is by selecting a single number that describes how much variation and diversity there is in the distribution. Numbers that describe diversity or variation are called measures of variability. Researchers often use measures of central tendency along with measures of variability to describe their data.

Measures of variability   Numbers that describe diversity or variability in the distribution of a variable.

In this chapter, we discuss five measures of variability: the index of qualitative variation, the range, the interquartile range, the standard deviation, and the variance. Before we discuss these measures, let's explore why they are important.

▣ THE IMPORTANCE OF MEASURING VARIABILITY

The importance of looking at variation and diversity can be illustrated by thinking about the differences in the experiences of U.S. women. Are women united by their similarities or divided by their differences? The answer is *both*. To address the similarities without dealing with differences is "to misunderstand and distort that which separates as well as that which binds women together."[1] Even when we focus on one particular group of women, it is important to look at the differences as well as the commonalities. Take, for example, Asian American women. As a group, they share a number of characteristics.

> Their participation in the workforce is higher than that of women in any other ethnic group. Many . . . live life supporting others, often allowing their lives to be subsumed by the needs of the extended family. . . . However, there are many circumstances when these shared experiences are not sufficient to accurately describe the condition of a particular Asian-American woman. Among Asian-American women there are those who were born in the United States . . . and . . . those who recently arrived in the United States. Asian-American women are diverse in their heritage or country of origin: China, Japan, the Philippines, Korea . . . and . . . India. . . . Although the majority of Asian-American women are working class—contrary to the stereotype of the "ever successful" Asians—there are poor, "middle-class," and even affluent Asian-American women.[2]

As this example illustrates, one basis of stereotyping is treating a group as if it were totally represented by its central value, ignoring the diversity within the group. Sociologists often contribute to this type of stereotyping when their empirical generalizations, based on a statistical difference between averages, are interpreted in an overly simplistic way. All this argues for the importance of using measures of variability as well as central tendency whenever we want to characterize or compare groups. Whereas the similarities and commonalities in the experiences of Asian American women are depicted by a measure of central tendency, the diversity of their experiences can be described only by using measures of variation.

The concept of variability has implications not only for describing the diversity of social groups such as Asian American women but also for issues that are important in your everyday life. One of the most important issues facing the academic community is how to reconstruct the curriculum to make it more responsive to the needs of students. Let's consider the issue of statistics instruction on the college level.

Statistics is perhaps the most anxiety-provoking course in any social science curriculum. Statistics courses are often the last "roadblock" preventing students from completing their major requirements. One factor, identified in numerous studies as a handicap for many students, is the "math anxiety syndrome." This anxiety often leads to a less than optimum learning environment, with students often trying to memorize every detail of a statistical procedure rather than understand the general concept involved.

Let's suppose that a university committee is examining the issue of how to better respond to the needs of students. In its attempt to evaluate statistics courses offered in different departments, the committee compares the grading policy in two courses. The first, offered in the sociology department, is taught by Professor Brown; the second, offered through the school of social work, is taught by Professor Yamato. The committee finds that over the years, the average grade for Professor Brown's class has been C+. The average grade in Professor Yamato's class is also C+. We could easily be misled by these statistics into thinking that the grading policy of both instructors is about the same. However, we need to look more closely into how the grades are distributed in each of the classes. The differences in the distribution of grades are illustrated in Figure 5.1, which displays the frequency polygon for the two classes.

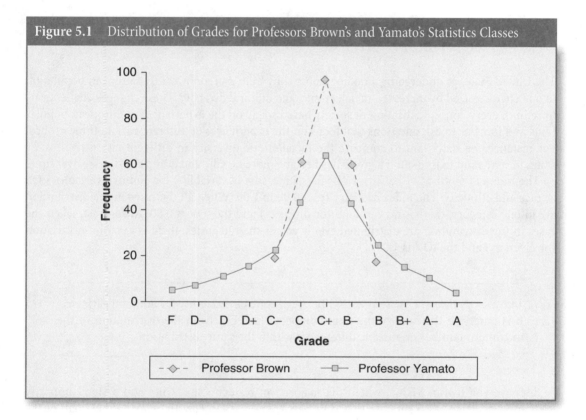

Figure 5.1 Distribution of Grades for Professors Brown's and Yamato's Statistics Classes

Compare the shapes of these two distributions. Notice that while both distributions have the same mean, they are shaped very differently. The grades in Professor Yamato's class are more spread out ranging from A to F, whereas the grades for Professor Brown's class are clustered around the mean and range only from B to C. Although the means for both distributions are identical, the grades in Professor Yamato's class vary considerably more than the grades given by Professor Brown. The comparison between the two classes is more complex than we first thought it would be.

As this example demonstrates, information on how scores are spread from the center of a distribution is as important as information about the central tendency in a distribution. This type of information is obtained by measures of variability.

Look closely at Figure 5.1. Whose class would you choose to take? If you were worried that you might fail statistics, your best bet would be Professor Brown's class where no one fails. However, if you want to keep up your GPA and are willing to work, Professor Yamato's class is the better choice. If you had to choose one of these classes based solely on the average grades, your choice would not be well informed.

▣ THE INDEX OF QUALITATIVE VARIATION: A BRIEF INTRODUCTION

The United States is undergoing a demographic shift from a predominantly European population to one characterized by increased racial, ethnic, and cultural diversity. These changes challenge us to rethink every conceptualization of society based solely on the experiences of European populations and force us to ask questions that focus on the experiences of different racial/ethnic groups. For instance, we may want to compare the racial/ethnic diversity in different cities, regions, or states or may want to find out if a group has become more racially and ethnically diverse over time.

The **index of qualitative variation (IQV)** is a measure of variability for nominal variables such as race and ethnicity. The index can vary from 0.00 to 1.00. When all the cases in the distribution are in one category, there is no variation (or diversity) and the IQV is 0.00. In contrast, when the cases in the distribution are distributed evenly across the categories, there is maximum variation (or diversity) and the IQV is 1.00.

Index of qualitative variation (IQV)   A measure of variability for nominal variables. It is based on the ratio of the total number of differences in the distribution to the maximum number of possible differences within the same distribution.

Suppose you live in Maine, where the majority of residents are white and a small minority are Latino or Asian. Also suppose that your best friend lives in Hawaii, where almost half of the population is either Asian or Native Hawaiian. The distributions for these two states are presented in Table 5.1. Which is more diverse? Clearly, Hawaii, where half the population is either Asian or Native Hawaiian, is more diverse than Maine, where Asians and Latinos are but a small minority.

Table 5.1   Top Five Racial/Ethnic Groups for Two States by Percentage, 2010

Racial/Ethnic Group	Maine	Hawaii
White	97.3	29.7
Latino	1.3	10.7

Racial/Ethnic Group	Maine	Hawaii
Asian	1.1	46.3
Native Hawaiian or Pacific Islander	—	11.9
Other*	0.3	1.5
Total	100.0	100.0

*The category "Other" counts as a racial/ethnic group.

Source: U.S. Census Bureau, Statistical Abstract of the United States: *2012* Tables 18–19.

Steps for Calculating the IQV

To calculate the IQV, we use this formula:

$$IQV = \frac{K(100^2 - \Sigma Pct^2)}{100^2(K-1)}$$ (5.1)

where

K = the number of categories

ΣPct^2 = the sum of all squared percentages in the distribution

In Table 5.2, we present the squared percentages for each racial/ethnic group for Maine and Hawaii.

Table 5.2 Squared Percentages for Five Racial/Ethnic Groups for Two States

Racial/Ethnic Group	Maine		Hawaii	
	%	(%)²	%	(%)²
White	97.3	9,467.29	29.7	882.09
Latino	1.3	1.69	10.7	114.49
Asian	1.1	1.21	46.3	2,143.69
Native Hawaiian or Pacific Islander	—	—	11.9	141.61
Other*	0.3	0.09	1.5	2.25
Total	100.0	9,470.28	100.0	3,284.13

* The category "Other" counts as a racial/ethnic group.

The IQV for Maine is

$$IQV = \frac{K(100^2 - \Sigma Pct^2)}{100^2(K-1)} = \frac{4(100^2 - 9,470.28)}{100^2(4-1)} = \frac{2,118.88}{30,000} = 0.07$$

The IQV for Hawaii is

$$IQV = \frac{K(100^2 - \Sigma Pct^2)}{100^2(K-1)} = \frac{5(100^2 - 3,284.13)}{100^2(5-1)} = \frac{33,579.35}{40,000} = 0.84$$

Note that the values of the IQV for the two states support our earlier observation: In Hawaii, where the IQV is 0.84, there is considerably more racial/ethnic variation than in Maine, where the IQV is 0.07.

It is important to remember that the IQV is partially a function of the number of categories. In this example, there were four and five racial/ethnic categories in Maine and Hawaii, respectively. Had we used more categories, the IQV for both states would have been considerably more.

To summarize, these are the steps we follow to calculate the IQV:

1. Construct a percentage distribution.

2. Square the percentages for each category.

3. Sum the squared percentages.

4. Calculate the IQV using the formula.

$$IQV = \frac{K(100^2 - \Sigma Pct^2)}{100^2(K-1)}$$

▣ A Closer Look 5.1
Statistics in Practice: Diversity at Berkeley Through the Years[*,†]

"Berkeley, Calif.—The photograph in Sproul Hall of the 10 Cal 'yell leaders' from the early 1960s, in their Bermuda shorts and letter sweaters, leaps out like an artifact from an ancient civilization. They are all fresh-faced, and in a way that is unimaginable now, they are all white."[‡]

On the flagship campus of the University of California system, the center of the affirmative action debate in higher education today, the ducktails and bouffant hairdos of those 1960s cheerleaders seem indeed out of date. The University of California's Berkeley campus was among the first of the nation's leading universities to embrace elements of affirmative action in its admission policies and now boasts that it has one of the most diverse campuses in the United States.

The following pie charts show the racial and ethnic breakdown of undergraduates at U.C. Berkeley for 1984 and 2012. The IQVs were calculated using the percentage distribution (as shown in the pie charts) for race and ethnicity for each year. Not only has the modal category of Berkeley's student body changed from white in 1984 to Asian in 2012, but the campus has become one of the most diverse in the United States.

Racial/Ethnic Composition of Student Body at U.C. Berkeley, 1984 and 2012

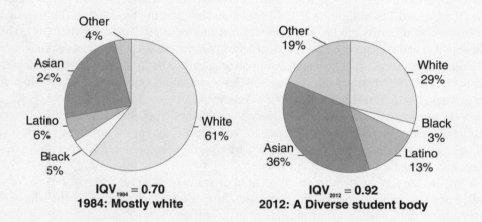

Source: *From The New York Times*, June 4. © 1995 *The New York Times.*

[†]2012 data are from the Office of Planning and Analysis, University of California, Berkeley, UC Berkeley Enrollment Data.

[‡]The Office of Planning and Analysis, University of California, Berkeley, *Cal Answers* 2012.

Expressing the IQV as a Percentage

The IQV can also be expressed as a percentage rather than a proportion: Simply multiply the IQV by 100. Expressed as a percentage, the IQV would reflect the percentage of racial/ethnic differences relative to the maximum possible differences in each distribution. Thus, an IQV of 0.07 indicates that the number of racial/ethnic differences in Maine is 7.0% (0.07 × 100) of the maximum possible differences. Similarly, for Hawaii, an IQV of 0.84 means that the number of racial/ethnic differences is 84.0% (0.84 × 100) of the maximum possible differences.

Examine A Closer Look 5.1 and consider the impact that the number of categories of a variable has on the IQV. What would happen to the Berkeley case if Asians were broken down into two categories with 19% Chinese Americans in one and 17% Other Asians in the other? (To answer this question you will need to recalculate the IQV with these new data.)

▣ STATISTICS IN PRACTICE: DIVERSITY IN U.S. SOCIETY

According to demographers' projections, by the middle of this century the United States will no longer be a predominantly white society. It is estimated that the combined population of the three largest minority groups—African Americans, Asian Americans, and Latino Americans—will reach an estimated 116 million by 2015.[3] Population shifts during the 1990s indicate geographic concentration of minority groups in specific regions and metropolitan areas of the United States.[4] Demographers call it chain migration: Essentially, migrants use social capital–specific knowledge of the migration process (i.e., to move from one area and settle in another).[5] For example, as of 2008, the Los Angeles metro area was home to 4.7 million Latino Americans, placing it first among cities in total growth in the number of Latino Americans.

How do you compare the amount of diversity in different cities, states, or regions? Diversity is a characteristic of a population many of us can sense intuitively. For example, the ethnic diversity of a large city is seen in the many members of various groups encountered when walking down its streets or traveling through its neighborhoods.[6]

We can use the IQV to measure the amount of diversity in different regions. Table 5.3 displays the 2011 percentage breakdown of the population by race for all four regions of the United States. Based on these data, and using Formula 5.1 as in our earlier example, we have also calculated the IQV for each region. The advantage of using a single number to express diversity is demonstrated in Figure 5.2, which depicts the regional variations in diversity as expressed by the IQVs from Table 5.3. Figure 5.2 shows the wide variation in racial diversity that exists in the United States. Note that the West, with an IQV of 0.79, is the most diverse region. At the other extreme, the Midwest, whose population is overwhelmingly white, is the most homogeneous region with an IQV of 0.48.

Table 5.3 Percentage Makeup of Population for Regions by Race, 2011

Region	White	Black	Latino	Asian	Other	IQV
Northeast	68.2	11.0	13.0	5.6	2.2	0.63
Midwest	77.5	10.2	7.1	2.6	2.6	0.48
South	59.5	19.0	16.2	2.8	2.5	0.73
West	52.3	4.4	29.0	9.2	5.0	0.79

Source: U.S. Census Bureau, American Community Survey, 2011.

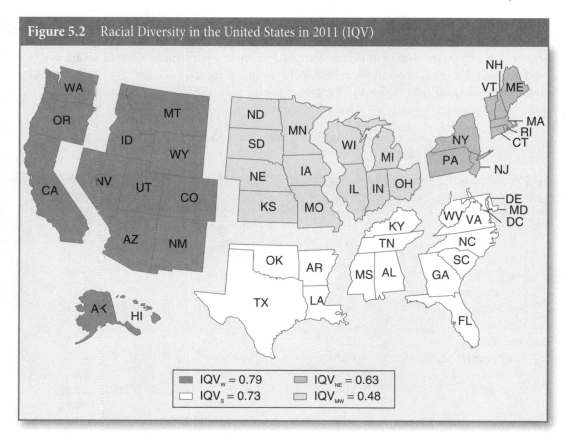

Figure 5.2   Racial Diversity in the United States in 2011 (IQV)

IQV_w = 0.79   IQV_NE = 0.63
IQV_s = 0.73   IQV_MW = 0.48

▣ THE RANGE

The simplest and most straightforward measure of variation is the **range**, which measures variation in interval-ratio variables. It is the difference between the highest (maximum) and the lowest (minimum) scores in the distribution:

$$\text{Range} = \text{Highest score} - \text{Lowest score}$$

In the 2010 General Social Survey (GSS), the oldest person included in the study was 89 years old and the youngest was 18. Thus, the range was $89 - 18 = 71$ years.

Range   A measure of variation in interval-ratio variables. It is the difference between the highest (maximum) and the lowest (minimum) scores in the distribution.

The range can also be calculated on percentages. For example, since the 1980s, relatively large communities of the elderly have become noticeable not just in the traditional retirement meccas of the Sun Belt[7] but also in the Ozarks of Arkansas and the mountains of Colorado and Montana. The number of elderly persons increased in every state during the 1990s and the 2000s (Washington, D.C., is the exception), but by different amounts. As the baby boomers age into retirement, we would expect this trend to continue. Table 5.4 displays the percentage change in the elderly population from 2008 to 2015 by region and by state as predicted by the U.S. Census Bureau.[8]

Table 5.4   Projected Percentage Change in the Population 65 Years and Over by Region and State, 2008–2015

Region, Division, and State	Percentage Change	Region, Division, and State	Percentage Change
Northeast	16.0	South (cont.)	
Connecticut	20.9	Georgia	21.1
Delaware	22.3	Kentucky	12.5
Maine	25.6	Louisiana	23.0
Massachusetts	17.7	Maryland	23.1
New Hampshire	28.4	Mississippi	16.4
New Jersey	20.4	North Carolina	20.7
New York	12.8	Oklahoma	12.8
Pennsylvania	12.5	South Carolina	22.1
Rhode Island	18.2	Tennessee	18.2
Vermont	31.4	Texas	25.9
		Virginia	26.8
Midwest	14.0	Washington, D.C.	−14.1
Indiana	11.3	West Virginia	15.4
Illinois	12.9		
Iowa	11.2	West	27.0
Kansas	14.2	Alaska	50.0
Michigan	15.5	Arizona	36.8
Minnesota	19.2	California	27.1
Missouri	14.5	Colorado	22.7
Nebraska	12.4	Hawaii	18.8
North Dakota	12.6	Idaho	20.2
Ohio	12.4	Montana	27.0
South Dakota	9.4	Nevada	42.1
Wisconsin	17.6	New Mexico	31.9
		Oregon	17.1
South	22.8	Utah	13.8
Alabama	15.1	Washington	23.2
Arkansas	14.7	Wyoming	36.9
Florida	29.7		

Source: U.S. Census Bureau, Statistical Abstract of the United States: 2010, Tables 16 and 18.

What is the range in the percentage change in state elderly population for the United States? To find the ranges in a distribution, simply pick out the highest and the lowest scores in the distribution and subtract. Alaska has the highest percentage change, with 50%, and Washington, D.C., has the lowest change, with −14.1%. The range is 64.1 percentage points, or 50% to −14.1%.

Although the range is simple and quick to calculate, it is a rather crude measure because it is based on only the lowest and the highest scores. These two scores might be extreme and rather atypical, which might make the range a misleading indicator of the variation in the distribution. For instance, note that among the 50 states and Washington, D.C., listed in Table 5.4, no state has a percentage decrease as that of Washington, D.C., and only Nevada has a percentage increase nearly as high as Alaska's. The range of 64.1 percentage points does not give us information about the variation in states between Washington, D.C., and Alaska.

✓ *Learning*
Check

> *Why can't we use the range to describe diversity in nominal variables? The range can be used to describe diversity in ordinal variables (e.g., we can say that responses to a question ranged from "somewhat satisfied" to "very dissatisfied"), but it has no quantitative meaning. Why not?*

▣ THE INTERQUARTILE RANGE: INCREASES IN ELDERLY POPULATIONS

To remedy the limitation of the range, we can employ an alternative—the *interquartile range*. The **interquartile range (IQR)**, a measure of variation for interval-ratio variables, is the width of the middle 50% of the distribution. It is defined as the difference between the lower and upper quartiles (Q_1 and Q_3).

$$IQR = Q_3 - Q_1$$

Recall that the first quartile (Q_1) is the 25th percentile, the point at which 25% of the cases fall below it and 75% above it. The third quartile (Q_3) is the 75th percentile, the point at which 75% of the cases fall below it and 25% above it. The IQR, therefore, defines variation for the middle 50% of the cases.

Interquartile range (IQR)   The width of the middle 50% of the distribution. It is defined as the difference between the lower and upper quartiles (Q_1 and Q_3).

Like the range, the IQR is based on only two scores. However, because it is based on intermediate scores, rather than on the extreme scores in the distribution, it avoids some of the instability associated with the range.

These are the steps for calculating the IQR

1. To find Q_1 and Q_3, order the scores in the distribution from the highest to the lowest score, or vice versa. Table 5.5 presents the data of Table 5.4 arranged in order from Alaska (50.0%) to Washington, D.C. (−14.1%).

2. Next, we need to identify the first quartile, Q_1 or the 25th percentile. We have to identify the percentage increase in the elderly population associated with the state that divides the distribution so that 25% of the states are below it and 75% of the states are above it. To find Q_1, we multiply N by 0.25:

$$(N)(0.25) = (51)(0.25) = 12.75$$

The first quartile falls between the 12th and the 13th states. Counting from the bottom, the 12th state is Illinois, and the percentage increase associated with it is 12.9. The 13th state is Utah, with a percentage increase of 13.8. To find the first quartile, we take the average of 12.9 and 13.8. Therefore, $(12.9 + 13.8)/2 = 13.35$ is the first quartile (Q_1).

3. To find Q_3, we have to identify the state that divides the distribution in such a way that 75% of the states are below it and 25% of the states are above it. We multiply N this time by 0.75:

$$(N)(0.75) = (51)(0.75) = 38.25$$

The third quartile falls between the 38th and the 39th states. Counting from the bottom, the 38th state is Washington, and the percentage increase associated with it is 23.2. The 39th state is Maine, with a percentage increase of 25.6. To find the third quartile, we take the average of 23.2 and 25.6. Therefore, $(23.2 + 25.6)/2 = 24.4$ is the third quartile (Q_3).

4. We are now ready to find the IQR:

$$IQR = Q_3 - Q_1 = 24.4 - 13.35 = 11.05$$

The IQR of percentage increase in the elderly population is 11.05 percentage points.

Notice that the IQR gives us better information than the range. The range gave us a 64.1-point spread, from 50% to −14.1%, but the IQR tells us that half the states are clustered between 24.4 and 13.35—a much narrower spread. The extreme scores represented by Alaska and Washington, D.C., have no effect on the IQR because they fall at the extreme ends of the distribution. This difference between the range and the interquartile range is also illustrated in Figure 5.3 where the extreme values of 10 children affects the value of the range but not of the IQR.

Why is the IQR better than the range as a measure of variability, especially when there are
extreme scores in the distribution? To answer this question, you may want to examine Figure 5.3.

Figure 5.3 The Range Versus the Interquartile Range: Number of Children Among Two
Groups of Women

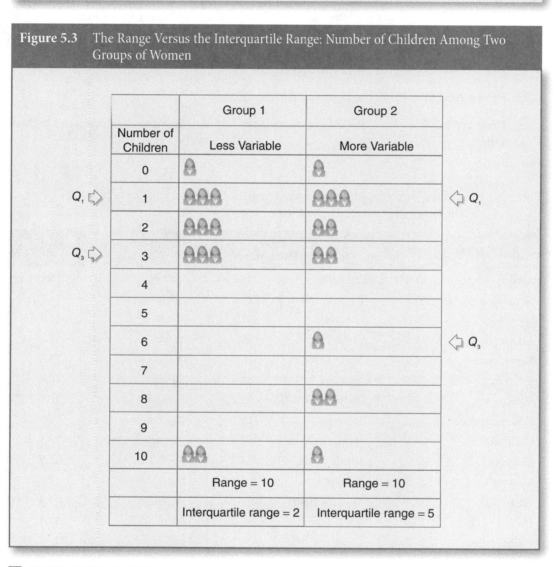

	Number of Children	Group 1	Group 2
		Less Variable	More Variable
	0		
Q_1 ⇨	1		
	2		
Q_3 ⇨	3		
	4		
	5		
	6		
	7		
	8		
	9		
	10		
		Range = 10	Range = 10
		Interquartile range = 2	Interquartile range = 5

⇦ Q_1

⇦ Q_3

▣ THE BOX PLOT

A graphic device called the *box plot* can visually present the range, the IQR, the median, the
lowest (minimum) score, and the highest (maximum) score. The box plot provides us with a

way to visually examine the center, the variation, and the shape of distributions of interval-ratio variables.

Figure 5.4 is a box plot of the distribution of the 2008–2015 projected percentage increase in the elderly population displayed in Table 5.5. To construct the box plot in Figure 5.4, we used the lowest and the highest values in the distribution, the upper and lower quartiles, and the median. We can easily draw a box plot by hand following these instructions:

1. Draw a box between the lower and upper quartiles.

2. Draw a solid line within the box to mark the median.

3. Draw vertical lines (called whiskers) outside the box, extending to the lowest and highest values.

Table 5.5   Projected Percentage Change in the Population 65 Years and Over, 2008–2015, by State, Ordered From the Highest to the Lowest

State	Percentage Change	State	Percentage Change	State	Percentage Change
Alaska	50.0	Delaware	22.3	Alabama	15.1
Nevada	42.1	South Carolina	22.1	Arkansas	14.7
Wyoming	36.9	Georgia	21.1	Missouri	14.5
Arizona	36.8	Connecticut	20.9	Kansas	14.2
New Mexico	31.9	North Carolina	20.7	Utah	13.8
Vermont	31.4	New Jersey	20.4	Illinois	12.9
Florida	29.7	Idaho	20.2	New York	12.8
New Hampshire	28.4	Minnesota	19.2	Oklahoma	12.8
California	27.1	Hawaii	18.8	Kentucky	12.5
Montana	27.0	Rhode Island	18.2	North Dakota	12.6
Virginia	26.8	Tennessee	18.2	Pennsylvania	12.5
Texas	25.9	Massachusetts	17.7	Nebraska	12.4
Maine	25.6	Wisconsin	17.6	Ohio	12.4
Washington	23.2	Oregon	17.1	Indiana	11.3
Maryland	23.1	Mississippi	16.4	Iowa	11.2
Louisiana	23.0	Michigan	15.5	South Dakota	9.4
Colorado	22.7	West Virginia	15.4	Washington, D.C.	−14.1

Source: U.S. Census Bureau, *Statistical Abstract of the United States: 2010*, Tables 16 and 18.

Figure 5.4 Box Plot of the Distribution of the Projected Percentage Increase in the Elderly Population, 2008–2015

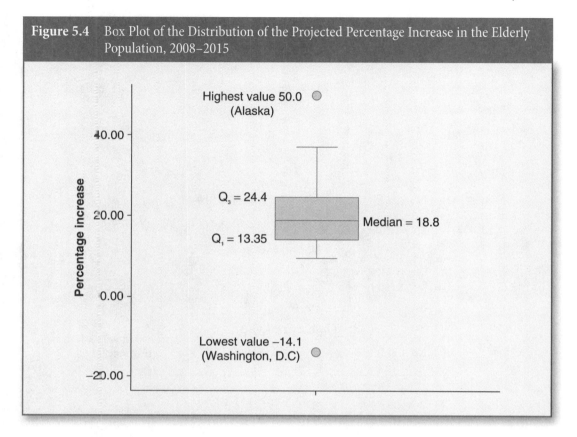

What can we learn from creating a box plot? We can obtain a visual impression of the following properties: First, the center of the distribution is easily identified by the solid line inside the box. Second, since the box is drawn between the lower and upper quartiles, the IQR is reflected in the height of the box. Similarly, the length of the vertical lines drawn outside the box (on both ends) represents the range of the distribution.[9] Both the IQR and the range give us a visual impression of the spread in the distribution. Finally, the relative position of the box and the position of the median within the box tell us whether the distribution is symmetrical or skewed. A perfectly symmetrical distribution would have the box at the center of the range as well as the median in the center of the box. When the distribution departs from symmetry, the box and/or the median will not be centered; it will be closer to the lower quartile when there are more cases with lower scores or to the upper quartile when there are more cases with higher scores.

Is the distribution shown in the box plot in Figure 5.4 symmetrical or skewed?

✓ *Learning Check*

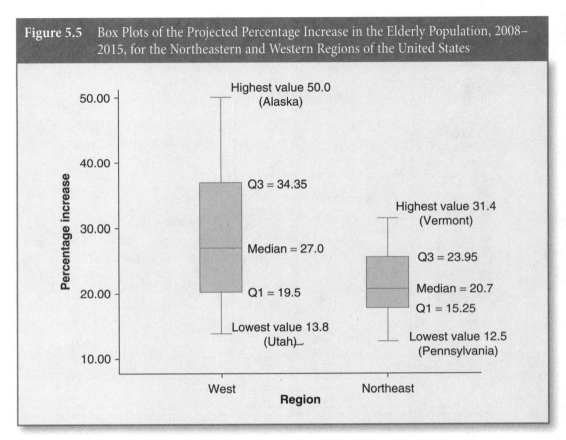

Figure 5.5   Box Plots of the Projected Percentage Increase in the Elderly Population, 2008–2015, for the Northeastern and Western Regions of the United States

Box plots are particularly useful for comparing distributions. To demonstrate box plots that are shaped quite differently, in Figure 5.5 we have used the data on the percentage increase in the elderly population (Table 5.5) to compare the pattern of change occurring between 2008 and 2015 in the northeastern and western regions of the United States.

As you can see, the box plots differ from each other considerably. What can you learn from comparing the box plots for the two regions? First, the positions of the medians highlight the dramatic increase in the elderly population in the western United States. While the Northeast (median = 20.7%) is projected to experience a steady rise in its elderly population, the West shows a much higher projected percentage increase (median = 27%). Second, both the range (illustrated by the position of the whiskers in each box plot) and the IQR (illustrated by the height of the box) are much wider in the West (range = 36.2%; IQR = 14.85%) than in the Northeast (range = 18.9%; IQR = 8.7%), indicating that there is more variability among states in the West than among those in the Northeast. Finally, the relative positions of the boxes tell us something about the different shapes of these distributions. Because its box is at about the center of its range, the northeast distribution is almost symmetrical. In contrast, with its box off center and closer to the lower end of the distribution, the distribution of percentage change in the elderly population for the western states is positively skewed.

▣ THE VARIANCE AND THE STANDARD DEVIATION: CHANGES IN THE ELDERLY POPULATION

As of 2010, the elderly population in the United States is 13 times as large as in 1900, and it is projected to continue to increase.[10] The pace and direction of these demographic changes will create compelling social, economic, and ethical choices for individuals, families, and governments.

Table 5.6 presents the projected percentage change in the elderly population for all regions of the United States.

Table 5.6   Projected Percentage Change in the Elderly Population by Region, 2008–2015

Region	Percentage
Northeast	16.0
South	22.8
Midwest	14.0
West	27.0
Mean ($\overline{Y}$)	19.95

Source: U.S. Census Bureau, *Statistical Abstract of the United States: 2010*, Tables 16 and 18.

These percentage changes were calculated by the U.S. Census Bureau using the following formula:

$$\text{Percentage change} = \left[\frac{(2015 \text{ population} - 2008 \text{ population})}{2008 \text{ population}} \right] \times 100$$

For example, the elderly population in the west region was 6,922,129 in 2008. In 2015, the elderly population will increase to 8,881,215. Therefore, the percentage change from 2008 to 2015 is

$$\text{Percentage change} = \left[\frac{(8,881,215 - 6,922,129)}{6,922,129} \right] \times 100 = 28.3$$

Table 5.6 shows that between 2008 and 2015, the size of the elderly population in the United States is projected to increase by an average of 19.95%. But this average increase does not inform us about the regional variation in the elderly population. For example, will the northeastern states show a smaller-than-average increase because of the out-migration of the elderly population to the warmer climate of the Sun Belt states? Is the projected increase higher in the South because of the immigration of the elderly?

Although it is important to know the average projected percentage increase for the nation as a whole, you may also want to know whether regional increases might differ from the national average. If the regional projected increases are close to the national average, the figures will cluster around the mean, but if the regional increases deviate much from the national average, they will be widely dispersed around the mean.

Table 5.6 suggests that there is considerable regional variation. The percentage change ranges from 27.0% in the West to 14.0% in the Midwest, so the range is 13.0% (27.0% − 14.0% = 13.0%). Moreover, most of the regions are projected to deviate considerably from the national average of 19.95%. How large are these deviations on the average? We want a measure that will give us information about the overall variations among all regions in the United States and, unlike the range or the IQR, will not be based on only two scores.

Such a measure will reflect how much, on the average, each score in the distribution deviates from some central point, such as the mean. We use the mean as the reference point rather than other kinds of averages (the mode or the median) because the mean is based on all the scores in the distribution. Therefore, it is more useful as a basis from which to calculate average deviation. The sensitivity of the mean to extreme values carries over the calculation of the average deviation, which is based on the mean. Another reason for using the mean as a reference point is that more advanced measures of variation require the use of algebraic properties that can be assumed only by using the arithmetic mean.

The *variance* and the *standard deviation* are two closely related measures of variation that increase or decrease based on how closely the scores cluster around the mean. The **variance** is the average of the squared deviations from the center (mean) of the distribution, and the **standard deviation** is the square root of the variance. Both measure variability in interval-ratio variables.

Variance   A measure of variation for interval-ratio variables; it is the average of the squared deviations from the mean.

Standard deviation   A measure of variation for interval-ratio variables; it is equal to the square root of the variance.

Calculating the Deviation From the Mean

Consider again the distribution of the percentage change in the elderly population for the four regions of the United States. Because we want to calculate the average difference of all the regions from the national average (the mean), it makes sense to first look at the difference between each region and the mean. This difference, called a deviation from the mean, is symbolized as $(Y - \bar{Y})$. The sum of these deviations can be symbolized as $\Sigma(Y - \bar{Y})$.

The calculations of these deviations for each region are displayed in Table 5.7 and Figure 5.6. We have also summed these deviations. Note that each region has either a positive or a negative deviation score. The deviation is positive when the percentage change in the elderly home population is above the mean. It is negative when the percentage change is below the mean. Thus, for example, the Northeast's deviation score of −3.95 means that its percentage change in the elderly population was 3.95 percentage points below the mean.

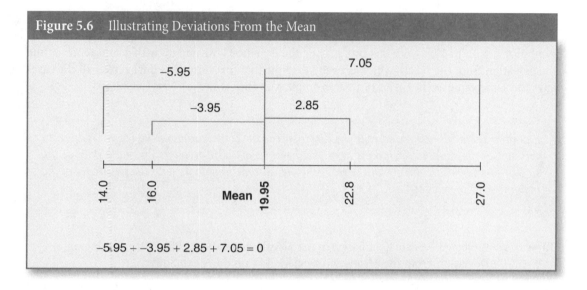

Figure 5.6   Illustrating Deviations From the Mean

Table 5.7   Projected Percentage Change in the Elderly Population, 2008–2015, by Region and Deviation From the Mean

Region	Percentage	$(Y - \overline{Y})$
Northeast	16.0	$16.0 - 19.95 = -3.95$
South	22.8	$22.8 - 19.95 = 2.85$
Midwest	14.0	$14.0 - 19.95 = -5.95$
West	27.0	$27.0 - 19.95 = 7.05$
	$\Sigma(Y) = 79.8$	$\Sigma(Y - \overline{Y}) = 0$

$$\overline{Y} = \frac{\Sigma Y}{N} = \frac{79.8}{4} = 19.95$$

You may wonder if we could calculate the average of these deviations by simply adding up the deviations and dividing them. Unfortunately we cannot, because the sum of the deviations of scores from the mean is always zero, or algebraically $\Sigma(Y - \overline{Y})$. In other words, if we were to subtract the mean from each score and then add up all the deviations as we did in Table 5.7, the sum would be zero, which in turn would cause the average deviation (i.e., average difference) to compute to zero. This is always true because the mean is the center of gravity of the distribution.

Mathematically, we can overcome this problem either by ignoring the plus and minus signs, using instead the absolute values of the deviations, or by squaring the deviations—that is, multiplying each deviation by itself to get rid of the negative sign. Since absolute values are difficult to work with mathematically, the latter method is used to compensate for the problem.

Table 5.8 presents the same information as Table 5.7, but here we have squared the actual deviations from the mean and added together the squares. The sum of the squared deviations is symbolized as $\Sigma(Y-\bar{Y})^2$. Note that by squaring the deviations, we end up with a sum representing the deviation from the mean, which is positive. (Note that this sum will equal zero if all the cases have the same value as the mean.) In our example, this sum is $\Sigma(Y-\bar{Y})^2 = 108.82$.

✓ Learning
Check

Examine Table 5.8 again and note the disproportionate contribution of the western region to the sum of the squared deviations from the mean (it actually accounts for about 45% of the sum of squares). Can you explain why? (Hint: It has something to do with the sensitivity of the mean to extreme values.)

Table 5.8   Projected Percentage Change in the Elderly Population, 2008–2015, by Region, Deviation From the Mean, and Deviation From the Mean Squared

Region	Percentage	$(Y-\bar{Y})$	$(Y-\bar{Y})^2$
Northeast	16.0	$16.0 - 19.95 = -3.95$	15.60
South	22.8	$22.8 - 19.95 = 2.85$	8.12
Midwest	14.0	$14.0 - 19.95 = -5.95$	35.40
West	27.0	$27.0 - 19.95 = 7.05$	49.70
	$\Sigma(Y) = 79.8$	$\Sigma(Y-\bar{Y}) = 0$	$\Sigma(Y-\bar{Y})^2 = 108.82$

$$\text{Mean} = \bar{Y} = \frac{\Sigma Y}{N} = \frac{79.8}{4} = 19.95$$

Calculating the Variance and the Standard Deviation

The average of the squared deviations from the mean is known as the *variance*. The variance is symbolized as S_Y^2. Remember that we are interested in the *average* of the squared deviations from the mean. Therefore, we need to divide the sum of the squared deviations by the number of scores (N) in the distribution. However, unlike the calculation of the mean, we will use $N - 1$ rather than N in the denominator.[11] The formula for the variance can be stated as

$$S_Y^2 = \frac{\Sigma\left(Y - \overline{Y}\right)^2}{N - 1}$$ (5.2)

where

S_Y^2 = the variance

$(Y - \overline{Y})$ = the deviation from the mean

$\Sigma(Y - \overline{Y})^2$ = the sum of the squared deviations from the mean

N = the number of scores

Note that the formula incorporates all the symbols we defined earlier. This formula means that the variance is equal to the average of the squared deviations from the mean.

Follow these steps to calculate the variance:

1. Calculate the mean, $\overline{Y} = \Sigma(Y)/N$.

2. Subtract the mean from each score to find the deviation, $Y - \overline{Y}$.

3. Square each deviation, $(Y - \overline{Y})^2$.

4. Sum the squared deviations, $\Sigma(Y - \overline{Y})^2$.

5. Divide the sum by $N - 1$, $\Sigma(Y - \overline{Y})^2/(N-1)$.

6. The answer is the variance.

To assure yourself that you understand how to calculate the variance, go back to Table 5.8 and follow this step-by-step procedure for calculating the variance. Now plug the required quantities into Formula 5.2. Your result should look like this:

$$S_Y^2 = \frac{\Sigma\left(Y - Y\right)^2}{\left(N - 1\right)} = \frac{108.82}{3} = 36.27$$

One problem with the variance is that it is based on squared deviations and therefore is no longer expressed in the original units of measurement. For instance, it is difficult to interpret the variance of 36.27, which represents the distribution of the percentage change in the elderly population, because this figure is expressed in squared percentages. Thus, we often take the square root of the variance and interpret it instead. This gives us the *standard deviation*, S_Y.

The standard deviation, symbolized as S_Y, is the square root of the variance, or

$$S_Y = \sqrt{S_Y^2}$$

The standard deviation for our example is

$$S_Y = \sqrt{S_Y^2} = \sqrt{36.27} = 6.02$$

The formula for the standard deviation uses the same symbols as the formula for the variance:

$$S_Y = \sqrt{\frac{\Sigma\left(Y - \bar{Y}\right)^2}{(N-1)}} \tag{5.3}$$

As we interpret the formula, we can say that the standard deviation is equal to the square root of the average of the squared deviations from the mean.

The advantage of the standard deviation is that unlike the variance, it is measured in the same units as the original data. For instance, the standard deviation for our example is 6.02. Because the original data were expressed in percentages, this number is expressed as a percentage as well. In other words, you could say, "The standard deviation is 6.02%." But what does this mean? The actual number tells us very little by itself, but it allows us to evaluate the dispersion of the scores around the mean.

In a distribution where all the scores are identical, the standard deviation is zero (0). Zero is the lowest possible value for the standard deviation; in an identical distribution, all the points would be the same, with the same mean, mode, and median. There is no variation or dispersion in the scores.

The more the standard deviation departs from zero, the more variation there is in the distribution. There is no upper limit to the value of the standard deviation. In our example, we can conclude that a standard deviation of 6.02% means that the projected percentage change in the elderly population for the four regions of the United States is widely dispersed around the mean of 19.95%.

The standard deviation can be considered a standard against which we can evaluate the positioning of scores relative to the mean and to other scores in the distribution. As we will see in more detail in Chapter 6, in most distributions, unless they are highly skewed, about 34% of all scores fall between the mean and 1 standard deviation above the mean. Another 34% of scores fall between the mean and 1 standard deviation below it. Thus, we would expect the majority of scores (68%) to fall within 1 standard deviation of the mean.

▣ FOCUS ON INTERPRETATION: GDP (PER CAPITA) FOR SELECT COUNTRIES

The table below shows considerable variability in GDP per capita for the selected countries. We can use the standard deviation to assess the variability around the mean GDP per capita.

GDP per Capita for Select Countries

Country	GDP per Capita[1]
Afghanistan	1,000
Brazil	12,000
Canada	41,500
Chile	18,400
Greece	25,100
Japan	36,200
Lebanon	15,900
Norway	55,300
Panama	15,300
Saudi Arabia	25,700
Singapore	60,900
Tunisia	9,700
United States	49,800
Vietnam	3,500
Zimbabwe	500

Source: GLOBAL13&SDS.

[1] Current U.S. dollar in millions.

The SPSS output showing the mean and standard deviation for GDP per capita is presented below.

Descriptive Statistics

	N	Minimum	Maximum	Mean	Std. Deviation
Gross Domestic Product per capita	70	400	80700	19247.14	1 7628.277
Valid N (listwise)	70				

The table titled "Descriptive Statistics" has six columns. In the first column, we see the name of the variable "Gross Domestic Product per capita" (GDP). The next several columns tell us that there were 70 countries in our sample and that the minimum GDP per capita was $400 and the maximum was $80,700. This is quite a gap between the poorest and richest countries in our sample. The mean and standard deviation are listed in the final two columns.

The mean GDP per capita is $19,247.14, with a standard deviation of $17,628.28. We can expect about 68% of these countries to have GDP per capita values within a range of $1,618.86 ($19,247.14 – $17,628.28) to $36,875.42 ($19,274.14 + $17,628.28). Hence, based on the mean and the standard deviation, we have a pretty good indication of what would be considered a typical GDP per capita value for the majority of countries in our sample. For example, we would consider a country with a GDP per capita value of $80,700 to be extremely wealthy in comparison to other countries. More than two thirds of all countries in our sample fall closer to the mean than the country with a GDP per capita value of $80,700.

Another way to interpret the standard deviation is to compare it with another distribution. For instance, Table 5.9 displays the means and standard deviations of employee age for two samples drawn from a *Fortune 100* corporation. Samples are divided into female clerical and female technical. Note that the mean ages for both samples are about the same—approximately 39 years of age. However, the standard deviations suggest that the distribution of age is dissimilar between the two groups. Figure 5.7 loosely illustrates this dissimilarity in the two distributions.

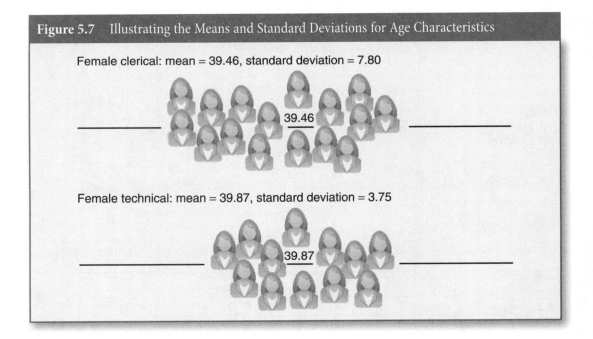

Figure 5.7   Illustrating the Means and Standard Deviations for Age Characteristics

Female clerical: mean = 39.46, standard deviation = 7.80

39.46

Female technical: mean = 39.87, standard deviation = 3.75

39.87

Table 5.9   Age Characteristics of Female Clerical and Technical Employees

Characteristics	Female Clerical N = 22	Female Technical N = 39
Mean age	39.46	39.87
Standard deviation	7.80	3.75

Source: Adapted from Marjorie Armstrong-Srassen, "The Effect of Gender and Organizational Level on How Survivors Appraise and Cope with Organizational Downsizing," *Journal of Applied Behavioral Science,* 34, no. 2 (June 1998): 125–142. Reprinted with permission.

The relatively low standard deviation for female technical indicates that this group is relatively homogenous in age. That is to say, most of the women's ages, while not identical, are fairly similar. The average deviation from the mean age of 39.87 is 3.75 years. In contrast, the standard deviation for female clerical employees is about twice the standard deviation for female technical. This suggests a wider dispersion or greater heterogeneity in the ages of clerical workers. We can say that the average deviation from the mean age of 39.46 is 7.80 years for clerical workers. The larger standard deviation indicates a wider dispersion of points below or above the mean. On average, clerical employees are farther in age from their mean of 39.46.[12]

Take time to understand the section on standard deviation and variance. You will see these statistics in more advanced procedures. Although your instructor may require you to memorize the formulas, it is more important for you to understand how to interpret standard deviation and variance and when they can be appropriately used. Many hand calculators and all statistical software programs will calculate these measures of diversity for you, but they won't tell you what they mean. Once you understand the meaning behind these measures, the formulas will be easier to remember.

▣ CONSIDERATIONS FOR CHOOSING A MEASURE OF VARIATION

So far, we have considered five measures of variation: (1) the IQV, (2) the range, (3) the IQR, (4) the variance, and (5) the standard deviation. Each measure can represent the degree of variability in a distribution. But which one should we use? There is no simple answer to this question. However, in general, we tend to use only one measure of variation, and the choice of the appropriate one involves a number of considerations. These considerations and how they affect our choice of the appropriate measure are presented in the form of a decision tree in Figure 5.8.

As in choosing a measure of central tendency, one of the most basic considerations in choosing a measure of variability is the variable's level of measurement. Valid use of any of the measures requires that the data are measured at the level appropriate for that measure or higher, as shown in Figure 5.8.

Nominal level: With nominal variables, your choice is restricted to the IQV as a measure of variability.

Ordinal level: The choice of measure of variation for ordinal variables is more problematic. The IQV can be used to reflect variability in distributions of ordinal variables, but because it is not sensitive to the rank ordering of values implied in ordinal variables, it loses some information. Another possibility is to use the IQR. However, the IQR relies on distance between two scores to express variation, information that cannot be obtained from ordinal-measured scores. The compromise is to use the IQR (reporting Q_1 and Q_3) alongside the median, interpreting the IQR as the range of rank-ordered values that includes the middle 50% of the observations.[13]

Interval-ratio level: For interval-ratio variables, you can choose the variance (or standard deviation), the range, or the IQR. Because the range, and to a lesser extent the IQR, is based on only two scores in the distribution (and therefore tends to be sensitive if either of the two points is extreme), the variance and/or standard deviation is usually preferred. However, if a distribution is extremely skewed so that the mean is no longer representative of the central tendency in the distribution, the

Figure 5.8 How to Choose a Measure of Variation

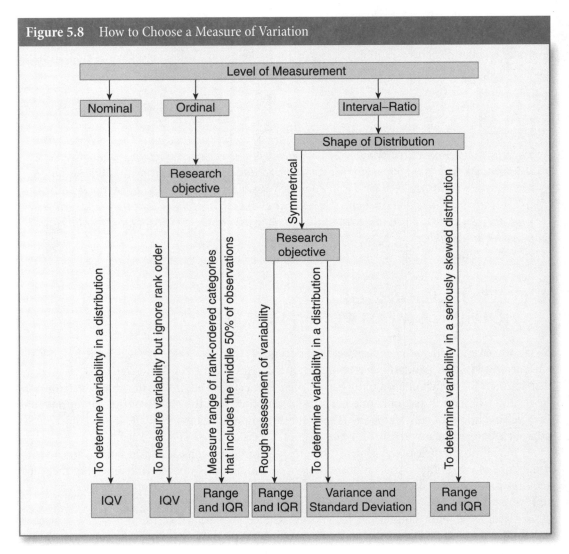

range and the IQR can be used. The range and the IQR will also be useful when you are reading tables or quickly scanning data to get a rough idea of the extent of dispersion in the distribution.

▣ READING THE RESEARCH LITERATURE: DIFFERENCES IN COLLEGE ASPIRATIONS AND EXPECTATIONS AMONG LATINO ADOLESCENTS

In Chapter 2, we discussed how frequency distributions are presented in the professional literature. We noted that most statistical tables presented in the social science literature are considerably more complex than those we describe in this book. The same can be said about measures of central tendency and variation. Most research articles use measures of central tendency and variation in ways that go beyond describing the central tendency and variation of a single variable. In this section, we refer to both the mean and the standard deviation because in most research reports the standard deviation is given along with the mean.

Table 5.10 displays data taken from a research article published in *Social Problems*.[14] This table illustrates a common research application of the mean and standard deviation. The authors of this article examine how ethnicity plays into one's college aspirations and expectations. Their major focus is to explore "potential differences in college aspirations and expectations across the three largest Latino groups and the potential sources of such differences."[15] We focus only on their data for Cubans and Mexicans to present a simplified example of the mean and standard deviation. Understanding the relationship between ethnicity and college aspirations and expectations is, nonetheless, critical in that the U.S. Latino population is growing faster than any other minority group, yet Latinos remain the least educated of all other people of color.

Table 5.10 Ethnicity and College Aspirations and Expectations

	Cubans		Mexicans	
	Mean	*Standard Deviation*	*Mean*	*Standard Deviation*
I. How much respondent wants to go to college	4.50	1.80	4.20	1.30
II. How likely respondent will go to college	4.30	2.00	3.70	1.40

Source: Adapted from Stephanie A. Bohon, Monica Kirkpatrick Johnson, and Bridget K. Gorman, "College Aspirations and Expectations Among Latino Adolescents in the United States," *Social Problems* 53, no. 2 (2006): 207–225. Published by the University of California Press.

Note: The authors examine variation among other ethnicities in this paper. However, to simplify this example, we focus on the descriptive for Cubans and Mexicans.

Data for this study come from the National Longitudinal Study of Adolescent Health survey. This survey is a representative sample of American adolescents in Grades 7 to 12. Complex sampling strategies are employed to ensure a representative sample. Thus, factors such as variation in geographic location, type of school, racial makeup, and so on are accounted for during data collection.

Respondents were asked a variety of questions, but the authors focused specifically on questions about college aspirations and expectations. Their measure of college aspirations is based on a scale of 1 to 5 derived from the question, "How much do you want to go to college?" An answer of 1 indicated a low desire to go to college, while an answer of 5 indicated a high desire to go to college. Their measure of college expectations was also based on the same scale ranging from 1 (*low*) to 5 (*high*). However, it was derived from the question, "How likely is it that you will go to college?"

What can we conclude from examining the means and standard deviations for these variables? The first thing we should look at is the means. Are they similar or different? For both the expectations and aspirations measure, we can see that Mexicans have slightly lower aspirations (4.20) and expectations (3.70) than Cubans (4.50 and 4.30, respectively). Furthermore, the standard deviations indicate that there is more variability in each of these measures for Cubans than for Mexicans.

The researchers of this study described the data displayed in Table 5.10 as follows:

They show strong aspirations for and expectations of college attendance across each of the five groups. Important differences across ethnic groups exist, however. As anticipated, Mexicans have weaker than average . . . and Cubans have stronger than average aspirations and expectations.[16]

Why might this be? The authors conclude their discussion of the data presented in Table 5.10 by arguing as follows:

Differential aspirations and expectations may be explained by the considerable differences in family and household characteristics, parental hopes for their child's educational success, and academic skills and disengagement.[17]

MAIN POINTS

- Measures of variability are numbers that describe how much variation or diversity there is in a distribution.

- The index of qualitative variation (IQV) is used to measure variation in nominal variables. It is based on the ratio of the total number of differences in the distribution to the maximum number of possible differences within the same distribution. IQV can vary from 0.00 to 1.00.

- The range measures variation in interval-ratio variables and is the difference between the highest (maximum) and the lowest (minimum) scores in the distribution. To find the range, subtract the lowest from the highest score in a distribution. For an ordinal variable, just report the lowest and the highest values without subtracting.

- The interquartile range (IQR) measures the width of the middle 50% of the distribution. It is defined as the difference between the lower and upper quartiles (Q_1 and Q_3). For an ordinal variable, just report Q_1 and Q_3 without subtracting.

- The box plot is a graphical device that visually presents the range, the IQR, the median, the lowest (minimum) score, and the highest (maximum) score. The box plot provides us with a way to visually examine the center, the variation, and the shape of a distribution.

- The variance and the standard deviation are two closely related measures of variation for interval-ratio variables that increase or decrease based on how closely the scores cluster around the mean. The variance is the average of the squared deviations from the center (mean) of the distribution; the standard deviation is the square root of the variance.

KEY TERMS

index of qualitative variation (IQV)

interquartile range (IQR)

measures of variability

range

standard deviation

variance

ⓈSAGE edge™

Sharpen your skills with SAGE edge at **edge.sagepub.com/frankfort7e**. **SAGE edge for students** provides a personalized approach to help you accomplish your coursework goals in an easy-to-use learning environment.

SPSS DEMONSTRATIONS

[GSS10SDSS]

Demonstration 1: Producing Measures of Variability With Frequencies

Except for the IQV, the SPSS Frequencies procedure can produce all the measures of variability we've reviewed in this chapter. (SPSS can be programmed to calculate the IQV, but the programming procedures are beyond the scope of our book.)

We'll begin with Frequencies and calculate various statistics for AGE. If we click on *Analyze*, *Descriptive Statistics*, *Frequencies*, then on the *Statistics* button, we can select the appropriate measures of variability.

The measures of variability available are listed in the Dispersion box at the bottom of the dialog box (see Figure 5.9). We've selected the standard deviation, variance, and range, plus the mean and median (in the Central Tendency box) for reference. In the Percentile Values box, we've selected Quartiles to tell SPSS to calculate the values for the 25th, 50th, and 75th percentiles. SPSS also allows us to specify exact percentiles in this section (such as the 34th percentile) by typing a number in the box after "Percentile(s)" and then clicking on the *Add* button.

Earlier, we had seen the frequency table for the variable AGE, so after clicking on *Continue*, we click on *Format* to turn off the display table. This is done by clicking on the button for "Suppress tables with many categories" (see Figure 5.10). There are other formatting options here that you may explore later when using SPSS.

Click on *Continue*, then *OK* to run the procedure. SPSS produces the mean and the other statistics we requested (Figure 5.11). The range of age is 71 years (from 18 to 89). The standard deviation is 17.557, which indicates that there is a moderate amount of dispersion in the ages (this can also be seen from the histogram of AGE in Chapter 3). The variance, 308.248, is the square of the standard deviation (17.557).

The value of the 25th percentile is 35, the value of the 50th percentile (which is also the median) is 49, and the value of the 75th percentile is 62. Although Frequencies does not calculate the IQR, it can easily be calculated by subtracting the value of the 25th percentile from the 75th percentile, which yields a value of 27 years. Compare this value with the standard deviation.

Exercises

Figure 5.9 Statistics Dialog Box

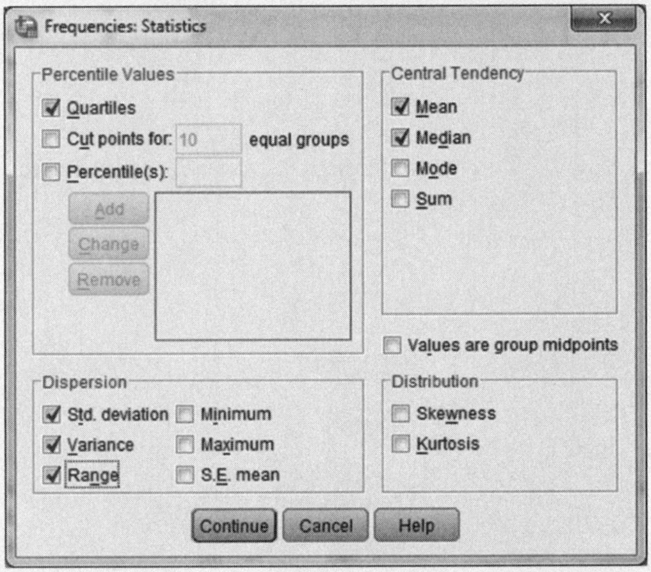

Figure 5.10 Format Dialog Box

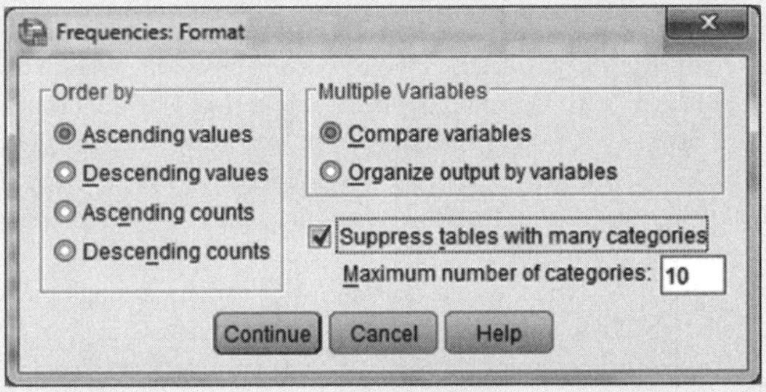

[GSS10SSDS]

Demonstration 2: Producing
Variability Measures and Box Plots With Explore

Another SPSS procedure that can produce the usual measures of variability is Explore, which also produces box plots. The Explore procedure is located in the *Descriptive Statistics* section of the *Analyze* menu.

Figure 5.11 Descriptive Statistics for AGE

Statistics

AGE OF RESPONDENT

N	Valid	1483
	Missing	17
Mean		49.21
Std. Deviation		17.557
Variance		308.248
Range		71
Percentiles	25	35.00
	50	49.00
	75	62.00

In its main dialog box (Figure 5.12), the variables for which you want statistics are placed in the Dependent List box. You have the option of putting one or more nominal variables in the Factor List box; Explore will display separate statistics for each category of the nominal variable(s) you've selected.

Figure 5.12 Explore Dialog Box

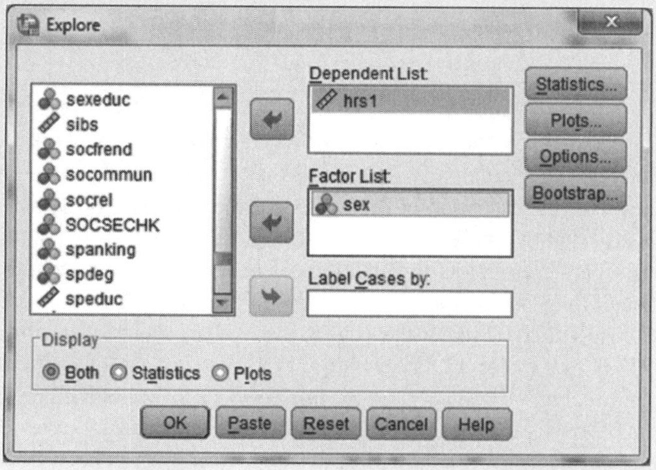

Place the variable HRS1 (number of hours worked last week) in the Dependent box and SEX in the Factor box to provide separate output for males and females. Click *OK*. By default, Explore will produce statistics and plots, so we don't need to make any other choices. Although our request will not produce percentiles or create a histogram, Explore has options to do both plus several other tasks.

Selected output for males is shown in Figure 5.13. Though not replicated here, you'll notice that the first table is the Case Processing Summary Table. It indicates that 390 males answered this question. The valid sample of females is also reported, 448. Based on the second table, Descriptives, we know that for males, the mean number of hours worked last week is 44.32; the median is 41.50. The standard deviation is 15.609, the range is 88, and the IQR is 12,[18] which is quite narrow compared with the range or standard deviation. (A stem-and-leaf plot—another way to visually present and review data—is also displayed by default. However, we will not cover stem-and-leaf plots in this textbook. The option for the stem-and-leaf plot can be changed so that it will not be displayed.)

Figure 5.13   Selected Output for Men's Number of Hours Worked Last Week

Descriptives

RESPONDENTS SEX				Statistic	Std. Error
NUMBER OF HOURS WORKED LAST WEEK	MALE	Mean		44.32	.790
		95% Confidence interval for mean	Lower Bound	42.76	
			Upper Bound	45.87	
		5% Trimmed Mean		44.41	
		Median		41.50	
		Variance		243.651	
		Std. Deviation		15.609	
		Minimum		1	
		Maximum		89	
		Range		88	
		Interquartile Range		12	
		Skewness		−.059	.124
		Kurtosis		.617	.247

Although not displayed here, the mean number of hours worked last week for females is 37.40; the median is 40. The standard deviation is 14.200, the IQR is 13, and the range, 88—values somewhat smaller than those for males with the exception of the range and the IQR. The variation in the number of hours worked last week is also slightly smaller for females than those for males.

Explore displays separate box plots for males and females in the same window for easy comparison (Figure 5.14). Although the SPSS box plot has some differences from those discussed in this chapter, some things are the same. The solid dark line is the value of the median. The width of the shaded box (in color on the screen) is the IQR (12 for males, 13 for females).

Note that SPSS only extends whiskers from the box edges to 1½ times the box width (the IQR). If there are additional values beyond 1½ times the IQR, SPSS displays the individual cases. Those that are somewhat extreme (1½ to 3 box widths from the edge of the box) are marked with an open circle; those considered very extreme (more than 3 box widths from the box edge) are marked with an asterisk.

Figure 5.14   Box Plots Displaying Men's and Women's Number of Hours Worked Last Week

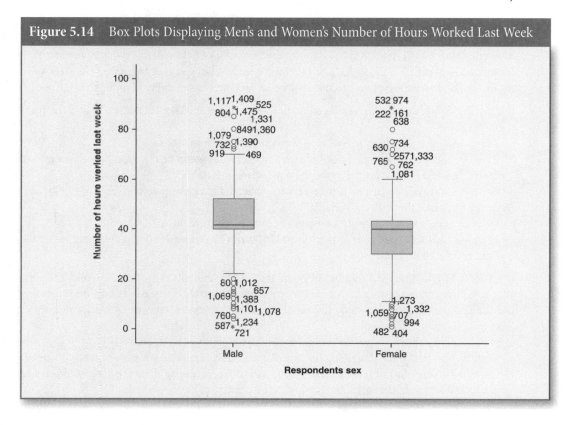

The box plot shows us that variability in hours worked last week is smaller for females than for males. Note that the box is slightly larger for females than for males. The IQR for males runs from 40 to 52, while the IQR for females runs from 30 to 43. Both genders have outlying cases beyond the edge of the whiskers.

SPSS PROBLEMS

[GSS10SSDS]

1. Use the Frequencies procedure to investigate the variability of the respondent's current age (AGE) and age when the respondent's first child was born (AGEKDBRN). Click on *Analyze, Descriptive Statistics, Frequencies,* and then *Statistics*. Select the appropriate measures of variability.

   a. Which variable has more variability? Use more than one statistic to answer this question.
   b. Why should one variable have more variability than the other from a societal perspective?

2. Using the Explore procedure, separate the statistics for AGEKDBRN for men and women, selecting SEX as a factor variable in the Explore window. Click on *Analyze, Descriptive Statistics, Explore,* and then insert AGEKDBRN into the Dependent List and SEX in the Factor List. What differences exist in the age of men and women at the birth of their first child? Assess the differences between men and women based on measures of central tendency and variability.

3. Repeat the procedure in Exercise 2, investigating the dispersion in the variables EDUC (education) and PRESTG80 (occupational prestige score). Select your own factor (nominal) variable to make the comparison (such as CLASS, RACECEN1, or some other factor). Click on *Analyze*, *Descriptive Statistics*, *Explore*, and insert EDUC and PRESTG80 into the Dependent List and your factor variable of choice in the Factor List. In a paragraph or two, use appropriate measures of variability to summarize the results.

4. Using GSS10SSDS, investigate respondents' confidence of the military (CONARMY) and the press (CONPRESS).
   a. First, use SPSS to identify the level of measurement for each variable.
   b. Based on the level of measurement for each variable, what would be the appropriate measures of central tendency? What are the appropriate measures of variability?
   c. Use SPSS and your calculator if necessary to calculate the appropriate measures of central tendency and variability for each variable.
   d. Do respondents more positively view press or military performance?
   e. Examine whether or not your answer toward (d) varies by gender. *Hint*: You may want to use the Data and Split File feature.

5. Use GSS10SSDS to study the number of hours that blacks and whites work each week. The variable HRS1 measures the number of hours a respondent worked the week before the interview. Use the Explore procedure to study the variability of hours worked, comparing blacks and whites (RACECEN1) in the GSS sample.
   a. Is there a difference between the two groups in the variability of work hours?
   b. Write a short paragraph describing the box plot that SPSS created as if you were writing a report and had included the box plot as a chart to support your conclusions about the difference between blacks and whites in the variability (and central tendency) of hours worked.

CHAPTER EXERCISES

1. Americans often think of themselves as quite diverse in their political opinions, within the continuum of liberal to conservative. Let's use data from the 2010 GSS to investigate the diversity of political views. The percentage distribution shown displays respondents' self-rating of their political position. (The statistics box is not displayed; cases with no response were removed for this example.)

Political Views	Percentage (%)
Extremely liberal	3.9
Liberal	11.5
Slightly liberal	12.8
Moderate	36.7
Slightly conservative	14.6
Conservative	16.4
Extremely conservative	4.0
Total	100.0

a. How many categories (K) are we working with?
b. Calculate the sum of the squared percentages, or ΣPct^2.
c. What is the IQV for this variable? Do you find it to be higher (closer to 1) or lower (closer to 0) than you might have expected for political views? Or to put it another way, did you expect that Americans would be diverse in their political views or more narrowly concentrated in certain categories? Does this IQV support your expectation and what you observe from the table?

2. Using the information listed below, answer the following questions to get an idea about the educational attainment, by percentage, of GSS respondents in 2010.

Highest Educational Degree	Male	Female
Less than high school	13.7	13.8
High school graduate	46.5	51.8
Junior college	6.5	8.2
Bachelor's degree	20.7	16.8
Graduate degree	12.7	9.4
Total[a]	100.0	100.0

[a] Totals do not equal 100% due to rounding.

a. What is the value of K?
b. Calculate the sum of the squared percentages, or ΣPct^2, for both males and females.
c. Use the values you calculated in (a) and (b) to calculate the IQV for males and females. Is there more diversity by degree for males or for females?

3. Public corruption continues to be a concern. Let's examine data from the U.S. Department of Justice to explore the variability in public corruption in the years 1990 and 2009. All the numbers below are of those convicted of public corruption.

Number of Public Corruption Convictions by Year

1990		2009	
Govt. Level	No. of Convictions	Govt. Level	No. of Convictions
Federal	583	Federal	426
State	79	State	102
Local	225	Local	257

Source: U.S. Census Bureau, *Statistical Abstract of the United States: 2012*, Table 338.

    a. What is the range of convictions in 1990? In 2009? Which is greater?

    b. What is the mean number of convictions in 1990 and 2009?

    c. Calculate the standard deviation for 1990 and 2009.

    d. Which year appears to have more variability in number of convictions as measured by the standard deviation? Are the results consistent with what you found using the range?

4. Your task is to construct a report regarding criminal offenses investigated by U.S. attorneys by offense and year using the following data from the U.S. Department of Justice. Your report should include the appropriate measures of central tendency, measures of variability, and a few sentences comparing the number of criminal offenses in 2005 with the number of criminal offenses in 2009. Also, include an explanation for any reported difference between 2005 and 2009.

2005		2009	
Type of Offense	No. of Suspects	Type of Offense	No. of Suspects
Violent	5,485	Violent	5,463
Property	25,570	Property	26,161
Drug	40,038	Drug	37,721
Public order	21,583	Public order	23,067
Weapon	13,689	Weapon	11,749
Immigration	36,559	Immigration	88,313

Source: U.S. Department of Justice, *Federal Justice Statistics 2009,* Table 4.

5. The output below depicts data for projected elderly population change in Midwestern and Western states between 2008 and 2015 from Table 5.4.

Descriptives

	Region		Statistic
Population_Change	Midwest	Mean	13.600
		Std. Deviation	2.7831
		Minimum	9.4
		Maximum	19.2
		Range	9.8
		Interquartile Range	3.7
	West	Mean	28.277
		Std. Deviation	10.6948
		Minimum	13.8
		Maximum	50.0
		Range	36.2
		Interquartile Range	17.3

a. Compare the range for the western states to that of the Midwest. Which region had a greater range?

b. Examine the IQR for each region. Which is greater?

c. Use the statistics to characterize the variability in population increase of the elderly in the two regions. Does one region have more variability than another? If yes, why do you think that is?

6. Occupational prestige is a statistic developed by sociologists to measure the status of one's occupation. Occupational prestige is also a component of what sociologists call socioeconomic status, a composite measure of one's status in society. On average, people with more education tend to have higher occupational prestige than people with less education. We investigate this using the 2010 GSS variable PRESTG80 and the Explore procedure to generate the selected SPSS output shown in Figure 5.15.

Figure 5.15   Descriptive Statistics for Occupational Prestige Score by Highest Degree Earned

PRESTG80			Statistic
RS OCCUFAIONAL PRESIGE SCORE (1980)	High School Diploma	Mean	40.59
		Median	40.00
		Std. Deviation	11.419
		Minimum	17
		Maximum	75
		Range	58
		Interquartile Range	17
	Bachelor's Degree	Mean	50.95
		Median	51.00
		Std. Deviation	12.930
		Minimum	23
		Maximum	75
		Range	52
		Interquartile Range	23

a. Note that SPSS supplies the IQR, the median, and the minimum and maximum values of each group. Looking at the values of the mean and median, do you think the distribution of prestige is skewed for respondents with a high school diploma? For respondents with a bachelor's degree? Why or why not?

b. Explain why you think there is more variability of prestige for either group, or why the variability of prestige is similar for the two groups.

7. The U.S. Census Bureau collects information about divorce rates. The following table summarizes the divorce rate for 10 U.S. states in 2007. Use the table to answer the questions that follow.

State	Divorce Rate per 1,000 Population
Alaska	4.3
Florida	4.7
Idaho	4.9

(Continued)

(Continued)

State	Divorce Rate per 1,000 Population
Maine	4.5
Maryland	3.1
Nevada	6.5
New Jersey	3.0
Texas	3.3
Vermont	3.8
Wisconsin	2.9

Source: U.S. Census Bureau, Statistical Abstract of the United States: 2010, Table 126.

   a. Calculate and interpret the range and the IQR. Which is a better measure of variability? Why?
   b. Calculate and interpret the mean and standard deviation.
   c. Identify two possible explanations for the variation in divorce rates across the 10 states.

8. The respondents of the 2007 HINTS reported their psychological distress on a scale between 0 and 24. In the table below, you will see separate data on two groups of respondents' distress scores: those who have ever been diagnosed as having cancer, and those who have not.

	Psychological Distress Score	
	Diagnosed	Not Diagnosed
$\bar{Y}$	3.9	4.87
ΣY	729	5,849
$\Sigma(Y-\bar{Y})^2$	3,059.14	25,180.20
N	187	1,200

   a. Calculate the variance and standard deviation from these statistics for both groups.
   b. What can you say about the variability in the distress scores for those respondents who have been diagnosed as having cancer and those who have not? Why might there be a difference? Why might there be more variability for one group than for the other?
   c. Was it necessary in this problem to provide you with the mean value to calculate the variance and standard deviation?

9. You are interested in studying the variability of crimes committed (including violent and property crimes) and police expenditures in the eastern and Midwestern United States. The U.S. Census Bureau collected the following statistics on these two variables for 21 states in the East and Midwest in 2008.

State	Number of Crimes per 100,000 Population	Police Protection Expenditures (in millions of dollars)
Maine	2,583	233
New Hampshire	2,384	317
Vermont	2,761	141
Massachusetts	2,860	1,843
Rhode Island	3,098	317
Connecticut	2,798	996
New York	2,407	8,164
New Jersey	2,618	3,087
Pennsylvania	2,842	2,840
Ohio	3,982	3,157
Indiana	3,947	1,223
Illinois[a]	3,498	4,242
Michigan	3,492	2,425
Wisconsin	3,047	1,552
Minnesota[b]	2,893	1,527
Iowa	2,820	614
Missouri	4,188	1,632
North Dakota	2,343	120
South Dakota	2,181	141
Nebraska	3,275	528
Kansas	3,800	684

Source: U.S. Census Bureau, *Statistical Abstract of the United States: 2012*, Tables 308 and 443.

[a] Limited data for Illinois during 2008 were available.

[b] Limited data for Minnesota during 2008 were available.

The SPSS output showing the mean and the standard deviation for both variables is presented below.

Descriptive Statistics

	N	Minimum	Maximum	Mean	Std. Deviation
Number of Crimes per 100,000 Population	21	2181	4188	3038.90	583.004
Police Protection Expenditures (in millions of dollars)	21	120	8164	1703.95	1895.214
Valid N (listwise)	21				

a. What are the means? The standard deviations?

b. Compare the mean with the standard deviation for each variable. Does there appear to be more variability in the number of crimes or in police expenditures per capita in these states? Which states contribute more to this greater variability?

c. Suggest why one variable has more variability than the other. In other words, what social forces would cause one variable to have a relatively large standard deviation?

10. Obtain a box plot for both variables in Exercise 9. Discuss how the box plot reinforces the conclusions you drew about the variability of crimes committed and police expenditures per capita.

11. You decide to use Monitoring the Future 2011 data to investigate how young Americans feel about alcohol (ATDRINK) and cigarette use (ATSMOKE). You obtain the data displayed below. You should note that ATDRINK measures how respondents feel about trying alcohol, while ATSMOKE measures how respondents feel about smoking one pack of cigarettes per day. These are substantially different questions, and you should consider that in your answer.

Adolescent Attitudes Toward Alcohol and Cigarettes	Trying Alcohol	Smoking One Pack of Cigarettes per Day
Don't disapprove	66.8%	26.2%
Disapprove	16.3%	35.7%
Strongly disapprove	16.9%	38.0%
Total	100.0%	100.0%
	$N = 1,194$	$N = 1,204$

a. What would an appropriate measure of variability be for these variables? Why?

b. Calculate the appropriate measure of variability for each variable.

c. Was there more variability in attitudes toward trying alcohol or smoking one pack of cigarettes per day? Offer an explanation for your findings.

12. Average life expectancy for females in 2010–2011 is reported for 10 countries. Calculate the appropriate measures of central tendency and variability for both European countries and non-European countries. Is there more variability in life expectancy for European countries or non-European countries? If so, what might explain these differences?

Country	Life Expectancy at Birth[a]
European countries	
France	84.8
Germany	82.6
Netherlands	82.7

Country	Life Expectancy at Birth[a]
Spain	84.7
Turkey	76.3
Non-European countries	
Japan	86.4
Australia	84.0
Mexico	79.2
Iceland	83.5
Israel	83.4

Source: GLOBAL13SSDS.

[a] Data for each country collected from either 2010 or 2011.

13. You have been asked to prepare a brief statement about labor force participation rate for males and females (percentage of population age 15–64). Using statistics from the following table obtained from the GLOBAL13SSDS data set, write a paragraph or two about labor force participation rates throughout the world. In your answer, be sure to identify at least two explanations for your findings.

Labor Force Participation Rates	Participating Countries	Mean	Standard Deviation
Males	70	79.44	6.20
Females	70	57.02	18.54

14. Public participation in election processes is a key to democracy. Let's examine voter turnout in the 2010 November elections by educational level.

Educational Level	Number That Voted (in thousands)
Less than high school graduate	29,837
High school graduate or general equivalency diploma	70,998
Some college or associate's degree	65,321
Bachelor's degree	41,703
Advanced degree	21,831

Source: U.S. Census Bureau, Current Population Survey, 2011.

a. Find the 20th and 80th percentile for the number of voters.
b. Write a few sentences explaining why the results from (a) need to be cautiously interpreted. (*Hint*: Consider the difference between raw frequencies and relative frequencies.)

15. The following table summarizes the racial differences in education and the ideal number of children for Chinese Americans and Filipino Americans. Based on the means and standard deviations (in parentheses), what conclusions can be drawn about differences in the ideal number of children?

	Chinese Americans	Filipino Americans
Education (years)	15.55 (3.643)	13.42 (3.704)
Ideal number of children	2.88 (2.167)	4.00 (2.098)

Source: GSS, 2010.

Chapter 6

The Normal Distribution

Chapter Learning Objectives

❖ Recognizing the importance and the use of the normal distribution in statistics
❖ Describing the properties of the normal distribution
❖ Transforming a raw score into standard (Z) score and vice versa
❖ Using the standard normal table
❖ Transforming a Z score into proportion (or percentage) and vice versa
❖ Finding and explaining the percentile rank of a score

I n the preceding chapters, we have learned some important things about distributions: how to organize them into frequency distributions, how to display them using graphs, and how to describe their central tendencies and variation using measures such as the mean and the standard deviation. We have also learned that distributions can have different shapes. Some distributions are symmetrical, and others are negatively or positively skewed. The distributions that we have described so far are all *empirical distributions*—that is, they are all based on real data.

The distribution that we describe in this chapter—known as the *normal curve* or the **normal distribution**—is a theoretical distribution. A *theoretical distribution* is similar to an empirical distribution in that it can be organized into frequency distributions, displayed using graphs, and described by its central tendency and variation using measures such as the mean and the standard deviation. However, unlike an empirical distribution, a theoretical distribution is based on theory rather than on real data. The value of the theoretical normal distribution lies in the fact that many empirical distributions that we study seem to approximate it. We can often learn a lot about the characteristics of these empirical distributions based on our knowledge of the theoretical normal distribution.

Normal distribution   A bell-shaped and symmetrical theoretical distribution with the mean, the median, and the mode all coinciding at its peak and with the frequencies gradually decreasing at both ends of the curve.

▣ PROPERTIES OF THE NORMAL DISTRIBUTION

The normal curve (Figure 6.1) looks like a bell-shaped frequency polygon. Because of this property, it is sometimes called the *bell-shaped curve*. One of the most striking characteristics of the normal distribution is its perfect symmetry. Notice that if you fold Figure 6.1 exactly in the middle, you have two equal halves, each the mirror image of the other. This means that precisely half the observations fall on each side of the middle of the distribution. In addition, the midpoint of the normal curve is the point having the maximum frequency. This is also the point at which three measures coincide: the mode (the point of the highest frequency), the median (the point that divides the distribution into two equal halves), and the mean (the average of all the scores). Notice also that most of the observations are clustered around the middle, with the frequencies gradually decreasing at both ends of the distribution.

Empirical Distributions Approximating the Normal Distribution

The normal curve is a theoretical ideal, and real-life distributions never match this model perfectly. However, researchers study many variables (e.g., standardized tests such as the SAT, ACT, or GRE; height; athletic ability; and numerous social and political attitudes) that closely resemble this theoretical model. When we say that a variable is "normally distributed," we mean that the graphic display will reveal an approximately bell-shaped and symmetrical distribution closely resembling the idealized model shown in Figure 6.1. This property makes it possible for us to describe many empirical distributions based on our knowledge of the normal curve.

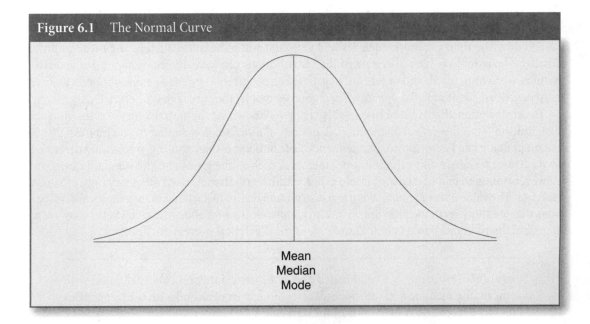

Figure 6.1   The Normal Curve

Mean
Median
Mode

An Example: Final Grades in Statistics

It is easier to understand the properties of a normal curve if we think in terms of a real distribution that is near normal. Let's examine the frequencies and the bar chart presented in Table 6.1. These data are the final scores of 1,200 students who took Professor Frankfort-Nachmias's social statistics class at the University of Wisconsin–Milwaukee between 1983 and 1993. To convince you that the variable *final score in statistics* is normally distributed, we overlaid a normal curve on the distribution shown in Table 6.1. Notice how closely our empirical distribution of statistics scores approximates the normal curve!

Note that 70 is the most frequent score obtained by the students, and therefore, it is the mode of the distribution. Because about half the students are either above (49.99%) or below (50.01%) this score (based on raw frequencies), both the mean (70.07) and the median (70) are approximately 70. Also shown in Table 6.1 is the gradual decrease in the number of students who scored either above or below 70. Very few students scored higher than 90 or lower than 50.

When we use the term *normal curve*, we are not referring to identical distributions. The shape of a normal distribution varies, depending on the mean and standard deviation of the particular distribution. (The symbol μ_y is the population notation for the mean while σ_y stands for the population

Table 6.1   Final Grades in Social Statistics of 1,200 Students (1983–1993): A Near Normal Distribution

Midpoint Score	Frequency Bar Chart	Freq	Cum Freq	%	Cum %
40		4	4	0.33	0.33
50	************	78	82	6.50	6.83
60	**************************	275	357	22.92	29.75
70	********************************	483	840	40.25	70.00
80	**************************	274	1,114	22.83	92.83
90	************	81	1,195	6.75	99.58
100		5	1,200	0.42	100.00
	0 50 100 200 300 400 500				

Mean $(\overline{Y}) = 70.07$ Median $= 70.00$ Mode $= 70.00$

Standard deviation $(S_y) = 10.27$

standard deviation. We will discuss these symbols in more detail in the next chapter.) For example, in Figure 6.2, we present two normally shaped distributions with identical means ($\mu_Y = 12$) but with different standard deviations ($\sigma_{y1} = 3$, $\sigma_{y2} = 5$). Note that the distribution with the larger standard deviation appears relatively wider and flatter.

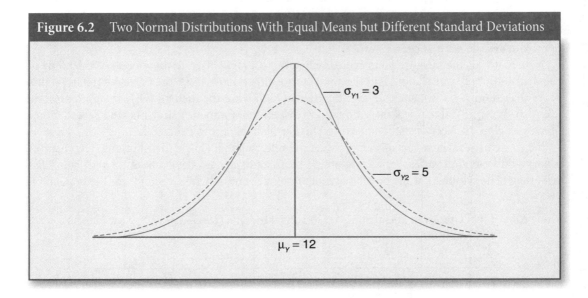

Figure 6.2   Two Normal Distributions With Equal Means but Different Standard Deviations

Areas Under the Normal Curve

Regardless of the precise shape of the distribution, in all normal or nearly normal curves we find a constant proportion of the area under the curve lying between the mean and any given distance from the mean when measured in standard deviation units. The area under the normal curve may be conceptualized as a proportion or percentage of the number of observations in the sample. Thus, the entire area under the curve is equal to 1.00 or 100% (1.00×100) of the observations. Because the normal curve is perfectly symmetrical, exactly 0.50 or 50% of the observations lie above or to the right of the center, which is the mean of the distribution, and 50% lie below or to the left of the mean.

In Figure 6.3, note the percentage of cases that will be included between the mean and 1, 2, and 3 standard deviations above and below the mean. The mean of the distribution divides it exactly into half; 34.13% is included between the mean and 1 standard deviation to the right of the mean, and the same percentage is included between the mean and 1 standard deviation to the left of the mean. The plus signs indicate standard deviations above the mean; the minus signs denote standard deviations below the mean. Thus, between the mean and ±1 standard deviation, 68.26% of all the observations in the distribution occur; between the mean and ±2 standard deviations, 95.46% of all observations in the distribution occur; and between the mean and ±3 standard deviations, 99.72% of the observations occur.

✓ *Learning Check*

Review and confirm the properties of the normal curve. What is the area underneath the curve equal to? What percentage of the distribution is within 1 standard deviation? Within 2 and 3 standard deviations? Verify the percentage of cases by summing the percentages in Figure 6.3.

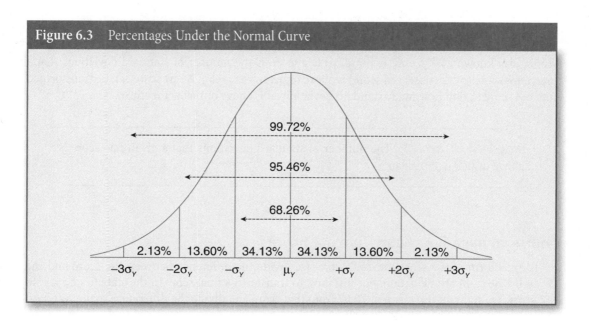

Figure 6.3 Percentages Under the Normal Curve

Interpreting the Standard Deviation

The fixed relationship between the distance from the mean and the areas under the curve represents a property of the normal curve that has highly practical applications. As long as a distribution is normal and we know the mean and the standard deviation, we can determine the relative frequency (proportion or percentage) of cases that fall between any score and the mean.

This property provides an important interpretation for the standard deviation of empirical distributions that are approximately normal. For such distributions, when we know the mean and the standard deviation, we can determine the percentage of scores that are within any distance, measured in standard deviation units, from that distribution's mean. For example, we know that college entrance tests such as the SAT and ACT are normally distributed. The SAT, for instance, has a mean of 500 and a standard deviation of 100. This means that approximately 68% of the students who take the test obtain a score between 400 (1 standard deviation below the mean) and 600 (1 standard deviation above the mean). We can also anticipate that approximately 95% of the students who take the test will score between 300 (2 standard deviations below the mean) and 700 (2 standard deviations above the mean).

Not every empirical distribution is normal. We've learned that the distributions of some common variables, such as income, are skewed and therefore not normal. The fixed relationship between the distance from the mean and the areas under the curve applies only to distributions that are normal or approximately normal.

▣ STANDARD (Z) SCORES

We can express the difference between any score in a distribution and the mean in terms of *standard scores*, also known as *Z scores*. A **standard (Z) score** is the number of standard deviations that a given raw score (or the observed score) is above or below the mean. A raw score can be transformed into a *Z* score to find how many standard deviations it is above or below the mean.

Standard (Z) score   The number of standard deviations that a given raw score is above or below the mean.

Transforming a Raw Score Into a Z Score

To transform a raw score into a *Z* score, we divide the difference between the score and the mean by the standard deviation. For instance, to transform a final score in the statistics class into a *Z* score, we subtract the mean of 70.07 from that score and divide the difference by the standard deviation of 10.27. Thus, the *Z* score of 80 is

$$\frac{80 - 70.07}{10.27} = 0.97$$

or 0.97 standard deviations above the mean. Similarly, the *Z* score of 60 is

$$\frac{60 - 70.07}{10.27} = -0.98$$

or 0.98 standard deviations below the mean; the negative sign indicates that this score is below the mean.

This calculation, in which the difference between a raw score and the mean is divided by the standard deviation, gives us a method of standardization known as *transforming a raw score into a Z score* (also known as a standard score). The *Z* score formula is

$$Z = \frac{Y - \overline{Y}}{S_Y} \tag{6.1}$$

A *Z* score allows us to represent a raw score in terms of its relationship to the mean and to the standard deviation of the distribution. It represents how far a given raw score is from the mean in standard deviation units. A positive *Z* indicates that a score is larger than the mean, and a negative *Z* indicates that it is smaller than the mean. The larger the *Z* score, the larger the difference between the score and the mean (Table 6.2).

Table 6.2   Final Social Science Statistics Scores Converted to Z Score

Final Score	Z Score
40	$Z = \dfrac{40 - 70.07}{10.27} = \dfrac{-30.07}{10.27} = -2.93$
50	$Z = \dfrac{50 - 70.07}{10.27} = \dfrac{-20.07}{10.27} = -1.95$
60	$Z = \dfrac{60 - 70.07}{10.27} = \dfrac{-10.07}{10.27} = -0.98$
70	$Z = \dfrac{70 - 70.07}{10.27} = \dfrac{-0.07}{10.27} = -0.01$
80	$Z = \dfrac{80 - 70.07}{10.27} = \dfrac{9.93}{10.27} = 0.97$
90	$Z = \dfrac{90 - 70.07}{10.27} = \dfrac{19.93}{10.27} = 1.94$
100	$Z = \dfrac{100 - 70.07}{10.27} = \dfrac{29.93}{10.27} = 2.91$
$\overline{Y} = 70.07$	$S_Y = 10.27$

Transforming a Z Score Into a Raw Score

For some normal curve applications, we need to reverse the process, transforming a Z score into a raw score instead of transforming a raw score into a Z score. A Z score can be converted to a raw score to find the score associated with a particular distance from the mean when this distance is expressed in standard deviation units. For example, suppose we are interested in finding out the final score in the statistics class that lies 1 standard deviation above the mean. To solve this problem, we begin with the Z score formula:

$$Z = \frac{Y - \overline{Y}}{S_Y}$$

Note that for this problem, we have the following values for Z ($Z = 1$), the mean, and the standard deviation $S_Y = 10.27$, but we need to determine the value of Y:

$$1 = \frac{Y - 70.07}{10.27}$$

Through simple algebra, we solve for Y:

$$Y = 70.07 + 1(10.27) = 70.07 + 10.27 = 80.34$$

The score of 80.34 lies 1 standard deviation (or 1 Z score) above the mean of 70.07. The general formula for transforming a Z score into a raw score is

$$Y = \overline{Y} + Z(S_Y) \tag{6.2}$$

Thus, to transform a Z score into a raw score, multiply the Z score by the standard deviation and add this product to the mean.

Now, what statistics score lies 1.5 standard deviations below the mean? Because the score lies below the mean, the Z score is negative. Thus,

$$Y = 70.07 + (-1.5)(10.27) = 70.07 - 15.41 = 54.66$$

The score of 54.66 lies 1.5 standard deviations below the mean of 70.07.

✓ *Learning*
Check

Transform the Z scores in Table 6.2 back into raw scores. Your answers should agree with the raw scores listed in the table.

THE STANDARD NORMAL DISTRIBUTION

When a normal distribution is represented in standard scores (Z scores), we call it the **standard normal distribution**. Standard scores, or Z scores, are the numbers that tell us the distance between an actual score and the mean in terms of standard deviation units. The standard normal distribution has a mean of 0.0 and a standard deviation of 1.0.

Standard normal distribution   A normal distribution represented in standard *(Z)* scores, with mean = 0 and standard deviation = 1.

Figure 6.4 shows a standard normal distribution with areas under the curve associated with 1, 2, and 3 standard scores above and below the mean. To help you understand the relationship between raw scores of a distribution and standard Z scores, we also show the raw scores in the statistics class that correspond to these standard scores. For example, notice that the mean for the statistics score distribution is 70.07 and the corresponding Z score—the mean of the standard normal distribution— is 0. The score of 80.34 is 1 standard deviation above the mean (70.07 + 10.27 = 80.34); therefore, its corresponding Z score is +1. Similarly, the score of 59.80 is 1 standard deviation below the mean (70.07 − 10.27 = 59.80), and its Z-score equivalent is −1.

THE STANDARD NORMAL TABLE

We can use Z scores to determine the proportion of cases that are included between the mean and any Z score in a normal distribution. The areas or proportions under the standard normal curve,

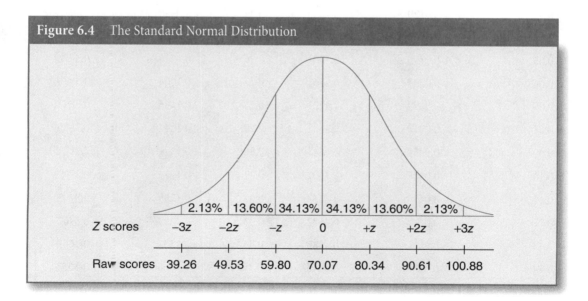

Figure 6.4   The Standard Normal Distribution

corresponding to any Z score or its fraction, are organized into a special table called the **standard normal table**. The table is presented in Appendix B. In this section, we discuss how to use this table.

Standard normal table   A table showing the area (as a proportion, which can be translated into a percentage) under the standard normal curve corresponding to any Z score or its fraction.

The Structure of the Standard Normal Table

Table 6.3 reproduces a small part of the standard normal table. Note that the table consists of three columns (rather than having one long table, we have moved the second half of the table next to the first half, so the three columns are presented in a six-column format).

Table 6.3   The Standard Normal Table

(A) Z	(B) Area Between Mean and Z	(C) Area Beyond Z	(A) Z	(B) Area Between Mean and Z	(C) Area Beyond Z
0.00	0.0000	0.5000	0.21	0.0832	0.4168
0.01	0.0040	0.4960	0.22	0.0871	0.4129
0.02	0.0080	0.4920	0.23	0.0910	0.4090
0.03	0.0120	0.4880	0.24	0.0948	0.4052
0.04	0.0160	0.4840	0.25	0.0987	0.4013
0.05	0.0199	0.4801	0.26	0.1026	0.3974
0.06	0.0239	0.4761	0.27	0.1064	0.3936
0.07	0.0279	0.4721	0.28	0.1103	0.3897
0.08	0.0319	0.4681	0.29	0.1141	0.3859
0.09	0.0359	0.4641	0.30	0.1179	0.3821
0.10	0.0398	0.4602	0.31	0.1217	0.3783
0.11	0.0438	0.4562	0.32	0.1255	0.3745
0.12	0.0478	0.4522	0.33	0.1293	0.3707
0.13	0.0517	0.4483	0.34	0.1331	0.3669
0.14	0.0557	0.4443	0.35	0.1368	0.3632

(A) Z	(B) Area Between Mean and Z	(C) Area Beyond Z	(A) Z	(B) Area Between Mean and Z	(C) Area Beyond Z
0.15	0.0596	0.4404	0.36	0.1406	0.3594
0.16	0.0636	0.4364	0.37	0.1443	0.3557
0.17	0.0675	0.4325	0.38	0.1480	0.3520
0.18	0.0714	0.4286	0.39	0.1517	0.3483
0.19	0.0753	0.4247	0.40	0.1554	0.3446
0.20	0.0793	0.4207			

Column A lists positive Z scores. Because the normal curve is symmetrical, the proportions that correspond to positive Z scores are identical to the proportions corresponding to negative Z scores.

Column B shows the area included between the mean and the Z score listed in Column A. Note that when Z is positive, the area is located on the right side of the mean (see Figure 6.5a), whereas for a negative Z score, the same area is located left of the mean (Figure 6.5b).

Column C shows the proportion of the area that is beyond the Z score listed in Column A. Areas corresponding to positive Z scores are on the right side of the curve (see Figure 6.5a). Areas corresponding to negative Z scores are identical except that they are on the left side of the curve (Figure 6.5b).

Transforming Z Scores Into Proportions (or Percentages)

We illustrate how to use Appendix B with some simple examples using our data on students' final statistics scores (see Table 6.1). The examples in this section are applications that require the transformation of Z scores into proportions (or percentages).

Figure 6.5   Areas Between Mean and Z (B) and Beyond Z (C)

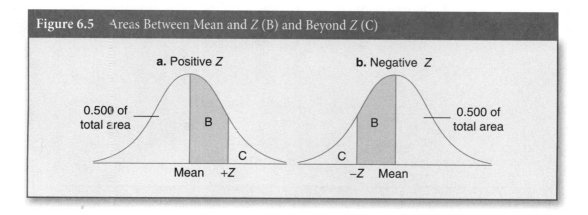

Finding the Area Between the Mean and a Specified Positive Z Score

Use the standard normal table to find the area between the mean and a specified positive Z score. To find the percentage of students whose scores range between the mean (70.07) and 85, follow these steps.

1. Convert 85 to a Z score:

$$Z = \frac{85 - 70.07}{10.27} = 1.45$$

2. Look up 1.45 in Column A (in Appendix B) and find the corresponding area in Column B, 0.4265. We can translate this proportion into a percentage ($0.4265 \times 100 = 42.65\%$) of the area under the curve included between the mean and a Z score of 1.45 (Figure 6.6).

3. Thus, 42.65% of the students scored between 70.07 and 85.

To find the actual number of students who scored between 70.07 and 85, multiply the proportion 0.4265 by the total number of students. Thus, approximately 512 students ($0.4265 \times 1,200 = 512$) obtained a score between 70.07 and 85.

Finding the Area Between the Mean and a Specified Negative Z Score

What is the percentage of students whose scores ranged between 65 and 70.07? We can use the standard normal table and the following steps to find out.

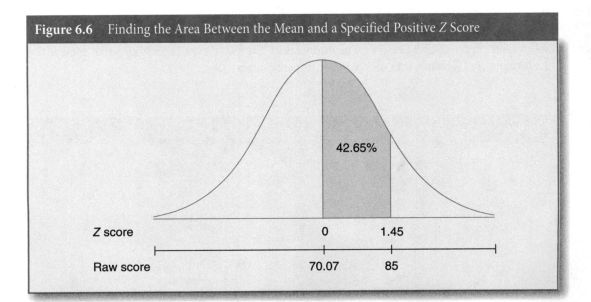

Figure 6.6   Finding the Area Between the Mean and a Specified Positive *Z* Score

1. Convert 65 to a Z score:

$$Z = \frac{65 - 70.07}{10.27} = -0.49$$

2. Because the proportions that correspond to positive Z scores are identical to the proportions corresponding to negative Z scores, we ignore the negative sign of Z and look up 0.49 in Column A. The area corresponding to a Z score of 0.49 is 0.1879. This indicates that 0.1879 of the area under the curve is included between the mean and a Z of -0.49 (Figure 6.7). We convert this proportion to 18.79% ($0.1879 \times 100 = 18.79\%$).

3. Thus, approximately 225 ($0.1879 \times 1,200 = 225$) students obtained a score between 65 and 70.07.

Finding the Area Above a Positive Z Score or Below a Negative Z Score

We can compare students who have done very well or very poorly to get a better idea of how they compare with other students in the class.

To identify students who did very well, we selected all students who scored above 85. To find how many students scored above 85, first convert 85 to a Z score

$$Z = \frac{85 - 70.07}{10.27} = 1.45$$

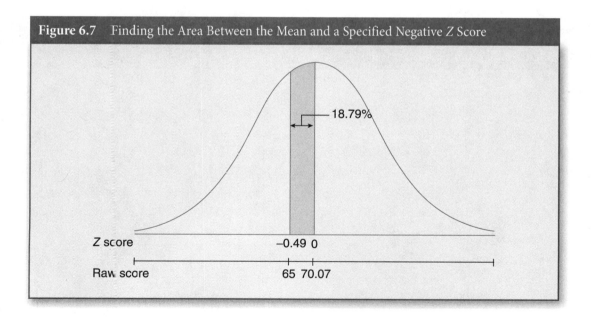

Figure 6.7   Finding the Area Between the Mean and a Specified Negative Z Score

Thus, the Z score corresponding to a final score of 85 in statistics is equal to 1.45.

The area beyond a Z of 1.45 includes all students who scored above 85. This area is shown in Figure 6.8. To find the proportion of students whose scores fall in this area, refer to the entry in Column C that corresponds to a Z of 1.45, 0.0735. This means that 7.35% (0.0735 × 100 = 7.35%) of the students scored above 85. To find the actual number of students in this group, multiply the proportion 0.0735 by the total number of students. Thus, there were 1,200 × 0.0735, or about 88 students, who scored above 85 over the 10-year period.

A similar procedure can be applied to identify the number of students who did not do well in the class. The cutoff point for poor performance in this class was the score of 50. To determine how many students did poorly, we first converted 50 to a Z score:

$$Z = \frac{50 - 70.07}{10.27} = -1.95$$

The Z score corresponding to a final score of 50 is equal to −1.95. The area beyond a Z of −1.95 includes all students who scored below 50. This area is also shown in Figure 6.8. Locate the proportion of students in this area in Column C in the entry corresponding to a Z of 1.95. (Remember that the proportions corresponding to positive or negative Z scores are identical.) This proportion is equal to 0.0256. Thus, 2.56% (0.0256 × 100 = 2.56%) of the group, or about 31 (0.0256 × 1,200) students, performed poorly in statistics.

Transforming Proportions (or Percentages) Into Z Scores

The examples in this section are applications that require transforming proportions (or percentages) into Z scores.

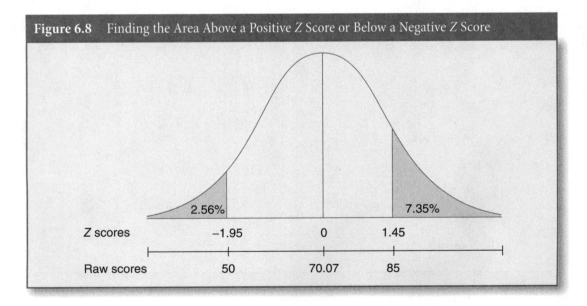

Figure 6.8   Finding the Area Above a Positive Z Score or Below a Negative Z Score

Finding a Z Score Bounding an Area Above It

Assuming that a grade of A is assigned to the top 10% of the students, what would it take to get an A in the class? To answer this question, we need to identify the cutoff point for the top 10% of the class. This problem involves two steps:

1. Find the Z score that bounds the top 10% or 0.1000 (0.1000 × 100 = 10%) of all the students who took statistics (Figure 6.9).

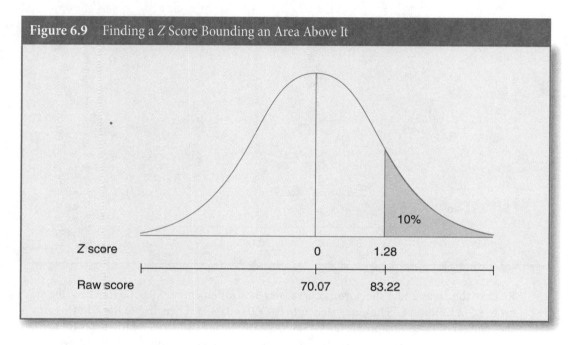

Figure 6.9   Finding a Z Score Bounding an Area Above It

Refer to the areas under the normal curve shown in Appendix B. First, look for an entry of 0.1000 (or the value closest to it) in Column C. The entry closest to 0.1000 is 0.1003. Then, locate the Z in Column A that corresponds to this proportion. The Z score associated with the proportion 0.1003 is 1.28.

2. Find the final score associated with a Z of 1.28.

This step involves transforming the Z score into a raw score. We learned earlier in this chapter (Formula 6.2) that to transform a Z score into a raw score we multiply the score by the standard deviation and add that product to the mean. Thus,

$$Y = 70.07 + 1.28(10.27) = 70.07 + 13.15 = 83.22$$

The cutoff point for the top 10% of the class is a score of 83.22.

Finding a Z Score Bounding an Area Below It

Now, let's assume that a grade of F was assigned to the bottom 5% of the class. What would be the cutoff point for a failing score in statistics? Again, this problem involves two steps:

1. Find the Z score that bounds the lowest 5% or 0.0500 of all the students who took the class (Figure 6.10).

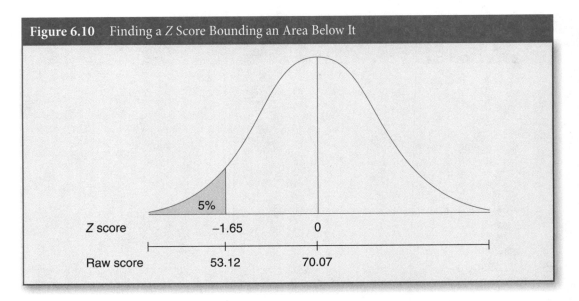

Figure 6.10 Finding a Z Score Bounding an Area Below It

Refer to the areas under the normal curve, and look for an entry of 0.0500 (or the value closest to it) in Column C. The entry closest to 0.0500 is 0.0495. Then, locate the Z in Column A that corresponds to this proportion, 1.65. Because the area we are looking for is on the left side of the curve—that is, below the mean—the Z score is negative. Thus, the Z associated with the lowest 0.0500 (or 0.0495) is −1.65.

2. To find the final score associated with a Z of −1.65, convert the Z score to a raw score:

$$Y = 70.07 + (-1.65)(10.27) = 70.07 - 16.95 = 53.12$$

The cutoff for a failing score in statistics is 53.12.

✓ *Learning*
  Check

Can you find the number of students who got a score of at least 90 in the statistics course? How many students got a score below 60?

Working With Percentiles in a Normal Distribution

In Chapter 4, we defined percentiles as scores below which a specific percentage of the distribution falls. For example, the 95th percentile is a score that divides the distribution so that 95% of the cases are below it and 5% of the cases are above it. How are percentile ranks determined? How do you convert a percentile rank to a raw score? To determine the percentile rank of a raw score requires transforming Z scores into proportions or percentages. Converting percentile ranks to raw scores is based on transforming proportions or percentages into Z scores. In the following examples, we illustrate both procedures based on our statistics scores example.

Finding the Percentile Rank of a Score Higher Than the Mean

Suppose you are one of the 1,200 students who took the statistics course. Your final score in the course was 85%. How well did you do relative to the other students who took the class? To evaluate your performance, you must translate your raw score into a percentile rank. Figure 6.11 illustrates this problem.

To find the percentile rank of a score higher than the mean, follow these steps:

1. Convert the raw score to a Z score:

$$Z = \frac{85 - 70.07}{10.27} = 1.45$$

The Z score corresponding to a raw score of 85 is 1.45.

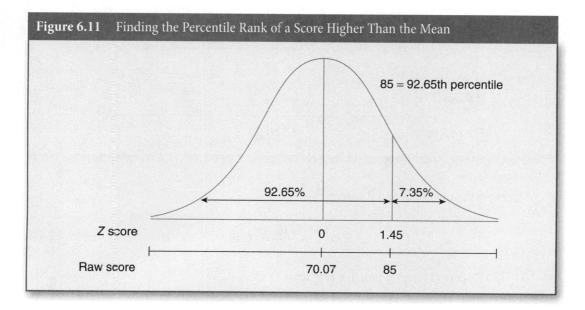

Figure 6.11   Finding the Percentile Rank of a Score Higher Than the Mean

85 = 92.65th percentile

92.65%

7.35%

Z score   0   1.45

Raw score   70.07   85

2. Find the area beyond Z in Appendix B, Column C. The area beyond a Z score of 1.45 is 0.0735.

3. Subtract the area from 1.00 and multiply by 100 to obtain the percentile rank:

$$\text{Percentile rank} = (1.0000 - .0735 = 0.9265)100 = 92.65\%$$

Being in the 92.65th percentile means that 92.65% of all the students enrolled in social statistics scored lower than 85 and 7.35% scored higher than 85%.

Finding the Percentile Rank of a Score Lower Than the Mean

Now, let's say that you were unfortunate enough to obtain a score of 65 in the class. What is your percentile rank? Again, to evaluate your performance, you must translate your raw score into a percentile rank. Figure 6.12 illustrates this problem.

To find the percentile rank of a score lower than the mean, follow these steps:

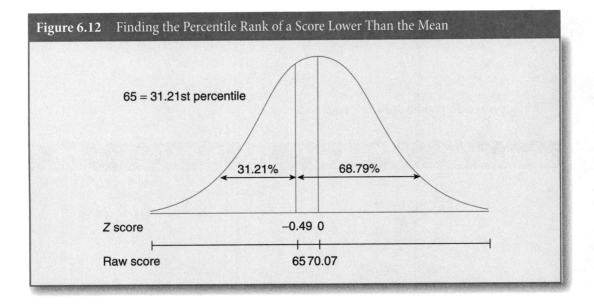

Figure 6.12 Finding the Percentile Rank of a Score Lower Than the Mean

1. Convert the raw score to a Z score:

$$Z = \frac{65 - 70.07}{10.27} = -0.49$$

The Z score corresponding to a raw score of 65 is −0.49.

2. Find the area beyond *Z* in Appendix B, Column C. The area beyond a *Z* score of −0.49 is 0.3121.

3. Multiply the area by 100 to obtain the percentile rank:

$$\text{Percentile rank} = 0.3121(100) = 31.21\%$$

The 31.21st percentile rank means that 31.21% of all the students enrolled in social statistics did worse than you (i.e., 31.21% scored lower than 65, but 68.79% scored higher than 65).

In Chapter 4, we learned to identify percentiles using cumulative percentages in a distribution. Examine Table 6.1 and find the 92nd percentile. Does your answer differ from the results that we obtained earlier (finding the percentile rank of a score higher than the mean)? If it does, explain why.

Finding the Raw Score Associated With a Percentile Higher Than 50

Now, let's assume that our graduate program in sociology will accept only students who scored at the 95th percentile. What is the cutoff point required for admission? Figure 6.13 illustrates this problem.

Figure 6.13 Finding the Raw Score Associated With a Percentile Higher Than 50

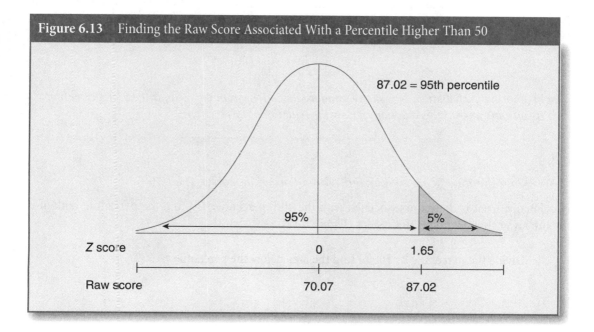

To find the score associated with a percentile higher than 50, follow these steps:

1. Divide the percentile by 100 to find the area below the percentile rank:

$$\frac{95}{100} = 0.95$$

2. Subtract the area below the percentile rank from 1.00 to find the area above the percentile rank:

$$1.00 - 0.95 = 0.05$$

3. Find the Z score associated with the area above the percentile rank.

   Refer to the area under the normal curve shown in Appendix B. First, look for an entry of 0.0500 (or the value closest to it) in Column C. The entry closest to 0.0500 is 0.0495. Now, locate the Z in Column A that corresponds to this proportion, 1.65.

4. Convert the Z score to a raw score:

$$Y = 70.07 + 1.65(10.27) = 70.07 + 16.95 = 87.02$$

The final statistics score associated with the 95th percentile is 87.02%. This means that you will need a score of 87.02 or higher to be admitted to the graduate program in sociology.

✓ *Learning*
Check

In a normal distribution, how many standard deviations from the mean is the 95th percentile? If you can't answer this question, review the material in this section.

Finding the Raw Score Associated With a Percentile Lower Than 50

Finally, what is the score associated with the 40th percentile? To find the percentile rank of a score lower than 50 follow these steps (Figure 6.14).

1. Divide the percentile by 100 to find the area below the percentile rank:

$$\frac{40}{100} = 0.40$$

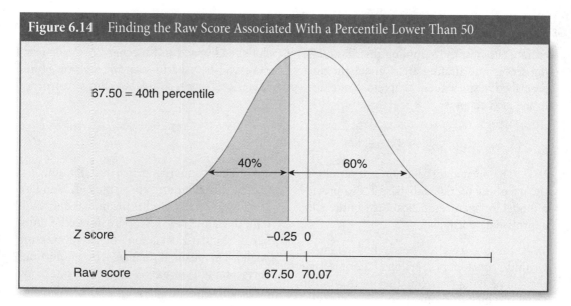

Figure 6.14 Finding the Raw Score Associated With a Percentile Lower Than 50

2. Find the *Z* score associated with this area.

   Refer to the area under the normal curve shown in Appendix B. First, look for an entry of 0.4000 (or the value closest to it) in Column C. The entry closest to 0.4000 is 0.4013. Now, locate the *Z* in Column A that corresponds to this proportion. The *Z* score associated with the proportion 0.4013 is −0.25.

3. Convert the *Z* score to a raw score:

$$Y = 70.07 + (-0.25)(10.27) = 70.07 - 2.568 = 67.50$$

   The final statistics score associated with the 40th percentile is 67.50. This means that 40% of the students scored below 67.50 and 60% scored above it.

What is the raw score in statistics associated with the 50th percentile?

✓ *Learning Check*

▣ A FINAL NOTE

In this chapter, we have learned how the properties of the theoretical normal curve can be applied to describe important characteristics of empirical distributions that are approximately normal. The normal curve has other practical applications as well, however, beyond the description of "real-life" distributions. In subsequent chapters, we will see that the normal distribution also enables us to describe the characteristics of a theoretical distribution of great significance in inferential statistics: the sampling distribution. The techniques learned in this chapter—transforming scores and finding areas under the normal curve—will be used in many of the procedures described in subsequent chapters. Make sure you understand these techniques before you proceed to the next chapter.

MAIN POINTS

- The normal distribution is central to the theory of inferential statistics. It also provides a model for many empirical distributions that approximate normality.

- In all normal or nearly normal curves, we find a constant proportion of the area under the curve lying between the mean and any given distance from the mean when measured in standard deviation units.

- The standard normal distribution is a normal distribution represented in standard scores, or Z scores, with mean = 0 and standard deviation = 1. Z scores express the number of standard deviations that a given score is above or below the mean. The proportions corresponding to any Z score or its fraction are organized into a special table called the standard normal table.

KEY TERMS

normal distribution
standard normal distribution

standard normal table
standard (Z) score

⑤SAGE edge™

Sharpen your skills with SAGE edge at **edge.sagepub.com/frankfort7e**. **SAGE edge for students** provides a personalized approach to help you accomplish your coursework goals in an easy-to-use learning environment.

SPSS DEMONSTRATION

[GSS10SSDS]

Producing Z Scores With SPSS

In this chapter, we have discussed the theoretical normal curve, Z scores, and the relationship between raw scores and Z scores. The SPSS Descriptives procedure can calculate Z scores for any distribution. We'll use it to study the distribution of occupational prestige in the 2010 GSS file. Locate the Descriptives procedure in the *Analyze* menu, under *Descriptive Statistics*, then click *Descriptives*. We can select one or more variables to place in the Variable(s) box; for now, we'll just place PRESTG80 (occupational prestige score) in this box (Figure 6.15). A checkbox in the bottom left corner tells SPSS to create standardized values, or Z

scores, as new variables. Any new variable is placed in a new Column in the Data View window and will then be available for additional analyses. Click on *OK* to run the procedure.

Figure 6.15 Descriptives Dialog Box

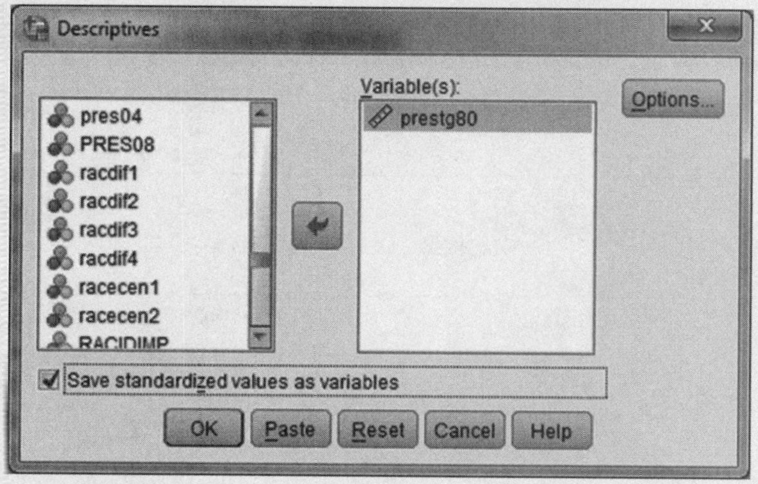

The output from Descriptives (Figure 6.16) is brief, listing the mean and standard deviation for PRESTG80, plus the minimum and maximum values and the number of valid cases.

Figure 6.16 Descriptives for Occupational Prestige Score

Descriptive Statistics

	N	Minimum	Maximum	Mean	Std. Deviation
RS OCCUPATIONAL PRESTIGE SCORE (1980)	1420	17	86	44.19	13.867
Valid N (listwise)	1420				

Though not indicated in the Output window, SPSS has created a new *Z* score variable for PRESTG80. To see this new variable, switch to the Data View screen. Then, go to the last Column, scrolling all the way to the right (Figure 6.17). By default, SPSS appends a *Z* to the variable name, so the new variable is called ZPRESTG80. The first case in the file has a *Z* score of 1.50056, so the prestige score for this person must be above the mean of 44.19. If we locate the respondent's PRESTG80 score, we see that the score for this person was 65 (not pictured), or above the mean as we expected. As seen in Figure 6.17, there are a number of missing values for ZPRESTG80. Simply put, the cells that contain only a "." indicate the respondent's answer was missing on the original variable (PRESTG80). Missing values include those that the question did not apply to, those that outright refused to provide occupational information, or those data entry errors that resulted in an invalid answer.

Figure 6.17   The Creation of the Z Score Variable for PRESTG80

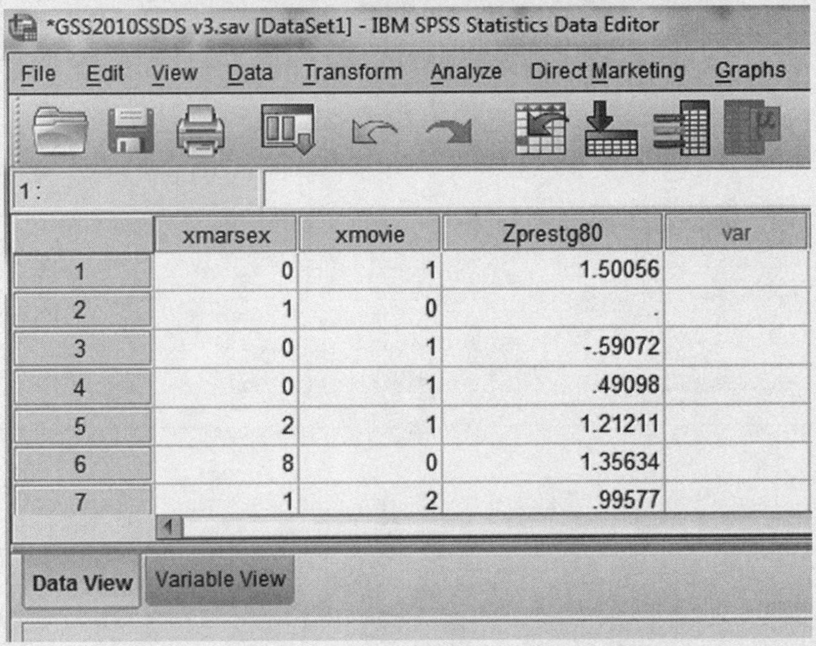

If the data file is saved, the new Z score variable will be saved along with the original data and then can be used in analyses. In addition, if we have SPSS calculate the mean and standard deviation of ZPRESTG80, we find that they are equal to 0 and 1.00, respectively.

SPSS PROBLEMS

[GSS10SSDS]

1. The majority of variables that social scientists study are not normally distributed. This doesn't typically cause problems in analysis when the goal of a study is to calculate means and standard deviations—as long as sample sizes are greater than about 50. (This will be discussed in later chapters.) However, when characterizing the distribution of scores in one sample, or in a complete population (if this information is

available), a non-normal distribution can cause complications. We can illustrate this point by examining the distribution of age in the GSS data file.

a. Create a histogram for AGE (click on *Graphs, Legacy Dialogs, Histogram;* insert the variable *age*) with a superimposed normal curve (click on the option *Display Normal Curve*). How does the distribution of AGE deviate from the theoretical normal curve?

b. Calculate the mean and standard deviation for AGE in this sample, using either the Frequencies or Descriptives procedure.

c. Assuming the distribution of AGE is normal, calculate the number of people who should be 25 years of age or less.

d. Use the Frequencies procedure to construct a table of the percentage of cases at each value of AGE. Compare the theoretical calculation in (c) with the actual distribution of age in the sample. What percentage of people in the sample are 25 years old or less? Is this value close to what you calculated? Why might there be a discrepancy?

2. SPSS will calculate standard scores for any distribution. Examine the distribution of EDUC (years of school completed).

a. Have SPSS calculate *Z* scores for EDUC. (See the SPSS Demonstration above if this is unclear.)

b. What is the equivalent *Z* score for someone who has completed 18 years of education?

c. Use the Frequencies procedure to find the percentile rank for a score of 18.

d. Does the percentile rank that you found from Frequencies correspond to the *Z* score for a value of 18? In other words, is the distribution for years of education normal? If so, then the *Z* score that SPSS calculates should be very close, after transforming it into an appropriate area, to the percentile rank for that same score.

e. Create histograms for EDUC and the new variable ZEDUC. Explain why they have the same shape.

3. Repeat the procedure in Problem 2, this time running separate analyses for men versus women (SEX) and blacks versus whites (RACECEN1) based on the variable EDUC. Remember, you can run separate analyses using the Data Split File command. Click on *Data, Split File, Organize Output by Groups* and select either SEX or RACECEN1. Is there a difference in EDUC among men/women and blacks/whites in the GSS sample? How would you describe the distribution of EDUC for the four groups?

CHAPTER EXERCISES

1. We discovered that 1,013 GSS respondents in 2010 watched television for an average of 3.01 hr/day, with a standard deviation of 2.65 hr. Answer the following questions assuming the distribution of the number of television hours is normal.

a. What is the *Z* score for a person who watches more than 8 hr/day?

b. What proportion of people watch television less than 5 hr/day? How many does this correspond to in the sample?

c. What number of television hours per day corresponds to a *Z* score of +1?

d. What is the percentage of people who watch between 1 and 6 hr of television per day?

2. If a particular distribution that you are studying is not normal, it may be difficult to determine the area under the curve of the distribution or to translate a raw score into a *Z* value. Is this statement true? Why or why not?

3. Let's assume that education is normally distributed. Using GSS data, we find the mean number of years of education is 13.47 with a standard deviation of 3.1. A total of 1,496 respondents were included in the survey. Use these numbers to answer the following questions.
   a. If you have 13.47 years of education, that is, the mean number of years of education, what is your Z score?
   b. If your friend is in the 60th percentile, how many years of education does she have?
   c. How many people have between your years of education (13.47) and your friend's years of education?

4. A criminologist developed a test to measure recidivism, where low scores indicated a lower probability of repeating the undesirable behavior. The test is normed so that it has a mean of 140 and a standard deviation of 40.
   a. What is the percentile rank of a score of 172?
   b. What is the Z score for a test score of 200?
   c. What percentage of scores falls between 100 and 160?
   d. What proportion of respondents should score above 190?
   e. Suppose an individual is in the 67th percentile in this test, what is his or her corresponding recidivism score?

5. The 2010 GSS provides the following statistics for the average years of education for lower-, working-, middle-, and upper-class respondents and their associated standard deviations.

	Mean	Standard Deviation	N
Lower class	11.61	2.67	123
Working class	12.80	2.85	697
Middle class	14.45	3.08	626
Upper class	15.45	2.98	38

   a. Assuming that years of education is normally distributed in the population, what proportion of working-class respondents have 12 to 16 years of education? What proportion of upper-class respondents have 12 to 16 years of education?
   b. What is the probability that a working-class respondent, drawn at random from the population, will have more than 16 years of education? What is the equivalent probability for a middle-class respondent drawn at random?
   c. What is the probability that a lower- or upper-class respondent will have less than 12 years of education?
   d. Find the upper and lower limits, centered on the mean that will include 50% of all working-class respondents.
   e. If years of education is actually positively skewed in the population, how would that change your other answers?

6. The following table displays unemployment information for each region of the United States in March 2013. The unemployment numbers listed in the table are in thousands. For example, the Midwest was home to 2,525,600 unemployed residents when data were collected.

Unemployment (in thousands) in the United States: 2013			
Midwest	2,525.6	West	3,004.6
Northeast	2,240.2	South	4,106.9

Source: U.S. Bureau of Labor Statistics, *News Release*, April 19, 2013, USDL-13-0672, Table 1.

  a. What are the mean and standard deviation unemployment numbers for all regions?
  b. Using information from (a), how many regions fall more than 1 standard above the mean? How does this number compare with the number expected from the theoretical normal curve distribution?
  c. Create a histogram representing the unemployment figures for all regions. Does the distribution appear to be normal? Explain your answer.

7. Information on the occupational prestige scores for blacks and whites are presented in the following table.

	Mean	Standard Deviation	N
Whites	45.03	13.93	1,100
Blacks	40.83	13.07	195

Source: GSS, 2010.

  a. What percentage of whites should have occupational prestige scores above 60? How many whites in the sample should have occupational prestige scores above 60?
  b. What percentage of blacks should have occupational prestige scores above 60? How many blacks should have occupational prestige scores above 60?
  c. What proportion of whites have prestige scores between 30 and 70? How many whites have prestige scores between 30 and 70?
  d. How many blacks in the sample should have an occupational prestige score between 30 and 60?

8. SAT scores are normed so that, in any year, the mean of the verbal or math test should be 500 and the standard deviation 100. Assuming this is true (it is only approximately true, both because of variation from year to year and because scores have decreased since the SAT tests were first developed), answer the following questions.
  a. What percentage of students score above 625 on the math SAT in any given year?
  b. What percentage of students score between 400 and 600 on the verbal SAT?
  c. A college decides to liberalize its admission policy. As a first step, the admissions committee decides to exclude only those applicants scoring below the 20th percentile on the verbal SAT. Translate this percentile into a Z score. Then, calculate the equivalent SAT verbal test score.

9. The Hate Crime Statistics Act of 1990 requires the Attorney General to collect national data about crimes that manifest evidence of prejudice based on race, religion, sexual orientation, or ethnicity, including the crimes of murder and non-negligent manslaughter, forcible rape, aggravated assault, simple assault, intimidation, arson, and destruction, damage or vandalism of property. The Hate Crime Data collected in 2007 reveals, based on a randomly selected sample of 300 incidents, that the mean number of victims in a particular type of hate crime was 1.28, with a standard deviation of 0.82. Assuming that the number of victims was normally distributed, answer the following questions.
   a. What proportion of crime incidents had more than 2 victims?
   b. What is the probability that there was more than 1 victim in an incident?
   c. What proportion of crime incidents had less than 4 victims?

10. The number of hours people work each week varies widely for many reasons. Using the 2010 GSS, you find that the mean number of hours worked last week was 40.62, with a standard deviation of 15.26 hr, based on a sample size of 838.
   a. Assume that hours worked is approximately normally distributed in the sample. What is the probability that someone in the sample will work 60 hr or more in a week? How many people in the sample of 894 should have worked 60 hr or more?
   b. What is the probability that someone will work 30 hr or fewer in a week (i.e., work part time)? How many people does this represent in the sample?
   c. What number of hours worked per week corresponds to the 60th percentile?

11. The National Collegiate Athletic Association (NCAA) has a public access database on each Division I sports team in the United States, which contains data on team-level Academic Progress Rates (APRs), eligibility rates, and retention rates. The mean APR of 359 men's basketball teams for the 2010–2011 academic year was 950.35 (based on a 1,000-point scale), with a standard deviation of 30.58. Assuming that the distribution of APRs for the teams is approximately normal,
   a. Would a team be at the upper quartile (the top 25%) of the APR distribution with an APR score of 975?
   b. What APR score should a team have to be more successful than 75% of all the teams?
   c. What is the Z value for this score?

12. According to the same NCAA data, the means and standard deviations of eligibility and retention rates (based on a 1,000-point scale) for the 2010–2011 academic year follow, along with the scores for two men's basketball teams, A and B. Assume that test scores are normally distributed.

	Mean	*Standard Deviation*	*Team A*	*Team B*
Eligibility	974.3	40.4	917	962
Retention	970.2	38.8	913	962

   a. On which criterion (eligibility or retention) did Team A do better, relative to the other teams? Calculate appropriate statistics to answer this question.
   b. On which criterion (eligibility or retention) did Team B do better, relative to the other teams? Calculate appropriate statistics to answer this question.

c. What proportion of the teams have retention rates below the retention rate of Team B?

d. What is the percentile rank of Team A's eligibility rate?

13. What is the value of the mean score for any standard normal distribution? What is the value of the standard deviation for any standard normal distribution? Explain why this is true for any standard normal distribution.

14. You are asked to do a study of shelters for abused and battered women to determine the necessary capacity in your city to provide housing for most of these women. After recording data for a whole year, you find that the mean number of women in shelters each night is 250, with a standard deviation of 75. Fortunately, the distribution of the number of women in the shelters each night is normal, so you can answer the following questions posed by the city council.

a. If the city's shelters have a capacity of 350, will that be enough places for abused women on 95% of all nights? If not, what number of shelter openings will be needed?

b. The current capacity is only 220 openings, because some shelters have been closed. What is the percentage of nights that the number of abused women seeking shelter will exceed current capacity?

15. Based on the chapter discussion,

a. What are the properties of the normal distribution? Why is it called "normal"?

b. What is the meaning of a positive (+) Z score? What is the meaning of a negative (−) Z score?

Chapter 7

Sampling and Sampling Distributions

Until now, we have ignored the question of who or what should be observed when we collect data or whether the conclusions based on our observations can be generalized to a larger group of observations. The truth is that we are rarely able to study or observe everyone or everything we are interested in. Although we have learned about various methods to analyze observations, remember that these observations represent only a tiny fraction of all the possible observations we might have chosen. Consider the following examples.

Example 1: The Muslim Student Association on your campus is interested in conducting a study of experiences with campus diversity. You only have enough funds to survey 300 students on your campus. Given that your campus is home to more than 20,000 students, what should you do?

Example 2: Local environmental activists want to assess recycling practices on your campus to develop a proposal to reduce unnecessary waste. Since the university serves more than 30,000 students, faculty, and staff, how should the activists proceed?

Example 3: The student union on your campus is trying to find out how it can better address the needs of commuter students and has commissioned you to conduct a needs assessment survey. You have been given enough money to survey about 500 students. Given that there are nearly 15,000 commuters on your campus, is this an impossible task?

What do these problems have in common? In all situations, the major problem is that there is too much information and not enough resources to collect and analyze all of it.

▣ AIMS OF SAMPLING[1]

Researchers in the social sciences almost never have enough time or money to collect information about the entire group that interests them. Known as the **population**, this group includes all the cases (individuals, objects, or groups) in which the researcher is interested. For example, in our first illustration, there are more than 20,000 students; the population in the second illustration consists of all 30,000 faculty, staff, and students; and in the third illustration, the population is all 15,000 commuter students.

Population   A group that includes all the cases (individuals, objects, or groups) in which the researcher is interested.

Fortunately, we can learn a lot about a population if we carefully select a subset of it. This subset is called a **sample**. Through the process of *sampling*—selecting a subset of observations from the population of interest—we attempt to generalize the characteristics of the larger group (population) based on what we learn from the smaller group (the sample). This is the basis of *inferential statistics*—making predictions or inferences about a population from observations based on a sample.

Sample   A subset of cases selected from a population.

The term **parameter**, associated with the population, refers to measures used to describe the distribution of the population we are interested in. For instance, the average commuting time for *all* of the 15,000 students on your campus is a population parameter because it refers to a population characteristic. In previous chapters, we have learned the many ways of describing a distribution, such as a proportion, a mean, or a standard deviation. When used to describe the population distribution, these measures are referred to as parameters. Thus, a population mean, a population proportion, and a population standard deviation are all parameters.

Parameter   A measure (e.g., mean or standard deviation) used to describe the population distribution.

We use the term **statistic** when referring to a corresponding characteristic calculated for the sample. For example, the average commuting time for a *sample* of commuter students is a sample statistic. Similarly, a sample mean, a sample proportion, and a sample standard deviation are all statistics.

Statistic   A measure (e.g., mean or standard deviation) used to describe the sample distribution.

In this chapter as well as in Chapters 8 and 9, we discuss some of the principles involved in generalizing results from samples to the population. In our discussion, we will use different notations when referring to sample statistics and population parameters. Table 7.1 presents the sample notation and the corresponding population notation.

The distinctions between a sample and a population and between a parameter and a statistic are illustrated in Figure 7.1. We've included for illustration the population parameter of 0.60—the proportion of white respondents in the population. However, since we almost never have enough resources to collect information about the population, it is rare that we know the value of

Table 7.1   Sample and Population Notations

Measure Notation	Sample Notation	Population
Mean	$\overline{Y}$	μ_Y
Proportion	p	π
Standard deviation	S_Y	σ_Y
Variance	S_Y^2	σ_Y^2

Figure 7.1   The Proportion of White Respondents in a Population and in a Sample

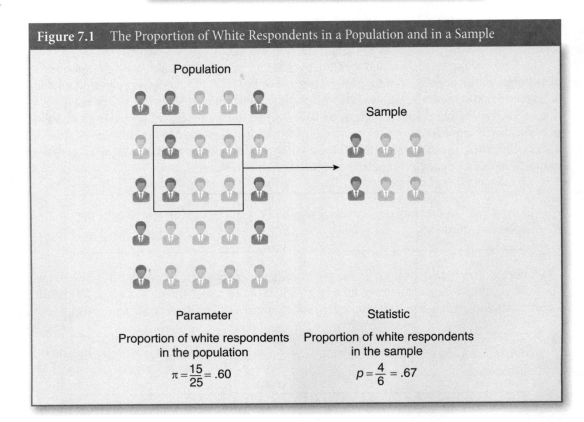

Population

Sample

Parameter

Proportion of white respondents in the population

$$\pi = \frac{15}{25} = .60$$

Statistic

Proportion of white respondents in the sample

$$p = \frac{4}{6} = .67$$

a parameter. The goal of most research is to find the population parameter. Researchers usually select a sample from the population to obtain an estimate of the population parameter. Thus, the major objective of sampling theory and statistical inference is to provide estimates of unknown parameters from sample statistics that can be easily obtained and calculated.

✓ *Learning Check*

It is important that you understand what the terms population, sample, parameter, and statistic mean. Use your own words so that the meaning makes sense to you. If you cannot clearly define these terms, review the preceding material. You will see these sample and population notations over and over again. If you memorize them, you will find it much easier to understand the formulas used in inferential statistics.

▣ SOME BASIC PRINCIPLES OF PROBABILITY

Probability Defined

We all use the concept of probability in everyday conversation. We might ask, "What is the probability that it will rain tomorrow?" or "What is the likelihood that we will do well on a test?" In everyday conversations, our answers to these questions are rarely systematic, but in the study of statistics, *probability* has a far more precise meaning.

In the following sections, we will discuss a variety of techniques adopted by social scientists to select samples from populations. The techniques all follow a general approach called *probability sampling*. Before we discuss these techniques, we will review some theories and principles of probability.

A probability is a quantitative measure of the chance that an event will occur. It is expressed as a ratio of the number of times a desired outcome will occur relative to the set of all possible and equally likely outcomes. Consider, for example, the outcome of rolling a 3 with a six-sided, equally weighted die. The probability of rolling a 3 is 1/6 or 0.17, because this outcome can occur only once out of a total of six possible outcomes: 1, 2, 3, 4, 5, 6. We can also say that the probability of rolling 3 is 17% (0.17 × 100).

The term *probability* is often applied to events where the outcome is uncertain, like the chance that you'll get an "A" on your statistics midterm. In this example, we don't know for sure what will happen. Probabilities are usually measured in terms of proportions that range in value from 0 to 1. The closer the proportion is to 1, the more likely it is that the desired outcome will occur. A proportion that is close to 0 means that the desired outcome will never occur, while 1 would mean that the event will always occur. Let's say that the chances you'll get an "A" on your statistics midterm are 50%. This means that you are just as likely to get an "A" or not get an "A."

The Relative Frequency Method

Sometimes we use information from past events to help us predict the likelihood of future events. Such a method is called the relative frequency method. Let's consider, for example, a sample of 1,266 respondents from the 2008 Monitoring the Future Survey. Respondents were asked their opinions regarding the job performance of the police; their responses are summarized in Table 7.2.

Table 7.2   Views on Police Performance

	Frequency	Proportion
Very poor	125	0.10
Poor	201	0.16
Fair	452	0.36
Good	380	0.30
Very good	108	0.09
Total	1,266	1.01

The ratio of respondents with the opinion that police do a "good" job is 380:1,266, or when reduced, approximately 1:3. To convert a ratio to a proportion, we divide the numerator (380) by the denominator (1,266), as shown in Table 7.2. Thus, the probability 380:1,266 is equivalent to 0.3 (380/1,266 = 0.3). Now, imagine that we wrote down each of the 1,266 respondents' names and placed them in a hat. Because the proportion of 0.3 is closer to 0 than it is to 1, there is a low likelihood that we would select a respondent with the opinion that police do a "good" job.

✓ *Learning Check*

> *What is the probability of drawing an ace out of a normal deck of 52 playing cards? It's not 1/52. There are four aces, so the probability is 4/52 or 1/13. The proportion is 0.08. The probability of drawing the ace of spades is 1/52 or 0.02.*

The observed relative frequencies are just an approximation of the true probability of selecting a respondent with a specific view on police performance. The true probabilities can only be determined if we were to repeat the study many times under the same conditions. Then, our long-run relative frequency (or probability) will approximate the true probability.

The Normal Distribution and Probabilities

In Chapter 6, you learned about the normal distribution and "areas" below it. We expressed these areas as proportions or percentages of the number of observations in a sample in terms of their distance from the mean expressed in standard deviation units. These proportions make it possible to estimate the probability of occurrence of these observations. For example, a study of 200 teen girls on the prevalence of texting found the average number of messages a teen girl texts per day to be 70 with a standard deviation of 10. We can estimate that the probability of randomly selecting a teen girl who texts between 70 and 80 messages per day is approximately .3413. (Do you know why? If not, review the material in Chapter 6.) You can also say that there is a 34.13% chance that any teen girl drawn randomly from the sample of 200 girls would text between 70 and 80 messages per day.

▣ PROBABILITY SAMPLING[2]

Social researchers are usually more systematic in their effort to obtain samples that are representative of the population than we are when we gather information in our everyday life. Such researchers have adopted a number of approaches for selecting samples from populations. Only one general approach, *probability sampling*, allows the researcher to use the principles of statistical inference to generalize from the sample to the population.

Probability sampling is a method that enables the researcher to specify for each case in the population the probability of its inclusion in the sample. The purpose of probability sampling is to select a sample that is as representative as possible of the population. The sample is selected in such a way as to allow the use of the principles of probability to evaluate the generalizations made from the sample to the population. A probability sample design enables the researcher to estimate the extent to which the findings based on one sample are likely to differ from what would be found by studying the entire population.

Probability sampling   A method of sampling that enables the researcher to specify for each case in the population the probability of its inclusion in the sample.

Although accurate estimates of sampling error can be made only from probability samples, social scientists often use nonprobability samples because they are more convenient and cheaper to collect. Nonprobability samples are useful under many circumstances for a variety of research purposes. Their main limitation is that they do not allow the use of the method of inferential statistics to generalize from the sample to the population. Because in this chapter and in Chapter 8 we deal only with inferential statistics, we do not discuss nonprobability sampling. In the following sections, we will learn about three sampling designs that follow the principles of probability sampling: (1) the simple random sample, (2) the systematic random sample, and (3) the stratified random sample.[3]

The Simple Random Sample

The *simple random sample* is the most basic probability sampling design, and it is incorporated into even more elaborate probability sampling designs. A **simple random sample** is a sample design chosen in such a way as to ensure that (1) every member of the population has an equal chance of being chosen and (2) every combination of N members has an equal chance of being chosen.

Simple random sample   A sample designed in such a way as to ensure that (1) every member of the population has an equal chance of being chosen and (2) every combination of N members has an equal chance of being chosen.

Let's take a very simple example to illustrate. Suppose we are conducting a cost-containment study of the 10 hospitals in our region, and we want to draw a sample of two hospitals to study intensively. We can put into a hat 10 slips of paper, each representing one of the 10 hospitals, and mix the slips carefully. We select one slip out of the hat and identify the hospital it represents. We then make the second draw and select another slip out of the hat and identify it. The two hospitals we identified on the two draws become the two members of our sample: (1) Assuming that we made sure the slips were really well mixed, pure chance determined which hospital was selected on each draw. The sample is a simple random sample because every hospital had the same chance of being selected as a member of our sample of two and (2) every combination of ($N = 2$) hospitals was equally likely to be chosen.

Researchers usually use computer programs or tables of random numbers in selecting random samples. An abridged table of random numbers is reproduced in Appendix A. To use a random number table, list each member of the population and assign the member a number. Begin anywhere on the table and read each digit that appears in the table in order—up, down, or sideways; the direction does not matter, as long as it follows a consistent path. Whenever we come across a digit in the table of random digits that corresponds to the number of a member in the population of interest, that member is selected for the sample. Continue this process until the desired sample size is reached.

Suppose now that, in your job as a hospital administrator, you are planning to conduct a cost-containment study by examining patients' records. Out of a total of 300 patients' records, you want to draw a simple random sample of five. You follow these steps:

1. Number the patient accounts, beginning with 001 for the first account and ending with 300, which represents the 300th account.

2. Use some random process to enter Appendix A (you might close your eyes and point a pencil). For our illustration, let's start with the first column of numbers. Note that each column lists five-digit numbers. Because your population contains only three-digit numbers (001 to 300), drop the last two digits of each number and read only the first three digits in each group of numbers. (Alternatively, you could choose any other group of three-digit numbers in this block—e.g., the last three digits in the block.)

3. Dropping the last two digits of each five-digit block and proceeding down the column, you obtain the following three-digit numbers:

104*	375	963	289*
223*	779	895	635
241*	995	854	094*
421			

Among these numbers, five correspond to numbers within the range of numbers assigned to the patient records. These are marked with asterisk symbols. The last number listed is 094 from Line 13. You do not need to list more numbers because you already have five different numbers that qualify for inclusion in the sample. The asterisked numbers represent the records you will choose for your sample because these are the only ones that fall between 001 and 300, the range you specified. We now have five records in our simple random sample. Let's list them: 104, 223, 241, 289, and 094.

The Systematic Random Sample

Now let's look at a sampling method that is easier to implement than a simple random sample. The *systematic random sample*, although not a true probability sample, provides results very similar to those obtained with a simple random sample. It uses a ratio, *K*, obtained by dividing the population size by the desired sample size:

$$K = \frac{\text{Population size}}{\text{Sample size}}$$

Systematic random sampling is a method of sampling in which every *K*th member in the total population is chosen for inclusion in the sample after the first member of the sample is selected at random from among the first *K* members in the population.

Systematic random sampling A method of sampling in which every *K*th member (*K* is a ratio obtained by dividing the population size by the desired sample size) in the total population is chosen for inclusion in the sample after the first member of the sample is selected at random from among the first *K* members in the population.

Recall our example in which we had a population of 15,000 commuting students and our sample was limited to 500. In this example,

$$K = \frac{15,000}{500} = 30$$

Using a systematic random sampling method, we first choose any one student at random from among the first 30 students on the list of commuting students. Then we select every 30th student after that until we reach 500, our desired sample size. Suppose that our first student selected at random happens to be the eighth student on the list. The second student in our sample is then 38th on the list (8 + 30 = 38). The third would be 38 + 30 = 68, the fourth, 68 + 30 = 98, and so on. An example of a systematic random sample is illustrated in Figure 7.2.

How does a systematic random sample differ from a simple random sample?

✓ *Learning Check*

Figure 7.2   Systematic Random Sampling

From a population of 40 students, let's select a systematic random sample of 8 students. Our value of *K* will be 5 (40 ÷ 8 = 5). Using a random number table, we first choose a number between 1 and 5. Let's say we choose 4. We then start with student 4 and pick every 5th student:

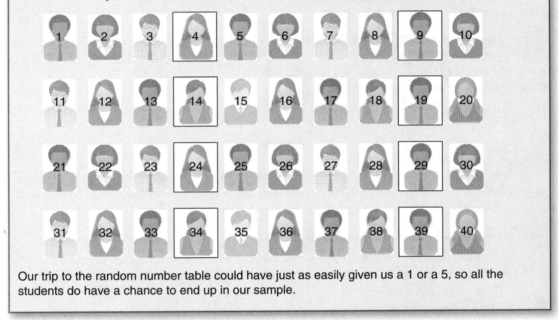

Our trip to the random number table could have just as easily given us a 1 or a 5, so all the students do have a chance to end up in our sample.

The Stratified Random Sample

A third type of probability sampling is the *stratified random sample*. We obtain a **stratified random sample** by (1) dividing the population into subgroups based on one or more variables central to our analysis and then (2) drawing a simple random sample from each of the subgroups. We could stratify by race/ethnicity, for example, by dividing the population into different racial/ethnic groups and then drawing a simple random sample from each group. For instance, suppose we want to compare the attitudes of Latinos toward abortion with the attitudes of white and black respondents. Our population of interest consists of 1,000 individuals, with 700 (or 70%) whites, 200 (or 20%) blacks, and 100 (10%) Latinos. In such a **proportionate stratified sample**, the size of the sample selected from each subgroup is proportional to the size of that subgroup in the entire population.

Stratified random sample   A method of sampling obtained by (1) dividing the population into subgroups based on one or more variables central to our analysis and (2) then drawing a simple random sample from each of the subgroups.

Proportionate stratified sample   The size of the sample selected from each subgroup is proportional to the size of that subgroup in the entire population.

In a **disproportionate stratified sample**, the size of the sample selected from each subgroup is deliberately made disproportional to the size of that subgroup in the population. For instance, for our example, we could select a sample ($N = 180$) consisting of 90 whites (50%), 45 blacks (25%), and 45 Latinos (25%). In such a sampling design, although the sampling probabilities for each population member are not equal (they vary between groups), they are *known*, and therefore, we can make accurate estimates of error in the inference process.[4] Disproportionate stratified sampling is especially useful when we want to compare subgroups with each other, and when the size of some of the subgroups in the population is relatively small. Proportionate sampling can result in the sample having too few members from a small subgroup to yield reliable information about them.

Disproportionate stratified sample   The size of the sample selected from each subgroup is disproportional to the size of the subgroup in the population.

🔲 A Closer Look 7.1
Disproportionate Stratified Samples and Diversity

Disproportionate stratified sampling is especially useful given the increasing diversity of American society. In a diverse society, factors such as race, ethnicity, class, and gender, as well as other categories of experience such as age, religion, and sexual orientation become central in shaping our experiences and defining the differences among us. These factors are an important dimension of the social structure, and they not only operate independently but also are experienced simultaneously by all of us.[5] For example, if you are a white woman, you may share some common experiences with a woman of color based on your gender, but your racial experiences are going to be different. Moreover, your experiences within the race/gender system are further conditioned by your social class. Similarly, if you are a man, your experiences are shaped as much by your class, race, and sexual orientation as they are by your gender. If you are a black gay man, for instance, you might not benefit equally from patriarchy compared with a classmate who is a white heterosexual male.

What are the research implications of an inclusive approach that emphasizes social differences? Such an approach will include women and men in a study of race, Latinos and people of color when considering class, and women and men of color when studying gender. Such an approach makes the experience of previously excluded groups more visible and central because it puts those who have been excluded at the center of the analysis so that we can better understand the experience of all groups, including those with privilege and power.

What are the sampling implications of such an approach? Let's think of an example. Suppose you are looking at the labor force experiences of black women and Latinas who are above 50 years of age and you want to compare these experiences with those of white women in the same age group. Both Latinas and black women comprise a small proportion of the population. A proportional sample probably would not include enough Latinas or black women to provide an adequate basis for comparison with white women. To make such comparisons, it would be desirable to draw a disproportionate stratified sample that deliberately overrepresents both Latinas and black women so that these subsamples will be of sufficient size (Figure 7.3).

(Continued)

(Continued)

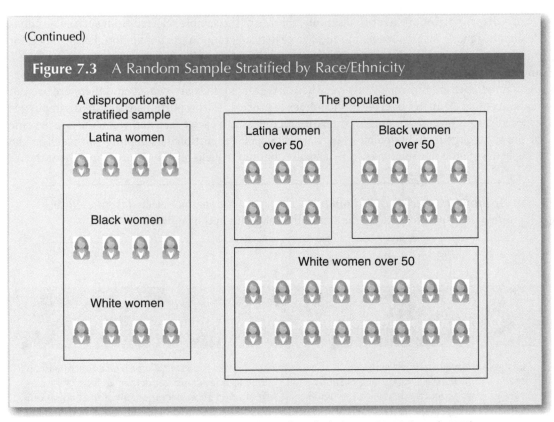

Figure 7.3   A Random Sample Stratified by Race/Ethnicity

*Margaret L. Andersen and Patricia Hill Collins, *Race, Class and Gender* (Belmont, CA: Wadsworth, 2009).

✓ *Learning*
Check

Can you think of some research questions that could best be studied using a disproportionate stratified random sample? When might it be important to use a proportionate stratified random sample?

◉ THE CONCEPT OF THE SAMPLING DISTRIBUTION

We began this chapter with a few examples illustrating why researchers in the social sciences almost never collect information on the entire population that interests them. Instead, they usually select a sample from that population and use the principles of statistical inference to estimate the characteristics, or parameters, of that population based on the characteristics, or statistics, of the sample. In this section, we describe one of the most important concepts in statistical inference—*sampling distribution*. The sampling distribution helps estimate the likelihood of our sample statistics and, therefore, enables us to generalize from the sample to the population.

The Population

To illustrate the concept of the sampling distribution, let's consider as our population the 20 individuals listed in Table 7.3.[5] Our variable, Y, is the income (in dollars) of these 20 individuals, and the parameter we are trying to estimate is the mean income.

Table 7.3   The Population: Personal Income (in dollars) for 20 Individuals (hypothetical data)

Individual	Income (Y)
Case 1	11,350 (Y_1)
Case 2	7,859 (Y_2)
Case 3	41,654 (Y_3)
Case 4	13,445 (Y_4)
Case 5	17,458 (Y_5)
Case 6	8,451 (Y_6)
Case 7	15,436 (Y_7)
Case 8	18,342 (Y_8)
Case 9	19,354 (Y_9)
Case 10	22,545 (Y_{10})
Case 11	25,345 (Y_{11})
Case 12	68,100 (Y_{12})
Case 13	9,368 (Y_{13})
Case 14	47,567 (Y_{14})
Case 15	18,923 (Y_{15})
Case 16	16,456 (Y_{16})
Case 17	27,654 (Y_{17})
Case 18	16,452 (Y_{18})
Case 19	23,890 (Y_{19})
Case 20	25,671 (Y_{20})
Mean (μ_Y) = 22,766	Standard deviation (σ_Y) = 14,687

We use the symbol μ_Y to represent the population mean; the Greek letter mu (μ) stands for the mean, and the subscript Y identifies the specific variable, income. Using Formula 4.1, we can calculate the population mean:

$$\mu_Y = \frac{\Sigma Y}{Y} = \frac{Y_1 + Y_2 + Y_3 + Y_4 + Y_5 + \ldots + Y_{20}}{20}$$

$$= \frac{11,350 + 7,859 + 41,654 + 13,445 + 17,458 + \ldots + 25,671}{20}$$

$$= 22,766$$

Using Formula 5.3, we can also calculate the standard deviation for this population distribution. We use the Greek symbol sigma (σ) to represent the population's standard deviation and the subscript Y to stand for our variable, income:

$$\sigma_Y = 14,687$$

Of course, most of the time, we do not have access to the population. So instead, we draw one sample, compute the mean—the statistic—for that sample, and use it to estimate the population mean—the parameter.

The Sample

Let's pretend that μ_Y is unknown and that we estimate its value by drawing a random sample of three individuals ($N = 3$) from the population of 20 individuals and calculate the mean income for that sample. The incomes included in that sample are as follows:

Case 8	18,342
Case 16	16,456
Case 17	27,654

Now let's calculate the mean for that sample:

$$\overline{Y} = \frac{18,342 + 16,456 + 27,654}{3} = 20,817$$

Note that our sample mean, $(\overline{Y}) = \$20,817$, differs from the actual population parameter, $\$22,766$. This discrepancy is due to sampling error. **Sampling error** is the discrepancy between a sample estimate of a population parameter and the real population parameter. By comparing the sample statistic with the population parameter, we can determine the sampling error. The sampling error for our example is 1,949 (22,766 − 20,817 = 1,949).

Sampling error   The discrepancy between a sample estimate of a population parameter and the real population parameter.

Now let's select another random sample of three individuals. This time, the incomes included are as follows:

Case 15	18,923
Case 5	17,458
Case 17	27,654

The mean for this sample is

$$\overline{Y} = \frac{18,923 + 17,458 + 27,654}{3} = 21,345$$

The sampling error for this sample is 1,421 (22,766 − 21,345 = 1,421), somewhat less than the error for the first sample we selected.

The Dilemma

Although comparing the sample estimates of the average income with the actual population average is a perfect way to evaluate the accuracy of our estimate, in practice, we rarely have information about the actual population parameter. If we did, we would not need to conduct a study! Moreover, few, if any, sample estimates correspond exactly to the actual population parameter. This, then, is our dilemma: If sample estimates vary and if most estimates result in some sort of sampling error, how much confidence can we place in the estimate? On what basis can we infer from the sample to the population?

The Sampling Distribution

The answer to this dilemma is to use a device known as the sampling distribution. The **sampling distribution** is a theoretical probability distribution of all possible sample values for the statistic in which we are interested. If we were to draw all possible random samples of the same size from our population of interest, compute the statistic for each sample, and plot the frequency distribution for that statistic, we would obtain an approximation of the sampling distribution. Every statistic—for example, a proportion, a mean, or a variance—has a sampling distribution. Because it includes all possible sample values, the sampling distribution enables us to compare our sample result with other sample values and determine the likelihood associated with that result.[6]

Sampling distribution   The sampling distribution is a theoretical probability distribution of all possible sample values for the statistics in which we are interested.

▣ THE SAMPLING DISTRIBUTION OF THE MEAN

Sampling distributions are theoretical distributions, which means that they are never really observed. Constructing an actual sampling distribution would involve taking all possible random samples of a fixed size from the population. This process would be very tedious because it would involve a very large number of samples. However, to help grasp the concept of the sampling distribution, let's illustrate how one could be generated from a limited number of samples.

An Illustration

For our illustration, we use one of the most common sampling distributions—the sampling distribution of the mean. The **sampling distribution of the mean** is a theoretical distribution of sample means that would be obtained by drawing from the population all possible samples of the same size.

Sampling distribution of the mean   A theoretical probability distribution of sample means that would be obtained by drawing from the population all possible samples of the same size.

Let's go back to our example in which our population is made up of 20 individuals and their incomes. From that population (Table 7.3), we now randomly draw 50 possible samples of size 3, computing the mean income for each sample and replacing it before drawing another.

In our first sample of size 3, we draw three incomes: \$8,451, \$41,654, and \$18,923. The mean income for this sample is

$$\overline{Y} = \frac{8,451 + 41,654 + 18,923}{3} = 23,009$$

Now we restore these individuals to the original list and select a second sample of three individuals. The mean income for this sample is

$$\overline{Y} = \frac{15,436 + 25,345 + 16,456}{3} = 19,079$$

We repeat this process 48 more times, each time computing the sample mean and restoring the sample to the original list. Table 7.4 lists the means of the first five and the 50th samples of $N = 3$ that were drawn from the population of 20 individuals. (Note that $\Sigma \overline{Y}$ refers to the sum of all the means computed for each of the samples and M refers to the total number of samples that were drawn.)

The grouped frequency distribution for all 50 sample means ($M = 50$) is displayed in Table 7.5; Figure 7.4 is a histogram of this distribution. This distribution is an example of a sampling

Table 7.4   Mean Income of 50 Samples of Size 3

Sample	*Mean ($\overline{Y}$)*
First	23,009
Second	19,079
Third	18,873
Fourth	26,885
Fifth	21,847
⋮	⋮
Fiftieth	26,645
Total (M) = 50	$\Sigma \overline{Y} = 1,237,482$

Table 7.5 Sampling Distribution of Sample Means for Sample Size $N = 3$ Drawn From the Population of 20 Individuals' Incomes

Sample Mean Intervals	Frequency	Percentage
11,500–15,500	6	12
15,500–19,500	7	14
19,500–23,500	14	28
23,500–27,500	4	8
27,500–31,500	9	18
31,500–35,500	7	14
35,500–39,500	1	2
39,500–43,500	2	4
Total (M)	50	100

Figure 7.4 Sampling Distribution of Sample Means for Sample Size $N = 3$ Drawn From the Population of 20 Individuals' Incomes

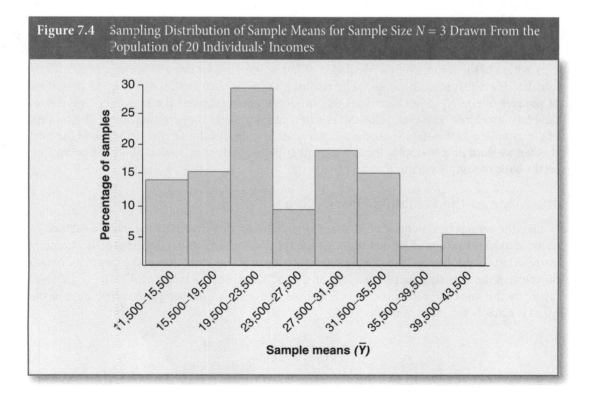

distribution of the mean. Note that in its structure, the sampling distribution resembles a frequency distribution of raw scores, except that here each score is a sample mean, and the corresponding frequencies are the number of samples with that particular mean value. For example, the third interval in Table 7.5 ranges from $19,500 to $23,500, with a corresponding frequency of 14, or 28%. This means that we drew 14 samples (28%) with means ranging between $19,500 and $23,500.

Remember that the distribution depicted in Table 7.5 and Figure 7.4 is an empirical distribution, whereas the sampling distribution is a theoretical distribution. In reality, we never really construct a sampling distribution. However, even this simple empirical example serves to illustrate some of the most important characteristics of the sampling distribution.

Review

Before we continue, let's take a moment to review the three distinct types of distribution.

The Population: We began with the *population distribution* of 20 individuals. This distribution actually exists. It is an empirical distribution that is usually unknown to us. We are interested in estimating the mean income for this population.

The Sample: We drew a sample from that population. The *sample distribution* is an empirical distribution that is known to us and is used to help us estimate the mean of the population. We selected 50 samples of $N = 3$ and calculated the mean income. We usually use the sample mean ($\overline{Y}$) as an estimate of the population mean (μ_Y).

The Sampling Distribution of the Mean: For illustration, we generated an approximation of the sampling distribution of the mean, consisting of 50 samples of $N = 3$. *The sampling distribution of the mean* does not really exist. It is a theoretical distribution.

To help you understand the relationship among the population, the sample, and the sampling distribution, we have illustrated in Figure 7.5 the process of generating an empirical sampling distribution of the mean. From a population of raw scores (Ys), we draw M samples of size N and calculate the mean of each sample. The resulting sampling distribution of the mean, based on M samples of size N, shows the values that the mean could take and the frequency (number of samples) associated with each value. Make sure you understand these relationships. The concept of the sampling distribution is crucial to understanding statistical inference. In this and the next chapter, we learn how to employ the sampling distribution to draw inferences about the population on the basis of sample statistics.

The Mean of the Sampling Distribution

Like the sample and population distributions, the sampling distribution can be described in terms of its mean and standard deviation. We use the symbol to represent the mean of the sampling distribution. The subscript indicates that the variable of this distribution is the mean. To obtain the mean of the sampling distribution, add all the individual sample means ($\Sigma \overline{Y} = 1,237,482$) and divide by the number of samples ($M = 50$). Thus, the mean of the sampling distribution of the mean is actually the mean of means:

$$\mu_{\overline{Y}} = \frac{\Sigma \overline{Y}}{M} = \frac{1,237,482}{50} = 24,750$$

Figure 7.5 Generating the Sampling Distribution of the Mean

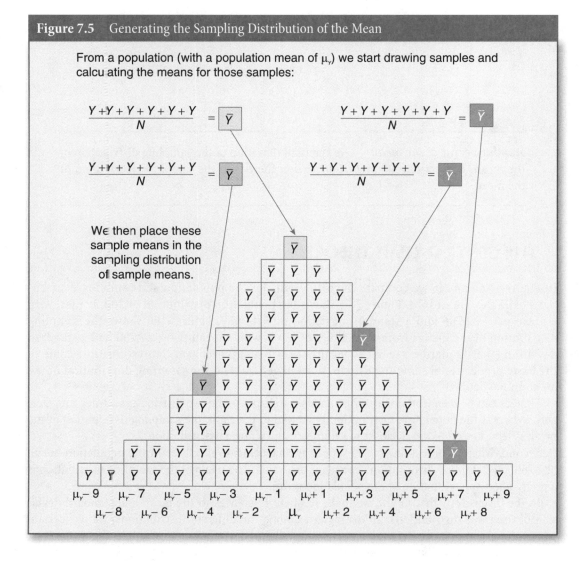

From a population (with a population mean of μ_y) we start drawing samples and calculating the means for those samples:

$$\frac{Y+Y+Y+Y+Y+Y}{N} = \bar{Y} \qquad\qquad \frac{Y+Y+Y+Y+Y+Y}{N} = \bar{Y}$$

$$\frac{Y+Y+Y+Y+Y+Y}{N} = \bar{Y} \qquad\qquad \frac{Y+Y+Y+Y+Y+Y}{N} = \bar{Y}$$

We then place these sample means in the sampling distribution of sample means.

The Standard Error of the Mean

The standard deviation of the sampling distribution is also called the **standard error of the mean**. The standard error of the mean, $\sigma_{\bar{Y}}$ describes how much dispersion there is in the sampling distribution, or how much variability there is in the value of the mean from sample to sample:

$$\sigma_{\bar{Y}} = \frac{\sigma_Y}{\sqrt{N}}$$

This formula tells us that the standard error of the mean is equal to the standard deviation of the population σ_Y divided by the square root of the sample size (N). For our example, because the population standard deviation is 14,687 and our sample size is 3, the standard error of the mean is

$$\sigma_{\bar{Y}} = \frac{14,687}{\sqrt{3}} = 8,480$$

Standard error of the mean   The standard deviation of the sampling distribution of the mean. It describes how much dispersion there is in the sampling distribution of the mean.

▣ THE CENTRAL LIMIT THEOREM

In Figures 7.6a and b, we compare the histograms for the population and sampling distributions of Tables 7.2 and 7.4. Figure 7.6a shows the population distribution of 20 incomes, with a mean $\mu_Y = 22,766$ and a standard deviation $\sigma_Y = 14,687$. Figure 7.6b shows the sampling distribution of the means from 50 samples of $N = 3$ with a mean $\mu_{\bar{Y}} = 24,750$ and a standard deviation (the standard error of the mean) $\sigma_{\bar{Y}} = 8,480$. These two figures illustrate some of the basic properties of sampling distributions in general and the sampling distribution of the mean in particular.

First, as can be seen from Figures 7.6a and b, the shapes of the two distributions differ considerably. Whereas the population distribution is skewed to the right, the sampling distribution of the mean is less skewed—that is, closer to symmetry and a normal distribution.

Second, whereas only a few of the sample means coincide exactly with the population mean, $22,766, the sampling distribution centers on this value. The mean of the sampling distribution is a pretty good approximation of the population mean.

In the discussions that follow, we make frequent references to the mean and standard deviation of the three distributions. To distinguish among the different distributions, we use certain conventional symbols to refer to the means and standard deviations of the sample, the population, and the sampling distribution. Note that we use Greek letters to refer to both the sampling and the population distributions.

The Population We began with the *population distribution* of 20 individuals. This distribution actually exists. It is an empirical distribution that is usually unknown to us. We are interested in estimating the mean income for this population.

The Sample We drew a sample from that population. The *sample distribution* is an empirical distribution that is known to us and is used to help us estimate the mean of the population. We selected 50 samples of $N = 3$ and calculated the mean income. We usually use the sample mean as an estimate of the population mean μ_Y.

The Sampling Distribution of the Mean For illustration, we generated an approximation of the sampling distribution of the mean, consisting of 50 samples of $N = 3$. *The sampling distribution of the mean* does not really exist. It is a theoretical distribution.

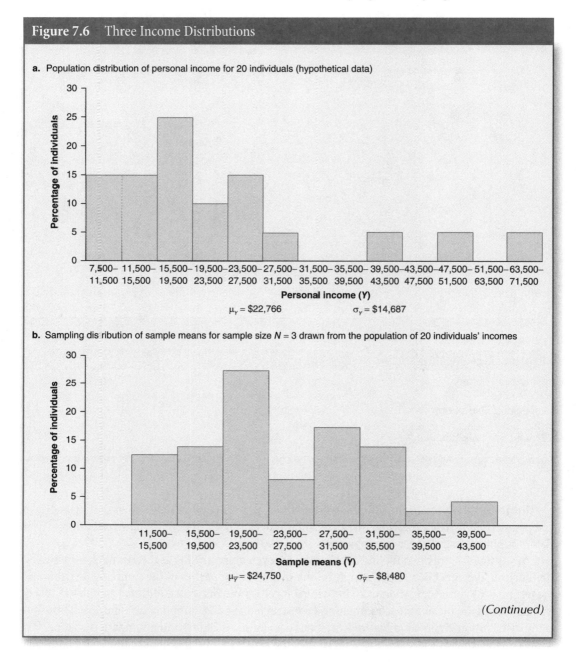

Figure 7.6   Three Income Distributions

a. Population distribution of personal income for 20 individuals (hypothetical data)

$\mu_Y = \$22,766$ $\sigma_Y = \$14,687$

b. Sampling distribution of sample means for sample size $N = 3$ drawn from the population of 20 individuals' incomes

$\mu_{\bar{Y}} = \$24,750$ $\sigma_{\bar{Y}} = \$8,480$

(Continued)

(Continued)

c. Sampling distribution of sample means for sample size $N = 6$ drawn from the population of 20 individuals' incomes

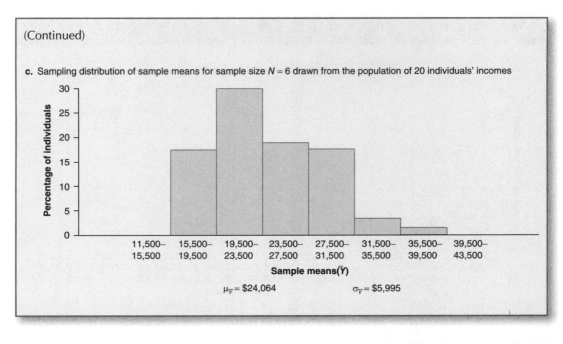

$\mu_{\bar{Y}} = \$24,064$ $\sigma_{\bar{Y}} = \$5,995$

	Mean	*Standard Deviation*
Sample distribution	$\bar{Y}$	S_Y
Population distribution	μ_Y	σ_Y
Sampling distribution of $\bar{Y}$	$\mu_{\bar{Y}}$	$\sigma_{\bar{Y}}$

Third, the variability of the sampling distribution is considerably smaller than the variability of the population distribution. Note that the standard deviation for the sampling distribution ($\sigma_{\bar{Y}} = 8,480$) is almost half that for the population ($\sigma_Y = 14,687$).

These properties of the sampling distribution are even more striking as the sample size increases. To illustrate the effect of a larger sample on the shape and properties of the sampling distribution, we went back to our population of 20 individual incomes and drew 50 additional samples of $N = 6$. We calculated the mean for each sample and constructed another sampling distribution. This sampling distribution is shown in Figure 7.6c. It has a mean $\mu_{\bar{Y}} = 24,064$ and a standard deviation $\sigma_{\bar{Y}} = 5,995$. Note that as the sample size increased, the sampling distribution became more compact. This decrease in the variability of the sampling distribution is reflected in a smaller standard deviation: With an increase in sample size from $N = 3$ to $N = 6$, the standard deviation of the sampling distribution decreased from 8,480 to 5,995. Furthermore, with a larger sample size, the sampling distribution of the mean is an even better approximation of the normal curve.

These properties of the sampling distribution of the mean are summarized more systematically in one of the most important statistical principles underlying statistical inference. It is called the **central limit theorem**, and it states that if all possible random samples of size N are drawn from a population with a mean μ_Y and a standard deviation σ_Y, then as N becomes larger, the sampling distribution of sample means becomes approximately normal, with mean $\mu_{\overline{Y}}$ equal to the population mean and a standard deviation equal to

$$\sigma_{\overline{Y}} = \frac{\sigma_Y}{\sqrt{N}}$$

Central limit theorem   If all possible random samples of size N are drawn from a population with a mean μ_Y and a standard deviation σ_Y, then as N becomes larger, the sampling distribution of sample means becomes approximately normal, with mean and standard deviation with mean $\mu_{\overline{Y}}$ equal to the population mean and a standard deviation equal to

$$\sigma_{\overline{Y}} = \frac{\sigma_Y}{\sqrt{N}}$$

The significance of the central limit theorem is that it tells us that with a *sufficient sample size* the sampling distribution of the mean will be normal regardless of the shape of the population distribution. Therefore, even when the population distribution is skewed, we can still assume that the sampling distribution of the mean is normal, given random samples of large enough size. Furthermore, the central limit theorem also assures us that (1) as the sample size gets larger, the mean of the sampling distribution becomes equal to the population mean and (2) as the sample size gets larger, the standard error of the mean (the standard deviation of the sampling distribution of the mean) decreases in size. The standard error of the mean tells how much variability in the sample estimates there is from sample to sample. The smaller the standard error of the mean, the closer (on average) the sample means will be to the population mean. Thus, the larger the sample, the more closely the sample statistic clusters around the population parameter.

✓ *Learning Check*

Make sure you understand the difference between the number of samples that can be drawn from a population and the sample size. Whereas the number of samples is infinite in theory, the sample size is under the control of the investigator.

The Size of the Sample

Although there is no hard-and-fast rule, a general rule of thumb is that when N is 50 or more, the sampling distribution of the mean will be approximately normal regardless of the shape of the distribution. However, we can assume that the sampling distribution will be normal even with samples as small as 30 if we know that the population distribution approximates normality.

> *What is a normal population distribution? If you can't answer this question, go back to Chapter 6. You must understand the concept of a normal distribution before you can understand the techniques involved in inferential statistics.*

The Significance of the Sampling Distribution and the Central Limit Theorem

In the preceding sections, we have covered a lot of abstract material. You may have a number of questions at this time. Why is the concept of the sampling distribution so important? What is the significance of the central limit theorem? To answer these questions, let's go back and review our 20 incomes example.

To estimate the mean income of a population of 20 individuals, we drew a sample of three cases and calculated the mean income for that sample. Our sample mean, $\overline{Y} = 20{,}817$, differs from the actual population parameter, $\mu_Y = 22{,}766$. When we selected different samples, we found each time that the sample mean differed from the population mean. These discrepancies are due to sampling errors. Had we taken a number of additional samples, we probably would have found that the mean was different each time because every sample differs slightly. Few, if any, sample means would correspond exactly to the actual population mean. Usually we have only one sample statistic as our best estimate of the population parameter.

So now let's restate our dilemma: If sample estimates vary and if most result in some sort of sampling error, how much confidence can we place in the estimate? On what basis can we infer from the sample to the population?

The solution lies in the sampling distribution and its properties. Because the sampling distribution is a theoretical distribution that includes all possible sample outcomes, we can compare our sample outcome with it and estimate the likelihood of its occurrence.

Since the sampling distribution is theoretical, how can we know its shape and properties so that we can make these comparisons? Our knowledge is based on what the central limit theorem tells us about the properties of the sampling distribution of the mean. We know that if our sample size is large enough (at least 50 cases), most sample means will be quite close to the true population mean. It is highly unlikely that our sample mean would deviate much from the actual population mean.

In Chapter 6, we saw that in all normal curves, a constant proportion of the area under the curve lies between the mean and any given distance from the mean when measured in standard deviation units, or Z scores. We can find this proportion in the standard normal table (Appendix B).

Knowing that the sampling distribution of the means is approximately normal, with a mean $\mu_{\overline{Y}}$ and a standard deviation $\sigma_Y / \sqrt{N}$ (the standard error of the mean), we can use Appendix B to determine the probability that a sample mean will fall within a certain distance—measured in standard deviation units, or Z scores—of $\mu_{\overline{Y}}$ or μ_Y. For example, we can expect approximately 68% (or we can say the probability is approximately 0.68) of all sample means to fall within ±1 standard error ($\sigma_{\overline{Y}} = \sigma_Y / \sqrt{N}$, or the standard deviation of the sampling distribution of the mean) of $\mu_{\overline{Y}}$ or μ_Y. Similarly, the probability is about 0.95 that the sample mean will fall within ±2 standard errors of $\mu_{\overline{Y}}$ or μ_Y. In the next chapter, we will see how this information helps us evaluate the accuracy of our sample estimates.

Suppose a population distribution has a mean $\mu_Y = 150$ and a standard deviation $\sigma_y = 30$, and you draw a simple random sample of N = 100 cases. What is the probability that the mean is between 147 and 153? What is the probability that the sample mean exceeds 153? Would you be surprised to find a mean score of 159? Why? (Hint: To answer these questions, you need to apply what you learned in Chapter 6 about Z scores and areas under the normal curve [Appendix B].) Remember, to translate a raw score into a Z score we used this formula:

$$Z = \frac{Y - \bar{Y}}{S_Y}$$

However, because here we are dealing with a sampling distribution, replace Y with the sample mean $\bar{Y}$, $\bar{Y}$ with the sampling distribution's mean $\mu_{\bar{Y}}$, and σ_y with the standard error of the mean

$$Z = \frac{\bar{Y} - \mu_{\bar{Y}}}{\sigma_Y / \sqrt{N}}$$

◙ STATISTICS IN PRACTICE: THE CENTRAL LIMIT THEOREM

There are numerous applications of the central limit theorem in research, business, and social policy. As varied as these applications may be, what they have in common is that the information and data they use is based on relatively small random samples taken from considerably larger and often varied populations. For example, a 2012 survey on higher education conducted by *TIME Magazine/Carnegie Corporation* reported that 80% of all U.S. adults believe that "At many colleges, the education students receive is not worth what they pay for it." This observation is based on a national random sample of only 1,000 adults and 540 senior administrators at public and private colleges and universities.[7] Similarly, a public opinion poll conducted in 2012 reported that 88% of Americans favor a federal law requiring background checks on all potential gun buyers. The researchers based their conclusion on a sample of 965 adults selected from a population of about 72,000.[8]

Election polls to predict presidential election results provide another example of the benefits of the sampling distribution and the central limit theorem. In November 2012, Barack Obama was reelected president of the United States with 51% of the votes. Mitt Romney, the republican candidate, received 47% of the vote. Weeks before the election took place, numerous polls called the election within two or three percentage points of the actual result. These predictions were based on interviews conducted with samples not larger than about 2,000 registered voters.

What is astounding about these polls (or other empirical studies based on random samples) is not only their accuracy, but that their observations about very large populations (such as all the eligible voters in the United States) are often based on a single sample. Moreover, the size of the sample can be limited to a few hundred respondents or even less, regardless of the size of the population! Thus, whether we study a population of 1,000, 10,000, or 100,000, we wouldn't necessarily have to increase the size of the sample.

MAIN POINTS

- Through the process of sampling, researchers attempt to generalize the characteristics of a large group (the population) from a subset (sample) selected from that group. The term parameter, associated with the population, refers to the information we are interested in finding out. Statistic refers to a corresponding calculated sample statistic.

- A probability sample design allows us to estimate the extent to which the findings based on one sample are likely to differ from what we would find by studying the entire population.

- A simple random sample is chosen in such a way as to ensure that every member of the population and every combination of N members have an equal chance of being chosen.

- In systematic sampling, every Kth member in the total population is chosen for inclusion in the sample after the first member of the sample is selected at random from the first K members in the population.

- A stratified random sample is obtained by (1) dividing the population into subgroups based on one or more variables central to our analysis and (2) then drawing a simple random sample from each of the subgroups.

- The sampling distribution is a theoretical probability distribution of all possible sample values for the statistic in which we are interested. The sampling distribution of the mean is a frequency distribution of all possible sample means of the same size that can be drawn from the population of interest.

- According to the central limit theorem, if all possible random samples of size N are drawn from a population with a mean μ_Y and a standard deviation σ_Y, then as N becomes larger, the sampling distribution of sample means becomes approximately normal, with mean σ_Y and standard deviation $\sigma_Y/\sqrt{N}$.

- The central limit theorem tells us that with sufficient sample size, the sampling distribution of the mean will be normal regardless of the shape of the population distribution. Therefore, even when the population distribution is skewed, we can still assume that the sampling distribution of the mean is normal, given a large enough randomly selected sample size.

KEY TERMS

central limit theorem
disproportionate
   stratified sample
parameter
population
probability sampling
proportionate
   stratified sample

sample
sampling
   distribution
sampling distribution
   of the mean
sampling error
simple random
   sample

standard error of the
   mean
statistic
stratified random
   sample
systematic random
   sampling

$SAGE edge™

Sharpen your skills with SAGE edge at **edge.sagepub.com/frankfort7e. SAGE edge for students** provides a personalized approach to help you accomplish your coursework goals in an easy-to-use learning environment.

SPSS DEMONSTRATION

[GSS10SSDS]

Selecting a Random Sample

In this chapter, we've discussed various types of samples and the definition of the standard error of the mean. Usually, data entered into SPSS have already been sampled from some larger population. However, SPSS does have a sampling procedure that can take random samples of data. Systematic samples and stratified samples can also be drawn with SPSS, but they require the use of the SPSS command language.

When might it be worthwhile to use the SPSS Sample procedure? One instance is when doing preliminary analysis of a very large data set. For example, if you worked for your local hospital and had complete data records for all patients (tens of thousands), there would be no need to use *all* the data during initial analysis. You could select a random sample of individuals and use the subset of data for preliminary analysis. Later, the complete patient data set could be used for completing your final analyses.

To use the Sample procedure, click on *Data* from the main menu, then click on *Select Cases*. The opening dialog box (Figure 7.7) has five choices that will select a subset of cases via various methods. By default, the *All cases* button is checked. We click on the *Random sample of cases* button, then on the *Sample* button to give SPSS our specification.

Figure 7.7 Select Cases Dialog Box

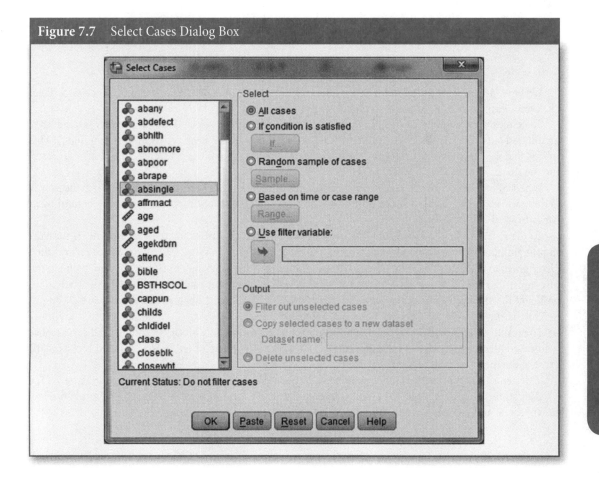

The next dialog box (Figure 7.8) provides two options to create a random sample. The most convenient one is normally the first, where we tell SPSS what percentage of cases to select from the larger file. Alternatively, we can tell SPSS to take an exact number of cases. The second option is available because SPSS will only take approximately the percentage specified in the first option.

Figure 7.8   Specifying Sample Size When Selecting Cases

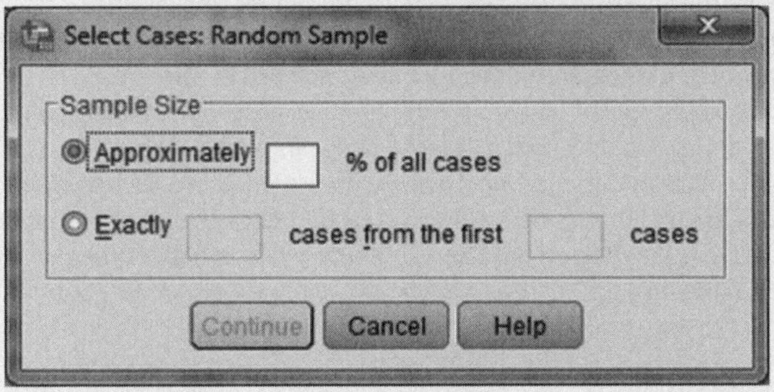

We type "10" in the box to ask for 10% of the original sample of 1,500 respondents from the GSS. Then click on *Continue* and *OK*, as usual, to process the request.

SPSS does not delete the cases from the active data file that aren't selected for the sample. Instead, they are filtered out (you can identify them in the Data View window by the slash across their row number). This means that we can always return to the full data file by going back to the Select Cases dialog box and selecting the *All cases* button.

When SPSS processes our request, it tells us that the data have been filtered by putting the words "Filter On" in the status area at the bottom of the SPSS window (the status area has many helpful messages from SPSS).

To demonstrate the effect of sampling, we ask for univariate statistics for the variable HRS1, measuring the number of hours a respondent worked last week. Click on *Analyze, Descriptive Statistics*, and then *Descriptives* to open this dialog box. Place HRS1 in the variable list. Click on the *Options* button to obtain the box shown in Figure 7.9. Select the mean, standard deviation, minimum, and maximum values. In addition, we'll add the standard error of the mean by clicking the *S.E. mean* box. Then click *Continue* and *OK* to put SPSS to work.

The results (Figure 7.10) show that the number of valid cases is exactly 83, or 10% of the valid cases (those who responded to the number of hours worked last week). The mean of HRS1 is 42.94, and the standard error of the mean is 1.738.

If we repeat the process, this time asking for a 25% sample, we obtain the results shown in Figure 7.11.

Your results may differ from the results presented here. We are asking SPSS to generate a random selection of cases, and you may not get the same selection of cases as we did.

How closely does the mean for HRS1 from these two random samples match that of the full file? The mean for all 838 respondents (the other 662 respondents did not have valid responses) is 40.62 years; so it certainly appears that SPSS did take a random sample of this larger file. Both samples produced means and standard deviations that are within the range of the population parameters.

Figure 7.9   Descriptive Statistics Dialog Box

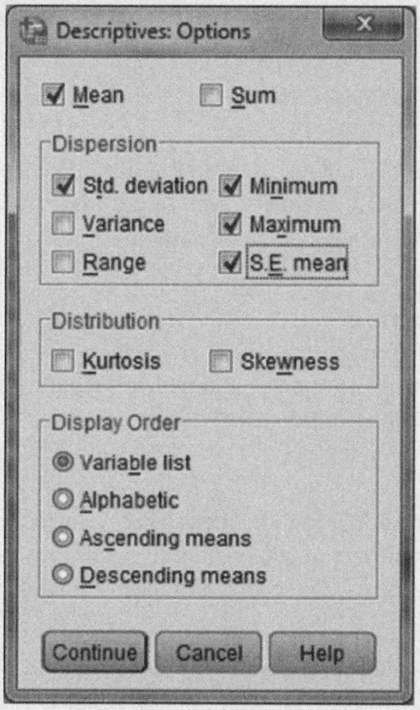

Figure 7.10   Descriptive Statistics for Number of Hours Worked Last Week, 10% Sample

Descriptive Statistics

	N	Minimum	Maximum	Mean		Std. Deviation
	Statistic	Statistic	Statistic	Statistic	Std. Error	Statistic
NUMBER OF HOURS WORKED LAST WEEK	83	8	89	42.94	1.738	15.835
Valid N (listwise)	83					

Figure 7.11 Descriptive Statistics for Number of Hours Worked Last Week, 25% Sample

Descriptive Statistics

	N	Minimum	Maximum	Mean		Std. Deviation
	Statistic	Statistic	Statistic	Statistic	Std. Error	Statistic
NUMBER OF HOURS WORKED LAST WEEK	187	1	89	41.28	1.139	15.577
Valid N (listwise)	187					

SPSS PROBLEM

Using GSS10SSDS, repeat the SPSS demonstration, selecting 25%, 50%, and 75% samples and requesting descriptives for MAEDUC and PAEDUC. Compare your descriptive statistics with descriptives for the entire sample. What can you say about the accuracy of your random samples?

CHAPTER EXERCISES

1. Explain which of the following is a statistic and which is a parameter.
   a. The mean age of Americans from the 2010 decennial census
   b. The unemployment rate for the population of U.S. adults, estimated by the government from a large sample
   c. The percentage of Texans opposed to the health care reform bill from a poll of 1,000 residents
   d. The mean salaries of employees at your school (e.g., administrators, faculty, maintenance)
   e. The percentage of students at your school who receive financial aid

2. The mayor of your city has been talking about the need for a tax hike. The city's newspaper uses letters sent to the editor to judge public opinion about this possible hike, reporting on their results in an article.
   a. Do you think that these letters represent a random sample? Why or why not?
   b. What alternative sampling method would you recommend to the mayor?

3. The following four common situation scenarios involve selecting a sample and understanding how a sample relates to a population.
   a. A friend interviews every 10th shopper who passes by her as she stands outside one entrance of a major department store in a shopping mall. What type of sample is she selecting? How might you define the population from which she is selecting the sample?
   b. A political polling firm samples 50 potential voters from a list of registered voters in each county in a state to interview for an upcoming election. What type of sample is this? Do you have enough information to tell?
   c. Another political polling firm in the same state selects potential voters from the same list of registered voters with a very different method. First, they alphabetize the list of last names, then pick the first 20 names that begin with an A, the first 20 that begin with a B, and so on until Z (the sample size is thus 20 × 26, or 520). Is this a probability sample?
   d. A social scientist gathers a carefully chosen group of 20 people whom she has selected to represent a broad cross-section of the population in New York City. She interviews them in depth for a study she is doing on race relations in the city. Is this a probability sample? What type of sample has she chosen?

4. An upper-level sociology class at a large urban university has 120 students, including 34 seniors, 57 juniors, 22 sophomores, and 7 freshmen.
   a. Imagine that you choose one random student from the classroom (perhaps by using a random number table). What is the probability that the student will be a junior?
   b. What is the probability that the student will be a freshman?
   c. If you are asked to select a proportionate stratified sample of size 30 from the classroom, stratified by class level (senior, junior, etc.), how many students from each group will there be in the sample?
   d. If instead you are to select a disproportionate sample of size 20 from the classroom, with equal numbers of students from each class level in the sample, how many freshmen will there be in the sample?

5. Can the standard error of a variable ever be larger than, or even equal in size to, the standard deviation for the same variable? Justify your answer by means of both a formula and a discussion of the relationship between these two concepts.

6. When taking a random sample from a very large population, how does the standard error of the mean change when
   a. the sample size is increased from 100 to 1,600?
   b. the sample size is decreased from 300 to 150?
   c. the sample size is multiplied by 4?

7. Many television news shows conduct "instant" polls by providing an 800 number and asking an interesting question of the day for viewers to call and answer.
   a. Is this poll a probability sample? Why or why not?
   b. Specify the population from which the sample of calls is drawn.

8. The following table shows the number of active military personnel in 2009, by region (including the District of Columbia).

Pacific	229,634	Mountain	89,816	West South Central	177,336
West North Central	64,564	East North Central	26,384	East South Central	68,440
South Atlantic	376,034	Middle Atlantic	41,441	New England	8,579

Sources: U.S. Census Bureau, *Statistical Abstract of the United States: 2012*, Table 508 (data) and U.S. Census Bureau, *Census Regions and Divisions of the United States* (regions).

   a. Calculate the mean and standard deviation for the population.
   b. Now take 10 samples of size 3 from the population. Use either simple random sampling or systematic sampling with the help of the table of random numbers in Appendix A. Calculate the mean for each sample.
   c. Once you have calculated the mean for each sample, calculate the mean of means (i.e., add up your 10 sample means and divide by 10). How does this mean compare with the mean for all states?
   d. How does the value of the standard deviation that you calculated in Exercise 8a compare with the value of the standard error (i.e., the standard deviation of the sampling distribution)?
   e. Construct two histograms, one for the distribution of values in the population and the other for the various sample means taken from Exercise 8b. Describe and explain any differences you observe between the two distributions.
   f. It is important that you have a clear sense of the population that we are working with in this exercise. What is the population?

Exercises

9. You've been asked to determine the percentage of students who would support gay marriage. You want to take a random sample of fellow students to make the estimate. Explain whether each of the following scenarios describes a random sample.
    a. You ask all students eating lunch in the cafeteria on a Tuesday at 12:30 p.m.
    b. You ask every 10th student from the list of enrolled students.
    c. You ask every 10th student passing by the student union.
    d. What sampling procedure would you recommend to complete your study?

10. The mean family income in Wisconsin, according to the 2011 data, is about $77,531[9], with a standard deviation (for the population) of approximately $59,750.
    a. Imagine that you are taking a subsample of 200 state residents. What is the probability that your sample mean is between $71,000 and $77,531?
    b. For this same sample size, what is the probability that the sample mean exceeds $85,000?

11. A small population of $N = 10$ has values of 4, 7, 2, 11, 5, 3, 4, 6, 10, and 1.
    a. Calculate the mean and standard deviation for the population.
    b. Take 10 simple random samples of size 3, and calculate the mean for each.
    c. Calculate the mean and standard deviation of all these sample means. How closely does the mean of all sample means match the population mean? How is the standard deviation of the means related to the standard deviation for the population?

12. Imagine that you are working with a total population of 21,473 respondents. You assign each respondent a value from 0 to 21,473 and proceed to select your sample using the random number table in Appendix A. Starting at Column 7, Line 1 in Appendix A and going down, which are the first five respondents that will be included in your sample?

13. The following data summarize the 2009 external debt (in millions of dollars) for seven countries.

Country	Debt (in millions of dollars)
Brazil	276,900
Chile	71,600
Colombia	52,200
India	237,700
Mexico	192,000
South Africa	42,100
Turkey	251,400

Source: U.S. Census Bureau, Statistical Abstract of the United States: 2012, Table 1404.

    a. Assume that $\sigma_Y = 93,500$. Calculate the standard error and interpret. (Hint: consider the formula for the standard error. Since you are provided with the population standard deviation, calculating the standard error requires only minor calculations.)
    b. Write a report wherein you discuss the following: the standard error compared with the standard deviation of the population, the shape of the sampling distribution, and suggestions for reducing the standard error.

Chapter 8

Estimation

> ## Chapter Learning Objectives
>
> ❖ Understanding the concept of estimation and the reasons for it
> ❖ Estimating confidence intervals for means
> ❖ Understanding the concept of risk and how to reduce it
> ❖ Estimating confidence intervals for proportions

In this chapter, we discuss the procedures involved in estimating population means and proportions. These procedures are based on the principles of sampling and statistical inference discussed in Chapter 7. Knowledge about the sampling distribution allows us to estimate population means and proportions from sample outcomes and to assess the accuracy of these estimates.

Example 1: Based on a random sample of 1,535 U.S. adults, a May 2013 Gallup poll found that Americans have become more accepting of gay or lesbian relations compared with 2001 poll results. In 2001, only 40 percent of Americans believed gay or lesbian relations were "morally acceptable," yet in 2013, the percentage had risen to 59 percent. One might presume that the legalization of same-sex marriages in several states between 2001 and 2013 as well as the increased attention via mass media outlets has persuaded more Americans to deem gay or lesbian relations appropriate. As more states continue to pass legislation legalizing same-sex marriage, it will be interesting to see how public opinion fluctuates.[1]

Example 2: Each month, the Bureau of Labor Statistics interviews a sample of about 50,000 adult Americans to determine job-related activities. Based on these interviews, monthly estimates are made of statistics such as the unemployment rate (the proportion who are unemployed), average earnings, the percentage of the workforce working part-time, and the percentage collecting unemployment benefits. These estimates are considered so vital that they cause fluctuations in the stock market and influence economic policies of the federal government.

Example 3: During the spring of 2013, the Obama administration received a significant amount of attention and criticism for three separate controversies that emerged within several weeks of one another, including the Internal Revenue Service's purported targeting of conservative nonprofit groups, supposed cover up of the September 11, 2012, Benghazi terrorist attack, and the Justice Department's subpoenaing of Associated Press journalist phone records. The Pew Research Center conducted a poll of 1,002 adults in May 2013 to estimate how much the American public was paying attention to each of these stories. What Pew found was that the percent of respondents paying close attention to these stories were very different from those relative to respondent political party identification. That is, a greater percentage of Republican respondents stated they were following each of the stories, compared with Democrats. For example, 34% of Republicans reported they were closely following the Benghazi investigations in comparison to 18% of Democrats.[2]

Example 4: Every other year, the National Opinion Research Center conducts the General Social Survey (GSS) on a representative sample of about 1,500 respondents. The GSS, from which many of the examples in this book are selected, is designed to provide social science researchers with a readily accessible database of socially relevant attitudes, behaviors, and attributes of a cross section of the U.S. adult population. For example, in analyzing the responses to the 2010 GSS, researchers found that the average respondent's education was about 13.47 years. This average probably differs from the average of the population from which the GSS sample was drawn. However, we can establish that in most cases the sample mean (in this case, 13.47 years) is fairly close to the actual true average in the population.

As you read these examples, you may have questioned the reliability of some of the numbers. Are Americans really becoming more accepting of gay and lesbian relations? What is the actual percentage of unemployed Americans? How closely do Americans follow controversial stories with White House connections? What is the actual average level of education in the United States?

▣ ESTIMATION DEFINED

The actual percentage of Americans who support gay and lesbian relations, the actual percentage of unemployed Americans, the varying valid percentages of Republicans and Democrats who closely follow controversial political news, and the actual average level of education in the United States are all population parameters. The percentage of Americans who favor gay and lesbian relations as approximated by the Gallup organization, the percentage of unemployed Americans as estimated by the Bureau of Labor Statistics, the attention Americans pay toward provocative news stories as assessed by the Pew Research Center, and the average level of education in the United States as calculated from the GSS are all sample estimates of population parameters. Sample estimates are used to calculate population parameters; the mean number of years of education of 13.47 calculated from the GSS sample can be used to estimate the mean education of all adults in the United States. Similarly, based on a national sample of adult Americans, the Gallup organization estimated the attitudes of Americans toward gay and lesbian relations.

These are all illustrations of estimation. **Estimation** is a process whereby we select a random sample from a population and use a sample statistic to estimate a population parameter. We can use sample proportions as estimates of population proportions, sample means as estimates of population means, or sample variances as estimates of population variances.

Estimation   A process whereby we select a random sample from a population and use a sample statistic to estimate a population parameter.

Reasons for Estimation

Why estimate? The goal of most research is to find the population parameter. Yet we hardly ever have enough resources to collect information about the entire population. We rarely know the value of the population parameter. On the other hand, we can learn a lot about a population by randomly selecting a sample from that population and obtaining an estimate of the population parameter. The major objective of sampling theory and statistical inference is to provide estimates of unknown population parameters from sample statistics.

Point and Interval Estimation

Estimates of population characteristics can be divided into two types: point estimates and interval estimates. **Point estimates** are sample statistics used to estimate the exact value of a population parameter. When the Gallup organization reports that 59% of Americans support gay and lesbian relations, they are using a point estimate. Similarly, if we reported the average level of education of the population of adult Americans to be exactly 13.47 years, we would be using a point estimate.

Point estimate   A sample statistic used to estimate the exact value of a population parameter.

The problem with point estimates is that sample statistics vary, usually resulting in some sort of sampling error. Thus, we never really know how accurate they are. As a result we rarely rely on them as estimators of population parameters such as average income or percentage of the population who are in favor of gay and lesbian relations.

One method of increasing accuracy is to use an interval estimate rather than a point estimate. In interval estimation, we identify a range of values within which the population parameter may fall. This range of values is called a **confidence interval** (CI). Instead of using a single value, 13.47 years, as an estimate of the mean education of adult Americans, we could say that the population mean is somewhere between 12 and 14 years.

Confidence interval (CI)   A range of values defined by the confidence level within which the population parameter is estimated to fall. Sometimes confidence intervals are referred to as margin of error.

When we use confidence intervals to estimate population parameters, such as mean educational levels, we can also evaluate the accuracy of this estimate by assessing the likelihood that any given interval will contain the mean. This likelihood, expressed as a percentage or a probability, is called a **confidence level**. Confidence intervals are defined in terms of confidence levels. Thus, by selecting a 95% confidence level, we are saying that there is a .95 probability—or 95 chances out of 100—that a specified interval will contain the population mean. Confidence intervals can be constructed for any level of confidence, but the most common ones are the 90%, 95%, and 99% levels. You should also know that confidence intervals are sometimes referred to in terms of **margin of error**. In short, margin of error is simply the radius of a confidence interval. If we select a 95% confidence level, we would have a 5% chance of our interval being incorrect.

Confidence level   The likelihood, expressed as a percentage or a probability, that a specified interval will contain the population parameter.

Margin of error   The radius of a confidence interval.

Confidence intervals can be constructed for many different parameters based on their corresponding sample statistics. In this chapter, we describe the rationale and the procedure for the construction of confidence intervals for means and proportions.

✓ *Learning Check*

What is the difference between a point estimate and a confidence interval?

▣ PROCEDURES FOR ESTIMATING CONFIDENCE INTERVALS FOR MEANS

To illustrate the procedure for establishing confidence intervals for means, we'll reintroduce one of the research examples mentioned in Chapter 7—assessing the needs of commuting students on our campus.

Recall that we have been given enough money to survey a random sample of 500 students. One of our tasks is to estimate the average commuting time of all 15,000 commuters on our campus—the population parameter. To obtain this estimate, we calculate the average commuting time for the sample. Suppose the sample average is $\bar{Y} = 7.5$ hrs/week, and we want to use it as an estimate of the true average commuting time for the entire population of commuting students.

Because it is based on a sample, this estimate is subject to sampling error. We do not know how close it is to the true population mean. However, based on what the central limit theorem tells us about the properties of the sampling distribution of the mean, we know that with a large enough sample size, most sample means will tend to be close to the true population mean.

Therefore, it is unlikely that our sample mean, $\overline{Y} = 7.5$ hrs/week, deviates much from the true population mean.

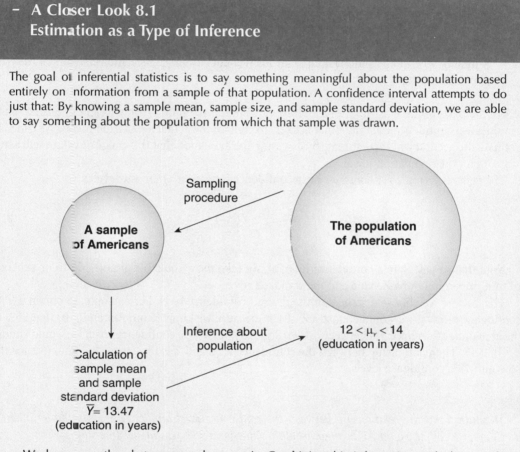

– A Closer Look 8.1
Estimation as a Type of Inference

The goal of inferential statistics is to say something meaningful about the population based entirely on information from a sample of that population. A confidence interval attempts to do just that: By knowing a sample mean, sample size, and sample standard deviation, we are able to say something about the population from which that sample was drawn.

Sampling procedure

A sample of Americans

The population of Americans

$12 < \mu_Y < 14$ (education in years)

Inference about population

Calculation of sample mean and sample standard deviation $\overline{Y} = 13.47$ (education in years)

We know exactly what our sample mean is. Combining this information with the sample standard deviation and sample size gives us a range within which we can confidently say that the population mean falls.

We know that the sampling distribution of the mean is approximately normal with a mean equal to the population mean μ_Y and a standard error $\sigma_{\overline{Y}}$ (standard deviation of the sampling distribution) as follows:

$$\sigma_{\overline{Y}} = \frac{\sigma_Y}{\sqrt{N}} \tag{8.1}$$

This information allows us to use the normal distribution to determine the probability that a sample mean will fall within a certain distance—measured in standard deviation (standard error) units or Z scores—of μ_Y or $\mu_{\bar{Y}}$. We can make the following assumptions:

- A total of 68% of all random sample means will fall within ±1 standard error of the true population mean.
- A total of 95% of all random sample means will fall within ±1.96 standard errors of the true population mean.
- A total of 99% of all random sample means will fall within ±2.58 standard errors of the true population mean.

On the basis of these assumptions and the value of the standard error, we can establish a range of values—a confidence interval—that is likely to contain the actual population mean. We can also evaluate the accuracy of this estimate by assessing the likelihood that this range of values will actually contain the population mean.

The general formula for constructing a confidence interval (CI) for any level is

$$CI = \bar{Y} \pm Z(\sigma_{\bar{Y}}) \tag{8.2}$$

Note that to calculate a confidence interval, we take the sample mean and add to or subtract from it the product of a Z value and the standard error.

The Z score we choose depends on the desired confidence level. For example, to obtain a 95% confidence interval we would choose a Z of 1.96 because we know (from Appendix B) that 95% of the area under the curve lies between ±1.96. Similarly, for a 99% confidence level, we would choose a Z of 2.58. The relationship between the confidence level and Z is illustrated in Figure 8.1 for the 95% and 99% confidence levels.

✓ *Learning*
Check

To understand the relationship between the confidence level and Z, review the material in Chapter 6. What would be the appropriate Z value for a 98% confidence interval?

Determining the Confidence Interval

To determine the confidence interval for means, follow these steps:

1. Calculate the standard error of the mean.

2. Decide on the level of confidence, and find the corresponding Z value.

3. Calculate the confidence interval.

4. Interpret the results.

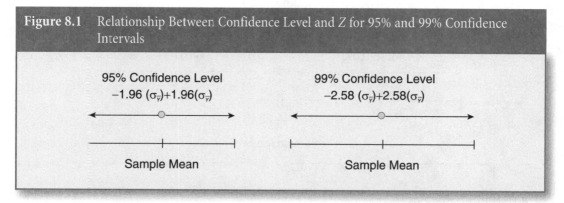

Figure 8.1 Relationship Between Confidence Level and Z for 95% and 99% Confidence Intervals

Source: David Freedman, Robert Pisani, Roger Purves, and Ani Akhikari, *Statistics*, 2nd ed. (New York: Norton, 1991).

Let's return to the problem of estimating the mean commuting time of the population of students on our campus. How would you find the 95% confidence interval?

Calculating the Standard Error of the Mean

Let's suppose that the standard deviation for our population of commuters is $\sigma_Y = 1.5$. We calculate the standard error for the sampling distribution of the mean:

$$\sigma_{\bar{Y}} = \frac{\sigma_Y}{\sqrt{N}} = \frac{1.5}{\sqrt{500}} = 0.07$$

Deciding on the Level of Confidence and Finding the Corresponding Z Value

We decide on a 95% confidence level. The Z value corresponding to a 95% confidence level is 1.96.

Calculating the Confidence Interval

The confidence interval is calculated by adding and subtracting from the observed sample mean the product of the standard error and Z:

$$95\% \text{ CI} = 7.5 \pm 1.96(0.07)$$

$$= 7.5 \pm 0.14$$

$$= 7.36 \text{ to } 7.64$$

The 95% CI for the mean commuting time is illustrated in Figure 8.2.

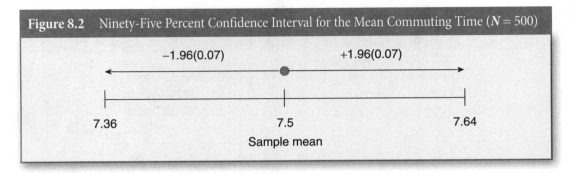

Figure 8.2 Ninety-Five Percent Confidence Interval for the Mean Commuting Time ($N = 500$)

Interpreting the Results

We can be 95% confident that the actual mean commuting time—the true population mean—is not less than 7.36 hrs and not greater than 7.64 hrs. In other words, if we collected a large number of samples ($N = 500$) from the population of commuting students, 95 times out of 100, the true population mean would be included within our computed interval. With a 95% confidence level, there is a 5% risk that we are wrong. Five times out of 100, the true population mean will not be included in the specified interval.

Remember that we can never be sure whether the population mean is actually contained within the confidence interval. Once the sample is selected and the confidence interval defined, the confidence interval either does or does not contain the population mean—but we will never be sure.

✓ **Learning Check**   *What is the 90% confidence interval for the mean commuting time? (Hint: First, find the Z value associated with a 90% confidence level.)*

To further illustrate the concept of confidence intervals, let's suppose that we draw 10 different samples ($N = 500$) from the population of commuting students. For each sample mean, we construct a 95% confidence interval. Figure 8.3 displays these confidence intervals. Each horizontal line represents a 95% confidence interval constructed around a sample mean (marked with a circle).

The vertical line represents the population mean. Note that the horizontal lines that intersect the vertical line are the intervals that contain the true population mean. Only 1 out of the 10 confidence intervals does not intersect the vertical line, meaning it does not contain the population mean. What would happen if we continued to draw samples of the same size from this population and constructed a 95% confidence interval for each sample? For about 95% of all samples the specified interval would contain the true population mean, but for 5% of all samples it would not.

Reducing Risk

One way to reduce the risk of being incorrect is by increasing the level of confidence. For instance, we can increase our confidence level from 95% to 99%. The 99% confidence interval for our commuting example is

Figure 8.3   Ninety-Five Percent Confidence Intervals for 10 Samples

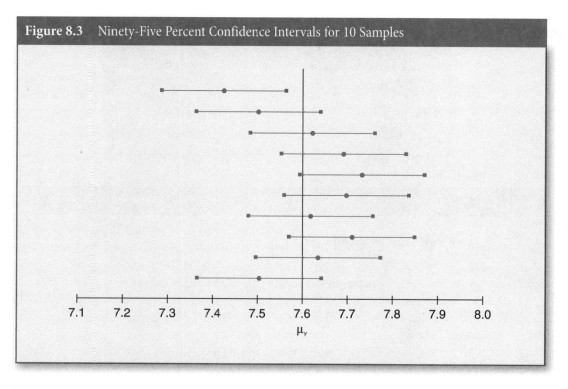

$$99\% \text{ CI} = 7.5 \pm 2.58(0.07)$$

$$= 7.5 \pm 0.18$$

$$= 7.32 \text{ to } 7.68$$

When using the 99% confidence interval, there is only a 1% risk that we are wrong and the specified interval does not contain the true population mean. We can be almost certain that the true population mean is included in the interval ranging from 7.32 to 7.68 hrs/week. Note that by increasing the confidence level, we have also increased the width of the confidence interval from 0.28 (7.36–7.64) to 0.36 hrs (7.32–7.68), thereby making our estimate less precise.

You can see that there is a trade-off between achieving greater confidence in an estimate and the precision of that estimate. Although using a higher level of confidence (e.g., 99%) increases our confidence that the true population mean is included in our confidence interval, the estimate becomes less precise as the width of the interval increases. Although we are only 95% confident that the interval ranging between 7.36 and 7.64 hrs includes the true population mean, it is a more precise estimate than the 99% interval ranging from 7.32 to 7.68 hrs. The relationship between the confidence level and the precision of the confidence interval is illustrated in Figure 8.4. Table 8.1 lists three commonly used confidence levels along with their corresponding Z values.

Table 8.1   Confidence Levels and Corresponding *Z* Values

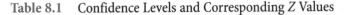

Confidence Level	Z Value
90%	1.65
95%	1.96
99%	2.58

Figure 8.4   Confidence Intervals, 95% Versus 99% (mean commuting time)

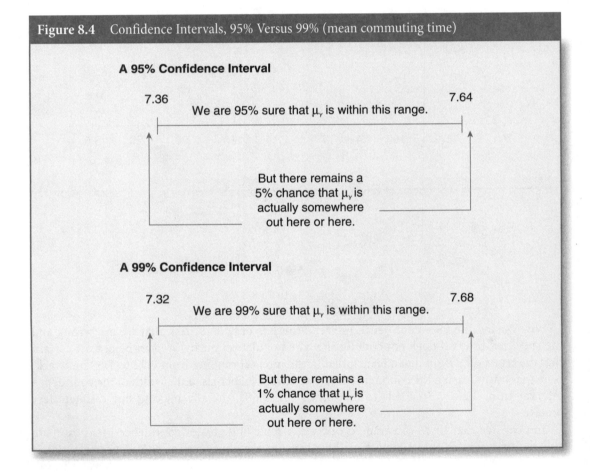

Estimating Sigma

To calculate confidence intervals, we need to know the standard error of the sampling distribution. The standard error is a function of the population standard deviation and the sample size:

$$\sigma_{\bar{Y}} = \frac{\sigma_Y}{\sqrt{N}}$$

In our commuting example, we have been using a hypothetical value, $\sigma_Y = 1.5$, for the population standard deviation. Typically, both the mean (μ_Y) and the standard deviation (σ_Y) of the population are unknown to us. When $N \geq 50$, however, the sample standard deviation, S_Y, is a good estimate of $\sigma_{\bar{Y}}$. The standard error is then calculated as follows:

$$S_{\bar{Y}} = \frac{S_Y}{\sqrt{N}} \tag{8.3}$$

As an example, we'll estimate the mean hours per day that Americans spend watching television based on the 2010 GSS. The mean hours per day spent watching television for a sample of $N = 1,013$ is $\bar{Y} = 3.01$, and the standard deviation $S_Y = 2.65$ hrs. Let's determine the 95% confidence interval for these data.

Calculating the Estimated Standard Error of the Mean

The estimated standard error for the sampling distribution of the mean is

$$S_{\bar{Y}} = \frac{S_Y}{\sqrt{N}} = \frac{2.65}{\sqrt{1,013}} = 0.08$$

Deciding on the Level of Confidence and Finding the Corresponding Z Value

We decide on a 95% confidence level. The Z value corresponding to a 95% confidence level is 1.96.

Calculating the Confidence Interval

The confidence interval is calculated by adding to and subtracting from the observed sample mean the product of the standard error and Z:

$$95\% \text{ CI} = 3.01 \pm 1.96(0.08)$$
$$= 3.01 \pm 0.16$$
$$= 2.85 \text{ to } 3.17$$

Interpreting the Results

We can be 95% confident that the actual mean hours spent watching television by Americans from which the GSS sample was taken is not less than 2.85 hrs and not greater than 3.17 hrs. In other words, if we drew a large number of samples ($N = 1,013$) from this population, then 95 times out of 100, the true population mean would be included within our computed interval.

Sample Size and Confidence Intervals

Researchers can increase the precision of their estimate by increasing the sample size. In Chapter 7, we learned that larger samples result in smaller standard errors and, therefore, sampling distributions are more clustered around the population mean (Figure 7.6). A more tightly clustered sampling distribution means that our confidence intervals will be narrower and more precise. To illustrate the relationship between sample size and the standard error, and thus the confidence interval, let's calculate the 95% confidence interval for our GSS data with (1) a sample of $N = 195$ and (2) a sample of $N = 1,987$.

With a sample size $N = 195$, the estimated standard error for the sampling distribution is

$$S_{\bar{Y}} = \frac{S_Y}{\sqrt{N}} = \frac{2.65}{\sqrt{195}} = 0.19$$

and the 95% confidence interval is

$$95\% \text{ CI} = 3.01 \pm 1.96(0.19)$$

$$= 3.01 \pm 0.37$$

$$= 2.64 \text{ to } 3.38$$

With a sample size $N = 1,987$, the estimated standard error for the sampling distribution is

$$S_{\bar{Y}} = \frac{S_Y}{\sqrt{N}} = \frac{2.65}{\sqrt{1,987}} = 0.06$$

and the 95% confidence interval is

$$95\% \text{ CI} = 3.01 \pm 1.96(0.06)$$

$$= 3.01 \pm 0.12$$

$$= 2.89 \text{ to } 3.13$$

In Table 8.2, we summarize the 95% confidence intervals for the mean number of hours watching television for these three sample sizes: $N = 195$, $N = 1,013$, and $N = 1,987$.

Table 8.2   Ninety-Five Percent Confidence Interval and Width for Mean Number of Hours per Day Watching Television for Three Different Sample Sizes

Sample Size (N)	Confidence Interval	Interval Width	S_Y	$S_{\bar{Y}}$
195	2.64–3.38	0.74	2.65	0.19
1,013	2.85–3.17	0.32	2.65	0.08
1,987	2.89–3.13	0.24	2.65	0.06

Note that there is an inverse relationship between sample size and the width of the confidence interval. The increase in sample size is linked with increased precision of the confidence interval. The 95% confidence interval for the GSS sample of 195 cases is 0.74 hrs. But the interval widths decrease to 0.32 and 0.24 hrs, respectively, as the sample sizes increase to $N = 1,013$ and then to $N = 1,987$. We had to nearly double the size of the sample (from 1,013 to 1,987) to reduce the confidence interval by about one-fourth (from 0.32 to 0.24 hrs). In general, although the precision of estimates increases steadily with sample size, the gains would appear to be rather modest after N reaches 1,987. An important factor to keep in mind is the increased cost associated with a larger sample. Researchers have to consider at what point the increase in precision is too small to justify the additional cost associated with a larger sample.

✓ *Learning Check*

Why do smaller sample sizes produce wider confidence intervals? (See Figure 8.5.) (Hint: Compare the standard errors of the mean for the three sample sizes.)

– A Closer Look 8.2
What Affects Confidence Interval Width? Summary

"Holding other factors constant . . ."

If the sample size goes up	↑	the confidence interval becomes more precise. → ←
If the sample size goes down	↓	the confidence interval becomes less precise. ← →
If the value of the sample standard deviation goes up	↑	the confidence interval becomes less precise. ← →
If the value of the sample standard deviation goes down	↓	the confidence interval becomes more precise. → ←
If the level of confidence goes up (from 95% to 99%)	↑	the confidence interval becomes less precise. ← →
If the level of confidence goes down (from 99% to 95%)	↓	the confidence interval becomes more precise. → ←

Figure 8.5 The Relationship Between Sample Size and Confidence Interval Width

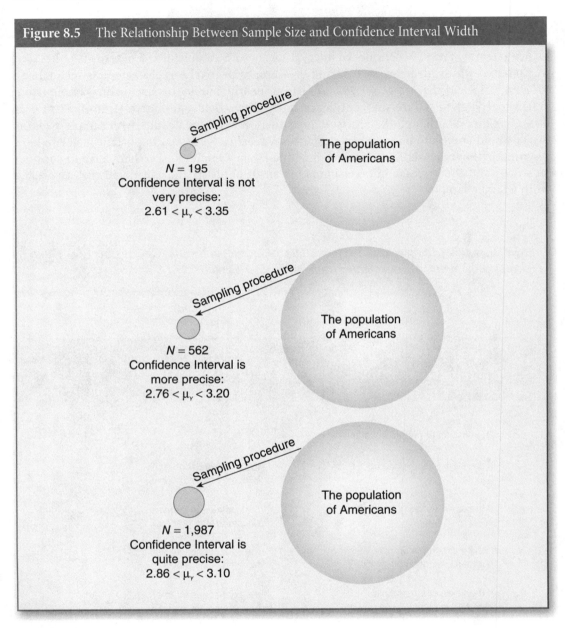

▣ STATISTICS IN PRACTICE:
HISPANIC MIGRATION AND EARNINGS

There were nearly 23 million people of Hispanic or Latino ethnicity in the U.S. in 2011. This represents 15 percent of the U.S. labor force.[3] This group is not homogeneous. Among its five major groups are individuals of Mexicans, Puerto Rican, and Cuban descent.[4]

During the last few decades, numerous studies have noted the discrepancy in earnings between these groups. The gap in earnings has been attributed mainly to differences in migration status and in level of education. Tienda and Wilson argued that Mexicans, Puerto Ricans, and Cubans varied markedly in socioeconomic characteristics because of differences in the timing and circumstances of their immigration to the United States.[6] The period of entry and the circumstances prompting migration affected the geographical distribution and the employment opportunities of each group. For example, Puerto Ricans were disproportionately located in the Northeast, where the labor market was characterized by the highest unemployment rates, whereas the majority of Cuban immigrants resided in the Southeast, where the unemployment rate was the lowest in the United States.

Tienda and Wilson also noted persistent differences in educational levels among Mexicans and Puerto Ricans compared with Cubans.[7] Only about 9% of Mexicans and 16% of Puerto Ricans have graduated college, compared with 25% of Cuban men.[8] These differences in migrant status and educational level were likely to be reflected in disparities in earnings among the three groups. We would anticipate that the earnings of Cubans would be higher than the earnings of Mexicans and Puerto Ricans.

We tested the ideas of Tienda and Wilson based on a sample of men from the 2000 Census that included 29,233 Cubans, 34,620 Mexican Americans, and 66,933 Puerto Ricans. As hypothesized, with average earnings of $24,018 ($S_Y = $36,298$), Cubans were at the top of the income hierarchy. Puerto Ricans were intermediate among the groups with earnings averaging $18,748 ($S_Y = $25,694$). Mexican men were at the bottom of the income hierarchy with average annual earnings of $16,537 ($S_Y = $23,502$). Although Tienda and Wilson did not calculate confidence intervals for their estimates we use the data from the 2000 Census to calculate a 95% confidence interval for the mean income of the three groups of Hispanic men.[9]

To find the 95% confidence interval for Cuban income, we first estimate the standard error:

$$S_{\bar{Y}} = \frac{S_Y}{\sqrt{N}} = \frac{36,298}{\sqrt{29,233}} = 212.29$$

Then, we calculate the confidence interval:

$$95\% \ CI = 24,018 \pm 1.96(212.29)$$

$$= 24,018 \pm 416$$

$$= 23,602 \ to \ 24,434$$

For Puerto Rican income, the estimated standard error is

$$S_{\bar{Y}} = \frac{S_Y}{\sqrt{N}} = \frac{25,694}{\sqrt{66,933}} = 99.32$$

and the 95% confidence interval is

$$95\% \; CI = 18{,}748 \pm 1.96(99.32)$$

$$= 18{,}748 \pm 195$$

$$= 18{,}553 \; to \; 18{,}943$$

Finally, for Mexican income, the estimated standard error is

$$S_{\bar{Y}} = \frac{S_Y}{\sqrt{N}} = \frac{23{,}502}{\sqrt{34{,}620}} = 126.31$$

and the 95% confidence interval is

$$95\% \; CI = 16{,}537 \pm 1.96(126.31)$$

$$= 16{,}537 \pm 248$$

$$= 16{,}289 \; to \; 16{,}785$$

The confidence intervals for mean annual income of Cuban, Puerto Rican, and Mexican immigrants are illustrated in Figure 8.6. We can say with 95% confidence that the true income mean for each Hispanic group lies somewhere within the corresponding confidence interval. Note that the

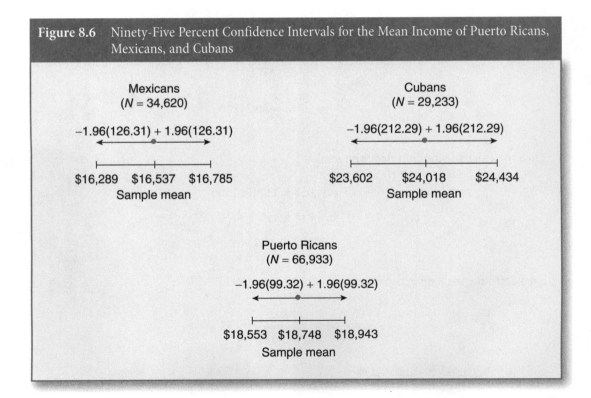

Figure 8.6   Ninety-Five Percent Confidence Intervals for the Mean Income of Puerto Ricans, Mexicans, and Cubans

confidence intervals do not overlap, thus revealing great disparities in earnings among the three groups. Highest interval estimates are for Cubans, followed by Mexicans and then Puerto Ricans.

回 CONFIDENCE INTERVALS FOR PROPORTIONS

Confidence intervals can also be computed for sample proportions or percentages to estimate population proportions or percentages. The procedures for estimating proportions and percentages are identical. Any of the formulas presented for proportions can be applied to percentages, and vice versa. We can obtain a confidence interval for a percentage by calculating the confidence interval for a proportion and then multiplying the result by 100.

The same conceptual foundations of sampling and statistical inference that are central to the estimation of population means—the selection of random samples and the special properties of the sampling distribution—are also central to the estimation of population proportions.

Earlier, we saw that the sampling distribution of the means underlies the process of estimating population means from sample means. Similarly, the *sampling distribution of proportions* underlies the estimation of population proportions from sample proportions. Based on the central limit theorem, we know that with sufficient sample size the sampling distribution of proportions is approximately normal, with mean μ_p equal to the population proportion π and with a standard error of proportions (the standard deviation of the sampling distribution of proportions) equal to

$$\sigma_p = \sqrt{\frac{(\pi)(1-\pi)}{N}} \tag{8.4}$$

where

σ_p = the standard error of proportions

π = the population proportion

N = the population size

However, since the population proportion, π, is unknown to us (that is what we are trying to estimate), we can use the sample proportion, p, as an estimate of π. The estimated standard error then becomes

$$S_p = \sqrt{\frac{(p)(1-p)}{N}} \tag{8.5}$$

where

S_p = the estimated standard error of proportions

p = the sample proportion

N = the sample size

As an example, let's calculate the estimated standard error for the survey by Gallup. Based on a random sample of 1,535 adults, the percentage who support gay and lesbian relations was estimated to be 59%. Based on Formula 8.5, with $p = 0.59$, $1 - p = (1 - 0.59) = 0.41$, and $N = 1,535$, the standard error is $S_p = \sqrt{(0.59)(1-0.59)/1,535} = 0.013$. We will have to consider two factors to meet the assumption of normality with the sampling distribution of proportions: (1) the sample size N and (2) the sample proportions p and $1 - p$. When p and $1 - p$ are about 0.50, a sample size of at least 50 is sufficient. But when $p > 0.50$ (or $1 - p < 0.50$), a larger sample is required to meet the assumption of normality. Usually, a sample of 100 or more is adequate for any single estimate of a population proportion.

Procedures for Estimating Proportions

Because the sampling distribution of proportions is approximately normal, we can use the normal distribution to establish confidence intervals for proportions in the same manner that we used the normal distribution to establish confidence intervals or means.

The general formula for constructing confidence intervals for proportions for any level of confidence is

$$CI = p \pm Z(S_p) \tag{8.6}$$

where

CI = the confidence interval

p = the observed sample proportion

Z = the Z corresponding to the confidence level

S_p = the estimated standard error of proportions

Let's examine this formula in more detail. Note that to obtain a confidence interval at a certain level, we take the sample proportion and add to or subtract from it the product of a Z value and the standard error. The Z value we choose depends on the desired confidence level. We want the area between the mean and the selected $\pm Z$ to be equal to the confidence level.

For example, to obtain a 95% confidence interval, we would choose a Z of 1.96 because we know (from Appendix B) that 95% of the area under the curve is included between ± 1.96. Similarly, for a 99% confidence level, we would choose a Z of 2.58. (The relationship between confidence level and Z values is illustrated in Figure 8.1.)

To determine the confidence interval for a proportion, we follow the same steps that were used to find confidence intervals for means:

1. Calculate the estimated standard error of the proportion.

2. Decide on the desired level of confidence, and find the corresponding Z value.

3. Calculate the confidence interval.

4. Interpret the results.

To illustrate these steps, we use the results of the Gallup survey on the percentage of Americans who support gay and lesbian relations.

Calculating the Estimated Standard Error of the Proportion

The standard error of the proportion 0.59 (59%) with a sample $N = 1,535$ is 0.013.

Deciding on the Desired Level of Confidence and Finding the Corresponding Z Value

We choose the 95% confidence level. The Z corresponding to a 95% confidence level is 1.96.

Calculating the Confidence Interval

We calculate the confidence interval by adding to and subtracting from the observed sample proportion the product of the standard error and Z:

$$95\% \ CI = 0.59 \pm 1.96(0.013)$$
$$= 0.59 \pm 0.025$$
$$= 0.565 \ to \ 0.615$$

Interpreting the Results

We are 95% confident that the true population proportion is somewhere between 0.565 and 0.615. In other words, if we drew a large number of samples from the population of adults, then 95 times out of 100, the confidence interval we obtained would contain the true population proportion. We can also express this result in percentages and say that we are 95% confident that the true population percentage of Americans who support gay and lesbian relations is included somewhere within our computed interval of 56.5% to 61.5%.

> *Calculate the confidence interval for the Gallup survey using percentages rather than proportions. Your results should be identical with ours except that they are expressed in percentages.*

✓ *Learning Check*

Note that with a 95% confidence level, there is a 5% risk that we are wrong. If we continued to draw large samples from this population, in 5 out of 100 samples the true population proportion would not be included in the specified interval.

We can decrease our risk by increasing the confidence level from 95% to 99%.

$$99\% \text{ CI} = 0.59 \pm 2.58(0.013)$$
$$= 0.59 \pm 0.034$$
$$= 0.556 \text{ to } 0.624$$

When using the 99% confidence interval, we can be almost certain (99 times out of 100) that the true population proportion is included in the interval ranging from 0.556 (55.6%) to 0.624 (62.4%). However, as we saw earlier, there is a trade-off between achieving greater confidence in making an estimate and the precision of that estimate. Although using a 99% level increased our confidence level from 95% to 99% (thereby reducing our risk of being wrong from 5% to 1%), the estimate became less precise as the width of the interval increased.[10,11]

▣ STATISTICS IN PRACTICE: THE 2012 BENGHAZI TERRORIST ATTACK INVESTIGATION

Poll or survey results may be limited to a single estimate of a parameter. For instance, political pollsters could estimate the percentage of Americans who closely follow controversial news stories. Most survey studies, however, are not limited to single estimates for the overall population. Often, separate estimates are reported for subgroups within the overall population of interest. In a report released on May 20, 2013, Gallup compared the percentage of Democrats and Republicans who were closely following the September 11, 2012, Benghazi terrorist attacks. They were interested in exploring whether or not there were differences across groups with different political affiliations.[12]

When estimates are reported for subgroups, the confidence intervals are likely to vary from subgroup to subgroup. Each confidence interval is based on the confidence level, the standard error of the proportion (which can be estimated from p), and the sample size. Even when a confidence interval is reported only for the overall sample, we can easily compute separate confidence intervals for each of the subgroups if the confidence level and the size of each of the subgroups are included.

To illustrate this, let's calculate the 95% confidence intervals for the proportions of Democrats and Republicans who were closely following the Benghazi terrorist attack investigation. Out of 317 Democrats in the sample, 0.18 (or 18%) were closely following the investigation. In contrast, of the 247 Republicans surveyed, 0.34 (or 34%) were closely following the same investigation.

Calculating the Estimated Standard Error of the Proportion

The estimated standard error for the proportion of Democrats is

$$S_p = \sqrt{\frac{(0.18)(1-0.18)}{317}} = 0.02$$

The estimated standard error for the proportion of Republicans is

$$S_p = \sqrt{\frac{(0.34)(1-0.34)}{247}} = 0.03$$

Deciding on the Desired Level of Confidence and Finding the Corresponding Z Value

We choose the 95% confidence level, with a corresponding Z value of 1.96.

Calculating the Confidence Interval

For Democrats,

$$95\% \text{ CI} = 0.18 \pm 1.96(0.02)$$
$$= 0.18 \pm 0.04$$
$$= 0.14 \text{ to } 0.22$$

and for Republicans,

$$95\% \text{ CI} = 0.34 \pm 1.96(0.03)$$
$$= 0.34 \pm 0.06$$
$$= 0.28 \text{ to } 0.40$$

The 95% confidence interval for the proportion of Democrats and Republicans surveyed who closely followed the Benghazi terrorist attack investigation is illustrated in Figure 8.7.

Interpreting the Results

We are 95% confident that the true population proportion that closely followed the Benghazi terrorist attack investigation was between 0.14 and 0.22 (or between 14% and 22%) for Democrats, and somewhere between 0.28 and 0.40 (or between 28% and 40%) for Republicans. Based on the

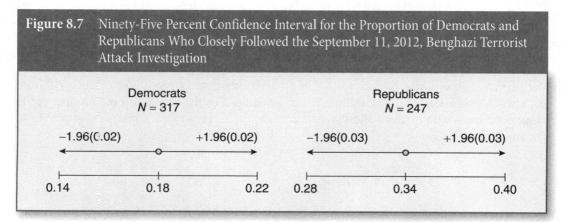

Figure 8.7 Ninety-Five Percent Confidence Interval for the Proportion of Democrats and Republicans Who Closely Followed the September 11, 2012, Benghazi Terrorist Attack Investigation

Source: "Partisan Interest, Reactions to IRS and AP Controversies," *Pew Research Center,* May 20, 2013.

sample, it is clear that among Americans there were partisan differences in how closely persons followed this investigation. Republicans were much more likely than Democrats to closely follow the Benghazi terrorist attack investigation.

⊡ A Closer Look 8.3
A Cautionary Note: The Margin of Error

The most common application of estimation using confidence intervals (also called the margin of error) is demonstrated in opinion and election polls. Pollsters usually interview a random sample representative of a defined population to assess their opinion on a certain issue or their voting preference in a particular election. For example, a 2013 Pew Research Center poll of 1,504 adults reported that 75% believe the U.S. immigration policy needs at least a major overhaul.[13] Also reported was the poll's margin of error of plus or minus 2.9 percentage points. The margin of error in a poll tells us how well a randomly selected sample represents the population from which it was selected. The Pew Research Center poll results indicate that we can be 95% confident that the true percentage of Americans who feel U.S. immigration policy is in need of at least a major overhaul is somewhere between 72.1% (75% − 2.9%) and 77.9% (75% + 2.9%).

A margin of error of 2.9% means that with a sample of 1,504 individuals, we can be 95% confident that the true value of 75% is within ±2.9 percentage points of what it would be if the entire American adult population had been polled.

MAIN POINTS

- The goal of most research is to find population parameters. The major objective of sampling theory and statistical inference is to provide estimates of unknown parameters from sample statistics.

- Researchers make point estimates and interval estimates. Point estimates are sample statistics used to estimate the exact value of a population parameter. Interval estimates are ranges of values within which the population parameter may fall.

- Confidence intervals can be used to estimate population parameters such as means or proportions. Their accuracy is defined with the confidence level. The most common confidence levels are 90%, 95%, and 99%.

- To establish a confidence interval for a mean or a proportion, add or subtract from the mean or the proportion the product of the standard error and the Z value corresponding to the confidence level.

KEY TERMS

Confidence interval   Confidence level   Margin of error
    (interval estimate)   Estimation   Point estimate

$SAGE edge™

Sharpen your skills with SAGE edge at **edge.sagepub.com/frankfort7e**. **SAGE edge for students** provides a personalized approach to help you accomplish your coursework goals in an easy-to-use learning environment.

SPSS DEMONSTRATION

[GSS10SSDS]

Producing Confidence Intervals Around a Mean

SPSS calculates confidence intervals around a sample mean or proportion with the Explore procedure. Let's investigate the average ideal number of children for men and women.

Activate the Explore procedure by selecting the *Analyze* menu, *Descriptive Statistics*, then *Explore*. The opening dialog box has spaces for both dependent and independent variables. Before running the Explore procedure, we defined the category of the variable CHILDIDEL "as many as want" (coded as 8) as missing. To do that, go to the *Data* menu, *Define Variable Properties*, find the variable CHILDIDEL in the variable list, place it in the box "Variables to Scan," and click on *Continue*; in the new dialog box that pops up, select the small square in the *Missing* column corresponding with category "as many as want," coded as 8 (the procedure is not visually represented here). Place CHLDIDEL in the Dependent List box, and SEX in the Factor List box, as shown in Figure 8.8. (For this analysis, we've eliminated response Categories 8 [as many as I want] and 9 [don't know or no answer].)

Click on the *Statistics* button. Note that the Descriptives choice also includes the confidence interval for the mean, which by default is calculated at the 95% confidence level. Let's change that to the 99% level by erasing the "95" and substituting "99" (Figure 8.9).

Figure 8.8 Explore Dialog Box

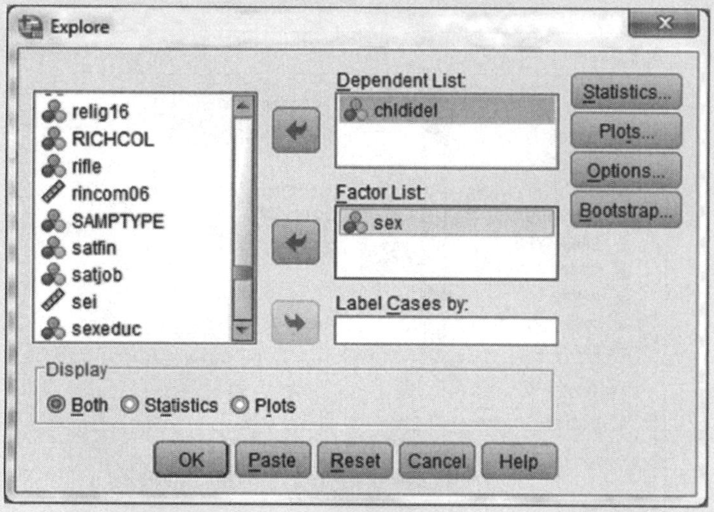

Click on *Continue* to return to the main dialog box. Recall that Explore produces several statistics and plots by default. For this example, we don't need to view the graphics, so click on the *Statistics* button in the *Display* section. Your screen should now look like Figure 8.10.

Click on *OK* to run the procedure.

Figure 8.9　Setting the Confidence Interval

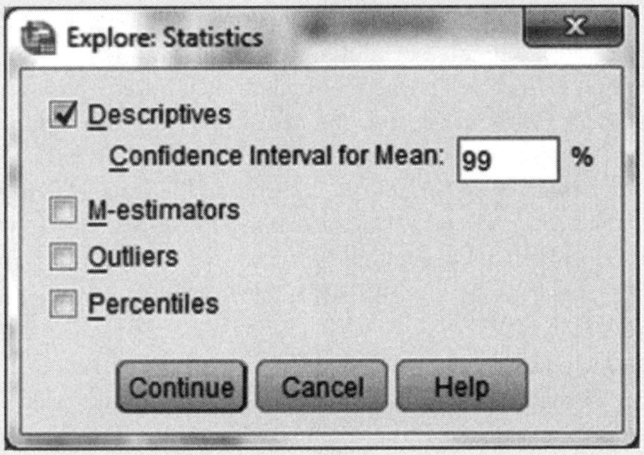

Figure 8.10　Explore Dialog Box

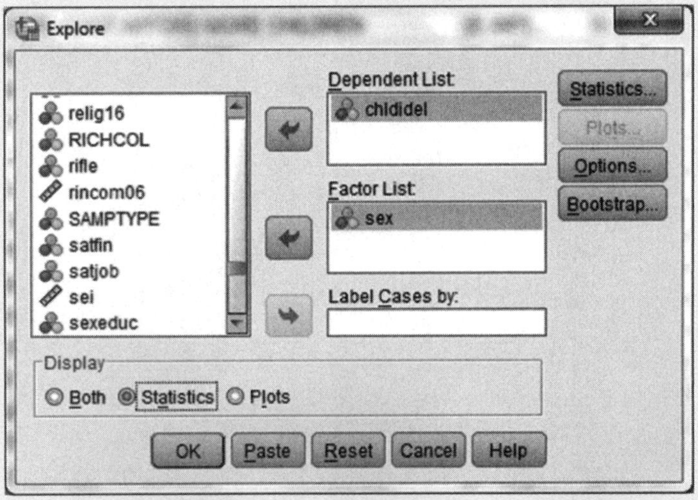

The output from the Explore procedure (Figure 8.11) is divided into two parts, one for males and one for females. The mean ideal number of children for males is 2.56; for females, it's 2.52. Our data indicate that, on average, the ideal number of children is slightly greater for men than it is for women.

Figure 8.11   SPSS Output for CHLDIDEL by Sex

Case Processing Summary

		Cases					
		Valid		Missing		Total	
	RESPONDENTS SEX	N	Percent	N	Percent	N	Percent
IDEAL NUMBER OF CHILDREN	MALE	391	60.3%	257	39.7%	648	100.0%
	FEMALE	474	55.6%	378	44.4%	852	100.0%

Descriptives

	RESPONDENTS SEX			Statistic	Std. Error
IDEAL NUMBER OF CHILDREN	MALE	Mean		2.56	.050
		99% Confidence Interval for Mean	Lower Bound	2.43	
			Upper Bound	2.69	
		5% Trimmed Mean		2.48	
		Median		2.00	
		Variance		.970	
		Std. Deviation		.985	
		Minimum		0	
		Maximum		7	
		Range		7	
		Interquartile Range		1	
		Skewness		1.626	.123
		Kurtosis		4.164	.246
	FEMALE	Mean		2.52	.041
		99% Confidence Interval for Mean	Lower Bound	2.41	
			Upper Bound	2.63	
		5% Trimmed Mean		2.49	
		Median		2.00	
		Variance		.813	
		Std. Deviation		.901	
		Minimum		0	
		Maximum		6	
		Range		6	
		Interquartile Range		1	
		Skewness		.804	.112
		Kurtosis		1.653	.224

Exercises

The 99% confidence interval for males runs from about 2.69 to 2.43 children. One way to interpret this result is to state that, in 100 samples each of size 391 males from the U.S. adult population, we would expect the confidence interval to include the true population value for the mean ideal number of children 99 times out of those 100. We can never be sure that in this particular sample the confidence interval includes the population mean. As explained in this chapter, the confidence interval of any one sample either does or does not contain the (unknown) population mean, so no probability value can be associated with a particular confidence interval. Still, our best estimate for the mean ideal number of children falls within a narrow range of only about 0.26. For females, the 99% confidence interval is almost the same, varying from about 2.63 to 2.41 children, or only 0.22.

SPSS PROBLEMS

[GSS10SSDS]

1. Recall that the GSS sample includes men and women from 18 to 89 years of age. Does it matter that we may have responses from men and women of diverse ages? Would our results change if we selected a younger sample of men and women?

   a. To take the SPSS demonstration one step further, use the Select Cases procedure to select respondents based on the variable AGE who are less than or equal to 35 years old. Do this by selecting *Data* and then *Select Cases*. Next, select *If Condition is satisfied* and then click on *If*. Find and highlight the variable AGE in the scroll-down box on the left of your screen. Click the arrow next to the scroll-down box. AGE will now appear in the box on the right. Now, tell SPSS that you want to select respondents who are 35 years of age or less. The box on the right should now read AGE <= 35. Click *Continue* and then *OK*.

   b. Using this younger sample, repeat the Explore procedure that we just completed in the demonstration. What differences exist between men and women in this younger sample on the ideal number of children? How do these results compare with those based on the entire sample?

2. Calculate the 90% confidence interval for the following variables, comparing lower, working, middle, and upper classes (CLASS) in the GSS sample. First, tell SPSS that we want to select all cases in the sample by selecting *Data, Select Cases*, and then *All Cases*, and then *OK*. Then, use the Explore procedure using CLASS as your factor variable (*Analyze, Descriptive Statistics, Explore*). Make a summary statement of your findings.

   a. CHILDS (Number of children in the household)
   b. EDUC (Respondent's highest year of school completed)
   c. PAEDUC (Father's highest year of school completed)
   d. PRESTG80 (Respondent's occupational prestige)
   e. MAEDUC (Mother's highest year of school completed)

CHAPTER EXERCISES

1. In the 2011 National Crime Victimization Study, the Federal Bureau of Investigation (FBI) found that 16.2% of Americans age 12 or older had been victims of crime during a 1-year period. This result was based on a sample of 143,120 persons.

   a. Estimate the percentage of U.S. adults who were victims at the 90% confidence level. State in words the meaning of the result.

   b. Estimate the percentage of victims at the 99% confidence level.

c. Imagine that the FBI cuts the sample size in half but finds the same value of 16.2% for the percentage of victims in the second sample. By how much would the 90% confidence interval increase? By how much would the 99% confidence interval increase?

d. Considering your answers to (a), (b), and (c), can you suggest why national surveys, such as those by Gallup, Roper, or *The New York Times*, typically take samples of size 1,000 to 1,500?

2. Use the data on education from Chapter 6, Exercise 5.

	Mean	*Standard Deviation*	N
Lower class	11.61	2.67	123
Working class	12.80	2.85	697
Middle class	14.45	3.08	626
Upper class	15.45	2.98	38

a. Construct the 95% confidence interval for the mean number of years of education for lower-class and middle-class respondents.

b. Construct the 99% confidence interval for the mean number of years of education for lower-class and middle-class respondents.

c. As our confidence in the result increases, how does the size of the confidence interval change? Explain why this is so.

3. There has been a great deal of discussion about global warming in recent years. In 2012, the Pew Research Center conducted a survey of 1,511 Americans to assess their opinion of global warming.[14] The data show that 589 respondents of the 1,511 surveyed felt global warming is a very serious problem.

a. Estimate the proportion of all adult Americans who felt global warming is a very serious problem at the 95% confidence interval.

b. Estimate the proportion of all adult Americans who felt global warming is a very serious problem at the 99% confidence interval.

c. If you were going to write a report on this poll result, would you prefer to use the 99% or 95% confidence interval? Explain why.

4. Use the data in Chapter 5, Exercise 6, about occupational prestige and education.

PRESTG80			*Statistic*
RS OCCUPATIONAL PRESTIGE SCORE (1980)	High School Diploma	Mean	40.59
		Median	40.00
		Std. Deviation	11.419

(Continued)

Exercises

(Continued)

PRESTG80			Statistic
		Minimum	17
		Maximum	75
		Range	58
		Interquartile Range	17
	Bachelor's Degree	Mean	50.95
		Median	51.00
		Std. Deviation	12.930
		Minimum	23
		Maximum	75
		Range	52
		Interquartile Range	23

a. Construct the 90% confidence interval for occupational prestige for respondents with only a high school diploma ($N = 702$).

b. Construct the 90% confidence interval for occupational prestige for respondents with a bachelor's degree ($N = 270$). State in words the meaning of the result.

c. Use these statistics to discuss differences in occupational prestige scores by educational attainment.

5. Gallup conducted a survey in April 1 to 25, 2010, to determine the congressional vote preference of the American voters.[15] They found that 51% of the male voters preferred a Republican candidate to a Democratic candidate in a sample of 5,490 registered voters. Gallup asks you, their statistical consultant, to tell them whether you could declare the Republican candidate as the likely winner of the votes coming from men if there was an election today. What is your advice? Why?

6. You have been doing research for your statistics class on the prevalence of severe binge drinking among teens. You have decided to use 2011 Monitoring the Future (MTF) data that has a scale (going from 0 to 14) measuring the number of times teens drank 10 or more alcoholic beverages in a single sitting in the past 2 weeks.

a. According to 2011 MTF data, the average severe binge drinking score, for this sample of 914 teens, is 1.27, with a standard deviation of 0.80. Construct the 95% confidence interval for the true average severe binge drinking score.

b. One of your classmates, who claims to be good at statistics, complains about your confidence interval calculation. She or he asserts that the severe binge drinking scores are not normally distributed, which in turn makes the confidence interval calculation meaningless. Assume that she or he is correct about the distribution of severe binge drinking scores. Does that imply that the calculation of a confidence interval is not appropriate? Why or why not?

7. From the 2010 GSS subsample, we find that 72.7% of respondents believe in some form of life after death ($N = 1,500$).
   a. What is the 95% confidence interval for the percentage of the U.S. population who believe in life after death?
   b. Without doing any calculations, make an educated guess at the lower and upper bounds of 90% and 99% confidence intervals.

8. A social service agency plans to conduct a survey to determine the mean income of its clients. The director of the agency prefers that you measure the mean income very accurately, to within ±$500. From a sample taken 2 years ago, you estimate that the standard deviation of income for this population is about $5,000. Your job is to figure out the necessary sample size to reduce sampling error to ±$500.
   a. Do you need to have an estimate of the current mean income to answer this question? Why or why not?
   b. What sample size should be drawn to meet the director's requirement at the 95% level of confidence? (*Hint:* Use the formula for a confidence interval and solve for N, the sample size.)
   c. What sample size should be drawn to meet the director's requirement at the 99% level of confidence?

9. Data from a 2010 GSS subsample show that the mean number of children per respondent was 1.97, with a standard deviation of 1.73. A total of 1,496 people answered this question. Estimate the population mean number of children per adult using a 90% confidence interval.

10. A sample of the 2011 MTF survey suggests that adolescents are divided in terms of their attitudes toward others trying marijuana at least once. In fact, 49.3% of the 1,202 respondents who answered the question reported that they don't disapprove of others trying marijuana at least once. Estimate at the 95% and 99% confidence levels the proportion of all adolescents who don't disapprove of others trying marijuana at least once.

11. According to a 2010 survey by the Pew Research Center, 61% of adult Americans use social networking websites such as Twitter and Facebook.[16] Interestingly, 21% of the 2,257 adults surveyed say that they used social network websites to access the 2010 midterm elections. What is the 95% confidence interval for the percentage of American adults that use social networking websites to connect to elections?

12. According to a report published by the Pew Research Center in February 2010, 61% of Millennials (Americans in their teens and 20s) think that their generation has a unique and distinctive identity ($N = 527$).[17]
   a. Calculate the 95% confidence interval to estimate the percentage of Millennials who believe that their generation has a distinctive identity as compared with the other generations (Generation X, baby boomers, or the Silent Generation).
   b. Calculate the 99% confidence interval.
   c. Are both these results compatible with the conclusion that the majority of Millennials believe that they have a unique identity that separates them from the previous generations?

13. Whether one views homosexual relations as wrong is closely related to whether one views homosexuality as a biological trait or the outcome of one's environment and/or socialization. Thus, it is not surprising that several religious groups that condemn homosexual relations have proclaimed their ability to "cure" gays of their sexual orientation. After all, their assumption is that homosexuality is not a trait that a person is born with. In 2010, GSS respondents ($N = 930$) were asked what they thought about homosexual relations. The data show that 50.2% believed that homosexual relations were always wrong, while 37.2% believed that homosexual relations were not wrong at all.

Exercises

    a. For each reported percentage, calculate the 95% confidence interval.

    b. Approximately 13% of GSS respondents were in the middle, some saying that homosexual relations were almost always wrong or sometimes wrong. Calculate the 95% confidence interval.

    c. What conclusions can you draw about the public's opinions of homosexual behavior based on your calculations?

14. A subsample of the 2011 MTF survey suggests that black adolescents don't perceive consuming four to five drinks per day as risky as do white adolescents. Of the 179 black adolescents who answered the question about alcohol consumption, 11.2% reported that consuming four to five drinks per day is "no risk." However, of the 783 white adolescents who answered the same question, only 4.7% reported that consuming four to five drinks per day is "no risk."

    a. Calculate the 95% confidence interval for each proportion reported.

    b. Write a summary based on your calculation suggesting at least two reasons for the observed difference.

15. Many women are raising their children while also working outside the home. Many have studied the impact this trend has on heterosexual families.

    a. How do you think Americans feel about this trend? Do you think there are differences among certain subgroups of the population? If yes, which subgroup(s) do you believe are most likely to view this trend favorably? If no, explain why you do not think there are differences among subgroups of the population.

    b. Researchers collecting data for the 2010 GSS offer insight into public attitudes toward this issue. They asked respondents to share their opinion about working mothers. Of the 459 male respondents who answered the question, 20% strongly agreed that a working mother does not hurt children. Construct a 90% confidence interval for this statistic.

    c. Of the 556 female respondents who answered the question, 36.9% strongly agreed that a working mother does not hurt children. Construct a 90% confidence interval for this statistic.

    d. Offer an explanation for why there is a difference between men and women on this issue.

Exercises

Chapter 9

Testing Hypotheses

Chapter Learning Objectives

❖ Understanding the assumptions of statistical hypothesis testing

❖ Defining and applying the components in hypothesis testing: the research and null hypotheses, sampling distribution, and test statistic

❖ Understanding what it means to reject or fail to reject a null hypothesis

❖ Applying hypothesis testing to two sample cases, with means or proportions

According to economist Ethan Harris, "People may not remember too many numbers about the economy, but there are certain signposts they do pay attention to. As a short hard way to assess how the economy is doing, everybody notices the price of gas."[1] In July 2008, the national record for a price of gasoline was set at $4.11 per gallon. The impact of high and volatile fuel prices is felt across the nation, affecting consumer spending and the economy, but the burden remains greater among distinct social economic groups and geographic areas.

Lower-income Americans spend eight times more of their disposable income on gasoline than wealthier Americans do.[2] For example, in Wilcox, Alabama, individuals spend 12.72% of their income to fuel one vehicle, while in Hunterdon Co., New Jersey, people spend 1.52%. Nationally, Americans spend 3.8% of their income fueling one vehicle. The first state to reach the $5 per gallon milestone was California in 2012. California's drivers were especially hit hard by the rising price of gas, due in part to their reliance on automobiles, especially for work commuters. Declines in consumer spending and confidence in the economy have been attributed in part to the high (and rising) cost of gasoline.

In 2013, gasoline prices remained higher for states along the West Coast, particularly in Alaska, California, and Hawaii. Let's say we drew a random sample of California gas stations ($N = 100$) and calculated the mean price for a gallon of regular gas. Based on consumer information,[3] we also know that nationally the mean price of a gallon was $3.53 with a standard deviation of 0.21 for the same week. We can thus compare the mean price of gas in California with the mean price of all gas stations in May 2013. By comparing these means, we are asking whether it is reasonable to consider our random sample of California gas as representative of the population of gas stations in the United States. Actually, we expect to find that the average price of gas from a sample of California gas stations will be unrepresentative of the population of gas stations because we assume higher gas prices in the state.

The mean price for our sample is $3.90. This figure is higher than $3.53, the mean price per gallon across the nation. But is the observed gap of 37 cents ($3.90–$3.53) large enough to convince us that the sample of California gas stations is not representative of the population?

The sample mean of $3.90 is higher than the population mean, but it is an estimate based on a single sample. Thus, it could mean one of two things: (1) the average price of gas in California is indeed higher than the national average or (2) the average price of gas in California is about the same as the national average, and this sample happens to show a particularly high mean.

How can we decide which of these explanations makes more sense? Because most estimates are based on single samples and different samples may result in different estimates, sampling results cannot be used directly to make statements about a population. We need a procedure that allows us to evaluate hypotheses about population parameters based on sample statistics. In Chapter 8, we saw that population parameters can be estimated from sample statistics. In this chapter, we will learn how to use sample statistics to make decisions about population parameters. This procedure is called **statistical hypothesis testing**.

Statistical hypothesis testing   A procedure that allows us to evaluate hypotheses about population parameters based on sample statistics.

▣ ASSUMPTIONS OF STATISTICAL HYPOTHESIS TESTING

Statistical hypothesis testing requires several assumptions. These assumptions include considerations of the level of measurement of the variable, the method of sampling, the shape of the population distribution, and the sample size. The specific assumptions may vary, depending on the test or the conditions of testing. However, without exception, *all* statistical tests assume random sampling. Tests of hypotheses about means also assume interval-ratio level of measurement and require that the population under consideration be normally distributed or that the sample size be larger than 50.

Based on our data, we can test the hypothesis that the average price of gas in California is higher than the average national price of gas. The test we are considering meets these conditions:

1. The sample of California gas stations was randomly selected.

2. The variable *price per gallon* is measured at the interval-ratio level.

3. We cannot assume that the population is normally distributed. However, because our sample size is sufficiently large ($N > 50$), we know, based on the central limit theorem, that the sampling distribution of the mean will be approximately normal.

▣ STATING THE RESEARCH AND NULL HYPOTHESES

Hypotheses are usually defined in terms of interrelations between variables and are often based on a substantive theory. Earlier, we defined *hypotheses* as tentative answers to research questions. They are tentative because we can find evidence for them only after being empirically tested. The testing of hypotheses is an important step in this evidence-gathering process.

The Research Hypothesis (H_1)

Our first step is to formally express the hypothesis in a way that makes it amenable to a statistical test. The substantive hypothesis is called the **research hypothesis** and is symbolized as H_1. Research hypotheses are always expressed in terms of population parameters because we are interested in making statements about population parameters based on our sample statistics.

Research hypothesis (H_1)   A statement reflecting the substantive hypothesis. It is always expressed in terms of population parameters, but its specific form varies from test to test.

In our research hypothesis (H_1), we state that the average price of gas in California is higher than the average price of gas nationally. Symbolically, we use μ_Y to represent the population mean; our hypothesis can be expressed as

$$H_1: \mu_Y > \$3.53$$

In general, the research hypothesis (H_1) specifies that the population parameter is one of the following:

1. Not equal to some specified value: $\mu_Y \neq$ some specified value
2. Greater than some specified value: $\mu_Y >$ some specified value
3. Less than some specified value: $\mu_Y <$ some specified value

The Null Hypothesis (H_0)

Is it possible that in the population there is no real difference between the mean price of gas in California and the mean price of gas in the nation and that the observed difference of 0.37 is actually due to the fact that this particular sample happened to contain California gas stations with higher prices? Since statistical inference is based on probability theory, it is not possible to prove or disprove the research hypothesis directly. We can, at best, estimate the *likelihood* that it is true or false.

To assess this likelihood, statisticians set up a hypothesis that is counter to the research hypothesis. The **null hypothesis**, symbolized as H_0, contradicts the research hypothesis and usually states that there is no difference between the population mean and some specified value. It is also referred to as the hypothesis of "no difference." Our null hypothesis can be stated symbolically as

$$H_0: \mu_Y = \$3.53$$

Rather than directly testing the substantive hypothesis (H_1) that there is a difference between the mean price of gas in California and the mean price nationally, we test the null hypothesis (H_0) that there is no difference in prices. In hypothesis testing, we hope to reject the null hypothesis to provide support for the research hypothesis. Rejection of the null hypothesis will strengthen our belief in the research hypothesis and increase our confidence in the importance and utility of the broader theory from which the research hypothesis was derived.

Null hypothesis (H_0) A statement of "no difference" that contradicts the research hypothesis and is always expressed in terms of population parameters.

More About Research Hypotheses: One- and Two-Tailed Tests

In a **one-tailed test**, the research hypothesis is directional; that is, it specifies that a population mean is either less than (<) or greater than (>) some specified value. We can express our research hypothesis as either

$$H_1: \mu_Y < \text{some specified value}$$

or

$$H_1: \mu_Y > \text{some specified value}$$

The research hypothesis we've stated for the average price of a gallon of regular gas in California is a one-tailed test.

When a one-tailed test specifies that the population mean is *greater than* some specified value, we call it a **right-tailed test** because we will evaluate the outcome at the right tail of the sampling distribution. If the research hypothesis specifies that the population mean is *less than* some specified value, it is called a **left-tailed test** because the outcome will be evaluated at the left tail of the sampling distribution. Our example is a right-tailed test because the research hypothesis states that the mean gas prices in California are higher than $3.53. (Refer to Figure 9.1 on page 272.)

Sometimes, we have some theoretical basis to believe that there is a difference between groups, but we cannot anticipate the direction of that difference. For example, we may have reason to believe that the average price of California gas is *different* from that of the general population, but we may not have enough research or support to predict whether it is *higher* or *lower*. When we have no theoretical reason for specifying a direction in the research hypothesis, we conduct a **two-tailed test**. The research hypothesis specifies that the population mean is not equal to some specified value. For example, we can express the research hypothesis about the mean price of gas as

$$H_1: \mu_Y \neq \$3.53$$

With both one- and two-tailed tests, our null hypothesis of no difference remains the same. It can be expressed as

$$H_0: \mu_Y = \text{some specified value}$$

One-tailed test　A type of hypothesis test that involves a directional research hypothesis. It specifies that the values of one group are either larger or smaller than some specified population value.

Right-tailed test　A one-tailed test in which the sample outcome is hypothesized to be at the right tail of the sampling distribution.

Left-tailed test　A one-tailed test in which the sample outcome is hypothesized to be at the left tail of the sampling distribution.

Two-tailed test　A type of hypothesis test that involves a nondirectional research hypothesis. We are equally interested in whether the values are less than or greater than one another. The sample outcome may be located at both the lower and the higher ends of the sampling distribution.

▣ DETERMINING WHAT IS SUFFICIENTLY IMPROBABLE: PROBABILITY VALUES AND ALPHA

Now let's put all our information together. We're assuming that our null hypothesis ($\mu_Y = \$3.53$) is true, and we want to determine whether our sample evidence casts doubt on that assumption, suggesting that there is evidence for research hypothesis, $\mu_Y > \$3.53$. What are the chances that we would have randomly selected a sample of California gas stations such that the average price per gallon is higher than $3.53, the average for the nation? We can determine the chances or probability because of what we know about the sampling distribution and its properties. We know, based on the central limit theorem, that if our sample size is larger than 50, the sampling distribution of the mean is approximately normal, with a mean and a standard deviation (standard error) of

$$\sigma_{\bar{Y}} = \frac{\sigma_Y}{\sqrt{N}}$$

We are going to assume that the null hypothesis is true and then see if our sample evidence casts doubt on that assumption. We have a population mean $\mu_Y = \$3.53$ and a standard deviation $\sigma_Y = 0.21$. Our sample size is $N = 100$, and the sample mean is $\$3.90$. We can assume that the distribution of means of all possible samples of size $N = 100$ drawn from this distribution would be approximately normal, with a mean of $\$3.53$ and a standard deviation of

$$\sigma_{\bar{Y}} = \frac{.21}{\sqrt{100}} = .02$$

This sampling distribution is shown in Figure 9.1. Also shown in Figure 9.1 is the mean gas price we observed for our sample of California gas stations.

Because this distribution of sample means is normal, we can use Appendix B to determine the probability of drawing a sample mean of $\$3.90$ or higher from this population. We will

Figure 9.1   Sampling Distribution of Sample Means Assuming H_0 Is True for a Sample $N = 100$

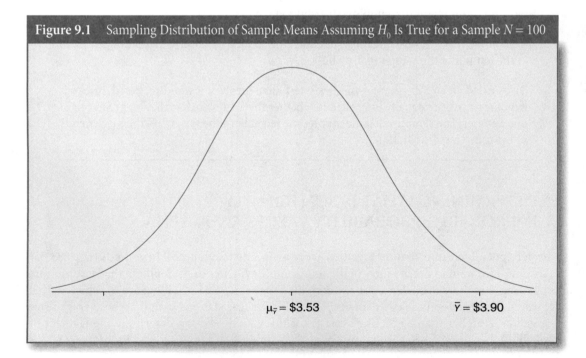

$$\mu_{\bar{Y}} = \$3.53 \qquad \bar{Y} = \$3.90$$

translate our sample mean into a Z score so that we can determine its location relative to the population mean. In Chapter 6, we learned how to translate a raw score into a Z score by using Formula 6.1:

$$Z = \frac{Y - \bar{Y}}{S_Y}$$

Because we are dealing with a sampling distribution in which our raw score is $\bar{Y}$, the mean, and the standard deviation (standard error) is $\sigma_Y / \sqrt{N}$, we need to modify the formula somewhat:

$$Z = \frac{\bar{Y} - \mu_{\bar{Y}}}{\sigma_Y / \sqrt{N}} \tag{9.1}$$

Converting the sample mean to a Z-score equivalent is called computing the *test statistic*. The Z value we obtain is called the **Z statistic (obtained)**. The obtained Z gives us the number of standard deviations (standard errors) that our sample is from the hypothesized value (μ_Y or $\mu_{\bar{Y}}$), assuming the null hypothesis is true. For our example, the obtained Z is

$$Z = \frac{3.90 - 3.53}{.21 / \sqrt{100}} = 18.50$$

Z statistic (obtained)   The test statistic computed by converting a sample statistic (such as the mean) to a Z score. The formula for obtaining Z varies from test to test.

Before we determine the probability of our obtained Z statistic, let's determine whether it is consistent with our research hypothesis. Recall that we defined our research hypothesis as a right-tailed test ($\mu_Y > \$3.53$), predicting that the difference would be assessed on the right tail of the sampling distribution. The positive value of our obtained Z statistic confirms that we will be evaluating the difference on the right tail. (If we had a negative obtained Z, it would mean the difference would have to be evaluated at the left tail of the distribution, contrary to our research hypothesis.)

To determine the probability of observing a Z value of 18.50, assuming that the null hypothesis is true, look up the value in Appendix B to find the area to the right of (above) the Z of 18.50. Our calculated Z value is not listed in Appendix B, so we'll need to rely on the last Z value reported in the table, 4.00. Recall from Chapter 6, where we calculated Z scores and their probability, that the Z values are located in Column A. The P value is the probability to the right of the obtained Z, or the "area beyond Z" in Column C. This area includes the proportion of all sample means that are \$3.90 or higher. The proportion is less than 0.0001 (Figure 9.2). This value is the probability of getting a result as extreme as the sample result if the null hypothesis is true; it is symbolized as P. Thus, for our example, $P \leq .0001$.

Figure 9.2   The Probability (*P*) Associated With *Z* ≥ 18.50

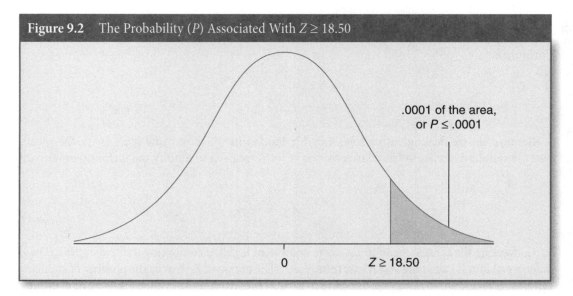

.0001 of the area,
or *P* ≤ .0001

0   *Z* ≥ 18.50

A *P value* can be defined as the actual probability associated with the obtained value of *Z*. It is a measure of how unusual or rare our obtained statistic is compared with what is stated in our null hypothesis. The smaller the *P* value, the more evidence we have that the null hypothesis should be rejected in favor of the research hypothesis.

P *value*   The probability associated with the obtained value of *Z*.

Researchers usually define in advance what a sufficiently improbable *Z* value is by specifying a cutoff point below which *P* must fall to reject the null hypothesis. This cutoff point, called **alpha** and denoted by the Greek letter α, is customarily set at the .05, .01, or .001 level. Let's say that we decide to reject the null hypothesis if $P \leq .05$. The value .05 is referred to as alpha (α); it defines for us what result is sufficiently improbable to allow us to take the risk and reject the null hypothesis. An alpha (α) of .05 means that even if the obtained *Z* statistic is due to sampling error, so that the null hypothesis is true, we would allow a 5% risk of rejecting it. Alpha values of .01 and .001 are more cautionary levels of risk. The difference between *P* and alpha is that *P* is the *actual probability* associated with the obtained value of *Z*, whereas alpha is the level of probability *determined in advance* at which the null hypothesis is rejected. The null hypothesis is rejected when $P \leq \alpha$.

Alpha (α)   The level of probability at which the null hypothesis is rejected. It is customary to set alpha at the .05, .01, or .001 level.

We have already determined that our obtained *Z* has a probability value less than .0001. Since our observed *P* is less than .05 ($P = .0001 < \alpha = .05$), we reject the null hypothesis. The value of .0001 means that fewer than 1 out of 10,000 samples drawn from this population are likely to have a mean that is 18.50 Z scores above the hypothesized mean of $3.53. Another way to say it is as follows: There is only 1 chance out of 10,000 (or .0001%) that we would draw a random sample with a $Z \geq 18.50$ if the mean price of California gas were equal to the national mean price.

Based on the P value, we can also make a statement regarding the "significance" of the results. If the P value is equal to or less than our alpha level, our obtained Z statistic is considered *statistically significant*—that is to say, it is very unlikely to have occurred by random chance or sampling error. We can state that the difference between the average price of gas in California and nationally is significantly different at the .05 level, or we can specify the actual level of significance by saying that the level of significance is less than .0001.

Recall that our hypothesis was a one-tailed test ($\mu_Y > \$3.53$). In a two-tailed test, sample outcomes may be located at both the higher and the lower ends of the sampling distribution. Thus, the null hypothesis will be rejected if our sample outcome falls either at the left or right tail of the sampling distribution. For instance, a .05 alpha or P level means that H_0 will be rejected if our sample outcome falls among either the lowest or the highest 5% of the sampling distribution.

Suppose we had expressed our research hypothesis about the mean price of gas as

$$H_1: \mu_Y \neq \$3.53$$

The null hypothesis to be directly tested still takes the form $H_0: \mu_Y = \$3.53$ and our obtained Z is calculated using the same formula (9.1) as was used with a one-tailed test. To find P for a two-tailed test, look up the area in Column C of Appendix B that corresponds to your obtained Z (as we did earlier) and then multiply it by 2 to obtain the two-tailed probability. Thus, the two-tailed P value for $Z = 18.50$ is $.0001 \times 2 = .0002$. This probability is less than our stated alpha (.05), and thus, we reject the null hypothesis.

▣ THE FIVE STEPS IN HYPOTHESIS TESTING: A SUMMARY

Regardless of the particular application or problem, statistical hypothesis testing can be organized into five basic steps. Let's summarize these steps:

1. Making assumptions

2. Stating the research and null hypotheses and selecting alpha

3. Selecting the sampling distribution and specifying the test statistic

4. Computing the test statistic

5. Making a decision and interpreting the results

Making Assumptions. Statistical hypothesis testing involves making several assumptions regarding the level of measurement of the variable, the method of sampling, the shape of the population distribution, and the sample size. In our example, we made the following assumptions:

1. A random sample was used.

2. The variable *price per gallon* is measured on an interval-ratio level of measurement.

3. Because $N > 50$, the assumption of normal population is not required.

Stating the Research and Null Hypotheses and Selecting Alpha. The substantive hypothesis is called the *research hypothesis* and is symbolized as H_1. Research hypotheses are always expressed in terms of population parameters because we are interested in making statements about population parameters based on sample statistics. Our research hypothesis was

$$H_1: \mu_Y > \$3.53$$

The *null hypothesis*, symbolized as H_0, contradicts the research hypothesis in a statement of no difference between the population mean and our hypothesized value. For our example, the null hypothesis was stated symbolically as

$$H_0: \mu_Y = \$3.53$$

We set alpha at .05, meaning that we would reject the null hypothesis if the probability of our obtained Z was less than or equal to .05.

Selecting the Sampling Distribution and Specifying the Test Statistic. The normal distribution and the Z statistic are used to test the null hypothesis.

Computing the Test Statistic. Based on Formula 9.1, our Z statistic is 18.50.

Making a Decision and Interpreting the Results. We confirm that our obtained Z is on the right tail of the distribution, consistent with our research hypothesis. We determine that the P value of 18.50 is less than .0001, less than our .05 alpha level. We have evidence to reject the null hypothesis of no difference between the mean price of California gas and the mean price of gas nationally. We thus conclude that the average price of California gas is significantly higher than the national average.

▣ ERRORS IN HYPOTHESIS TESTING

We should emphasize that because our conclusion is based on sample data, we will never really know if the null hypothesis is true or false. In fact, as we have seen, there is a 0.01% chance that the null hypothesis is true and that we are making an error by rejecting it.

The null hypothesis can be either true or false, and in either case, it can be rejected or not rejected. If the null hypothesis is true and we reject it nonetheless, we are making an incorrect decision. This type of error is called a Type I error. Conversely, if the null hypothesis is false but we fail to reject it, this incorrect decision is a Type II error.

Type I error The probability associated with rejecting a null hypothesis when it is true.

Type II error The probability associated with failing to reject a null hypothesis when it is false.

In Table 9.1, we show the relationship between the two types of errors and the decisions we make regarding the null hypothesis. The probability of a Type I error—rejecting a true hypothesis—is equal to the chosen alpha level. For example, when we set alpha at the .05 level, we know that the probability that the null hypothesis is in fact true is .05 (or 5%).

Table 9.1 Type I and Type II Errors

Decision made	True State of Affairs	
	H_0 *is true*	H_0 *is false*
Reject H_0	Type I error (α)	Correct decision
Do not reject H_0	Correct decision	Type II error

We can control the risk of rejecting a true hypothesis by manipulating alpha. For example, by setting alpha at .01, we are reducing the risk of making a Type I error to 1%. Unfortunately, however, Type I and Type II errors are inversely related; thus, by reducing alpha and lowering the risk of making a Type I error, we are increasing the risk of making a Type II error (Table 9.1).

As long as we base our decisions on sample statistics and not population parameters, we have to accept a degree of uncertainty as part of the process of statistical inference.

✓ *Learning Check*

The implications of research findings are not created equal. For example, researchers might hypothesize that eating spinach increases the strength of weight lifters. Little harm will be done if the null hypothesis that eating spinach has no effect on the strength of weight lifters is rejected in error. The researchers would most likely be willing to risk a high probability of a Type I error, and all weight lifters would eat spinach. However, when the implications of research have important consequences (funding of social programs or medical testing), the balancing act between Type I and Type II errors becomes more important. Can you think of some examples where researchers would want to minimize Type I errors? When might they want to minimize Type II errors?

The *t* Statistic and Estimating the Standard Error

The Z statistic we have calculated (Formula 9.1) to test the hypothesis involving a sample of California gas stations assumes that the population standard deviation σ_Y is known. The value of σ_Y is required to calculate the standard error

$$\sigma_Y \big/ \sqrt{N}$$

In most situations, σ_Y will not be known, and we will need to estimate it using the sample standard deviation S_Y. We then use the t statistic instead of the Z statistic to test the null hypothesis. The formula for computing the t statistic is

$$t = \frac{\overline{Y} - \mu_Y}{S_Y \big/ \sqrt{N}} \tag{9.2}$$

The t value we calculate is called the *t* **statistic (obtained)**. The obtained t represents the number of standard deviation units (or standard error units) that our sample mean is from the hypothesized value of μ_Y, assuming that the null hypothesis is true.

---

t *statistic (obtained)*   The test statistic computed to test the null hypothesis about a population mean when the population standard deviation is unknown and is estimated using the sample standard deviation.

The *t* Distribution and Degrees of Freedom

To understand the t statistic, we should first be familiar with its distribution. The *t* **distribution** is actually a family of curves, each determined by its *degrees of freedom*. The concept of degrees of freedom is used in calculating several statistics, including the t statistic. The **degrees of freedom** (*df*) represent the number of scores that are free to vary in calculating each statistic.

---

t *distribution*   A family of curves, each determined by its degrees of freedom *(df)*. It is used when the population standard deviation is unknown and the standard error is estimated from the sample standard deviation.

Degrees of freedom (df)   The number of scores that are free to vary in calculating a statistic.

To calculate the degrees of freedom, we must know the sample size and whether there are any restrictions in calculating that statistic. The number of restrictions is then subtracted from the sample size to determine the degrees of freedom. When calculating the t statistic for a one-sample test, we start with the sample size N and lose 1 degree of freedom for the population standard deviation we estimate.[4] Note that the degrees of freedom will increase as the sample size increases. In the case of a single-sample mean, the *df* is calculated as follows:

$$df = N - 1 \tag{9.3}$$

Comparing the *t* and *Z* Statistics

Notice the similarities between the formulas for the *t* and *Z* statistics. The only apparent difference is in the denominator. The denominator of *Z* is the standard error based on the population standard deviation σ_Y. For the denominator of *t*, we replace $\sigma_Y / \sqrt{N}$ with $S_Y / \sqrt{N}$, the estimated standard error based on the sample standard deviation.

However, there is another important difference between the *Z* and *t* statistics: Because it is estimated from sample data, the denominator of the *t* statistic is subject to sampling error. The sampling distribution of the test statistic is not normal, and the standard normal distribution cannot be used to determine probabilities associated with it.

In Figure 9.3, we present the *t* distribution for several *df*s. Like the standard normal distribution, the *t* distribution is bell shaped. The *t* statistic, similar to the *Z* statistic, can have positive and negative values. A positive *t* statistic corresponds to the right tail of the distribution; a negative value corresponds to the left tail. Note that when the *df* is small, the *t* distribution is much flatter than the normal curve. But as the degrees of freedom increases, the shape of the *t* distribution gets closer to the normal distribution, until the two are almost identical when *df* is greater than 120.

Appendix C summarizes the *t* distribution. Note that the *t* table differs from the normal (*Z*) table in several ways First, the column on the left side of the table shows the degrees of freedom. The *t*

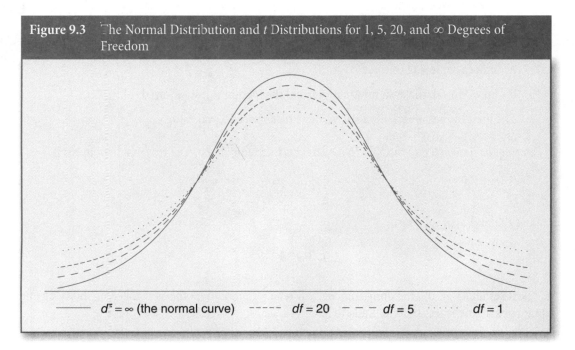

Figure 9.3   The Normal Distribution and *t* Distributions for 1, 5, 20, and ∞ Degrees of Freedom

——— $df = \infty$ (the normal curve)   - - - - - $df = 20$ - - - $df = 5$ · · · · · · $df = 1$

statistic will vary depending on the degrees of freedom, which must first be computed ($df = N - 1$). Second, the probabilities or alpha, denoted as significance levels, are arrayed across the top of the table in two rows, the first for a one-tailed and the second for a two-tailed test. Finally, the values of t, listed as the entries of this table, are a function of (1) the degrees of freedom, (2) the level of significance (or probability), and (3) whether the test is a one- or a two-tailed test.

To illustrate the use of this table, let's determine the probability of observing a t value of 2.021 with 40 degrees of freedom and a two-tailed test. Locating the proper row ($df = 40$) and column (two-tailed test), we find the t statistic of 2.021 corresponding to the .05 level of significance. Restated, we can say that the probability of obtaining a t statistic of 2.021 is .05, or that there are less than 5 chances out of 100 that we would have drawn a random sample with an obtained t of 2.021 if the null hypothesis were correct.

▣ STATISTICS IN PRACTICE: THE EARNINGS OF WHITE WOMEN

To illustrate the application of the t statistic, let's test a two-tailed hypothesis about a population mean μ_Y. Let's say we drew a random sample of 320 white females who worked full time in 2009. We found their mean earnings to be \$36,471, with a standard deviation $S_Y = \$28,563$. Based on data from the U.S. Census Bureau,[5] we also know that the 2009 mean earnings nationally for all women was $\mu_Y = \$33,797$. However, we do not know the value of the population standard deviation. We want to determine whether the sample of white women was representative of the population of all full-time women workers in 2009. Although we suspect that white American women experienced a relative advantage in earnings, we are not sure enough to predict that their earnings were indeed higher than the earnings of all women nationally. Therefore, the statistical test is two tailed.

Let's apply the five-step model to test the hypothesis that the average earnings of white women differed from the average earnings of all women working full time in the United States in 2009.

Making Assumptions. Our assumptions are as follows:

1. A random sample is selected.

2. Because $N > 50$, the assumption of normal population is not required.

3. The level of measurement of the variable *income* is interval ratio.

Stating the Research and the Null Hypotheses and Selecting Alpha. The research hypothesis is

$$H_1: \mu_Y \neq \$33,797$$

and the null hypothesis is

$$H_0: \mu_Y = \$33,797$$

We'll set alpha at .05, meaning that we will reject the null hypothesis if the probability of our obtained statistic is less than or equal to .05.

Selecting the Sampling Distribution and Specifying the Test Statistic. We use the t distribution and the t statistic to test the null hypothesis.

Computing the Test Statistic. We first calculate the df associated with our test:

$$df = (N-1) = (320 - 1) = 319$$

To evaluate the probability of obtaining a sample mean of $36,471, assuming the average earnings of white women were equal to the national average of $33,797, we need to calculate the obtained t statistic by using Formula 9.2:

$$t = \frac{\overline{Y} - \mu_Y}{S_Y / \sqrt{N}} = \frac{36,471 - 33,797}{28,563 / \sqrt{320}} = 1.67$$

Making a Decision and Interpreting the Results. Given our research hypothesis, we will conduct a two-tailed test. To determine the probability of observing a t value of 1.67 with 319 degrees of freedom, let's refer to Appendix C. From the first column, we can see that 319 degrees of freedom is not listed, so we'll have to use the last row, $df = \infty$, to assess the significance of our obtained t statistic.

Though our obtained t statistic of 1.67 is not listed in the last row, we can see that it lies somewhere between 1.645 (for .05 one-tailed test) and 1.960 (for .025 one-tailed test). The probability of 1.67 can be estimated as $.05 > p < .025$, allowing us to determine that we can reject the null hypothesis. We can also note how the t-obtained statistic of 1.67 is greater than the t critical of 1.645 and make the same decision. We have sufficient evidence to reject the null hypothesis and conclude that the 2009 average earnings of white women were significantly higher than the average earnings of all women. The difference of $2,674 is significant at the .05 level.

▣ TESTING HYPOTHESES ABOUT TWO SAMPLES

The two examples that we reviewed at the beginning of this chapter dealt with data from one sample compared with data from the population. In practice, social scientists are often more interested in situations involving two (sample) parameters than those involving one, such as the differences between men and women, Democrats and Republicans, whites and nonwhites, or high school or college graduates. Specifically, we may be interested in finding out whether the average years of education for one racial/ethnic group is the same, lower, or higher than another group.

U.S. data on educational attainment reveal that Asian and Pacific Islanders have more years of education than any other racial/ethnic groups; this includes the percentage of those earning a high school degree or higher or a college degree or higher. Though years of education have steadily increased for blacks and Hispanics since 1990, their numbers remain behind Asian and Pacific Islanders and whites.

Using data from the 2010 General Social Survey (GSS) we examine the difference in white and black educational attainment. From the GSS sample, white respondents reported an average of 13.66 years of education and blacks, an average of 12.89 years as shown in Table 9.2. These sample averages could mean either (1) the average number of years of education for whites is higher than the average for blacks or (2) the average for whites is actually about the same as for blacks, but our sample just happens to indicate a higher average for whites. What we are applying here is a bivariate analysis (for more information, refer to Chapter 10), a method to detect and describe the relationship between two variables—race/ethnicity and educational attainment.

Table 9.2   Years of Education for White and Black Men and Women, GSS 2010

	Whites (Sample 1)	Blacks (Sample 2)
Mean	13.66	12.89
Standard deviation	3.16	3.03
Variance	9.99	9.18
N	584	118

The statistical procedures discussed in the following sections allow us to test whether the differences that we observe between two samples are large enough for us to conclude that the populations from which these samples are drawn are different as well. We present tests for the significance of the differences between two groups. Primarily, we consider differences between sample means and differences between sample proportions.

Hypothesis testing with two samples follows the same structure as for one-sample tests: The assumptions of the test are stated, the research and null hypotheses are formulated and the alpha level selected, the sampling distribution and the test statistic are specified, the test statistic is computed, and a decision is made whether or not to reject the null hypothesis.

The Assumption of Independent Samples

One important difference between one- and two-sample hypothesis testing involves sampling procedures. With a two-sample case, we assume that the samples are independent of each other. The choice of sample members from one population has no effect on the choice of sample members from the second population. In our comparison of whites and blacks, we are assuming that the selection of whites is independent of the selection of black individuals. (The requirement of independence is also satisfied by selecting one sample randomly, then dividing the sample into appropriate subgroups. For example, we could randomly select a sample and then divide it into groups based on gender, religion, income, or any other attribute that we are interested in.)

Stating the Research and Null Hypotheses

The second difference between one- and two-sample tests is in the form taken by the research and the null hypotheses. In one-sample tests, both the null and the research hypotheses are statements about a single population parameter, μ_Y. In contrast, with two-sample tests, we compare two population parameters.

Our research hypothesis (H_1) is that the average years of education for whites is not equal to the average years of education for black respondents. We are stating a hypothesis about the relationship between race/ethnicity and education in the general population by comparing the mean educational attainment of whites with the mean educational attainment of blacks. Symbolically, we use μ to represent the population mean; the subscript 1 refers to our first sample (whites) and subscript 2 to our second sample (blacks). Our research hypothesis can then be expressed as

$$H_1: \mu_1 \neq \mu_2$$

Because H_1 specifies that the mean education for whites is not equal to the mean education for blacks, it is a nondirectional hypothesis. Thus, our test will be a two-tailed test. Alternatively, if there were sufficient basis for deciding which population mean score is larger (or smaller), the research hypothesis for our test would be a one-tailed test:

$$H_1: \mu_1 < \mu_2 \text{ or } H_1: \mu_1 > \mu_2$$

In either case, the null hypothesis states that there are no differences between the two population means:

$$H_0: \mu_1 = \mu_2$$

We are interested in finding evidence to reject the null hypothesis of no difference so that we have sufficient support for our research hypothesis.

✓ *Learning*
Check

For the following research situations, state your research and null hypotheses:

- *There is a difference between the mean statistics grades of social science majors and the mean statistics grades of business majors.*
- *The average number of children in two-parent black families is lower than the average number of children in two-parent nonblack families.*
- *Grade point averages are higher among girls who participate in organized sports than among girls who do not.*

▣ THE SAMPLING DISTRIBUTION OF THE DIFFERENCE BETWEEN MEANS

The sampling distribution allows us to compare our sample results with all possible sample outcomes and estimate the likelihood of their occurrence. Tests about differences between two sample means are based on the **sampling distribution of the difference between means**. The sampling distribution of the difference between two sample means is a theoretical probability distribution that would be obtained by calculating all the possible mean differences by drawing all possible independent random samples of size N_1 and N_2 from two populations.

Sampling distribution of the difference between means A theoretical probability distribution that would be obtained by calculating all the possible mean differences that would be obtained by drawing all the possible independent random samples of size N_1 and N_2 from two populations where N_1 and N_2 are both greater than 50.

The properties of the sampling distribution of the difference between two sample means are determined by a corollary to the central limit theorem. This theorem assumes that our samples are independently drawn from normal populations, but that with sufficient sample size ($N_1 > 50$, $N_2 > 50$) the sampling distribution of the difference between means will be approximately normal, even if the original populations are not normal. This sampling distribution has a mean $\mu_{\bar{Y}_1} - \mu_{\bar{Y}_2}$ -and a standard deviation (standard error)

$$\sigma_{\bar{Y}_1 - \bar{Y}_2} = \sqrt{\frac{\sigma_{Y_1}^2}{N_1} + \frac{\sigma_{Y_2}^2}{N_2}} \tag{9.4}$$

which is based on the variances in each of the two populations ($\sigma_{Y_1}^2$ and $\sigma_{Y_2}^2$).

Estimating the Standard Error

Formula 9.4 assumes that the population variances are known and that we can calculate the standard error $\sigma_{\bar{Y}_1 - \bar{Y}_2}$ (the standard deviation of the sampling distribution). However, in most situations, the only data we have are based on sample data, and we do not know the true value of the population variances, $\sigma_{Y_1}^2$ and $\sigma_{Y_2}^2$. Thus, we need to estimate the standard error from the sample variances, $S_{Y_1}^2$ and $S_{Y_2}^2$. The estimated standard error of the difference between means is symbolized as $S_{\bar{Y}_1 - \bar{Y}_2}$ (instead of $\sigma_{\bar{Y}_1 - \bar{Y}_2}$).

Calculating the Estimated Standard Error

When we can assume that the two population variances are equal, we combine information from the two sample variances to calculate the estimated standard error.

$$S_{\bar{Y}_1 - \bar{Y}_2} = \sqrt{\frac{(N_1 - 1)S_{Y_1}^2 + (N_2 - 1)S_{Y_2}^2}{(N_1 + N_2) - 2}} \sqrt{\frac{N_1 + N_2}{N_1 N_2}} \tag{9.5}$$

where $S_{\bar{Y}_1 - \bar{Y}_2}$ is the estimated standard error of the difference between means, and $S_{Y_1}^2$ and $S_{Y_2}^2$ are the variances of the two samples. As a rule of thumb, when either sample variance is more than *twice* as large as the other, we can no longer assume that the two population variances are equal and would need to use Formula 9.8 in A Closer Look 9.1.

The *t* Statistic

As with single sample means, we use the *t* distribution and the *t* statistic whenever we estimate the standard error for a difference between means test. The *t* value we calculate is the obtained *t*. It represents the number of standard deviation units (or standard error units) that our mean difference $\left(\overline{Y}_1 - \overline{Y}_2 \right)$ is from the hypothesized value of $\mu_1 - \mu_2$, assuming that the null hypothesis is true.

The formula for computing the *t* statistic for a difference between means test is

$$t = \frac{\overline{Y}_1 - \overline{Y}_2}{S_{\overline{Y}_1 - \overline{Y}_2}} \tag{9.6}$$

where $S_{\overline{Y}_1 - \overline{Y}_2}$ is the estimated standard error.

Calculating the Degrees of Freedom for a Difference Between Means Test

To use the *t* distribution for testing the difference between two sample means, we need to calculate the degrees of freedom. As we saw earlier, the degrees of freedom (*df*) represent the number of scores that are free to vary in calculating each statistic. When calculating the *t* statistic for the two-sample test, we lose 2 degrees of freedom, one for every population variance we estimate. When population variances are assumed to be equal or if the size of both samples is greater than 50, the *df* is calculated as follows:

$$df = (N_1 + N_2) - 2 \tag{9.7}$$

When we cannot assume that the population variances are equal and when the size of one or both samples is equal to or less than 50, we use Formula 9.9 in A Closer Look 9.1 to calculate the degrees of freedom.

▣ A Closer Look 9.1
Calculating the Estimated Standard Error and the Degrees of Freedom (*df*) When the Population Variances Are Assumed to Be Unequal

If the variances of the two samples ($S_{Y_1}^2$ and $S_{Y_2}^2$) are very different (one variance is twice as large as the other), the formula for the estimated standard error becomes

$$S_{\overline{Y}_1 - \overline{Y}_2} = \sqrt{\frac{S_{Y_1}^2}{N_1} + \frac{S_{Y_2}^2}{N_2}} \tag{9.8}$$

(Continued)

(Continued)

When the population variances are unequal and the size of one or both samples is equal to or less than 50, we use another formula to calculate the degrees of freedom associated with the t statistic:[6]

$$df = \frac{(S_{Y_1}^2/N_1 + S_{Y_2}^2/N_2)^2}{(S_{Y_1}^2/N_1)^2/(N_1-1) + (S_{Y_2}^2/N_2)^2/(N_2-1)} \qquad (9.9)$$

▣ THE FIVE STEPS IN HYPOTHESIS TESTING ABOUT DIFFERENCE BETWEEN MEANS: A SUMMARY

As with single-sample tests, statistical hypothesis testing involving two sample means can be organized into five basic steps. Let's summarize these steps:

1. Making assumptions
2. Stating the research and null hypotheses and selecting alpha
3. Selecting the sampling distribution and specifying the test statistic
4. Computing the test statistic
5. Making a decision and interpreting the results

Making Assumptions. In our example, we made the following assumptions:

1. Independent random samples are used.
2. The variable *years of education* is measured at an interval-ratio level of measurement.
3. Because $N_1 > 50$ and $N_2 > 50$, the assumption of normal population is not required.
4. The population variances are assumed to be equal.

Stating the Research and Null Hypotheses and Selecting Alpha. Our research hypothesis is that the mean education of whites is different from the mean education of blacks, indicating a two-tailed test. Symbolically, the research hypothesis is expressed as

$$H_1: \mu_1 \neq \mu_2$$

with μ_1 representing the mean education of whites and μ_2 the mean education of blacks. The null hypothesis states that there are no differences between the two population means, or

$$H_0: \mu_1 = \mu_2$$

We are interested in finding evidence to reject the null hypothesis of no difference so that we have sufficient support for our research hypothesis. We will reject the null hypothesis if the probability of t (obtained) is less than or equal to .05 (our alpha value).

Selecting the Sampling Distribution and Specifying the Test Statistic. The t distribution and the t statistic are used to test the significance of the difference between the two sample means.

Computing the Test Statistic. To test the null hypothesis about the differences between the mean education of whites and blacks, we need to translate the ratio of the observed differences to its standard error into a t statistic (based on data presented in Table 9.2). The obtained t statistic is calculated using Formula 9.6:

$$t = \frac{\overline{Y}_1 - \overline{Y}_2}{S_{\overline{Y}_1 - \overline{Y}_2}}$$

where $S_{\overline{Y}_1 - \overline{Y}_2}$ is the estimated standard error of the sampling distribution. Because the population variances are assumed to be equal, df is $(N_1 + N_2) - 2 = (584 + 118) - 2 = 700$ and we can combine information from the two sample variances to estimate the standard error (Formula 9.5):

$$S_{\overline{Y}_1 - \overline{Y}_2} = \sqrt{\frac{(584-1)(3.16)^2 + (118-1)(3.03)^2}{(584+118)-2}} \sqrt{\frac{584+118}{584(118)}} = 3.14(.10) = .31$$

We substitute this value into the denominator for the t statistic (Formula 9.6):

$$t = \frac{13.66 - 12.89}{.31} = \frac{.77}{.31} = 2.48$$

Making a Decision and Interpreting the Results. We confirm that our obtained t is on the right tail of the distribution. Since our obtained t statistic of 2.48 is greater than $t = 2.326$ ($df = \infty$, two tailed; see Appendix C), we can state that its probability is less than .02. This is less than our .05 alpha level and we can reject the null hypothesis of no difference between the educational attainment of whites and blacks. We conclude that white men and women, on average, have significantly higher years of education than black men and women do.

▣ FOCUS ON INTERPRETATION: CIGARETTE USE AMONG TEENS

Administered annually since 1975, the Monitoring the Future (MTF) survey measures the extent of and beliefs regarding drug use among 8th, 10th, and 12th graders. In recent years, data collected from the MTF surveys revealed decreases or stability in drug use among youths, particularly for cigarettes, alcohol, marijuana, cocaine, and methamphetamine.[7]

Let's examine data from the MTF 2011 survey, comparing first-time cigarette use between black and white students.

The survey results indicate that black students are more likely to smoke cigarettes later (in later grades) than white students. The mean grade of first use of cigarettes is 6.38 for white students and 7.15 for black students.

We will rely on SPSS to calculate the t obtained for the data. We will not present the complete five-step model and t-test calculation because we want to focus on interpreting the SPSS output. However, we will need a research hypothesis and an alpha level to guide our interpretation. SPSS always estimates a two-tailed test, namely does the gap of 0.77 (7.15 − 6.38) indicate a difference in when black and white adolescents first smoke cigarettes? We'll set alpha at .05.

Table 9.3   Grade When First Smoked Cigarettes by Race, MTF 2011

	Black Students	White Students
Mean	7.15	6.38
Standard Deviation	1.99	2.29
N	156	748

The output includes two tables. The Group Statistics table (Figure 9.4) presents descriptive statistics for each group. In the second table (Figure 9.5), labeled Independent Samples Test, t statistics are presented for equal variances assumed (3.891) and equal variances not assumed (4.266). In order to determine which t statistic to use, review the results of the Levene's Test for Equality of Variances. The Levene's Test (a calculation that we will not cover in this text) tests the null hypothesis that the population variances are equal. If the significance of the reported F statistic is equal to or less than .05 (the baseline alpha for the Levene's Test), we can reject the null hypothesis that the variances are equal; if the significance is greater than .05, we fail to reject the null hypothesis. [To say it another way: if the significance for the Levene's Test is greater than .05, refer to the t obtained for equal variances assumed; if the significance is less than .05, refer to the t obtained for equal variances not assumed.] Since the significance of F is .000 < .05, we reject the null hypothesis and conclude that the variances are unequal. Thus, the t obtained that we will use for this model is 4.266 (the one corresponding to equal variances not assumed).

Figure 9.4   Group Statistics

Group Statistics

	race Respondent's race (trichotomized B/W/H)	N	Mean	Std. Deviation	Std. Error Mean
grsmoke What grade when first smoked cigarettes?	1 BLACK: (1)	156	7.15	1.990	.159
	2 WHITE: (2)	748	6.38	2.291	.084

Figure 9.5   Independent Samples Test

Independent Samples Test

		Levene's Test for Equality of Variances	
		F	Sig.
grsmoke What grade when first smoked cigarettes?	Equal variances assumed	34.238	.000
	Equal variances not assumed		

	t-test for Equality of Means						
			Sig. (2-tailed)	Mean Difference	Std. Error Difference	95% Confidence interval of the Difference	
	t	df				Lower	Upper
Equal variances assumed	3.891	902	.000	.768	.197	.380	1.155
Equal variances not assumed	4.266	248.610	.000	.768	.180	.413	1.122

SPSS calculates the probability of the *t* obtained for a two-tailed test. There is no need to estimate it based on Appendix C. The significance of 4.266 is .000, which is less than our alpha level of .05. We reject the null hypothesis of no difference for grade of first time cigarette use between white and black students. On average, black students first use cigarettes at a later grade (.77 grades later) than white students.

> *Would you change your decision in the previous example if alpha was .01? Why or why not?*

✓ *Learning Check*

▣ TESTING THE SIGNIFICANCE OF THE DIFFERENCE BETWEEN TWO SAMPLE PROPORTIONS

In the preceding sections, we have learned how to test for the significance of the difference between two population means when the variable is measured at an interval-ratio level. Yet numerous variables in the social sciences are measured at a nominal or an ordinal level. These variables are often described in terms of proportions or percentages. For example, we might be interested in comparing the proportion of those who support immigrant policy reform among Hispanics and non-Hispanics or the proportion of men and women who supported the Democratic candidate during the last presidential election. In this section, we present statistical inference techniques to test for significant differences between two sample proportions.

Hypothesis testing with two sample proportions follows the same structure as the statistical tests presented earlier: The assumptions of the test are stated, the research and null hypotheses are formulated, the sampling distribution and the test statistic are specified, the test statistic is calculated, and a decision is made whether or not to reject the null hypothesis.

▣ STATISTICS IN PRACTICE: COMPARING FIRST- AND SECOND-GENERATION HISPANIC AMERICANS

In 2013 the Pew Research Center[8] presented a comparison of first-generation Americans (immigrants who were foreign born) and second-generation Americans (adults who have at least one immigrant parent) on several key demographic variables. Based on several measures of success, the Center documented social mobility between the generations, confirming that second-generation Americans were doing better than the first-generation Americans. The statistical question we examine here is whether the difference between the generations is significant.

For example, according to the Center's report, the proportion of first-generation Hispanic Americans who earned a bachelor's degree or higher was 0.11 (p_1); the proportion of second-generation Hispanic Americans with the same response was 0.21 (p_2). A total of 899 first-generation Hispanic Americans (N_1) and 351 second-generation Hispanic Americans (N_2) answered this question. We use the five-step model to determine whether the difference between the two proportions is significant.

Making Assumptions. Our assumptions are as follows:

1. Independent random samples of $N_1 > 50$ and $N_2 > 50$ are used.

2. The level of measurement of the variable is nominal.

Stating the Research and Null Hypotheses and Selecting Alpha. We propose a two-tailed test that the population proportions for first-generation and second-generation Hispanic Americans are not equal.

$$H_1: \pi_1 \neq \pi_2$$
$$H_0: \pi_1 = \pi_2$$

We decide to set alpha at .05.

Selecting the Sampling Distribution and Specifying the Test Statistic. The population distributions of dichotomies are not normal. However, based on the central limit theorem, we know that the sampling distribution of the difference between sample proportions is normally distributed when the sample size is large (when $N_1 > 50$ and $N_2 > 50$), with mean μ_{p1-p2} and the estimated standard error S_{p1-p2}. Therefore, we can use the normal distribution as the sampling distribution, and we can calculate Z as the test statistic.[9]

The formula for computing the Z statistic for a difference between proportions test is

$$Z = \frac{p_1 - p_2}{S_{p_1 - p_2}} \tag{9.10}$$

where p_1 and p_2 are the sample proportions for first- and second-generation Hispanic Americans, and S_{p1-p2} is the estimated standard error of the sampling distribution of the difference between sample proportions.

The estimated standard error is calculated using the following formula:

$$S_{p_1 - p_2} = \sqrt{\frac{p_1(1 - p_1)}{N_1} + \frac{p_2(1 - p_2)}{N_2}} \tag{9.11}$$

Calculating the Test Statistic. We calculate the standard error using Formula 9.11:

$$S_{p_1 - p_2} = \sqrt{\frac{.11(1 - .11)}{899} + \frac{.21(1 - .21)}{351}} = .\sqrt{.000581547} = .02$$

Substituting this value into the denominator of Formula 9.10, we get

$$Z = \frac{.11 - .21}{.02} = -5.00$$

Making a Decision and Interpreting the Results. Our obtained Z of -5.00 indicates that the difference between the two proportions will be evaluated at the left tail (the negative side) of the Z distribution. To determine the probability of observing a Z value of -5.00 if the null hypothesis is true, look up the value in Appendix B (Column C) to find the area to the right of (above) the obtained Z.

Note that a Z score of 5.00 is not listed in Appendix B; however, the value exceeds the largest Z reported in the table, 4.00. The P value corresponding to a Z score of -5.00 would be less than

.0001. For a two-tailed test, we'll have to multiply *P* by 2 (.0001 × 2 = .0002). If this were a one-tailed test, we would not have to multiply the *P* value by 2. The probability of −5.00 for a two-tailed test is less than our alpha level of .05 (.0002 < .05).

Thus, we reject the null hypothesis of no difference and conclude that there is a significant difference in the proportion of college graduates among first- and second-generation Hispanic Americans. There is a significantly higher proportion of college graduates among second-generation Hispanic Americans compared with first-generation Hispanic Americans.

回 FOCUS ON INTERPRETATION: FIRST- AND SECOND-GENERATION ASIAN AMERICANS

We continue our analysis of the 2013 Pew Research Center data, this time examining the difference in educational attainment between first- and second-generation Asian Americans presented in Table 9.4. Our research hypothesis is whether there is a lower proportion of college graduates among first-generation Asian Americans than second-generation Asian Americans, indicating a one-tailed test. We'll set alpha at .05.

Table 9.4 Proportion of College Graduates Among First-Generation and Second-Generation Asian Americans

First-Generation Asian Americans	Second-Generation Asian Americans
$p_1 = 0.50$	$p_2 = 0.55$
$N_1 = 2,684$	$N_2 = 566$

Source: Pew Research Center, *Second-Generation Americans: A Portrait of the Adult Children of Immigrants,* February 7, 2013.

The final calculation for Z is:

$$Z = \frac{.50 - .55}{.02} = -2.50$$

The one-tailed probability of −2.50 is .0062 (Column C for Z = 2.50). Comparing .0062 to our alpha, we reject the null hypothesis of no difference. We conclude that a significantly higher proportion of second-generation Asian Americans (55%) have a bachelor's degree or higher compared with first-generation Asian Americans (50%). The 5% difference is significant at the .0062 level.

State the null and research hypotheses for this example. Confirm the calculations presented here.

✓ Learning Check

◉ A Closer Look 9.2
   A Cautionary Note: Is There a Significant Difference?

The news media made note of a 2010 Centers for Disease Control (CDC) study that examined the difference in length of marriage between couples in 2005 who first cohabited before marriage and couples who did not cohabit before marriage. Several news services released stories noting the "troubles" associated with living together. As reported, the percentage of marriages surviving to the 10th anniversary, among those who cohabited before marriage, was lower than those who did not cohabit before their first marriage. A closer look at the report reveals important (overlooked) details.

CDC researchers Goodwin, Mosher, and Chandra (2010) reported that previous cohabitation experience was significantly associated with marriage survival probabilities for men. Conversely, though the probability that a woman's marriage would last at least 10 years was lower than for those who cohabited before marriage (60%) than for women who did not (66%), the researchers wrote, "However, in the 2002 data, the difference was not significant at the 5% level" (p. 13).[10]

Throughout this chapter, we've assessed the difference between two means and two proportions, attempting to determine whether the difference between them is due to real effects in the population or due to sampling error. A significant difference is one that confirms that effects of the independent variable, such as cohabiting before marriage, are real. As in the case of marriage survival rate, cohabitation before marriage makes a significant difference in marital outcomes for men, but not for women in the CDC sample. Take caution in accepting comparative statements that fail to mention significance. There may be a difference, but you have to ask, is it a significant difference?

◉ READING THE RESEARCH LITERATURE: REPORTING THE RESULTS OF STATISTICAL HYPOTHESIS TESTING

Let's conclude with an example of how the results of statistical hypothesis testing are presented in the social science research literature. Keep in mind that the research literature does not follow the same format or the degree of detail that we've presented in this chapter. For example, most research articles do not include a formal discussion of the null hypothesis or the sampling distribution. The presentation of statistical analyses and detail will vary according to the journal's editorial policy or the standard format for the discipline.

It is not uncommon for a single research article to include the results of 10 to 20 statistical tests. Results have to be presented succinctly and in summary form. An author's findings are usually presented in a summary table that may include the sample statistics (e.g., the sample means), the obtained test statistics (t or Z), the P level, and an indication of whether or not the results are statistically significant.[11]

Robert Emmet Jones and Shirley A. Rainey (2006) examined the relationship between race, environmental attitudes, and perceptions about environmental health and justice.[12] Researchers have documented how people of color and the poor are more likely than whites and more affluent groups to live in areas with poor environmental quality and protection, exposing them to greater health risks. Yet little is known about how this disproportional exposure and risk are perceived by those affected. Jones and Rainey studied black and white residents from the Red River community in Tennessee, collecting data from interviews and a mail survey during 2001 to 2003.

They created a series of index scales measuring residents' attitudes pertaining to environmental problems and issues. The Environmental Concern (EC) Index measures public concern for specific environmental problems in the neighborhood. It includes questions on drinking water quality, landfills, loss of trees, lead paint and poisoning, the condition of green areas, and stream and river conditions. EC-II measures public concern (very unconcerned to very concerned) for the overall environmental quality in the neighborhood. EC-III measures the seriousness (not serious at all to very serious) of environmental problems in the neighborhood. Higher scores on all EC indicators indicate greater concern for environmental problems in their neighborhood. The Environmental Health (EH) Index measures public perceptions of certain physical side effects, such as headaches, nervous disorders, significant weight loss or gain, skin rashes, and breathing problems. The EH Index measures the likelihood (very unlikely to very likely) that the person believes that he or she or a household member experienced health problems due to exposure to environmental contaminants in his or her neighborhood. Higher EH scores reflect a greater likelihood that respondents believe that they have experienced health problems from exposure to environmental contaminants. Finally, the Environmental Justice (EJ) Index measures public perceptions about environmental justice, measuring the extent to which they agreed (or disagreed) that public officials had informed residents about environmental problems, enforced environmental laws, or held meetings to address residents' concerns. A higher mean EJ score indicates a greater likelihood that respondents think public officials failed to deal with environmental problems in their neighborhood. Index score comparisons between black and white respondents are presented in Table 9.5.

Table 9.5   Environmental Concern (EC), Environmental Health (EH), and Environmental Justice (EJ)

Indicator	Group	Mean	Standard Deviation	t	Significance (one tailed)
EC Index	Blacks	56.2	13.7	6.2	<0.001
	Whites	42.6	15.5		
EC-II	Blacks	4.4	1.0	5.6	<0.001
	Whites	3.5	1.3		
EC-III	Blacks	3.4	1.1	6.7	<0.001
	Whites	2.3	1.0		
EH Index	Blacks	23.0	10.5	5.1	<0.001
	Whites	16.0	7.3		
EJ Index	Blacks	31.0	7.3	3.8	<0.001
	Whites	27.2	6.3		

Source: Robert E. Jones and Shirley A. Rainey, "Examining Linkages Between Race, Environmental Concern, Health and Justice in a Highly Polluted Community of Color," *Journal of Black Studies* 36, no. 4 (2006): 473–496.

Note: N = 78 blacks, 113 whites.

> *Review the information provided in Table 9.5. What would be the t critical at the .05 level for the first indicator, EC Index? Assume a two-tailed test.*

Let's examine the table carefully. Each row represents a single index measurement, reporting means and standard deviations separately for black and white residents. Obtained *t*-test statistics are reported in the second to last column. The probability of each *t* test is reported in the last column ($P < .001$), indicating a significant difference in responses between the two groups. All index score comparisons are significant at the .001 level.

While not referring to specific differences in index scores or to *t*-test results, Jones and Rainey use data from this table to summarize the differences between black and white residents on the three environmental index measurements:

> The results presented [in Table 1] suggest that as a group, Blacks are significantly more concerned than Whites about local environmental conditions (EC Index). . . . The results . . . also indicate that as a group, Blacks believe they have suffered more health problems from exposure to poor environmental conditions in their neighborhood than Whites (EH Index). . . . [T]here is greater likelihood that Blacks feel local public agencies and officials failed to deal with environmental problems in their neighborhood in a fair, just, and effective manner (EJ Index). (p. 485)

MAIN POINTS

- Statistical hypothesis testing is a decision-making process that enables us to determine whether a particular sample result falls within a range that can occur by an acceptable level of chance. The process of statistical hypothesis testing consists of five steps: (1) making assumptions, (2) stating the research and null hypotheses and selecting alpha, (3) selecting a sampling distribution and a test statistic, (4) computing the test statistic, and (5) making a decision and interpreting the results.

- Statistical hypothesis testing may involve a comparison between a sample mean and a population mean or a comparison between two sample means. If we know the population variance(s) when testing for differences between means, we can use the Z statistic and the normal distribution. However, in practice, we are unlikely to have this information.

- When testing for differences between means when the population variance(s) are unknown, we use the t statistic and the t distribution.

- Tests involving differences between proportions follow the same procedure as tests for differences between means when population variances are known. The test statistic is Z, and the sampling distribution is approximated by the normal distribution.

KEY TERMS

alpha (α)	one-tailed test	right-tailed test
degrees of freedom (*df*)	*P* value	sampling distribution
left-tailed test	research hypothesis	of the difference
null hypothesis (H_0)	(H_1)	between means

statistical hypothesis	*t* statistic (obtained)	Type II error
testing	two-tailed test	*Z* statistic (obtained)
t distribution	Type I error	

$SAGE edge™

SPSS DEMONSTRATIONS

[GSS10SSDS]

Demonstration 1: Producing a One-Sample T Test

In this chapter we discussed methods of testing differences in means between a sample and a population value. SPSS includes a One-Sample T Test procedure to do this test. SPSS does not do the test with the *Z* statistic; instead, it uses the *t* statistic to test for all mean differences. The One-Sample T Test procedure can be found under the *Analyze* menu choice, then under *Compare Means,* where it is labeled *One-Sample T Test.* The opening dialog box (Figure 9.6) requires that you place at least one variable in the Test Variable(s) box. Then a test value must be specified.

We'll use the 2010 GSS data for this demonstration. The standard workweek is thought to be 40 hours, so let's test to see whether American adults work that many hours each week. In this example, place HRS1 in the Test Variable(s) box and "40" in the Test Value box. Then click on *OK* to run the procedure.

Figure 9.6   One-Sample T Test Dialog Box

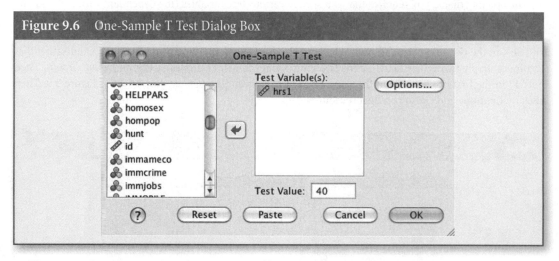

The output from the One-Sample T Test procedure is not very extensive (see Figure 9.7). A total of 838 people answered the question about number of hours worked per week. The mean number of hours worked is 40.62, with a standard deviation of 15.259. Below this, SPSS lists the test value, 40. It includes the two-tailed significance, or probability, for the one-sample test. This value is .242, given the calculated *t* statistic of 1.170, with 837 degrees of freedom. Thus, at the .01 significance level, we would fail to reject the null hypothesis and conclude that American adults work 40 hrs/week.

SPSS also supplies a 95% confidence interval for the mean difference between the test value and the sample mean. Here, the confidence interval runs from −.42 to 1.65, providing estimates of how much more than 40 hrs/week Americans work.

Figure 9.7   One-Sample T Test Output

One-Sample Statistics

	N	Mean	Std. Deviation	Std. Error Mean
hrs 1 NUMBER OF HOURS WORKED LAST WEEK	838	40.62	15.259	.527

One-Sample Test

	Test Value = 40					
					95% Confidence interval of the Difference	
	t	df	Sig. (2-tailed)	Mean Difference	Lower	Upper
hrs 1 NUMBER OF HOURS WORKED LAST WEEK	1.170	837	.242	.617	−.42	1.65

Demonstration 2: Producing a Test of Mean Differences

In this chapter, we have also discussed methods of testing differences in means or proportions between two samples (or groups). The Two-Sample T Test procedure can be found under the *Analyze* menu choice, then under *Compare Means*, where it is labeled *Independent-Samples T Test*.

The opening dialog box requires that you specify various test variables (the dependent variable) and one independent or grouping variable (Figure 9.8). We'll test the null hypothesis that men and women work the same number of hours each week by using the variable HRS1. Place that variable in the Test Variable(s) box and SEX in the Grouping Variable box. When you do so, question marks appear next to SEX indicating that you must supply two values to define the two groups (independent samples). Click on *Define Groups*. Then put "1" in the first box and "2" in the second box (1 = *male* and 2 = *female*), as shown in Figure 9.9. Then click on *Continue* and *OK* to run the procedure.

Figure 9.8   Independent-Samples T Test Dialog Box

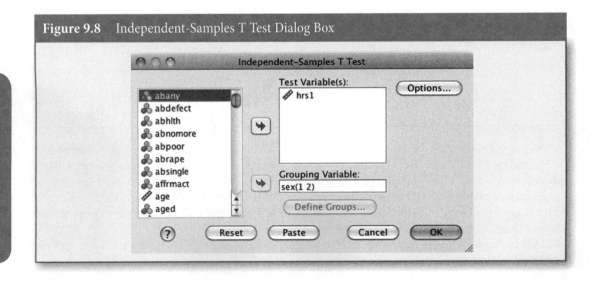

Exercises

Figure 9.9 Define Groups Dialog Box

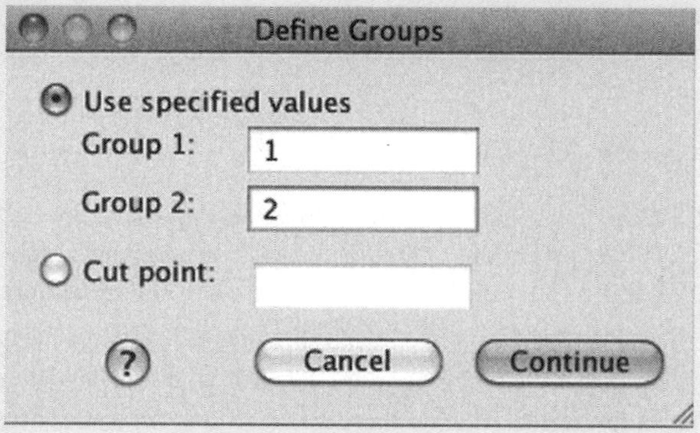

The output from Independent Samples T test (Figure 9.10) is detailed and contains more information than we have reviewed in this chapter. The first part of the output displays the mean number of hours worked for whites and blacks, the number of respondents in each group, the standard deviation, and the standard error of the mean. We see that males worked 6.92 hours more per week than females (44.32 − 37.40 = 6.92).

Figure 9.10 Independent-Samples T Test Output

Group Statistics

	sex RESPONDENTS SEX	N	Mean	Std. Deviation	Std. Error Mean
hrs 1 NUMBER OF HOURS WORKED LAST WEEK	1 MALE	390	44.32	15.609	.790
	2 FEMALE	448	37.40	14.200	.671

Independent Samples Test

		Levene's Test for Equality of Variances		t-test for Equality of Means					95% Confidence interval of the Difference	
		F	Sig.	t	df	Sig. (2-tailed)	Mean Difference	Std. Error Difference	Lower	Upper
hrs 1 NUMBER OF HOURS WORKED LAST WEEK	Equal variances assumed	4.202	.041	6.717	836	.000	6.918	1.030	4.896	8.940
	Equal variances not assumed			6.673	793.150	.000	6.918	1.037	4.883	8.953

Earlier in the chapter, we reviewed the Levene's Test and how to determine whether the variances of the two groups are equal. In this case, we reject the null hypothesis of equal variances (the significance of *F* is .045 < .05 alpha). The *t* obtained is 6.673 (equal variances not assumed) with a probability of .000 (smaller than .05 or .01). We can reject the null hypothesis of no difference and conclude that men work significantly more hours per week than women. The difference of 6.92 hours is significant at the .000 level.

What if we wanted to do a one-tailed test instead? SPSS does not directly list the probability for a one-tailed test, but it is easy to calculate. If we had specified a directional research hypothesis—such as that men work more hours than women—we would simply take the probability reported by SPSS and divide it into half for a one-tailed test. Because the probability is so large in this case, our conclusion will be the same whether we do a one- or a two-tailed test.

Exercises

The last portion of output on each line is the 95% confidence interval for the mean difference in hours worked between the two groups. (Confidence intervals were reviewed in Chapter 8.) It is helpful information when testing mean differences because the actual mean difference measured (6.92 hours) is a sample mean, which will vary from sample to sample. The 95% confidence interval gives us a range over which the sample mean differences are likely to vary.

SPSS PROBLEMS

1. Use the GSS10SSDS file to investigate whether or not Americans have at least two children per person. Use the One Sample T Test procedure to do this test with the variable CHILDS. Do the test at the .01 significance level. What did you find? Do Americans have two children, more, or less?

2. Investigate the difference between individuals who support legalization of marijuana from those who do not based on data from the GSS. Use the variable GRASS as your independent or grouping variable (1 = *legal* and 2 = *not legal*). Investigate whether there is a significant difference between these two groups in terms of their age (AGE), number of children (CHILDS), and education (EDUC). Assume that α is .05 for a two-tailed test. Based on your analysis, write three Step 5–type statements summarizing your findings.

3. Extend your analysis in Exercise 2, this time by comparing individuals who support/do not support gun permits (GUNLAW). Use the same dependent variables, AGE, CHILDS, and EDUC, to estimate *t* tests. Assume α is .05 for a two-tailed test. Prepare a statement to summarize your findings.

4. The GSS10SSDS includes a measure of highest educational degree completed (DEGREE). Test whether there is a significant difference between those with less than high school (coded 0) and those with a bachelor's degree (coded 3) in the number of hours they watch television (TVHOURS) and in the number of hours on the Internet per week (WWWHR). Assume α is .05 for a two-tailed test. Prepare a statement to summarize your findings.

5. In this exercise, we will use data from the MTF2011 survey, comparing GPA between two racial/ethnic student groups. First, you'll need to run frequencies of the variable RACE, taking note of what each racial/ethnic group is coded (e.g., black students are coded as "1"). The MTF 2011 includes three categories for RACE; you'll need to select two as your independent (factor) variables. Use GPA as your dependent variable. Calculate the *t*-test models for two sets of GPA comparisons, for example, white versus black and black versus Hispanic. Assume α is .05 for a two-tailed test. Prepare a statement to summarize your findings.

CHAPTER EXERCISES

1. It is known that, nationally, doctors working for health maintenance organizations (HMOs) average 13.5 years of experience in their specialties, with a standard deviation of 7.6 years. The executive director of an HMO in a Western state is interested in determining whether or not its doctors have less experience than the national average. A random sample of 150 doctors from HMOs shows a mean of only 10.9 years of experience.
   a. State the research and the null hypotheses to test whether or not doctors in this HMO have less experience than the national average.
   b. Using an alpha level of .01, make this test.

2. Consider the problem facing security personnel at a military facility in the Southwest. Their job is to detect infiltrators (spies trying to break in). The facility has an alarm system to assist the security officers. However, sometimes the alarm doesn't work properly, and sometimes the officers don't notice a real alarm. In general, the security personnel must decide between these two alternatives at any given time:

H_0: Everything is fine; no one is attempting an illegal entry.

H_1: There are problems; someone is trying to break into the facility.

Based on this information, fill in the blanks in these statements:

a. A "missed alarm" is a Type ___ error, and its probability of occurrence is denoted as ___.

b. A "false alarm" is a Type ___ error.

3. For each of the following situations determine whether a one- or a two-tailed test is appropriate. Also, state the research and the null hypotheses.

a. You are interested in finding out if the average household income of residents in your state is different from the national average household. According to the U.S. Census, for 2011, the national average household income is $50,054.

b. You believe that students in small liberal arts colleges attend more parties per month than students nationwide. It is known that nationally undergraduate students attend an average of 3.2 parties per month. The average number of parties per month will be calculated from a random sample of students from small liberal arts colleges.

c. A sociologist believes that the average income of elderly women is lower than the average income of elderly men.

d. Is there a difference in the amount of study time on-campus and off-campus students devote to their schoolwork during an average week? You prepare a survey to determine the average number of study hours for each group of students.

e. Reading scores for a group of third graders enrolled in an accelerated reading program are predicted to be higher than the scores for non-enrolled third graders.

f. Stress (measured on an ordinal scale) is predicted to be lower for adults who own dogs (or other pets) than for non-pet owners.

4. a. For each situation in Exercise 3, describe the Type I and Type II errors that could occur.

b. What are the general implications of making a Type I error? Of making a Type II error?

c. When would you want to minimize Type I error? Type II error?

5. One way to check on how representative a survey is of the population from which it was drawn is to compare various characteristics of the sample with the population characteristics. A typical variable used for this purpose is age. The 2010 GSS of the American adult population found a mean age of 49.28 and a standard deviation of 17.21 for its sample of 4,857 adults. Assume that we know from census data that the mean age of all American adults is 37.2. Use this information to answer these questions.

a. State the research and the null hypotheses for a two-tailed test.

b. Calculate the t statistic and test the null hypothesis at the .001 significance level. What did you find?

c. What is your decision about the null hypothesis? What does this tell us about how representative the sample is of the American adult population?

6. In the chapter, we examined the difference between white and black students in the timing of when they first tried cigarettes. In this SPSS output based upon MTF11SSDS, we examine the grade when black and Hispanic students first tried alcohol. Present Step 5 (final decision) for this data. Assume alpha = .05, two-tailed test.

Figure 9.11   T Test Output for RACE and GRDRINK

Group Statistics

	race Respondent's race (trichoromized B/W/H)	N	Mean	Std. Deviation	Std. Error Mean
grdrink What grade when first tried alcohol, even a few sips?	1 BLACK:(1)	148	5.74	2.269	.187
	3 HISPANIC:(3)	166	4.78	2.390	.185

Independent Samples Test

		Levene's Test for Equality of Variances		t-test for Equality of Means						
		F	sig.	t	df	Sig. (2–Tailed)	Mean Difference	Std. Error Difference	95% Confidence Interval of the Difference	
									Lower	Upper
grdrink What grade when first tried alcohol, even a few sips?	Equal variances assumed	.590	.443	3.614	312	.000	.953	.264	.434	1.472
	Equal variances not assumed			3.625	310.753	.000	.953	.263	.436	1.471

7.   In this exercise, we will examine the attitudes of liberals and conservatives toward affirmative action policies in the workplace. Data from the 2010 GSS reveal that 12% of conservatives ($N = 336$) and 27% of liberals ($N = 267$) indicate that they "strongly support" or "support" affirmative action policies for African Americans in the workplace.
   a.   What is the appropriate test statistic? Why?
   b.   Test the null hypothesis with a one-tailed test (conservatives are less likely to support affirmative action policies than liberals); $\alpha = .05$. What do you conclude about the difference in attitudes between conservatives and liberals?
   c.   If you conducted a two-tailed test with $\alpha = .05$, would your decision have been different?

8.   The GSS 2010 measures the amount of hours individuals spend on the Internet per week. Males use the Internet 10.17 hrs per week (standard deviation = 11.71, $N = 118$), while women use the Internet 9.08 hours per week (standard deviation = 12.26, $N = 157$).
   a.   Test the research hypothesis that men use the Internet more hours than women, set alpha at .05.
   b.   Would your decision have been different if alpha were set at .01?

9.   During the 2012 Presidential campaign, pollsters consistently reported how Obama's supporters were mostly women, with men less likely to support his candidacy. In surveys conducted during March 2012 (months before the election), the Pew Research Center reported that among 762 men, 49% indicated that they supported President Obama. Among 741 women, 58% reported the same. Do these differences reflect a significant gender gap among Obama supporters?[13]
   a.   If you wanted to test the research hypothesis that the proportion of male voters supporting President Obama is less than the proportion of female voters, would you conduct a one- or a two-tailed test?
   b.   Test the research hypothesis at the .05 alpha level. What do you conclude?
   c.   If alpha were changed to .01, would your decision remain the same?

10.   Is there a significant difference in the level of community service participation between college and high school graduates? According to the 2010 GSS, 38% of 160 college graduates reported volunteering in the previous month compared with 29% of 210 high school graduates.

a. What is the research hypothesis? Should you conduct a one- or a two-tailed test? Why?

b. Present the five-step model, testing your hypothesis at the .05 level. What do you conclude?

11. We will continue to examine media usage in two additional categories: e-mail hours per week and hours per day watching television. We compare usage among high school and college graduates from the GSS 2010.

Media Use Means and Standard Deviations for High School and College Graduates

	E-mail Hours Per Week	*Television Watching Hours per Day*
High School Graduates	Mean = 5.71 *Standard Deviation* = 7.26 *N* = 84	Mean = 3.25 *Standard Deviation* = 2.60 *N* = 246
College Graduates	Mean = 7.32 *Standard Deviation* = 7.23 *N* = 41	Mean = 2.41 *Standard Deviation* = 1.74 *N* = 111

a. Determine whether high school graduates have significantly lower e-mail hours per week than then college graduates. Test at the .05 alpha level.

b. Test whether there is a significant difference in hours of television viewing between high school and college graduates. Assume alpha = .01.

12. GSS 2010 male and female respondents reported the age when their first child was born. Based on the SPSS output, determine whether there is a significant difference between the two groups. Assume a two-tailed test; α = .05.

Figure 9.12   T Test Output for SEX and AGEKDBRN

Group Statistics

	sex RESPONDENT SEX	N	Mean	Std. Deviation	Std. Error Mean
agekdbrn R'S AGE WHEN 1ST CHILD BORN	1 MALE	379	25.78	6.561	.337
	2 FEMALE	583	22.42	5.155	.214

Independent Samples Test

		Levene's Test for Equality of Variances		t-test for Equality of Means					95% Confidence Interval of the Difference	
		F	sig.	t	df	Sig. (2–Tailed)	Mean Difference	Std. Error Difference	Lower	Upper
agekdbrn R'S AGE WHEN 1ST CHILD BORN	Equal variances assumed	15.334	.000	8.858	960	.000	3.361	.379	2.616	4.105
	Equal variances not assumed			8.424	672.029	.000	3.361	.399	2.577	4.144

13. We calculate the *t*-test for high school and college graduates measuring the average age when their first child was born. Results, based on the GSS10SSDS, are presented below.

Figure 9.13　T Test Output for DEGREE and AGEKDBRN

Group Statistics

	degree RS HIGHEST DEGREE	N	Mean	Std. Deviation	Std. Error Mean
agekdbrn R'S AGE WHEN 1ST CHILD BORN	1 HIGH SCHOOL	485	22.66	5.111	.232
	3 BACHELOR	159	26.75	5.510	.437

Independent Samples Test

		Levene's Test for Equality of Variances		t-test for Equality of Means						
									95% Confidence Interval of the Difference	
		F	sig.	t	df	Sig. (2–Tailed)	Mean Difference	Std. Error Difference	Lower	Upper
agekdbrn R'S AGE WHEN 1ST CHILD BORN	Equal variances assumed	2.054	.152	–8.593	642	.000	–4.093	.476	–5.028	–3.158
	Equal variances not assumed			–8.272	253.116	.000	–4.093	.495	–5.067	–3.158

Based on a two-tailed test, $\alpha = .05$, present step 5 (final decision). What do you conclude?

14. In the chapter we examined the difference in educational attainment between first- and second-generation Hispanic and Asian Americans based on the proportion of each group with a bachelor's degree. We present additional data from the Pew Research Center's 2013 report, measuring the percent of each group that owns a home.

	Percent Owning a Home
First-Generation Hispanic Americans $N = 899$	43
Second-Generation Hispanic Americans $N = 351$	50
First-Generation Asian Americans $N = 2,684$	58
Second-Generation Asian Americans $N = 566$	51

Source: Pew Research Center, *Second-Generation Americans: A Portrait of the Adult Children of Immigrants*, February 7, 2013.

a. Test whether there is a significant difference in the proportion of homeowners between first- and second-generation Hispanic Americans. Set alpha at .05.

b. Test whether there is a significant difference in the proportion of homeowners between first- and second-generation Asian Americans. Set alpha at .01.

Chapter 10

Bivariate Tables

Chapter Learning Objectives

❖ Constructing a bivariate table

❖ Dealing with ambiguous relationships between variables

❖ Determining the properties of a bivariate relationship: existence, strength, and direction

❖ Understanding how to elaborate the relationship between variables: nonspuriousness, intervening, and conditional relationships

One of the main objectives of social science is to make sense out of human and social experience by uncovering regular patterns among events. Therefore, the language of *relationships* is at the heart of social science inquiry. Consider the following examples from articles and research reports:

Example 1: Americans 50 years and older are more likely to oppose creating a path to citizenship for illegal immigrants than are younger Americans.[1] (This example indicates a relationship between age and immigration reform.)

Example 2: Contrary to the stereotype, whites use government safety net programs more than blacks or Latinos, and they are more likely than minorities to be lifted out of poverty by the taxpayer money that they get.[2] (This example indicates a relationship between race and receipt of government aid.)

Example 3: On average, blacks, Asians, and Hispanics are more likely than whites not to have health insurance.[3] (This example indicates a relationship between race and access to health care.)

In each of these examples, a relationship means that certain values of one variable tend to "go together" with certain values of the other variable. In Example 1, age "goes together" with immigration reform and being younger is associated with support of a path to citizenship. In Example

2, being white "goes together" with frequent use of government aid and being black or Latino goes with less frequent use of government aid. Finally, in Example 3, white "goes together" with a higher likelihood of access to health insurance and being black, Asian, or Hispanic "goes together" with a lower likelihood of access to health insurance.

In this chapter, we introduce one of the most common techniques used in the analysis of relationships between two variables: *cross-tabulation*. **Cross-tabulation** is a technique for analyzing the relationship between two variables that have been organized in a table. A cross-tabulation is a type of **bivariate analysis**, a method designed to detect and describe the relationship between two nominal or ordinal variables. We demonstrate not only how to detect whether two variables are associated but also how to determine the strength of the association and, when appropriate, its direction. We will also see how these methods are applied in "real" research situations. We have already applied bivariate analysis in Chapter 9, using *t* tests and *Z* tests to determine the difference between two means or proportions.[4]

Cross-tabulation   A technique for analyzing the relationship between two nominal or ordinal variables that have been organized in a table.

Bivariate analysis   A statistical method designed to detect and describe the relationship between two nominal or ordinal variables.

▣ INDEPENDENT AND DEPENDENT VARIABLES

In the social sciences, an important aspect in research design and statistics is the distinction between the *independent variable* and the *dependent variable*. These terms, first introduced in Chapter 1, are used throughout this chapter as well as in the following chapters, and therefore, it is important that you understand the distinction between them. Let's consider, for example, the relationship between environmental concern and willingness to take a cut in one's standard of living, in which environmental concern—whether a person is concerned with the current state of the environment—has some influence on the level of willingness to take a cut in one's standard of living. Even though environmental concern is not necessarily a direct cause of willingness to take a cut in one's standard of living, environmental concern is assumed to be connected to willingness to take a cut in one's standard of living through a complex set of experiences—such as education, employment, and other socialization experiences—all of which do have an influence on the acquisition of attitudes and opinions. If we hypothesize that willingness to take a cut in one's standard of living (which is the variable to be explained by the researcher) varies by whether a person is concerned about the state of the environment (which is the variable assumed to influence willingness to take a cut in one's standard of living), then environmental concern is the independent variable, and willingness to take a cut in one's standard of living is the dependent variable.

In each of the illustrations given, there are two variables: an independent and a dependent variable. In Example 1, the purpose of the research is to explain support for immigration reform laws. One of the variables hypothesized as being connected to support for immigration reform is age. Therefore, support for immigration reform is the dependent variable, and age is the independent variable. In Example 2, the object of the investigation is to examine the common stereotype that people of color use government aid more than white Americans. The investigator is trying to explain differences in utilization of government aid using race as an explanatory variable. Therefore, utilization of government aid is the dependent variable, and race is the independent variable. Similarly, in Example 3, access to health care is the dependent variable because it is the variable to be explained, whereas race, the explanatory variable, is the independent variable.

The statistical techniques discussed in this and Chapters 11 through 13 help the researcher decide the strength of the relationship between the independent and dependent variables.

✓ *Learning* *Check*

For some variables, whether it is the independent or dependent variable depends on the research question. If you are still having trouble distinguishing between an independent and a dependent variable, go back to Chapter 1 for a detailed discussion.

▣ HOW TO CONSTRUCT A BIVARIATE TABLE: RACE AND HOME OWNERSHIP

A **bivariate table** displays the distribution of one variable across the categories of another variable. It is obtained by classifying cases based on their joint scores on two nominal or ordinal variables. It can be thought of as a series of frequency distributions joined to make one table. The data in Table 10.1 represent a sample of General Social Survey (GSS) respondents by race and whether they own or rent their home (in this case, both variables are nominal-level measurements).

Table 10.1   Race and Home Ownership for 17 GSS Respondents

Respondent	Race	Home Ownership
1	Black	Own
2	Black	Own
3	White	Rent
4	White	Rent
5	White	Own
6	White	Own
7	White	Own

(Continued)

Table 10.1 (Continued)

Respondent	Race	Home Ownership
8	Black	Rent
9	Black	Rent
10	Black	Rent
11	White	Own
12	White	Own
13	White	Rent
14	White	Own
15	Black	Rent
16	White	Own
17	Black	Rent

To make sense out of these data, we must first construct the table in which these individual scores will be classified. In Table 10.2, the 17 respondents have been classified according to joint scores on race and home ownership.

Table 10.2 Home Ownership by Race (absolute frequencies), GSS

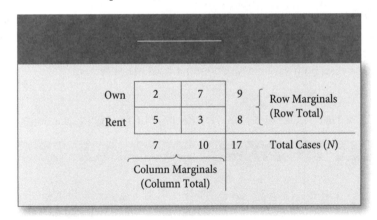

The table has the following features typical of most bivariate tables:

1. The table's title is descriptive, identifying its content in terms of the two variables.

2. It has two dimensions, one for race and one for home ownership. The variable *home ownership* is represented in the rows of the table, with one row for owners and another for renters. The variable *race* makes up the columns of the table, with one column for each racial group.

A table may have more columns and more rows, depending on how many categories the variables represent. For example, had we included a group of Latinos, there would have been three columns (not including the Row Total column). Usually, the independent variable is the **column variable** and the dependent variable is the **row variable**.

3. The intersection of a row and a column is called a **cell**. For example, the two individuals represented in the upper left cell are blacks who are also homeowners.

4. The column and row totals are the frequency distribution for each variable, respectively. The column total is the frequency distribution for *race,* the row total for *home ownership.* Row and column totals are sometimes called **marginals**. The total number of cases (N) is the number reported at the intersection of the row and column totals. (These elements are all labeled in the table.)

5. The table is a 2×2 table because it has two rows and two columns (not counting the marginals). We usually refer to this as an $r \times c$ table, in which r represents the number of rows and c the number of columns. Thus, a table in which the row variable has three categories and the column variable has two categories would be designated as a 3×2 table.

6. The source of the data should also be clearly noted in a source note to the table. This is consistent with what we reviewed in Chapter 2, Organization of Information.

Bivariate table A table that displays the distribution of one variable across the categories of another variable.

Column variable A variable whose categories are the columns of a bivariate table.

Row variable A variable whose categories are the rows of a bivariate table.

Cell The intersection of a row and a column in a bivariate table.

Marginals The row and column totals in a bivariate table.

✓ *Learning Check*

Examine Table 10.2. Make sure you can identify all the parts just described and that you understand how the numbers were obtained. Can you identify the independent and dependent variables in the table? You will need to know this to convert the frequencies to percentages.

▣ HOW TO COMPUTE PERCENTAGES IN A BIVARIATE TABLE

To compare home ownership status for blacks and whites, we need to convert the raw frequencies to percentages because the column totals are not equal. Recall from Chapter 2 that percentages are especially useful for comparing two or more groups that differ in size. There are two basic rules for computing and analyzing percentages in a bivariate table:

1. Calculate percentages within each category of the independent variable.

2. Interpret the table by comparing the percentage point difference for different categories of the independent variable.

Calculating Percentages Within Each Category of the Independent Variable

The first rule means that we have to calculate percentages within each category of the variable that the investigator defines as the independent variable. When the independent variable is arrayed in the *columns*, we compute percentages within each column separately. The frequencies within each cell and the row marginals are divided by the total of the column in which they are located, and the column totals should sum to 100%. When the independent variable is arrayed in the *rows*, we compute percentages within each row separately. The frequencies within each cell and the column marginals are divided by the total of the row in which they are located, and the row totals should sum to 100%.

In our example, we are interested in *race* as the independent variable and in its relationship with *home ownership*. Therefore, we are going to calculate percentages by using the column total of each racial group as the base of the percentage. For example, the percentage of black respondents who own their homes is obtained by dividing the number of black homeowners by the total number of blacks in the sample:

Table 10.3   Home Ownership by Race (in percentages)

Home Ownership	Race		
	Black	White	Total
Own	28.6%	70.0%	52.9%
Rent	71.4%	30.0%	47.1%
Total	100%	100%	100%
(N)	(7)	(10)	(17)

Table 10.3 presents percentages based on the data in Table 10.2. Notice that the percentages in each column add up to 100%, including the total column percentages. Always show the Ns that are used to compute the percentages—in this case, the column totals.

Comparing the Percentages Across Different Categories of the Independent Variable

The second rule tells us to compare how home ownership varies between blacks and whites. Comparisons are made by examining differences between percentage points across different categories of the independent variable. Some researchers limit their comparisons to categories with at least a

10 percentage point difference. In our comparison, we can see that there is a 41.4 percentage point difference between the percentage of white homeowners (70%) and black homeowners (28.6%). In other words, in this group, whites are more likely to be homeowners than blacks.[5] Therefore, we can conclude that one's race appears to be associated with the likelihood of being a homeowner.

Note that the same conclusion would be drawn had we compared the percentage of black and white renters. However, since the percentages of homeowners and renters within each racial group sum to 100%, we need to make only one comparison. In fact, for any 2 × 2 table, only one comparison needs to be made to interpret the table. For a larger table, more than one comparison can be made and used in interpretation.

✓ *Learning Check*

Practice constructing a bivariate table. Use Table 10.1 to create a percentage bivariate table. Compare your table with Table 10.3. Did you remember all the parts? Are your calculations correct? If not, go back and review this section. It might be helpful to examine A Closer Look 10.1 below. It illustrates the process of constructing and percentaging bivariate tables. Remember, you must correctly identify the independent variable so that you know whether to percentage across the rows or down the columns.

🔲 A Closer Look 10.1
Percentaging a Bivariate Table

1. Black and white homeowners and renters:

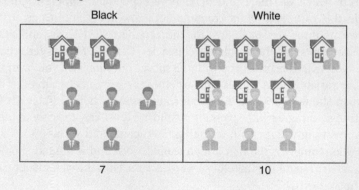

2. Divide respondents into two groups by race (the independent variable); count the number in each group to get the column totals.

(Continued)

(Continued)

3. Divide each group into homeowners and renters (the dependent variable); count the number in each group to get the row totals.

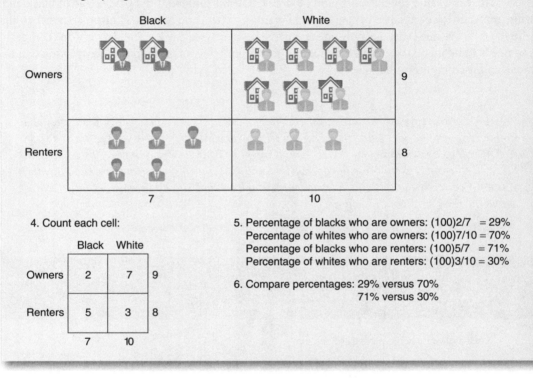

4. Count each cell:

	Black	White	
Owners	2	7	9
Renters	5	3	8
	7	10	

5. Percentage of blacks who are owners: (100)2/7 = 29%
   Percentage of whites who are owners: (100)7/10 = 70%
   Percentage of blacks who are renters: (100)5/7 = 71%
   Percentage of whites who are renters: (100)3/10 = 30%

6. Compare percentages: 29% versus 70%
   71% versus 30%

▣ HOW TO DEAL WITH AMBIGUOUS RELATIONSHIPS BETWEEN VARIABLES

Sometimes it isn't apparent which variable is independent or dependent; sometimes the data can be viewed either way. In this case, you might compute both row and column percentages. For example, Table 10.4 presents three sets of figures for the variables SPANKING and FEFAM for a sample of 127 GSS respondents: (a) the absolute frequencies, (b) the column percentages, and (c) the row percentages. SPANKING is measured with the survey question "Do you favor spanking to discipline a child?" The variable FEFAM measures whether the respondent agrees or disagrees with the statement "a man should work and a woman should stay at home." Table 10.4b shows that respondents who strongly disagree with spanking a child are less likely to agree to the FEFAM statement than those who strongly agree with spanking (10% compared with 50%). Table 10.4c shows that individuals who strongly agree that a man should work and a woman should stay at home are more likely to agree to spanking than those who disagree with the statement on men and women's roles (94% compared with 63%).

Table 10.4   The Different Ways Percentages Can Be Computed: SPANKING by FEFAM

FEFAM	SPANKING		Row Total
	Strongly Agree	*Strongly Disagree*	*Row Total*
a. Absolute frequencies			
Strongly agree	48	3	51
Strongly disagree	48	28	76
Column total	96	31	127
b. Column percentages (column totals as base)			
Strongly agree	50%	10%	40%
Strongly disagree	50%	90%	60%
Column total	100% (96)	100% (31)	100% (127)
c. Row percentages (row totals as base)			
Strongly agree	94%	6%	100% (51)
Strongly disagree	63%	37%	100% (76)
Column total	76%	24%	100% (127)

Thus, percentaging within each *column* (Table 10.4b) allows us to examine the hypothesis that spanking (the independent variable) is associated with agreement to the FEFAM statement (dependent variable). When we percentage within each *row* (Table 10.4c), the hypothesis is that agreement or disagreement with the FEFAM statement (the independent variable) may be related to SPANKING (the dependent variable).[6] Figures 10.1a and b are simple bar charts illustrating the two methods of calculating and comparing percentages depicted in Tables 10.4b and c.

Finally, it is important to understand that ultimately what guides the construction and interpretation of bivariate tables is the theoretical question posed by the researcher. Although the particular example in Table 10.4 makes sense if interpreted using row or column percentages, not all data can be interpreted this way. For example, a table comparing women's and men's attitudes toward sexual harassment in the workplace could provide a sensible explanation in only one direction. Gender might influence a person's attitude toward sexual harassment; however, a person's attitude toward sexual harassment certainly couldn't influence her or his gender. Therefore, either row or column percentages are appropriate, depending on the way the variables are arrayed, but not both.

Figure 10.1 A Comparison of Column Versus Row Percentages

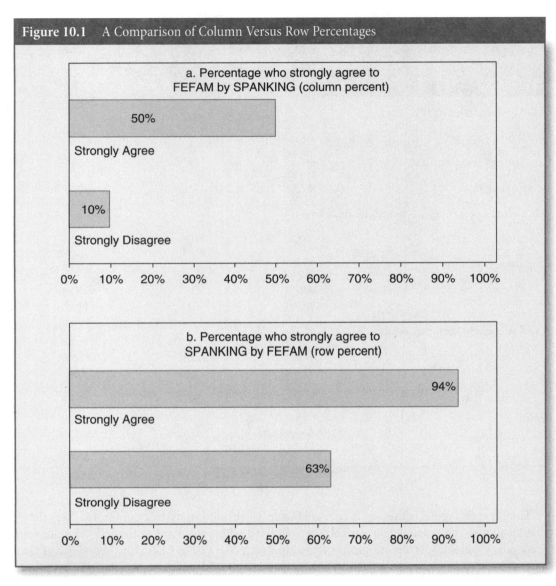

▣ READING THE RESEARCH LITERATURE: PLACE OF DEATH IN AMERICA

The guidelines for constructing and interpreting bivariate tables discussed in this chapter are not always strictly followed. Most bivariate tables presented in the professional literature are a good deal more complex than those we have just been describing. Let's conclude this section with a typical example of how bivariate tables are presented in social science literature. The following example is drawn from a 2007 study by Andrea Gruneir, Vincent Mor, Sherry Weitzen,

Rachael Truchill, Joan Teno, and Jason Roy on understanding variations on the sites of death in America.

According to the researchers, driven in part by the increasing aging of the U.S. population, there has been an increase in the level of public and professional concern about the quality of end-of-life care. Though public surveys confirm that most would prefer to die at home, the majority of Americans die in an institutional setting, such as a hospital or care facility. Acute care hospitals are still the number one site of death for people with chronic illnesses. In this study, Gruneir and her colleagues explored the likelihood of home versus hospital or nursing home death, explaining that

> where individuals spend their last days of life is influenced by individual demographic and clinical characteristics as well as to the degree which their community has an interest in and sufficient wealth to invest in service resources such as hospitals, nursing homes, or home and hospice care services. (p. 359)

The study examines differences in the place of death by gender, age, marital status, race/ethnicity, education, and cause of death. Researchers relied on data from the 1997 National Vital Statistics System (NVSS). The data set includes death certificates for 1,402,167 deaths, identifying place of death as either acute care hospital, nursing care facility, home, or other.

Table 10.5 shows the results of the survey.

Follow these steps in examining it:

1. Identify the dependent variable and the type of unit of analysis it describes (such as individual, city, or child). Here the dependent variable is *place of death in 1997.* The categories for this variable are "hospital," "home," or "nursing home." The type of unit used in this table is individual.

2. Identify the independent variables included in the table and the categories of each. There are five independent variables: gender, age, marital status, race/ethnicity, and education. For the first variable, gender, the categories include "male" and "female." Review table to determine the categories for the remaining variables.

3. Clarify the structure of the table. Note that the independent variables are arrayed in the rows of the table and the dependent variable, *place of death,* is arrayed in the columns. The table is divided into five panels, one for each independent variable. There are actually five bivariate tables here—one for each independent variable.

   Since the independent variables are arrayed in the rows, percentages are calculated within each row separately, with the row totals (not shown) serving as the base for the percentages. From the table, we know that the largest number of 1997 deaths occurred in a hospital—740,405 died in a hospital compared with 330,447 who died at home and 331,315 who died in a nursing home. Combining categories for hospital and nursing home, as Gruneir and colleagues explained, the majority of Americans died in an institutional setting rather than at home. Though not calculated, the row percentages should total 100%.

4. Using Table 10.5, we can make a number of comparisons, depending on which independent variable we are examining. For example, to determine the relationship between gender and

Table 10.5 Place of Death 1997, by Gender, Age, Marital Status, Race/Ethnicity, and Education (percentages reported)

| | *Place of Death, 1997* | | |
	Hospital (N = 740,405)	*Home (N = 330,447)*	*Nursing home (N = 331,315)*
Gender			
Male	57.3	25.5	17.2
Female	48.7	21.8	29.5
Age			
<65	64.4	29.2	6.4
65–74	59.3	28.1	12.6
75–84	52.7	22.7	24.6
85–94	40.8	16.9	42.3
95+	28.0	14.5	57.6
Marital status			
Never married	55.9	21.5	22.7
Married	59.0	26.9	14.1
Widowed	45.2	19.9	34.9
Divorced	54.6	26.1	19.2
Not stated	57.1	24.9	18.0
Race/ethnicity			
White	49.7	24.2	26.1
Black	66.4	20.2	13.5
Hispanic	65.2	22.7	12.1
Other/unknown	63.4	21.7	14.9
Education (years)			
<9	50.8	20.3	29.0
9-11	54.7	23.0	22.3
12	53.5	23.8	22.7
13-15	51.9	26.4	21.7
16+	50.8	27.7	21.6
Unknown	56.8	18.8	24.4

Source: Andrea Gruneir, Vincent Mor, Sherry Weitzen, Rachael Truchil, Joan Teno, and Jason Roy, "Where People Die: A Multilevel Approach to Understanding Influences on Site of Death in America," *Medical Care Research Review 64* (2007): 351–378.

place of death, compare the percentages between males and females. For example, we know that the largest percentages for both male and females are in the category "died in hospital." Yet looking at each place of death category, we see that the percentages are about the same for those who died at home (25.5 males, 21.8 females), but greater differences exist between the percentage of those who died in a nursing home (17.2 males, 29.5 females) and in hospitals (57.3 males, 48.7 females). A higher percentage of females than males were reported dying in a nursing home, while a higher percentage of males than females were reported dying in a hospital.

You can make similar comparisons to determine the association between age, marital status, race/ethnicity, and education.

5. Finally, what conclusions can you draw about variations in place of death? The researchers offer this interpretation of the findings presented in the table.

The frequency of nursing home death increased with age and among the oldest adults, nursing homes were the most common site of death. A greater percentage of women than men died in the nursing home (29.5% vs. 17.2%) but the converse was seen in other sites of death. Married and divorced decedents showed the greatest frequency of home death (26.9% and 26.1%, respectively) while widowed decedents showed the greatest frequency of nursing home death (34.9%). Approximately half of all white decedents died in hospital but well over 60% of each other racial/ethnic group died in hospital. Of those who died outside the hospital, white decedents were equivalently split between home and nursing home while other groups more frequently died at home than in nursing home. (p. 363)

> ✓ *Learning Check*
>
> *Use Table 10.5 to verify each of the following conclusions drawn by the researchers about the place of death: (1) Among the oldest adults, nursing homes were the most common site of death. (2) A greater percentage of women died in nursing homes than men. (3) Marital status is related to home death. (4) Approximately half of all white respondents died at a hospital, while more than 60% of all other racial/ethnic groups died in a hospital. Can you explain these patterns? What other questions do these patterns raise about place of death?*

▣ THE PROPERTIES OF A BIVARIATE RELATIONSHIP

So far, we have looked at the general principles of a bivariate relationship as well as the more specific "mechanics" involved in examining bivariate tables. In this section, we present some detailed observations that we may want to make about the "properties" of a bivariate association. These properties can be expressed as three questions to ask when examining a bivariate relationship:[7]

1. Does there appear to be a relationship?

2. How strong is it?

3. What is the direction of the relationship?

The Existence of the Relationship

We have seen earlier in this chapter that calculating percentages and comparing them are the two operations necessary to analyze a bivariate table. Based on Table 10.6, we want to examine whether the frequency of church attendance by respondents had an effect on their support for abortion. Support for abortion was measured with the following question: "Please tell me whether or not you think it should be possible for a pregnant woman to obtain a legal abortion if the woman wants it for any reason." Frequency of church attendance was determined by asking respondents to indicate how often they attend religious services.[8]

Table 10.6   Support for Abortion by Church Attendance

| Abortion | Church Attendance | | | Total |
	Never	Infrequently	Frequently	
Yes	55%	50%	26%	43%
No	45%	50%	74%	57%
Total	100%	100%	100%	100%
(N)	(111)	(212)	(157)	(480)

Let's hypothesize that those who attend church frequently are more likely to be pro-life. We are not suggesting that church attendance necessarily "causes" pro-life attitudes, but that perhaps, there is an indirect connection between the two. For example, perhaps those who attend church less frequently are more likely to want decisions about the body to be made on an individual basis through the right to choose an abortion. (Indirect associations often can be elaborated further by looking at other variables. We discuss elaboration in more detail later in this chapter.)

In this formulation, church attendance is said to "influence" attitudes toward abortion, so it is the independent variable; therefore, percentages are calculated within each category of church attendance (church attendance is the column variable). We now want to establish whether a relationship exists between the two variables.

A relationship is said to exist between two variables in a bivariate table if the percentage distributions vary across the different categories of the independent variable, in this case church attendance. We can easily see that the percentage that supports abortion changes across the different levels of church attendance. Of those who never attend church, 55% are pro-choice; of those who infrequently attend church, 50% are pro-choice; and of those who frequently attend church, 26% are pro-choice.

Table 10.6 indicates that church attendance and support for abortion are associated as hypothesized.

If church attendance were unrelated to attitudes toward abortion among GSS respondents, then we would expect to find equal percentages of respondents who are pro-choice (or anti-choice) regardless of the level of church attendance. Table 10.7 is a fictional representation of a strictly hypothetical pattern of no association between abortion attitudes and church attendance.

Table 10.7   Support for Abortion by Church Attendance (a hypothetical
illustration of no relationship)

Abortion	Church Attendance			
	Never	Infrequently	Frequently	Total
Yes	43%	43%	43%	43%
No	57%	57%	57%	57%
Total	100%	100%	100%	100%
(N)	(111)	(212)	(157)	(480)

The percentage of respondents who are pro-choice in each category of church attendance is equal to the overall percentage of respondents in the sample who are pro-choice (43%).

The Strength of the Relationship

In the preceding section, we saw how to establish whether an association exists in a bivariate table. If it does, how do we determine the strength of the association between the two variables? A quick method is to examine the percentage difference across the different categories of the independent variable. The larger the percentage difference across the categories, the stronger the association.

In the hypothetical example of no relationship between church attendance and attitude toward abortion (Table 10.7), there is a 0% difference between the columns. At the other extreme, if all respondents who never attended church were pro-choice and none of the respondents who frequently attended church were pro-choice, a perfect relationship would be manifested in a 100% difference. Most relationships, however, will be somewhere in between these two extremes. In fact, we rarely see a situation with either a 0% or a 100% difference. Going back to the observed percentages in Table 10.6, we find the largest percentage difference between respondents who never attend church and respondents who frequently attend church (55% − 26% = 29%). The difference between respondents who infrequently attend church and respondents who frequently attend church (50% − 26% = 24%), though not as large, is nonetheless substantial, indicating a moderate relationship between church attendance and attitudes toward abortion.

Percentage differences are a rough indicator of the strength of a relationship between two variables. In later chapters, we discuss measures of association that provide a more standardized indicator of the strength of an association.

The Direction of the Relationship

When both the independent and dependent variables in a bivariate table are measured at the ordinal level or the interval-ratio level, we can talk about the relationship between the variables as being either positive or negative. A **positive** bivariate relationship exists when the variables vary in the same direction. Higher values of one variable "go together" with higher values of the other variable. In a negative bivariate relationship, the variables vary in opposite directions: higher values of one variable "go together" with lower values of the other variable (and the lower values of one go together with the higher values of the other).

Positive relationship   A bivariate relationship between two variables measured at the ordinal level or higher in which the variables vary in the same direction.

Negative relationship   A bivariate relationship between two variables measured at the ordinal level or higher in which the variables vary in opposite directions.

Table 10.8, from the International Social Survey Programme, displays a positive relationship between willingness to pay higher taxes and willingness to pay higher prices. Examine each category separately. For respondents who are unwilling to pay higher prices, an unwillingness to pay higher taxes is most typical (91.5%). For respondents who are indifferent to paying higher prices, the most common response is to be indifferent to paying higher taxes (55.1%); and finally, for respondents who are willing to pay higher prices, a willingness to pay higher taxes is most typical (57.8%). This is a positive relationship, with a willingness to pay higher prices associated with a willingness to pay higher taxes and an unwillingness to pay higher prices associated with an unwillingness to pay higher taxes.

Table 10.9, also from the International Social Survey Programme, shows a negative association between educational level and attendance of religious services for a sample of about 400 international respondents.[9] Individuals with no education typically attended religious services two to three times per month or more (66.2%). Individuals with a secondary degree (i.e., roughly, the U.S. equivalent to high school) typically attended religious services infrequently, ranging from monthly to several times a year (35.0%); and for individuals who had completed work at a university, the most common category was "never," meaning they never attend religious services (37.3%). The relationship is a negative one because as educational level increases, the frequency of attendance of religious services decreases.

Table 10.8   Willingness to Pay Higher Taxes by Willingness to Pay Higher Prices: A Positive Relationship

	Willingness to Pay Higher Prices		
Willingness to Pay Higher Taxes	*Unwilling*	*Indifferent*	*Willing*
Unwilling	91.5%	36.4%	23.6%
Indifferent	5.1%	55.1%	18.6%
Willing	3.4%	8.5%	57.8%
Total	100%	100%	100%
(*N*)	(529)	(352)	(532)

Table 10.9   Support for Attendance of Religious Services by Educational Level: A Negative Relationship

Attendance of Religious Services	Educational Level		
	None	*Secondary Degree*	*University Degree*
Never	5.2%	32.5%	37.3%
Infrequently	28.6%	35.0%	34.9%
2 to 3 Times per Month or More	66.2%	32.5%	27.8%
Total	100%	100%	100%
(*N*)	(77)	(237)	(126)

▣ ELABORATION

In the preceding sections, we have looked at relationships between two variables—an independent and a dependent variable. The examination of a possible relationship between two variables, however, is only a first step in data analysis. Having established through bivariate analysis that the independent and dependent variables are associated, we seek to further interpret and understand the nature of this relationship. In this section, we discuss a procedure called *elaboration*. **Elaboration** is a process designed to further explore a bivariate relationship, involving the introduction of additional variables, called **control variables**. By adding a control variable to our analysis, we are considering or "controlling" for the variable's effect on the bivariate relationship. Each potential control variable represents an alternative explanation for the bivariate relationship under consideration.

Elaboration   A process designed to further explore a bivariate relationship; it involves the introduction of control variables.

Control variable   An additional variable considered in a bivariate relationship. The variable is controlled for when we take into account its effect on the variables in the bivariate relationship.

The introduction of additional control variables into a bivariate relationship serves three primary goals in data analysis.

- Elaboration allows us to test for nonspuriousness. Establishing cause-and-effect relations requires not only showing that an independent and a dependent variable are associated but also establishing the time order between them and providing theoretical and empirical evidence that the association is nonspurious—that is, it cannot be "explained away" by other variables.

- Elaboration clarifies the causal sequence of bivariate relationships by introducing variables hypothesized to intervene between the independent and dependent variables.
- Elaboration specifies the different conditions under which the original bivariate relationship might hold.

In the preceding sections, we learned how to establish that two variables are associated; in this section, we explore the theoretical and statistical considerations involved in elaborating bivariate relationships. We illustrate the process of elaboration using three examples. The first is an example of testing for nonspuriousness, the second is a research example illustrating a causal sequence in which a third variable intervenes between the independent and dependent variables, and, finally, the third research example illustrates how elaboration can uncover conditional relationships.

Testing for Nonspuriousness: Firefighters and Property Damage

Let's begin with a favorite example of a spurious relationship. Researchers have confirmed a strong bivariate relationship between *number of firefighters* (the independent variable) at a fire site and *amount of property damage* (the dependent variable). The more firefighters at the site, the greater the amount of damage. This association might lead you to the embarrassing conclusion (depicted in Figure 10.2) that firefighters cause property damage at fire sites.

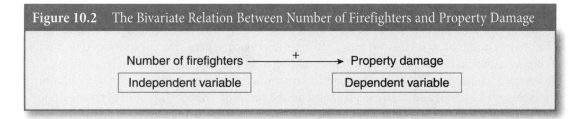

Figure 10.2   The Bivariate Relation Between Number of Firefighters and Property Damage

Figure 10.2 depicts what might be a *direct causal relationship* between firefighters and the amount of damage. The relationship between two variables is said to be a **direct causal relationship** when it cannot be accounted for by other theoretically relevant variables. Clearly, in this case, the relationship between the number of firefighters and amount of damage can be accounted for by a third, causally prior variable—the size of the fire. When the fire is large, more firefighters are sent to the site, and there is a great deal of property damage. Similarly, when the fire is small, fewer firefighters are at the site, and there is probably very little damage.

Direct causal relationship   A bivariate relationship that cannot be accounted for by other theoretically relevant variables.

This alternative explanation is shown in Figure 10.3. Note that according to the hypothesized causal order suggested in Figure 10.3, the number of firefighters and the extent of property damage are both related to the variable *size of fire* but are not related to each other. The size of the fire is called a *control variable*, and the relation between the number of firefighters and property damage as depicted in Figure 10.2 is *spurious*. A **spurious relationship** is a relationship between two variables in which both the independent and dependent variables are influenced by a causally prior control variable, and there is no causal link between them. The bivariate relationship between the independent and dependent variables can thus be "explained away" through the introduction of the control variable.

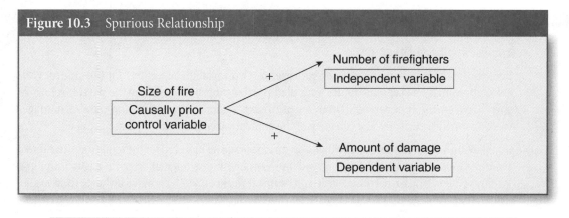

Figure 10.3 Spurious Relationship

Spurious relationship   A relationship in which both the independent and dependent variables are influenced by a causally prior control variable, and there is no causal link between them. The relationship between the independent and dependent variables is said to be "explained away" by the control variable.

Researchers have adopted the following rule of thumb for determining whether a relationship between two variables is either direct (causal) or spurious: If the bivariate relationship between the two variables remains about the same after controlling for the effect of one or more causally prior and theoretically relevant variables, then the original bivariate relationship is said to be a direct (causal relationship) association. Conversely, if the original bivariate relationship decreases considerably (or vanishes), then the bivariate relationship is said to be spurious.

Let's see how we can apply this rule of thumb to the firefighter example. One way to control for the effect of the size of the fire on the relationship between the number of firefighters and the extent of damage is to divide the fire sites into large and small fires and then reexamine the bivariate association between the other two variables within each group of fire sites. If the original bivariate relationship vanishes (or diminishes considerably), then the explanation suggested by Figure 10.3 would seem more likely. If, however, the original relationship is maintained, then we may need to hold on to the original explanation suggested by Figure 10.2 or go back to the drawing board and think of other alternative explanations for the puzzling relationship between the number of firefighters and the extent of property damage.

Figure 10.4 illustrates the bivariate association between the number of firefighters and the extent of property damage (10.4a) and the process of controlling for the variable *size of fire* (10.4b). Note that the control *for size of fire* resulted in a substantial decrease (from 40% to 12% difference) in the size of the relationship between the number of firefighters and property damage. This result supports the notion, as depicted in Figure 10.3, that the size of the fire explains both the number of firefighters and the extent of property damage and that the relationship between the number of firefighters and property damage is therefore spurious.

The introduction of the control variable *size of fire* into the original bivariate relationship between *number of firefighters* and *amount of damage* illustrates the process of elaboration. These are the steps:

1. Divide the observations into subgroups on the basis of the control variable. We have as many subgroups as there are categories in the control variable. (In our case, there were two subgroups: small and large fires.)

2. Reexamine the relationship between the original two variables separately for the control variable subgroups. The separate tables are called **partial tables**; they display the **partial relationship** between the independent (number of firefighters) and dependent (amount of damage) variables within each specific category of the control variable (small vs. large fire size).

3. Compare the partial relationships with the original bivariate relationship for the total group. In a direct causal pattern, the partial relationships will be very close to the original bivariate relationship. In a spurious pattern, the partial relationship will be much weaker than the original bivariate relationship.

Partial tables   Bivariate tables that display the relationship between the independent and dependent variables while controlling for a third variable.

Partial relationship   The relationship between the independent and dependent variables shown in a partial table.

Figure 10.4   Elaborating a Bivariate Relationship

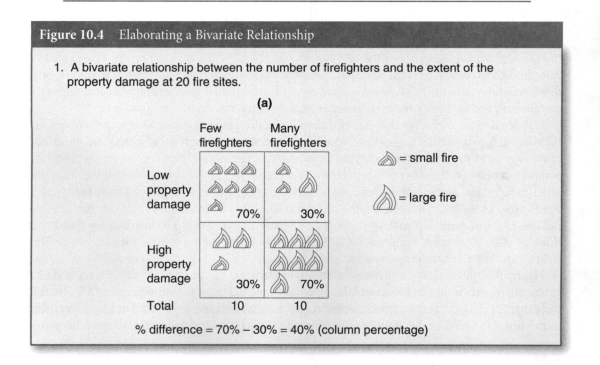

1. A bivariate relationship between the number of firefighters and the extent of the property damage at 20 fire sites.

(a)

% difference = 70% − 30% = 40% (column percentage)

2. Control for size of fire: divide fire sites into small and large fires. In each group, recalculate the bivariate relationship between the number of firefighters and the extent of the property damage.

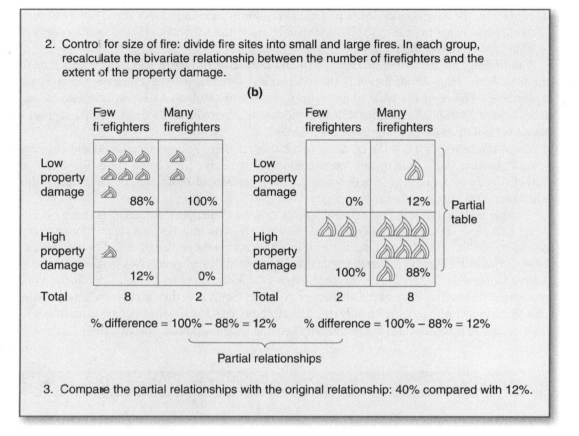

(b)

% difference = 100% − 88% = 12%   % difference = 100% − 88% = 12%

Partial relationships

3. Compare the partial relationships with the original relationship: 40% compared with 12%.

We have employed the elaboration procedure to test for a spurious relationship between the number of firefighters and the amount of property damage. Now, let's see how elaboration is used to interpret the causal sequence of bivariate relationships by introducing a control variable hypothesized to *intervene* between the independent and dependent variables.

An Intervening Relationship: Religion and Attitude Toward Abortion

The research on the relationship between religious affiliation and attitudes toward abortion has shown a consistent pattern: Religious affiliation is related to the level of support for abortion.[10] In particular, it has been shown that Catholics oppose abortion more than Protestants or Jews do.[11]

To test the hypothesis that religion and abortion attitudes are related, we used data from the 1988 to 1991 GSS sample. We limited our analysis to Catholics and Protestants because of the small numbers of respondents with other religious affiliation. Attitudes toward abortion are measured in terms of respondents' approval or disapproval of the following three situations: (1) the woman does not want the baby because the family has a very low income and cannot afford more children; (2) the woman is not married and does not want to marry the father; and (3) the woman does not want to have more children.[12]

The findings are presented in Table 10.10 and illustrated in Figure 10.5. Since, according to the hypothesis, religious affiliation is the independent variable, we use column percentages for our analysis. The results provide some support for the hypothesis that religion is related to attitudes toward abortion. We see that 45% of Protestants compared with 34% of Catholics support a woman's right to an abortion for these cited reasons.

These results may suggest the existence of a causal relationship between religion and attitudes toward abortion. According to this interpretation of the relationship, being either Protestant or Catholic leads to a different abortion orientation regardless of other factors. Graphically, this hypothesized relationship is shown in Figure 10.6.

Another body of research findings dealing with religion challenges the conclusion that there is a direct causal link (as suggested by Figure 10.6) between religious affiliation and support for abortion. According to this research literature, some of the differences between Catholics and Protestants can be explained by the variable *preferred family size*.[13] It is argued that religion is systematically related to desired family size: Catholics prefer larger numbers of children than non-Catholics. Similarly, if one conceptualizes abortion as an alternative device to control family size, then support for abortion may also be associated with preferred family size. Therefore, preferred family size operates as an intervening mechanism through which the relationship between religion and abortion attitudes occurs.

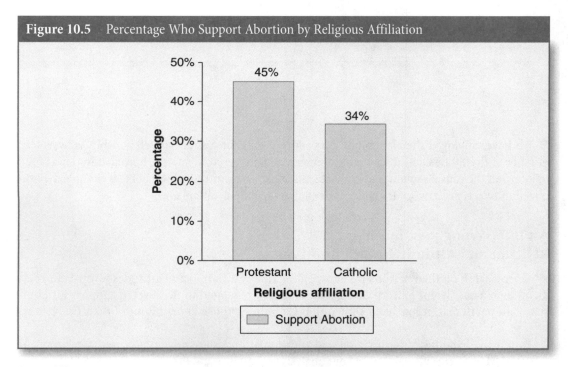

Figure 10.5 Percentage Who Support Abortion by Religious Affiliation

Source: GSS, 1988–1991.

Table 10 10   Religious Affiliation and Support for Abortion

Support	Preferred Family Size		Total
	More Than 2 Children	2 or Fewer Children	
Yes	25%	50%	41%
	(38)	(127)	
No	75%	50%	59%
	(112)	(126)	
Total	100%	100%	100%
(N)	(150)	(253)	(403)

Source: GSS 1988–1991.

Figure 10.6   The Bivariate Relationship Between Religion and Support for Abortion

Religion ————————→ Support for abortion

Independent variable   Dependent variable

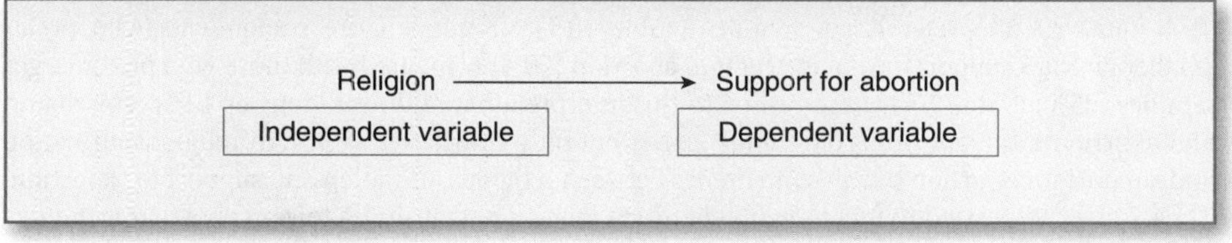

To check these ideas, we analyzed the bivariate associations between preferred family size and religion (Table 10.11) and between preferred family size and support for abortion (Table 10.12).[14] Note that because the theory suggests that preferred family size operates as an intervening mechanism between religious affiliation and support for abortion, it is analyzed as the dependent variable in Table 10.11 and as the independent variable in Table 10.12.

Table 10.11   Religious Affiliation and Preferred Family Size

Support	Religious Affiliation		Total
	Catholic	Protestant	
Yes	34%	45%	41%
	(56)	(109)	
No	66%	55%	59%
	(107)	(131)	
Total	100%	100%	100%
(N)	(163)	(240)	(403)

Source: GSS, 1988–1991.

Table 10.12   Preferred Family Size and Support for Abortion

| Preferred Family Size | Religious Affiliation | | Total |
	Catholic	Protestant	
More than 2 children	52% (85)	27% (65)	37%
2 or fewer children	48% (78)	73% (175)	63%
Total (N)	100% (163)	100% (240)	100% (403)

Source: GSS, 1988–1991.

The data in Tables 10.11 and 10.12 confirm the linkages between preferred family size and religion and preferred family size and support for abortion. First, more Catholics (52%) than Protestants (27%) prefer larger families (Table 10.11). Second, more respondents who prefer smaller families support a woman's right to abortion (50%) compared with those who prefer larger families (25%) (Table 10.12). According to this interpretation of the relationship between religion and abortion attitudes, preferred family size is not only associated with both religious affiliation and support for abortion but also intervenes between religious affiliation and support for abortion. Thus, it is hypothesized that the relation between religion and attitudes toward abortion is *indirect* and *linked* via the control variable—preferred family size.

The hypothetical causal sequence suggested by this interpretation is shown in Figure 10.7. In this formulation, the control variable (preferred family size) is called an *intervening variable*. An **intervening variable** is a control variable that follows an independent variable but precedes the dependent variable in a causal sequence. Because preferred family size follows the independent variable, religion, but precedes the dependent variable, abortion attitudes, it is considered an intervening variable. The relationship between religion and support for abortion shown in Figure 10.7 is called an *intervening relationship*. An **intervening relationship** is one between two variables in which a control variable intervenes between the independent and dependent variables.

Intervening variable   A control variable that follows an independent variable but precedes the dependent variable in a causal sequence.

Intervening relationship   A relationship in which the control variable intervenes between the independent and dependent variables.

We can test the model shown in Figure 10.7 by controlling for preferred family size and repeating the original bivariate analysis between religious affiliation and support for abortion. We control for preferred family size by separating the respondents who indicated that they preferred larger families from those who preferred smaller families. If the causal sequence hypothesized by

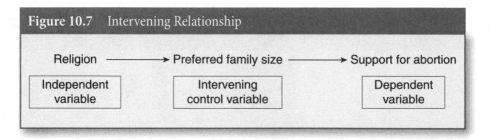

Figure 10.7 Intervening Relationship

Religion ⟶ Preferred family size ⟶ Support for abortion

Independent variable — Intervening control variable — Dependent variable

Figure 10.7 is correct, then the association between religion and abortion attitudes should disappear or diminish considerably once preferred family size has been controlled.

The results presented in Table 10.13 and Figure 10.8 support the notion, as depicted in Figure 10.7, that preferred family size intervenes between religion and abortion attitudes. The associations between religion and abortion attitudes in the two partial tables are smaller than the original bivariate table (Table 10.10). Among respondents who prefer larger families, there are smaller differences between Catholics and Protestants regarding a woman's right to an abortion. A total of 28% of Protestants and 24% of Catholics support legal abortion. Among those who prefer smaller families, there are also small differences between the two religious groups. A total of 52% of Protestants and 46% of Catholics are in support of abortion. Thus, we would conclude that Catholics are less favorable to abortion (than Protestants) because they prefer larger families. These findings increase our understanding of the original bivariate relationship between religious affiliation and attitudes toward abortion.

Table 10.13 Religious Affiliation and Support for Abortion After Controlling for Preferred Family Size

| Support | Religious Affiliation | | Total |
	Catholic	Protestant	
Preferred family size: 2 or fewer children			
Yes	46% (36)	52% (91)	50%
No	54% (42)	48% (84)	50%
Total (*N*)	100% (78)	100% (175)	100% (253)
Preferred family size: more than 2 children			
Yes	24% (20)	28% (18)	25%
No	76% (65)	72% (47)	75%
Total (*N*)	100% (85)	100% (65)	100% (150)

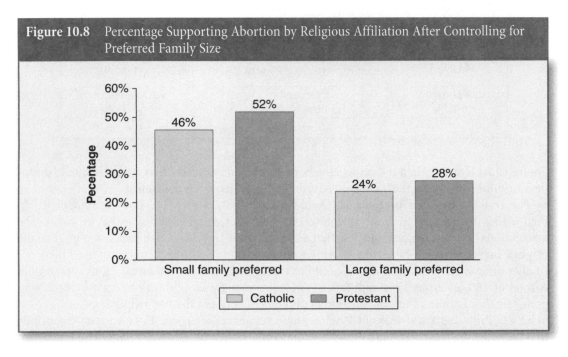

Figure 10.8   Percentage Supporting Abortion by Religious Affiliation After Controlling for Preferred Family Size

✓ *Learning*
Check

You may have noticed that the tests for spuriousness and for an intervening relationship are identical: They both require that the partial associations disappear or diminish considerably! So how can you differentiate between the two? The differentiation is made on theoretical rather than empirical grounds. When a relationship is spurious, there is no causal link between the independent and dependent variables; both are influenced by a causally prior control variable. In an intervening relationship, there is an indirect causal link between the independent and dependent variables; the control variable follows the independent variable but precedes the dependent variable in the causal sequence.

Conditional Relationships: More on Abortion

What other variables may explain the relationship between religion and attitudes toward abortion? One possible variable is *religious participation*. In their research on abortion attitudes, Arney and Trescher[15] found that when religious participation is controlled for, there is little difference in abortion attitudes between Catholics and Protestants who attend church less than once a month. In contrast, among Catholics and Protestants who attend church more than once a month, Catholics were more likely than Protestants to oppose abortion.[16] Other researchers note that age and gender may also influence the relationship between religion and abortion attitudes.

What do these examples have in common? They all specify different conditions under which the relationship between religion and abortion attitudes is expected to hold. For example, Arney and Trescher indicate that the differences in abortion attitudes between Protestants and Catholics might hold under one condition (attend church more than once a month) of the control variable *religious participation* but not under another (attend church less than once a month). Similarly, the relationship may differ for men and women or for older and younger individuals. When a bivariate relationship differs for different conditions of the control variable, we say that it is a **conditional relationship**. Another way to describe a conditional relationship is to say that there is a *statistical interaction* between the control variable and the independent variable.

Conditional relationship   A relationship in which the control variable's effect on the dependent variable is conditional on its interaction with the independent variable. The relationship between the independent and dependent variables will change according to the different conditions of the control variable.

Table 10.14   Abortion Morality and Stance on Legal Abortion

	Stance on Legal Abortion		
Abortion Morality	*Pro-Choice*	*Pro-Life*	*Total*
Always wrong or depends	37%	98%	57%
Not wrong	63%	2%	43%
Total	100%	100%	100%
(*N*)	(337)	(162)	(499)

Source: Adapted from Jacqueline Scott, "Conflicting Belief About Abortion: Legal Approval and Moral Doubts," *Social Psychology Quarterly* 52, no. 4 (1989): 319–326. Copyright © 1989 by the American Sociological Association. Published by SAGE.

Because conditional relationships are very common, sociology offers many research examples illustrating this pattern of elaboration. One such example comes from a study by Jacqueline Scott on the relationship between stance on legal abortion and opinions about the morality of abortion. The study shows that although nearly all opponents of legal abortion view abortion as morally wrong, not all pro-choice supporters view abortion as morally right. Instead, many pro-choice supporters favor legal abortion despite personal moral reservations.[17] This bivariate relationship between abortion morality and stance on legal abortion is displayed in Table 10.14.

Because stance on legal abortion is the independent variable, percentages are calculated in the columns. The results of this analysis support Scott's hypothesis. Among those who oppose abortion, there is almost unanimous agreement (98%) that abortion is morally wrong. Among those who favor legal abortion, however, the level of incongruence is relatively high: A total of 37% support legal abortion despite viewing it as morally wrong or ambiguous.[18]

Although there is little difference between men's and women's attitudes toward the legality of abortion, some argue that women are far more likely to feel that abortion is morally wrong. For example,

Carol Gilligan[19] argues that whereas men tend to be more concerned with rights and rules, women are more concerned with caring and relationships. Abortion, therefore, may pose a greater moral dilemma for women than for men. To examine the hypothesis that women are more likely than men to favor legal abortion despite moral reservations, Scott controlled for gender and compared the original relationship between stance on legal abortion and abortion morality among men and women. The cross-tabulation of abortion morality by stance on legal abortion, controlling for gender, is given in Table 10.15. The table shows a marked gender difference in the relationship between abortion morality and stance on legal abortion. Although we can still conclude from Table 10.15 that the stance on legal abortion and the stance on abortion morality are associated, we need to qualify this conclusion by saying that this association is stronger for men (the percentage difference is 96% − 29% = 67%) than for women (the percentage difference is 100% − 46% = 54%).

Because the relationship between the independent and dependent variables is different in each of the partial tables, the relationship is said to be a conditional relationship—that is, the original bivariate relationship depends on the control variable. In our example, the strength of the relationship between abortion morality and stance on legal abortion is conditioned on gender. The conditional relationship between stance on abortion and abortion morality is depicted in Figure 10.9.

The Limitations of Elaboration

The elaboration examples discussed in this section point to the complexity of the social world. We started this chapter by stating that most things around us "go together." It is more accurate to say that most things around us are "tangled," and one of the goals of social science is to "untangle" them. Elaboration is a procedure that helps us "untangle" bivariate relations.

In the illustrations presented in this section, we looked at bivariate relationships that were clarified and reinterpreted when a control variable was introduced. How do we know which variables to control for? In reality, theory provides significant guidance as to the relationships that we look for and the sorts of variables that should be introduced as controls. Without theory as a guide, elaboration

Table 10.15   Abortion Morality and Stance on Legal Abortion After Controlling for Gender

| Abortion Morality | Men | | | Abortion Morality | Women | | |
| | Stance on Legal Abortion | | | | Stance on Legal Abortion | | |
	Pro-Choice	Pro-Life	Total		Pro-Choice	Pro-Life	Total
Always wrong or depends	29%	96%	50%	Always wrong or depends	46%	100%	64%
Not wrong	71%	4%	50%	Not wrong	54%	0%	36%
Total	100%	100%	100%	Total	100%	100%	100%
(N)	(172)	(78)	(250)	(N)	(165)	(84)	(249)

Source: Adapted from Jacqueline Scott, "Conflicting Belief About Abortion: Legal Approval and Moral Doubts," *Social Psychology Quarterly* 52, no. 4 (1989): 319–326. Copyright © 1989 by the American Sociological Association. Published by SAGE.

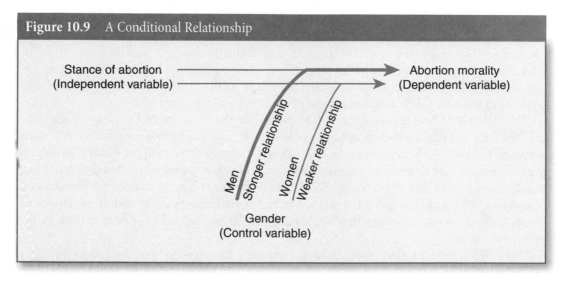

Figure 10.9   A Conditional Relationship

can become a series of exercises that more closely resembles random shots in the dark than scientific analysis. Even with theory as our guide, the statistical analysis is often more complex than the presentation in this section may suggest. In our examples, when the control variable was introduced, the "real" nature of the relationship "jumped right out at us." It's not always that easy. In fact, most often there is a perilous gap between theory and analysis. This does not mean that you have to abandon your effort to "untangle" bivariate relationships, only that you should be aware of both the importance of theory as a guide to your analysis and the limitations of the statistical analysis.

In this section, you have been introduced to a number of important new terms. See if you can write out definitions for the following terms: elaboration, control variable, intervening variable, causally prior variable, spurious relationship, partial relationship, partial table, and conditional relationship.

✓ *Learning Check*

▣ STATISTICS IN PRACTICE: FAMILY SUPPORT FOR THE TRANSITION FROM HIGH SCHOOL

In earlier chapters, we saw that statistics helps us analyze how race, class, age, or gender shapes our experiences. However, we focused primarily on how these categories of experience operate separately (we compared men and women, young and old, working class and middle class, etc.). Now, we need to think about how these systems interlock in shaping our experience as individuals in society.[20] Everyone has his or her own particular combination of race, social class, age, and gender. These factors act as lenses through which we experience the world. Through analysis of the intersecting effects of these factors, we can understand the ways in which others experience the world from their different or similar perspectives.

When we start to see race, class, and gender as intersecting systems of experience, we see, for example, that while white women and women of color may share some common experiences based on their gender, their racial experiences are distinct. Similarly, depending on their race and class, men experience gender differently. For example, we know that the removal of manufacturing jobs has increased the job loss of black and Hispanic males. At the same time, many women of color have found their work opportunities expanded in service and high-tech jobs.[21]

The methods of bivariate analysis and, in particular, the statistical techniques of elaboration are especially suitable for the examination of how race, class, and gender are linked with social behavior. In Table 10.16, we present the findings of a study that examined the kind of family support women, who are now in professional and managerial positions, received when they made their transition from high school to college. This example illustrates how to analyze the simultaneous operation of race and class using the method of elaboration. The example also demonstrates the drastic differences in conclusions that would have been drawn had either or both of these factors been ignored.[22]

Table 10.16 includes five types of family support, representing five dependent variables: (1) information on entrance examinations and colleges, (2) information on admission requirements, (3) financial support in paying tuition and fees, (4) emotional support, and (5) encouragement for career. Only one category is given for each dependent variable. This category represents the percentage of women who received family support in each of the specified areas. For example, 42% of black women who were raised in middle-class families ($N = 50$) reported that family members had helped them in procuring information on entrance examinations and colleges. The remaining 58% of this group (not shown) did not receive family help in this area.

Race and class origin are the two independent variables in this analysis. To estimate the effect of class on family support, we compare middle-class-raised women with working-class-raised women among black and white women. The data show that there are large class differences in all types of family support provided to these women by their families. For example, whereas 90% of black middle-class families paid tuition for their daughters, only 56% of black working-class families did so. A similar pattern is observed among the white women. Similarly, more middle-class families, both black (86%) and white (70%), provided emotional support to their daughters during the transition from high school to college.

The second step involved in looking at a table such as this one is to examine whether there are racial differences in family support. To estimate the effect of race, we compare black and white women who were raised in working-class and middle-class families. This comparison reveals virtually no relationship between race and either procurement of information or financial support. For instance, 20% of working-class blacks and 20% of working-class whites received help with information on college admissions requirements; similarly, 34% of middle-class blacks and 30% of middle-class whites received support in this category. However, examination of the emotional support category reveals fairly substantial race differences: A total of 86% of middle-class-raised black respondents report that their families provided emotional support compared with only 70% of the middle-class-raised whites. Similarly, more working-class black families (64% vs. 56%) provided emotional support to their daughters in the transition from high school to college.

The group that differs most from the others on both emotional support and encouragement for career is black middle-class women, who received the highest degree of family support in each of these categories.

Table 10.16 Race and Class Origin Differences in Percentage of Women Reporting Family Support for the Transition from High School to College

Type of Family Support	Black		White	
	Working Class (N = 50)	*Middle Class* (N = 50)	*Working Class* (N = 50)	*Middle Class* (N = 50)
Information				
Entrance exams and colleges	22%	42%	24%	40%
Admission requirements	20%	34%	20%	30%
Financial				
Paid tuition and fees	56%	90%	62%	88%
Emotional				
Emotional support	64%	86%	56%	70%
Encouragement for career	56%	60%	40%	52%

Source. Adapted from Lynn Weber, Elizabeth Higginbotham, and Marianne L. A. Leung, "Race and Class Bias in Research on Women: A Methodological Note," Research paper 5, presented at the Center for Research on Women, University of Memphis, 1987.

In conclusion, the data reveal a strong relationship between class origin and both information and financial support provided by the family. In addition, the data show relationships between both race and class and emotional encouragement and support. Had the study failed to address both the race and class background of these professional and managerial women, we would have drawn very different conclusions about the role of families in supporting women as they moved from high school to college.[23]

This is another example of the pattern of elaboration examined earlier. In this case, class origin is used as a control variable to elaborate on the relationship between race and family support. In American society, race is associated with class (blacks are more likely to be raised in a working-class family), and class is associated with family support (working-class families are less likely to provide family support). Had we not analyzed the effect of the class background of the women as well as their race, we would have concluded that black women receive far less support in all areas than white women. Such a conclusion could have reinforced a stereotype—that black families are less supportive of their children's education. Such a conclusion would represent a distortion of the real process since it is working-class women, both black and white, who receive less family support.[24]

Finally, this example demonstrates the importance of looking at the simultaneous effects of race and class on the lives of women. This is only one among many ways in which race, class, and gender comparisons can be incorporated in a statistical analysis. Moreover, examining the linkages between race, class, and gender cannot be limited to women. While integrating these variables into our analysis introduces complexity to our research, it also suggests new possibilities for thinking that will enrich us all.

MAIN POINTS

- Bivariate analysis is a statistical technique designed to detect and describe the relationship between two variables. A relationship is said to exist when certain values of one variable tend to "go together" with certain values of the other variable.

- A bivariate table displays the distribution of one variable across the categories of another variable. It is obtained by classifying cases based on their joint scores for two variables.

- Percentaging bivariate tables are used to examine the relationship between two variables that have been organized in a bivariate table. The percentages are always calculated within each category of the independent variable.

- Bivariate tables are interpreted by comparing percentages across different categories of the independent variable. A relationship is said to exist if the percentage distributions vary across the categories of the independent variable.

- Variables measured at the ordinal or interval-ratio levels may be positively or negatively associated. With a positive association, higher values of one variable correspond to higher values of the other variable. When there is a negative association between variables, higher values of one variable correspond to lower values of the other variable.

- Elaboration is a technique designed to clarify bivariate associations. It involves the introduction of control variables to interpret the links between the independent and dependent variables.

- In a spurious relationship, both the independent and dependent variables are influenced by a causally prior control variable, and there is no causal link between them.

- In an intervening relationship, the control variable follows the independent variable but precedes the dependent variable in the causal sequence.

- In a conditional relationship, the bivariate relationship between the independent and dependent variables is different in each of the partial tables.

KEY TERMS

bivariate
   analysis
bivariate table
cell
column variable
conditional
   relationship
control variable
cross-tabulation

direct causal
   relationship
elaboration
intervening
   relationship
intervening variable
marginals
negative relationship
partial relationship

partial tables
positive relationship
row variable
spurious relationship

⑤SAGE edge™

Sharpen your skills with SAGE edge at **edge.sagepub.com/frankfort7e**. **SAGE edge for students** provides a personalized approach to help you accomplish your coursework goals in an easy-to-use learning environment.

SPSS DEMONSTRATIONS

[GSS10SSDS]

Demonstration 1: Producing Bivariate Tables

SPSS has a separate procedure designed specifically to produce cross-tabulation tables. It is called the Crosstabs procedure and can be found under *Descriptive Statistics* in the *Analyze* menu. The dialog box for Crosstabs (Figure 10.10) requires us to specify both a variable that will define the rows and one that defines the columns of a table. We will investigate the relationship between support for a legal abortion for a woman who is married but does not want any more children (ABNOMORE) and recoded religious affiliation (NRELIG). For this illustration, RELIG categories 5 through 13 were recoded to 5—Other.

By default, SPSS displays the count in each cell of the table. Normally, then, you should click on the *Cells* button to request percentages (Figure 10.11). As usual, we percentage the table based on the independent or predictor variable, which is religious affiliation. The independent variable is placed in the columns, while the dependent variable is placed in rows. We click on the checkbox for "Column" to percentage the table by religious affiliation. (Note that "Observed" is already checked by default in the Counts section. In the Noninteger Weights section, "Round cell counts" is checked by default.)

Click on *Continue*, then *OK*, to obtain the table shown in Figure 10.12. SPSS displays both the count and the column percentage in each cell. In the upper left corner of the table, the labels "Count" and "% within RELIG" are displayed as a reminder of what SPSS has placed in each cell. Row totals and column totals are supplied automatically, as is the overall total (930 respondents gave valid responses to both questions). The number of missing responses on one or both variables may also be displayed.

The table shows great differences in support across religious categories for a legal abortion for a married woman who does not want any more children. A majority of Protestants and Catholics oppose abortion in this instance, but a majority of Jews, others (Hindus, Buddhists, Muslims, and others[25]), and the nonreligious support abortion. Do you find these differences surprising, or are they consistent with your understanding of the social world?

Demonstration 2: Producing Tables With a Control Variable

As we've seen in this chapter, the analysis of data is enhanced when a third variable—a control variable—is added to a bivariate table. In the Crosstabs procedure, the third variable is added in the Layer section of the main dialog box (Figure 10.13). (This box is labeled "Layer 1 of 1" because it is possible to have additional levels of control, which are accessed by clicking on the *Next* button.) We will keep the same dependent variable, ABNOMORE, but make RACECEN1 the column variable and SEX the control variable. There is no need to change the numbers displayed in the cells: The observed count and column percentages are still correct choices. Figure 10.14 shows the bivariate tables of support for legal abortions for married women by race separately for males and females (males are listed first).[26] SPSS labels each table with the value of the control variable for easy reference.

Exercises

Figure 10.10 Crosstabs Dialog Box

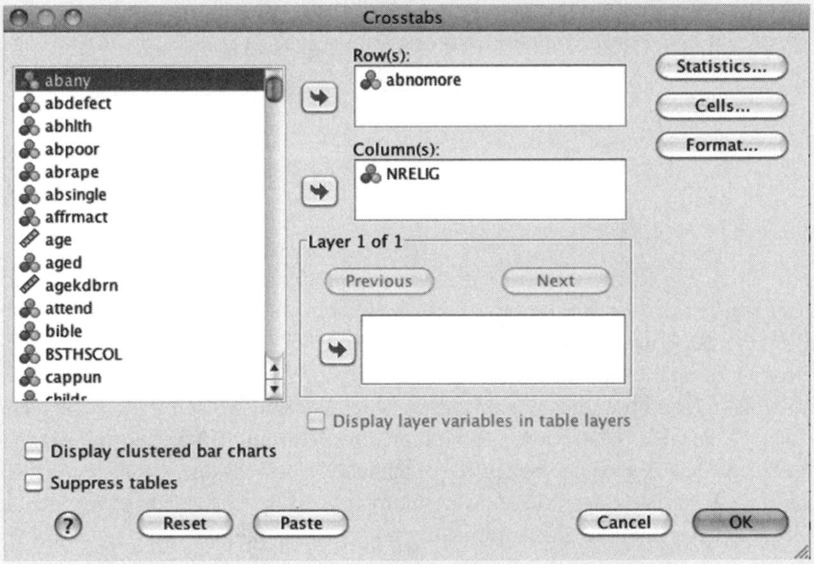

Figure 10.11 Crosstabs: Cell Display Dialog Box

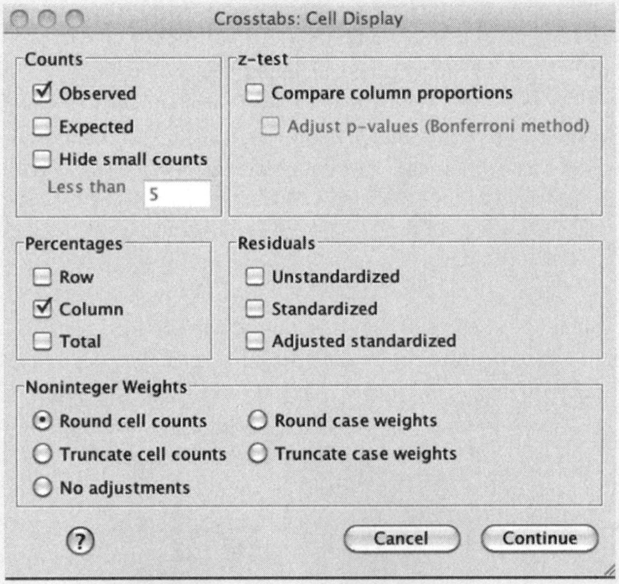

Figure 10.12 Cross-Tabulation Output: ABNOMORE by NRELIG

abnomore MARRIED—WANTS NO MORE CHILDREN * NRELIG New Religion Recode Crosstabulation

			NRELIG New Religion Recode					Total
			1.00 Protestant	2.00 Catholic	3.00 Jewish	4.00 None	5.00 Other	
abnomore MARRIED—WANTS NO MORE CHILDREN	1 YES	Count	173	69	12	96	34	384
		% within NRELIG New Religion Recode	35.3%	33.8%	75.0%	64.0%	48.6%	41.3%
	2 NO	Count	317	135	4	54	36	546
		% within NRELIG New Religion Recode	64.7%	66.2%	25.0%	36.0%	51.4%	58.7%
Total		Count	490	204	16	150	70	930
		% within NRELIG New Religion Recode	100.0%	100.0%	100.0%	100.0%	100.0%	100.0%

Figure 10.13 Crosstabs Dialog Box

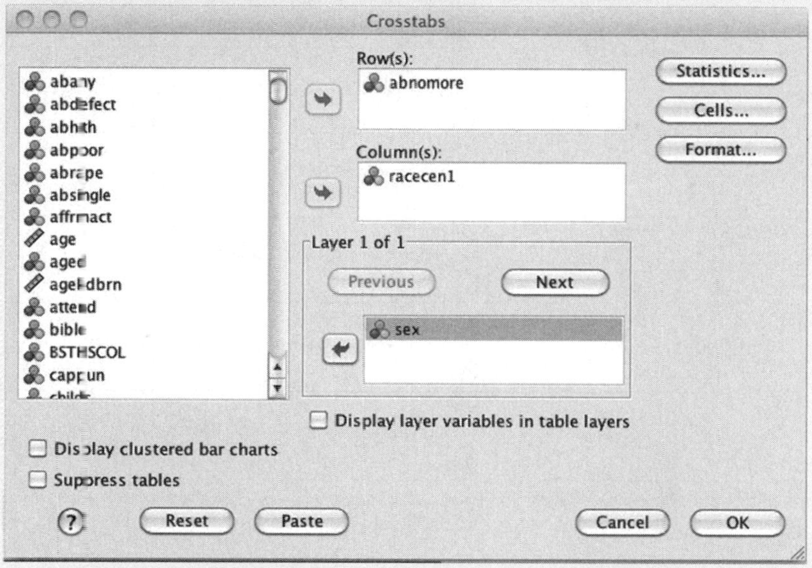

SPSS will report frequencies for all races as reported, but we'll focus on the results for the first two categories: whites and blacks or African Americans. We see that the percentage of male respondents who do not support abortion (those who responded "no" to ABNOMORE) is highest for whites (57.7%) compared with blacks (48.9%). Black males are more likely than white males to support abortion (responded "yes") in this circumstance (51.1% vs. 42.3%). In the table for females, a majority of both races oppose abortion, with a higher percentage of black women opposing than white females (63.4% vs. 59.9%). Finding differences such as these is one reason why researchers use control variables in analyses. These tables display a conditional relationship between race and support for abortion for married women when sex is introduced as a control variable.

In later chapters, we will use the Statistics button in the Crosstabs dialog box to request additional output to further interpret and evaluate bivariate tables.

Exercises

Figure 10.14 Cross-Tabulation Output: ABNOMORE by RACECEN1 Controlling for SEX

abnomore MARRIED—WANTS NO MORE CHILDREN * racecen1 WHAT IS RS RACE 1ST MENTION * sex
RESPONDENTS SEX Crosstabulation

sex RESPONDENTS SEX				racecen1 WHAT IS RS RACE 1ST MENTION		Total
				1 WHITE	2 BLACK OR AFRICAN AMERICAN	
1 MALE	abnomore MARRIED—WANTS NO MORE CHILDREN	1 YES	Count	127	23	150
			% within racecen1 WHAT IS RS RACE 1ST MENTION	42.3%	51.1%	43.5%
		2 NO	Count	173	22	195
			% within racecen1 WHAT IS RS RACE 1ST MENTION	57.7%	48.9%	56.5%
	Total		Count	300	45	345
			% within racecen1 WHAT IS RS RACE 1ST MENTION	100.0%	100.0%	100.0%
2 FEMALE	abnomore MARRIED—WANTS NO MORE CHILDREN	1 YES	Count	166	30	196
			% within racecen1 WHAT IS RS RACE 1ST MENTION	40.1%	36.6%	39.5%
		2 NO	Count	248	52	300
			% within racecen1 WHAT IS RS RACE 1ST MENTION	59.9%	63.4%	60.5%
	Total		Count	414	82	496
			% within racecen1 WHAT IS RS RACE 1ST MENTION	100.0%	100.0%	100.0%
Total	abnomore MARRIED—WANTS NO MORE CHILDREN	1 YES	Count	293	53	346
			% within racecen1 WHAT IS RS RACE 1ST MENTION	41.0%	41.7%	41.1%
		2 NO	Count	421	74	495
			% within racecen1 WHAT IS RS RACE 1ST MENTION	59.0%	58.3%	58.9%
	Total		Count	714	127	841
			% within racecen1 WHAT IS RS RACE 1ST MENTION	100.0%	100.0%	100.0%

SPSS PROBLEMS

[GSS10SSDS and MTF11SSDS]

1. The GSS data set includes responses to questions about the respondent's general happiness (HAPPY) and his or her subjective class identification (CLASS). Analyze the relationship between responses to these two questions with the SPSS Crosstabs procedure, requesting counts and appropriate cell percentages. (Click on Analyze, Descriptive Statistics, and Crosstabs to get started.)

   a. What percentage of working-class people responded that they were "very happy"?
   b. What percentage of lower-class people were "very happy"?
   c. What percentage of those who were "pretty happy" were also from the middle and upper classes?
   d. Most of the people who said that they were "very happy" were from which two classes?

e. Is there a relationship between perceived class and perceived happiness? If there is a relationship, describe it. Is it strong or weak? (*Hint:* Use perceived class as the independent variable.)

f. Rerun your analysis, this time adding RACECEN1 as a control variable. Is there a difference in the relationship between perceived class and happiness for whites and blacks in the sample? (Because of the large number of racial categories, just compare blacks and whites.)

2. Analyze the relationship between self-reported health condition and general happiness.
   a. Use SPSS to construct a table showing the relationship between health condition (HEALTH) and reported general happiness (HAPPY). (*Hint:* Use HEALTH as the dependent variable.) Next, use SPSS to construct tables showing the same relationship controlling for sex.
   b. Overall, are women or men more likely to report "excellent" health?
   c. Do women and men with higher levels of happiness report poor or excellent health? Is there a relationship between happiness and health? Make sure to support your answer with data from your cross-tabulation.

3. Is there a difference in attitudes about abortion depending on the circumstance of the woman's pregnancy or her reason for an abortion? Separately assess the relationship between SEX and two abortion items, ABPOOR (Should a woman have an abortion if she can't afford any more children?) and ABHLTH (Should a woman have an abortion if her health is seriously endangered?). What do you conclude?

4. For the GSS2010, respondents were asked to report which candidate they voted for in the 2004 and 2008 presidential elections (PRES04 and PRES08) and their feelings about the Bible (BIBLE). Does a relationship exist between a respondent's 2008 vote and her or his feelings about the Bible? For example, if someone thinks that the Bible is a "book of fables," did the individual vote for Senator John Kerry or President George W. Bush in 2004? If the respondent believes the Bible is the word of God, how did the respondent vote in 2004 or 2008?
   a. Which variable should be defined as the dependent variable? Explain your answer.
   b. Using SPSS Crosstabs, create two tables with BIBLE and each of the PRES variables. Explain the relationship between the two variables for 2004 and 2008. (Remember, when you discuss your findings, you should exclude those respondents who did not vote.)
   c. Examine the relationship between BIBLE and one of the PRES variables with a control variable of your choice.

5. Based on the MTF11SSD, examine the relationship between a teen's race (RACE) and the number of friends who drink alcohol (FRDRINK) and smoke cigarettes (FRSMOKE). Using SPSS Crosstabs, create two tables with RACE and each friend variable. What is the relationship between these variables?

CHAPTER EXERCISES

1. Use the following GSS data on fear, race, and home ownership for this exercise. Variables measure respondents race, whether the respondent fears walking alone at night, and his or her home ownership.

Respondent	Race	Fear of Walking Alone	Rent/Own
1	W	N	R
2	B	N	R
3	W	Y	R
4	B	N	R
5	W	N	R
6	B	Y	O
7	W	Y	R
8	W	Y	R
9	W	N	O
10	W	N	O
11	W	Y	R
12	W	N	R
13	B	Y	O
14	W	N	R
15	B	N	O
16	B	N	R
17	W	N	O
18	W	N	O
19	B	N	R
20	W	N	O
21	B	Y	R

Notes: Race: B = black, W = white; Fear: Y = yes, N = no; Rent/Own: R = rent, O = own.

a. Construct a bivariate table of frequencies for race and fear of walking alone at night. Which is the independent variable?

b. Calculate percentages for the table based on the independent variable. Describe the relationship between race and fear of walking alone using the table. What sampling issues are involved here?

c. Use the data to construct a bivariate table to compare fear of walking alone at night between people who own their homes and those who rent. Use percentages to show whether there is a difference between homeowners and renters in fear of walking alone.

2. Do women and men have different opinions about affirmative action? Based on data from the GSS2010, the output in Figure 10.15 shows respondent's sex (SEX) and attitudes toward affirmative action (DIS-CAFF: Are whites hurt by affirmative action?).

Figure 10.15   DISCAFF by SEX Cross-Tabulation

discaff WHITES HURT BY AFF. ACTION * sex RESPONDENTS SEX Crosstabulation

Count

		sex RESPONDENTS SEX		
		1 MALE	2 FEMALE	Total
discaff WHITES HURT BY AFF. ACTION	1 VERY LIKELY	56	103	159
	2 SOMEWHAT LIKELY	171	255	426
	3 NOT VERY LIKELY	168	193	361
Total		395	551	946

a. Which is the independent variable?

b. What are the differences in attitudes between men and women?

c. What might be some other reasons that influence attitudes about affirmative action? Suggest at least two reasons.

3. Advocates of gay rights often argue that homosexuality is not a "preference" or a choice but rather an "orientation" that cannot be changed. One of your classmates argues that attitudes about homosexuality often influence political views. Those who think homosexual relations are wrong tend to be more conservative compared with those who do not think that homosexual relations are wrong. Use the following table based on the GSS 2010 to answer the questions.

	Homosexual Relations		
Political Views	Always Wrong	Not Wrong at All	Total
Liberal	82	155	237
	18.2%	45.4%	29.9%
Moderate	140	120	260
	31%	35.2%	32.8%
Conservative	229	66	295
	50.8%	19.4%	37.2%
Total	451	341	792
	100.0%	100.0%	99.9%

Note: Original GSS categories have been recoded for illustration purposes.

a. Based on your classmate's argument, what is the dependent variable? The independent variable?

b. What percentage of those polled think that homosexual relations are always wrong?

c. Using the percentages in the table, describe the relationship between views about homosexual relations and political orientation?

4. We continue our examination of attitudes regarding homosexuality. Suppose that a classmate of yours suggests that views about homosexual relations can be explained by the frequency of church attendance. Your classmate shows you the following table taken from the 2010 GSS sample. (Frequencies are shown below.)

| Homosexual Relations | Church Attendance | | | |
	Never	Several Times a Year	Every Week	Total
Always wrong	50	52	136	238
Not wrong at all	111	36	38	185
Total	161	88	174	423

   a. Which is the dependent variable in this table? Which is the independent variable?
   b. Calculate the percentages using church attendance as the independent variable for each cell in the table. Is there a relationship between church attendance and views about homosexual relations? If so, how strong is it?
   c. Suppose that you respond to your classmate by stating that it is not church attendance that explains views about homosexual relations; rather, it is one's opinion about the nature of right and wrong (i.e., morality) that explains attitudes about homosexual relations. Why might there be a potential problem with your argument? Think in terms of assigning variables to the independent and dependent categories.

5. Youth were asked in the MTF 2011 survey to report how drunk they get when they consume alcohol. Responses for 361 males are reported by race.

| Alchhowdrunk | Race | | | |
	Black	White	Hispanic	Total
Not at all	10	71	14	95
A little	4	64	16	84
Moderate	10	108	19	137
Very	5	35	5	45
Total	29	278	54	361

   Calculate the percentages using race as the independent variable. Is there a relationship between student race and level of drunkenness?

6. The educational level of Americans has increased throughout the 20th century. The following U.S. Census data show the level of education attained by American adults over the age of 25 years at several points in time.

Year	Educational Level	
	High School Graduate or More (%)	College Graduate or More (%)
1980	66.5	16.2
1990	77.6	21.3
1995	81.7	23.0
2000	84.1	25.6
2005	85.2	27.7
2010	87.1	30.3

Source: U.S. Census Bureau, *Statistical Abstract of the United State: 2012,* Table 229.

    a. What is the direction of the relationship between each year and level of education?

    b. Use percentage differences to describe the relationship. Why don't the percentages add to 100% by year? Is there a problem in analyzing the table?

    c. Do these data support the idea that Americans were more educated in 2010 than in previous years?

7. In 2004, high school seniors were surveyed about their postsecondary expectations and plans. U.S. Department of Education data are presented for male and female students. Which group of students has higher educational expectations? Refer to the data to support your answer. [The row total for males will not equal to 100% due to rounding.]

Sex	Students' Educational Expectations (percentages reported)				
	Do not know yet	High school or less	Some college	Bachelor's degree	Graduate/Advanced degree
Males	9.4	6.9	20.5	34.4	28.9
Females	7.4	3.1	15.6	32.6	41.3

Source: Xianglei Chen, Joanna Wu, Shayna Tasoff, and Thomas Weko, *Postsecondary Expectations and Plans of the High School Senior Class of 2003–2004,* U.S. Department of Education NCES 2010–070 rev, 2010.

8. In Exercise 1, you found that more blacks than whites are likely to fear walking alone in their neighborhoods. You now wonder if this difference exists because whites are more likely to own their own homes and so live in safer neighborhoods. In other words, you want to try some elaboration.

    a. Use the data from Exercise 1 to construct tables showing the relationship between fear of walking alone and race, controlling for whether the individual rents or owns his or her dwelling.

    b. Does renting versus owning one's dwelling "explain" the difference in fear between whites and blacks? (Use percentage differences to support your answer.)

    c. Has introducing home ownership shown that the relationship between race and fear is spurious or is home ownership an intervening variable? Explain.

9. Segregation in schools appears to be increasing, due in part to class (and racial) separation between public and private schools. The table below summarizes the percentage of students who are white versus students of color in public versus private elementary schools. Data are provided by the U.S. Census Bureau. Describe the relationship between racial composition of students and type of institution. Over time, does this relationship change?

A Typical Black Student's Classmates Are	Elementary School (Public)			Elementary School (Private)		
	1980	1990	2005	1980	1990	2005
White students (%)	80.9	78.9	75.2	90.7	88.2	83.0
Students of color (%)	19.1	21.1	24.8	9.3	11.8	17.0

Source: U.S. Census Bureau, *Statistical Abstract of the United State: 2008*, Table 213.

10. Based on MTF2011 data, we present the cross-tabulation for student race and how many of their friends smoke marijuana. [In SPSS Exercise 5, we examined the relationship between student race and friends who smoke cigarettes or drink alcohol.]

Figure 10.16   FRWEED by Race Cross-Tabulation

frweed How many friends smoke marijuana? * race Respondent's race (trichotomized B/W/H) Crosstabulation

Count

		race Respondent's race (trichotomized B/W/H)			Total
		1 BLACK:(1)	2 WHITE:(2)	3 HISPANIC: (3)	
frweed How many friends smoke marijuana?	1 NONE:(1)	50	138	33	221
	2 A FEW:(2)	34	208	36	278
	3 SOME:(3)	40	229	53	322
	4 MOST:(4)	47	184	53	284
	5 ALL:(5)	8	30	11	49
Total		179	789	186	1154

a. Identify the dependent and independent variables for this table.
b. What proportion of black, white, and Hispanic respondents reported that most or all of their friends smoke marijuana? Calculate these proportions separately.
c. Explain the relationship between student race and the number of friends who smoke marijuana.

11. We continue our examination of high school senior educational expectations (Exercise 7), this time examining the relationship between highest level of parents' education and seniors' educational expectations. How would you characterize the relationship between the two variables?

Highest Level of Parents' Education	Students' Educational Expectations (percentages reported)				
	Do Not Know Yet	High School or Less	Some College	Bachelor's Degree	Graduate/Advanced Degree
High school or less	11.4	9.4	27.2	30.0	22.0
Some college	9.0	5.1	21.0	35.4	29.5
College graduation	6.2	2.6	12.6	38.5	40.1
Graduate/ Professional degree	5.7	1.5	6.7	28.2	57.9

Source: Xianglei Chen, Joanna Wu, Shayna Tasoff, and Thomas Weko, *Postsecondary Expectations and Plans of the High School Senior Class of 2003–2004*, U.S. Department of Education NCES 2010–070 rev, 2010.

12. We consider one more variable—2001 family income—and its relationship with students' educational expectations. What direction is the relationship between the two variables? Explain your answer. [Note: Some row percentages will not equal 100% due to rounding.]

Family Income in 2001	Students' Educational Expectations (percentages reported)				
	Do Not Know Yet	High School or Less	Some College	Bachelor's Degree	Graduate/ Advanced Degree
$35,000 or lower	11.3	7.8	24.3	30.2	26.3
$35,001–75,000	8.4	5.1	18.7	35.0	32.9
More than $75,000	5.1	1.8	10.3	34.8	48.0

Source: Xianglei Chen, Joanna Wu, Shayna Tasoff, and Thomas Weko, *Postsecondary Expectations and Plans of the High School Senior Class of 2003–2004*, U.S. Department of Education NCES 2010–070 rev, 2010.

13. In Exercise 5 we presented MTF2011 data for male students. In this exercise, we present the data for 373 female students and their self-report of drunkenness by race.

Alchhowdrunk	Race			
	Black	White	Hispanic	Total
Not at all	24	82	23	129
A little	24	71	12	107
Moderate	13	83	18	114
Very	3	14	6	23
Total	64	250	59	373

Exercises

Compare this table to the one presented in Exercise 5. Do females report the same level of drunkenness as male students? Explain your answer.

14. In 2000, respondents in several European countries were asked whether they chose to avoid driving a car for environmental reasons. Their responses are listed below. (Frequencies are shown below.)

Avoid Driving Car for Environmental Reasons	Country					
	Great Britain	Spain	Austria	Ireland	Netherlands	Norway
Always	33	15	40	19	47	53
Often	96	51	165	71	287	206
Sometimes	260	122	297	225	541	507
Never	343	413	268	655	411	515
Total	732	601	770	970	1,286	1,281

Source: International Social Survey Programme, 2000.

a. Is there a relationship between a respondent's country of residence and whether or not he or she abstains from driving a car for environmental reasons?

b. Approximately 27% of Austrian respondents and 26% of Dutch respondents say that they always or often avoid driving a car for environmental reasons, whereas for Irish respondents, this figure is only 9%. Provide some sociological insight as to why these figures are so different.

Chapter 11

The Chi-Square Test and Measures of Association

┌───┐
│ ### Chapter Learning Objectives

❖ Understanding hypothesis testing and statistical independence with chi-square

❖ Recognizing the limitations of chi-square test—sample size and statistical significance

❖ Understanding the concept of PRE (proportional reduction of error) and how to interpret measures of association

❖ Calculating and interpreting lambda, gamma, and Kendall's tau-*b*

❖ Interpreting Cramer's *V*: a chi-square-related measure of association
└───┘

Figures collected by the U.S. Census Bureau indicate that educational attainment is increasing in the United States. The percentage of Americans who completed 4 years of high school or more increased from 52.3% in 1970 to 87.1% in 2010. In 1970, only about 11% of Americans completed 4 years or more of college compared with 30% in 2010.[1] Despite this overall increase, educational attainment and one's educational experience still vary by demographic factors such as race/ethnicity, class, or gender.

We extend our examination of the educational experience by focusing on first-generation college students—that is, students whose parents never completed a postsecondary education. The proportion of first-generation students has declined within the total population of first-year, full-time-entering college freshmen, reflecting the overall increase in educational attainment in the U.S. population. However, racial/ethnic differences in the rate of first-generation college students continue to exist. Hispanics have a higher percentage of first-generation college students (38.2%) at 4-year colleges than any other racial/ethnic group.[2]

Most first-generation students begin college at 2-year programs or at community colleges. According to W. Elliot Inman and Larry Mayes (1999), since first-generation college students represent a large segment of the community college population, they bring with them a set of distinct goals and constraints. Understanding their experiences and their demographic backgrounds may allow for more intentional recruiting, retention, and graduation efforts. Inman and Mayes set out to examine first-generation college students' experiences, but they began first by determining who was most likely to be a first-generation college student.

Data from Inman and Mayes's study are presented in Table 11.1, a bivariate table, which includes *gender* and *first-generation college status*. From the table, we know that a higher percentage of women than men reported being first-generation college students, 46.6% versus 35.4%.

Table 11.1 Percentage of Men and Women Who Are First-Generation College Students

First Generation	Men	Women	Total
Firsts	35.4%	46.6%	41.9%
	(691)	(1,245)	(1,936)
Nonfirsts	64.6%	53.4%	58.1%
	(1,259)	(1,425)	(2,684)
Total (N)	100.0%	100.0%	100.0%
	(1,950)	(2,670)	(4,620)

Source: Adapted from W. Elliot Inman and Larry Mayes, "The Importance of Being First: Unique Characteristics of First Generation Community College Students," *Community College Review* 26, no. 3 (1999): 8. Copyright © North Carolina State University. Published by SAGE Publications.

The percentage differences between males and females in first-generation college status, shown in Table 11.1, suggest that there is a relationship. In inferential statistics, we base our statements about the larger population on what we observe in our sample. How do we know whether the gender differences in Table 11.1 reflect a real difference in first-generation college status among the larger population? How can we be sure that these differences are not just a quirk of sampling? If we took another sample, would these differences be wiped out or be even reversed?

Let's assume that men and women are equally likely to be first-generation college students—that in the population from which this sample was drawn, there are no real differences between them. What would be the expected percentages of men and women who are first-generation college students versus those who are not?

If gender and first-generation college status were not associated, we would expect the same percentage of men and women to be first-generation college students. Similarly, we would expect to see the same percentage of men and women who are nonfirsts. These percentages should be equal to the percentage of "firsts" and "nonfirsts" respondents in the sample as a whole (categories used by Inman and Mayes). The last column of Table 11.1—the row marginals—displays these percentages: 41.9% of all respondents were first-generation students, whereas 58.1% were non-firsts. Therefore, if there were no association between gender and first-generation college status, we would expect to see 41.9% of the men and 41.9% of the women in the sample as first-generation students. Similarly, 58.1% of the men and 58.1% of the women would not be.

Table 11.2 shows these hypothetical expected percentages. Because the percentage distributions of the variable *first-generation college status* are identical for men and women, we can say that Table 11.2 demonstrates a perfect model of "no association" between the variable *first-generation college status* and the variable *gender.*

If there is an association between gender and first-generation college status, then at least some of the observed percentages in Table 11.1 should differ from the hypothetical expected percentages shown in Table 11.2. Conversely, if gender and first-generation college status are not associated, the observed percentages should approximate the expected percentages shown in Table 11.2. In a cell-by-cell comparison of Tables 11.1 and 11.2, you can see that there is quite a disparity between the observed percentages and the hypothetical percentages. For example, in Table 11.1, 35.4% of the men reported that they were first-generation college students, whereas the corresponding cell for Table 11.2 shows that 41.9% of the men reported the same. The remaining three cells reveal similar discrepancies.

Are the disparities between the observed and expected percentages large enough to convince us that there is a genuine pattern in the population? The *chi-square* statistic helps us answer this question. It is obtained by comparing the actual observed frequencies in a bivariate table with the frequencies that are generated under an assumption that the two variables in the cross-tabulation are not associated with each other. If the observed and expected values are very close, the chi-square statistic will be small. If the disparities between the observed and expected values are large, the chi-square statistic will be large. In the following sections, we will learn how to compute the chi-square statistic to determine whether the differences between men's and women's first-generation college status could have occurred simply by chance.

Table 11.2   Percentage of Men and Women Who Are First-Generation College Students: Hypothetical Data Showing No Association

First Generation	Men	Women	Total
Firsts	41.9%	41.9%	41.9%
			(1,936)
Nonfirsts	58.1%	58.1%	58.1%
			(2,684)
Total (N)	100.0%	100.0%	100.0%
	(1,950)	(2,670)	(4,620)

◙ THE CONCEPT OF CHI-SQUARE AS A STATISTICAL TEST

The **chi-square test** (pronounced kai-square and written as χ^2) is an inferential statistical technique designed to test for significant relationships between two variables organized in a bivariate table. The test has a variety of research applications and is one of the most widely used tests in the social sciences. Chi-square requires no assumptions about the shape of the population distribution from which a sample is drawn. It can be applied to nominally or ordinally measured variables (including grouped interval-level data).

Chi-square test   An inferential statistical technique designed to test for significant relationships between two nominal or ordinal variables organized in a bivariate table.

The chi-square test can also be applied to the distribution of scores for a single variable. Also referred to as the goodness-of-fit test, the chi-square can compare the actual distribution of a variable with a set of expected frequencies. This application is not presented in this chapter.

◙ THE CONCEPT OF STATISTICAL INDEPENDENCE

When two variables are not associated (as in Table 11.2), one can say that they are **statistically independent**. That is, an individual's score on one variable is independent of his or her score on the second variable. We identify statistical independence in a bivariate table by comparing the distribution of the dependent variable in each category of the independent variable. When two variables are statistically independent, the percentage distributions of the dependent variable within each category of the independent variable are identical. The hypothetical data presented in Table 11.2 illustrate the notion of statistical independence. Based on Table 11.2, we would say that first-generation college status is independent of one's gender.[3]

Statistical independence   The absence of association between two cross-tabulated variables. The percentage distributions of the dependent variable within each category of the independent variable are identical.

✓ *Learning Check*

The data we will use to practice calculating chi-square are also from Inman and Mayes's research. We will examine the relationship between age (independent variable) and first-generation college status (the dependent variable), as shown in the following bivariate table:

Age and First-Generation College Status

	Years of Age		
First-Generation Status	19 Years or Younger	20 Years or Older	Total
Firsts	916 (33.7%)	1,018 (53.6%)	1,934 (41.9%)
Nonfirsts	1,802 (66.3%)	881 (46.4%)	2,683 (58.1%)
Total (N)	2,718 (100.0%)	1,899 (100.0%)	4,617 (100.0%)

Source: Adapted from W. Elliot Inman and Larry Mayes, "The Importance of Being First: Unique Characteristics of First Generation Community College Students," *Community College Review* 26, no. 3 (1999): 8.

Construct a bivariate table (in percentages) showing no association between age and first-generation college status.

THE STRUCTURE OF HYPOTHESIS TESTING WITH CHI-SQUARE

The chi-square test follows the same five basic steps as the statistical tests presented in Chapter 9: (1) making assumptions, (2) stating the research and null hypotheses and selecting alpha, (3) selecting the sampling distribution and specifying the test statistic, (4) computing the test statistic, and (5) making a decision and interpreting the results. Before we apply the five-step model to a specific example, let's discuss some of the elements that are specific to the chi-square test.

The Assumptions

The chi-square test requires no assumptions about the shape of the population distribution from which the sample was drawn. However, like all inferential techniques, it assumes random sampling. It can be applied to variables measured at a nominal and/or an ordinal level of measurement.

Stating the Research and the Null Hypotheses

The research hypothesis (H_1) proposes that the two variables are related in the population.

H_1: The two variables are related in the population. (Gender and first-generation college status are statistically dependent.)

Like all other tests of statistical significance, the chi-square is a test of the null hypothesis. The null hypothesis (H_0) states that no association exists between two cross-tabulated variables in the population, and therefore, the variables are statistically independent.

H_0: There is no association between the two variables in the population. (Gender and first-generation college status are statistically independent.)

> *Refer to the data in the previous Learning Check. Are the variables age and first-generation college status statistically independent? Write out the research and the null hypotheses for your practice data.*

The Concept of Expected Frequencies

Assuming that the null hypothesis is true, we compute the cell frequencies that we would expect to find if the variables are statistically independent. These frequencies are called expected frequencies (and are symbolized as f_e). The chi-square test is based on cell-by-cell comparisons between the expected frequencies (f_e) and the frequencies actually observed (observed frequencies are symbolized as f_o).

Expected frequencies (f_e)   The cell frequencies that would be expected in a bivariate table if the two variables were statistically independent.

Observed frequencies (f_o)   The cell frequencies actually observed in a bivariate table.

Calculating the Expected Frequencies

The difference between f_o and f_e will determine the likelihood that the null hypothesis is true and that the variables are, in fact, statistically independent. When there is a large difference between f_o and f_e, it is unlikely that the two variables are independent, and we will probably reject the null hypothesis. On the other hand, if there is little difference between f_o and f_e, the variables are probably independent of each other, as stated by the null hypothesis (and therefore, we will not reject the null hypothesis).

The most important element in using chi-square to test for the statistical significance of cross-tabulated data is the determination of the expected frequencies. Because chi-square is computed on actual frequencies instead of on percentages, we need to calculate the expected frequencies based on the null hypothesis.

In practice, the expected frequencies are more easily computed directly from the row and column frequencies than from the percentages. We can calculate the expected frequencies using this formula:

$$f_e = \frac{(Column\ marginal)(Row\ marginal)}{N} \tag{11.1}$$

To obtain the expected frequencies for any cell in any cross-tabulation in which the two variables are assumed independent, multiply the row and column totals for that cell and divide the product by the total number of cases in the table.

Let's use this formula to recalculate the expected frequencies for our data on gender and first-generation college status as displayed in Table 11.1. Consider the men who were first-generation college students (the upper left cell). The expected frequency for this cell is the product of the column total (1,950) and the row total (1,936) divided by all the cases in the table (4,620):

$$f_e = \frac{(1,936)(1,950)}{4,620} = 817.14$$

For men who are nonfirsts (the lower left cell), the expected frequency is

$$f_e = \frac{(2,684)(1,950)}{4,620} = 1,132.86$$

Next, let's compute the expected frequencies for women who are first-generation college students (the upper right cell):

$$f_e = \frac{(1,936)(2,670)}{4,620} = 1,118.86$$

Finally, the expected frequency for women who are nonfirsts (the lower right cell) is

$$f_e = \frac{(2,684)(2,670)}{4,620} = 1,551.14$$

These expected frequencies are displayed in Table 11.3.

Note that the table of expected frequencies contains identical row and column marginals as the original table (Table 11.1). Although the expected frequencies usually differ from the observed frequencies (depending on the degree of relationship between the variables), the row and column marginals must always be identical with the marginals in the original table.

Table 11.3   Expected Frequencies of Men and Women and First-Generation College Status

First Generation	Men	Women	Total
Firsts	817.14	1,118.86	1,936
Nonfirsts	1,132.86	1,551.14	2,684
Total (N)	1,950	2,670	4,620

Refer to the data in the Learning Check on page 351. Calculate the expected frequencies for age and first-generation college status and construct a bivariate table. Are your column and row marginals the same as in the original table?

Calculating the Obtained Chi-Square

The next step in calculating chi-square is to compare the differences between the expected and observed frequencies across all cells in the table. In Table 11.4, the expected frequencies are shown next to the corresponding observed frequencies. Note that the difference between the observed and expected frequencies in each cell is quite large. Is it large enough to be significant? The way we decide is by calculating the **obtained chi-square** statistic:

$$\chi^2 = \Sigma \frac{(f_o - f_e)^2}{f_e} \tag{11.2}$$

Where

f_o = observed frequencies

f_e = expected frequencies

Chi-square (obtained)   The test statistic that summarizes the differences between the observed (f_o) and the expected (f_e) frequencies in a bivariate table.

According to this formula, for each cell, subtract the expected frequency from the observed frequency, square the difference, and divide by the expected frequency. After performing this operation for every cell, sum the results to obtain the chi-square statistic.

Table 11.4   Observed and Expected Frequencies of Men and Women Who Are First-Generation College Students

First Generation	Men		Women		Total
	f_o	f_e	f_o	f_e	
Firsts	691	817.14	1,245	1,118.86	1,936
Nonfirsts	1,259	1,132.86	1,425	1,551.14	2,684
Total (N)	1,950		2,670		4,620

Let's follow these procedures using the observed and expected frequencies from Table 11.4. Our calculations are displayed in Table 11.5. The obtained chi-square statistic, 57.99, summarizes the differences between the observed frequencies and the frequencies that we would expect to see if the null hypothesis were true and the variables—gender and first-generation college status—were not associated. Next, we need to interpret our obtained chi-square statistic and decide whether it is large enough to allow us to reject the null hypothesis.

Table 11.5   Calculating Chi-Square

Gender and First-Generation College Status	f_o	f_e	$f_o - f_e$	$(f_o - f_e)^2$	$\dfrac{(f_o - f_e)^2}{f_e}$
Men/firsts	691	817.14	−126.14	15,911.2996	19.47
Men/nonfirsts	1,259	1,132.86	126.14	15,911.2996	14.04
Women/firsts	1,245	1,118.86	126.14	15,911.2996	14.22
Women/nonfirsts	1,425	1,551.14	−126.14	15,911.2996	10.26

$$\chi^2 = \sum \frac{(f_o - f_e)^2}{f_e} = 57.99$$

Using the format of Table 11.5, construct a table to calculate chi-square for age and educational attainment.

✓ *Learning Check*

The Sampling Distribution of Chi-Square

In Chapter 9, we learned that test statistics such as Z and t have characteristic sampling distributions that tell us the probability of obtaining a statistic, assuming that the null hypothesis is true. In the same way, the sampling distribution of chi-square tells the probability of getting values of chi-square, assuming no relationship exists in the population.

Like other sampling distributions, the chi-square sampling distributions depend on the degrees of freedom. In fact, the chi-square sampling distribution is not one distribution, but—like the t distribution—is a family of distributions. The shape of a particular chi-square distribution depends on the number of degrees of freedom. This is illustrated in Figure 11.1, which shows chi-square distributions for 1, 5, and 9 degrees of freedom. Here are some of the main properties of the chi-square distributions that can be observed in this figure:

- The distributions are positively skewed. The research hypothesis for the chi-square is always a one-tailed test.

- Chi-square values are always positive. The minimum possible value is zero, with no upper limit to its maximum value. A chi-square of zero means that the variables are completely independent and the observed frequencies in every cell are equal to the corresponding expected frequencies.
- As the number of degrees of freedom increases, the chi-square distribution becomes more symmetrical and, with degrees of freedom greater than 30, begins to resemble the normal curve.

Determining the Degrees of Freedom

In Chapter 9, we defined degrees of freedom (df) as the number of values that are free to vary. With cross-tabulation data, we find the degrees of freedom by using the following formula:

$$df = (r-1)(c-1)$$

where

r = the number of rows

c = the number of columns

Thus, Table 11.1 with 2 rows and 2 columns has $(2 - 1)(2 - 1)$ or 1 degree of freedom. If the table had 3 rows and 2 columns, it would have $(3 - 1)(2 - 1)$ or 2 degrees of freedom.

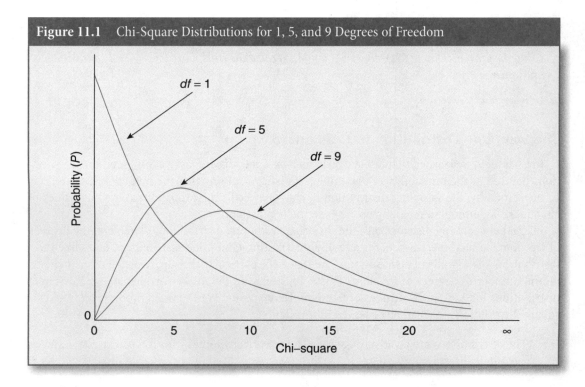

Figure 11.1   Chi-Square Distributions for 1, 5, and 9 Degrees of Freedom

Appendix D shows values of the chi-square distribution for various degrees of freedom. Notice how the table is arranged with the degrees of freedom listed down the first column and the level of significance (or *P* values) arrayed across the top. For example, with 5 degrees of freedom, the probability associated with a chi-square as large as 15.086 is .01. An obtained chi-square as large as 15.086 would occur only once in 100 samples.

The degrees of freedom in a bivariate table can be interpreted as the number of cells in the table for which the expected frequencies are free to vary, given that the marginal totals are already set. Based on our data in Table 11.3, suppose we first calculate the expected frequencies for men who are first-generation college students (f_e = 817.14). Because the sum of the expected frequencies in the first column is set at 1,950, the expected frequency of men who are nonfirsts has to be 1,132.86 (1,950 – 817.14). Similarly, all other cells are predetermined by the marginal totals and are not free to vary. Therefore, this table has only 1 degree of freedom.

Data in a bivariate table can be distorted if by chance one cell is over- or undersampled and may influence the chi-square calculation. Calculation of the degrees of freedom compensates for this, but in the case of a 2 × 2 table with just 1 degree of freedom, the value of chi-square should be adjusted by applying the Yates's correction for continuity. The formula reduces the absolute value of each ($f_o - f_e$) by .5, then the difference is squared and then divided by the expected frequency for each cell. The formula for the Yates's correction for continuity is as follows:

$$\chi^2_c = \sum \frac{(|f_o - f_e| - 0.5)^2}{f_e}$$ (11.4)

✓ *Learning Check*

Based on Appendix D, identify the probability for each chi-square value (df in parentheses):

- *12.307 (15)*
- *20.337 (21)*
- *54.052 (24)*

Making a Final Decision

With the Yates's correction, the corrected chi-square is 57.54. Refer to Table 11.6 for calculations.

We can see that 57.54 does not appear on the first row (df = 1); in fact, it exceeds the largest chi-square value of 10.827 (P = .001). We can establish that the probability of obtaining a chi-square of 57.54 is less than 001 if the null hypothesis were true. If our alpha was preset at .05, the probability of 10.827 would be well below this. Therefore, we can reject the null hypothesis that gender and first-generation college status are not associated in the population from which our sample was drawn. Remember, the larger the chi-square statistic, the smaller the *P* value providing us with more evidence to reject the null hypothesis. We can be very confident of our conclusion that there is a relationship between gender and first-generation college status in the population because the probability of this result occurring owing to sampling error is less than .001, a very rare occurrence.

Table 11.6   Calculating Yates's Correction

Gender and First-Generation College Status	$\|f_o - f_e\|$	$(\|f_o - f_e\| - .50)^2$	f_e	$\dfrac{(\|f_o - f_e\| - .5)^2}{f_e}$
Men firsts	126.14	$(125.64)^2 = 15{,}785.41$	817.14	19.32
Men nonfirsts	126.14	$(125.64)^2 = 15{,}785.41$	1,132.86	13.93
Women firsts	126.14	$(125.64)^2 = 15{,}785.41$	1,118.86	14.11
Women nonfirsts	126.14	$(125.64)^2 = 15{,}785.41$	1,551.14	10.18
Total				57.54

Review

To summarize our discussion, let's apply the five-step process of hypothesis testing. *Making Assumptions.* Our assumptions are as follows:

1. A random sample of $N = 4{,}620$ was selected.

2. The level of measurement of the variable gender is nominal.

3. The level of measurement of the variable first-generation college status is nominal.

Stating the Research and Null Hypotheses and Selecting Alpha. The research hypothesis, H_1, is that there is a relationship between gender and first-generation college status (i.e., gender and first-generation college status are statistically dependent). The null hypothesis, H_0, is that there is no relationship between gender and first-generation college status in the population (i.e., gender and first-generation college status are statistically independent). Alpha is set at .05.

Selecting the Sampling Distribution and Specifying the Test Statistic. Both the sampling distribution and the test statistic are chi-square.

Computing the Test Statistic. We should first determine the degrees of freedom associated with our test statistic:

$$df = (r - 1)(c - 1) = (2 - 1)(2 - 1) = (1)(1) = 1$$

Next, to calculate chi-square, we calculate the expected frequencies under the assumption of statistical independence. To obtain the expected frequencies for each cell, we multiply its row and column marginal totals and divide the product by N. The expected frequencies are displayed in Table 11.3.

Are these expected frequencies different enough from the observed frequencies presented in Table 11.1 to justify rejection of the null hypothesis? To find out, we calculate the chi-square statistic of 57.54 (with the Yates's correction). The calculations are shown in Table 11.6.

Making a Decision and Interpreting the Results. To determine the probability of obtaining our chi-square of 57.54, we refer to Appendix D. With 1 degree of freedom, the probability of obtaining 57.54 is less than .001 (less than our alpha of .05). We reject the null hypothesis that there is no difference in first-generation college status among men and women. Thus, we can conclude that in the population from which our sample was drawn, first-generation college status does vary by gender. Based on our sample data, we know that women are more likely to report being first-generation college students than men.

What decision can you make about the association between age and first-generation college status? Should you reject the null hypothesis at the .05 alpha level or at the .01 level?

✓ *Learning Check*

▣ A Closer Look 11.1
A Cautionary Note: Sample Size and Statistical Significance for Chi-Square

Although we found the relationship between gender and first-generation college status to be statistically significant, this in itself does not give us much information about the *strength* of the relationship or its *substantive significance* in the population. Statistical significance only helps us evaluate whether the argument (the null hypothesis) that the observed relationship occurred by chance is reasonable. It does not tell us anything about the relationship's theoretical importance or even if it is worth further investigation.

The distinction between statistical and substantive significance is important in applying any of the statistical tests discussed in Chapter 9. However, this distinction is of particular relevance for the chi-square test because of its sensitivity to sample size. The size of the calculated chi-square is directly proportional to the size of the sample, independent of the strength of the relationship between the variables.

For instance, suppose that we cut the observed frequencies for every cell in Table 11.1 exactly into half—which is equivalent to reducing the sample size by one half. This change will not affect the percentage distribution of firsts among men and women; therefore, the size of the percentage difference and the strength of the association between gender and first-generation college status will remain the same. However, reducing the observed frequencies by half will cut down our calculated chi-square by exactly half, from 57.54 to 28.77. (Can you verify this calculation?) Conversely, had we doubled the frequencies in each cell, the size of the calculated chi-square would have doubled, thereby making it easier to reject the null hypothesis.

This sensitivity of the chi-square test to the size of the sample means that a relatively strong association between the variables may not be significant when the sample size is small. Similarly, even when the association between variables is very weak, a large sample may result in a statistically significant relationship. However, just because the calculated chi-square is large and we are able to reject the null hypothesis by a large margin does not imply that the relationship between the variables is strong and substantively important.

(Continued)

(Continued)

Another limitation of the chi-square test is that it is sensitive to small expected frequencies in one or more of the cells in the table. Generally, when the expected frequency in one or more of the cells is below 5, the chi-square statistic may be unstable and lead to erroneous conclusions. There is no hard-and-fast rule regarding the size of the expected frequencies. Most researchers limit the use of chi-square to tables that either have no f_e values below 5 or have no more than 20% of the f_e values below 5.

Testing the statistical significance of a bivariate relationship is only a small step, although an important one, in examining a relationship between two variables. A significant chi-square suggests that a relationship, weak or strong, probably exists in the population and is not due to sampling fluctuation. However, to establish the strength of the association, we need to employ measures of association such as gamma, lambda (both covered later in this chapter), or Pearson's r (refer to Chapter 13). Used in conjunction, statistical tests of significance and measures of association can help determine the importance of the relationship and whether it is worth additional investigation.

▣ FOCUS ON INTERPRETATION: EDUCATION AND HEALTH ASSESSMENT

For the General Social Survey, individuals were asked to identify their highest educational degree and their level of health (poor, moderate, good, and excellent). These data are shown in Table 11.7. The bivariate table shows a clear pattern of positive association between education (the independent variable) and health assessment (the dependent variable). For instance, whereas 35% of individuals with some college or more reported excellent health, 12.5% of those with less than a high school degree reported the same. Similarly, whereas only 2.1% of respondents with some college or more reported poor health, 12.5% of respondents with less than a high school degree fell into that category.

The differences in the levels of health among the three educational groups seem sizable. However, it is not clear whether these differences are owing to chance or to sampling fluctuations, or whether they reflect a real pattern of association in the population. In the following discussion, we will not review our calculations (though they are presented in Table 11.8). Rather, our focus will be on the five-step model and drawing conclusions about the relationship between health and educational degree.

Making Assumptions. Our assumptions are as follows:

1. A random sample of $N = 844$ is selected.

2. The level of measurement of the variable *education* is ordinal.

3. The level of measurement of the variable *health* is ordinal.

Stating the Research and Null Hypotheses and Selecting Alpha. Our hypotheses are as follows:

H_1: There is a relationship between education and health in the population. (Education and health are statistically dependent.)

Table 11.7   Health by Educational Level, General Social Survey

	Educational Level			
Health	Less Than High School	High School Degree	Some College or More	Total
Poor	16	26	6	48
	(12.5%)	(6.0%)	(2.1%)	(5.7%)
Moderate	44	79	39	162
	(34.4%)	(18.1%)	(13.9%)	(19.2%)
Good	52	213	137	402
	(40.6%)	(48.9%)	(48.9%)	(47.6%)
Excellent	16	118	98	232
	(12.5%)	(27.1%)	(35.0%)	(27.5%)
Total	128	436	280	844
	(100%)	(100.1%)	(99.9%)	(100%)

H_0: There is no relationship between education and health in the population. (Education and health are statistically independent.)

For this test, we'll select an alpha of .01.

Selecting the Sampling Distribution and Specifying the Test Statistic. The sampling distribution is chi-square; the test statistic is also chi-square.

Computing the Test Statistic. The degrees of freedom for Table 11.7 is

$$df = (r-1)(c-1) = (4-1)(3-1) = (3)(2) = 6$$

The chi-square obtained is 53.96. The detailed calculations are shown in Table 11.8.

Making a Decision and Interpreting the Results. To determine if the observed frequencies are significantly different from the expected frequencies, we compare our calculated chi-square with Appendix D. With 6 degrees of freedom, our chi-square of 53.96 exceeds the largest listed chi-square value of 22.457 ($P = .001$). We determine that the probability of observing our obtained chi-square of 53.96 is less than .001, and less than our alpha of .01. We can reject the null hypothesis that there are no differences in health among the different educational groups. Thus, we conclude that in the population from which our sample was drawn, health does vary by educational attainment. The positive relationship between the two variables is significant.

Table 11.8   Calculating Chi-Square for Education and Health

Education and Health	f_o	f_e	$f_o - f_e$	$(f_o - f_e)^2$	$\dfrac{(f_o - f_e)^2}{f_e}$
Less than high school/poor	16	7.3	8.7	75.69	10.37
Less than high school/moderate	44	24.6	19.4	376.36	15.30
Less than high school/good	52	61.0	−9.0	81.0	1.33
Less than high school/excellent	16	35.2	−19.2	368.64	10.47
High school/poor	26	24.8	1.2	1.44	0.06
High school/moderate	79	83.7	−4.7	22.09	0.26
High school/good	213	207.7	5.3	28.09	0.13
High school/excellent	118	119.8	−1.8	3.24	0.03
Some college or more/poor	6	15.9	−9.9	98.01	6.16
Some college or more/moderate	39	53.7	−14.7	216.09	4.02
Some college or more/good	137	133.4	3.6	12.96	0.10
Some college or more/excellent	98	77.0	21	441	5.73

$$\chi^2 = \Sigma \frac{(f_o - f_e)^2}{f_e} = 53.96$$

▣ READING THE RESEARCH LITERATURE: VIOLENT OFFENSE ONSET BY GENDER, RACE, AND AGE

Paul Mazerolle, Alex Piquero, and Robert Brame (2010)[4] investigate whether violent onset offenders have distinct career dimensions from offenders whose initial offending involves nonviolence. In Table 11.9, the researchers examine the relationship between gender, race, and age, and nonviolent versus violent onset using chi-square analysis. Their data are based on 1,503 juvenile offenders in Queensland, Australia.

Note that the obtained chi-square and its probability are reported for each pair of variables. There are two significant models, violent offense by gender and violent offense by age. For each cell, the N and percentage are reported.

According to the researchers' report, first, while males, in absolute terms, contribute many more violent onset youth to the overall total, in proportional terms, females exhibit a higher prevalence rate. The findings show that 18.32% of females exhibit violent onset compared with 11.71% of males.

Moreover, and perhaps unexpectedly, no differences were observed in the prevalence of violent onset across indigenous (11.83%) and nonindigenous groups (12.83%). However, in proportional terms, a higher prevalence of violent onset was observed for late-onset (14.74%) as opposed to early-onset offenders (9.67%), which was significant at $P < .01$.[5]

Table 11.9   Violent Offense Onset by Gender, Race, and Age

	Nonviolent Onset N (%)	*Violent Onset* N (%)	*Total* N (%)
Gender			
Male	1,146 (88.29)	152 (11.71)	1,298 (100)
Female	156 (81.68)	35 (18.32)	191 (100)
Total	1,302	187	1,489
			$\chi^2 = 6.331$**
Indigenous status			
Nonindigenous	815 (87.17)	120 (12.83)	935 (100)
Indigenous	477 (88.17)	64 (11.83)	541 (100)
			$\chi^2 = 0.317$
Age at first offense			
Less than 14 years	579 (90.33)	62 (9.67)	641 (100)
14 years and older	723 (85.26)	125 (14.74)	848 (100)
			$\chi^2 = 8.539$**

Note: **$P < .01$.

✓ *Learning Check*

For the bivariate table with age and first-generation college status, the value of the obtained chi-square is 181.15 with 1 degree of freedom. Based on Appendix D, we determine that its probability is less than .001. This probability is less than our alpha level of .05. We reject the null hypothesis of no relationship between age and first-generation college status. If we reduce our sample size by half, the obtained chi-square is 90.58. Determine the P value for 90.58. What decision can you make about the null hypothesis?

▣ PROPORTIONAL REDUCTION OF ERROR: A BRIEF INTRODUCTION

Earlier, we introduced cross-tabulation where the relationship between two variables was analyzed by making a number of percentage comparisons. Using the chi-square statistic, we also examined whether two variables are statistically related. Now we review special measures of association for nominal and ordinal variables. These measures enable us to use a single summarizing measure or number for analyzing the pattern of relationship between two variables. Unlike chi-square, measures of association reflect the strength of the relationship and, at times, its direction (whether it is positive or negative). They also indicate the usefulness of predicting the dependent variable from the independent variable.

In this section, we discuss four measures of association: lambda (measures of association for nominal variables), gamma and Kendall's tau-*b* (measures of association between ordinal variables), and Cramer's *V* (a chi-square related measure of association). In Chapter 13, we introduce Pearson's correlation coefficient, which is used for measuring bivariate association between interval-ratio variables.

Measure of association   A single summarizing number that reflects the strength of a relationship, indicates the usefulness of predicting the dependent variable from the independent variable, and often shows the direction of the relationship.

All the measures of association discussed here and in Chapter 13 are based on the concept of the proportional reduction of error, often abbreviated as PRE. According to the concept of PRE, two variables are associated when information about one can help us improve our prediction of the other.

Proportional reduction of error (PRE)   The concept that underlies the definition and interpretation of several measures of association. PRE measures are derived by comparing the errors made in predicting the dependent variable while ignoring the independent with errors made when making predictions that use information about the independent variable.

Table 11.10 may help us grasp intuitively the general concept of PRE. Using General Social Survey (GSS) 2010 data, Table 11.10 shows a moderate relationship between the independent variable, *educational attainment*, and the dependent variable, *support for abortion if the woman is poor and can't afford any more children*. The table shows that 69.0% of the respondents who did not receive a bachelor's degree were antiabortion, compared with only 45.9% of the respondents who had a bachelor's degree or more.

The conceptual formula for all[6] PRE measures of association is

$$PRE = \frac{E_1 - E_2}{E_1} \tag{11.5}$$

where

E_1 = errors of prediction made when the independent variable is ignored (Prediction 1)

E_2 = errors of prediction made when the prediction is based on the independent variable (Prediction 2)

Table 11.10   Support for Abortion by Degree

| Support for Abortion | Degree | | Total |
	Less Than Bachelor's	Bachelor's or More	
No	462	124	586
	69.0%	45.9%	62.3%
Yes	208	146	354
	31.0%	54.1%	37.7%
Total	670	270	940
	100.0%	100.0%	100.0%

Source: GSS, 2010.

All PRE measures are based on comparing predictive error levels that result from each of the two methods of prediction. Let's say that we want to predict a respondent's position on abortion, but we do not know anything about the degree he or she has. Based on the row totals in Table 11.10, we could predict that every respondent in the sample is antiabortion because this is the modal category of the variable *abortion position*. With this prediction, we would make 354 errors because in fact 586 respondents in this group are antiabortion but 354 respondents are pro-choice. Thus,

$$E_1 = 940 - 586 = 354$$

How can we improve this prediction by using the information we have on each respondent's educational attainment? For our new prediction, we will use the following rule: If a respondent has less than a bachelor's degree, we predict that he or she will be antiabortion; if a respondent has a bachelor's degree or more, we predict that he or she is pro-choice. It makes sense to use this rule because we know, based on Table 11.10, that respondents with a lower educational attainment are more likely to be antiabortion, while respondents who have a bachelor's degree or more are more likely to be pro-choice. Using this prediction rule, we will make 332 errors (instead of 354) because 124 of the respondents who have a bachelor's degree or more are actually antiabortion, whereas 208 of the respondents who have less than a bachelor's degree are pro-choice (124 + 208 = 332). Thus,

$$E_2 = 124 + 208 = 332$$

Our first prediction method, ignoring the independent variable (educational attainment), resulted in 354 errors. Our second prediction method, using information we have about the independent variable (educational attainment), resulted in 332 errors. If the variables are *associated*, the second method will result in fewer errors of prediction than the first method. The stronger the relationship is between the variables, the larger will be the reduction in the number of errors of prediction.

Let's calculate the proportional reduction of error for Table 11.10 using Formula 11.5. The proportional reduction of error resulting from using educational attainment to predict position on abortion is

$$PRE = \frac{354 - 332}{354} = 0.06$$

PRE measures of association can range from 0.0 to ±1.0. A PRE of zero indicates that the two variables are not associated; information about the independent variable will not improve predictions about the dependent variable. A PRE of ±1.0 indicates a perfect positive or negative association between the variables; we can predict the dependent variable without error using information about the independent variable. Intermediate values of PRE will reflect the strength of the association between the two variables and therefore the utility of using one to predict the other. The more the measure of association departs from 0.00 in either direction, the stronger the association. PRE measures of association can be multiplied by 100 to indicate the percentage improvement in prediction.

▣ A Closer Look 11.2
What Is Strong? What Is Weak? A Guide to Interpretation

The more you work with various measures of association, the better feel you will have for what particular values mean. Until you develop this skill, here are some guidelines regarding what is generally considered a strong relationship and what is considered a weak relationship.

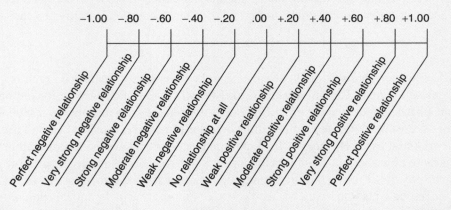

Keep in mind that these are only rough guidelines. Often, the interpretation for a measure of association will depend on the research context. A +0.30 in one research field will mean something a little different from a +0.30 in another research field. Zero, however, always means the same thing: no relationship.

A PRE of 0.06 indicates that there is a weak relationship between respondents' educational attainment and their position on abortion. (Refer to A Closer Look 11.2 for a discussion of the strength of a relationship.) A PRE of 0.06 means that we have improved our prediction of respondents' position on abortion by just 6% (0.06 × 100 = 6.0%) by using information on their educational attainment.

▣ LAMBDA: A MEASURE OF ASSOCIATION FOR NOMINAL VARIABLES

In June of 2013, Edward Snowden, a former National Security Agency employee, leaked confidential information to certain members of the American and international press, revealing that the federal government collected personal data on approximately one third of American citizens after September 11, 2001 in a supposed effort to monitor potential terrorist attacks. Brought on by the passing of the USA PATRIOT Act in 2001, the federal government was more easily able to collect personal data (e.g., phone and Internet conversations) from U.S. civilians and noncivilians. Many citizens believed personal data surveillance and collection was reserved specifically for individuals suspected of engaging in terrorism. However, a significant amount of controversy emerged when Americans learned they had a one-in-three chance of being monitored by the federal government, including such things as their social media and e-mail accounts. Further controversy emerged when it was made known that the U.S. government had illegally tapped the European Union offices, in addition to infiltrating EU internal computer networks.[7]

In light of this controversial event, let's examine the relationship between party identification, the independent variable, and approval/disapproval of the federal government's collection of phone and Internet data for antiterrorism efforts, the dependent variable. Table 11.11 displays results from the Pew Research Center based on a nationally representative survey taken during June 12–16, 2013. We can see 840 U.S. citizens classified by their party identification and their stance on collection of personal data for antiterrorism efforts. We will consider a respondent's party identification to be the independent variable and approval/disapproval of the federal government's collection of phone and Internet data for antiterrorism efforts to be the dependent variable.

Because party identification and approval/disapproval are nominal variables, we need to apply a measure of association suitable for calculating relationships between nominal variables. Such a measure will help us determine how strongly associated party identification is with one's position on the collection of phone and Internet data as part of antiterrorism efforts. Lambda is such a PRE measure.

Table 11.11   Position on Government Collection of Phone and Internet Data by Party Identification

	Party Identification		
Collection of Data for Antiterrorism Efforts	*Republican*	*Democrat*	*Row Total*
Approve	175	282	457
Disapprove	198	185	383
Column total	373	467	840

Source: Pew Research Center, "Public Split over Impact of NSA Leak, But Most Want Snowden Prosecuted," June 17, 2013.

Lambda   An asymmetrical measure of association, lambda is suitable for use with nominal variables and may range from 0.0 to 1.0. It provides us with an indication of the strength of an association between the independent and dependent variables.

A Method for Calculating Lambda

Take a look at Table 11.11 and examine the row totals, which show the distribution of the variable collection of data for antiterrorism efforts. If we had to predict whether Democrats would approve or disapprove of these data collection efforts, our best bet would be to guess the mode, which is that everyone approved of phone and Internet data collection. This prediction will result in the smallest possible error. The number of wrong predictions we make using this method is actually 383, since only 457 (the mode) out of 840 indicated they approved of the collection of phone and Internet data for antiterrorism efforts ($840 - 457 = 383$).

Now take another look at Table 11.11, but this time let's consider party identification when we predict approval/disapproval of phone and Internet data. Again, we can use the mode, but this time we apply it separately for Republicans and Democrats. The mode for Republicans is "Disapprove" (198); therefore, we can predict that all Republicans disapprove of the collection of phone and Internet data for antiterrorism efforts. With this method of prediction, we make 175 errors, since 175 out of 373 Republicans approve of phone and Internet data collection ($373 - 198 = 175$). Next, we look at the group of Democrats. The mode for this group is "Approve"; this will be our prediction for this group. This method of prediction results in 185 errors ($467 - 282 = 185$). The total number of errors is thus $175 + 185$, or 360 errors.

Let's now put it all together and state the procedure for calculating lambda in more general terms.

1. Find E_1, the errors of prediction made when the independent variable is ignored. To find E_1, find the mode of the dependent variable and subtract its frequency from N. For Table 11.11,

$$E_1 = N - \text{Modal frequency}$$

$$E_1 = 840 - 457 = 383$$

2. Find E_2, the errors made when the prediction is based on the independent variable. To find E_2, find the modal frequency for each category of the independent variable, subtract it from the category total to find the number of errors, and then add up all the errors. For Table 11.11,

$$\text{Republicans} = 373 - 198 = 175$$

$$\text{Democrats} = 467 - 282 = 185$$

$$E_2 = 175 + 185 = 360$$

3. Calculate lambda using Formula 11.5

$$Lambda = \frac{E_1 - E_2}{E_1} = \frac{383 - 360}{383} = 0.06$$

Lambda may range in value from 0.0 to 1.0. Zero indicates that there is nothing to be gained by using the independent variable to predict the dependent variable. A lambda of 1.0 indicates that by using the independent variable as a predictor, we are able to predict the dependent variable without any error. In our case, a lambda of 0.06 is less than one quarter of the distance between 0.0 and 1.0, indicating that for this sample of respondents, party identification and approval/disapproval of the government's collection of phone and Internet data for antiterrorism efforts are only slightly associated.

The proportional reduction of error indicated by lambda, when multiplied by 100, can be interpreted as follows: By using information on respondents' party identification to predict one's position on the collection of phone and Internet data, we have reduced our error of prediction by 6% ($0.06 \times 100 = 6\%$). In other words, if we rely on respondents' party identification to predict whether they approve or disapprove of the government's collection of phone and Internet data for antiterrorism efforts, we would reduce our error of prediction by 6 out of 100, or 6% (0.06×100).

Some Guidelines for Interpreting Lambda

Lambda is an asymmetrical measure of association. This means that lambda will vary depending on which variable is considered the independent variable and which the dependent variable. In our example, we considered one's approval/disapproval of the government's collection of phone and Internet data on behalf of antiterrorism efforts as the dependent variable and party identification as the independent variable, and not vice versa. Had we considered, instead, party identification as the dependent variable and one's approval/disapproval of the government's collection of phone and Internet data as the independent variable, we would have obtained a slightly different lambda value.

Asymmetrical measure of association   A measure whose value may vary depending on which variable is considered the independent variable and which the dependent variable.

The method of calculation follows the same guidelines even when the variables are switched. However, exercise caution in calculating lambda, especially when the independent variable is arrayed in the rows rather than in the columns. To avoid confusion, it is safer to switch the variables and follow the convention of arraying the independent variable in the columns; then follow the exact guidelines suggested for calculating lambda. Remember, however, that although lambda can be calculated either way, ultimately what guides the decision of which variables to consider as independent or dependent is the theoretical question posed by the researcher.

Lambda is always zero in situations in which the mode for each category of the independent variable falls into the same category of the dependent variable. A problem with interpreting lambda arises in situations in which lambda is zero, but other measures of association indicate that the variables are associated. To avoid this potential problem, examine the percentage differences in the table whenever lambda is exactly equal to zero. If the percentage differences are very small (usually 5% or less), lambda is an appropriate measure of association for the table. However, if the percentage differences are larger, indicating that the two variables may be associated, lambda will be a poor choice as a measure of association. In such cases, we may want to discuss the association in terms of the percentage differences or select an alternative measure of association.

▣ CRAMER'S *V*: A CHI-SQUARE–RELATED MEASURE OF ASSOCIATION FOR NOMINAL VARIABLES

Cramer's *V* is an alternative measure of association that can be used for nominal variables. It is based on the value of chi-square (discussed earlier in this chapter) and ranges between 0 to 1, with 0 indicating no association and 1 indicating perfect association. Because it cannot take negative values, it is considered a nondirectional measure. Unfortunately Cramer's *V* is somewhat limited because the results cannot be interpreted using the PRE framework. It is calculated using the following formula:

$$Cramer's\ V = \sqrt{\frac{\chi^2}{N \times m}} \tag{11.6}$$

where m = smaller of $(r-1)$ or $(c-1)$.

Earlier, we tested the hypothesis that education and health assessment are related in the population (Tables 11.7 and 11.8). The analysis yielded a chi-square value of 53.96, leading us to reject the null hypothesis that there are no differences in health among different educational groups. We concluded that in the population from which our sample was drawn, health does vary by educational attainment.

We can use Cramer's *V* to measure the relative strength of the association between health assessment and level of education using Formula 11.6.

$$Cramer's\ V = \sqrt{\frac{\chi^2}{N \times m}} = \sqrt{\frac{53.96}{844 \times 2}} = \sqrt{0.032} = 0.18$$

A Cramer's *V* of 0.18 tells us that there is a weak association between health assessment and level of education.

▣ FOCUS ON INTERPRETATION: GAMMA AND KENDALL'S TAU-*b*

In this section, we discuss a way to measure and interpret an association between two *ordinal* variables. If there is an association between the two variables, knowledge of one variable will enable us to make better predictions of the other variable.

Ordinal variables are very common in social science research. The GSS contains many questions that ask people to indicate their responses on an ordinal scale—for example, "very often," "fairly often," "occasionally," or "almost never."

Let's look at a research example in which the association between two ordinal variables is considered. We want to examine the hypothesis that the higher one's educational level, the more satisfied he or she is with his or her financial situation. To examine this hypothesis, we selected two variables from the 2010 GSS: the variable education (EDUC), with those indicating that they had 11 or fewer years of education in one category and those reporting that they had 12 or more years of education into a second category. The variable satisfaction with financial situation (SATFIN) has two categories: "satisfied" and "unsatisfied."

Table 11.12   Financial Satisfaction by Education

| Financial Satisfaction (Y) | Education (X) | | Total |
	High School or More	Less Than High School	
Satisfied	25.8%	19.3%	24.9%
	(332)	(40)	(372)
Unsatisfied	74.2%	80.7%	75.1%
	(957)	(167)	(1,124)
Total	100%	100%	100%
(N)	(1,289)	(207)	(1,496)

Source: GSS, 2010.

Table 11.12 displays the cross-tabulation of these two variables, with education as the independent variable and satisfaction with financial situation as the dependent variable. We find that 80.7% of those with less than a high school degree are unsatisfied with their financial situation, as compared with 74.2% of those with at least a high school degree. The percentage difference (80.7% − 74.2% = 6.5%) suggests that the variables are related. We can examine the percentage difference across those who are satisfied with their financial situation (25.8% − 19.3% = 6.5%), and reach the same conclusion.

The next step in analyzing the relationship between education and financial satisfaction is to select a measure that will enable us to assess the strength and the direction (sign) of that relationship. We selected gamma because our variables (education and financial satisfaction) are ordinal variables. We will focus on interpreting gamma rather than calculating it.

The SPSS output showing the value of gamma is presented below. It reports that the gamma for the table is .183, indicating a weak positive relationship between education and financial satisfaction. The positive sign of gamma indicates that as education increases, so does the level of financial satisfaction. A gamma of .183 indicates that by using education to predict financial satisfaction, we've reduced our prediction error by 18.3%.

Symmetric Measures

		Value	Asymp. Std. Error[a]	Approx. T[b]	Approx. Sig.
Ordinal by Ordinal	Kendall's tau-b	.051	.024	2.128	.033
	Gamma	.183	.090	2.128	.033
N of Valid Cases		1496			

a. Not assuming the null hypothesis.

b. Using the asymptotic standard error assuming the null hypothesis.

Gamma and Kendall's tau-*b* are symmetrical measures of association suitable for use with ordinal variables or with dichotomous nominal variables. This means that their value will be the same regardless of which variable is the independent variable or the dependent variable. Thus, if we had wanted to predict education from financial satisfaction rather than the opposite, we would have obtained the same gamma. Both gamma and Kendall's tau-*b* can vary from 0.0 to ±1.0 and provide us with an indication of the strength and direction of the association between the variables. Gamma and Kendall's tau-*b* can be positive or negative. A Gamma or Kendall's tau-*b* of 1.0 indicates that the relationship between the variables is positive and that the dependent variable can be predicted without any errors based on the independent variable. A gamma of −1.0 indicates a perfect, negative association between the variables. A gamma or a Kendall's tau-*b* of zero reflects no association between the two variables; hence there is nothing to be gained by using the independent variable to predict the dependent variable.

Gamma   A symmetrical measure of association suitable for use with ordinal variables or with dichotomous nominal variables. It can vary from 0.0 to ±1.0 and provides us with an indication of the strength and direction of the association between the variables.

Kendall's tau-b   A symmetrical measure of association suitable for use with ordinal variables. It can vary from 0.0 to ±1.0. It provides an indication of the strength and direction of the association between the variables. Kendall's tau-*b* will always be lower than gamma.

Symmetrical measure of association   A measure whose value will be the same when either variable is considered the independent variable or the dependent variable.

▣ USING ORDINAL MEASURES WITH DICHOTOMOUS VARIABLES

Measures of association for ordinal data are not influenced by the modal category as is lambda. Consequently, an ordinal measure of association might be preferable for tables when an association cannot be detected by lambda. We can use an ordinal measure for some tables where one or both variables would appear to be measured on a nominal scale. Dichotomous variables (those with only two categories) can be treated as ordinal variables for most purposes. In this chapter, we calculated lambda to examine the association between abortion attitudes and educational attainment (Table 11.10). Although both variables might be considered as nominal variables—because both are dichotomized (yes/no; high school or less/more than high school)—they could also be treated as ordinal variables. Thus, the association might also be examined using gamma, an ordinal measure of association.[8]

FOCUS ON INTERPRETATION: THE GENDER GAP IN GUN CONTROL

Is there a gender gap in attitude towards gun control? Surveys have shown that women are generally more in favor of stricter gun laws than men.

Let's examine data from the GSS 2010 survey comparing men and women's attitudes towards requiring gun permits. The table below shows that more women (83.2%) than men (67.0%) are in favor of gun permits. These findings confirm the results obtained by most public opinion polls.

| | | | RESPONDENTS SEX | | Total |
			MALE	FEMALE	
FAVOR OR OPPOSE GUN PERMITS	FAVOR	Count	272	469	741
		% within RESPONDENTS SEX	67.0%	83.2%	76.4%
	OPPOSE	Count	134	95	229
		% within RESPONDENTS SEX	33.0%	16.8%	23.6%
Total		Count	406	564	970
		% within RESPONDENTS SEX	100.0%	100.0%	100.0%

The observed percentage difference between men and women is a useful indicator that there is a gender gap in opinions about gun control. However, we are seeking a measure that will enable us to assess the strength of that relationship. We can select gamma for our purposes because the independent and dependent variables are dichotomous.

The SPSS output showing the value of gamma is presented below. It reports that the gamma for the table is −0.417,[9] indicating a moderate relationship between sex and opinions about requiring gun permits. By using sex to predict men and women's opinion about requiring gun permits, we've reduced our prediction error by almost half (41.7%).

Symmetric Measures

		Value	Asymp. Std. Error[a]	Approx. T[b]	Approx. Sig.
Ordinal by Ordinal	Gamma	-.417	.064	-5.728	.000
N of Valid Cases		970			

a. Not assuming the null hypothesis.

b. Using the asymptotic standard error assuming the null hypothesis.

MAIN POINTS

- The chi-square test is an inferential statistical technique designed to test for a significant relationship between nominal or ordinal variables organized in a bivariate table. The test is conducted by testing the null hypothesis that no association exists between two cross-tabulated variables in the population, and therefore, the variables are statistically independent.

- The obtained chi-square (χ^2) statistic summarizes the differences between the observed frequencies (f_o) and the expected frequencies (f_e)—the frequencies we would have expected to see if the null hypothesis were true and the variables were not associated. The Yates's correction for continuity is applied to all 2 × 2 tables.

- The sampling distribution of chi-square tells the probability of getting values of chi-square, assuming no relationship exists in the population. The shape of a particular chi-square sampling distribution depends on the number of degrees of freedom.

- Measures of association are single summarizing numbers that reflect the strength of the relationship between variables, indicate the usefulness of predicting the dependent from the independent variable, and often show the direction of the relationship.

- Proportional reduction of error (PRE) underlies the definition and interpretation of several measures of association. PRE measures are derived by comparing the errors made in predicting the dependent variable while ignoring the independent variable with errors made when making predictions that use information about the independent variable.

- Measures of association may be symmetrical or asymmetrical. When the measure is symmetrical, its value will be the same regardless of which of the two variables is considered the independent or dependent variable. In contrast, the value of asymmetrical measures of association may vary depending on which variable is considered the independent variable and which the dependent variable.

- Lambda is an asymmetrical measure of association suitable for use with nominal variables. It can range from 0.0 to 1.0 and gives an indication of the strength of an association between the independent and the dependent variables.

- Gamma is a symmetrical measure of association suitable for ordinal variables or for dichotomous nominal variables. It can vary from 0.0 to ±1.0 and reflects both the strength and direction of the association between two variables.

- Kendall's tau-*b* is a symmetrical measure of association suitable for use with ordinal variables. Unlike gamma, it accounts for pairs tied on the independent and dependent variable. It can vary from 0.0 to ±1.0. It provides an indication of the strength and direction of the association between two variables.

- Cramer's *V* is a measure of association for nominal variables. It is based on the value of chi-square and ranges between 0.0 to 1.0. Because it cannot take negative values, it is considered a nondirectional measure.

KEY TERMS

asymmetrical measure
    of association
chi-square (obtained)
chi-square test
expected
    frequencies (f_e)

gamma
Kendall's tau-*b*
lambda
measure of association
observed
    frequencies (f_o)

proportional
    reduction of error
statistical
    independence
symmetrical measure
    of association

$SAGE edge™

Sharpen your skills with SAGE edge at **edge.sagepub.com/frankfort7e**. **SAGE edge for students** provides a personalized approach to help you accomplish your coursework goals in an easy-to-use learning environment.

SPSS DEMONSTRATION

[GSS10SSDS]

Demonstration 1: Producing the Chi-Square Statistic for Cross-Tabulations

The SPSS Cross-tabs procedure was previously demonstrated in Chapter 10. This procedure can also be used to calculate a chi-square value for a bivariate table.

Click on *Analyze, Descriptive Statistics,* and *Crosstabs,* then on the *Statistics* button. You will see the Dialog box shown in Figure 11.2. To request the chi-square statistic, click on the Chi-square box in the upper left corner. You can also request expected frequencies via the Cells button.

Click on *Continue.* In this demonstration, we will look at the relationship between educational degree (DEGREE) and political views (POLVIEWS). Place POLVIEWS in the Row(s) box and DEGREE in the Column(s) box. Then click on *OK* to run the procedure.

The resulting output includes the chi-square statistics as shown in Figure 11.3. SPSS produces quite a bit of output, perhaps more than what is expected. We will concentrate on the first row of information, the Pearson chi-square.

The Pearson chi-square has a value of 58.708 with 24 degrees of freedom. SPSS calculates the significance of this chi-square to be .000. The interpretation is that educational degree and political views are related.

Exercises

Figure 11.2   Crosstabs Statistics Dialog Box

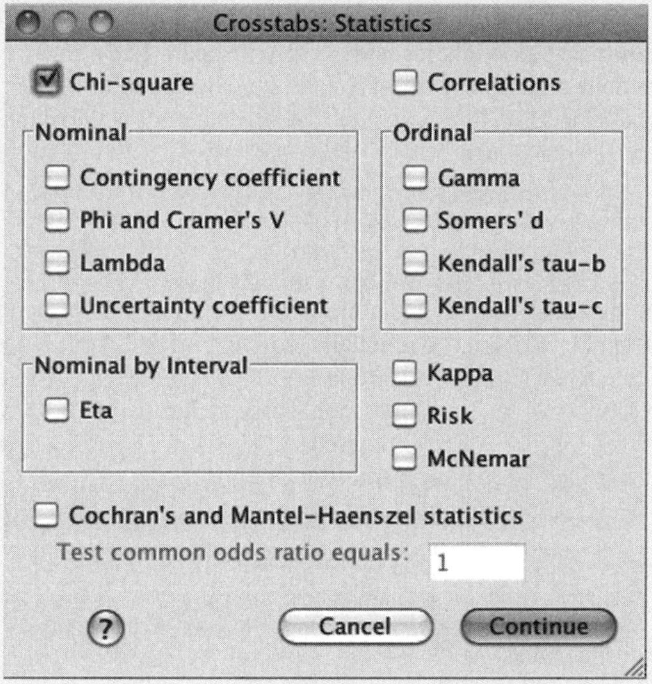

Figure 11.3   Chi-Square Test Output for DEGREE by POLVIEWS

Chi-Square Tests

	Value	df	Asymp. Sig. (2-sided)
Pearson Chi-Square	58.708[a]	24	.000
Likelihood Ratio	57.527	24	.000
Linear-by-Linear Association	2.766	1	.096
N of Valid Cases	1457		

a. 2 cells (5.7%) have expected count less than 5. The minimum expected count is 4.30.

Specifically, as educational degree increases (graduate degree attainment), it appears that men and women are more likely to report being "extremely liberal."

The last portion of the output from SPSS allows us to check for the assumption that all expected values in each cell of the table are 5 or greater. The output indicates that two of the cells or 5.7% have a value less than 5. This is lower than our threshold of 20%.

Demonstration 2: Producing Nominal and Ordinal Measures of Association for Bivariate Tables

In Chapter 10, we used the Crosstabs procedure in SPSS to create bivariate tables. The same procedure is used to request measures of association. We'll begin by investigating the relationship between belief in the Bible (BIBLE) and support for legal abortions for women for any reason (ABANY) in the 2010 GSS.

Click on *Analyze, Descriptive Statistics*, then *Crosstabs* to get to the Crosstabs dialog box. Put ABANY in the Row(s) box and BIBLE in the Column(s) box. Then click on the Statistics button. The Statistics dialog box (Figure 11.4) has about a dozen statistics from which to choose. Note that four statistics are listed in separate categories for "Nominal" and "Ordinal" data. Lambda is listed in the former, and gamma and Kendall's tau-*b* in the latter. Cramer's *V* can be easily obtained by checking the Phi and Cramer's *V* box. The other measures of association, such as Somer's *d* and Phi, will not be discussed in this textbook.

Figure 11.4 The Statistics Dialog Box

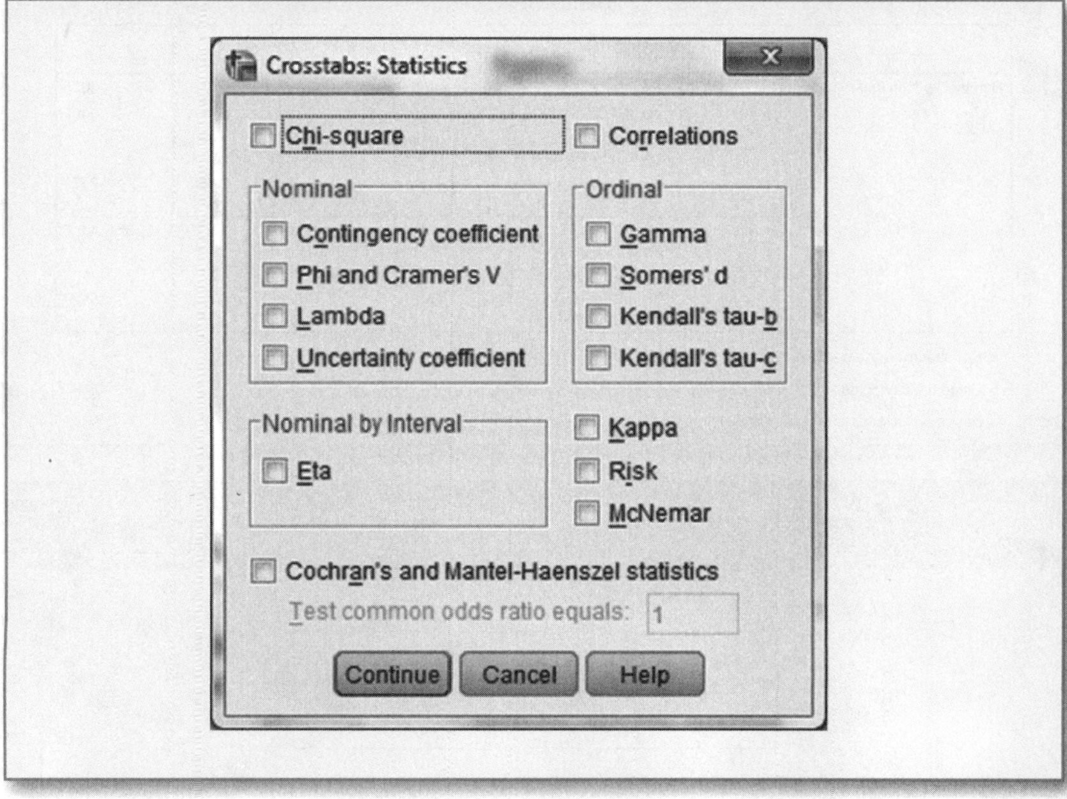

Since both variables are nominal, check the box for lambda. It is critical that we, as users of statistical programs, understand which statistics to select in any procedure. SPSS, like most programs, can't help us select the appropriate statistic for an analysis. Now click on Continue and then OK to create the table (Figure 11.5).

The first table is Case Processing Summary showing the number of valid and missing cases (not shown here). The second table should be a bivariate table of our two variables (not shown). Below this table is a table labeled "Directional Measures." For now, we will only concern ourselves with the first two columns. Lambda is listed with three values. We've learned that the value of lambda depends on which variable is considered the dependent variable. In our example, attitude toward abortion for any reason is dependent, so lambda is .139. This indicates a weak relationship between the two variables. We can conclude that knowing the respondent's belief about the Bible increases the ability to predict his or her abortion attitude by just 13.9%.

SPSS also calculates a symmetrical lambda for those tables, where there is no independent or dependent variable. This calculation goes beyond the scope of this book. (It is not simply an average of the two other values of lambda.) In addition, as a kind of bonus, SPSS provides the Goodman and Kruskal tau statistic, another nominal measure of association, even though it was not requested. These measures will always be produced when lambda is requested.

If we checked the box for the Phi and Cramer's *V* in the Statistics dialog box, we would also get the output shown in Figure 11.6.

Figure 11.5 SPSS Output Displaying the Relationship Between BIBLE and ABANY

Directional Measures

			Value	Asymp. Std. Error[a]	Approx. T[b]	Approx. Sig.
Nominal by Nominal	Lambda	Symmetric	.106	.029	3.515	.000
		ABORTION IF WOMAN WANTS FOR ANY REASON Dependent	.139	.034	3.798	.000
		FEELINGS ABOUT THE BIBLE Dependent	.083	.043	1.863	.062
	Goodman and kruskal tau	ABORTION IF WOMAN WANTS FOR ANY REASON Dependent	.148	.021		.000[c]
		FEELINGS ABOUT THE BIBLE Dependenet	.068	.010		.000[c]

a. Not assuming the null hypothesis.

b. Using the asymptotic standard error assuming the null hypothesis.

c. Based on chi-square approximation

Figure 11.6 SPSS Output Displaying the Cramer's *V* for the Relationship Between BIBLE and ABANY

Symmetric Measures

		Value	Approx. Sig.
Nominal by Nominal	Phi	.385	.000
	Cramer's V	.385	.000
N of Valid Cases		930	

Cramer's *V* is .385, which indicates a moderate association between belief in the Bible and support for legal abortions for women for any reason.

We can also use the same procedures to calculate gamma for ordinal measures. For this demonstration, we'll examine the relationship between educational attainment (DEGREE) and attitudes toward same-sex relations (HOMOSEX). Respondents were asked whether same-sex relations were wrong (i.e., always wrong, almost always wrong, sometimes wrong, or not wrong at all). Both variables are ordinal measurements.

Click on *Analyze*, *Descriptive Statistics*, then *Crosstabs* to get to the Crosstabs dialog box. Put HOMOSEX in the Row(s) box and DEGREE in the Column(s) box. Then click on the Statistics button. The Statistics dialog box has about a dozen statistics from which to choose. Click on gamma and Kendall's tau-*b* listed in the ordinal box. SPSS produces two separate tables (other than Case Processing Summary), the first is the bivariate table between HOMOSEX and DEGREE and the second is the table of symmetric measures, gamma and Kendall's tau-*b*, which we requested (Figure 11.7).

Figure 11.7   SPSS Output Displaying the Relationship Between DEGREE and HOMOSEX

Symmetric Measures

		Value	Asymp. Std. Error[a]	Approx. T[b]	Approx. Sig.
Ordinal by Ordinal	Kendall's tau-b	.171	.027	6.186	.000
	Gamma	.262	.042	6.186	.000
N of Valid Cases		930			

a. Not assuming the null hypothesis.

b. Using the asymptotic standard error assuming the null hypothesis

The Kendall's tau-*b* statistic is in the first row under the column labeled "Value" followed by the gamma statistic. For this bivariate table, both the Kendall's tau-*b* statistic (.171) and the gamma statistic (.262) indicate a weak to moderate positive relationship between educational level and attitudes toward same-sex relations. Using Kendall's tau-*b*, we can reduce about 17% of our error in predicting attitudes toward same-sex relations by using information about respondent's education. Using gamma, about 26% of the error in predicting attitudes toward same-sex relations would be reduced if we had information about respondent's educational attainment. Note that given how HOMOSEX is coded, the positive gamma indicates that as DEGREE increases, respondents are more likely to indicate that same sex relations is not wrong at all (coded 4)

SPSS PROBLEMS

[GSS10SSDS and MTF11SSDS]

1. The GSS 2010 contains a series of questions about the role of women at home and at work. It is very likely that the responses to these questions vary by sex—or do they?
   a. Use SPSS to investigate the relationship between SEX and FECHLD (a working mother does not hurt her children). Create a bivariate table and ask for appropriate percentages and expected

values. Does the table have a large number of cells with expected values less than 5? Are there any surprises in the data?

b. Have SPSS calculate chi-square for the table.

c. Test the null hypothesis at the .05 significance level. What do you conclude?

d. Select another demographic variable (DEGREE or CLASS) and investigate its relationship with (FECHLD).

2. Is it better for a man to work and a woman to stay at home? Women and men were asked this question in the GSS 2010. Investigate the relationship between marital status (MARITAL) and responses to this question (FEFAM). Have SPSS calculate the cross-tabulation of both variables, along with chi-square (set alpha at .05). What can you conclude?

3. The MTF data set includes teens' attitudes toward different types of drug use—alcohol (ATDRINK), marijuana (ATWEED), and cigarettes (ATSMOKE). Create bivariate tables with these drug variables, along with demographic variables such as sex, race, or age. Have SPSS calculate the appropriate percentages and chi-squares (set alpha at .05). What relationship exists between your selected demographic variable and attitudes toward trying these drugs?

4. Use GSS 2010 to examine the relationship between respondent's health (HEALTH) and social class (CLASS). Treat social class as the independent variable.

a. Request the appropriate measures of associations to describe the relationship.

b. Add SEX as a control variable and calculate the association measure for each partial table. Is the relationship stronger for women or men? Can you think of reasons why this might be so?

c. What other control variables may be appropriate? Continue to examine the relationship between HEALTH and CLASS with one additional control variable.

5. Investigate the relationship between the abortion attitudes in GSS 2010 (e.g., ABANY) and various demographic variables (you might begin with gender, age, or race). Examine the relationship of these variables based on the appropriate measures of association. For example, you might examine whether attitude toward each of the abortion items has a similar relationship to gender. That is, if females are supportive of abortion for rape victims, are they also supportive of abortion in other circumstances? Try exploring these relationships further by adding control variables. You might create tables of abortion attitude by race and by gender. When you have finished the analysis, write a short report summarizing the findings. Suggest possible causes for the relationships you found.

CHAPTER EXERCISES

1. We examine the relationship between gender and fear of walking at night in their neighborhood (FEAR) based on GSS 2010 data.

Afraid to Walk at Night in Your Neighborhood	Men	Women	Total
Yes	94	242	336
No	343	295	638
Total	437	537	974

    a. What is the number of degrees of freedom for this table?

    b. Test the null hypothesis that gender and fear of walking alone are independent (alpha = .05). What do you conclude?

    c. If alpha were set at .01, would your decision change? Explain.

2. Illegal immigration in the United States is a complex matter, and people have diverse and conflicting ideas on how to best address it. The 2010 GSS contains several questions on this topic. For this exercise, we present the SPSS analysis of political party identification and the variable UNDOCKID, which measures support of the statement whether children of illegal immigrants should qualify for citizenship.

    a. What percent of Democrats indicate that children of immigrants should qualify for citizenship? What percent of Republicans?

    b. Based on an alpha of .01, what can you conclude about the relationship between political party identification and UNDOCKID?

Figure 11.8   Cross-Tabulation and Chi-Square for NPARTYID and UNDOCKID

npartyid Recoded party id * undockid US CITIZENSHIP FOR CHILDREN OF ILLEGAL IMMIGRANTS Crosstabulation

Count

		undockid US CITIZENSHIP FOR CHILDREN OF ILLEGAL IMMIGRANTS		Total
		1 YES, QUALIFY	2 NO, NOT QUALIFY	
npartyid Recoded party id	1.00 democrat	172	53	225
	2.00 independent	42	30	72
	3.00 republican	80	75	155
Total		294	158	452

Chi-Square Tests

	Value	df	Asymp. Sig. (2-sided)
Pearson Chi-Square	26.586[a]	2	.000
Likelihood Ratio	26.869	2	.000
Linear-by-Linear Association	25.670	1	.000
N of Valid Cases	452		

a. 0 cells (0.0%) have expected count less than 5. The minimum expected count is 25.17.

---

3. We extend our analysis of fear and gender, from Exercise 1, with the addition of a control variable, race. Bivariate tables for whites and blacks are presented.

For Whites

Afraid to Walk at Night in Your Neighborhood	Men	Women	Total
Yes	59	160	219
No	253	224	477
Total	312	384	696

For Blacks

Afraid to Walk at Night in Your Neighborhood	Men	Women	Total
Yes	7	52	59
No	41	38	79
Total	48	90	138

    a. Which racial group has a higher percentage of respondents indicating that they are afraid to walk at night in their neighborhood?

    b. Regardless of race, are women more likely to report than men that they are afraid to walk at night in their neighborhood?

    c. For each table, test the hypothesis that gender and fear to walk at night are independent (alpha = .01). What do you conclude?

4. We continue our analysis from Exercise 2, this time examining the relationship between educational attainment (DEGREE) and citizenship for children of illegal immigrants (UNDOCKID). Refer to Figure 11.9. Based on an alpha of .05, do you reject the null hypothesis? Explain the reason for your answer.

5. Does access to marijuana vary by the size of the community a teenager lives in? The MTF (2012) survey asked teens how easy it was to obtain marijuana (GWEED). Their responses are shown by residence size—small town, medium-sized city, and large city. Refer to Figure 11.10. Based on an alpha of .05, what would you conclude? Does marijuana access vary by residential city size?

6. Teens were asked in the MTF 2012 survey to report their level of happiness (how are things these days?). The bivariate table includes responses organized by teen's race. Based on an alpha of .05, test whether race and happiness are independent.

How are things these days?	Race of Respondent			Total
	Black	White	Hispanic	
Not happy	33	93	30	156
Pretty happy	116	488	119	723
Very happy	32	214	40	286
Total	181	795	189	1,165

Figure 11.9 Cross-Tabulation and Chi-Square for DEGREE and UNDOCKID

degree RS HIGHEST DEGREE * undockid US CITIZENSHIP FOR CHILDREN OF ILLEGAL IMMIGRANTS Crosstabulation

Count

		undockid US CITIZENSHIP FOR CHILDREN OF ILLEGAL IMMIGRANTS		Total
		1 YES, QUALIFY	2 NO, NOT QUALIFY	
degree RS HIGHEST DEGREE	0 LT HIGH SCHOOL	53	14	67
	1 HIGH SCHOOL	144	82	226
	2 JUNIOR COLLEGE	22	18	40
	3 BACHELOR	56	32	88
	4 GRADUATE	28	18	46
Total		303	164	467

Chi–Square Tests

	Value	df	Asymp. Sig. (2–sided)
Pearson Chi–Square	8.182[a]	4	.085
Likelihood Ratio	8.641	4	.071
Linear–by–Linear Association	2.829	1	.093
N of Valid Cases	467		

a. 0 cells (0.0%) have expected count less than 5. The minimum expected count is 14.05.

7. Earlier in this chapter, we reviewed Inman and Mayes (1999) research on first-generation college students. The researchers also examined the relationship between student race and first-generation college status. Based on their data, test whether race is independent of first-generation college status (alpha = .01).

First-Generation College Status	Student Race					Total
	White	Black	Native American	Hispanic	Asian American	
Firsts	1,742	102	41	19	6	1,910
Nonfirsts	2,392	119	45	25	22	2,603
Total	4,134	221	86	44	28	4,513

Exercises

Figure 11.10   Cross-Tabulation and Chi-Square for NGREWUP and GWEED

Ngrewup Recoded grew up * gweed how easy is it to obtain marijuana? Crosstabulation

| | | | gweed How easy is it do obtain marijuana? | | | | | |
			1 PROB IMP: (1)	2 VRY DIFF: (2)	3 FRLY DIF: (3)	4 FRLY EAS: (4)	5 VRY EASY: (5)	Total
Ngrewup Recoded grew up	1.00 small town	Count	35	22	35	131	320	543
		% within Ngrewup Recoded grew up	6.4%	4.1%	6.4%	24.1%	58.9%	100.0%
	2.00 medium city	Count	14	8	18	87	183	310
		% within Ngrewup Recoded grew up	4.5%	2.6%	5.8%	28.1%	59.0%	100.0%
	3.00 large cityy	Count	17	14	24	99	232	386
		% within Ngrewup Recoded grew up	4.4%	3.6%	6.2%	25.6%	60.1%	100.0%
Total		Count	66	44	77	317	735	1239
		% within Ngrewup Recoded grew up	5.3%	3.6%	6.2%	25.6%	59.3%	100.0%

Chi-Square Tests

	Value	df	Asymp.Sig. (2-sided)
Pearson Chi-Squre	4.872[a]	8	.771
Likelihood Ratio	4.909	8	.767
Linear-by-Linear Association	1.492	1	.222
N of Valid Cases	1239		

a. 0 cells (0.0%) have expected count less than 5. The minimum expected count is 11.01.

8. Is there a relationship between the race of violent offenders and their victims? Data from the U.S. Department of Justice (Expanded Homicide Data Table 6, 2011) are presented below.

| | Characteristics of Offender | | |
Characteristics of Victim	White	Black	Other
White	2,630	448	33
Black	193	2,447	9
Other	180	45	99

a. Let's treat race of offenders as the independent variable and race of victims as the dependent variable. If we first ignore the independent variable and try to predict race of victim, how many errors will we make?

b. If we now take into account the independent variable, how many errors of prediction will we make for those offenders who are white? Black offenders? Other offenders?

c. Combine the answers in (a) and (b) to calculate the proportional reduction in error for this table based on the independent variable. How does this statistic improve our understanding of the relationship between the two variables?

9. Let's continue our analysis of offenders and victims of violent crime. In the following table, data for the sex of offenders and the sex of victims are reported (U.S. Department of Justice, Expanded Homicide Data Table 6, 2011).

	Sex of Offender	
Sex of Victim	Male	Female
Male	3,760	450
Female	1,590	140

a. Treating sex of offender as the independent variable, how many errors of prediction will be made if the independent variable is ignored?
b. How many fewer errors will be made if the independent variable is taken into account?
c. Combine your answers in (a) and (b) to calculate lambda. Discuss the relationship between these two variables.
d. Which lambda is stronger, the one for sex of offenders/victims or race of offenders/victims?

10. Does the belief that women are not suited for politics vary by gender and/or educational attainment? GSS 2010 respondents were asked if they believe that women were not suited for politics (FEPOL). Examine how this variable is associated with respondent's sex (SEX). Examine and interpret the output below. Would lambda be appropriate as a measure of association? Why or why not? Would gamma and Kendall's tau-b be appropriate measures? Why or why not?

WOMEN NOT SUITED FOR POLITICS * RESPONDENTS SEX Crosstabulation

Count

		RESPONDENTS SEX		
		MALE	FEMALE	Total
WOMEN NOT SUITED FOR POLITICS	AGREE	83	112	195
	DISAGREE	349	421	770
Total		432	533	965

Directional Measures

			Value	Asymp. Std. Error	Approx. T	Approx. Sig.
Nominal by Nominal	Lambda	Symmetric	.000	.000	.	.
			.000	.000	.	.
			.000	.000	.	.

Symmetric Measures

		Value	Asymp. Std. Error	Approx. T	Approx. Sig.
Ordinal by Ordinal	Kendall's tau-b	-.022	.032	-.695	.487
	Gamma	-.056	.081	-.695	.487
N of Valid Cases		965			

11. The GSS asked respondents to report their opinion on spanking as a method to discipline a child (SPANKING). Examine how respondents' attitudes toward spanking a child are associated with SEX, CLASS, and MARITAL (marital status). Using the SPSS output below, interpret the measures of association for each of the variable pairs.

SPANKING and SEX

Crosstab

Count

		RESPONDENTS SEX		Total
		MALE	FEMALE	
FAVOR SPANKING TO DISCIPLINE CHILD	STRONGLY AGREE	120	121	241
	AGREE	217	260	477
	DISAGREE	104	126	230
	STRONGLY DISAGREE	15	44	59
Total		456	551	1007

Symmetric Measures

		Value	Asymp. Std. Error	Approx. T	Approx. Sig.
Ordinal by Ordinal	Kendall's tau-b	.067	.029	2.305	.021
	Gamma	.118	.051	2.305	.021
N of Valid Cases		1007			

SPANKING and CLASS

Count

		SUBJECTIVE CLASS IDENTIFICATION (RECODED)				
		Upper Class	Middle Class	Working Class	Lower Class	Total
FAVOR SPANKING TO DISCIPLINE CHILD	STRONGLY AGREE	3	85	128	23	239
	AGREE	15	195	224	39	473
	DISAGREE	4	121	84	19	228
	STRONGLY DISAGREE	2	33	19	5	59
Total		24	434	455	86	999

Symmetric Measures

		Value	Asymp. Std. Error	Approx. T	Approx. Sig.
Ordinal by Ordinal	Kendall's tau-b	-.113	.028	-4.014	.000
	Gamma	-.178	.044	-4.014	.000
N of Valid Cases		999			

SPANKING and MARITAL STATUS

Crosstab

Count

		MARITAL STATUS					
		MARRIED	WIDOWED	DIVORCED	SEPARATED	NEVER MARRIED	Total
FAVOR SPANKING TO DISCIPLINE CHILD	STRONGLY AGREE	120	20	29	8	64	241
	AGREE	245	33	70	12	117	477
	DISAGREE	99	23	43	9	56	230
	STRONGLY DISAGREE	31	6	6	2	14	59
Total		495	82	148	31	251	1007

Directional Measures

			Value	Asymp. Std. Error	Approx. T	Approx. Sig.
Nominal by Nominal	Lambda	Symmetric	.000	.000	.	.
			.000	.000	.	.
			.000	.000	.	.

Analysis of Variance

M any research questions require us to look at multiple samples or groups, at least more than two at a time. We may be interested in studying the influence of ethnic identity (white, African American, Asian American, Latino/a) on church attendance, the influence of social class (lower, working, middle, and upper) on President Barack Obama's job-approval ratings, or the effect of educational attainment (less than high school, high school graduate, some college, and college graduate) on household income. Note that each of these examples requires a comparison between multiple demographic or ethnic groups, more than the two-group comparisons that we reviewed in Chapter 9. While it would be easy to confine our analyses between two groups, our social world is much more complex and diverse.

Let's say that we're interested in examining educational attainment—on average, how many years of education do Americans achieve? For 2010, the U.S. Census reported that 87% of adults (25 years and older) completed at least a high school degree, and 30% of all adults attained at least a bachelor's degree.[1] During his first term of office, President Obama pledged that the United States would have the world's highest proportion of college graduates by 2020. Special attention has been paid to the educational achievement of Latino students. Data from the U.S. Census, as well as from the U.S. Department of Education, confirm that Latino students continue to have lower levels of educational achievement than other racial or ethnic groups.

In Chapter 9, Testing Hypotheses, we introduced statistical techniques to assess the difference between two sample means or proportions. For our example in Table 9.2, we compared the difference in educational attainment for blacks and whites. But what if we wanted to examine separate groups of men and women by their race or ethnicity? Is there a significant variation in educational attainment among black women, Hispanic women, black men, and Hispanic men?

Table 12.1   Educational Attainment (measured in years) for Four GSS Groups

Black Males n₁ = 6	Hispanic Males n₂ = 4	Black Females n₃ = 6	Hispanic Females n₄ = 5
16	14	16	14
12	12	18	12
14	11	16	12
12	11	14	13
12		16	14
12		12	

We've taken a random sample of 21 men and women from the General Social Survey (GSS), grouped them into four demographic categories, and included their educational attainment in Table 12.1. With the *t*-test statistic we covered in Chapter 9, we could analyze only two samples at a time. We would have to analyze the mean educational attainment of black women versus Hispanic women, black women versus black men, and black women versus Hispanic men, and so on. (Confirm that we would have to analyze six different pairs.) In the end, we would have a tedious series of *t*-test statistic calculations, and we still wouldn't be able to answer our original question: Is there a difference in educational attainment among all *four* demographic groups?

There is a statistical technique that will allow us to examine all the four groups or samples simultaneously. This technique is called **analysis of variance** (ANOVA). ANOVA follows the same five-step model of hypothesis testing that we used with *t* test and *Z* test for proportions (in Chapter 9) and chi-square (in Chapter 11). In this chapter, we review the calculations for ANOVA and discuss two applications of ANOVA from the research literature.

Analysis of variance (ANOVA)   An inferential statistics technique designed to test for a significant relationship between two variables in two or more groups or samples.

▣ UNDERSTANDING ANALYSIS OF VARIANCE

Recall that the *t* test examines the difference between two means, $\overline{Y}_1 - \overline{Y}_2$, while the null hypothesis assumed that there was no difference between them: $\mu_1 = \mu_2$. Rejecting the null hypothesis meant that there was a significant difference between the two mean scores (or the populations from which the samples were drawn). In our Chapter 9 example, we analyzed the difference between mean years of education for blacks and whites. Based on our t-test statistic, we rejected the null hypothesis, concluding that white men and women, on average, have significantly more years of education than black men and women do.

The logic of ANOVA is the same but extending to two or more groups. For the data presented in Table 12.1, ANOVA will allow us to examine the variation among four means $\left(\overline{Y}_1, \overline{Y}_2, \overline{Y}_3, \overline{Y}_4 \right)$, and the null hypothesis can be stated as follows: $\mu_1 = \mu_2 = \mu_3 = \mu_4$. Rejecting the null hypothesis for ANOVA indicates that there is a significant variation among the four samples (or the four populations from which the samples were drawn) and that at least one of the sample means is significantly different from the others. In our example, it suggests that years of education (dependent variable) do vary by group membership (independent variable). When ANOVA procedures are applied to data with one dependent and one independent variable, it is called a **one-way ANOVA**.

One-way ANOVA   Analysis of variance application with one dependent and one independent variable.

The means, standard deviations, and variances for the samples have been calculated and are shown in Table 12.2. Note that the four mean educational years are not identical, with black women having the highest educational attainment. Also, based on the standard deviations, we can tell that the samples are relatively homogeneous with deviations within 1.00 to 2.07 years of the mean. We already know that there is a difference between the samples, but the question remains: Is this difference significant? Do the samples reflect a relationship between demographic group membership and educational attainment in the general population?

✓ *Learning Check*

We've calculated the mean and standard deviation scores for each group in Table 12.2. Compute each mean (Chapter 4) and standard deviation (Chapter 5) and confirm that our statistics are correct.

Table 12.2   Means, Variances, and Standard Deviations for Four GSS 2006 Groups

Black Males $n_1 = 6$	Hispanic Males $n_2 = 4$	Black Females $n_3 = 6$	Hispanic Females $n_4 = 5$
16	14	16	14
12	12	18	12
14	11	16	12
12	11	14	13
12		16	14
12		12	

Black Males $n_1 = 6$	Hispanic Males $n_2 = 4$	Black Females $n_3 = 6$	Hispanic Females $n_4 = 5$
$\overline{Y}_1 = 13.00$	$\overline{Y}_2 = 12.00$	$\overline{Y}_3 = 15.33$	$\overline{Y}_4 = 13.00$
$S_1 = 1.67$	$S_2 = 1.41$	$S_3 = 2.07$	$S_4 = 1.00$
$S_1^2 = 2.79$	$S_2^2 = 1.99$	$S_3^2 = 4.28$	$S_4^2 = 1.00$
$\overline{Y} = 13.48$			

To determine whether the differences are significant, ANOVA examines the differences *between* our four samples, as well as the differences *within* a single sample. The differences can also be referred to as variance or variation, which is why ANOVA is the analysis of *variance*. What is the difference between one sample's mean score and the overall mean? What is the variation of individual scores within one sample? Are all the scores alike (no variation), or is there a broad variation in scores? ANOVA allows us to determine whether the variance between samples is larger than the variance within the samples. If the variance is larger between samples than the variance within samples, we know that educational attainment varies significantly across the samples. It would support the notion that group membership explains the variation in educational attainment.

▣ THE STRUCTURE OF HYPOTHESIS TESTING WITH ANOVA

The Assumptions

ANOVA requires several assumptions regarding the method of sampling, the level of measurement, the shape of the population distribution, and the homogeneity of variance.

1. Independent random samples are used. Our choice of sample members from one population has no effect on the choice of sample members from the second, third, or fourth population. For example, the selection of Hispanic men has no effect on the selection of any other sample.

2. The dependent variable, years of education, is an interval-ratio level of measurement. Some researchers also apply ANOVA to ordinal-level measurements.

3. The population is normally distributed. Although we cannot confirm whether the populations are normal, given that our N is so small, we must assume that the population is normally distributed to proceed with our analysis.

4. The population variances are equal. Based on our calculations in Table 12.2, we see that the sample variances, although not identical, are relatively homogeneous.[2]

Stating the Research and the Null Hypotheses and Setting Alpha

The research hypothesis (H_1) proposes that at least one of the means is different. We do not identify which one(s) will be different, or larger or smaller, we only predict that a difference does exist.

H_1: At least one mean is different from the others.

ANOVA is a test of the null hypothesis of no difference between any of the means. Since we're working with four samples, we include four μs in our null hypothesis.

H_0: $\mu_1 = \mu_2 = \mu_3 = \mu_4$

As we did in other models of hypothesis testing, we'll have to set our alpha. Alpha is the level of probability at which we'll reject our null hypothesis. For this example, we'll set alpha at .05.

The Concepts of Between and Within Total Variance

A word of caution before we proceed: Since we're working with four different samples and a total of 21 respondents, we'll have a lot of calculations. It's important to be consistent with your notations (don't mix up numbers for the different samples) and be careful with your calculations.

Our primary set of calculations has to do with the two types of variance: between-group variance and within-group variance. The estimate of each variance has two parts, the sum of squares and degrees of freedom (*df*).

The **between-group sum of squares** or *SSB* measures the difference in average years of education between our four groups. Sum of squares is the short form for "sum of squared deviations." For *SSB*, what we're measuring is the sum of squared deviations between each sample mean to the overall mean score. The formula for the *SSB* can be presented as follows:

$$SSB = \sum n_k \left(\overline{Y}_k - \overline{Y} \right)^2 \qquad (12.1)$$

where

n_k = the number of cases in a sample (*k* represents the number of different samples)

$\overline{Y}_k$ = the mean of a sample

$\overline{Y}$ = the overall mean

SSB can also be understood as the amount of variation in the dependent variable (years of education) that can be attributed to or explained by the independent variable (the four demographic groups).

Between-group sum of squares or SSB   The sum of squared deviations between each sample mean to the overall mean score.

Within-group sum of squares or *SSW* measures the variation of scores within a single sample or, as in our example, the variation in years of education within one group. *SSW* is also referred to as the amount of unexplained variance, since this is what remains after we consider the effect of the specified independent variable. The formula for *SSW* measures the sum of squared deviations within each group: between each individual score with its sample mean.

$$SSW = \sum \left(Y_i - \overline{Y}_k \right)^2 \tag{12.2}$$

where

Y_i = each individual score in a sample

$\overline{Y}_k$ = the mean of a sample

Even with our small sample size, if we were to use Formula 12.2, we'd have a tedious and cumbersome set of calculations. Instead, we suggest using the following computational formula for within-group variation or *SSW*:

$$SSW = \sum Y_i^2 - \sum \frac{\left(\sum Y_k \right)^2}{n_k} \tag{12.3}$$

where

Y_i^2 = the squared scores from each sample

$\sum Y_k$ = the sum of the scores of each sample

n_k = the number of cases in a sample

Within-group sum of squares or SSW   Sum of squared deviations within each group, calculated between each individual score and the sample mean.

Together, the explained (*SSB*) and unexplained (*SSW*) variances compose the amount of total variation in scores. The **total sum of squares** or *SST* can be represented by

$$SST = \sum \left(Y_i - \overline{Y} \right)^2 = SSB + SSW \tag{12.4}$$

where

Y_i = each individual score

$\overline{Y}$ = the overall mean

Total sum of squares or SST   The total variation in scores, calculated by adding *SSB* and *SSW*.

The second part of estimating the between-group and within-group variances is calculating the degrees of freedom. Degrees of freedom are also discussed in Chapters 9 and 11. For ANOVA, we have to calculate two degrees of freedom. For *SSB*, the degrees of freedom are determined by

$$df_b = k - 1$$

(12.5)

where k is the number of samples.

For *SSW*, the degrees of freedom are determined by

$$df_w = N - k$$

(12.6)

where

N = total number of cases

k = number of samples

Finally, we can estimate the between-group variance by calculating mean square between. Simply stated, mean squares are averages computed by dividing each sum of squares by its corresponding degrees of freedom. Mean square between can be represented by

$$\text{Mean square between} = SSB / df_b$$

(12.7)

and the within-group variance or mean square within can be represented by

$$\text{Mean square within} = SSW / df_w$$

(12.8)

Mean square between   Sum of squares between divided by its corresponding degrees of freedom.

Mean square within   Sum of squares within divided by its corresponding degrees of freedom.

▣ A Closer Look 12.1
Decomposition of *SST*

According to Formula 12.4, sum of squares total (*SST*) is equal to

$$SST = \sum (Y_i - \bar{Y})^2 = SSB + SSW$$

You can see that the between sum of squares (explained variance) and within sum of squares (unexplained variance) account for the total variance (*SST*) in a particular dependent variable. How does that apply to a single case in our educational attainment example? Let's take the first black female in Table 12.1 with 16 years of education.

Her total deviation (corresponding to *SST*) is based on the difference between her score from the overall mean (Formula 12.4). Her score is quite a bit higher than the overall mean education of 13.48 years. The difference of her score from the overall mean is 2.52 years (16 − 13.48). Between-group deviation (corresponding to *SSB*) can be determined by measuring the difference between her group average from the overall mean (Formula 12.1). We've already commented on the higher educational attainment for black females (average of 15.33 years) when compared with the other three demographic groups. The deviation between the group average and overall average for black females is 1.85 years (15.33 − 13.48). Finally, the within-group deviation (corresponding to *SSW*, Formula 12.2) is based on the difference between the first black female's years of education and the group average for black females: 0.67 years (16 − 15.33). So for the first black female in our sample, *SSB* + *SSW* = *SST* or 1.85 + 0.67 = 2.52. In a complete ANOVA problem, we're computing these two sources of deviation (*SSB* and *SSW*) to obtain *SST* (Formula 12.4) for everyone in the sample.

The *F* Statistic

Together the mean square between (Formula 12.7) and mean square within (Formula 12.8) compose the *F* ratio obtained or *F* statistic. Developed by R. A. Fisher, the *F* statistic is the ratio of between-group variance to within-group variance and is determined by Formula 12.9:

$$F = \frac{\text{Mean square between}}{\text{Mean square within}} = \frac{SSB/df_b}{SSW/df_w} \tag{12.9}$$

We know that a larger *F* obtained statistic means that there is more between-group variance than within-group variance, increasing the chances of rejecting our null hypothesis. In Table 12.3, we present additional calculations to compute *F*.

Let's calculate between-group sum of squares and degrees of freedom based on Formulas 12.1 and 12.5. The calculation for *SSB* is

$$\sum n_k \left(\overline{Y}_k - \overline{Y} \right)^2 = 6(13.00 - 13.48)^2 + 4(12.00 - 13.48)^2 + 6(15.33 - 13.48)^2 + 5(13.00 - 13.48)^2$$
$$= 31.83$$

The degrees of freedom for *SSB* is $k - 1$ or $4 - 1 = 3$. Based on Formula 12.7, the mean square between is

$$\text{Mean square between} = \frac{31.83}{3} = 10.61$$

Table 12.3   Computational Worksheet for ANOVA

Black Males	Hispanic Males	Black Females	Hispanic Females
$n_1 = 6$	$n_2 = 4$	$n_3 = 6$	$n_4 = 5$
16	14	16	14
12	12	18	12
14	11	16	12
12	11	14	13
12		16	14
12		12	
$\bar{Y}_1 = 13.00$	$\bar{Y}_2 = 12.00$	$\bar{Y}_3 = 15.33$	$\bar{Y}_4 = 13.00$
$S_1 = 1.67$	$S_2 = 1.41$	$S_3 = 2.07$	$S_4 = 1.00$
$S_1^2 = 2.79$	$S_2^2 = 1.99$	$S_3^2 = 4.28$	$S_4^2 = 1.00$
$\Sigma Y_1 = 78$	$\Sigma Y_2 = 48$	$\Sigma Y_3 = 92$	$\Sigma Y_4 = 65$
$\Sigma Y_1^2 = 1028$	$\Sigma Y_2^2 = 582$	$\Sigma Y_3^2 = 1432$	$\Sigma Y_4^2 = 849$

$$\bar{Y} = 13.48$$

The within-group sum of squares and degrees of freedom are based on Formulas 12.3 and 12.6. The calculation for SSW is

$$SSW = \Sigma Y_i^2 - \Sigma \frac{\left(\Sigma Y_k\right)^2}{n_k} = (1{,}028 + 582 + 1{,}432 + 849) - \left(\frac{78^2}{6} + \frac{48^2}{4} + \frac{92^2}{6} + \frac{65^2}{5}\right)$$

$$= 3{,}891 - 3{,}845.67$$

$$= 45.33$$

The degrees of freedom for SSW is $N - k = 21 - 4 = 17$. Based on Formula 12.8, the mean square within is

$$\text{Mean square within} = \frac{45.33}{17} = 2.67$$

Finally, our calculation of F is based on Formula 12.9:

$$F = \frac{10.61}{2.67} = 3.97$$

F *ratio or* F *statistic* The test statistic for ANOVA, calculated by the ratio of mean square between to mean square within.

Making a Decision

To determine the probability of calculating an *F* statistic of 3.97, we rely on Appendix E, the distribution of the *F* statistic. Appendix E lists the corresponding values of the *F* distribution for various degrees of freedom and two levels of significance, .05 and .01.

Since we set alpha at .05, we'll refer to the table marked "*P* = .05." Note that Appendix E includes two *df*s. These refer to our degrees of freedom, $df_1 = df_b$ and $df_2 = df_w$.

Because of the two degrees of freedom, we'll have to determine the probability of our *F* obtained differently than we did with *t* test or chi-square. For this ANOVA example, we'll have to determine the corresponding *F*, also called the *F* critical, when $df_b = 3$ and $df_w = 17$, and $\alpha = .05$.

Based on Appendix E, the *F* critical is 3.20, while our *F* obtained (the one that we calculated) is 3.97. Since our *F* obtained is greater than the *F* critical (3.97 > 3.20), we know that its probability is <.05, extending into the shaded area. (If our *F* obtained was <3.20, we could determine that its probability was greater than our alpha [α] of .05, in the unshaded area of the *F* distribution curve. Refer to Figure 12.1.) We can reject the null hypothesis of no difference and conclude that there is a significant difference in educational attainment between the four groups.

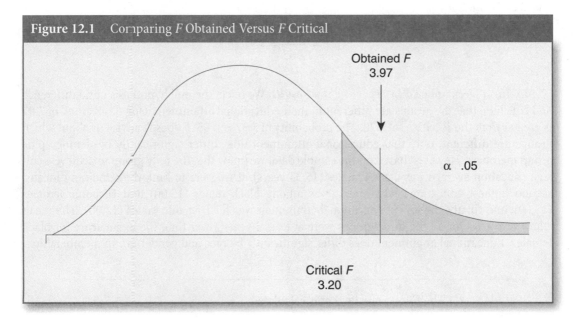

Figure 12.1 Comparing *F* Obtained Versus *F* Critical

▣ THE FIVE STEPS IN HYPOTHESIS TESTING: A SUMMARY

To summarize, we've calculated an analysis of variance test examining the difference between four demographic groups and their average years of education.

Making Assumptions.

1. Independent random samples are used.

2. The dependent variable, years of education, is an interval-ratio level of measurement.

3. The population is normally distributed.

4. The population variances are equal.

Stating the Research and Null Hypothesis and Selecting Alpha.

H_1: At least one mean is different from the others.

H_0: $\mu_1 = \mu_2 = \mu_3 = \mu_4$

$$\alpha = .05$$

Selecting the Sampling Distribution and Specifying the Test Statistic. The *F* distribution and *F* statistic are used to test the significance of the difference between the four sample means.

Computing the Test Statistic. We need to calculate the between-group and within-group variation (sum of squares and degrees of freedom). We estimate $SSB = 10.61$ ($df_b = 3$) and $SSW = 2.67$ ($df_w = 17$). Based on Formula 14.9,

$$F = \frac{10.61}{2.67} = 3.97$$

Making a Decision and Interpreting the Results. We reject the null hypothesis of no difference and conclude that the groups are different in their educational attainment. Our *F obtained* of 3.97 is greater than the *F critical* of 3.20. The probability of 3.97 is <.05. *F* doesn't advise us about which groups are different, only that educational attainment does differ significantly by demographic group members. However, based on the sample data, we know that the only group to achieve a college education average was black females (15.33 years). If we were to rank the remaining means, second highest educational attainment was among black males (13.00) and Hispanic females (13.00), and finally, the lowest educational attainment was for Hispanic males (12.00). The mean education years for all the three groups were at least 2 years lower than the mean score for black females. Educational attainment does differ significantly by race and gender group membership.

F *obtained*   The *F*-test statistic that is calculated.

F *critical*   The *F*-test statistic that corresponds to the alpha level, df_w, and df_b (as in Appendix E).

A Closer Look 12.2
Assessing the Relationship Between Variables

Based on our five-step model of *F*, we've determined that there is a significant difference between the four demographic groups in their educational attainment. We rejected the null hypothesis and concluded that the years of education (our dependent variable) do vary by group membership (our independent variable). But can we say anything about how strong the relationship is between the variables?

The correlation ratio or eta square (η^2) allows us to make a statement about the strength of the relationship. Eta square is determined by the following:

$$\eta^2 = \frac{SSB}{SST} \tag{12.10}$$

The ratio of *SSB* to *SST* (*SSB* + *SSW*) represents the proportion of variance that is explained by the group (or independent) variable. Eta square indicates the strength of the relationship between the independent and dependent variables, ranging in value from 0 to 1.0. As eta square approaches 0, the relationship between the variables is weaker, and as eta square approaches 1, the relationship between the variables is stronger.

Based on our ANOVA example,

$$\eta^2 = \frac{10.61}{10.61 + 2.67} = \frac{10.61}{13.28} = 0.80$$

We can state that 80% of the variation in educational attainment can be attributed to demographic group membership. Or, phrased another way, 80% of the variation in the dependent variable (educational attainment) can be explained by the independent variable (group membership). So how strong is this relationship? We can base our determination of the strength on A Closer Look 12.1 from Chapter 12, the same scale that we used to assess gamma. Based on A Closer Look 12.1, we can conclude that there is a very strong relationship between group membership and educational attainment.

FOCUS ON INTERPRETATION: ARE IMMIGRANTS GOOD FOR AMERICA'S ECONOMY?

We rely on SPSS to examine the relationship between respondent's political views (three ordinal categories: liberal, moderate, and conservative) and their level of agreement to the statement: Immigrants are generally good for America's economy. The variable IMMAMECO has five ordinal categories: 1—agree strongly; 2—agree; 3—neither; 4—disagree; and 5—disagree strongly. We will set alpha at .05 to assess our results. SPSS output are presented as Figure 12.2.

Figure 12.2   SPSS ANOVA Output: Political Views and IMMAMECO

Descriptives

Immameco IMMIGRANTS GOOD FOR AMERICA

	N	Mean	Std. Deviation	Std. Error	95% Confidence interval for Mean		Minimum	Maximum
					Lower Bound	Upper Bound		
1.00 liberal	76	2.42	.868	.100	2.22	2.62	1	4
2.00 moderate	75	2.76	.998	.115	2.53	2.99	1	5
3.00 conservative	75	2.76	.984	.114	2.53	2.99	1	5
Total	226	2.65	.961	.064	2.52	2.77	1	5

ANOVA

Immameco IMMIGRANTS GOOD FOR AMERICA

	Sum of Squares	df	Mean Square	F	Sig.
Between Groups	5.795	2	2.898	3.201	.043
Within Groups	201.886	223	.905		
Total	207.681	225			

The ANOVA output includes two tables, Descriptives and ANOVA. In the Descriptives table, the N, mean, and standard deviation are reported for each group and the entire sample, along with the 95% confidence interval for each mean.

The F obtained is reported in the ANOVA table, along with its level of significance (or probability). For this data, F obtained is 3.201 with a significance of .043. Since the level of significance is less than our alpha (.043 < .05), we reject the null hypothesis and conclude that at least one of the means is significantly different. Notice that the lowest IMMAMECO score is 2.42 for those in the liberal group. Moderates and conservatives are tied at 2.76 out of the five-point scale.

✓ *Learning*
Check

Calculate eta-squared for this model.

▣ READING THE RESEARCH LITERATURE: SELF-IMAGE AND ETHNIC IDENTIFICATION

Like bivariate, t test, or chi-square analyses, ANOVA can help us understand how the categories of experience—race, age, class, and/or gender—shape our social lives. As we did in our first example, comparing the impact of race and gender on educational attainment, ANOVA allows us to investigate a variety of social categories by comparing the differences between them. We conclude our ANOVA discussion with two examples of how ANOVA is presented and interpreted in the social science literature. As a statistical method, ANOVA is most commonly used in the field of social psychology. Both our research examples come from social psychology journals.

Our first example is based on Elirea Bornman's 1999 research on ethnic identification in South Africa.[3] Politics, language, ethnicity, race, and culture all play an important role in defining self-image and ethnic identity in South Africa. But more important, according to Bornman, the relationship between ethnic identity and self-image is highly relevant in a society characterized by "complex pluralization on the basis of racial and ethnic differences."[4] Bornman hypothesized that "each group's attitude toward their ingroup as well as the socioeconomic and political changes in South Africa since the 1990s may have influenced the relationship between ethnic identification and self-image."[5]

Bornman examined the differences in self-image and ethnic identity, comparing Afrikaans-speaking whites, blacks, and English-speaking whites. Based on a survey conducted by the Human Sciences Research Council, Bornman analyzed a sample of South Africans' responses to several scales measuring self-image and ethnic identity. The Rosenberg Self-Esteem Scale (1965) measured both negative and positive self-image. For negative self-image, a higher score indicated a more negative self-image; for the positive self-image scale, a higher score indicated a more positive self-image.[6] Bornman created three measures of ethnic identification: (1) ethnic identification (higher score indicates stronger identification, loyalty, respect, and pride with one's own ethnic group); (2) exploration, identity achievement, and involvement (high score reflected higher levels of exploration, achievement of a well-defined identity, and involvement with and participation in cultural and other activities); and (3) ambivalence versus protection (a higher score indicated a greater willingness to protect and preserve the identity of the group and less uncertainty about the membership in one's ethnic group).[7] Table 12.4 shows the means and standard deviations for Bornman's three South African groups. Degrees of freedom, along with the *F* statistic, are reported in the last two columns of the table. All *F* statistics are significant at the .01 level, indicated by the asterisks.

Based on her data analysis, Bornman writes,

> On average, the Afrikaans-speaking Whites had the most positive self-image. Their mean score for negative self-image was the lowest, and they also had the highest mean score or positive self-image. In contrast, the Black respondents had the highest mean score for negative self-image and the lowest mean score for positive self-image, an indication that they had, on average, a more negative self-image than members of the two White groups. The results of the ANOVAs indicated that statistically significant differences existed between the mean scores of the various groups; for negative self-image, $F(2, 291) = 99.47$, $p = .0001$; for positive self-image, $F(2, 921) = 32.47$, $p = .0001$. . . . The Afrikaans-speaking Whites had the highest mean score for ethnic identification; the mean score for the English-speaking Whites was the lowest. The results of an ANOVA indicated the existence of significant differences, $F(2, 922) = 8.52$, $p = .0002$. . . . The Afrikaans-speaking Whites had the highest mean scores for the other two variables associated with ethnic identification (i.e., exploration, identity achievement, and involvement and ambivalence versus protection). However, the Black respondents had the lowest mean scores for these variables. The results of the ANOVAs were as follows: $F(2, 921) = 16.79$, $p = .0001$, for exploration, identity achievement, and involvement; $F(2, 922) = 61.71$, $p = .0001$, for ambivalence versus protection [8]

Note that in her discussion, Bornman reports each significant *F* statistic, along with its degrees of freedom and probability. While she does not specifically mention the mean scores, she does identify which groups have the highest or lowest scores on the measures for self-image and ethnic identification.

Table 12.4   Mean Scores and the Results of ANOVA for the Various Scales

	Afrikaans-Speaking Whites	Blacks	English-Speaking Whites	df	F
Self-image scales					
Negative self-image	6.66	9.21	7.35	2, 921	99.47**
	(2.39)	(2.89)	(2.89)		
Positive self-image	17.49	15.97	17.30	2, 921	32.47**
	(2.08)	(3.31)	(2.29)		
Scales associated with ethnic identity					
Ethnic identification	37.92	36.71	35.01	2, 922	8.52**
	(6.45)	(6.97)	(6.67)		
Exploration, identity achievement, and involvement	22.84	20.73	21.13	2, 921	16.79**
	(4.76)	(5.64)	(4.43)		
Ambivalence versus protection	15.36	12.64	13.42	2, 922	61.71**
	(3.33)	(3.65)	(3.14)		

Notes: Standard deviation in parentheses.

**$P < .01$.

▣ READING THE RESEARCH LITERATURE: STRESSES AND STRAINS AMONG GRANDMOTHER CAREGIVERS

Musil and colleagues (2009) examined the family life stresses and strains affecting grandmothers involved in caregiving to grandchildren.[9] Previous studies suggested that grandmother caregivers have more depressive symptoms than their noncaregiving peers. The sample comprises grandmothers, divided into three caregiving groups: primary, multigenerational, or noncaregiver. The groups were defined as

> Primary caregiver grandmothers had responsibility for raising their grandchildren without parents living in the home. Multigenerational grandmothers lived in a home with one or more grandchildren and the grandchild(ren)'s parent(s). Noncaregiver grandmothers did not live with or provide regular babysitting for grandchildren but lived within 1 hour or 50 miles of grandchildren and had an ongoing relationship with them. (p. 395)[10]

The researchers measured family life stresses and strains based on several existing scales.

- The level of strain and stresses (conflict, difficulty) was measured for general intrafamily strain (conflict among children, difficulty in managing children), family life stresses, financial (increasing financial debts), transitions (a member lost or quit a job, moved into a new home), family legal (incidents of physical abuse or aggression), family loss (child died), family care (child became seriously ill or injured), and pregnancy (teenager became pregnant).
- Social support was assessed based on the Duke Social Support Index, measuring both subjective and instrumental dimensions of support. Instrumental support items measured the extent to which friends and family offered assistance or help in specific situations. A higher score indicates high instrumental support. Subjective support was measured by items about feelings of support and involvement with friends and family. A higher score indicates a high level of subjective support.
- Resourcefulness was measured by the Self-Control Schedule. A higher score indicates greater resourcefulness.
- Depressive symptoms were evaluated based on a 20-item Center for Epidemiological Studies—Depression Scale. Higher scores indicate an increased clinical depression.

A portion of Musil and her colleagues' findings are presented in Table 12.5. In the table, they report the mean score and standard deviation for each stress/strain area, social support, resourcefulness, and depressive symptoms, using analysis of variance to compare the results for each grandmother group. They highlight the significant differences in the following paragraph.

There were significant differences between groups in intrafamily strain: Primary caregivers reported the most strain [Table 1, Table 12.5, this chapter]; there were no differences in the family life stresses summary score. There were significant differences between grandmother caregiver groups on specific family life stresses. . . . Post hoc tests showed that noncaregivers reported fewer financial strains than primary and multigenerational grandmothers, and primary caregivers reported significantly more family legal problems. Multigenerational grandmothers reported more transitions than primary caregivers. There were no significant between-group differences on family-care strains, loss, or pregnancy strain. There were significant between-group differences in support, but not resourcefulness. Noncaregivers reported more subjective support than primary caregivers. Grandmothers in multigenerational homes reported the most instrumental support and primary caregivers reported the least. Primary caregivers reported higher depressive symptoms than grandmothers in the other two groups. (p. 399)[11]

Notice how *F* test results are not reported in their summary. However, we know from Table 12.5 which model was significant. For example, the ANOVA model for intrafamily strain produced an *F* obtained of 18.4 (significant at the .001 level). As we review the mean scores for each group, the highest level of intrafamily strain was reported by primary caregivers (a mean score of 4.4), followed by multigenerational caregivers (3.9). Musil and colleagues conclude that these results reflect the "more complex family situations in these homes." Apart from the need to coordinate the schedules of grandchildren and the adults in the household, they identify the additional relationship strains of lack of privacy, less discretionary time, and conflict with birth parents as sources of intrafamily strain.

Table 12.5   Means, Standard Deviations, and ANOVA Results by Caregiver Group

Variables	Primary (n = 183)		Multigenerational (n = 136)		Noncaregivers (n = 167)		F Test
	M	SD	M	SD	M	SD	
Intrafamily strain	4.4	2.8	3.9	2.9	2.7	2.3	18.4***
Family life stresses (aggregate)	5.2	3.2	5.4	3.1	4.6	2.9	4.1
Financial	1.2	0.8	1.1	0.8	0.9	0.8	5.8*
Transitions	1.7	1.5	2.3	1.7	1.9	1.5	4.7**
Family legal	0.7	0.9	0.4	0.7	0.4	0.7	9.9***
Family loss	0.7	0.7	0.7	0.7	0.6	0.7	0.2
Family care	0.8	1.1	0.8	1.0	0.7	1.0	0.2
Pregnancy	0.1	0.2	0.1	0.2	0.0	0.2	2.0
Support— Instrumental	7.7	3.4	9.7	2.2	8.6	2.8	19.2***
Support— Subjective	11.1	3.1	11.8	2.4	12.2	2.6	7.9***
Resourcefulness	3.2	0.6	3.2	0.6	3.3	0.6	2.2
Depressive symptoms	15.8	11.3	12.4	10.4	11.5	10.6	8.0***

Note: $*P < = .05$, $**P < .01$, $***P < .001$.

✓ *Learning Check*

> *For the ANOVA model for Intrafamily Strain, what is the F critical? What information do you need to determine the F critical? Assume alpha = .05.*

MAIN POINTS

- Analysis of variance (ANOVA) procedures allow us to examine the variation in means in more than two samples. To determine whether the difference in mean scores is significant, ANOVA examines the differences between multiple samples, as well as the differences within a single sample.

• One-way ANOVA is a procedure using one dependent variable and one independent variable. The five-step hypothesis testing model is applied to one-way ANOVA.

• The test statistic for ANOVA is F. The F statistic is the ratio of between-group variance to within-group variance.

KEY TERMS

analysis of variance (ANOVA)
between-group sum of squares (SSB)
F critical

F obtained
F ratio or F statistic
mean square between
mean square within
one-way ANOVA

total sum of squares (SST)
within-group sum of squares (SSW)

$SAGE edge™

Sharpen your skills with SAGE edge at **edge.sagepub.com/frankfort7e**. **SAGE edge for students** provides a personalized approach to help you accomplish your coursework goals in an easy-to-use learning environment.

SPSS DEMONSTRATION

[GSS10SSDS]

Computing Analysis of Variance Models

Social scientists have examined the association between a woman's fertility decisions (deciding whether and/or when to have a child) and her wages, employment status, and education, along with other socioeconomic and demographic factors. Research has indicated that different social groups may have different norms and values about fertility.[12]

In this example, we'll investigate the relationship between a woman's educational attainment and the age at which her first child was born. Using education as the independent variable and age at which her first child was born as the dependent variable, we can assess whether there is a relationship between educational attainment and age at first childbirth.

We'll use two variables for our analysis, the variable DEGREE (five categories of educational attainment) and AGEKDBRN (respondent's age when her first child was born). But first, we'll restrict our analysis to women in the GSS sample (using *Data—Select Cases* command. You will have to select the option "If the condition is satisfied," then type SEX = 2 to restrict your analysis to women).

We can compute the ANOVA model by clicking on *Analyze, Compare Means*, then *One-Way ANOVA*. The opening dialog box requires that we insert AGEKDBRN in the box labeled "Dependent List" and in the box labeled "Factor" insert DEGREE (see Figure 12.3).

Click on the *Options* button at the upper right. Click on *Descriptive* in the Statistics box. This will produce a table of means and standard deviations along with the ANOVA statistics (Figure 12.4). Click on *Continue* in the Options box, then *OK* in the One-Way ANOVA box.

Figure 12.3 One-Way ANOVA Dialog Box

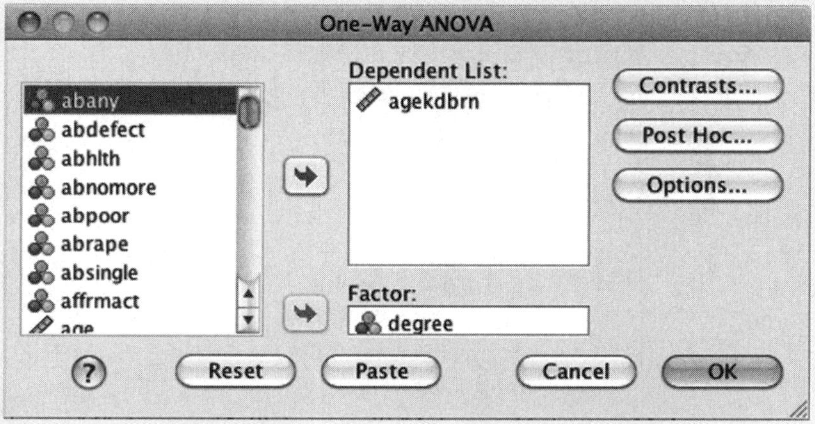

Figure 12.4 One-Way ANOVA Options Dialog Box

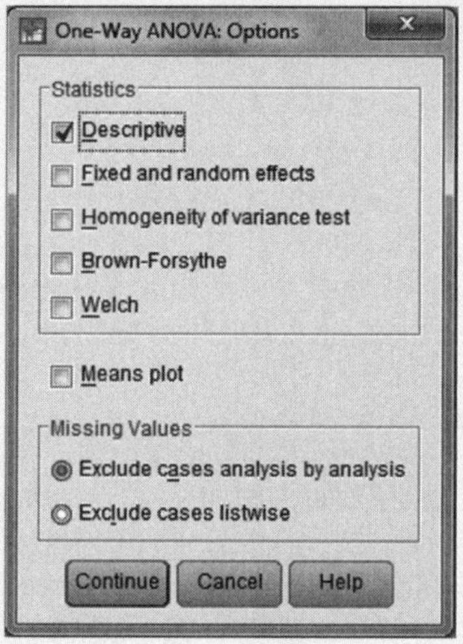

We're interested in the *F* statistic and significance in the ANOVA table (Figure 12.5). Based on the output, *F* is 39.897 with a significance of .000. We can conclude that the difference between the educational groups is significant. The higher one's educational attainment, the higher the age of first childbirth. The oldest average age at first childbirth is for women with graduate degrees (28.13 years of age), followed by women with bachelor's degrees (25.35 years of age). The youngest group of first-time mothers is women with less than a high school diploma. On average, women with less than a high school diploma had their first child at 19.63 years of age. When compared with the age of graduate-degree first-time mothers, there is a difference of 8.50 years.

Figure 12.5 ANOVA Output for Age at First Childbirth and Education, Women Only

Descriptives

agekdbrn R'S AGE WHEN 1ST CHILD BORN

	N	Mean	Std. Deviation	Std. Error	95% Confidence interval for Mean		Minimum	Maximum
					Lower Bound	Upper Bound		
0 LT HIGH SCHOOL	106	19.63	4.369	.424	18.79	20.47	13	38
1 HIGH SCHOOL	361	21.71	4.531	.238	21.24	22.18	14	38
2 JUNIOR COLLEGE	56	22.52	4.464	.597	21.32	23.71	16	35
3 BACHELOR	96	25.35	4.971	.507	24.35	26.36	16	40
3 GRADUATE	52	28.13	6.101	.846	26.44	29.83	16	43
Total	671	22.47	5.222	.202	22.07	22.86	13	43

ANOVA

agekdbrn R'S AGE WHEN 1ST CHILD BORN

	Sum of Squares	df	Mean Square	F	Sig.
Between Groups	3531.471	4	882.868	39.897	.000
Within Groups	14737.524	666	22.128		
Total	18268.996	670			

SPSS PROBLEMS

[GSS10SSDS]

1. Let's continue to examine the relationship between fertility decisions and education. But this time, we'll analyze the relationship for men.
   a. Run a Select Cases, selecting only men for the analysis.
   b. Compute an ANOVA model for men, using age at first-born child (AGEKDBRN) as the dependent variable and educational degree (DEGREE) as the independent variable. Based on the SPSS output, what can you conclude about the relationship between degree attainment and AGEKDBRN for men? How do these results compare with the results for women in the SPSS demonstration?
   c. Compute a second ANOVA model for men, using number of children (CHILDS) as the dependent variable and educational degree (DEGREE) as the independent variable. Based on your results, what conclusions can you make about the relationship between the two variables?

2. Repeat Exercise 1b, substituting respondent's social class (CLASS) as the independent variable in separate models for men and women. What can you conclude about the relationship between CLASS and AGEKDBRN?

3. We'll continue our analysis of fertility decisions, examining responses to the question, What is the ideal number of children a family should have (variable CHLDIDEL)? Use CHLDIDEL as your dependent variable and DEGREE as your independent variable. Is there a significant difference in the number of ideal children among different educational groups? (Option: You can run three sets of analyses—first, for all GSS respondents; second, an ANOVA model for women only; and finally, a model for men.)

4. Examine attitudes toward affirmative action based on two variables: AFFRMACT and DISCAFF. AFFR-MACT measures respondents' support of preferential hiring and promotion of blacks (a higher score indicates opposition). For the variable DISCAFF, individuals reported how likely it is that a white person won't get a job or promotion while an equally or less qualified black person gets one (a higher score indicates "not very likely"). Using AFFRMACT and DISCAFF as your dependent variables, determine whether there are significant differences in attitudes by social class (CLASS)? (You should have two ANOVA models, with CLASS as the independent variable in both models.)

CHAPTER EXERCISES

1. In Chapter 11 we analyzed the relationship between social class and health assessment. We continue the analysis here for a random sample of 32 GSS cases. Health is measured according to a four-point scale: 1 = excellent, 2 = good, 3 = fair, and 4 = poor. Four social classes are reported here: lower, working, middle, and upper. Present the five-step model for these data, using alpha = .05.

Lower Class	Working Class	Middle Class	Upper Class
3	2	2	2
2	1	3	1
2	3	1	1
2	2	1	2
3	2	2	1
3	2	3	1
4	3	3	1
4	3	1	2

2. We take another look at health, this time examining the relationship between educational attainment and perceived quality of health care. Data for three groups are presented based on the HINTS2012 data set. Present the five-step model for these data, using alpha = .01. QUALITYCARE is measured on a five-point scale: 1—excellent, 2—very good, 3—good, 4—fair, and 5—poor. Note how a lower score indicates a higher quality of care.

Present the five-step model for these data, using alpha = .05.

Less Than High School	Some College	College Graduate
1	2	1
4	3	1
2	2	1
2	2	2
3	4	1
3	2	2

3. In this exercise, let's examine the relationship between educational degree and church attendance. We selected a sample of 30 International Social Science Programme respondents, noting their educational status (no degree, secondary degree, and university degree) and their level of church attendance (0 = never, 1 = infrequently, and 2 = two to three times per month or more).

Complete the five-step model for these data, using alpha = .01.

No Degree	Secondary Degree	University Degree
2	2	0
1	2	0
1	2	0
2	1	0
2	1	1
2	0	1
0	2	0
2	1	1
2	1	2
2	2	1

4. Based on data from the GSS10SDSS, we examine the relationship between highest educational degree and agreement to the statement, "Financial dependence on others is one of my greatest fears about old age." The variable FINDEPND is measured on an ordinal scale: 1—strongly agree, 2—agree, 3—neither, 4—disagree, and 5—strongly disagree. Is there a relationship between educational attainment and level of agreement to the statement?
   a. Set alpha at .01 and test the null hypothesis of equal means.
   b. What is the eta-squared for this model?

Figure 12.6   ANOVA Output for FINDEPND and DEGREE

Descriptives

FINDEPND WORRY ABOUT DEPENDENCE

	N	Mean	Std. Deviation	Std. Error	95% Confidence interval for Mean Lower Bound	Upper Bound	Minimum	Maximum
0 LT HIGH SCHOOL	32	2.53	1.218	.215	2.09	2.97	1	5
1 HIGH SCHOOL	156	2.63	1.214	.097	2.44	2.82	1	5
2 JUNIOR COLLEGE	26	2.88	1.243	.244	2.38	3.39	1	5
3 BACHELOR	50	2.88	1.304	.184	2.51	3.25	1	5
3 GRADUATE	45	3.49	1.199	.179	3.13	3.85	1	5
Total	309	2.81	1.259	.072	2.66	2.95	1	5

Anova

FINDEPND WORRY ABOUT DEPENDENCE

	Sum of Squares	df	Mean Square	F	Sig.
Between Groups	28.767	4	7.192	4.757	.001
Within Groups	459.583	304	1.512		
Total	488.350	308			

Exercises

5. GSS 2010 respondents were asked their agreement to the following statement: "Parents ought to provide financial help to their adult children when the children are having financial difficulty." Their responses to HELPKIDS were measured on the same agreement scale (as FINDEPND in Question 4). Set alpha at .05 and test the null hypothesis of equal group means.

Figure 12.7 ANOVA Output for HELPKIDS and DEGREE

Descriptives

HELPKIDS PARENTS ADULT CHILDREN FINANCIALLY

	N	Mean	Std. Deviation	Std. Error	95% Confidence interval for Mean Lower Bound	Upper Bound	Minimum	Maximum
0 LT HIGH SCHOOL	32	2.53	1.270	.224	2.07	2.99	1	5
1 HIGH SCHOOL	155	2.59	.811	.065	2.46	2.72	1	5
2 JUNIOR COLLEGE	26	2.65	1.056	.207	2.23	3.08	1	5
3 BACHELOR	50	2.60	1.030	.146	2.31	2.89	1	5
3 GRADUATE	45	2.62	.984	.147	2.33	2.92	1	5
Total	308	2.60	.945	.054	2.49	2.70	1	5

Anova

HELPKIDS PARENTS ADULT CHILDREN FINANCIALLY

	Sum of Squares	df	Mean Square	F	Sig.
Between Groups	.253	4	.063	.070	.991
Within Groups	273.825	303	.904		
Total	274.078	307			

6. We examine the relationship between educational attainment and agreement to the statement, "Immigrants take jobs away from people who were born in America" as measured in the GSS 2010. Responses to IMMJOBS are measured according to the same five-point scale (as FINDEPND in Question 4).
   a. Set alpha at .05 and test the null hypothesis of equal means.
   b. If alpha were set at .01, would your decision remain the same?

Figure 12.8 ANOVA Output for IMMJOBS and DEGREE

Descriptives

Immjobs IMMIGRANTS TAKE JOBS AWAY

	N	Mean	Std. Deviation	Std. Error	95% Confidence interval for Mean Lower Bound	Upper Bound	Minimum	Maximum
0 LT HIGH SCHOOL	53	2.96	1.315	.181	2.60	3.32	1	5
1 HIGH SCHOOL	189	2.63	1.081	.079	2.48	2.79	1	5
2 JUNIOR COLLEGE	35	2.97	1.071	.181	2.60	3.34	1	5
3 BACHELOR	70	3.27	1.020	.122	3.03	3.51	1	5
3 GRADUATE	36	3.42	1.079	.180	3.05	3.78	1	5
Total	383	2.90	1.137	.058	2.79	3.02	1	5

ANOVA

Immjobs IMMIGRANTS TAKE JOBS AWAY

	Sum of Squares	df	Mean Square	F	Sig.
Between Groups	32.931	4	8.233	6.746	.000
Within Groups	461.298	378	1.220		
Total	494.230	382			

7. Based on a sample of 21 MTF respondents, we present their racial/ethnic background and the numbers of school days missed in the past 4 weeks.
   a. Complete the five-step model for these data, set alpha at .05.
   b. If alpha were set at .01, would your decision change? Explain.

White	Black	Hispanic
4	1	4
5	2	3
3	2	5
4	1	1
4	3	5
4	4	2
6	3	2

8. We selected a sample of 14 MTF respondents. We present their number of moving (traffic) violations in the last 12 months along with their residential area (residential area is the independent variable). Complete the five-step model for these data, using alpha = .05.

Small Town	Medium-Sized City	Large City
0	2	3
0	3	4
1	1	4
2	1	3
1		2

9. Nan Sook Park and her colleagues (2012) investigated racial/ethnic differences in predictors of self-rating health and the use of sociocultural resources. Their data is based on the Survey of Older Floridians, a statewide sample of white, African American, Cuban, and non-Cuban Hispanic seniors.

We present ANOVA results for two sociocultural resources. Social support was measured with the question: In times of trouble, can you count on at least some of your family and friends? (1—hardly ever, 2—some of the time, and 3—most of the time). Religious attendance was measured according to the scale: 1—never or almost never to 5—more than once a week. Mean scores are presented for each racial/ethnic group, along with the standard deviation in parentheses.

| | Racial/Ethnic Group Mean (Standard Deviation) | | | | |
Variable	Whites (n = 503)	African Americans (n = 360)	Cubans (n = 328)	Non-Cuban Hispanics (n = 241)	F
Social Support	2.85 (0.47)	2.75 (0.57)	2.73 (0.60)	2.58 (0.70)	12.17***
Religious Attendance	2.79 (1.57)	3.94 (1.21)	2.74 (1.49)	3.37 (1.43)	56.43***

Source: Park, Nan Sook, Yuri Jan, Beom Lee and David Chiriboga. "Racial/Ethnic Differences in Predictors of Self-Rated Health: Findings from the Survey of Older Floridians." *Research on Aging* 35, no. 1 (2012): 207.

*** $P < .001$

Review each measure of sociocultural resource and determine whether the null hypothesis would be rejected. Set alpha at .05 for each.

10. Is there a significant difference in Internet use per week between different educational groups? Using data from the GSS10SSDS, we ran an ANOVA model using DEGREE (educational attainment) as the independent variable and WWHR (WWW hours per week) as the dependent variable. Based on an alpha of .05, what can you conclude?

Figure 12.9 ANOVA Output for WWWHR and DEGREE

Descriptives

wwwhr WWW HOURS PER WEEK

	N	Mean	Std. Deviation	Std. Error	95% Confidence Interval for Mean		Minimum	Maximum
					Lower Bound	Upper Bound		
0 LT HIGH SCHOOL	18	3.56	5.772	1.361	.69	6.43	0	25
1 HIGH SCHOOL	165	8.90	12.166	.947	7.03	10.77	0	80
2 JUNIOR COLLEGE	22	7.14	8.817	1.880	3.23	11.05	0	40
3 BACHELOR	84	11.18	10.404	1.135	8.92	13.44	0	50
4 GRADUATE	34	11.32	14.954	2.565	6.11	16.54	0	66
Total	323	9.33	11.689	.650	8.05	10.61	0	80

ANOVA

wwwhr WWW HOURS PER WEEK

	Sum of Squares	df	Mean Square	F	Sig.
Between Groups	1158.308	4	289.577	2.150	.075
Within Groups	42835.246	318	134.702		
Total	43993.554	322			

Regression and Correlation

M any research questions require the analysis of relationships between interval-ratio variables. Social scientists, for instance, frequently measure variables such as educational attainment, family size, and household income. Let's say that we're interested in the relationship between median household income and educational attainment. Bivariate regression analysis provides us with the tools to express a relationship between two interval-ratio variables in a concise way.[1]

The United States of America has long been viewed as a land of opportunity where everyone is positioned to succeed. However, stratification scholars have long argued that opportunity is limited based on the social class one was born into. An individual born into a higher social class background is likely to have more opportunities than one born into a lower social class background. With this in mind, let's examine whether or not such a relationship exists at the state level.

The U.S. Census Bureau collects and reports an array of information about the United States and its residents. Annual household income and educational attainment are two of the many characteristics regularly monitored. Table 13.1 displays the percentage of state residents with a bachelor's degree in 2009 for the 10 most populated states. Also presented are the mean, variance, and range for these data.

Table 13.1   Percentage of State Residents With a Bachelor's Degree, 2009

State	Percentage of State Residents With a Bachelor's Degree
California	29.90
Texas	25.50
New York	32.40
Florida	25.30
Illinois	30.60
Pennsylvania	26.40
Ohio	24.10
Michigan	24.60
Georgia	27.50
New Jersey	34.50

$$\text{Mean } X = \overline{X} = \frac{\sum X}{N} = \frac{280.8}{10} = 28.08$$

$$\text{Variance } X = S_X^2 = \frac{\sum(X - \overline{X})^2}{N-1} = \frac{115.04}{9} = 12.78$$

$$\text{Range } X = 34.5 - 24.1 = 10.4$$

Source: U.S. Census Bureau, *Statistical Abstract of the United States*, 2012, Table 233.

In examining Table 13.1 and the descriptive statistics, notice the variability in educational attainment. The percentage of state residents with a bachelor's degree ranges from a low of 24.10% for the state of Ohio to a high of 34.50% for the state of New Jersey.

One possible explanation for the differences in educational attainment is the economic condition of these states. Stratification scholars have long argued that limited economic resources can affect educational attainment. Since an important indicator of economic condition is median household income, we would expect states with a higher household income to also have a larger percentage of its residents attain a college degree. Table 13.2 displays the median household income in 2009 for 10 of the most populated states. Note that the median household income ranges widely from a low of $44,736 for the state of Florida (third lowest in terms of percentage of residents with a bachelor's degree amongst the 10 most populated states) to a high of $68,342 for the state of New Jersey.

▣ THE SCATTER DIAGRAM

Let's examine the possible relationship between the interval-ratio variables *percentage of state residents with a bachelor's degree* and *median household income*. One quick visual method used to display such a relationship between two interval-ratio variables is the **scatter diagram** (or **scatterplot**). Often used as a first exploratory step in regression analysis, a scatter diagram can suggest whether two variables are associated.

Scatter diagram (scatterplot)   A visual method used to display a relationship between two interval-ratio variables.

Table 13.2   Median Household Income ($)

State	Median Household Income ($)
California	58,931
Texas	48,259
New York	54,659
Florida	44,736
Illinois	53,966
Pennsylvania	49,520
Ohio	45,395
Michigan	45,255
Georgia	47,590
New Jersey	68,342

Mean $X = \overline{X} = \dfrac{\sum X}{N} = \dfrac{516{,}653}{10} = \$51{,}665.30$

Variance $X = S_X^2 = \dfrac{\sum\left(X - \overline{X}\right)^2}{N-1} = \dfrac{506{,}395{,}248}{9} = \$56{,}266{,}139$

Range $X = \$68{,}342 - \$44{,}736 = \$23{,}606$

Source: U.S. Census Bureau, *American Community Survey,* 2009.

The scatter diagram showing the relationship between educational attainment and household income for the 10 states is shown in Figure 13.1. In a scatter diagram, the scales for the two variables form the vertical and horizontal axes of a graph. Usually, the independent variable, X, is arrayed along the horizontal axis and the dependent variable, Y, along the vertical axis. Because differences in the median household income are hypothesized to account for differences in the percentage of state residents with a bachelor's degree, household income is assumed as the independent variable and is arrayed along the horizontal axis. Educational attainment, the dependent variable, is arrayed along the vertical axis. In Figure 13.1, each dot represents a state; its location lies at the exact intersection of that state's percentage of residents with a bachelor's degree and its median household income.

Note that there is an apparent tendency for states with a lower median household income (e.g., Ohio and Texas) to also have a lower percentage of residents with a bachelor's degree, whereas in states with a higher median household income (e.g., New Jersey and California), there are a higher percentage of residents with a bachelor's degree. In other words, we can say that median household income and educational attainment are positively associated.

Scatter diagrams can also illustrate a negative association between two variables. For example, Figure 13.2 displays the association between median household income and larceny/theft crime rates for the 10 most populated states using data from the *Statistical Abstract of the United States*.

Figure 13.1   Scatter Diagram of Educational Attainment and Median Household Income

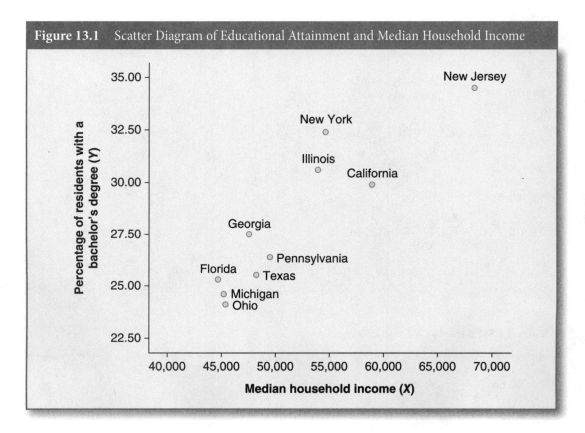

Figure 13.2 suggests that a low median household income is associated with a higher rate of larceny/theft. Conversely, high median household income seems to be associated with a lower larceny/theft rate (see Table 13.5 for data).

LINEAR RELATIONS AND PREDICTION RULES

Scatter diagrams provide a useful but only preliminary step in exploring a relationship between two interval-ratio variables. We need a more systematic way to express this relationship. Let's examine Figures 13.1 and 13.2 again. They allow us to understand how household income is related to educational attainment (Figure 13.1) and larceny (Figure 13.2). The relationships displayed are by no means perfect, but the trends are apparent. In the first case (Figure 13.1), as state income increases, so does the percentage of its residents with a bachelor's degree. In the second case (Figure 13.2), as state income increases, larceny/theft crime rate decreases.

One way to evaluate these relationships is by expressing them as *linear relationships*. A **linear relationship** allows us to approximate the observations displayed in a scatter diagram with a straight line. In a perfectly linear relationship, all the observations (the dots) fall along a straight line (a perfect relationship is sometimes called a **deterministic relationship**), and the line itself

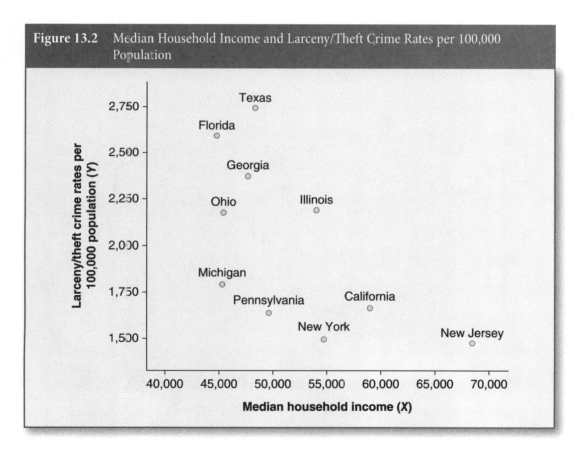

Figure 13.2 Median Household Income and Larceny/Theft Crime Rates per 100,000 Population

provides a predicted value of Y (the vertical axis) for any value of X (the horizontal axis). For example, in Figure 13.3, we have superimposed a straight line on the scatterplot originally displayed in Figure 13.1. Using this line, we can obtain a predicted value of the percentage of state residents with a bachelor's degree for any value of household income, by reading up to the line from the income axis and then over to the percentage with a bachelor's degree axis (indicated by the dotted lines). For example, the predicted value of the percentage of state residents with a bachelor's degree in a state with a $50,000 median household income is approximately 27%. Similarly, for a state with a $55,000 median household income, we would predict that approximately 29% of its residents would have a bachelor's degree.

Linear relationship   A relationship between two interval-ratio variables in which the observations displayed in a scatter diagram can be approximated with a straight line.

Deterministic (perfect) linear relationship   A relationship between two interval-ratio variables in which all the observations (the dots) fall along a straight line. The line provides a predicted value of Y (the vertical axis) for any value of X (the horizontal axis).

Figure 13.3   A Straight-Line Graph for Median Household Income and Percentage of Residents With a Bachelor's Degree

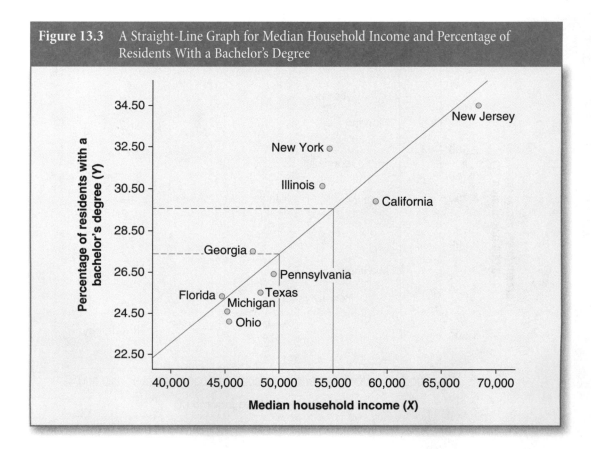

As indicated in Figure 13.3, for the 10 states surveyed, the actual relationship between income and the percentage of state residents with a bachelor's degree is not perfectly linear. Although some of the states lie very close to the line, none fall exactly on the line and some deviate from it considerably. Are there other lines that provide a better description of the relationship between income and the percentage of state residents with a bachelor's degree?

In Figure 13.4, we have drawn two additional lines that approximate the pattern of relationship shown by the scatter diagram. In each case, notice that even though some of the states lie close to the line, all fall considerably short of perfect linearity. Is there one line that provides the best linear description of the relationship between median household income and the percentage of residents with a bachelor's degree? How do we choose such a line? What are its characteristics? Before we describe a technique for finding the straight line that most accurately describes the relationship between two variables, we first need to review some basic concepts about how straight-line graphs are constructed.

✓ *Learning Check*

Use Figure 13.3 to predict the percentage of residents with a bachelor's degree in a state with a median household income of $47,500 and one with a median household income of $50,000.

Figure 13.4   Alternative Straight-Line Graph for Median Household Income and Percentage of Residents With a Bachelor's Degree

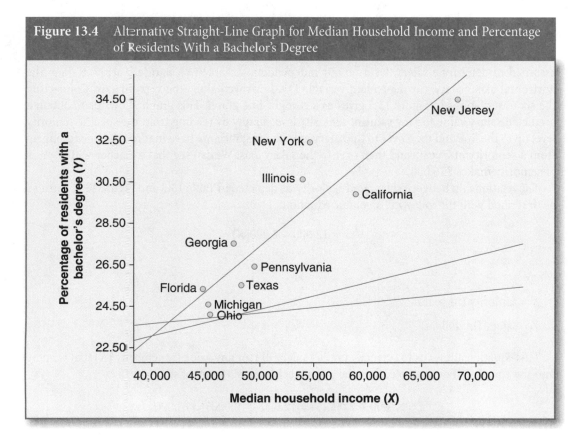

Constructing Straight-Line Graphs

To illustrate the fundamentals of straight-line graphs, let's take a simple example. Suppose that in a local school system, teachers' salaries are completely determined by seniority. New teachers begin with an annual salary of $12,000, and for each year of seniority, their salary increases by $2,000. The seniority and annual salary of six hypothetical teachers are presented in Table 13.3.

Table 13.3   Seniority and Salary of Six Teachers (hypothetical data)

Seniority (in years) X	Salary (in dollars) Y
0	12,000
1	14,000
2	16,000
3	18,000
4	20,000
5	22,000

Now, let's plot the values of these two variables on a graph (Figure 13.5). Because seniority is assumed to determine salary, let it be our independent variable (X), and let's array it along the horizontal axis. Salary, the dependent variable (Y), is arrayed along the vertical axis. Connecting the six observations in Figure 13.5 gives us a straight-line graph. This graph allows us to obtain a predicted salary value for any value of seniority level simply by reading from the specific seniority level up to the line and then over to the salary axis. For instance, we have marked the lines going up from a seniority of 7 years and then over to the salary axis. We can see that a teacher with 7 years of seniority makes $26,000.

The relationship between salary and seniority, as depicted in Table 13.3 and Figure 13.5, can also be described with the following algebraic equation:

$$Y = 12,000 + 2,000(X)$$

where

X = seniority (in years)

Y = salary (in dollars)

This equation allows us to correctly predict salary (Y) for any value for seniority (X) that we plug into the equation. For example, the salary of a teacher with 5 years of seniority is

$$Y = 12,000 + 2,000(5) = 12,000 + 10,000 = \$22,000$$

Figure 13.5 A Perfect Linear Relationship Between Seniority (in years) and Annual Salary (in thousand dollars) of Six Teachers (hypothetical)

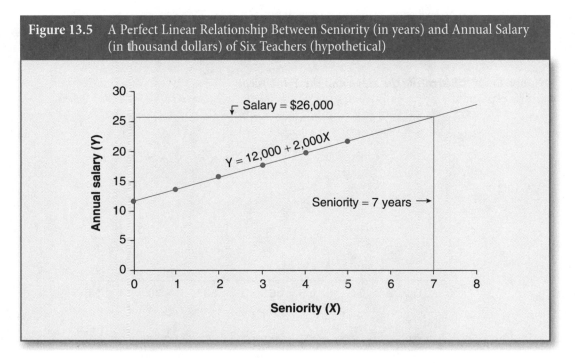

Note that we can also plug in values of X that are not shown in Table 13.3. For example, the salary of a teacher with 10 years of seniority is

$$Y = 12,000 + 2,000(10) = 12,000 + 20,000 = \$32,000$$

The equation describing the relationship between seniority and salary is an equation for a straight line. The equations for all straight-line graphs have the same general form:

$$Y = a + b(X) \tag{13.1}$$

where

Y = the predicted score on the dependent variable

X = the score on the independent variable

a = the Y-intercept, or the point where the line crosses the Y-axis; therefore, a is the value of Y when X is 0

b = the slope of the regression line, or the change in Y with a unit change in X. In our example, a = 12,000 and b = 2,000. That is, a teacher will make \$12,000 with 0 years of seniority but then her or his salary will go up by \$2,000 with each year of seniority.

✓ *Learning*
Check

For each of these four lines, as X goes up by 1 unit, what does Y do? Be sure you can answer this question using both the equation and the line.

Four Lines: Illustrating the Slope and the Y-Intercept

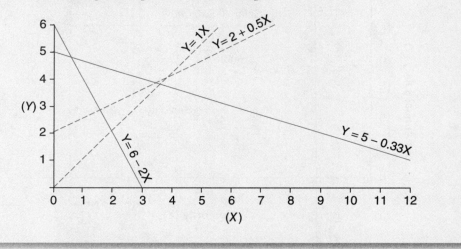

Slope (b) The change in variable Y (the dependent variable) with a unit change in variable X (the independent variable).

Y-intercept (a) The point where the line crosses the Y-axis, or the value of Y when X is 0.

✓ *Learning*
Check

Use the linear equation describing the relationship between seniority and salary of teachers to obtain the predicted salary of a teacher with 12 years of seniority.

Finding the Best-Fitting Line

The straight line displayed in Figure 13.5 and the linear equation representing it ($Y = 12,000 + 2,000\{X\}$) provide a very simple depiction of the relationship between seniority and salary because salary (the Y variable) is completely determined by seniority (the X variable). When each value of Y is completely determined by X, all the points (observations) lie on the line, and the relationship between the two variables is a deterministic, or perfectly linear, relationship.

However, most relationships we study in the social sciences are not deterministic, and we are not able to come up with a linear equation that allows us to predict Y from X with perfect accuracy. We are much more likely to find relationships approximating linearity, but in which numerous cases don't follow this trend perfectly. For instance, in reality, teachers' salaries are not completely determined by seniority, and therefore, knowing years of seniority will not provide us with a perfect prediction of their salary level.

When the dependent variable (*Y*) is not completely determined by the independent variable (*X*), not all (sometimes none) of the observations will lie exactly on the line. Look back at Figure 13.4, our example of the percentage of state residents with a bachelor's degree in relation to the state's median household income. Though each line represents a linear equation showing us how the percentage of state residents with a bachelor's degree rises with a state's median household income, we do not have a perfect prediction in any of the lines. Although all three lines approximate the linear trend suggested by the scatter diagram, very few of the observations lie exactly on any of the lines, and some deviate from them considerably.

Given that none of the lines is perfect, our task is to choose one line—the *best-fitting line*. But which is the best-fitting line?

Defining Error

The best-fitting line is the one that generates the least amount of error, also referred to as the *residual*. Let's think about how the residual is defined. Look again at Figure 13.3. For each income level, the line (or the equation that this line represents) predicts a value of *Y*. Texas, for example, with a median household income of $48,259, gives us a predicted value for *Y* of 26.7%. But the actual value for Texas is 25.5% (see also Table 13.1). Thus, we have two values for *Y*: (1) a predicted *Y*, which we symbolize as $\hat{Y}$ and which is generated by the prediction equation, also called the *linear regression equation Y=a + b(X)* and (2) the observed *Y*, symbolized simply as *Y*. Thus, for Texas, $\hat{Y}$=26.7%, whereas *Y* = 25.5%.

We can think of the residual as the difference between the observed *Y*(*Y*) and the predicted *Y*($\hat{Y}$). If we symbolize the residual as *e*, then

$$e = Y - \hat{Y}$$

The residual for Texas is 25.5% – 26.7% = –1.2 percentage points.

The Residual Sum of Squares (Σe^2)

We want a line or a prediction equation that minimizes *e* for each individual observation. However, any line we choose will minimize the residual for some observations but may maximize it for others. We want to find a prediction equation that minimizes the residuals over all observations.

There are many mathematical ways of defining the residuals. For example, we may take the algebraic sum of residuals $\Sigma(Y - \hat{Y})$, the sum of the absolute residuals $\Sigma(|Y - \hat{Y}|)$, or the sum of the squared residuals $\Sigma(Y - \hat{Y})^2$. For mathematical reasons, statisticians prefer to work with the third method—squaring and summing the residuals over all observations. The result is the *residual sum of squares*, or Σe^2. Symbolically, Σe^2 is expressed as

$$\Sigma e^2 = \Sigma(Y - \hat{Y})^2$$

The Least Squares Line

The best-fitting regression line is that line where the sum of the squared residuals, or Σe^2, is at a minimum. Such a line is called the **least squares line** (or **best-fitting line**), and the technique that produces this line is called the **least squares method**. The technique involves choosing a and b for the equation such that Σe^2 will have the smallest possible value. In the next section, we use the data from the 10 states to find the least squares equation. But before we continue, let's review where we are so far.

Least squares line (best-fitting line)   A line where the residual sum of squares, or Σe^2, is at a minimum.

Least squares method   The technique that produces the least squares line.

Review

1. We examined the relationship between a state's median household income and the percentage of its residents with a bachelor's degree for 10 different states. We used a *scatter diagram (scatterplot)* to display the relationship between these variables.

2. The scatter diagram indicated that the relationship between these variables might be *linear*, as a state's median household income increases, so does the percentage of its residents with a bachelor's degree.

3. A more systematic way to analyze the relationship is to develop a *straight-line equation* to predict the percentage of state residents with a bachelor's degree based on median household income. We saw that there are a number of straight lines that can approximate the data.

4. The *best-fitting line* is one that minimizes Σe^2. Such a line is called the *least squares line*, and the technique that produces this line involves choosing the a and b for the equation $\hat{Y} = a + bx$ that minimize Σe^2.

Computing *a* and *b* for the Prediction Equation

Through the use of calculus, it can be shown that to figure out the values of a and b in a way that minimizes Σe^2, we need to apply the following formulas:

$$b = \frac{S_{YX}}{S_X^2} \tag{13.2}$$

$$a = \bar{Y} - b(\bar{X}) \tag{13.3}$$

where

S_{YX} = the covariance of X and Y

S_X^2 = the variance of X

$\overline{Y}$ = the mean of Y

$\overline{X}$ = the mean of X

a = the Y-intercept

b = the slope of the line

These formulas assume that X is the independent variable and Y is the dependent variable.

Before we compute a and b, let's examine these formulas. The denominator for b is the variance of the variable X. It is defined as follows:

$$\text{Variance } (X) = S_X^2 = \frac{\Sigma\left(X - \overline{X}\right)^2}{N - 1}$$

This formula should be familiar to you from Chapter 5. The numerator (S_{YX}), however, is a new term. It is the covariance of X and Y and is defined as

$$\text{Covariance } (X,Y) = S_{YX} = \frac{\Sigma(X - \overline{X})(Y - \overline{Y})}{N - 1} \tag{13.4}$$

The covariance is a measure of how X and Y vary together. Basically, the covariance tells us to what extent higher values of one variable "go together" with higher values on the second variable (in which case we have a positive covariation) or with lower values on the second variable (which is a negative covariation). Take a look at this formula. It tells us to subtract the mean of X from each X score and the mean of Y from each Y score, and then take the product of the two deviations. The results are then summed for all the cases and divided by $N - 1$.

In Table 13.4, we show the computations necessary to calculate the values of a and b for our 10 states. The means for median household income and percentage of state residents with a bachelor's degree are obtained by summing Column 1 and Column 2, respectively, and dividing each sum by N. To calculate the covariance, we first subtract from each X score (Column 3) and from each Y score (Column 5) to obtain the mean deviations. We then multiply these deviations for every observation. The products of the mean deviations are shown in Column 7. For example, for the first observation, California, the mean deviation for median household income is 7,265.7 (58,931 − 51,665.3 = 7,265.37); for the percentage of residents with a bachelor's degree, it is 1.82 (29.90 − 28.08 = 1.82). The product of these deviations, 13,233.57 $(7,265.7 \times 1.82 = 13,223.57)$, is shown in Column 7. The sum of these products, shown at the bottom of Column 7, is 220,301.66. Dividing it by 9 ($N - 1$), we get the covariance of 24,477.96.

Table 13.4   Worksheet for Calculating *a* and *b* for the Regression Equation

	(1)	*(2)*	*(3)*	*(4)*	*(5)*	*(6)*	*(7)*
	Median Household Income	*Percentage With a Bachelor's Degree*					
State	X	Y	$(X-\bar{X})$	$(X-\bar{X})^2$	$(Y-\bar{Y})$	$(Y-\bar{Y})^2$	$(X-\bar{X})(Y-\bar{Y})$
California	58,931	29.9	7,265.7	52,790,396	1.82	3.31	13,223.57
Texas	48,259	25.5	−3,406.3	11,602,880	−2.58	6.66	8,788.25
New York	54,659	32.4	2,993.7	8,962,240	4.32	18.66	12,932.78
Florida	44,736	25.3	−6,929.3	48,015,198	−2.78	7.73	19,263.45
Illinois	53,966	30.6	2,300.7	5,293,220	2.52	6.35	5,797.76
Pennsylvania	49,520	26.4	−2,145.3	4,602,312	−1.68	2.82	3,604.10
Ohio	45,395	24.1	−6,270.3	39,316,662	−3.98	15.84	24,955.79
Michigan	45,255	24.6	−6,410.3	41,091,946	−3.48	12.11	22,307.84
Georgia	47,590	27.5	−4,075.3	16,608,070	−0.58	0.34	2,363.67
New Jersey	68,342	34.5	16,676.7	278,112,323	6.42	41.22	107,064.41
	ΣX=516,653	ΣY=280.8	0[a]	506,395,248	0[a]	115.0	220,301.66

$$\text{Mean } X = \bar{X} = \frac{\Sigma X}{N} = \frac{516,653}{10} = 51,665.3$$

$$\text{Mean } Y = \bar{Y} = \frac{\Sigma Y}{N} = \frac{280.8}{10} = 28.08$$

$$\text{Variance}(X) = S_X^2 = \frac{\Sigma(X-\bar{X})^2}{N-1} = \frac{506,395,248}{9} = 56,266,139$$

$$\text{Standard Deviation}(X) = S_X = \sqrt{56,266,139} = 7,501.08$$

$$\text{Variance}(Y) = S_Y^2 = \frac{\Sigma(Y-\bar{Y})^2}{N-1} = \frac{115.0}{9} = 12.78$$

$$\text{Standard Deviation}(Y) = S_Y = \sqrt{12.78} = 3.57$$

$$\text{Covariance}(X,Y) = S_{XY} = \frac{\Sigma(X-\bar{X})(Y-\bar{Y})}{N-1} = \frac{220,301.66}{9} = 24,477.96$$

a. Answers may differ due to rounding; however, the exact value of these column totals, properly calculated, will always be equal to zero.

The covariance is a measure of the linear relationship between two variables, and its value reflects both the strength and the direction of the relationship. The covariance will be close to zero when X and Y are unrelated; it will be larger than zero when the relationship is positive and smaller than zero when the relationship is negative.

Now, let's substitute the values for the covariance and the variance from Table 13.4 to calculate b:

$$b = \frac{S_{YX}}{S_X^2} = \frac{24,477.96}{56,266,139} = 0.0004$$

Once b has been calculated, finding a, the intercept, is simple:

$$a = \overline{Y} - b(\overline{X}) = 28.08 - 0.0004(51,665.3) = 7.41$$

The prediction equation is therefore

$$\hat{Y} = 7.41 + 0.0004(X)$$

This equation can be used to obtain a predicted value for the percentage of state residents who have a bachelor's degree given a state's median household income. For example, for a state with a median household income of $48,000, the predicted percentage is

$$\hat{Y} = 7.41 + 0.0004(48,000) = 26.61$$

Similarly, for a state with a median household income of $56,000, the predicted value is

$$\hat{Y} = 7.41 + 0.0004(56,000) = 29.81$$

Now, we can plot the straight-line graph corresponding to the regression equation. To plot a straight line, we need only two points, where each point corresponds to an X, Y value predicted by the equation. We can use the two points we just obtained: (1) $X = \$48,000$, $\hat{Y} = 26.61\%$ and (2) $X = \$56,000$, $\hat{Y} = 29.81\%$. In Figure 13.6, the regression line is plotted over the scatter diagram we first displayed in Figure 13.1.

> *Use the prediction equation to calculate the predicted values of Y for New York, Georgia, and Ohio. Verify that the regression line in Figure 13.6 passes through these points.*

✓ *Learning Check*

Interpreting *a* and *b*

Now, let's interpret the coefficients a and b in our equation. The b coefficient is equal to 0.0004%. This tells us that the percentage of state residents with a bachelor's degree will increase by 0.0004% for every $1 increment in their state's median household income. Similarly, an increase of $10,000 in a state's median household income corresponds to a 4% increase in the percentage of state residents with a bachelor's degree.

Note that because the relationships between variables in the social sciences are inexact, we don't expect our regression equation to make perfect predictions for every individual case. However, even though the pattern suggested by the regression equation may not hold for every individual state, it gives us a tool by which to make the best possible guess about how a state's median household income is associated, on average, with the percentage of state residents with a bachelor's degree. We can say that the slope of 0.0004% is the estimate of this underlying relationship.

The *Y* intercept *a* is the predicted value of *Y*, when *X* = 0. Thus, it is the point at which the regression line and the *Y*-axis intersect. With *a* = 7.41, we would predict that very few residents (7.41%) of a state with a median household income equal to zero would have obtained a bachelor's degree. Note, however, that no state has an income as low as zero. As a general rule, be cautious when making predictions for *Y* based on values of *X* that are outside the range of the data. Thus, when the lowest value for *X* is far above zero, the intercept may not have a clear substantive interpretation.

Figure 13.6   The Best-Fitting Line for Median Household Income and Percentage of State Residents With a Bachelor's Degree

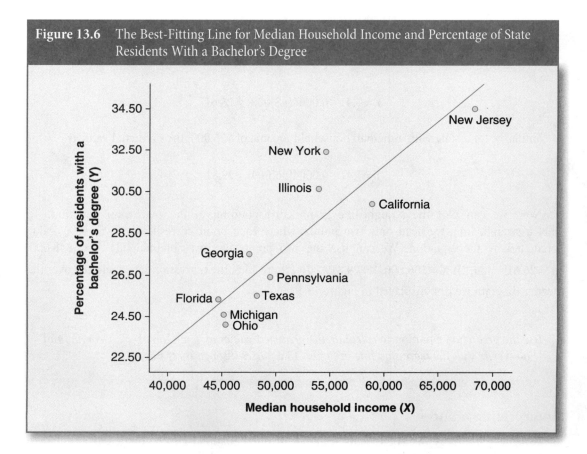

Y intercept (a)   The point where the regression line crosses the *Y* axis and where *X* = 0.

▣ STATISTICS IN PRACTICE: MEDIAN HOUSEHOLD INCOME AND CRIMINAL BEHAVIOR

In our ongoing example, we have looked at the association between median household income and educational attainment measured by the percentage of state residents with a bachelor's degree. The regression equation we have estimated from the data collected by the U.S. Census Bureau in 10 states shows that as a state's median household income rises, so does its percentage of residents with a bachelor's degree. This finding confirms that household income is related to educational attainment.

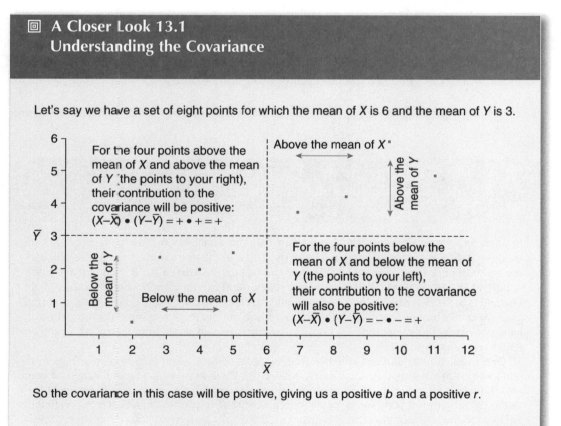

▣ A Closer Look 13.1
Understanding the Covariance

Let's say we have a set of eight points for which the mean of *X* is 6 and the mean of *Y* is 3.

For the four points above the mean of *X* and above the mean of *Y* (the points to your right), their contribution to the covariance will be positive:
$(X-\bar{X}) \bullet (Y-\bar{Y}) = + \bullet + = +$

Above the mean of *X*

Above the mean of *Y*

For the four points below the mean of *X* and below the mean of *Y* (the points to your left), their contribution to the covariance will also be positive:
$(X-\bar{X}) \bullet (Y-\bar{Y}) = - \bullet - = +$

Below the mean of *Y*

Below the mean of *X*

So the covariance in this case will be positive, giving us a positive *b* and a positive *r*.

(Continued)

(Continued)

Now let's say we have a set of eight points that look like this:

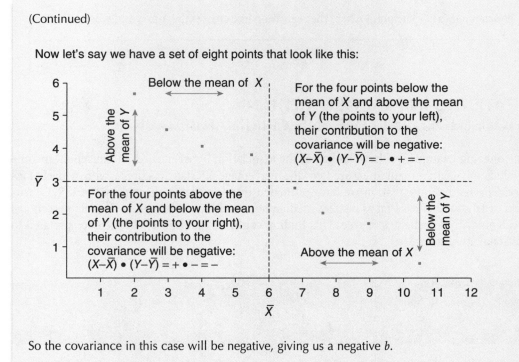

So the covariance in this case will be negative, giving us a negative *b*.

🔲 A Closer Look 13.2
A Note on Nonlinear Relationships

In analyzing the relationship between median household income and the percentage of state residents with a bachelor's degree, we have assumed that the two variables are linearly related. For the most part, social science relationships can be approximated using a linear equation. It is important to note, however, that sometimes a relationship cannot be approximated by a straight line and is better described by some other, nonlinear function. For example, the following scatter diagram shows a nonlinear relationship between age and hours of reading (hypothetical data). Hours of reading increase with age until the twenties, remain stable until the forties, and then tend to decrease with age.

One quick way to find out whether your variables form a linear or a nonlinear pattern of relationship (or whether the variables are related at all!) is to make a scatter diagram of your data. If there is a significant departure from linearity, it would make no sense to fit a straight line to the data. Statistical techniques for analyzing nonlinear relationships between two variables are beyond the scope of this book. Nonetheless, at the very least, you should check for possible departures from linearity when examining your scatter diagram.

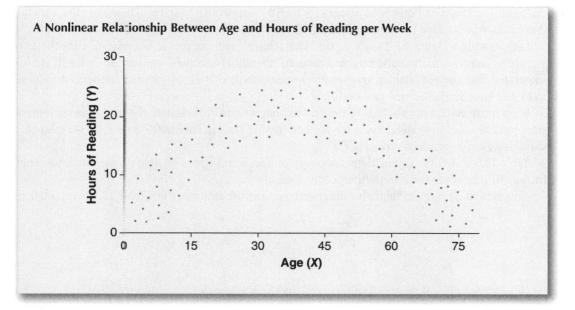

A Nonlinear Relationship Between Age and Hours of Reading per Week

In an attempt to understand criminal behavior, let's examine the relationship between median household income and criminal behavior. The U.S. Census Bureau regularly collects a variety of information from U.S. residents. In the most recent *Statistical Abstract of the United States*, crime rates were tabulated and reported for all the 50 states, including the District of Columbia. Let's focus on the larceny/theft crime rate per 100,000 population. Table 13.5 displays the larceny/theft

Table 13.5   Larceny/Theft Crime Rate per 100,000 Population and Median Household Income for 10 States

State	Median Household Income X	Larceny/Theft Crime Rate Y
California	58,931	1,663
Texas	48,259	2,741
New York	54,659	1,494
Florida	44,736	2,589
Illinois	53,966	2,188
Pennsylvania	49,520	1,636
Ohio	45,395	2,173
Michigan	45,255	1,791
Georgia	47,590	2,369
New Jersey	68,342	1,473

Source: U.S. Census Bureau, *Statistical Abstract of the United States: 2012,* Table 308; U.S.Census Bureau, American Community Survey, 2009.

crime rate and median household income for the 10 most populated states. The scatter diagram for these data was displayed earlier, in Figure 13.2.

Let's examine Figure 13.2 once again. The scatter diagram seems to indicate that the two variables—larceny/theft crime rate and median household income—are linearly related. It also illustrates that these variables are negatively associated; that is, as median household income rises, the larceny/theft crime rate declines.

For a more systematic analysis of the association, we need to estimate the least squares regression equation for these data. Since we want to predict the larceny/theft crime rate, we treat this variable as our dependent variable (Y).

Table 13.6 shows the calculations necessary to find a and b for our data on median household income in relation to the larceny/theft crime rate.

Now, let's substitute the values for the covariance and the variance from Table 13.6 to calculate b:

$$b = \frac{S_{XY}}{S_X^2} = \frac{-2,154,753}{56,266,139} = -0.04$$

Once b has been calculated, finding a, the intercept, is simple:

$$a = \overline{Y} - b(\overline{X}) = 2,011.7 - (-0.04)(51,665.3) = 4,078$$

The prediction equation is therefore

$$\hat{Y} = 4,078 + (-0.04)X$$

This equation can be used to obtain a predicted value for a state's larceny/theft crime rate given a state's median household income.

▣ METHODS FOR ASSESSING THE ACCURACY OF PREDICTIONS

So far, we have developed two regression equations that are helping us make state-level predictions about educational attainment and criminal behavior. But in both cases, our predictions are far from perfect. If we examine Figures 13.6 and 13.7, we can see that we fail to make accurate predictions in every case. Though some of the states lie pretty close to the regression line, hardly any lie directly on the line—an indication that some error of prediction was made. You must be wondering by now, "Okay, I understand that the model helps us make predictions, but how can I assess the accuracy of these predictions?"

We saw earlier that one way to judge the accuracy of the predictions is to "eyeball" the scatterplot. The closer the observations are to the regression line, the better the "fit" between the predictions and the actual observations. Still we want a more systematic method for making such a judgment. We need a measure that tells us how accurate a prediction the regression model provides. The *coefficient of determination*, or r^2, is such a measure. It tells us how well

Table 13.6   Median Household Income and the Larceny/Theft Crime Rate for 10 States

	(1)	(2)	(3)	(4)	(5)	(6)	(7)
	Median Household Income	*Larceny/ Theft Crime Rate*					
State	X	Y	$(X-\bar{X})$	$(X-\bar{X})^2$	$(Y-\bar{Y})$	$(Y-\bar{Y})^2$	$(X-\bar{X})(Y-\bar{Y})$
California	58 931	1,663	7,265.7	52,790,396	−348.7	121,592	−2,533,550
Texas	48 259	2,741	−3,406.3	11,602,880	729.3	531,878	−2,484,215
New York	54 659	1,494	2,993.7	8,962,240	−517.7	268,013	−1,549,838
Florida	44 736	2,589	−6,929.3	48,015,198	577.3	333,275	−4,000,285
Illinois	53 966	2,188	2,300.7	5,293,220	176.3	31,082	405,613
Pennsylvania	49 520	1,636	−2,145.3	4,602,312	−375.7	141,150	805,989
Ohio	45 395	2,173	−6,270.3	39,316,662	161.3	26,018	−1,011,399
Michigan	45 255	1,791	−6,410.3	41,091,946	−220.7	48,708	1,414,753
Georgia	47 590	2,369	−4,075.3	16,608,070	357.3	127,663	−1,456,105
New Jersey	68 342	1,473	16,676.7	278,112,323	−538.7	290,198	−8,983,738
	$\Sigma X=516,653$	$\Sigma Y=20,117$	0[a]	506,395,248	0[a]	1,919,578	−19,392,774

$$\text{Mean } X = \bar{X} = \frac{\Sigma X}{N} = \frac{516,653}{10} = 51,665.3$$

$$\text{Mean } Y = \bar{Y} = \frac{\Sigma Y}{N} = \frac{20,117}{10} = 2,011.7$$

$$\text{Variance}(X) = S_X^2 = \frac{\Sigma(X-\bar{X})^2}{N-1} = \frac{506,395,248}{9} = 56,266,139$$

$$\text{Standard Deviation}(X) = S_X = \sqrt{56,266,139} = 7,501.08$$

$$\text{Variance}(Y) = S_Y^2 = \frac{\Sigma(Y-\bar{Y})^2}{N-1} = \frac{1,919,578}{9} = 213,286$$

$$\text{Standard Deviation}(Y) = S_Y = \sqrt{213,286} = 462$$

$$\text{Covariance}(X,Y) = S_{XY} = \frac{\Sigma(X-\bar{X})(Y-\bar{Y})}{N-1} = \frac{-19,392,774}{9} = -2,154,753$$

a. Answers may differ due to rounding; however, the exact value of these column totals, properly calculated, will always be equal to zero.

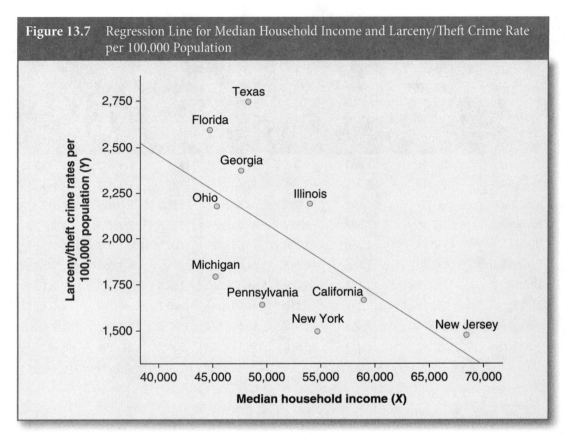

Figure 13.7   Regression Line for Median Household Income and Larceny/Theft Crime Rate per 100,000 Population

the bivariate regression model fits the data. Both r^2 and r measure the strength of the association between two interval-ratio variables. Before we discuss these measures, let's first examine the notion of prediction errors.

Prediction Errors

Examine Figure 13.8. It displays the regression line for the variables median household income (X) and the percentage of state residents with a bachelor's degree (Y). This regression line and the scatter diagram for the 10 states were originally presented in Figure 13.6.

In Figure 13.8, we consider the prediction of Y for one state, New York, out of the 10 states presented. (The X and Y scores for all 10 states, including New York, are presented in Table 13.4.)

Suppose we didn't know the actual Y, the percentage of New York residents who had a bachelor's degree. Suppose further that we did not have knowledge of X, New York's median household income. Because the mean minimizes the sum of the squared errors for a set of scores, our best guess for Y would be the mean of Y, or 28.08%. The horizontal line in Figure 13.8 represents this mean. Now, let's compare New York's actual Y, 32.40%, with this prediction:

$$Y - \overline{Y} = 32.40 - 28.08 = 4.32$$

Figure 13.8 Error Terms for New York

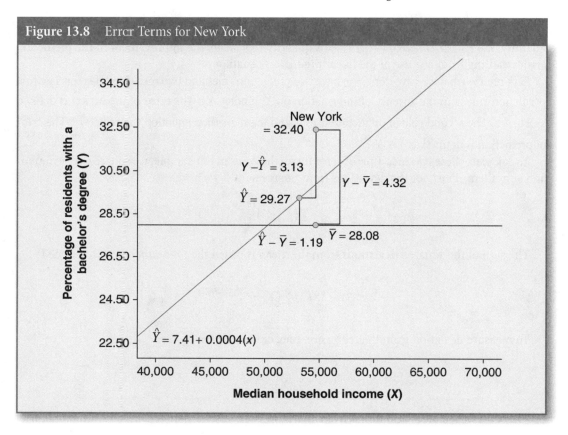

With an error of 4.32, our prediction of the average score for New York is not very accurate.

Now, let's see if our predictive power can be improved by using our knowledge of *X*—the median household income for New York—and its linear relationship with *Y*. If we plug New York's median household income of $54,659 into our prediction equation, as follows

$$\hat{Y} = 7.41 + 0.0004(X)$$

$$\hat{Y} = 7.41 + 0.0004(54,659) = 29.27$$

we obtain a predicted $\hat{Y}$ of 29.27.

We can now recalculate our new error of prediction by comparing the predicted $\hat{Y}$ with the actual *Y*:

$$Y - \hat{Y} = 32.40 - 29.27 = 3.13$$

Although this prediction is by no means perfect, it is a slight improvement of 1.19 (4.32 – 3.13 = 1.19) over our earlier prediction.

This improvement is illustrated in Figure 13.8. Note that this improvement of 1.19 is equal to the quantity $\hat{Y} - \overline{Y} = 29.27 - 28.08 = 1.19$. This quantity represents the improvement in the prediction error resulting from our use of the linear prediction equation.

Let's review what we have done. We have two prediction rules and two measures of error. The first prediction rule is in the absence of information on X, predict $\overline{Y}$. The error of prediction is defined as $Y - \overline{Y}$. The second rule of prediction uses X and the regression equation to predict $\hat{Y}$. The error of prediction is defined as $Y - \hat{Y}$.

To calculate these two measures of error for all the cases in our sample, we square the deviations and sum them. Thus, for the deviations from the mean of Y we have

$$\sum \left(Y - \overline{Y} \right)^2$$

The sum of the squared deviations from the mean is called the *total sum of squares*, or *SST*:

$$SST = \sum \left(Y - \overline{Y} \right)^2$$

To measure deviation from the regression line, or $\hat{Y}$, we have

$$\sum (Y - \hat{Y})^2$$

The sum of squared deviations from the regression line is denoted as the *residual sum of squares*, or *SSE*:

$$SSE = \sum (Y - \hat{Y})^2$$

(We discussed this error term, the residual sum of squares, earlier in the chapter.)

The predictive value of the linear regression equations can be assessed by the extent to which the residual sum of squares, or *SSE*, is smaller than the total sum of squares, *SST*. By subtracting *SSE* from *SST* we obtain the *regression sum of squares*, or *SSR*, which reflects improvement in the prediction error resulting from our use of the linear prediction equation. *SSR* is defined as

$$SSR = SST - SSE$$

Let's calculate these terms for our data on median household income (X) and the percentage of state residents with a bachelor's degree (Y). We already have from Table 13.4 the total sum of squares:

$$SST = \sum (Y - \overline{Y})^2 = 115.0$$

To calculate the errors sum of squares, we will calculate the predicted $\hat{Y}$ for each state, subtract it from the observed Y, square the differences, and sum these for all states. These calculations are presented in Table 13.7.

The residual sum of squares is thus

$$SSE = \sum (Y - \hat{Y})^2 = 19.81$$

The regression sum of squares is then

$$SSR = SST - SSE = 115.0 - 19.81 = 95.19$$

The Coefficient of Determination (r²) as a PRE Measure

The coefficient of determination, r^2, measures the improvement in the prediction error resulting from our use of the linear prediction equation. The coefficient of determination is a PRE measure of association. We saw in Chapter 12 that all PRE measures adhere to the following formula:

Table 13.7   Worksheet for Calculating Errors Sum of Squares (*SSE*)

	(1)	*(2)*	*(3)*	*(4)*	*(5)*
	Median Household Income	*Percentage With a Bachelor's Degree*	*Predicted* Y		
State	X	Y	$\hat{Y}$	$(Y - \hat{Y})$	$(Y - \hat{Y})^2$
California	58,931	29.9	30.98	−1.08	1.17
Texas	48,259	25.5	26.71	−1.21	1.46
New York	54,659	32.4	29.27	3.13	9.80
Florida	44,736	25.3	25.30	0.00	0.00
Illinois	53,966	30.6	29.00	1.60	2.56
Pennsylvania	49,520	26.4	27.22	−0.82	0.67
Ohio	45,395	24.1	25.57	−1.47	2.16
Michigan	45,255	24.6	25.51	−0.91	0.83
Georgia	47,590	27.5	26.45	1.05	1.10
New Jersey	68,342	34.5	34.75	−0.25	0.06
	$\sum X = 516{,}653$	$\sum Y = 280.8$			$\sum (Y - \hat{Y})^2 = 19.81$

$$PRE = \frac{E_1 - E_2}{E_1}$$

where

E_1 = prediction errors made when the independent variable is ignored

E_2 = prediction errors made when the prediction is based on the independent variable

We have all the elements we need to construct a PRE measure. Because the total sum of squares (*SST*) measures the prediction errors when the independent variable is ignored, we can define

$$E_1 = SST$$

Similarly, because the residual sum of squares (*SSE*) measures the prediction errors resulting from using the independent variable, we can define

$$E_2 = SSE$$

We are now ready to define the coefficient of determination r^2. It measures the proportional reduction of error associated with using the linear regression equation as a rule for predicting Y:

$$PRE = \frac{E_1 - E_2}{E_1} = \frac{\Sigma\left(Y - \overline{Y}\right)^2 - \Sigma\left(Y - \hat{Y}\right)^2}{\Sigma\left(Y - \overline{Y}\right)^2} \qquad (13.5)$$

For our example,

$$r^2 = \frac{115.0 - 19.81}{115.0} = \frac{95.19}{115.0} = 0.83$$

The **coefficient of determination** (r^2) reflects the proportion of the total variation in the dependent variable, Y, explained by the independent variable, X. An r^2 of 0.83 means that by using median household income and the linear prediction rule to predict Y—the percentage of state residents with a bachelor's degree—we have reduced the error of prediction by 83% (0.83×100). We can also say that the independent variable (median household income) explains about 83% of the variation in the dependent variable (the percentage of state residents with a bachelor's degree), as illustrated in Figure 13.9.

Coefficient of determination (r^2)   A PRE measure reflecting the proportional reduction of error that results from using the linear regression model. It reflects the proportion of the total variation in the dependent variable, Y, explained by the independent variable, X.

Figure 13.9   A Pie Graph Approach to r^2

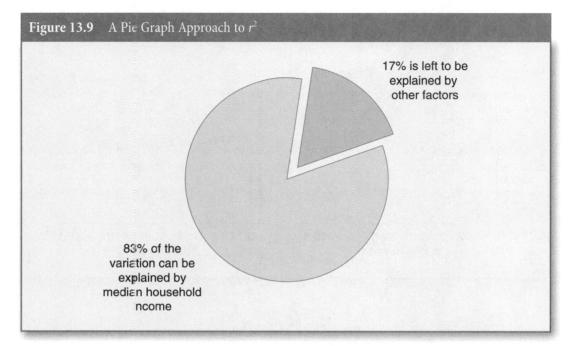

17% is left to be explained by other factors

83% of the variation can be explained by median household income

The coefficient of determination ranges from 0.0 to 1.0. An r^2 of 1.0 means that by using the linear regression model, we have reduced uncertainty by 100%. It also means that the independent variable accounts for 100% of the variation in the dependent variable. With an r^2 of 1.0, all the observations fall along the regression line, and the prediction error is equal to 0.0. An r^2 of 0.0 means that using the regression equation to predict Y does not improve the prediction of Y. Figure 13.10 shows r^2 values near 0.0 and near 1.0. In Figure 13.10a, where r^2 is approximately 1.0, the regression model provides a good fit. In contrast, a very poor fit is evident in Figure 13.10b, where r^2 is near zero. An r^2 near zero indicates either poor fit or a well-fitting line with a b of zero.

Calculating r^2

Another method for calculating r^2 uses the following equation:

$$r^2 = \frac{\left[Covariance(X,Y)^2 \right]}{\left[Variance\,(X) \right]\left[Variance(Y) \right]} = \frac{S^2_{YX}}{S^2_X S^2_Y} \tag{13.6}$$

This formula tells us to divide the square of the covariance of X and Y by the product of the variance of X and the variance of Y.

To calculate r^2 for our example, we can go back to Table 13.4, where the covariance and the variances for the two variables have already been calculated:

$$S_{XY} = 24{,}477.96$$

Figure 13.10   Examples Showing r^2 (a) Near 1.0 and (b) Near 0

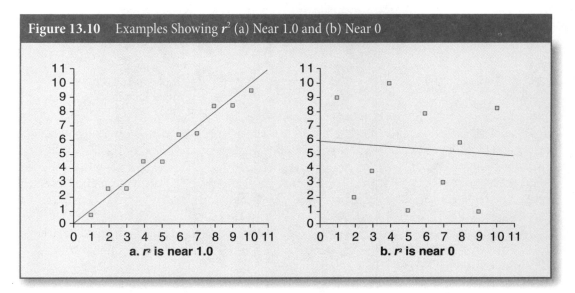

a. r^2 is near 1.0

b. r^2 is near 0

$$S_X^2 = 56,266,139$$

$$S_Y^2 = 12.78$$

Therefore,

$$r^2 = \frac{(24,477.96)^2}{(56,266,139)(12.78)} = \frac{599,170,526}{719,081,256} = 0.83$$

Since we are working with actual values for median household income, its metric, or measurement, values are different from the metric values for the dependent variable, the percentage of state residents with a bachelor's degree. While this hasn't been an issue until now, we must account for this measurement difference if we elect to use the variances and covariance to calculate r^2 (Formula 13.6). The remedy is actually quite simple. All we have to do is multiply our obtained r^2, 0.83, by 100 to obtain 83. You might be wondering, "Why multiply the obtained r^2 by 100?" The answer is we multiply by 100 because the dependent variable, percentage of residents with a bachelor's degree, is measured as a percentage ranging from 1 to 100. You will note that we've now obtained the exact value as obtained earlier with Formula 13.5.

We can multiply r^2 by 100 to obtain the percentage of variation in the dependent variable explained by the independent variable. An r^2 of 0.83 means that by using median household income and the linear prediction rule to predict Y, the percentage of state residents with a bachelor's degree—we have reduced uncertainty of prediction by 83% (0.83×100). We can also say that the independent variable (median household income) explains 83% of the variation in the dependent variable (the percentage of state residents with a bachelor's degree), as illustrated in Figure 13.9.

▣ TESTING THE SIGNIFICANCE OF R^2 USING ANOVA

Like other descriptive statistics, r^2 is an estimate based on sample data. Once r^2 is obtained, we should assess the probability that the linear relationship between median household income and the percentage of state residents with a bachelor's degree, as expressed in r^2, is really zero in the population (given the observed sample coefficient). In other words, we must test r^2 for statistical significance. ANOVA, presented earlier in Chapter 12, can easily be applied to determine the statistical significance of the regression model as expressed in r^2. In fact, when you look closely, ANOVA and regression analysis can look very much the same. In both methods, we attempt to account for variation in the dependent variable in terms of the independent variable, except that in ANOVA the independent variable is a categorical variable (nominal or ordinal, e.g., gender or social class) and with regression, it is an interval-ratio variable (e.g., income measured in dollars).

With ANOVA, we decomposed the total variation in the dependent variable into portions explained (*SSB*) and unexplained (*SSW*) by the independent variable. Next, we calculated the mean squares between (SSB/df_b) and mean squares within (SSW/df_w). The statistical test, F, is the ratio of the mean squares between to the mean squares within Formula 13.7.

$$F = \frac{\text{Mean squares between}}{\text{Mean squares within}} = \frac{SSB/df_b}{SSW/df_w} \tag{13.7}$$

With regression analysis, we decomposed the total variation in the dependent variable into portions explained, *SSR* (**regression sum of squares**), and unexplained, *SSE* (**residual sum of squares**). Similar to ANOVA, the mean squares regression and the mean squares residual are calculated by dividing each sum of squares by its corresponding degrees of freedom (df). The degrees of freedom associated with *SSR* (df_r) are equal to K, which refers to the number of independent variables in the regression equation.

$$\text{Mean squares regression} = \frac{SSR}{df_r} = \frac{SSR}{K} \tag{13.8}$$

For *SSE*, degrees of freedom (df_e) is equal to $[N - (K + 1)]$, with N equal to the sample size.

$$\text{Mean squares residual} = \frac{SSE}{df_e} = \frac{SSE}{[N - (K + 1)]} \tag{13.9}$$

Regression sum of squares (SSR)   Reflects the improvement in the prediction error resulting from using the linear prediction equation, SST – SSE.

Residual sum of squares (SSE)   Sum of squared differences between observed and predicted Y.

In Table 13.8 for example, we present the ANOVA summary table for median household income and the percentage of state residents with a bachelor's degree.

In the table, under the heading *Source of Variation* are displayed the regression, residual, and total sums of squares. The column marked *df* shows the degrees of freedom associated with both the *regression* and *residual* sum of squares. In the bivariate case, *SSR* has 1 degree of freedom associated with it. The degrees of freedom associated with *SSE* is $[N – (K + 1)]$, where K refers to the number of independent variables in the regression equation. In the bivariate case, with one independent variable—median household income—*SSE* has $N – 2$ degrees of freedom associated with it $[N – (1 + 1)]$. Finally, the **mean squares regression** (*MSR*) and the **mean squares residual** (*MSE*) are calculated by dividing each sum of squares by its corresponding degrees of freedom. For our example,

$$\text{Mean squares regression} = \frac{SSR}{1} = \frac{95.19}{1} = 95.19$$

$$\text{Mean squares residual} = \frac{SSE}{8} = \frac{19.81}{8} = 2.48$$

Mean squares regression   An average computed by dividing the regression sum of squares (*SSR*) by its corresponding degrees of freedom.

Mean squares residual   An average computed by dividing the residual sum of squares (*SSE*) by its corresponding degrees of freedom.

Table 13.8   Analysis of Variance Summary Table for Median Household Income and the Percentage of State Residents With a Bachelor's Degree

Source of Variation	Sum of Squares	df	Mean Squares	F
Regression	95.19	1	95.19	38.38
Residual	19.81	8	2.48	
Total	115.0	9		

The F statistic together with the mean squares regression and the mean squares residual compose the obtained *F* ratio or *F* statistic. The *F* statistic is the ratio of the mean squares regression to the mean squares residual:

$$F = \frac{\text{Mean squares regression}}{\text{Mean squares residual}} = \frac{SSR / df_r}{SSE / df_e} \qquad (13.10)$$

The *F* ratio, thus, represents the size of the mean squares regression relative to the size of the mean squares residual. The larger the mean squares regression relative to the mean squares residual, the larger the *F* ratio and the more likely that r^2 is significantly larger than zero in the population. We are testing the null hypothesis that r^2 is zero in the population.

Let's calculate the *F* ratio for our example of median household income and the percentage of state residents with a bachelor's degree:

$$F = \frac{\text{Mean squares regression}}{\text{Mean squares residual}} = \frac{95.19}{2.48} = 38.38$$

Making a Decision

To determine the probability of calculating an *F* statistic of 38.38, we rely on Appendix E, Distribution of *F*. Appendix E lists the corresponding values of the *F* distribution for various degrees of freedom and two levels of significance, .05 and .01. We will set alpha at .05, and thus, we will refer to the table marked "*F* = .05." Note that Appendix E includes two *df*s. For the numerator, df_1 refers to the df_r associated with the mean squares regression; for the denominator, df_2 refers to the df_e associated with the means squares residual. For our example, we compare our obtained *F* (38.38) to the *F* critical. When the *df*s are 1 (numerator) and 8 (denominator), and α = .05, the *F* critical is 5.32. Since our obtained *F* is larger than the *F* critical (38.38 > 5.32), we can reject the null hypothesis that r^2 is zero in the population. We conclude that the linear relationship between median household income and the percentage of state residents with a bachelor's degree as expressed in r^2 is probably greater than zero in the population (given our observed sample coefficient).

✓ *Learning*
Check

Test the null hypothesis that there is a linear relationship between median household income and a state's larceny/theft crime rate. The mean squares regression is 916,504.82 with 1 degree of freedom. The mean squares residual is 174,732.41 with 8 degrees of freedom. Calculate the F statistic and assess its significance.

Pearson's Correlation Coefficient (r)

In the social sciences, it is the square root of r^2, or *r*—known as Pearson's correlation coefficient—that is most often used as a measure of association between two interval-ratio variables:

$$r = \sqrt{r^2}$$

Pearson's correlation coefficient (r)   The square root of r^2; it is a measure of association for interval-ratio variables, reflecting the strength of the linear association between two interval-ratio variables. It can be positive or negative in sign.

Pearson's r is usually computed directly by using the following definitional formula:

$$r = \frac{\left[Covariance(X,Y) \right]}{\left[Standard\,deviation(X) \right]\left[Standard\,deviation(Y) \right]} = \frac{S_{YX}}{S_X S_Y}$$

Thus, r is defined as the ratio of the covariance of X and Y to the product of the standard deviations of X and Y.

Characteristics of Pearson's r

Pearson's r is a measure of relationship or association for interval-ratio variables. Like gamma (introduced in Chapter 11), it ranges from 0.0 to ±1.0, with 0.0 indicating no association between the two variables. An r of +1.0 means that the two variables have a perfect positive association; –1.0 indicates that it is a perfect negative association. The absolute value of r indicates the strength of the linear association between two variables. (Refer back to A Closer Look 12.1 for an interpretational guide.) Thus, a correlation of –0.75 demonstrates a stronger association than a correlation of 0.50. Figure 13.11 illustrates a strong positive relationship, a strong negative relationship, a moderate positive relationship, and a weak negative relationship.

Unlike the b coefficient, r is a symmetrical measure. That is, the correlation between X and Y is identical to the correlation between Y and X. In contrast, b may be different when the variables are switched—for example, when we use Y as the independent variable rather than as the dependent variable.

To calculate r for our example of the relationship between median household income and the percentage of state residents with a bachelor's degree, let's return to Table 13.4, where the covariance and the standard deviations for X and Y have already been calculated:

$$r = \frac{S_{XY}}{S_X S_Y} = \frac{24,477.96}{(7,501.08)(3.57)} = \frac{24,477.96}{26,778.86} = 0.91$$

A correlation coefficient of 0.91 indicates that there is a strong positive linear relationship between median household income and the percentage of state residents with a bachelor's degree.

Note that we could have just taken the square root of r^2 to calculate r, because $r = \sqrt{r^2}$ or $\sqrt{0.83} = 0.91$. Similarly, if we first calculate r, we can obtain r^2 simply by squaring r (be careful not to lose the sign of r^2).

Figure 13.11 Scatter Diagrams Illustrating Weak, Moderate, and Strong Relationships as Indicated by the Absolute Value of *r*

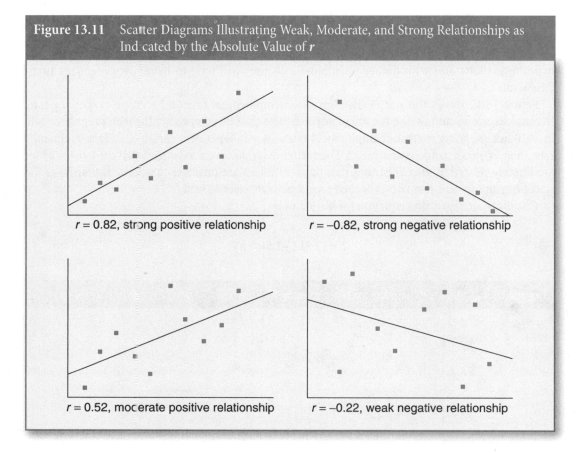

r = 0.82, strong positive relationship

r = –0.82, strong negative relationship

r = 0.52, moderate positive relationship

r = –0.22, weak negative relationship

▣ STATISTICS IN PRACTICE: TEEN PREGNANCY AND SOCIAL INEQUALITY

The United States has by far the highest rate of teenage pregnancy of any industrialized nation. The pregnancy rate for U.S. teens aged between 15 and 19 years was 95.9 pregnancies per 1,000 women in 1990. Although, in 2010, teen pregnancy rates reached its lowest point in more than 70 years (34.2 per 1,000 women aged 15–19),[2] this rate is still higher than any other industrialized nation. These high rates have been attributed, among other factors, to the high rate of poverty and inequality in the United States.

The association between teen pregnancy and poverty and social inequality has been well documented both nationally and internationally. Teen pregnancy rates are higher among people living in poverty, and industrial societies that have done the most to reduce social inequality tend to have the lowest rates of teen pregnancy.[3] The noted sociologist William Wilson has claimed that the disappearance of hundreds of low-skilled jobs in the past 25 years and the resulting increase in unemployment, especially in the inner cities, has led to the increase in teenage pregnancy rates and to welfare dependency.[4] Teenagers living in areas of high unemployment, poverty, and lack of opportunities are six to seven times more likely to become unwed parents.[5]

To examine the degree to which economic factors influence teenage pregnancy rates, we analyze state-by-state data on unemployment rates in 2009 and teenage pregnancy rates in 2010. Using unemployment rate and pregnancy rate, both interval-ratio variables, we can examine the hypothesis that states with higher unemployment rates will tend to have higher teenage pregnancy rates.

Figure 13.12 shows the scatter diagram for unemployment rate and teenage pregnancy rate. Because we are assuming that the unemployment rate in 2009 can predict the teen pregnancy rate in 2010, we are going to treat unemployment rate as our independent variable, *X*. Teen pregnancy rate, then, is our dependent variable, *Y*. The scatter diagram seems to suggest that the two variables are linearly related. It also illustrates that these variables are positively associated; that is, as the state's unemployment rate rises, the teen pregnancy rate rises as well.

Our bivariate regression equation for 40[6] states is

$$\hat{Y} = 17.312 + 1.567(X)$$

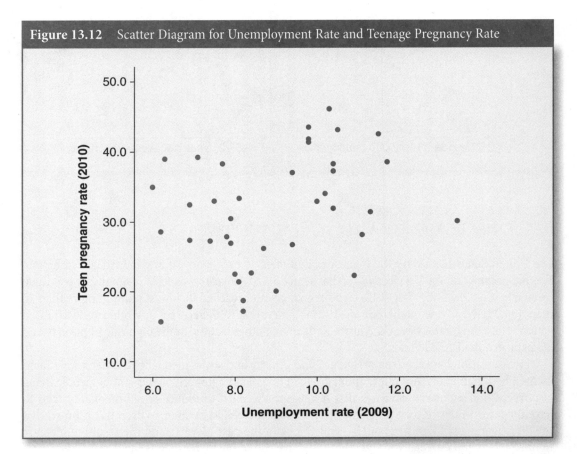

Figure 13.12   Scatter Diagram for Unemployment Rate and Teenage Pregnancy Rate

Sources: Center for Disease Control, "Births: Final Data for 2010," *National Vital Statistics Report*: 61(1), August 28, 2012.

Bureau of Labor Statistics, "Unemployment Rates for States Annual Average Rankings Year: 2009"

In this prediction equation, the **slope** (*b*) is 1.567 and the intercept (*a*) is 17.312. The positive slope, 1.567, confirms our earlier impression, based on the scatter diagram, that the relationship between the unemployment rate and teenage pregnancy rate is positive. In other words, the higher the unemployment rate, the higher the pregnancy rate. A *b* equal to 1.567 means that for every 1 percentage point increase in the unemployment rate, the pregnancy rate for teens aged 15 to 19 years will increase by 1.567 pregnancies per 1,000 women. The intercept, *a*, of 17.312 indicates that with full employment (an unemployment rate of 0), the teen pregnancy rate will be 17.312 pregnancies per 1,000 women. The regression line corresponding to this linear regression equation is shown in Figure 13.13.

Slope (b)   The amount of change in a dependent variable per unit change in an independent variable.

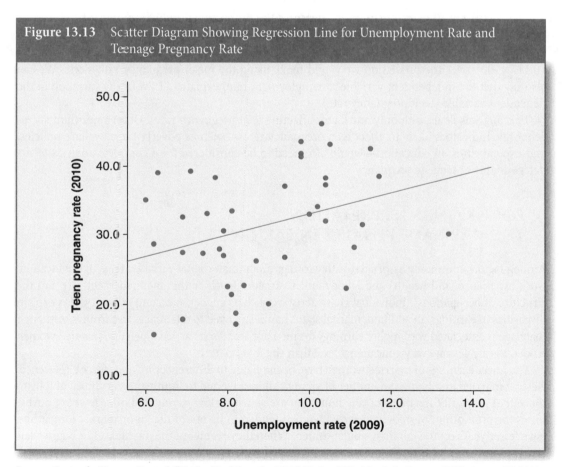

Figure 13.13   Scatter Diagram Showing Regression Line for Unemployment Rate and Teenage Pregnancy Rate

Sources: Center for Disease Control, "Births: Final Data for 2010," *National Vital Statistics Report:* 61(1), August 28, 2012.

Bureau of Labor Statistics, "Unemployment Rates for States Annual Average Rankings Year: 2009."

Based on the linear regression equation, we could predict the teenage pregnancy rate for any state based on its unemployment rate in 2009. For example, with a 2009 unemployment rate of 9.8%, Alabama's predicted 2010 teen pregnancy rate is

$$\hat{Y} = 17.312 + 1.567(9.8) = 32.67$$

With a higher unemployment rate of 13.4%, the predicted 2010 teen pregnancy rate for Michigan is

$$\hat{Y} = 17.312 + 1.567(13.4) = 38.31$$

We also calculated r and r^2 for these data. We obtained an r of 0.342 and an r^2 of $0.342^2 = 0.117$. An r of 0.342 indicates that there is a moderate positive relationship between the unemployment rate in 2009 and the teen pregnancy rate in 2010.

The coefficient of determination, r^2, measures the proportional reduction of error that results from using the linear regression model to predict teen pregnancy rates. An r^2 of 0.117 means that by using the regression equation, our prediction of teen pregnancy rates is improved by 11.7% (0.117×100) over the prediction we would make using the mean pregnancy rate alone. We can also say that the independent variable (unemployment rate) explains 11.7% of the variation in the dependent variable (teen pregnancy rate).

This analysis deals with only one factor affecting teen pregnancy rates. Other important socio-economic indicators likely to affect teen pregnancy rates—such as poverty rates, welfare policies, and expenditures on education—would also need to be considered for a complete analysis of the determinants of teenage pregnancy.

▣ FOCUS ON INTERPRETATION: THE MARRIAGE PENALTY IN EARNING

Among factors commonly associated with earnings are human capital variables (e.g., age, education, work experience, and health) and labor market variables (such as the unemployment rate and the structure of occupations). Individual characteristics, such as gender, race, and ethnicity, also explain disparities in earnings. In addition, marital status has been linked to differences in earnings. Although marriage is associated with higher earnings for men, for women it carried a penalty; married women tended to earn less at every educational level than single women.

The lower earnings of married women have been related to differences in labor force experience. Getting married and being the mother of young children tended to limit women's choice of jobs to those that may offer flexible working hours but are generally low paying and offer fewer opportunities for promotion. Moreover, married women tended to be out of the labor market longer and have fewer years on the job than single women. When they reentered the job market or begin their career after their children are grown, they competed with coworkers with considerably more work experience and on-the-job training. (Women who need to become financially independent after divorce or widowhood may share some of the same liabilities as married women.)

Past studies have shown that the returns for formal education were generally lower for married women and that single women earned more for each year of formal education than married women. However, evolving family dynamics over the past decades have resulted in an increase in the proportion of married women who are the sole primary provider.[7] Forty percent of American households with children under age 18 now include a mother who is either the sole or primary earner for her family. These changes have manifested in increasing wages for women who have entered primary earning roles.

We explore this issue by analyzing the bivariate relationship between level of education and personal income among 307 single and married females (working full-time) included in the 2010 GSS.[8] We are assuming that level of education (measured in years) can predict personal income, and therefore, we treat education as our independent variable, X. Personal income (measured in dollars), then, is the dependent variable, Y. Since both are interval-ratio variables, we can use bivariate regression analysis to examine the difference in returns for education.

We will rely on SPSS to calculate the bivariate regression equations for both single and married females working full time. We will not present the calculations of a, b, and r^2 because we want to focus on interpreting the SPSS output. The output for single females includes two tables. The output for married women is not shown here.

The regression equation coefficients are listed in the Coefficients table, under the column labeled "B." The coefficient for EDUC, or b, is 2,637.41; the intercept term, or a, identified in the "(Constant)" row, is −11,810.19. Using these terms, we can express the bivariate relationship between education and income for single females working full time as

$$\hat{Y}(\text{single}) = -11,810.19 + 2,637.41(X)$$

Figure 13.14 SPSS Regression Output for Single Females

Model Summary[a]

Model	R	R Square	Adjusted R Square	Std. Error of the Estimate
1	.436[b]	.190	.176	15391.651

a. MARITAL STATUS = NEVER MARRIED

b. Predictors: (Constant), HIGHEST YEAR OF SCHOOL COMPLETED

Coefficients[a,b]

Model		Unstandardized Coefficients B	Unstandardized Coefficients Std. Error	Standardized Coefficients Beta	t	Sig.
1	(Constant)	-11810.194	10835.606		-1.090	.280
	HIGHEST YEAR OF SCHOOL COMPLETED	2637.410	714.091	.436	3.693	.000

a. MARITAL STATUS = NEVER MARRIED

b. Dependent Variable: RS INCOME IN CONSTANT $

The regression equation tells us that for every one year increase in education we can predict an increase of $2,637.41 in the annual income of single women in our sample who work full time.

The bivariate regression equation for married females working full time is (output not shown here) is:

$$\hat{Y}(\text{married}) = -32{,}946.04 + 4{,}155.15(X)$$

This analysis shows that in fact it is married women who benefit more from the effect of education on their income. For single women one year of education is worth $2,637.41; for married women it is $4,155.15. These results are puzzling and contradict literature that has suggested that married women were placed at a disadvantage when compared to single women because of their prolonged absence from the labor market due to child rearing responsibilities. However, with evolving family patterns, many more married women remain in the labor force even when their children are very young. This may account for the larger return for education for married women.

One should be extremely cautious when interpreting these data. In all likelihood, the difference in earnings between single and married women is due to numerous other factors such as occupation, family size, ethnicity, and race. To test some of this idea, we would need to use more advanced statistical techniques not covered in this text.

SPSS also calculates r-squared for these data. These results are presented in the table titled "Model Summary." The coefficient of determination (r^2) is labeled "R square." For single women, r^2 is 0.190; for married women, it is 0.275 (not shown). These coefficients indicate that for both groups there is a weak-to-moderate relationship between education and earnings (the relationship is substantially stronger for married women).

Using the regression equation, our prediction of income for single women is improved by 19.0% (0.190×100) over the prediction we would make using the mean alone. For married women, there is more of an improvement in prediction, 27.5% (0.275×100).

We can use these regression equations to predict the difference in annual income between a single woman and a married woman, both with 16 years of education and working full time:

$$\hat{Y}(\text{single}) = -11{,}810.19 + 2{,}637.41(16) = 30{,}388.37$$

$$\hat{Y}(\text{married}) = -32{,}946.04 + 4{,}155.15(16) = 33{,}536.36$$

This analysis deals with only one factor affecting earnings—the level of education. Other important factors associated with earnings—including occupation, seniority, race/ethnicity, and age—would need to be considered for a complete analysis of the differences in earnings between single and married women.

▣ MULTIPLE REGRESSION

Thus far, we have used examples that involved only two variables: a dependent variable and an independent variable. For example, in an earlier section, we attempted to account for variations in teen pregnancy rates on the basis of unemployment rates. We employed a linear bivariate regression equation in which unemployment rate was the independent variable and teen pregnancy rate, the dependent variable. Whereas this equation gave us a relatively accurate prediction, it seems reasonable that other variables besides the state's unemployment rate might affect the rate of teen-age pregnancy.

For example, we know from theoretical and empirical accounts that lack of educational opportunities also accounts for the rate of teen pregnancy. We might be able to provide a better explanation of teen pregnancy rates if we also included a measure of educational resources in addition to unemployment rates.

Multiple regression is an extension of bivariate regression. It allows us to examine the effect of two or more independent variables on the dependent variable. The calculations involved in multiple regression are quite elaborate but are easily accomplished using SPSS or other statistical software.

Multiple regression An extension of bivariate regression in which the effects of two or more independent variables on the dependent variable are examined. The general form of the multiple regression equation involving two independent variables is

$$\hat{Y} = a + b_1(X_1) + b_2(X_2)$$

The general form of the multiple regression equation involving two independent variables is

$$\hat{Y} = a + b_1(X_1) + b_2(X_2) \tag{13.8}$$

where

$\hat{Y}$ = the predicted score on the dependent variable

X_1 = the score on independent variable X_1

X_2 = the score on independent variable X_2

a = the Y-intercept, or the value of Y when both X_1 and X_2 are equal to zero

b_1 = the change in Y with a unit change in X_1, when the other independent variable X_2 is controlled

b_2 = the change in Y with a unit change in X_2, when the other independent variable X_1 is controlled

To illustrate, let's expand our investigation of teen pregnancy and add a second independent variable—the state's 2009 expenditure per pupil in elementary and secondary schools. We are hypothesizing that the higher the state's expenditure, the lower the teen pregnancy rate. We are also hypothesizing, as we did earlier, that the higher the state's unemployment rate, the higher the teen pregnancy rate. The multiple linear equation that incorporates both the unemployment rate and the level of educational expenditures as predictors of teen pregnancy rates is

$$\hat{Y} = 39.661 + 0.823(X_1) - 0.001(X_2)$$

where

$\hat{Y}$ = predicted pregnancy rate, 2010

X_1 = state unemployment rate, 2009

X_2 = expenditure per pupil, 2009

This equation tells us that a state's pregnancy rate goes up by 0.823 per 1,000 women for each 1% increase in the unemployment rate (X_1), holding expenditure per pupil (X_2) constant. Similarly, the state's pregnancy rate goes down by 0.001 with each 1-dollar increase in the state's expenditure per pupil (X_2), holding the unemployment rate (X_1) constant.

Controlling for the effect of one variable, while examining the effect of the other, allows us to separate out the effects of each predictor independently of the other. For example, given two states with the same unemployment rate, the state with $1 additional expenditure per pupil is expected to have a teen pregnancy rate that is 0.001 lower. Similarly, given two states with the same level of expenditure per pupil, the state where the unemployment rate is 1 percentage point higher will have 0.823 more pregnancies per 1,000 women. Finally, the value of a (39.661) reflects the state's teen pregnancy rate when both the unemployment rate and the state's expenditure per pupil are equal to zero. Although it seems unlikely that any state will ever have rates as low as zero, the value of a is a baseline that must be added to the equation for pregnancy rate to be properly estimated.

Using our prediction equation for rates of teen pregnancy, we can predict the teen pregnancy rates for states with given levels of unemployment and expenditures per pupil. For example, with an unemployment rate of 9.80% and an expenditure per pupil of $7,848, Arizona's predicted pregnancy rate for 2010 is

$$\hat{Y} = 39.661 + 0.823(9.80) - 0.001(7,848) = 39.88$$

Like bivariate regression, multiple regression analysis yields a **coefficient of determination,** symbolized as R^2 (corresponding to r^2 in the bivariate case). R^2 measures the proportional reduction of error that results from using the linear regression model. It reflects the proportion of the total variation in the dependent variable that is explained jointly by two or more independent variables. We obtained an R^2 of 0.330. This means that by using states' unemployment rates and expenditures per pupil to predict pregnancy rates, we have reduced error of prediction by 33.0% (0.330×100). We can also say that the independent variables, *unemployment rates* and *expenditures per pupil*, in combination explain 33% of the variation in states' pregnancy rates.

Multiple coefficient of determination (R^2)   Measure that reflects the proportion of the total variation in the dependent variable that is explained jointly by two or more independent variables.

The inclusion of expenditure per pupil greatly improved our prediction of teen pregnancy rates. As we saw earlier, unemployment rate accounted for 11.7% of the variation in teen pregnancy rate. The addition of expenditure per pupil to the prediction equation resulted in an increase of 21.3% ($33.0\% - 11.7\% = 21.3\%$) in the percentage of explained variation in teen pregnancy rate.

As in the bivariate case, the square root of R^2, or R, is Pearson's multiple correlation coefficient. It measures the linear relationship between the dependent variable and the combined effect of two or more independent variables. For our example, $R = 0.574$. It indicates that there is a moderate-to-strong relationship between the dependent variable, *teen pregnancy rate*, and both independent variables, *unemployment rate* and *expenditure per pupil*.

Pearson's multiple correlation coefficient (R)   Measure of the linear relationship between the independent variable and the combined effect of two or more independent variables.

✓ *Learning Check*

Use the prediction equation describing the relationship between teen pregnancy and both unemployment and expenditures on education to calculate the 2010 predicted teen pregnancy rate for a state with an unemployment rate of 3% and an expenditure per pupil of $6,000.

▣ ANOVA FOR MULTIPLE LINEAR REGRESSION

The ANOVA summary table for multiple regression is nearly identical to the one for simple linear regression, except that the degrees of freedom are adjusted to reflect the number of independent variables in the model.

We conducted an ANOVA test to assess the probability that the linear relationship between teen pregnancy and the combined effect of expenditure per pupil and the unemployment rate, as expressed by R^2, is really zero. The results of this test are summarized in Table 13.9 . The obtained F statistic of 9.107 is shown in this table. With 2 and 37 degrees of freedom, we would need an F of 5.18 to reject the null hypothesis that $R^2 = 0$ at the .01 level. Since our obtained F exceeds that value ($9.107 > 5.18$), we can reject the null hypothesis with $P < .01$.

Table 13.9   Analysis of Variance Summary Table for Teen Pregnancy Rate With Expenditure per Pupil and Unemployment Rate

Source of Variation	Sum of Squares	df	Mean Squares	F
Regression	857.194	2	428.597	9.107
Error	1,741.304	37	47.062	
Total	2,598.498	39		

▣ A Closer Look 13.3
A Cautionary Note: Spurious Correlations and Confounding Effects

In this chapter, we introduced the correlation coefficient, r, a frequently used measure of association between two variables. For example, we found that the correlation between the unemployment rate and the teen pregnancy rate in a state is $r = 0.342$. We interpreted this correlation to mean that there is a moderate association between the two variables.

It is important to note that the existence of a correlation only denotes that the two variables are associated (they occur together or covary) and *not* that they are causally related. The well-known phrase "correlation is not causation" points to the fallacy of inferring that one variable causes the other based on the correlation between the variables. Such relationship is sometimes said to be "spurious" because both variables are influenced by a causally prior control variable, and there is no causal link between them. We can also say that a relationship between the independent and dependent variables is "confounded" by a third variable.

In Chapter 10, we described a favorite example of spurious relationship between the *number of firefighters* (the independent variable) at a fire site and *amount of property damage* (the dependent variable). The more firefighters are at the site, the greater the amount of damage. This association might lead to the embarrassing conclusion that firefighters cause property damage at fire sites. Clearly, in this case, the relationship between the number of firefighters and amount of damage can be accounted for by a third, causally prior variable—*the size of the fire*. When the fire is large, more firefighters are sent to the site, and there is a great deal of property damage. Similarly, when the fire is small, fewer firefighters are at the site, and there is probably very little damage.

The number of firefighters and the extent of property damage are both related to the variable size of fire but are not related to each other. The size of the fire is called a control variable, and the relation between the number of firefighters and property damage is *spurious*. The bivariate relationship between the independent and dependent variables can thus be "explained away" through the introduction of the control variable.

There are numerous examples in the research literature of spurious or confounded relationships. For instance, in a 2004 article, Michael Benson and his colleagues[9,10] discuss the issue of domestic violence as a correlate of race. Studies and reports have consistently found that rates of domestic abuse are higher in communities with a higher percentage of African American residents. Would this correlation indicate that race and domestic violence are causally related? To suggest that African Americans are more prone to engage in domestic violence would be erroneous if not outright racist. Benson and colleagues argue that the correlation between race and domestic violence is confounded by the level of economic distress in the community. Economically distressed communities are typically occupied by a higher percentage of African Americans. Also, rates of domestic violence tend to be higher in such communities. We can say that the relationship between race and domestic violence is confounded by a third variable—level of economic distress in the community.

How do we know that an observed correlation is spurious? As we saw in Chapter 10, we have to "control" for the potentially confounding effect of causally prior and theoretically relevant variables. By reexamining the relationship between number of firefighters and extent of damage in groups of small and large fires, we were "controlling" for the effect of fire size. We expected the original relationship to disappear or diminish considerably, indicating that it is spurious or confounded by the size of the fire.

Similarly, to test for the confounding effect of community economic distress on the relationship between race and domestic violence, Benson and Fox[11] calculated rates of domestic violence for African Americans and whites in communities with high and low levels of economic distress. They found that the relationship between race and domestic violence is not significant when the level of economic distress is constant. That is, the difference in the base rate of domestic violence for African Americans and whites is reduced by almost 50% in communities with high distress levels. Similarly, in communities with low distress level (and high income), the rate of domestic violence of African Americans is virtually identical to that of whites. The results showed that the correlation between race and domestic violence is accounted for in part by the level of economic distress of the community.

Uncovering spurious or confounded relations between an independent and a dependent variable can also be accomplished by using multiple regression. Multiple regression, an extension of bivariate regression, helps us examine the effect of an independent variable on a dependent variable while holding constant one or more additional variables. For example, in the previous section, we were able to identify the effect of a state's unemployment rate on its teen pregnancy rate while holding constant its level of expenditure per pupil and the effect of expenditure per pupil while holding constant the state's unemployment rate.

MAIN POINTS

- A scatter diagram (also called scatterplot) is a quick visual method used to display relationships between two interval-ratio variables.

- Equations for all straight lines have the same general form:

$$\hat{Y} = a + b(X)$$

- The best-fitting regression line is that line where the residual sum of squares, or Σe^2, is at a minimum. Such a line is called the least squares line, and the technique that produces this line is called the least squares method.

- The coefficient of determination (r^2) and Pearson's correlation coefficient (r) measure how well the regression model fits the data. Pearson's r also measures the strength of the association between the two variables.

- The general form of the multiple regression equation involving two independent variables is

$$\hat{Y} = a + b_1(X_1) + b_2(X_2)$$

KEY TERMS

coefficient of
    determination *(r²)*
F critical
least squares line
    (best-fitting line)
linear relationship
multiple coefficient
    of determination
    (R²)

Pearson's correlation
    coefficient *(r)*
scatter diagram
    (scatterplot)
slope *(b)*
Y-intercept *(a)*
deterministic (perfect)
    linear relationship
least squares method

regression sum of squares
residual sum of squares
mean squares
    regression
mean squares residual
multiple regression
Pearson's multiple
    correlation
    coefficient

$SAGE edge™

Sharpen your skills with SAGE edge at **edge.sagepub.com/frankfort7e**. **SAGE edge for students** provides a personalized approach to help you accomplish your coursework goals in an easy-to-use learning environment.

SPSS DEMONSTRATIONS

[GSS10SSDS]

Demonstration 1: Producing Scatterplots (Scatter Diagrams)

Do people with more education work more hours per week? Some may argue that those with lower levels of education are forced to work low-paying jobs, thereby requiring them to work more hours per week to make ends meet. Others may rebut this argument by saying those with higher levels of education are in greater positions of authority, which requires more time to ensure operations run smoothly. This question can be explored with SPSS using the techniques discussed in this chapter for interval-ratio data because *hours worked last week* (HRS1) and *number of years of education* (EDUC) are both coded at an interval-ratio level in the GSS10SSDS file.

We begin by looking at a scatterplot of these two variables. The Scatter procedure can be found under the *Graphs* menu choice. In the opening dialog box, click *Legacy Dialogs* then *Scatter/Dot* (which means we want to produce a standard scatterplot with two variables), select the icon for *Simple Scatter*, and then click *Define*.

The Scatterplot dialog box (Figure 13.15) requires that we specify a variable for both the *X*- and *Y*-axes. We place EDUC (number of years of education) on the *X*-axis because we consider it the independent variable and HRS1 (number of hours worked last week) on the *Y*-axis because it is the dependent variable. Then, click *OK*.

SPSS creates the requested graph (Figure 13.16). You can edit it to change its appearance by double-clicking on the chart in the viewer. The action of double-clicking displays the chart in a chart window. You can edit the chart from the menus, from the toolbar, or by double-clicking on the object you want to edit.

It is difficult to tell whether a relationship exists just by looking at points in the scatterplot, so we will ask SPSS to include the regression line. To add a regression line to the plot, we start by double-clicking on the scatterplot to open the Chart Editor. Click *Elements* from the main menu, then *Fit Line at Total*. In the section of the dialog box headed "Fit Method," select *Linear*. Click *Apply* and then *Close*. Finally, in the Chart Editor, click *File* and then *Close*. The result of these actions is shown in Figure 13.17.

Since the regression line clearly rises as number of years of education increases, we observe that there appears to be a positive relationship between education and number of hours worked last week. The predicted value for those with 20 years of education is about 43 hours, compared with slightly more than 39 hours for those with 10 years of education. However, because there is a lot of scatter around the line, the predictive power of the model is weak.

Demonstration 2: Producing Correlation Coefficients

To further quantify the effect of education on hours worked, we request a correlation coefficient. This statistic is available in the Bivariate procedure, which is located by clicking on *Analyze, Correlate*, then *Bivariate* (Figure 13.18). Place the variables you are interested in correlating, EDUC and HRS1, in the Variable(s) box, then click *OK*.

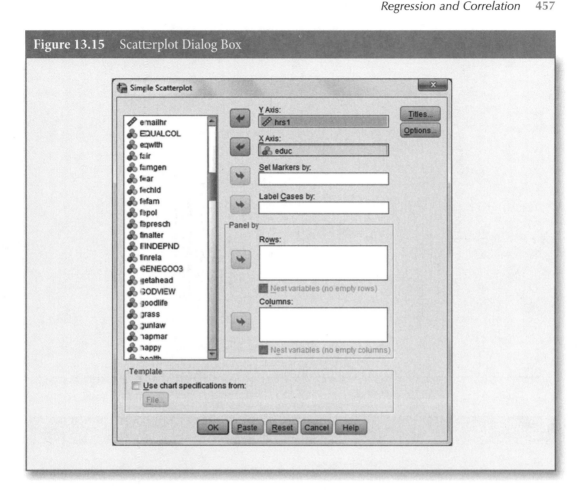

Figure 13.15 Scatterplot Dialog Box

SPSS produces a matrix of correlations, shown in Figure 13.19. We are interested in the correlation in the bottom left-hand cell, .074. We see that this correlation is closer to 0 than to 1, which tells us that education is not a very good predictor of hours worked, even if it is true that those with more education work more hours per week. The number under the correlation coefficient, 837, is the number of valid cases (N)—those respondents who gave a valid response to both questions. The number is reduced because not everyone in the sample is working.

Correlation is significant at the .05 level (two-tailed).

Demonstration 3: Producing a Regression Equation

Next, we will use SPSS to calculate the best-fitting regression line and the coefficient of determination. This procedure is located by clicking on *Analyze*, *Regression*, then *Linear*. The Linear Regression dialog box (Figure 13.20) provides boxes in which to enter the dependent variable, HRS1, and the independent variable, EDUC (regression allows more than one). After you place the variables in their appropriate places, click *OK*

Figure 13.16 Scatterplot of Education by Hours Worked Last Week

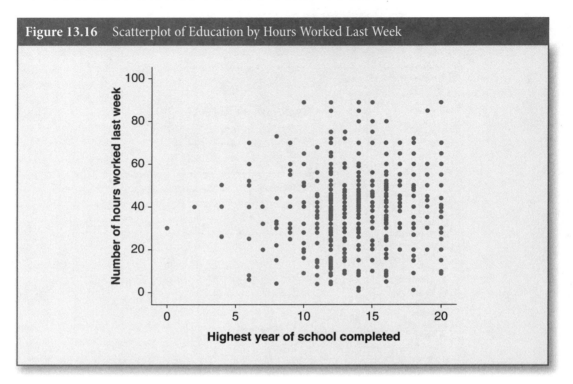

Figure 13.17 Scatterplot of Education by Hours Worked, With a Regression Line

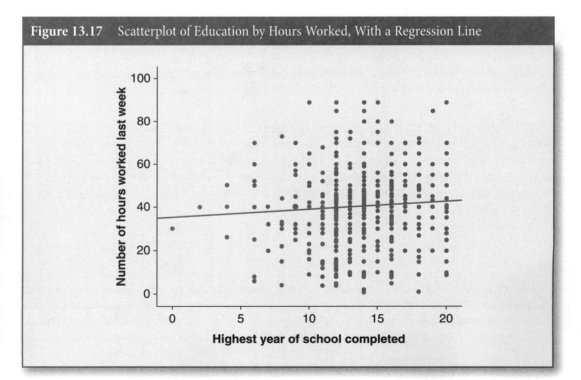

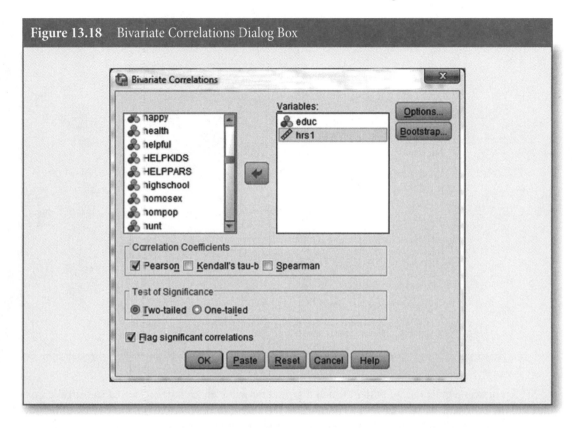

Figure 13.18 Bivariate Correlations Dialog Box

Figure 13.19 SPSS Output Specifying the Correlation Between Education and Number of Hours Worked Last Week

Correlations

		HIGHEST YEAR OF SCHOOL COMPLETED	NUMBER OF HOURS WORKED LAST WEEK
HIGHEST YEAR OF SCHOOL COMPLETED	Pearson Correlation	1	.074[*]
	Sig. (2-tailed)		.033
	N	1496	837
NUMBER OF HOURS WORKED LAST WEEK	Pearson Correlation	.074[*]	1
	Sig. (2-tailed)	.033	
	N	837	838

*. Correlation is significant at the 0.05 level (2-tailed).

to generate the output. The Linear Regression dialog box offers many other choices, but the default output from the procedure contains all that we need.

Figure 13.20 Linear Regression Dialog Box

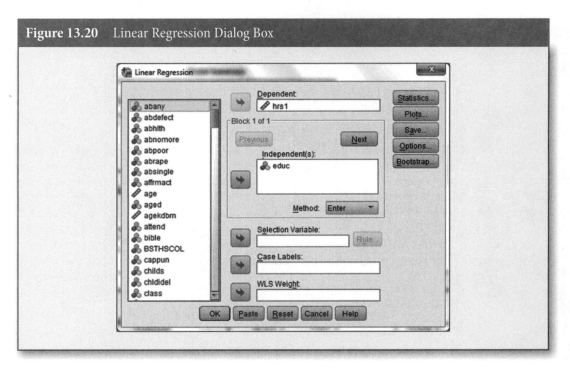

SPSS produces a great deal of output, which is typical for many of the more advanced statistical procedures in the program. We've selected two portions of the output to review here (Figure 13.21). Under the Model Summary, the coefficient of determination is labeled "R square." Its value is .005, which is very weak. Educational attainment explains little of the variation in hours worked, less than 1%.

Figure 13.21 Linear Regression Output Specifying the Relationship Between Education and Number of Hours Worked Last Week

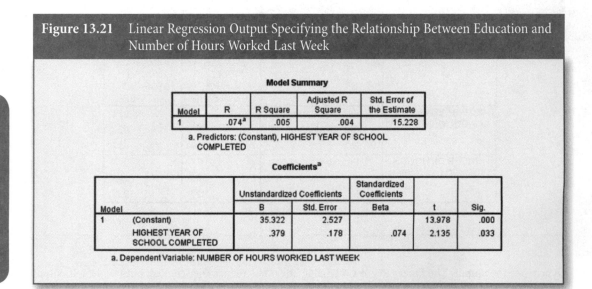

Model Summary

Model	R	R Square	Adjusted R Square	Std. Error of the Estimate
1	.074[a]	.005	.004	15.228

a. Predictors: (Constant), HIGHEST YEAR OF SCHOOL COMPLETED

Coefficients[a]

Model		Unstandardized Coefficients		Standardized Coefficients	t	Sig.
		B	Std. Error	Beta		
1	(Constant)	35.322	2.527		13.978	.000
	HIGHEST YEAR OF SCHOOL COMPLETED	.379	.178	.074	2.135	.033

a. Dependent Variable: NUMBER OF HOURS WORKED LAST WEEK

The regression equation coefficients are presented in the Coefficients table. The regression equation coefficients are listed in the column headed "B." The coefficient for EDUC, or *b*, is about .379; the intercept term, or *a*, identified in the "(Constant)" row, is 35.322. Thus, we would predict that every additional year of education increases the number of hours worked each week by about 23 minutes. Or we could predict that those with a high school level of education work, on average, 35.322 + (.379)(12) hours, or about 40 hours.

Demonstration 4: Computing Analysis of Variance Models

We'll use the same dependent variable—HRS1—for our ANOVA analysis, but instead of using EDUC as our independent variable, we'll use DEGREE (respondent's highest degree). We can compute the ANOVA model by clicking on *Analyze, Compare Means*, then *One-Way ANOVA*. The opening dialog box requires that we insert HRS1 in the box labeled "Dependent List" and in the box labeled "Factor" insert DEGREE (see Figure 13.22).

We're interested in the *F* statistic and significance in the ANOVA table (Figure 13.24). Based on the output, *F* is 2.895 with a significance of .021. We know that the difference between the educational groups is significantly different. The higher one's educational attainment, the more hours they work per week. The most hours worked per week is for persons with a junior college level of education (44.79 hrs/week), followed by the group of respondents with a graduate degree (42.36). The group of respondents who worked the fewest amount of hours per week are those with less than a high school diploma. On average, persons with less than a high school diploma work 37.47 hrs/week; when compared with those with a junior-college level of education, there is a difference of 7.32 hrs/week.

Demonstration 5: Producing an ANOVA Table, Regression-Bivariate

For this Demonstration, we can once again use the variables presented in Demonstrations 1–3 (EDUC and HRS1). You should have produced output for ANOVA in Demonstration 3 along with the regression

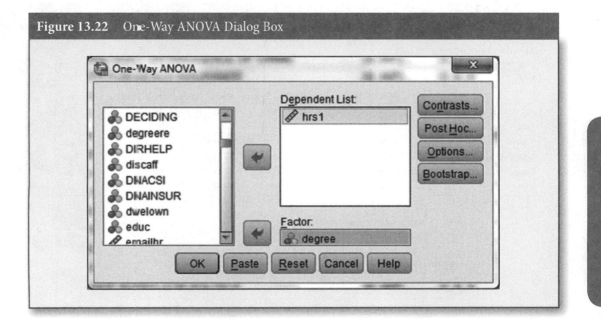

Figure 13.22   One-Way ANOVA Dialog Box

Figure 13.23   One-Way ANOVA Options Dialog Box

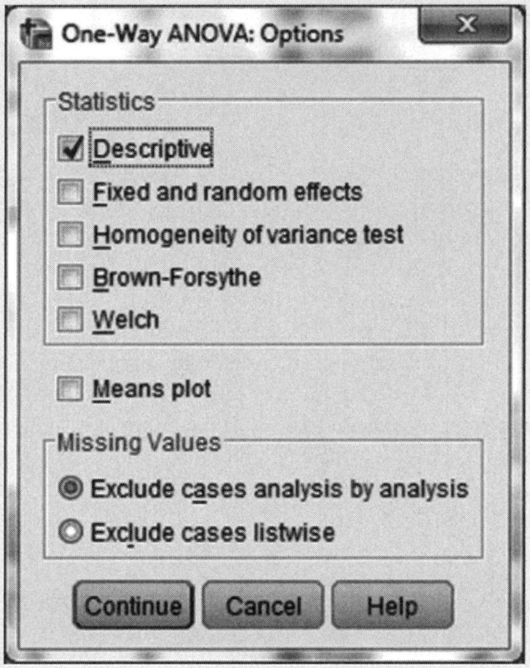

Figure 13.24   ANOVA Output for Hours Worked Last Week and Degree

Descriptives

NUMBER OF HOURS WORKED LAST WEEK

	N	Mean	Std. Deviation	Std. Error	95% Confidence interval for Mean		Minimum	Maximum
					Lower Bound	Upper Bound		
LT HIGH SCHOOL	81	37.47	16.014	1.779	33.93	41.01	4	73
HIGH SCHOOL	401	39.77	15.297	.764	38.26	41.27	2	89
JUNIOR COLLEGE	67	44.79	16.616	2.030	40.74	48.84	1	89
BACHELOR	188	41.37	13.160	.960	39.47	43.26	5	80
GRADUATE	101	42.36	16.584	1.650	39.08	45.63	1	89
Total	838	40.62	15.259	.527	39.58	41.65	1	89

ANOVA

NUMBER OF HOURS WORKED LAST WEEK

	Sum of Squares	df	Mean Square	F	Sig.
Between Groups	2671.983	4	667.996	2.895	.021
Within Groups	192220.056	833	230.756		
Total	194892.039	837			

Exercises

output. However, if you've misplaced that output, simply follow the directions listed in Demonstration 3 once more.

The ANOVA table provides the results of the analysis of variance test (Figure 13.25). The table includes regression and residual sum of squares, as well as mean squares. To test the null hypothesis that r^2 is zero, you will only need the statistic shown in the last column labeled "Sig." This is the P value associated with the F ratio listed in the column head "F." The F statistic is 4.559, and its associated P value is .033. This means that there is a little probability (.033) that r^2 is really zero in the population, given the observed r^2 of .005. We are therefore able to reject the null hypothesis at the .05 level.

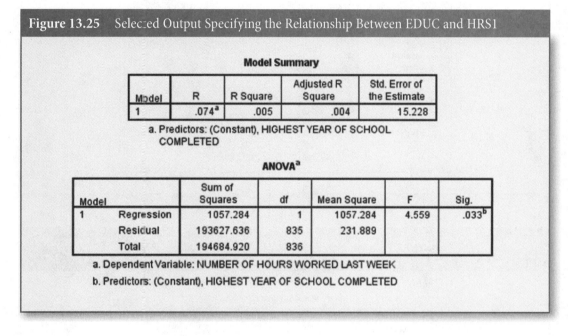

Figure 13.25   Selected Output Specifying the Relationship Between EDUC and HRS1

Model Summary

Model	R	R Square	Adjusted R Square	Std. Error of the Estimate
1	.074[a]	.005	.004	15.228

a. Predictors: (Constant), HIGHEST YEAR OF SCHOOL COMPLETED

ANOVA[a]

Model		Sum of Squares	df	Mean Square	F	Sig.
1	Regression	1057.284	1	1057.284	4.559	.033[b]
	Residual	193627.636	835	231.889		
	Total	194684.920	836			

a. Dependent Variable: NUMBER OF HOURS WORKED LAST WEEK

b. Predictors: (Constant), HIGHEST YEAR OF SCHOOL COMPLETED

Demonstration 6: Producing a Multiple Regression Equation

What other variables, in addition to education, affect the number of hours worked per week? One possible answer to this question is that age (AGE) has something to do with the number of hours worked per week. To answer this question, we will use SPSS to calculate a multiple regression equation and a multiple coefficient of determination. This procedure is similar to the one used to generate the bivariate regression equation. Click *Analyze*, *Regression*, then *Linear*. The Linear Regression dialog box (Figure 13.26) provides boxes in which to enter the dependent variable, HRS1, and the independent variables, EDUC and AGE. We place EDUC (number of years of education) and AGE (age in years) in the box for the independent variables and HRS1 (the number of hours worked last week) in the box for the dependent variable, and click *OK*.

SPSS produces a great deal of output. We've selected two portions of the output to review here (Figure 13.27).

Under the Model Summary, the multiple correlation coefficient labeled "R" is .074. This tells us that education and age are weakly associated with hours worked last week. The coefficient of determination is labeled "R square." Its value is .006. An R^2 of .006 means that educational attainment and age jointly explain

Figure 13.26   Linear Regression Dialog Box Incorporating Multiple Independent Variables

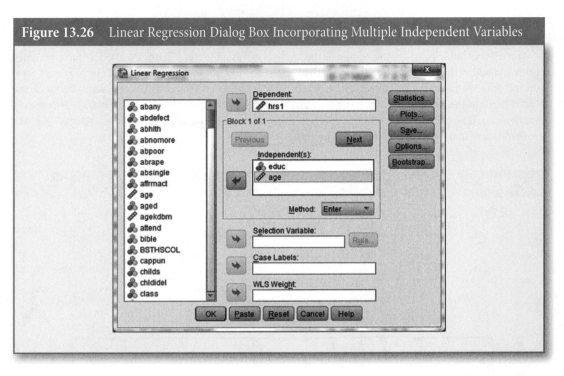

Figure 13.27   Multiple Regression Output Specifying the Relationship Between Education, Age, and Number of Hours Worked Last Week

Model Summary

Model	R	R Square	Adjusted R Square	Std. Error of the Estimate
1	.074[a]	.006	.003	15.286

a. Predictors: (Constant), AGE OF RESPONDENT, HIGHEST YEAR OF SCHOOL COMPLETED

Coefficients[a]

Model		Unstandardized Coefficients		Standardized Coefficients	t	Sig.
		B	Std. Error	Beta		
1	(Constant)	35.938	3.099		11.598	.000
	HIGHEST YEAR OF SCHOOL COMPLETED	.378	.179	.073	2.112	.035
	AGE OF RESPONDENT	-.013	.039	-.012	-.341	.733

a. Dependent Variable: NUMBER OF HOURS WORKED LAST WEEK

less than 1% of the variation in hours worked last week. In addition, SPSS provides an "Adjusted R square," which is .003. The "adjusted R square" adjusts the R^2 coefficient for the number of predictors in the equation. Generally, the adjusted R^2 will be lower, relative to R^2, the larger the number of predictors.

The regression equation coefficients are listed in the in the Coefficients table. The regression equation coefficients are listed in the column headed "B." The coefficient for EDUC is about .378, and for AGE it is −.013. The intercept term, or *a*, identified in the "(Constant)" row, is 35.938. Thus, we would predict that, holding age constant, every additional year of education increases the number of hours worked the previous week by about 23 minutes. However, as is shown in the far right column in the Coefficients section, age is not significant at $P < .05$. In other words, the age of person in conjunction with one's education does a poor job of predicting the number of hours worked last week. This makes sense, in that the 40-hour work week is the standard for all persons in the United States, no matter what their age.

SPSS PROBLEMS

[GSS10SSDS]

1. Use the GSS10SSDS data file to study the relationship between the number of siblings a respondent has (SIBS) and his or her number of children (CHILDS).
   a. Construct a scatterplot of these two variables in SPSS, and place the best-fit linear regression line on the scatterplot. Describe the relationship between the number of siblings a respondent has (SIBS) and the number of his or her children (CHILDS).
   b. Have SPSS calculate the regression equation predicting CHILDS with SIBS. What are the intercept and the slope? What are the coefficient of determination and the correlation coefficient?
   c. What is the predicted number of children for someone with three siblings?
   d. What is the predicted number of children for someone without any siblings?
   e. Can you find a way for SPSS to calculate the error of prediction and predicted value for each respondent and save them as new variables?

2. Use the same variables as in Exercise 1, but do the analysis separately for men and women. Begin by locating the variable SEX. Click *Data, Split File,* and then select *Organize Output by Groups.* Insert SEX into the box and click *OK.* Now, SPSS will split your results by sex.
   a. Have SPSS calculate the regression equation for men and women. (*Note:* You will need to scroll down through your output to find the results for men and women.) How similar are they?
   b. What is the predicted number of children for a man with two siblings? Six siblings? For a woman with the same number of siblings? Which is greater?

3. Use the same variables as in Exercise 1, but do the analysis separately for whites and blacks. Click *Data, Split File,* and then select *Organize Output by Groups.* Insert RACECEN1 into the box and click *OK.* (*Note:* Be sure to remove SEX from the box if it is still there from the previous exercise.) Now, SPSS will split your results by RACECEN1.
   a. Is there any difference between the regression equations for whites and blacks?
   b. What is the predicted number for whites and blacks with the same number of siblings: one sibling, four siblings, and seven siblings?

4. Use the same variables as in Exercise 1, but do the analysis separately for married and divorced respondents. Begin by locating the variable MARITAL. Click *Data, Split File,* and then select *Organize Output by Groups.* Insert MARITAL into the box and click *OK.* (*Note:* Be sure to remove SEX and/or

RACECEN1 from the box if they are still there from the previous exercises.) Now, SPSS will split your results by marital status.

a. Is there any difference between the regression equations for married and divorced respondents?

b. What is the predicted number of children for married and divorced respondents with the following number of siblings: one sibling, four siblings, and seven siblings?

c. What differences, if any, do you find? Is the number of siblings a better predictor of number of children for married respondents or for women?

5. Use the 2010 GSS file (GSS10SSDS) to investigate the relationship between the respondent's education (EDUC) and the education received by his or her father and mother (PAEDUC and MAEDUC, respectively).

a. Use SPSS to find the correlation coefficient, the coefficient of determination, and the regression equation predicting the respondent's education with father's education only. Interpret your results.

b. Use SPSS to find the multiple correlation coefficient, the multiple coefficient of determination, and the regression equation predicting the respondent's education with father's and mother's education. Interpret your results.

c. Did taking into account the respondent's mother's education improve our prediction? Discuss this on the basis of the results from 5b.

d. Using the regression equation from 5a, calculate the predicted number of years of education for a person with a father with 12 years of education. Then, repeat this procedure, adding in a mother's 12 years of education and using the regression equation from 5b.

6. In Problem 3, we looked at the linear relationship between SIBS and CHILDS for whites and blacks. In this problem, we continue with this comparison except that now we want to look at ANOVA and the F statistic. What is the F statistic? What is its p level? Are there differences between whites and blacks? Are we able to reject the null hypothesis that $r^2 = 0$? Compare these hypotheses between whites and blacks.

CHAPTER EXERCISES

Country	Percentage Concerned	Percentage Donating Money
Austria	35.5	27.8
Denmark	27.2	22.3
Netherlands	30.1	44.8
Philippines	50.1	6.8
Russia	29.0	1.6
Slovenia	50.3	10.7
Spain	35.9	7.4
United States	33.8	22.8

Source: International Social Survey Programme, 2000.

1. For a variety of reasons, a larger percentage of people are concerned today about the state of the environment than in years past. This has led to the formation of environmental action groups that attempt to alter environmental policies nationally and around the globe. A large number of environmental action groups subsist on the donations of concerned citizens. Based on the following eight countries, examine the data to determine the extent of the relationship between simply being concerned about the environment and actually giving money to environmental groups.

   a. Construct a scatterplot of the two variables, placing percentage concerned about the environment on the horizontal or *X*-axis and the percentage donating money to environmental groups on the vertical or *Y*-axis.

   b. Does the relationship between the two variables seem linear? Describe the relationship.

   c. Find the value of the Pearson correlation coefficient that measures the association between the two variables and offer an interpretation.

2. There is often thought to be a relationship between a person's educational attainment and the number of children he or she has. The hypothesis is that as one's educational level increases, he or she has fewer children. Investigate this conjecture with the following scatterplot and regression output produced from the 2010 GSS and interpret the results (see Figures 13.28 and 13.29).

Figure 13.28   Scatterplot of Number of Children by Education

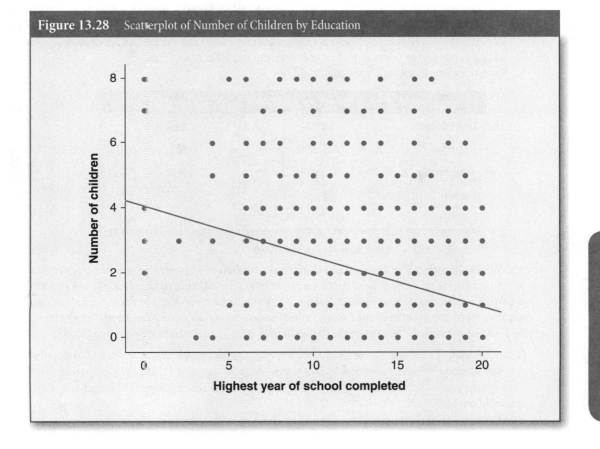

Figure 13.29   Linear Regression Output Specifying the Relationship Between Education and Number of Children

Coefficients[a]

Model		Unstandardized Coefficients		Standardized Coefficients	t	Sig.
		B	Std. Error	Beta		
1	(Constant)	4.060	.191		21.220	.000
	HIGHEST YEAR OF SCHOOL COMPLETED	-.155	.014	-.279	-11.203	.000

a. Dependent Variable: NUMBER OF CHILDREN

Model Summary

Model	R	R Square	Adjusted R Square	Std. Error of the Estimate
1	.279[a]	.078	.077	1.667

a. Predictors: (Constant), HIGHEST YEAR OF SCHOOL COMPLETED

3. The condition and health of our environment is a growing concern. Let's examine the relationship between a country's gross national product (GNP) and the percentage of respondents willing to pay higher prices for goods to protect the environment. The following table displays information for five countries selected at random.

   a. Calculate the correlation coefficient between a country's GNP and the percentage of its residents willing to pay higher prices to protect the environment. What is its value?

   b. Provide an interpretation for the coefficient.

Country	GNP per Capita	Percentage Willing to Pay
United States	29.24	44.9
Ireland	18.71	53.3
Netherlands	24.78	61.2
Norway	34.31	40.7
Sweden	25.58	32.6

Source: International Social Survey Programme, 2000.

4. The SPSS output shown in Figure 13.30 displays the relationship between education (measured in years) and television viewing per day (measured in hours) based on 2010 GSS data. We can hypothesize that as educational attainment increases, hours of television viewing will decrease, indicating a negative relationship between the two variables. Discuss the significance of the overall model based on F and its P values. Is the relationship between education and television viewing significant?

5. Before calculating a correlation coefficient or a regression equation, it is always important to examine a scatter diagram between two variables to see how well a straight line fits the data. If a straight line does not appear to fit, other curves can be used to describe the relationship (this subject is not discussed in our text).

   The SPSS scatterplot in Figure 13.31 and output shown in Figure 13.32 display the relationship between education (measured in years) and television viewing (measured in hours) based on 2010 GSS data. We can hypothesize that as educational attainment increases, hours of television viewing will decrease, indicating a negative relationship between the two variables.

Interpret the results of the scatterplot, as well as the "Coefficients" and "Model Summary" output.

Figure 13.30 ANOVA Output for Education and Television Viewing

Model Summary

Model	R	R Square	Adjusted R Square	Std. Error of the Estimate
1	.268[a]	.072	.071	2.553

a. Predictors: (Constant), HIGHEST YEAR OF SCHOOL COMPLETED

ANOVA[a]

Model		Sum of Squares	df	Mean Square	F	Sig.
1	Regression	506.785	1	506.785	77.757	.000[b]
	Residual	6563.151	1007	6.518		
	Total	7069.937	1008			

a. Dependent Variable: HOURS PER DAY WATCHING TV

b. Predictors: (Constant), HIGHEST YEAR OF SCHOOL COMPLETED

Figure 13.31 Scatterplot of Hours of Television Viewing per Day by Highest Year of School Completed

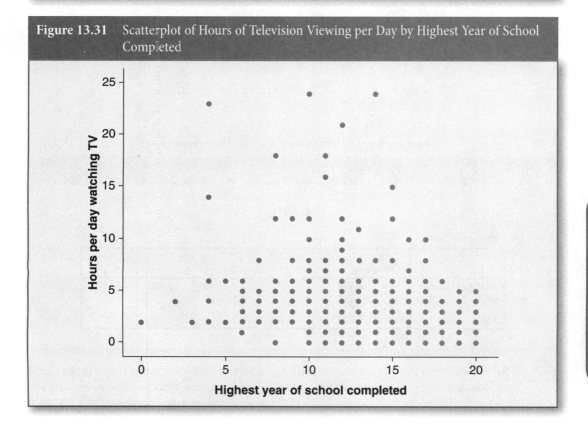

Figure 13.32   Linear Regression Output Specifying the Relationship Between Education and Hours Spent per Day Watching Television

Coefficients[a]

Model		Unstandardized Coefficients		Standardized Coefficients	t	Sig.
		B	Std. Error	Beta		
1	(Constant)	6.130	.363		16.884	.000
	HIGHEST YEAR OF SCHOOL COMPLETED	-.231	.026	-.268	-8.818	.000

a. Dependent Variable: HOURS PER DAY WATCHING TV

Model Summary

Model	R	R Square	Adjusted R Square	Std. Error of the Estimate
1	.268[a]	.072	.071	2.553

a. Predictors: (Constant), HIGHEST YEAR OF SCHOOL COMPLETED

6. We selected a sample of 14 respondents from the 2006 MTF. We present their number of moving (traffic) violations in the last 12 months along with their residential area (residential area is the independent variable). Use the proceeding output to discuss the significance of the F and P values. Is the relationship between city size and traffic violations significant?

Small Town	Medium-Sized City	Large City
0	2	3
0	3	4
1	1	4
2	1	3
1		2

Figure 13.33   ANOVA Output for Residential Area and Traffic Violations

ANOVA

Traffic Violations

	Sum of Squares	df	Mean Square	F	Sig.
Between Groups	14.579	2	7.289	9.603	.004
Within Groups	8.350	11	.759		
Total	22.929	13			

7. Social scientists have long been interested in the aspirations and achievements of people in the United States. Research on social mobility, status, and educational attainment has provided convincing evidence on the relationship between parents' and children's socioeconomic achievement. The GSS 2010

data set has information on the educational level of respondents and their mothers. Use the scatterplot and regression output below to interpret the relationship between mothers' level of education and one's own level of education (see figures 13.34 and 13.35).

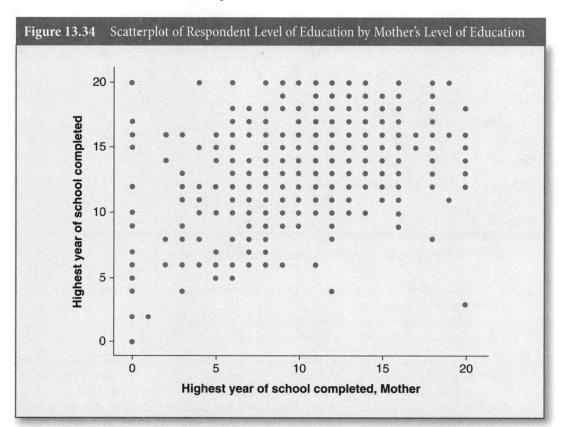

Figure 13.34 Scatterplot of Respondent Level of Education by Mother's Level of Education

Figure 13.35 Linear Regression Output Specifying the Relationship Between Respondent Level of Education by Mother's Level of Education

Coefficients[a]

Model		Unstandardized Coefficients		Standardized Coefficients	t	Sig.
		B	Std. Error	Beta		
1	(Constant)	9.988	.262		38.138	.000
	HIGHEST YEAR SCHOOL COMPLETED, MOTHER	.326	.022	.383	15.018	.000

a. Dependent Variable: HIGHEST YEAR OF SCHOOL COMPLETED

Model Summary

Model	R	R Square	Adjusted R Square	Std. Error of the Estimate
1	.383[a]	.146	.146	2.762

a. Predictors: (Constant), HIGHEST YEAR SCHOOL COMPLETED, MOTHER

8. In this exercise, we will investigate the relationship between GDP per capita and birth rates in South America.

Country	GDP per Capita in 2008 (U.S. Dollars)	Birth Rate in 2010 (estimated)
Argentina	8,236	18
Bolivia	1,720	25
Brazil	8,205	18
Chile	10,084	15
Colombia	5,416	18
Ecuador	4,056	20
Paraguay	2,561	18
Peru	4,477	19
Uruguay	9,654	14
Venezuela	11,246	13

Sources: World Bank, *World Development Indicators*, 2010; *The World Factbook*, 2010.

a. Construct a scatterplot for GDP and birth rate. Do you think the scatterplot can be characterized by a linear relationship?
b. Calculate the coefficient of determination and correlation coefficient.
c. Use this information to describe the relationship between the variables.

9. In 2010, a U.S. Census Bureau report revealed that approximately 13% of all Americans were living below the poverty line in 2007. This figure is higher than in 2000, when the poverty rate was 12.2%. This translates to an increase of approximately 4.75 million Americans living below the poverty line. Individuals and families living below the poverty line face many obstacles, the least of which is access to health care. In many cases, those living below the poverty line are without any form of health insurance. Using data from the U.S. Census Bureau, analyze the relationship between living below the poverty line and access to health care.

State	Percentage Below Poverty Line (2007)	Percentage Without Health Insurance (2007)
Alabama	16.9	12.0
California	12.4	18.2
Idaho	12.1	13.9
Louisiana	18.6	18.5
New Jersey	8.6	15.8
New York	13.7	13.2
Pennsylvania	11.6	9.5

State	Percentage Below Poverty Line (2007)	Percentage Without Health Insurance (2007)
Rhode Island	12.0	10.8
South Carolina	15.0	16.4
Texas	16.3	25.2
Washington	11.4	11.3
Wisconsin	10.8	8.2

Source: U.S. Census Bureau, *The 2010 Statistical Abstract*, 2010, Tables 693 and 150.

a. Construct a scatterplot, predicting the percentage without health insurance with the percentage living below the poverty level. Does it appear that a straight-line relationship will fit the data?

b. Calculate the regression equation with percentage of the population without health insurance as the dependent variable, and draw the regression line on the scatterplot. What is its slope? What is the intercept? Has your opinion changed about whether a straight line seems to fit the data? Are there any states that fall far from the regression line? Which one(s)?

c. What percentage of the population must be living below the poverty line to obtain a predicted value of 5% without health insurance?

d. Predicting a value that falls beyond the observed range of the two variables in a regression is problematic at best, so your answer in (c) isn't necessarily statistically believable. However, what is a nonstatistical, or substantive, reason? Why might making such a prediction be important?

10. Let's examine the relationship between GNP per capita and the percentage of respondents willing to pay more in taxes.

a. In this chapter, we used Table 13.4 to illustrate how to calculate the slope and intercept in the regression table. Using Table 13.4 as a model, create a similar table using the data below for GNP per capita and the percentage willing to pay higher taxes.

b. From the table that you created in 10a, calculate a and b and write out the regression equation (i.e., prediction equation).

c. Calculate and interpret error type, E_2.

d. Using your answer from 10c, calculate the PRE measure, r^2. Interpret.

e. About what percentage of citizens are willing to pay higher taxes for a country with a GNP per capita of 3.0 (i.e., $3,000)? For a GNP per capita of 30.0 (i.e., $30,000)?

Country	GNP per Capita	Percentage Willing to Pay Higher Taxes
Canada	19.71	24.0
Chile	4.99	29.1
Finland	24.28	12.0

(Continued)

Exercises

(Continued)

Country	GNP per Capita	Percentage Willing to Pay Higher Taxes
Ireland	18.71	34.3
Japan	32.35	37.2
Latvia	2.42	17.3
Mexico	3.84	34.7
Netherlands	24.78	51.9
Norway	14.60	22.8
Portugal	34.31	17.1
Russia	10.67	29.9
Spain	2.66	22.2
Sweden	14.10	19.5
Switzerland	25.58	33.5
United States	39.98	31.6

Sources: The World Bank Group, *Development Education Program; Learning Module: Economics, GNP per Capita,* 2004; International Social Survey Programme, 2000.

11. In Exercise 5, we examined the relationship between years of education and hours of television watched per day. We saw that as education increases, hours of television viewing decreases. The number of children a family has could also affect how much television is viewed per day. Having children may lead to more shared and supervised viewing and thus increases the number of viewing hours. The SPSS output in Figure 13.36, based on 2010 GSS data, displays the relationship between television viewing (measured in hours per day) and both education (measured in years) and number of children. We hypothesize that whereas more education may lead to less viewing, the number of children has the opposite effect: Having more children will result in more hours of viewing per day.

   a. What is the b coefficient for education? For number of children? Interpret each coefficient. Is the relationship between education and hours of viewing as hypothesized? How about number of children and television viewing?

   b. Using the multiple regression equation with both education and number of children as independent variables, calculate the number of hours of television viewing for a person with 16 years of education and two children. Using the equation from Exercise 5, how do the results compare between a person with 16 years of education (number of children not included in the equation) and a person with 16 years of education with two children?

   c. Compare the r^2 value from Exercise 5 with the R^2 value from this regression. Does using education and number of children jointly reduce the amount of error involved in predicting hours of television viewed per day?

Figure 13.36 Multiple Regression Output Specifying the Relationship Between Education, Number of Children, and Hours Spent per Day Watching Television

Coefficients[a]

Model		Unstandardized Coefficients		Standardized Coefficients	t	Sig.
		B	Std. Error	Beta		
1	(Constant)	5.857	.412		14.218	.000
	HIGHEST YEAR OF SCHOOL COMPLETED	-.220	.027	-.255	-8.081	.000
	NUMBER OF CHILDREN	.066	.049	.043	1.352	.177

a. Dependent Variable: HOURS PER DAY WATCHING TV

Model Summary

Model	R	R Square	Adjusted R Square	Std. Error of the Estimate
1	.270[a]	.073	.071	2.553

a. Predictors: (Constant), NUMBER OF CHILDREN, HIGHEST YEAR OF SCHOOL COMPLETED

12. In 2011, the U.S. Census published a report saying that the number of Americans living below the federal poverty line was at an all-time high. We want to know if the percentage of residents in each state living below the federal poverty line can be predicted by taking into account both states' racial composition and residents' educational attainment. Figure 13.37 displays the results of multiple

Figure 13.37 Multiple Regression Predicting the Percentage Living Below Poverty by Racial Composition and Educational Attainment

Coefficients[a]

Model		Unstandardized Coefficients		Standardized Coefficients	t	Sig.
		B	Std. Error	Beta		
1	(Constant)	75.613	9.254		8.171	.000
	% Black Residents	-.015	.037	-.047	-.410	.684
	% W/ HS Diploma	-.710	.104	-.788	-6.836	.000

a. Dependent Variable: % Below Poverty

Model Summary

Model	R	R Square	Adjusted R Square	Std. Error of the Estimate
1	.762[a]	.581	.563	2.0308

a. Predictors: (Constant), % W/ HS Diploma, % Black Residents

Exercises

regression ($N = 50$ states), predicting the percentage of a state's residents living below the federal poverty line between 2009 and 2010 using the percentage of black residents in each state in 2010 and percentage of residents in each state with at least a high school diploma in 2009. Use these results to answer the questions below.

a. What is the b coefficient for the percentage of black residents in each state? For the percentage of states' residents with at least a high school diploma? Interpret each coefficient. Do these results support the idea that poverty can be explained, at least in part, by considering the racial composition and education level of states' residents? Why or why not? Use the appropriate statistics to make your argument.

b. Use the regression results to predict the percentage of a state's residents living below the federal poverty line. Use the 2010 mean value of 10.3% for the percentage of black residents in each state and the 2009 mean value of 86.9% for the percentage of states' residents with at least a high school diploma. Is the predicted value below or above the mean value of 13.8% living below the federal poverty line between 2009 and 2010?

c. What is the coefficient of determination? By how much has our prediction of the percentage living below the federal poverty line improved by employing the multiple regression equation?

13. On completing this chapter, you should be able to correctly answer the following questions.

a. True or false: It is possible, in fact it often is the case, that your slope b, will be a positive value and your correlation coefficient, r, will be a negative value.

b. Both a and b refer to changes in which variable, the independent or dependent?

c. The coefficient of determination, r^2, is a PRE measure. What does this mean?

d. True or false: All regression equations reflect *causal* relationships expressed as linear functions.

APPENDIX A
TABLE OF RANDOM NUMBERS

A Table of 14,000 Random Units

Line/Col.	(1)	(2)	(3)	(4)	(5)	(6)	(7)	(8)	(9)	(10)	(11)	(12)	(13)	(14)
1	10480	15011	01536	02011	81647	91646	69179	14194	62590	36207	20969	99570	91291	90700
2	22368	46573	25595	85393	30995	89198	27982	53402	93965	34095	52666	19174	39615	99505
3	24130	48360	22527	97265	76393	64809	15179	24830	49340	32081	30680	19655	63348	58629
4	42167	93093	06243	61680	07856	16376	39440	53537	71341	57004	00849	74917	97758	16379
5	37570	39975	81837	16656	06121	91782	60468	81305	49684	60672	14110	06927	01263	54613
6	77921	06907	11008	42751	27756	53498	18602	70659	90655	15053	21916	81825	44394	42880
7	99562	72905	56420	69994	98872	31016	71194	18738	44013	48840	63213	21069	10634	12952
8	96301	91977	05463	07972	18876	20922	94595	56869	69014	60045	18425	84903	42508	32307
9	89579	14342	63661	10281	17453	18103	57740	84378	25331	12566	58678	44947	05585	56941
10	85475	36857	43342	53988	53060	59533	38867	62300	08158	17983	16439	11458	18593	64952
11	28918	69578	88231	33276	70997	79936	56865	05859	90106	31595	01547	85590	91610	78188
12	63553	40961	48235	03427	49626	69445	18663	72695	52180	20847	12234	90511	33703	90322
13	09429	93969	52636	92737	88974	33488	36320	17617	30015	08272	84115	27156	30613	74952
14	10365	61129	87529	85689	48237	52267	67689	93394	01511	26358	85104	20285	29975	89868
15	07119	97336	71048	08178	77233	13916	47564	81056	97735	85977	29372	74461	28551	90707
16	51085	12765	51821	51259	77452	16308	60756	92144	49442	53900	70960	63990	75601	40719
17	02368	21382	52404	60268	89368	19885	55322	44819	01188	65255	64835	44919	05944	55157
18	01011	54092	33362	94904	31273	04146	18594	29852	71585	85030	51132	01915	92747	64951
19	52162	53916	46369	58586	23216	14513	83149	98736	23495	64350	94738	17752	35156	35749
20	07056	97628	33787	09998	42698	06691	76988	13602	51851	46104	88916	19509	25625	58104
21	48663	91245	85828	14346	09172	30168	90229	04734	59193	22178	30421	61666	99904	32812
22	54164	58492	22421	74103	47070	25306	76468	26384	58151	06646	21524	15227	96909	44592
23	32639	32363	05597	24200	13363	38005	94342	28728	35806	06912	17012	64161	18296	22851
24	29334	27001	87637	87308	58731	00256	45834	15398	46557	41135	10367	07684	36188	18510
25	02488	33062	28834	07351	19731	92420	60952	61280	50001	67658	32586	86679	50720	94953

(Continued)

(Continued)

Line/Col.	(1)	(2)	(3)	(4)	(5)	(6)	(7)	(8)	(9)	(10)	(11)	(12)	(13)	(14)
26	81525	72295	04839	96423	24878	82651	66566	14778	76797	14780	13300	87074	79666	95725
27	29676	20591	68086	26432	46901	20849	89768	81536	86645	12659	92259	57102	80428	25280
28	00742	57392	39064	66432	84673	40027	32832	61362	98947	96067	64760	64584	96096	98253
29	05366	04213	25669	26422	44407	44048	37937	63904	45766	66134	75470	66520	34693	90449
30	91921	26418	64117	94305	26766	25940	39972	22209	71500	64568	91402	42416	07844	69618
31	00582	04711	87917	77341	42206	35126	74087	99547	81817	42607	43808	76655	62028	76630
32	00725	69884	62797	56170	86324	88072	76222	36086	84637	93161	76038	65855	77919	88006
33	69011	65797	95876	55293	18988	27354	26575	08625	40801	59920	29841	80150	12777	48501
34	25976	57948	29888	88604	67917	48708	18912	82271	65424	69774	33611	54262	85963	03547
35	09763	83473	73577	12908	30883	18317	28290	35797	05998	41688	34952	37888	38917	88050
36	91567	42595	27958	30134	04024	86385	29880	99730	55536	84855	29080	09250	79656	73211
37	17955	56349	90999	49127	20044	59931	06115	20542	18059	02008	73708	83317	36103	42791
38	46503	18584	18845	49618	02304	51038	20655	58727	28168	15475	56942	53389	20562	87338
39	92157	89634	94824	78171	84610	82834	09922	25417	44137	48413	25555	21246	35509	20468
40	14577	62765	35605	81263	39667	47358	56873	56307	61607	49518	89656	20103	77490	18062
41	98427	07523	33362	64270	01638	92477	66969	98420	04880	45585	46565	04102	46880	45709
42	34914	63976	88720	82765	34476	17032	87589	40836	32427	70002	70663	88863	77775	69348
43	70060	28277	39475	46473	23219	53416	94970	25832	69975	94884	19661	72828	00102	66794
44	53976	54914	06990	67245	68350	82948	11398	42878	80287	88267	47363	46634	06541	97809
45	76072	29515	40980	07391	58745	25774	22987	80059	39911	96189	41151	14222	60697	59583
46	90725	52210	83974	29992	65831	38857	50490	83765	55657	14361	31720	57375	56228	41546
47	64364	67412	33339	31926	14883	24413	59744	92351	97473	89286	35931	04110	23726	51900
48	08962	00358	31662	25388	61642	34072	81249	35648	56891	69352	48373	45578	78547	81788
49	95012	68379	93526	70765	10593	04542	76463	54328	02349	17247	28865	14777	62730	92277
50	15664	10493	20492	38391	91132	21999	59516	81652	27195	48223	46751	22923	32261	85653
51	16408	81899	04153	53381	79401	21438	83035	92350	36693	31238	59649	91754	72772	02338
52	18629	81953	05520	91962	04739	13092	97662	24822	94730	06496	35090	04822	86772	98289
53	73115	35101	47498	87637	99016	71060	88824	71013	18735	20286	23153	72924	35165	43040
54	57491	16703	23167	49323	45021	33132	12544	41035	80780	45393	44812	12515	98931	91202
55	30405	83946	23792	14422	15059	45799	22716	19792	09983	74353	68668	30429	70735	25499
56	16631	35006	85900	98275	32388	52390	16815	69298	82732	38480	73817	32523	41961	44437
57	96773	20206	42559	78985	05300	22164	24369	54224	35083	19687	11052	91491	60383	19746
58	38935	64202	14349	82674	66523	44133	00697	35552	35970	19124	63318	29686	03387	59846
59	31624	76384	17403	53363	44167	64486	64758	75366	76554	31601	12614	33072	60332	92325
60	78919	19474	23632	27889	47914	02584	37680	20801	72152	39339	34806	08930	85001	87820
61	03931	33309	57047	74211	63445	17361	62825	39908	05607	91284	68833	25570	38818	46920
62	74426	33278	43972	10119	89917	15665	52872	73823	73144	88662	88970	74492	51805	99378
63	09066	00903	20795	95452	92648	45454	09552	88815	16553	51125	79375	97596	16296	66092

Line/Col.	(1)	(2)	(3)	(4)	(5)	(6)	(7)	(8)	(9)	(10)	(11)	(12)	(13)	(14)
64	42238	12426	87025	14267	20979	04508	64535	31355	86064	29472	47689	05974	52468	16834
65	16153	08002	26504	41744	81959	65642	74240	56302	00033	67107	77510	70625	28725	34191
66	21457	40742	29820	96783	29400	21840	15035	34537	33310	06116	95240	15957	16572	06004
67	21581	57802	02050	89728	17937	37621	47075	42080	97403	48626	68995	43805	33386	21597
68	55612	78095	83197	33732	05810	24813	86902	60397	16489	03264	88525	42786	05269	92532
69	44657	66999	99324	51281	84463	60563	79312	93454	68876	25471	93911	25650	12682	73572
70	91340	84979	46949	81973	37949	61023	43997	15263	80644	43942	89203	71795	99533	50501
71	91227	21199	31935	27022	84067	05462	35216	14486	29891	68607	41867	14951	91696	85065
72	50001	38140	56321	19924	72163	09538	12151	06878	91903	18749	34405	56087	82790	70925
73	65390	05224	72958	28609	81406	39147	25549	48542	42627	45233	57202	94617	23772	07896
74	27504	96131	83944	41575	10573	08619	64482	73923	36152	05184	94142	25299	84387	34925
75	37169	94851	39117	89632	00959	16487	65536	49071	39782	17095	02330	74301	00275	48280
76	11508	70225	51111	38351	19444	66499	71945	05422	13442	78675	84081	66938	93654	59894
77	37449	30362	06694	54690	04052	53115	62757	95348	78662	11163	81651	50245	34971	52924
78	46515	70331	85922	38329	57015	15765	97161	17869	45349	61796	66345	81073	49106	79860
79	30986	81223	42416	58353	21532	30502	32305	86482	05174	07901	54339	58861	74818	46942
80	63798	64995	46583	09765	44160	78128	83991	42865	92520	83531	80377	35909	81250	54238
81	82486	84846	99254	67632	43218	50076	21361	64816	51202	88124	41870	52689	51275	83556
82	21885	32906	92431	09060	64297	51674	64126	62570	26123	05155	59194	52799	28225	85762
83	60336	98782	07408	53458	13564	59089	26445	29789	85205	41001	12535	12133	14645	23541
84	43937	46891	24010	25560	86355	33941	25786	54990	71899	15475	95434	98227	21824	19585
85	97656	63175	89303	16275	07100	92063	21942	18611	47348	20203	18534	03862	78095	50136
86	03299	01221	05418	38982	55758	92237	26759	86367	21216	98442	08303	56613	91511	75928
87	79626	06486	03574	17668	07785	76020	79924	25651	83325	88428	85076	72811	22717	50585
88	85636	68335	47539	03129	65651	11977	02510	26113	99447	68645	34327	15152	55230	93448
89	18039	14367	61337	06177	12143	46609	32989	74014	64708	00533	35398	58408	13261	47908
90	08362	15656	60627	36478	65648	16764	53412	09013	07832	41574	17639	82163	60859	75567
91	79556	29068	04142	16268	15387	12856	66227	38358	22478	73373	88732	09443	82558	05250
92	92608	82674	27072	32534	17075	27698	98204	63863	11951	34648	88022	56148	34925	57031
93	23982	25835	40055	67006	12293	02753	14827	22235	35071	99704	37543	11601	35503	85171
94	09915	96306	05908	97901	28395	14186	00821	80703	70426	75647	76310	88717	37890	40129
95	50937	33300	26695	62247	69927	76123	50842	43834	86654	70959	79725	93872	28117	19233
96	42488	78077	69882	61657	34136	79180	97526	43092	04098	73571	80799	76536	71255	64239
97	46764	86273	63003	93017	31204	36692	40202	35275	57306	55543	53203	18098	47625	88684
98	03237	45430	55417	63282	90816	17349	88298	90183	36600	78406	06216	95787	42579	90730
99	86591	81482	52667	61583	14972	90053	89534	76036	49199	43716	97548	04379	46370	28672
100	38534	01715	94964	87288	65680	43772	39560	12918	86537	62738	19636	51132	25739	56947

Source: William H. Beyer, ed., Handbook for Probability and Statistics, 2nd ed. Copyright © 1966 CRC Press, Boca Raton, Florida. Used by permission.

APPENDIX B
THE STANDARD NORMAL TABLE

The values in column A are Z scores. Column B lists the proportion of area between the mean and a given Z. Column C lists the proportion of area beyond a given Z. Only positive Z scores are listed. Because the normal curve is symmetrical, the areas for negative Z scores will be exactly the same as the areas for positive Z scores.

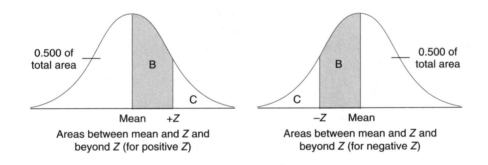

Areas between mean and Z and beyond Z (for positive Z)

Areas between mean and Z and beyond Z (for negative Z)

A Z	B Area Between Mean and Z	C Area Beyond Z	A Z	B Area Between Mean and Z	C Area Beyond Z	A Z	B Area Between Mean and Z	C Area Beyond Z
0.00	0.0000	0.5000	0.11	0.0438	0.4562	0.21	0.0832	0.4168
0.01	0.0040	0.4960	0.12	0.0478	0.4522	0.22	0.0871	0.4129
0.02	0.0080	0.4920	0.13	0.0517	0.4483	0.23	0.0910	0.4090
0.03	0.0120	0.4880	0.14	0.0557	0.4443	0.24	0.0948	0.4052
0.04	0.0160	0.4840	0.15	0.0596	0.4404	0.25	0.0987	0.4013
0.05	0.0199	0.4801	0.16	0.0636	0.4364	0.26	0.1026	0.3974
0.06	0.0239	0.4761	0.17	0.0675	0.4325	0.27	0.1064	0.3936
0.07	0.0279	0.4721	0.18	0.0714	0.4286	0.28	0.1103	0.3897
0.08	0.0319	0.4681	0.19	0.0753	0.4247	0.29	0.1141	0.3859
0.09	0.0359	0.4641	0.20	0.0793	0.4207	0.30	0.1179	0.3821
0.10	0.0398	0.4602						

A Z	B Area Between Mean and Z	C Area Beyond Z	A Z	B Area Between Mean and Z	C Area Beyond Z	A Z	B Area Between Mean and Z	C Area Beyond Z
0.31	0.1217	0.3783	0.71	0.2611	0.2389	1.11	0.3665	0.1335
0.32	0.1255	0.3745	0.72	0.2642	0.2358	1.12	0.3686	0.1314
0.33	0.1293	0.3707	0.73	0.2673	0.2327	1.13	0.3708	0.1292
0.34	0.1331	0.3669	0.74	0.2703	0.2297	1.14	0.3729	0.1271
0.35	0.1368	0.3632	0.75	0.2734	0.2266	1.15	0.3749	0.1251
0.36	0.1406	0.3594	0.76	0.2764	0.2236	1.16	0.3770	0.1230
0.37	0.1443	0.3557	0.77	0.2794	0.2206	1.17	0.3790	0.1210
0.38	0.1480	0.3520	0.78	0.2823	0.2177	1.18	0.3810	0.1190
0.39	0.1517	0.3483	0.79	0.2852	0.2148	1.19	0.3830	0.1170
0.40	0.1554	0.3446	0.80	0.2881	0.2119	1.20	0.3849	0.1151
0.41	0.1591	0.3409	0.81	0.2910	0.2090	1.21	0.3869	0.1131
0.42	0.1628	0.3372	0.82	0.2939	0.2061	1.22	0.3888	0.1112
0.43	0.1664	0.3336	0.83	0.2967	0.2033	1.23	0.3907	0.1093
0.44	0.1700	0.3300	0.84	0.2995	0.2005	1.24	0.3925	0.1075
0.45	0.1736	0.3264	0.85	0.3023	0.1977	1.25	0.3944	0.1056
0.46	0.1772	0.3228	0.86	0.3051	0.1949	1.26	0.3962	0.1038
0.47	0.1808	0.3192	0.87	0.3078	0.1992	1.27	0.3980	0.1020
0.48	0.1844	0.3156	0.88	0.3106	0.1894	1.28	0.3997	0.1003
0.49	0.1879	0.3121	0.89	0.3133	0.1867	1.29	0.4015	0.0985
0.50	0.1915	0.3085	0.90	0.3159	0.1841	1.30	0.4032	0.0968
0.51	0.1950	0.3050	0.91	0.3186	0.1814	1.31	0.4049	0.0951
0.52	0.1985	0.3015	0.92	0.3212	0.1788	1.32	0.4066	0.0934
0.53	0.2019	0.2981	0.93	0.3238	0.1762	1.33	0.4082	0.0918
0.54	0.2054	0.2946	0.94	0.3264	0.1736	1.34	0.4099	0.0901
0.55	0.2088	0.2912	0.95	0.3289	0.1711	1.35	0.4115	0.0885
0.56	0.2123	0.2877	0.96	0.3315	0.1685	1.36	0.4131	0.0869
0.57	0.2157	0.2843	0.97	0.3340	0.1660	1.37	0.4147	0.0853
0.58	0.2190	0.2810	0.98	0.3365	0.1635	1.38	0.4162	0.0838
0.59	0.2224	0.2776	0.99	0.3389	0.1611	1.39	0.4177	0.0823
0.60	0.2257	0.2743	1.00	0.3413	0.1587	1.40	0.4192	0.0808
0.61	0.2291	0.2709	1.01	0.3438	0.1562	1.41	0.4207	0.0793
0.62	0.2324	0.2676	1.02	0.3461	0.1539	1.42	0.4222	0.0778
0.63	0.2357	0.2643	1.03	0.3485	0.1515	1.43	0.4236	0.0764
0.64	0.2389	0.2611	1.04	0.3508	0.1492	1.44	0.4251	0.0749
0.65	0.2422	0.2578	1.05	0.3531	0.1469	1.45	0.4265	0.0735
0.66	0.2454	0.2546	1.06	0.3554	0.1446	1.46	0.4279	0.0721
0.67	0.2486	0.2514	1.07	0.3577	0.1423	1.47	0.4292	0.0708
0.68	0.2517	0.2483	1.08	0.3599	0.1401	1.48	0.4306	0.0694
0.69	0.2549	0.2451	1.09	0.3621	0.1379	1.49	0.4319	0.0681
0.70	0.2580	0.2420	1.10	0.3643	0.1357	1.50	0.4332	0.0668

(Continued)

(Continued)

A	B	C	A	B	C	A	B	C
	Area	Area		Area	Area		Area	Area
	Between	Beyond		Between	Beyond		Between	Beyond
Z	Mean and Z	Z	Z	Mean and Z	Z	Z	Mean and Z	Z
1.51	0.4345	0.0655	1.91	0.4719	0.0281	2.31	0.4896	0.0104
1.52	0.4357	0.0643	1.92	0.4726	0.0274	2.32	0.4898	0.0102
1.53	0.4370	0.0630	1.93	0.4732	0.0268	2.33	0.4901	0.0099
1.54	0.4382	0.0618	1.94	0.4738	0.0262	2.34	0.4904	0.0096
1.55	0.4394	0.0606	1.95	0.4744	0.0256	2.35	0.4906	0.0094
1.56	0.4406	0.0594	1.96	0.4750	0.0250	2.36	0.4909	0.0091
1.57	0.4418	0.0582	1.97	0.4756	0.0244	2.37	0.4911	0.0089
1.58	0.4429	0.0571	1.98	0.4761	0.0239	2.38	0.4913	0.0087
1.59	0.4441	0.0559	1.99	0.4767	0.0233	2.39	0.4916	0.0084
1.60	0.4452	0.0548	2.00	0.4772	0.0228	2.40	0.4918	0.0082
1.61	0.4463	0.0537	2.01	0.4778	0.0222	2.41	0.4920	0.0080
1.62	0.4474	0.0526	2.02	0.4783	0.0217	2.42	0.4922	0.0078
1.63	0.4484	0.0516	2.03	0.4788	0.0212	2.43	0.4925	0.0075
1.64	0.4495	0.0505	2.04	0.4793	0.0207	2.44	0.4927	0.0073
1.65	0.4505	0.0495	2.05	0.4798	0.0202	2.45	0.4929	0.0071
1.66	0.4515	0.0485	2.06	0.4803	0.0197	2.46	0.4931	0.0069
1.67	0.4525	0.0475	2.07	0.4808	0.0192	2.47	0.4932	0.0068
1.68	0.4535	0.0465	2.08	0.4812	0.0188	2.48	0.4934	0.0066
1.69	0.4545	0.0455	2.09	0.4817	0.0183	2.49	0.4936	0.0064
1.70	0.4554	0.0466	2.10	0.4821	0.0179	2.50	0.4938	0.0062
1.71	0.4564	0.0436	2.11	0.4826	0.0174	2.51	0.4940	0.0060
1.72	0.4573	0.0427	2.12	0.4830	0.0170	2.52	0.4941	0.0059
1.73	0.4582	0.0418	2.13	0.4834	0.0166	2.53	0.4943	0.0057
1.74	0.4591	0.0409	2.14	0.4838	0.0162	2.54	0.4945	0.0055
1.75	0.4599	0.0401	2.15	0.4842	0.0158	2.55	0.4946	0.0054
1.76	0.4608	0.0392	2.16	0.4846	0.0154	2.56	0.4948	0.0052
1.77	0.4616	0.0384	2.17	0.4850	0.0150	2.57	0.4949	0.0051
1.78	0.4625	0.0375	2.18	0.4854	0.0146	2.58	0.4951	0.0049
1.79	0.4633	0.0367	2.19	0.4857	0.0143	2.59	0.4952	0.0048
1.80	0.4641	0.0359	2.20	0.4861	0.0139	2.60	0.4953	0.0047
1.81	0.4649	0.0351	2.21	0.4864	0.0136	2.61	0.4955	0.0045
1.82	0.4656	0.0344	2.22	0.4868	0.0132	2.62	0.4956	0.0044
1.83	0.4664	0.0336	2.23	0.4871	0.0129	2.63	0.4957	0.0043
1.84	0.4671	0.0329	2.24	0.4875	0.0125	2.64	0.4959	0.0041
1.85	0.4678	0.0322	2.25	0.4878	0.0122	2.65	0.4960	0.0040
1.86	0.4686	0.0314	2.26	0.4881	0.0119	2.66	0.4961	0.0039
1.87	0.4693	0.0307	2.27	0.4884	0.0116	2.67	0.4962	0.0038
1.88	0.4699	0.0301	2.28	0.4887	0.0113	2.68	0.4963	0.0037
1.89	0.4706	0.0294	2.29	0.4890	0.0110	2.69	0.4964	0.0036
1.90	0.4713	0.0287	2.30	0.4893	0.0107	2.70	0.4965	0.0035

A	B	C	A	B	C	A	B	C
Z	Area Between Mean and Z	Area Beyond Z	Z	Area Between Mean and Z	Area Beyond Z	Z	Area Between Mean and Z	Area Beyond Z
2.71	0.4966	0.0034	3.01	0.4987	0.0013	3.31	0.4995	0.0005
2.72	0.4967	0.0033	3.02	0.4987	0.0013	3.32	0.4995	0.0005
2.73	0.4968	0.0032	3.03	0.4988	0.0012	3.33	0.4996	0.0004
2.74	0.4969	0.0031	3.04	0.4988	0.0012	3.34	0.4996	0.0004
2.75	0.4970	0.0030	3.05	0.4989	0.0011	3.35	0.4996	0.0004
2.76	0.4971	0.0029	3.06	0.4989	0.0011	3.36	0.4996	0.0004
2.77	0.4972	0.0028	3.07	0.4989	0.0011	3.37	0.4996	0.0004
2.78	0.4973	0.0027	3.08	0.4990	0.0010	3.38	0.4996	0.0004
2.79	0.4974	0.0026	3.09	0.4990	0.0010	3.39	0.4997	0.0003
2.80	0.4974	0.0026	3.10	0.4990	0.0010	3.40	0.4997	0.0003
2.81	0.4975	0.0025	3.11	0.4991	0.0009	3.41	0.4997	0.0003
2.82	0.4976	0.0024	3.12	0.4991	0.0009	3.42	0.4997	0.0003
2.83	0.4977	0.0023	3.13	0.4991	0.0009	3.43	0.4997	0.0003
2.84	0.4977	0.0023	3.14	0.4992	0.0008	3.44	0.4997	0.0003
2.85	0.4978	0.0022	3.15	0.4992	0.0008	3.45	0.4997	0.0003
2.86	0.4979	0.0021	3.16	0.4992	0.0008	3.46	0.4997	0.0003
2.87	0.4979	0.0021	3.17	0.4992	0.0008	3.47	0.4997	0.0003
2.88	0.4980	0.0020	3.18	0.4993	0.0007	3.48	0.4997	0.0003
2.89	0.4981	0.0019	3.19	0.4993	0.0007	3.49	0.4998	0.0002
2.90	0.4981	0.0019	3.20	0.4993	0.0007	3.50	0.4998	0.0002
2.91	0.4982	0.0018	3.21	0.4993	0.0007	3.60	0.4998	0.0002
2.92	0.4982	0.0018	3.22	0.4994	0.0006	3.70	0.4999	0.0001
2.93	0.4983	0.0017	3.23	0.4994	0.0006	3.80	0.4999	0.0001
2.94	0.4984	0.0016	3.24	0.4994	0.0006	3.90	0.4999	<0.0001
2.95	0.4984	0.0016	3.25	0.4994	0.0006	4.00	0.4999	<0.0001
2.96	0.4985	0.0015	3.26	0.4994	0.0006			
2.97	0.4985	0.0015	3.27	0.4995	0.0005			
2.98	0.4986	0.0014	3.28	0.4995	0.0005			
2.99	0.4986	0.0014	3.29	0.4995	0.0005			
3.00	0.4986	0.0014	3.30	0.4995	0.0005			

APPENDIX C
DISTRIBUTION OF *t*

df	Level of Significance for One-Tailed Test					
	.10	.05	.025	.01	.005	.0005
	Level of Significance for Two-Tailed Test					
	.20	.10	.05	.02	.01	.001
1	3.078	6.314	12.706	31.821	63.657	636.619
2	1.886	2.920	4.303	6.965	9.925	31.598
3	1.638	2.353	3.182	4.541	5.841	12.941
4	1.533	2.132	2.776	3.747	4.604	8.610
5	1.476	2.015	2.571	3.365	4.032	6.859
6	1.440	1.943	2.447	3.143	3.707	5.959
7	1.415	1.895	2.365	2.998	3.499	5.405
8	1.397	1.860	2.306	2.896	3.355	5.041
9	1.383	1.833	2.262	2.821	3.250	4.781
10	1.372	1.812	2.228	2.764	3.169	4.587
11	1.363	1.796	2.201	2.718	3.106	4.437
12	1.356	1.782	2.179	2.681	3.055	4.318
13	1.350	1.771	2.160	2.650	3.012	4.221
14	1.345	1.761	2.145	2.624	2.977	4.140
15	1.341	1.753	2.131	2.602	2.947	4.073
16	1.337	1.746	2.120	2.583	2.921	4.015
17	1.333	1.740	2.110	2.567	2.898	3.965
18	1.330	1.734	2.101	2.552	2.878	3.922
19	1.328	1.729	2.093	2.539	2.861	3.883
20	1.325	1.725	2.086	2.528	2.845	3.850
21	1.323	1.721	2.080	2.518	2.831	3.819
22	1.321	1.717	2.074	2.508	2.819	3.792
23	1.319	1.714	2.069	2.500	2.807	3.767
24	1.318	1.711	2.064	2.492	2.797	3.745
25	1.316	1.708	2.060	2.485	2.787	3.725

df	Level of Significance for One-Tailed Test					
	.10	.05	.025	.01	.005	.0005
	Level of Significance for Two-Tailed Test					
	.20	.10	.05	.02	.01	.001
26	1.315	1.706	2.056	2.479	2.779	3.707
27	1.314	1.703	2.052	2.473	2.771	3.690
28	1.313	1.701	2.048	2.467	2.763	3.674
29	1.311	1.699	2.045	2.462	2.756	3.659
30	1.310	1.697	2.042	2.457	2.750	3.646
40	1.303	1.684	2.021	2.423	2.704	3.551
60	1.296	1.671	2.000	2.390	2.660	3.460
120	1.289	1.658	1.980	2.358	2.617	3.373
∞	1.282	1.645	1.960	2.326	2.576	3.291

Source: Abridged from R. A. Fisher and F. Yates, *Statistical Tables for Biological, Agricultural and Medical Research*, 6th ed. Copyright © R. A. Fisher and F. Yates 1963. Reprinted by permission of Pearson Education Limited.

APPENDIX D
DISTRIBUTION OF CHI-SQUARE

df	.99	.98	.95	.90	.80	.70	.50	.30	.20	.10	.05	.02	.01	.001
1	.03157	.03628	.00393	.0158	.0642	.148	.455	1.074	1.642	2.706	3.841	5.412	6.635	10.827
2	.0201	.0404	.103	.211	.446	.713	1.386	2.408	3.219	4.605	5.991	7.824	9.210	13.815
3	.115	.185	.352	.584	1.005	1.424	2.366	3.665	4.642	6.251	7.815	9.837	11.341	16.268
4	.297	.429	.711	1.064	1.649	2.195	3.357	4.878	5.989	7.779	9.488	11.668	13.277	18.465
5	.554	.752	1.145	1.610	2.343	3.000	4.351	6.064	7.289	9.236	11.070	13.388	15.086	20.517
6	.872	1.134	1.635	2.204	3.070	3.828	5.348	7.231	8.558	10.645	12.592	15.033	16.812	22.457
7	1.239	1.564	2.167	2.833	3.822	4.671	6.346	8.383	9.803	12.017	14.067	16.622	18.475	24.322
8	1.646	2.032	2.733	3.490	4.594	5.527	7.344	9.524	11.030	13.362	15.507	18.168	20.090	26.125
9	2.088	2.532	3.325	4.168	5.380	6.393	8.343	10.656	12.242	14.684	16.919	19.679	21.666	27.877
10	2.558	3.059	3.940	4.865	6.179	7.267	9.342	11.781	13.442	15.987	18.307	21.161	23.209	29.588
11	3.053	3.609	4.575	5.578	6.989	8.148	10.341	12.899	14.631	17.275	19.675	22.618	24.725	31.264
12	3.571	4.178	5.226	6.304	7.807	9.034	11.340	14.011	15.812	18.549	21.026	24.054	26.217	32.909
13	4.107	4.765	5.892	7.042	8.634	9.926	12.340	15.119	16.985	19.812	22.362	25.472	27.688	34.528
14	4.660	5.368	6.571	7.790	9.467	10.821	13.339	16.222	18.151	21.064	23.685	26.873	29.141	36.123
15	5.229	5.985	7.261	8.547	10.307	11.721	14.339	17.322	19.311	22.307	24.996	28.259	30.578	37.697
16	5.812	6.614	7.962	9.312	11.152	12.624	15.338	18.418	20.465	23.542	26.296	29.633	32.000	39.252
17	6.408	7.255	8.672	10.085	12.002	13.531	16.338	19.511	21.615	24.769	27.587	30.995	33.409	40.790
18	7.015	7.906	9.390	10.865	12.857	14.440	17.338	20.601	22.760	25.989	28.869	32.346	34.805	42.312
19	7.633	8.567	10.117	11.651	13.716	15.352	18.338	21.689	23.900	27.204	30.144	33.687	36.191	43.820
20	8.260	9.237	10.851	12.443	14.578	16.266	19.337	22.775	25.038	28.412	31.410	35.020	37.566	45.315
21	8.897	9.915	11.591	13.240	15.445	17.182	20.337	23.858	26.171	29.615	32.671	36.343	38.932	46.797
22	9.542	10.600	12.338	14.041	16.314	18.101	21.337	24.939	27.301	30.813	33.924	37.659	40.289	48.268
23	10.196	11.293	13.091	14.848	17.187	19.021	22.337	26.018	28.429	32.007	35.172	38.968	41.638	49.728
24	10.856	11.992	13.848	15.659	18.062	19.943	23.337	27.096	29.553	33.196	36.415	40.270	42.980	51.179
25	11.524	12.697	14.611	16.473	18.940	20.867	24.337	28.172	30.675	34.382	37.652	41.566	44.314	52.620
26	12.198	13.409	15.379	17.292	19.820	21.792	25.336	29.246	31.795	35.563	38.885	42.856	45.642	54.052
27	12.879	14.125	16.151	18.114	20.703	22.719	26.336	30.319	32.912	36.741	40.113	44.140	46.963	55.476
28	13.565	14.847	16.928	18.939	21.588	23.647	27.336	31.391	34.027	37.916	41.337	45.419	48.278	56.893
29	14.256	15.574	17.708	19.768	22.475	24.577	28.336	32.461	35.139	39.087	42.557	46.693	49.588	58.302
30	14.953	16.306	18.493	20.599	23.364	25.508	29.336	33.530	36.250	40.256	43.773	47.962	50.892	59.703

Source: R. A. Fisher & F. Yates, *Statistical Tables for Biological, Agricultural and Medical Research,* 6th ed. Copyright © R. A. Fisher and F. Yates 1963. Reprinted by permission of Pearson Education Limited.

Appendix E
Distribution of F

df_2	df_1									
	1	2	3	4	5	6	8	12	24	∞
1	161.4	199.5	215.7	224.6	230.2	234.0	238.9	243.9	249.0	254.3
2	18.51	19.00	19.16	19.25	19.30	19.33	19.37	19.41	19.45	19.50
3	10.13	9.55	9.28	9.12	9.01	8.94	8.84	8.74	8.64	8.53
4	7.71	6.94	6.59	6.39	6.26	6.16	6.04	5.91	5.77	5.63
5	6.61	5.79	5.41	5.19	5.05	4.95	4.82	4.68	4.53	4.36
6	5.99	5.14	4.76	4.53	4.39	4.28	4.15	4.00	3.84	3.67
7	5.59	4.74	4.35	4.12	3.97	3.87	3.73	3.57	3.41	3.23
8	5.32	4.46	4.07	3.84	3.69	3.58	3.44	3.28	3.12	2.93
9	5.12	4.26	3.86	3.63	3.48	3.37	3.23	3.07	2.90	2.71
10	4.96	4.10	3.71	3.48	3.33	3.22	3.07	2.91	2.74	2.54
11	4.84	3.98	3.59	3.36	3.20	3.09	2.95	2.79	2.61	2.40
12	4.75	3.88	3.49	3.26	3.11	3.00	2.85	2.69	2.50	2.30
13	4.67	3.80	3.41	3.18	3.02	2.92	2.77	2.60	2.42	2.21
14	4.60	3.74	3.34	3.11	2.96	2.85	2.70	2.53	2.35	2.13
15	4.54	3.68	3.29	3.06	2.90	2.79	2.64	2.48	2.29	2.07
16	4.49	3.63	3.24	3.01	2.85	2.74	2.59	2.42	2.24	2.01
17	4.45	3.59	3.20	2.96	2.81	2.70	2.55	2.38	2.19	1.96
18	4.41	3.55	3.16	2.93	2.77	2.66	2.51	2.34	2.15	1.92
19	4.38	3.52	3.13	2.90	2.74	2.63	2.48	2.31	2.11	1.88
20	4.35	3.49	3.10	2.87	2.71	2.60	2.45	2.28	2.08	1.84
21	4.32	3.47	3.07	2.84	2.68	2.57	2.42	2.25	2.05	1.81
22	4.30	3.44	3.05	2.82	2.66	2.55	2.40	2.23	2.03	1.78
23	4.28	3.42	3.03	2.80	2.64	2.53	2.38	2.20	2.00	1.76
24	4.26	3.40	3.01	2.78	2.62	2.51	2.36	2.18	1.98	1.73
25	4.24	3.38	2.99	2.76	2.60	2.49	2.34	2.16	1.96	1.71
26	4.22	3.37	2.98	2.74	2.59	2.47	2.32	2.15	1.95	1.69
27	4.21	3.35	2.96	2.73	2.57	2.46	2.30	2.13	1.93	1.67
28	4.20	3.34	2.95	2.71	2.56	2.44	2.29	2.12	1.91	1.65
29	4.18	3.33	2.93	2.70	2.54	2.43	2.28	2.10	1.90	1.64
30	4.17	3.32	2.92	2.69	2.53	2.42	2.27	2.09	1.89	1.62
40	4.08	3.23	2.84	2.61	2.45	2.34	2.18	2.00	1.79	1.51
60	4.00	3.15	2.76	2.52	2.37	2.25	2.10	1.92	1.70	1.39
120	3.92	3.07	2.68	2.45	2.29	2.17	2.02	1.83	1.61	1.25
∞	3.84	2.99	2.60	2.37	2.21	2.09	1.94	1.75	1.52	1.00

					$\alpha = .01$					
					df_1					
df_2	1	2	3	4	5	6	8	12	24	∞
1	4052	4999	5403	5625	5764	5859	5981	6106	6234	6366
2	98.49	99.01	99.17	99.25	99.30	99.33	99.36	99.42	99.46	99.50
3	34.12	30.81	29.46	28.71	28.24	27.91	27.49	27.05	26.60	26.12
4	21.20	18.00	16.69	15.98	15.52	15.21	14.80	14.37	13.93	13.46
5	16.26	13.27	12.06	11.39	10.97	10.67	10.27	9.89	9.47	9.02
6	13.74	10.92	9.78	9.15	8.75	8.47	8.10	7.72	7.31	6.88
7	12.25	9.55	8.45	7.85	7.46	7.19	6.84	6.47	6.07	5.65
8	11.26	8.65	7.59	7.01	6.63	6.37	6.03	5.67	5.28	4.86
9	10.56	8.02	6.99	6.42	6.06	5.80	5.47	5.11	4.73	4.31
10	10.04	7.56	6.55	5.99	5.64	5.39	5.06	4.71	4.33	3.91
11	9.65	7.20	6.22	5.67	5.32	5.07	4.74	4.40	4.02	3.60
12	9.33	6.93	5.95	5.41	5.06	4.82	4.50	4.16	3.78	3.36
13	9.07	6.70	5.74	5.20	4.86	4.62	4.30	3.96	3.59	3.16
14	8.86	6.51	5.56	5.03	4.69	4.46	4.14	3.80	3.43	3.00
15	8.68	6.36	5.42	4.89	4.56	4.32	4.00	3.67	3.29	2.87
16	8.53	6.23	5.29	4.77	4.44	4.20	3.89	3.55	3.18	2.75
17	8.40	6.11	5.18	4.67	4.34	4.10	3.79	3.45	3.08	2.65
18	8.28	6.01	5.09	4.58	4.25	4.01	3.71	3.37	3.00	2.57
19	8.18	5.93	5.01	4.50	4.17	3.94	3.63	3.30	2.92	2.49
20	8.10	5.85	4.94	4.43	4.10	3.87	3.56	3.23	2.86	2.42
21	8.02	5.78	4.87	4.37	4.04	3.81	3.51	3.17	2.80	2.36
22	7.94	5.72	4.82	4.31	3.99	3.76	3.45	3.12	2.75	2.31
23	7.88	5.66	4.76	4.23	3.94	3.71	3.41	3.07	2.70	2.26
24	7.82	5.61	4.72	4.22	3.90	3.67	3.36	3.03	2.66	2.21
25	7.77	5.57	4.68	4.18	3.86	3.63	3.32	2.99	2.62	2.17
26	7.72	5.53	4.64	4.14	3.82	3.59	3.29	2.96	2.58	2.13
27	7.68	5.49	4.60	4.11	3.78	3.56	3.26	2.93	2.55	2.10
28	7.64	5.45	4.57	4.07	3.75	3.53	3.23	2.90	2.52	2.06
29	7.60	5.42	4.54	4.04	3.73	3.50	3.20	2.87	2.49	2.03
30	7.56	5.39	4.51	4.02	3.70	3.47	3.17	2.84	2.47	2.01
40	7.31	5.18	4.31	3.83	3.51	3.29	2.99	2.66	2.29	1.80
60	7.08	4.98	4.13	3.65	3.34	3.12	2.82	2.50	2.12	1.60
120	6.85	4.79	3.95	3.48	3.17	2.96	2.66	2.34	1.95	1.38
∞	6.64	4.60	3.78	3.32	3.02	2.80	2.51	2.18	1.79	1.00

APPENDIX F
A BASIC MATH REVIEW

by James Harris

Y ou have probably already heard that there is a lot of math in statistics, and for this reason you are somewhat anxious about taking a statistics course. Although it is true that courses in statistics can involve a great deal of mathematics, you should be relieved to hear that this course will stress interpretation rather than the ability to solve complex mathematical problems. With that said, however, you will still need to know how to perform some basic mathematical operations as well as understand the meanings of certain symbols used in statistics. Following is a review of the symbols and math you will need to know to successfully complete this course.

▣ SYMBOLS AND EXPRESSIONS USED IN STATISTICS

Statistics provides us with a set of tools for describing and analyzing *variables*. A variable is an attribute that can vary in some way. For example, a person's age is a variable because it can range from just born to more than one hundred years old. "Race" and "gender" are also variables, though with fewer categories than the variable "age." In statistics, variables you are interested in measuring are often given a symbol. For example, if we wanted to know something about the age of students in our statistics class, we would use the symbol Y to represent the variable "age." Now let's say for simplicity we asked only the students sitting in the first row their ages—19, 21, 23, and 32. These four ages would be scores of the Y variable.

Another symbol that you will frequently encounter in statistics is Σ, or uppercase sigma. Sigma is a Greek letter that stands for summation in statistics. In other words, when you see the symbol Σ, it means you should sum all of the scores. An example will make this clear. Using our sample of students' ages represented by Y, the use of sigma as in the expression ΣY (read as: the sum of Y) tells us to sum all the scores of the variable Y. Using our example, we would find the sum of the set of scores from the variable "age" by adding the scores together:

$$19 + 21 + 23 + 32 = 95$$

So, for the variable "age," $\Sigma Y = 95$.

Sigma is also often used in expressions with an exponent, as in the expression ΣY^2 (read as: the sum of squared scores). This means that we should first square all the scores of the Y variable and then sum the squared products. So using the same set of scores, we would solve the expression by squaring each score first and then adding them together:

$$19^2 + 21^2 + 23^2 + 32^2 = 361 + 441 + 529 + 1{,}024 = 2{,}355$$

So, for the variable "age," $\Sigma Y^2 = 2{,}355$.

A similar, but slightly different, expression, which illustrates the function of parentheses, is $(\Sigma Y)^2$ (read as: the sum of scores, squared). In this expression, the parentheses tell us to first sum all the scores and then square this summed total. Parentheses are often used in expressions in statistics, and they always tell us to perform the expression within the parentheses first and then the part of the problem that is outside of the parentheses. To solve this expression, we need to sum all the scores first. However, we already found that $\Sigma Y = 95$, so to solve the expression $(\Sigma Y)^2$, we simply square this summed total,

$$95^2 = 9{,}025$$

So, for the variable "age," $(\Sigma Y)^2 = 9{,}025$.

You should also be familiar with the different symbols that denote multiplication and division. Most students are familiar with the times sign ($\times$); however, there are several other ways to express multiplication. For example,

$$3(4) \quad (5)6 \quad (4)(2) \quad 7{\cdot}8 \quad 9*6$$

all symbolize the operation of multiplication. In this text, the first three are most often used to denote multiplication. There are also several ways division can be expressed. You are probably familiar with the conventional division sign ($\div$), but division can also be expressed in these other ways:

$$4/6 \quad \frac{6}{3}$$

This text uses the latter two forms to express division.

In statistics you are likely to encounter greater than and less than signs ($>$, $<$), greater than or equal to and less than or equal to signs ($\geq$, $\leq$), and not equal to signs ($\neq$). It is important you understand what each sign means, though admittedly it is easy to confuse them. Use the following expressions for review. Notice that numerals and symbols are often used together:

$4 > 2$ means 4 is greater than 2

$H_1 > 10$ means H_1 is greater than 10

$7 < 9$ means 7 is less than 9

$a < b$ means a is less than b

$Y \geq 10$ means that the value for Y is a value greater than or equal to 10

$a \leq b$ means that the value for a is less than or equal to the value for b

$8 \neq 10$ means 8 does not equal 10

$H_1 \neq H_2$ means H_1 does not equal H_2

▣ PROPORTIONS AND PERCENTAGES

Proportions and percentages are commonly used in statistics and provide a quick way to express information about the relative frequency of some value. You should know how to find proportions and percentages.

Proportions are identified by P; to find a proportion apply this formula:

$$P = \frac{f}{N}$$

where f stands for the frequency of cases in a category and N the total number of cases in all categories. So, in our sample of four students, if we wanted to know the proportion of males in the front row, there would be a total of two categories, female and male. Because there are 3 females and 1 male in our sample, our N is 4; and the number of cases in our category "male" is 1. To get the proportion, divide 1 by 4:

$$P = \frac{f}{N} \qquad P = \frac{1}{4} = .25$$

So, the proportion of males in the front row is .25. To convert this to a percentage, simply multiply the proportion by 100 or use the formula for percentaging:

$$\% = \frac{f}{N} \times 100 \qquad \% = \frac{1}{4} \times 100 = 25\%$$

▣ WORKING WITH NEGATIVES

Addition, subtraction, multiplication, division, and squared numbers are not difficult for most people; however, there are some important rules to know when working with negatives that you may need to review.

1. When adding a number that is negative, it is the same as subtracting:

$$5 + (-2) = 5 - 2 = 3$$

2. When subtracting a negative number, the sign changes:

$$8 - (-4) = 8 + 4 = 12$$

3. When multiplying or dividing a negative number, the product or quotient is always negative:

$$6 \times -4 = -24 \qquad -10 \div 5 = -2$$

4. When multiplying or dividing two negative numbers, the product or quotient is always positive:

$$-3 \times -7 = 21 \qquad -12 \div -4 = 3$$

5. Squaring a number that is negative always gives a positive product because it is the same as multiplying two negative numbers:

$$-5^2 = 25 \text{ is the same as } -5 \times -5 = 25$$

▣ ORDER OF OPERATIONS AND COMPLEX EXPRESSIONS

In statistics you are likely to encounter some fairly lengthy equations that require several steps to solve. To know what part of the equation to work out first, follow two basic rules. The first is called the rules of precedence. They state that you should solve all squares and square roots first, then multiplication and division, and finally, all addition and subtraction from left to right. The second rule is to solve expressions in parentheses first. If there are brackets in the equation, solve the expression within parentheses first and then the expression within the brackets. This means that parentheses and brackets can override the rules of precedence. In statistics, it is common for parentheses to control the order of calculations. These rules may seem somewhat abstract here, but a brief review of their application should make them more clear.

To solve this problem,

$$4 + 6 \cdot 8 = 4 + 48 = 52$$

do the multiplication first and then the addition. Not following the rules of precedence will lead to a substantially different answer:

$$4 + 6 \cdot 8 = 10 \cdot 8 = 80$$

which is incorrect.

To solve this problem,

$$6 - 4(6)/3^2$$

first, find the square of 3,

$$6 - 4(6)/9$$

then do the multiplication and division from left to right,

$$6 - \frac{24}{9} = 6 - 2.67$$

and finally, work out the subtraction,

$$6 - 2.67 = 3.33$$

To work out the following equation, do the expressions within parentheses first:

$$(4 + 3) - 6(2)/(3 - 1)^2$$

First, solve the addition and subtraction in the parentheses,

$$(7) - 6(2)/(2)^2$$

Now that you have solved the expressions within parentheses, work out the rest of the equation based on the rules of precedence, first squaring the 2,

$$(7) - 6(2)/4$$

Then do the multiplication and division next:

$$(7) - \frac{12}{4} = (7) - 3$$

Finally, work out the subtraction to solve the equation:

$$7 - 3 = 4$$

The following equation may seem intimidating at first, but by solving it in steps and following the rules, even these complex equations should become manageable:

$$\sqrt{\left(8(4-2)^2\right) \Big/ \left(12/4\right)^2}$$

For this equation, work out the expressions within parentheses first; note that there are parentheses within parentheses. In this case, work out the inner parentheses first,

$$\sqrt{\left(8(2)^2\right) \Big/ 3^2}$$

Now do the outer parentheses, making sure to follow the rules of precedence within the parentheses—square first and then multiply:

$$\sqrt{\frac{32}{3^2}}$$

Now, work out the square of 3 first and then divide:

$$\sqrt{\frac{32}{9}} = \sqrt{3.55}$$

Last, take the square root:

$$1.88$$

LEARNING CHECK SOLUTIONS

◉ CHAPTER 1

(p. 7)

Learning Check. Review the definitions of exhaustive and mutually exclusive. Now look at Figure 1.2. What other categories could be added to the variable religion to be exhaustive and mutually exclusive? What other categories could be added to social class? To income?

Answer:

To the variable social class, we could add "lower class" as a category. Monthly income requires many additional categories and could be recoded as an ordinal measure: 0 – $25,000, $25,001 – $50,000, $50,001 – 75,000, $75,001 and higher. For religion, we can also include "Protestant" and those without a religion.

(p. 10)

Learning Check. Identify the independent and dependent variables in the following hypotheses:

- *Younger Americans are more likely to support stricter gun control laws than older Americans.*
- *People who attend church regularly are more likely to oppose abortion than people who do not attend church regularly.*
- *Elderly women are more likely to live alone than elderly men.*
- *Individuals with postgraduate education are likely to have fewer children than those with less education.*

What are the independent and dependent variables in your hypothesis?

Answer:

Independent	Dependent
Age	Support for stricter gun control
Church attendance	Opposition to abortion
Gender	Living arrangement
Educational attainment	Number of children

◉ CHAPTER 2

(p. 30)

Learning Check. Compare Group A with Group B in Figure 2.1 and answer the following questions: Which group has the greater number of women? Which group has the larger proportion of women?

Answer:

Group A: 5 women, Group B: 3 women

Group A: 5/10 = .50, Group B: 3/5 = .60

(p. 34)

Learning Check. Examine Table 2.4 and answer the following questions: What is the percentage of white non-Hispanics who are employed? What is the base (N) for this percentage? What is the percentage of Hispanics who are not in the labor force? What is the base (N) for this percentage?

Answer:

For white non-Hispanics: 56.2%, N = 7,363
For Hispanics: 29.2%, N = 17,162

(p. 50)

Learning Check. Inspect Table 2.15 and answer the following questions:

- *What is the source of this table?*
- *How many variables are presented? What are their names?*
- *What is represented by the numbers presented in the second column? In the last row of the table?*

Answer:

The source for the data is noted at the bottom of the table.

There are nine variables, listed in the first column of the table. The first variable name is "Prenatal care in first three months of pregnancy."

The second column corresponds to mothers who are Mexican immigrants. The numbers correspond to the percentage of these mothers who utilized each health and public assistance program.

The last row corresponds to WIC (Women, Infants and Children Program) utilization.

▣ CHAPTER 4

(p. 99)

Learning Check. Listed below are the political party affiliations of 15 individuals. Find the mode.

Democrat	Republican	Democrat	Republican	Republican
Independent	Democrat	Democrat	Democrat	Republican
Independent	Democrat	Independent	Republican	Democrat

Answer:

The mode is "Democrat," because this category has the highest frequency, which is 7.

(p. 104)

Learning Check. Find the median of the following distribution of an interval-ratio variable: 22, 15, 18, 33, 17, 5, 11, 28, 40, 19, 8, 20.

Answer:

First, we need to arrange the numbers: 5, 8, 11, 15, 17, 18, 19, 20, 22, 28, 33, 40.

(N + 1)/2 = (12 + 1)/2 = 6.5. So the median is the average of the sixth and the seventh numbers, which are 18 and 19.

$$\text{Median} = \frac{18+19}{2} = 18.5$$

So the median is 18.5.

(p. 106)

Learning Check. Examine Figure 4.4 and contrast the median incomes of women and men over the three decades. What can you learn about gender and income?

Answer:

Since the early 1970s, the median income of women increased more rapidly than that of men. While there was a 17.1% increase in men's median income in 2011 as compared with 1973, the median income of women increased more than 50% over the same period. Still, however, men, on average, have a much higher income than women in the United States, which suggests that there may be an association between gender and income.

(p. 113)

Learning Check. The following distribution is the same as the one you used to calculate the median in an earlier Learning Check: 22, 15, 18, 33, 17, 5, 11, 28, 40, 19, 8, 20. Can you calculate the mean? Is it the same as the median, or is it different?

Answer:

$$\text{Mean} = \frac{22+15+18+33+17+5+11+28+40+19+8+20}{12} = 19.67$$

So the mean, 19.67, is larger than the median, 18.5.

▣ CHAPTER 5

(p. 142)

Learning Check. Examine A Closer Look 5.1 and consider the impact that the number of categories of a variable has on the IQV. What would happen to the Berkeley case if Asians were divided into two categories with 19% Chinese American in one and 17% Other Asian in the other? (To answer this question, you will need to recalculate the IQV with these new data.)

Answer:

If Asians were divided into two categories that comprised 19% and 17% of the total undergraduate students at U.C. Berkeley in 2012, we would have 6 racial/ethnic categories instead of 5. Then, the IQV would be calculated as follows:

$$IQV = \frac{K(100^2 - \Sigma Pct^2)}{100^2(K-1)} = \frac{6(100^2 - 2,030)}{100^2(6-1)} = \frac{47,820}{50,000} = 0.96$$

When we increased the number of categories in our race/ethnicity variable, the IQV also increased from 0.92 (the IQV with 5 racial/ethnic categories) to 0.96. So, other things being equal, the larger the number of categories, the larger the IQV.

(p. 145)

Learning Check. Why can't we use the range to describe diversity in nominal variables? The range can be used to describe diversity in ordinal variables (e.g., we can say that responses to a question ranged from "somewhat satisfied" to "very dissatisfied"), but it has no quantitative meaning. Why not?

Answer:

In nominal variables, the numbers are used only to represent the different categories of a variable without implying anything about the magnitude or quantitative difference between these categories. Therefore, the range, being a measure of variability that gives the quantitative difference between two values that a variable takes, is not an appropriate measure for nominal variables. Similarly, in ordinal variables, numbers corresponding with the categories of a variable are only used to rank order these categories without having any meaning in terms of the quantitative difference between these categories. Therefore, the range does not convey any quantitative meaning when used to describe the diversity in ordinal variables.

(p. 147)

Learning Check. Why is the IQR better than the range as a measure of variability, especially when there are extreme scores in the distribution? To answer this question, you may want to examine Figure 5.3.

Answer:

Extreme scores directly impact the range, which is by definition the difference between the highest and the lowest scores. Therefore, if a distribution has extreme (very high and/or very low) scores, the range does not provide an accurate description of the distribution. IQR, on the other hand, is not affected by extreme scores. Thus, it is a better measure of variability than the range when there are extreme scores in the distribution.

(p. 154)

Learning Check. Examine Table 5.8 again and note the disproportionate contribution of the Western region to the sum of the squared deviations from the mean (it actually accounts for about 45% of the sum of squares). Can you explain why? (Hint: It has something to do with the sensitivity of the mean to extreme values.)

Answer:

The Western region has the highest projected percentage change in the elderly population between 2008 and 2015, which is 27%. Therefore, it deviates more from the mean than the other regions. The more a category of a variable deviates from the mean, the larger the square of the deviation gets, and hence the more this category contributes to the sum of the squared deviations from the mean.

▣ CHAPTER 6

(p. 184)

Learning Check. Transform the Z scores in Table 6.2 back into raw scores. Your answers should agree with the raw scores listed in the table.

Answer:

Z Score	Raw Score
−2.93	$Y = 70.07 − 2.93(10.27) = 40$
−1.95	$Y = 70.07 − 1.95(10.27) = 50$
−0.98	$Y = 70.07 − 0.98(10.27) = 60$
−0.01	$Y = 70.07 − 0.01(10.27) = 70$
0.97	$Y = 70.07 + 0.97(10.27) = 80$
1.94	$Y = 70.07 + 1.94(10.27) = 90$
2.91	$Y = 70.07 + 2.91(10.27) = 100$

(p. 195)

Learning Check. In Chapter 4, we learned to identify percentiles using cumulative percentages in a distribution. Examine Table 6.1 and find the 92nd percentile. Does your answer differ from the results that we obtained earlier (finding the percentile rank of a score higher than the mean)? If it does, explain why.

Answer:

According to Table 6.1, the 92nd percentile is 80 because 92% of all the students fall somewhere in this category (see the cumulative percentage associated with the score of 80). However, if we calculate the percentile rank of 80, we find it to be 83.4, not 92:

$$Z = \frac{(80 - 70.07)}{10.27} = 0.97$$

The area beyond a Z score of 0.97 is 0.1660. So the percentile rank = $(1 - 0.1660)100 = 83.4$, which means that 83.4% of all the students enrolled in social statistics scored lower than 80. The percentile rank identified according to Table 6.1 is different from the percentile rank of 80 calculated above because while the former method relies on the cumulative percentages, the latter incorporates mean and standard deviation to give an exact location of a percentile.

(p. 196)

Learning Check. In a normal distribution, how many standard deviations from the mean is the 95th percentile? If you can't answer this question, review the material in this section.

Answer:

The number of standard deviations from the mean is what we call a Z score. The Z score associated with the 95th percentile is 1.65. So a score at the 95th percentile is 1.65 standard deviations above the mean.

(p. 197)

Learning Check. What is the raw score in statistics associated with the 50th percentile?

Answer:

The raw score associated with the 50th percentile is the median.

▣ CHAPTER 7

(p. 229)

Learning Check. Suppose a population distribution has a mean $\mu_Y = 150$ and a standard deviation $\sigma_Y = 30$ and you draw a simple random sample of N = 100 cases. What is the probability that the mean is between 147 and 153? What is the probability that the sample mean exceeds 153? Would you be surprised to find a mean score of 159? Why? (Hint: To answer these questions, you need to apply what you learned in Chapter 6 about Z scores and areas under the normal curve [Appendix B].) Remember, to translate a raw score into a Z score we used this formula:

$$Z = \frac{Y - \bar{Y}}{S_Y}$$

However, because here we are dealing with a sampling distribution, replace Y with the sample mean $\bar{Y}$, $\bar{Y}$ with the sampling distribution's mean $\mu_{\bar{Y}}$ and S_Y with the standard error of the mean $\sigma_Y / \sqrt{N}$

$$Z = \frac{\bar{Y} - \mu_{\bar{Y}}}{\sigma_Y / \sqrt{N}}$$

Answer:

Z score equivalent of 147 is

$$Z = \frac{\bar{Y} - \mu_{\bar{Y}}}{\sigma_Y / \sqrt{N}} = \frac{147 - 150}{30 / \sqrt{100}} = \frac{-3}{3} = -1$$

Z score equivalent of 153 is

$$Z = \frac{\overline{Y} - \mu_{\overline{Y}}}{\sigma_Y / \sqrt{N}} = \frac{153 - 150}{30 / \sqrt{100}} = \frac{3}{3} = 1$$

Using the standard normal table (Appendix B), we can see that the probability of the area between the mean and a score 1 standard deviation above or below the mean is 0.3413. So the probability that the mean is between 147 and 153, both of which deviate from the mean by 1 standard deviation, is 0.6826 (0.3413 + 0.3413), or 68.26%.

The probability of the area beyond 1 standard deviation from the mean is 0.1587. So the probability that the mean exceeds 153 is 0.1587, or 15.87%.

Z score equivalent of 159 is

$$Z = \frac{\overline{Y} - \mu_{\overline{Y}}}{\sigma_Y / \sqrt{N}} = \frac{159 - 150}{30 / \sqrt{100}} = \frac{9}{3} = 3$$

The probability of the area beyond 3 standard deviations from the mean, according to the standard normal table, is 0.0014. Therefore, it would be surprising to find a mean score of 159, as the probability is very low (0.14%).

▣ CHAPTER 8

(p. 240)

Learning Check. What is the difference between a point estimate and a confidence interval?

Answer:

When the estimate of a population parameter is a single number, it is called a point estimate. When the estimate is a range of scores, it is called an interval estimate. Confidence intervals are used for interval estimates.

(p. 242)

Learning Check. To understand the relationship between the confidence level and Z, review the material in Chapter 6. What would be the appropriate Z value for a 98% confidence interval?

Answer:

The appropriate Z value for a 98% confidence interval is 2.33.

(p. 244)

Learning Check. What is the 90% confidence interval for the mean commuting time? (Hint: First, find the Z value associated with a 90% confidence level.)

Answer:

$$90\% \text{ CI} = 7.5 \pm 1.65(0.07)$$

$$= 7.5 \pm 0.12$$

$$= 7.38 \text{ to } 7.62$$

(p. 249)

Learning Check. Why do smaller sample sizes produce wider confidence intervals? (See Figure 8.5.) (Hint: Compare the standard errors of the mean for the three sample sizes.)

Answer:

As the sample size gets smaller, the standard error of the mean gets larger, which, in turn, results in a wider confidence interval.

(p. 255)

Learning Check. Calculate the confidence interval for the Gallup survey using percentages rather than proportions. Your results should be identical with ours except that they are expressed in percentages.

Answer:

$$\text{Standard error} = \sqrt{59(100-59)/1{,}535} = 1.26$$

$$95\% \text{ CI} = 59 \pm 1.96(1.26)$$

$$= 59 \pm 2.47$$

$$= 56.53 \text{ to } 61.47$$

The confidence interval we calculated using percentages is almost identical with the confidence interval we calculated using proportions except for a small difference that is due to rounding off of the numbers.

CHAPTER 9

(p. 283)

Learning Check. For the following research situations, state your research and null hypotheses:

- *There is a difference between the mean statistics grades of social science majors and the mean statistics grades of business majors.*
- *The average number of children in two-parent black families is lower than the average number of children in two-parent nonblack families.*
- *Grade point averages are higher among girls who participate in organized sports than among girls who do not.*

Answer:

Null Hypothesis	Research Hypothesis
Means are presumed equal for all statements.	Two-tailed test. No direction is stated.
	One-tailed test, left.
	One-tailed test, right.

(p. 289)

Learning Check. Would you change your decision in the previous example if alpha were .01? Why or why not?

Answer:

The significance of 4.266 is .000, which is less than .01. Our decision to reject the null hypothesis would not change.

(p. 291)

Learning Check. State the null and research hypothesis for this example.

Answer:

The null hypothesis is: $\pi_1 = \pi_2$

The research hypothesis is: $\pi_1 \neq \pi_2$

(p. 294)

Learning Check. Review the information provided in Table 9.5. What would be the t critical at the .05 level for the first indicator, EC Index? Assume a two-tailed test.

Answer:

The *N*'s are reported as a Note in the bottom of the table. The *df* calculation would be $(78 + 113) - 2 = 189$. Based on Appendix C, $df = \infty$, *t* critical is 1.960.

▣ CHAPTER 10

(p. 307)

Learning Check. Examine Table 10.2. Make sure that you can identify all the parts just described and that you understand how the numbers were obtained. Can you identify the independent and dependent variables in the table? You will need to know this to convert the frequencies to percentages.

Answer:

The independent variable is race, and home ownership is the dependent variable.

▣ CHAPTER 11

(p. 351)

Learning Check. Construct a bivariate table (in percentages) showing no association between age and first-generation college status.

Answer:

Age and First-Generation College Status

	19 Years or Younger	*20 Years or Older*	
Firsts	41.9%	41.9%	41.9% (1,934)
Nonfirsts	58.1%	58.1%	58.1% (2,683)
	100.0%	100.0%	4,617

(p. 352)

Learning Check. Refer to the data in the previous Learning Check. Are the variables age and first-generation college status statistically independent? Write out the research and the null hypotheses for your practice data.

Answer:

Null hypothesis: There is no association between age and first-generation college status.
Research hypothesis: Age and first-generation college status are statistically dependent.

(p. 354)

Learning Check. Refer to the data in the Learning Check on page 351. Calculate the expected frequencies for age and first-generation college status and construct a bivariate table. Are your column and row marginals the same as in the original table?

Answer:

Using the format of Table 11.5, construct a table to calculate chi-square for age and educational attainment.

	f_o	f_e	$f_o - f_e$	$(f_o - f_e)^2$	$(f_o - f_e)^2 / f_e$
19/Firsts	916	1138.53	−222.53	49519.60	43.49
19/Nonfirsts	1802	1579.47	222.53	49519.60	31.35
20/Firsts	1018	795.47	222.53	49519.60	62.25
20/Nonfirsts	−881	1103.53	−222.53	49519.60	44.87

Chi-square = 181.96, with Yates correction = 181.15.

(p. 357)

Learning Check. *Based on Appendix D, identify the probability for each chi-square value (df in parentheses)*

Answer:

- *12.307 (15)* Between .70 and .50
- *20.337 (21)* Exactly .50
- *54.052 (24)* Less than .001

(p. 359)

Learning Check. *What decision can you make about the association between age and first-generation college status? Should you reject the null hypothesis at the .05 alpha level or at the .01 level?*

Answer:

We would reject the null hypothesis of no difference. Our calculated chi-square is significant at the .05 and the .01 levels. We have evidence that age is related to first-generation college status—older students are more likely to be first-generation students than younger students. Fifty-four percent of students 20 years or older are first-generation students versus 33.7% of students 19 years or younger.

(p. 363)

Learning Check. *For the bivariate table with age and first-generation college status, the value of the obtained chi-square is 181.15 with 1 degree of freedom. Based on Appendix D, we determine that its probability is less than .001. This probability is less than our alpha level of .05. We reject the null hypothesis of no relationship between age and first-generation college status. If we reduce our sample size by half, the obtained chi-square is 90.58. Determine the P value for 90.58. What decision can you make about the null hypothesis?*

Answer:

Even if we reduce the chi-square by half, we would still reject the null hypothesis.

▣ CHAPTER 12

(p. 400)

Learning Check. *Calculate eta² for this model.*

Answer:

Based on the output eta^2 = 5.795/207.681 = .028 = .03. If we know the respondent's political views, we can predict their IMMAMECO response with 3% accuracy.

(p. 404)

Learning Check. *For the ANOVA model for Intrafamily Strain, what is the F critical? What information do you need to determine the F critical? Assume alpha = .05.*

Answer:

You would need to determine k and N. In this case, $k = 3$ and $N = 486$. There are two degrees of freedom to calculate: df (between) $= k - 1 = 3 - 1 = 2$ and df(within) $= N - k = 486 - 3 = 483$. For an alpha of .05, the F critical is 2.99 (based on Appendix E).

▣ CHAPTER 13

(p. 419)

Learning Check. *Use Figure 13.3 to predict the percentage of residents with a bachelor's degree in a state with a median household income of $47,500 and one with a median household income of $50,000.*

Answer:

The percentage of residents with a bachelor's degree in a state with a median household income of $47,500 is about 26%. The comparable percentage in a state with a median household income of $50,000 is about 27%.

(p. 422)

Learning Check. For each of these four lines, as X goes up by 1 unit, what does Y do? Be sure you can answer this question using both the equation and the line.

Answer:

For the line $Y = 1X$, as X goes up by 1 unit, Y also goes up by 1 unit. In the second line, $Y = 2 + 0.5X$, Y increases by 0.5 units as a result of 1-unit increase in X. The line $Y = 6 - 2X$ tells that every 1-unit increase in X results in 2-unit decrease in Y. Finally, in the fourth line, Y decreases by 0.33 units as a result of 1-unit increase in X.

(p. 422)

Learning Check. Use the linear equation describing the relationship between seniority and salary of teachers to obtain the predicted salary of a teacher with 12 years of seniority.

Answer:

The predicted salary of a teacher with 12 years of seniority is $36,000 ($Y = 12{,}000 + 2{,}000(12)$).

(p. 427)

Learning Check. Use the prediction equation to calculate the predicted values of Y for New York, Georgia, and Ohio. Verify that the regression line in Figure 13.6 passes through these points.

Answer:

$$\text{New York: } \hat{Y} = 7.41 + 0.0004(54{,}659) = 29.27\%$$

$$\text{Georgia: } \hat{Y} = 7.41 + 0.0004(47{,}590) = 26.45\%$$

$$\text{Ohio: } \hat{Y} = 7.41 + 0.0004(45{,}395) = 25.57\%$$

(p. 453)

Learning Check. Use the prediction equation describing the relationship between teen pregnancy and both unemployment and expenditures on education to calculate the 2010 predicted teen pregnancy rate for a state with an unemployment rate of 3% and an expenditure per pupil of $6,000.

Answer:

$$\hat{Y} = 39.661 + 0.823(3) - 0.001(6{,}000) = 36.13$$

ANSWERS TO ODD-NUMBERED EXERCISES

◙ CHAPTER 1

1. Once our research question, the hypothesis, and the study variables have been selected, we move on to the next stage of the research process—measuring and collecting the data. The choice of a particular data collection method or instrument depends to our study objective. After our data have been collected, we have to find a systematic way to organize and analyze our data and set up some set of procedures to decide what we mean.

3. a. Interval ratio
   b. Nominal
   c. Interval ratio
   d. Ordinal
   e. Nominal
   f. Interval ratio
   g. Interval ratio
   h. Nominal

5. There are many possible variables from which to choose. Some of the most common selections by students will probably be: type of occupation or industry, work experience, and educational training or expertise. Students should first address the relationship between these variables and gender. For example, men have more years of work experience than women in the same occupation. Students may also consider measuring structural bias or discrimination.

7. In general, the difficulty with studying criminal acts is that the criminal act needs to be reported first. It is estimated that the majority of crimes are not reported to authorities. Data on reported crimes are routinely collected by the Federal Bureau of Investigation and the Bureau of Justice.

9. Individual age: This variable could be measured as an interval-ratio variable, with actual age in years reported. As discussed in the chapter, interval ratio variables are the highest level of measurement and can also be measured at ordinal or nominal levels.

   Annual income: This variable could be measured as an interval-ratio variable, with actual dollar earnings reported.

   Religiosity: This variable could be measured in several ways. For example, as church attendance, the variable could be ordinal (number of times attended church in a month: every week, at least twice a month, less than two times a month, none at all).

   Student performance: This could be measured as an interval-ratio variable as GPA or test score.

Social class: This variable is an ordinal variable, with categories low, working, middle, and upper.

Attitude toward gun control: This variable is an ordinal variable, with categories strongly disagree, disagree, neutral, agree, and strongly agree.

▣ CHAPTER 2

1. a. Race is a nominal variable. Class is an ordinal variable, since the categories can be ordered from lower to higher status.
   b.

Frequency Table for Race

Race	Frequency (f)
White	17
Nonwhite	13
Total (N)	30

Frequency Table for Class

Class	Frequency (f)
Lower	3
Working	15
Middle	11
Upper	1
Total (N)	30

3.

Number of traumas	Frequency (f)
0	15
1	11
2	4
Total (N)	30

Trauma is an interval or ratio-level variable, since it has a real zero point and a meaningful numeric scale.

   b. People in this survey are more likely to have experienced no traumas last year (50% of the group).
   c. The proportion who experienced one or more traumas is calculated by first adding 36.7% and 13.3% = 50%. Then divide that number by 100 to obtain the proportion, 0.50, or half the group.

5. Ranking them from highest to lowest level of support: Strong Democrats, Strong Republicans, and Independents. Support does vary by group, however, the majority of strong Democrats (56.8%) and strong

Republicans (50%) agree/strongly agree with the statement. The group with the lowest level of support is Independents with 42.3%.

7.   a.
For whites.

Education	f	%	C%
Less than high school	72	12.3	12.3
High school graduate	272	46.5	58.8
Junior college	46	7.9	66.7
Bachelor	118	20.2	86.9
Graduate	77	13.2	100.1
TOTAL	585		

For blacks.

Education	f	%	C%
Less than high school	26	22.0	22.0
High school graduate	59	50	72.0
Junior college	10	8.5	80.5
Bachelor	16	13.6	94.1
Graduate	7	5.9	100.0
TOTAL	118		

For males.

Education	f	%	C%
Less than high school	46	14.0	14.0
High school graduate	151	45.9	59.9
Junior college	24	7.3	67.2
Bachelor	65	19.8	87
Graduate	43	13.1	100.1
TOTAL	329		

For females.

Education	f	%	C%
Less than high school	67	15.0	15.0
High school graduate	214	47.8	62.8
Junior college	37	8.2	71.0
Bachelor	81	18.1	89.1
Graduate	49	10.9	100.0
TOTAL	448		

  b. 40.2% of males attended school beyond high school. A lower percentage of females (37.2%) did the same.
  c. 58.8% for whites and 72.0% for blacks.
  d. Cumulative percentages are more similar for men and women than for white and blacks. Inequality appears to be larger between racial groups. A larger percentage of whites complete bachelor or graduate degrees than do blacks.

9. a. Interval-ratio
  b. 33.7% of males and 34.9% of females had 3 children or more.
  c. Based on the cumulative percentages, a higher percentage of males have fewer children (0–1) than females (44.6% vs. 36.7%).

	Males			Females		
	(f)	*%*	*C(%)*	*(f)*	*%*	*C(%)*
0	94	28.7	28.7	92	20.6	20.6
1	52	15.9	44.6	72	16.1	36.7
2	71	21.7	66.3	127	28.4	65.1
3	47	14.4	80.7	91	20.4	85.5
4	30	9.2	89.9	38	8.5	94
5 or more	33	10.1	100	27	6.0	100
Total (*N*)	327			447		

11. a. Victimization rates are highest for those 12–17 years of age.
  b. Victimization rates have been declining since 1994–1998. In the last time period, 2005–2010, all rates are below 5 per 1,000 females. Across the three time periods, victimization rates are highest for females ages 12–17 (11.3–4.1). Second highest rates are among females ages 18–34 years (7.0–3.7).

13. a. SEX: nominal
     RACE: nominal
     AGE: ordinal
     EDUCATION: ordinal

INCOME LEVEL: ordinal

RELIGIOUS AFFILIATION: nominal

b. Based on the Gallup data, we know that the majority of female voters, total nonwhite and non-Hispanic black voters, young (18–29) voters, voters with postgraduate degrees, and lower income voters supported President Obama and Vice President Biden. Governor Romney and Senator Ryan had strongest support among men, non-Hispanic whites, seniors (65 years and older), college graduates or those with some college, and voters who earned $36,000 or more.

▣ CHAPTER 3

1. The group with the largest increase in voting rates is blacks, from 53% in 1996 to 66.2% in 2012. Blacks are the only group that did not experience a decline in voting rates for the years presented. Hispanic voting rates exceeded the voting rates for Asians in 2000 and remained higher than Asians through 2012. Hispanics and Asians have the lowest voting rates for all groups. As noted in the exercise, in the 2012 presidential election, blacks had the highest voting rates for all groups, followed by non-Hispanic whites, Hispanics, and Asians. White voting rates declined by 2% from 2008 to 2012. The highest voting rate for whites was in 2004 (67.2%), 2008 for Hispanics (49.9%), and for Asians (47.6%).

3. According to the graph, the largest group of seniors (15.2%) reported a household income of $25,999–$34,999, followed by 14.6% at $35,000–$49,999. The smallest income group was under $5,000 (2.3%).

5. b. More than 10% of females reported a household size of 7. The largest household size for males is 5.

    c. Frequencies don't control or adjust for the total number of people in each group. There are more males (17) than females (13), so percentages must be used to make the bars comparable.

7. The data is an ordinal measure and can be presented in a bar graph or histogram. Notice that percentages are reported for comparison between the two groups.

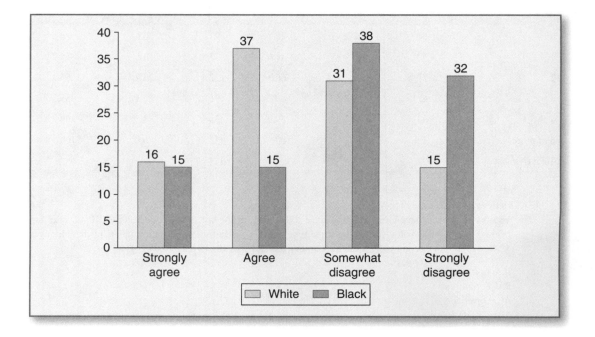

9. a. Years of education is an interval-ratio variable. Thus a histogram, which is suitable for graphing interval-ratio data, can be used for years of education.

    b. The following educational categories were created for this chart: 0–4, 5–8, 9–12, 13–16, and 17–20 years.

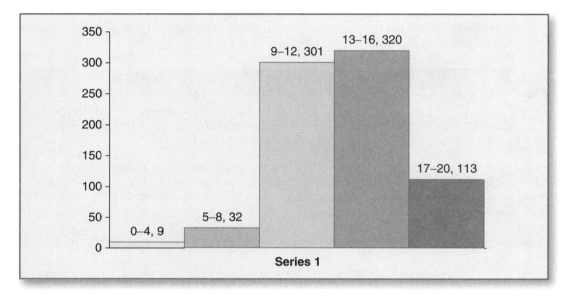

11. E-mail hours per week is an interval measurement, suitable for a line graph.

13. a. The data is interval and should be presented in either a bar chart or histogram.

    b. Number of children by gender, GSS 2010, frequencies reported.

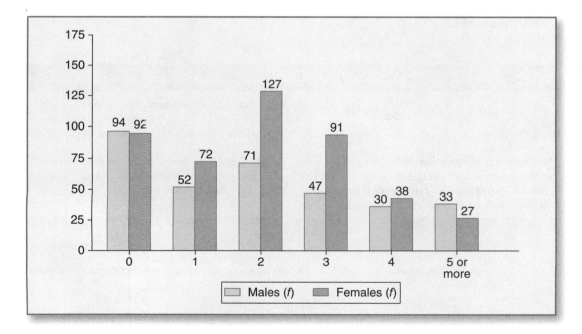

▣ CHAPTER 4

1. a. The mode can be found two ways: looking for either the highest frequency (470) or the highest percentage (48.3). The mode is the category that corresponds to these values, "Exciting."
   b. The median can be found two ways: by using either the frequencies column or the cumulative percentages.

Using Frequencies	Using Cumulative Percentages
$$\frac{N+1}{2} = \frac{974+1}{2} = 487.5\text{th case}$$	Notice that 48.3% of the observations fall in the "Exciting" percentage category; 93.9% fall in or before the "Routine" category.
Starting with the frequency in the first category (470), add up the frequencies until you find where the 487th and 488th cases fall. Both of these cases correspond to the category "Routine," which is the median.	The 50% mark, or the median, is located somewhere within the "Routine" category. So the median is "Routine."

   c. The mode is simply the category with the highest frequency (or percentage) in the distribution. The median divides the distribution into two equal parts so that half the cases are below it and half are above it.
   d. Because this variable is an ordinal-level variable.

3. a. Interval-ratio. The mode can be found two ways: by looking either for the highest frequency (14) or the highest percentage (43.8%). The mode is the category that corresponds to the value "40 hours worked last week." The median can be found two ways: by using either the frequencies column or the cumulative percentages.

Using Frequencies	Using Cumulative Percentages
$$\frac{N+1}{2} = \frac{32+1}{2} = 16.5\text{th case}$$	Notice that 34.4% of the observations fall in or below the "32 hours worked last week" category; 78.1% fall in or below the "40 hours worked last week" category.
Starting with the frequency in the first category (1), add up the frequencies until you find where the 16th and 17th cases fall. Both of these cases correspond to the category "40 hours worked last week," which is the median.	The 50% mark, or the median, is located somewhere within the "40 hours worked last week" category. So the median is "40 hours worked last week."

   b. Since the median is merely a synonym for the 50th percentile, we already know that its value is 40 hours worked last week.

   25th percentile = (32 × 0.25) = 8th case = 30 hours worked last week
   75th percentile = (32 × 0.75) = 24th case = 40 hours worked last week

5. a. The mode can be found by looking for the highest frequency in each column; the mode for each group is listed below:

   18–29: Good
   30–39: Good
   40–49: Good
   50–59: Good

   The median can be found two ways: by using either the frequencies column or the cumulative percentages. However, since the problem only gives the frequencies, we'll use those to solve for the median.

Age Group			
18–29	*30–39*	*40–49*	*50–59*
$\frac{N+1}{2} = \frac{164+1}{2} = 82.5\text{th case}$	$\frac{N+1}{2} = \frac{169+1}{2} = 85\text{th case}$	$\frac{N+1}{2} = \frac{168+1}{2} = 84.5\text{th case}$	$\frac{N+1}{2} = \frac{173+1}{2} = 87\text{th case}$
Starting with the frequency in the first category (56), add up the frequencies until you find where the 82nd and 83rd cases fall. Both cases correspond to "Good," which is the median.	Starting with the frequency in the first category (55), add up the frequencies until you find where the 85th case falls. This case corresponds to "Good," which is the median.	Starting with the frequency in the first category (41), add up the frequencies until you find where the 84th and 85th cases fall. Both cases correspond to "Good," which is the median.	Starting with the frequency in the first category (38), add up the frequencies until you find where the 87th case falls. It corresponds to "Good," which is the median.

   b. Since the mode and median for all four age groups was "Good," it has to do with how respondents interpreted the question. For instance, it is possible that one's health status was assessed relative to his or her age. Neither the median nor the mode provides a better description of the data since they provide the same information.

7. We begin by multiplying each household size by its frequency.

Household Size	Frequency	Frequency × Y (fY)
1	381	381
2	526	1,052
3	227	681
4	200	800
5	96	480
6	42	252
7	19	133
8	5	40
9	2	18
10	2	20
Total	$N = 1,500$	$\Sigma fy = 3,857$

$$\bar{Y} = \frac{\Sigma fy}{N} = \frac{3,857}{1,500} = 2.57$$

So, the mean number of people per household is 2.57.

9.

a. There appear to be a few outliers (i.e., extremely high values); this leads us to believe that the distribution is skewed in the positive direction.

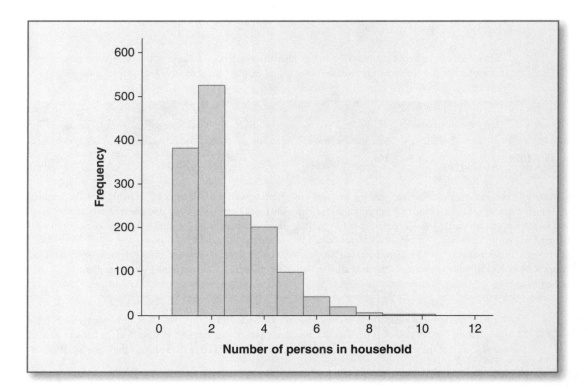

b. The median can be found two ways: by using either the frequencies column or the cumulative percentages. The data are in frequencies; we'll use those to solve the median. Since the median (2) is less than the mean (2.57), we can conclude that the distribution is skewed in a positive direction. Our answer to question 9a is further supported.

Using Frequencies

$$\frac{N+1}{2} = \frac{1,500+1}{2} = 750.5\text{th case}$$

Starting with the frequency in the first category (381), add up the frequencies until you find where the 750th and 751st cases fall. Both of these cases correspond to the category "2," which is the median.

11. Yes, both politicians can be correct, at least in a technical sense. One politician can be referring to the mean; the other could be using the median. It would be unusual if these two statistics were exactly equal. The average or mean income of Americans can be greater than the median if the distribution of income is positively skewed, which is certainly true.

13. First, let's order each set of scores from lowest to highest.

2008–2010 Male Murder Rate per 100,000			
Top 10 by Population	*Murder Rate*	*Bottom 10 by Population*	*Murder Rate*
Japan	0.4	Germany	0.9
China	2.2	Italy	1.6
India	3.9	United Kingdom	1.7
Pakistan	4.3	France	1.9
United States	6.6	Egypt	2.2
Indonesia	13.9	South Korea	2.2
Nigeria	18.2	Iran	2.3
Mexico	23.0	Vietnam	2.6
Russia	29.1	Turkey	8.6
Brazil	54.7	Democratic Republic of the Congo	35.8
	$\Sigma = 156.3$		$\Sigma = 59.8$

The median is simply the number in the middle. Since we have 10 countries in each group, we want the 5.5th case ($[10 + 1]/2$). For the countries in the top 10, the 5.5th case falls between the United States and Indonesia. So the median is 10.3 ($[6.6+13.9]/2$). For the countries in the bottom 10, the 5.5th case falls between Egypt and South Korea. So the median is 2.2. ($[2.2+2.2]/2$).

The mean for each group is calculated using the following formula:

$$\bar{Y} = \frac{\Sigma Y}{N}$$

For countries in the top 10 for murder rates, the mean is 15.63 (156.3/10). For countries in the bottom 10, the mean is 5.98 (59.8/10). Brazil has the highest murder rate (54.7) among these countries. On average, countries with higher populations (i.e., top 10) had higher murder rates. The distribution of murder rates for countries in the bottom 10 is skewed in a positive direction because only one country (i.e., Democratic Republic of the Congo) had a very high murder rate. The pattern is similar for the countries in the top 10 due to Brazil's high murder rate, as well as the fairly high murder rates for Mexico and Russia.

15. a. We begin by ordering the countries from lowest to highest rate of infant mortality.

Country	Infant Mortality Rates
Finland	3.40
Luxembourg	4.39
Canada	4.85
United States	6.00
Panama	11.32

Country	Infant Mortality Rates
Syria	15.12
Colombia	15.92
Turkey	23.07
Zimbabwe	28.23
Rwanda	62.51
Afghanistan	121.63

Since we are working with an odd number of cases (11), the median is simply the frequency associated with the sixth case, Syria. Therefore, the median is 15.12. To calculate the mean, we total the number of infant mortality rates for the eleven countries.

Country	Infant Mortality Rates
Finland	3.40
Luxembourg	4.39
Canada	4.85
United States	6.00
Panama	11.32
Syria	15.12
Colombia	15.92
Turkey	23.07
Zimbabwe	28.23
Rwanda	62.51
Afghanistan	121.63
	$\Sigma = 296.44$

$$\bar{Y} = \frac{\Sigma f Y}{N} = \frac{296.44}{11} = 26.95$$

b. Since the median value (15.12) is much lower than the mean value (26.95), we know that the data listed above are positively skewed.
c. Two reasons for the varying infant mortality rates are the types of health services available to women as well as the average level of education of women.

▣ CHAPTER 5

1. a. The table reveals seven response categories for political views.
    b. The sum of the squared percentages, ΣPct^2, is equal to 2,156.31.

Political Views	Percentage (%)	Percentage Squared (%²)
Extremely liberal	3.9	15.21
Liberal	11.5	132.25
Slightly liberal	12.8	163.84
Moderate	36.7	1,346.89
Slightly conservative	14.6	213.16
Conservative	16.4	268.96
Extremely conservative	4.0	16.00
Total	100.0	$\Sigma = 2,156.31$

c. Using the formula, we calculate the IQV as follows:

$$IQV = \frac{K(100^2 - \sum Pct^2)}{100^2(K-1)} = \frac{7(100^2 - 2,156.31)}{100^2(7-1)} = \frac{54,905.83}{60,000} = 0.92$$

The IQV we calculated (0.92) is close to 1.0 and suggests that Americans are in fact fairly diverse in their political views. The IQV does support our observations from the table.

3. a. The range of convictions in 1990 is (583 – 79) = 504. The range of convictions in 2009 is (426 – 102) = 324. The range of convictions is larger in 1990 than 2009.
    b. The mean number of convictions is 295.67 in 1990 and 261.67 in 2009.
    c.

1990

Government Level	# of Convictions	$(Y - \bar{Y})$	$(Y - \bar{Y})^2$
Federal	583	287.33	82,558.53
State	79	−216.67	46,945.89
Local	225	−70.67	4,994.25
Total	887	−0.01	134,498.67
	$\bar{Y} = 295.67$		

$$S_Y = \sqrt{S_Y^2} = \sqrt{\frac{\sum(Y-\bar{Y})^2}{N-1}} = \sqrt{\frac{134,498.67}{2}} = 259.32$$

2009

Government Level	# of Convictions	$(Y - \bar{Y})$	$(Y - \bar{Y})^2$
Federal	426	164.33	27,004.35
State	102	−159.67	25,494.51
Local	257	−4.67	21.81
Total	785	−0.01	52,520.67

$\bar{Y} = 261.67$

$$S_Y = \sqrt{S_Y^2} = \sqrt{\frac{\sum(Y-\bar{Y})^2}{N-1}} = \sqrt{\frac{52,520.67}{2}} = 162.05$$

d. The standard deviation is larger in 1990 than in 2009, thus indicating more variability in number of convictions in 1990 than in 2009. This supports our results from 3a.

5. a. The range of projected increase in the elderly population for the Western states is 36.2%. The range of percent increase for the Midwestern states is 9.8%. The Western states have a much larger range.
   b. The IQR for the Western states is 17.3%. The IQR for the Midwestern states is 3.7%. Again, the value for the Western states is greater.
   c. There is great variability in the projected increase in the elderly population in Western states, chiefly caused by the large increases in Nevada, Arizona, Wyoming, and Alaska, as measured by either the range or the IQR.

7. a. The range is 3.6 (6.5 − 2.9). The 25th percentile, 3.05, means that 25% of cases fall below 3.05 divorce rate per 1,000 population. Likewise, the 75th percentile means that 75% of all cases fall below 4.6 divorce rate per 1,000 population.

25th percentile	10(0.25) = 2.5th case	So (3.0 + 3.1)/2 = 3.05
75th percentile	10(0.75) = 7.5th case	So (4.5 + 4.7)/2 = 4.6

The IQR is thus 4.6 − 3.05 = 1.55. Both measures of variability are appropriate, but the range is somewhat better, as the value for the IQR is fairly small. In other words, the range gives us a better picture of the variability of divorce rates for all states in our sample.
   b.

State	Divorce Rate per 1,000 Population	$Y - \bar{Y}$	$(Y - \bar{Y})^2$
Alaska	4.3	0.2	0.04
Florida	4.7	0.6	0.36
Idaho	4.9	0.8	0.64

(Continued)

State	Divorce Rate per 1,000 Population	$Y - \bar{Y}$	$(Y - \bar{Y})^2$
Maine	4.5	0.4	0.16
Maryland	3.1	−1.0	1.00
Nevada	6.5	2.4	5.76
New Jersey	3.0	−1.1	1.21
Texas	3.3	−0.8	0.64
Vermont	3.8	−0.3	0.09
Wisconsin	2.9	−1.2	1.44
Total	41	0.00	11.34

$$\bar{Y} = \frac{\sum Y}{N} = \frac{41}{10} = 4.1$$

$$S_Y = \sqrt{S_Y^2} = \sqrt{\frac{\sum(Y - \bar{Y})^2}{N-1}} = \sqrt{\frac{11.34}{9}} = 1.12$$

   c. Divorce rates may vary by state due to factors such as variation in religiosity, state policy (i.e., no-fault divorce laws), or employment opportunities.

9. a. The mean numbers of crimes is 3,038.9 and the standard deviation is 583.004. The mean amount of dollars (in millions) spent on police protection is $1,704.0 and the standard deviation is $1,895.214.
   b. Because the number of crimes and police protection expenditures is measured according to different scales, it isn't appropriate to directly compare the mean and standard deviation for one variable with the other. But we can talk about each distribution separately. We know from examining the mean (3,038.90) and standard deviation (583.00) for the number of crimes that the standard deviation is large, indicating a wide dispersion of scores from the mean. For the number of crimes, states such as Missouri and South Dakota contribute more to its variability because they have values far from the mean (both above and below). With respect to police protection expenditures, we can see that there is a large dispersion from the mean of $1,703.95, as the standard deviation is $1,895.21. States such as New York and North Dakota contribute more to its variability because they have values far from the mean (both above and below).
   c. Among other considerations, we need to consider the economic conditions in each state. A downturn in the local and state economy may play a part in the number of crimes and police expenditures per capita.

11. a. Seeing as this is nominal variable, the most appropriate measure of variability would be the index of qualitative variation.
   b. Alcohol IQV

$$IQV = \frac{K(100^2 - \sum Pct^2)}{100^2(K-1)} = \frac{3(100^2 - 5,013.54)}{100^2(3-1)} = \frac{14.959.38}{20,000} = 0.75$$

The IQV for trying alcohol is 0.75.

Adolescent Attitudes Toward Alcohol	Trying Alcohol	Percentage Squared (%²)
Don't disapprove	66.8%	4,462.24
Disapprove	16.3%	265.69
Strongly disapprove	16.9%	285.61
Total	100.0%	Σ = 5,013.54

Cigarettes IQV

Adolescent Attitudes Toward Cigarettes	Pack per Day	Percentage Squared (%²)
Don't disapprove	26.2%	686.44
Disapprove	35.7%	1,274.49
Strongly disapprove	38.0%	1,444.00
Total	100.0%	Σ = 3,404.93

$$IQV = \frac{K(100^2 - \sum Pct^2)}{100^2(K-1)} = \frac{3(100^2 - 3,404.93)}{100^2(3-1)} = \frac{19,785.21}{20,000} = 0.99$$

The IQV for smoking a pack of cigarettes per day is 0.99.

c. Essentially, these two variables are measuring an unspecified amount of alcohol at any time compared with an entire pack of cigarettes during one day. If the quantity of alcohol were likened to that of a pack of cigarettes and was specified to be consumed during a single day, we might see similar values for the IQVs.

13. Of the 70 countries in our sample, males had a higher rate of labor force participation than females, according to the mean values. That is, 79.44 percent of men ages 15–64 were formally employed while 57.02 women abided by the same conditions. Women had greater variation in labor force participation, such that the standard deviation for women (18.54) was approximately three times the standard deviation for men (6.20). One possible reason for the lower rates of labor force participation for females would be their gender role as homemakers, in that some countries socialize their women to stay at home in order to take care of children. However, the standard deviation for women also suggests that labor force participation varies widely throughout the world. In some countries, women are encouraged to work in the formal labor force as much as men (e.g., the United States), while others strictly forbid women from working (e.g., Saudi Arabia).

15. We should be cautious when making generalized statements about the relationship between education and ideal number of children because we only have statistics for two groups. We would need more data from a number of groups in order to make specific statements about this relationship. Therefore, we must restrict our discussion to Chinese Americans and Filipino Americans. On average, Chinese Americans are more educated than Filipino Americans (15.55 years versus 13.42 years), and both groups have about the same standard deviation (3.643 for

Chinese Americans and 3.704 for Filipino Americans). Additionally, Chinese Americans report a lower number of ideal children (2.88) than Filipino Americans (4.00). Again, for this variable, both groups have about the same standard deviation (2.167 for Chinese Americans and 2.098 for Filipino Americans). Based on these findings, we might suggest that as level of education increases, the ideal number of children decreases (but remember: we can't be certain this is the case for all Americans!).

▣ CHAPTER 6

1.
   a. The Z score for a person who watches more than 8 hrs/day:

$$Z = \frac{8 - 3.01}{2.65} = 1.88$$

   b. We first need to calculate the Z score for a person who watches 5 hrs/day:

$$Z = \frac{5 - 3.01}{2.65} = 0.75$$

The area between Z and the mean is 0.2734. We then need to add 0.50 to 0.2734 to find the proportion of people who watch television less than 5 hrs/day. Thus, we conclude that the proportion of people who watch television less than 5 hrs/day is 0.7734. This corresponds to 783.45 (0.7734 × 1,013).

   c. 5.66 television hours per day corresponds to a Z score of +1.

$$Y = \overline{Y} + Z(S_Y) = 3.01 + 1(2.65) = 5.66$$

   d. The Z score for a person who watches 1 hr of television per day is

$$Z = \frac{1 - 3.01}{2.65} = -0.76$$

The area between the mean and Z is 0.2764.
The Z score for a person who watches 6 hrs of television per day is

$$Z = \frac{6 - 3.01}{2.65} = 1.13$$

The area between the mean and Z is 0.3708.
Therefore, the percentage of people who watch between 1 and 6 hrs of television per day is 64.72% (0.2764 + 0.3708 = 0.6472 × 100).

3. a. For an individual with 13.47 years of education, his or her Z score would be

$$Z = \frac{13.47 - 13.47}{3.1} = 0.0$$

b. Since our friend's number of years of education completed is associated with the 60th percentile, we need to solve for Y. However, we must first use the logic of the normal distribution to find Z. For any normal distribution, 50% of all cases will fall above the mean. Since our friend is in the 60th percentile, we know that the area between the mean and our friend's score is 0.10. Similarly, the area beyond our friend's score is 0.40. We can now look in Appendix B column "B" for 0.10 or in column "C" for 0.40. We find that the Z associated with these values is 0.25. Now, we can solve for Y:

$$Y = \bar{Y} + Z(S_Y) = 13.47 + 0.25(3.1) = 14.25$$

c. Since we already know that the proportion between our number of years of education (13.47) and our friend's number of years of education (14.25) is 0.10, we can multiply N (1,496) by this proportion. Thus, 149.6 people have between 13.47 and 14.25 years of education.

5. a. Among working-class respondents:
The Z score for a value of 12 is

$$Z = \frac{12 - 12.80}{2.85} = -0.28$$

The Z score for a value of 16 is

$$Z = \frac{16 - 12.80}{2.85} = 1.12$$

The area between a Z of -0.28 and the mean is 0.1103. The area between a Z of 1.12 and the mean is 0.3686, so the total area between the scores is

$$Area = 0.1103 + 0.3686 = 0.4789$$

So the proportion of working-class respondents with 12 to 16 years of education is 0.4789.

Among upper-class respondents:
The Z score for a value of 12 is

$$Z = \frac{12 - 15.45}{2.98} = -1.16$$

The Z score for a value of 16 is

$$Z = \frac{16 - 15.45}{2.98} = 0.18$$

The area between a Z of -1.16 and the mean is 0.3770. The area between a Z of 0.18 and the mean 0.0714, so the total area between the scores is

$$Area = 0.3770 + 0.0714 = 0.4484$$

So the proportion of upper-class respondents with 12 to 16 years of education is 0.4484.

b. Among working-class respondents:
The Z score for a value of 16 is

$$Z = \frac{16 - 12.80}{2.85} = 1.12$$

The area between a Z of 1.12 and the tail of the distribution (Column C) is 0.1314. So the probability of a working-class respondent having more than 16 years of education is 0.1314.

Among middle-class respondents:
The Z score for a value of 16 is

$$Z = \frac{16 - 14.45}{3.08} = 0.50$$

The area between a Z of 0.50 and the tail of the distribution (Column C) is 0.3085. So the probability of a middle-class respondent having more than 16 years of education is 0.3085.

c. Among lower-class respondents:
The Z score for a value of 12 is

$$Z = \frac{12 - 11.61}{2.67} = 0.15$$

The area between a Z of 0.15 and the mean (Column B) is 0.0596. To this, we must add 0.50 (the lower half of the distribution) to 0.0596. So the probability of a lower-class respondent having less than 12 years of education is 0.5596 (0.0596 + 0.50).

Among upper-class respondents:
The Z score for a value of 12 is

$$Z = \frac{12 - 15.45}{2.98} = -1.16$$

The area between a Z of −1.16 and the tail of the distribution (Column C) is 0.1230.
Remember, in this case, the fact that the Z score is a negative value tells us that we are working on the lower half of the distribution. So unlike our previous answer, we do not need to add 0.50. So the probability of an upper-class respondent having less than 12 years of education is 0.1230.

d. First, we find the Z score that has 25%, or 0.25, of the area between it and the mean. This is a Z score of about 0.68. The lower limit is

$$Y = \overline{Y} + Z(S_Y) = 12.80 + -0.68(2.85) = 10.86$$

And the upper limit is

$$Y = \overline{Y} + Z(S_Y) = 12.80 + 0.68(2.85) = 14.74$$

So the middle 50% of working-class respondents falls between 10.86 and 14.74 years of education.

e. If years of education is positively skewed, then the proportion of cases with high levels of education will be less than for a normal distribution. This means, for example, that the probabilities associated with high levels of education will be smaller.

7. a. An occupational prestige score of 60 corresponds to a Z score of

$$Z = \frac{60 - 45.03}{13.93} = 1.07$$

The area between a Z of 1.07 and the tail of the distribution is 0.1423. So about 14% of whites should have occupational prestige scores above 60. This corresponds to approximately 157 whites (0.1423 × 1,100) in our sample who should have occupational prestige scores above 60.

b.　An occupational prestige score of 60 corresponds to a Z score of

$$Z = \frac{60 - 40.83}{13.07} = 1.47$$

The area between a Z of 1.47 and the tail of the distribution is 0.0708. So about 7% of Blacks should have occupational prestige scores above 60. This corresponds to approximately 14 blacks (0.0708 × 195) in our sample who should have occupational prestige scores above 60.

c.　An occupational prestige score of 30 corresponds to a Z of score of

$$Z = \frac{30 - 45.03}{13.93} = -1.08$$

The area between a Z of −1.08 and the mean is 0.3599.
An occupational prestige score of 70 corresponds to a Z score of

$$Z = \frac{70 - 45.03}{13.93} = 1.79$$

The area between a Z of 1.79 and the mean is 0.4633. So the proportion of whites with occupational prestige scores between 30 and 70 is 0.8232 (0.3599 + 0.4633). Thus, approximately 906 whites (0.8232 × 1,100) in the sample should have occupational prestige scores between 30 and 70.

d.　An occupational prestige score of 30 corresponds to a Z score of

$$Z = \frac{30 - 40.83}{13.07} = -0.83$$

The area between a Z of −0.83 and the mean is 0.2967.
An occupational prestige score of 60 corresponds to Z score of

$$Z = \frac{60 - 40.83}{13.07} = 1.47$$

The area between a Z of 1.47 and the mean is 0.4292. So the proportion of blacks with occupational prestige scores between 30 and 60 is 0.7259 (0.2967 + 0.4292). Thus, approximately 142 blacks (0.7259 × 195) in the sample should have occupational prestige scores between 30 and 60.

9.　a.　About 0.1894 of the distribution falls above the Z score, so that is the proportion of crime incidents with more than 2 victims.

$$Z = \frac{2 - 1.28}{0.82} = 0.88$$

b.　The area between the mean and the Z score is about 0.1331, so the total area above 1 victim is 0.50 + 0.1331 = 0.6331, or 63.31%.

$$Z = \frac{1 - 1.28}{0.82} = -0.34$$

c. The area between the mean and the Z score is about 0.4995, so the total area below 4 victims is 0.50 + 0.4995 = 0.9995.

$$Z = \frac{4 - 1.28}{0.82} = 3.32$$

11. a. For a team with an APR score of 975

$$Z = \frac{975 - 950.35}{30.58} = 0.81$$

From Appendix B, the area beyond 0.81 is 0.2090, or about the 79th percentile. The team is at the upper quartile because it is above the 75th percentile.

b. The Z value which corresponds to a cutoff score with an area of about 0.25 toward the tail of the distribution is 0.67. This is translated into a cutoff score by

$$\frac{\text{Cutoff Score} - 950.35}{30.58} = 0.67$$

$$\text{Cutoff score} = 970.84$$

Students should round off to the whole number that has a value closest to a Z of 0.67.

c. The Z value is 0.67.

13. For any Z distribution, the value of the mean is 0. The standard deviation of a Z distribution is 1. Z distributions are based on the mean of a variable and are centered on that value, so they have a mean of 0 by definition. A Z score of 1 or −1 is equivalent to a score in the original distribution that is 1 standard deviation above or below the mean, respectively. This direct mapping from the original distribution to a Z score means that the standard deviation of a Z distribution must be equal to 1.

15. a. The normal curve is a perfectly symmetrical *bell-shaped curve*. This means that precisely half the observations fall on each side of the middle of the distribution. The midpoint of the normal curve is the point at which the mode (the point of the highest frequency), the median (the point that divides the distribution into two equal halves), and the mean (the average of all the scores) coincide. Also, most of the observations in a normal distribution are clustered around the middle, with the frequencies gradually decreasing at both ends of the distribution. This distribution is called normal because many empirical distributions seem to approximate it, and thus, we can learn a lot about the characteristics of the empirical distribution based on our knowledge of our theoretical normal distribution.

b. In general, standardized scores or Z scores provide a means to express the distance between the mean and a particular point or score. A Z score is the number of standard deviation units a raw score is from the mean. A negative Z score indicates that it is lower than the mean (or to the left of the mean), while a positive Z score indicates that it is higher than the mean (or to the right of the mean).

▣ CHAPTER 7

1. a. Although there are problems with the collection of data from all Americans, the census is assumed to be complete, so the mean age would be a parameter.

  b. A statistic because it is estimated from a sample.
  c. A statistic because it is estimated from a sample.
  d. A parameter because the school has information on all employees.
  e. A parameter because the school would have information on all its students.

3. a. Assuming that the population is defined as all persons shopping at that shopping mall that day of the week, she is selecting a systematic random sample. A more precise definition might limit it to all persons passing by the department store at the mall that day.
  b. This is a stratified sample because voters were first grouped by county, and unless the counties have the same number of voters, it is a disproportionate stratified sample because the same number is chosen from each county. We can assume that it was a probability sample, but we are not told exactly how the 50 voters were chosen from the lists. However, assuming that the population is defined as all Americans, this sort of sampling technique would qualify as nonprobability sampling.
  c. This is neither a simple random sample nor a systematic random sample. It might be thought of as a sample stratified on last name, but even then, choosing the first 20 names is not a random selection process.
  d. This is not a probability sample. Instead, it is a purposive sample chosen to represent a cross section of the population in New York City.

5. The relationship between the standard error and the standard deviation is $\sigma_{\bar{Y}} = \sigma_Y / \sqrt{N}$ where $\sigma_{\bar{Y}} = \sigma_Y / \sqrt{N}$ is the standard error of the mean and σ_Y is the standard deviation. Since σ_Y is divided by $\sqrt{N}$, $\sigma_{\bar{Y}} = \sigma_Y / \sqrt{N}$ must always be smaller than σ_Y, except in the trivial case where $N = 1$. Theoretically, the dispersion of the mean must be less than the dispersion of the raw scores. This implies that the standard error of the mean is less than the standard deviation.

7. a. These polls are definitely not probability samples. No sampling is done by the television station to choose who calls the 800 number.
  b. The population is all those people who watch the television station and see the 800 number advertised.

9. a. This is not a random sample. The students eating lunch on Tuesday are not necessarily representative of all students at the school, and you have no way of calculating the probability of inclusion of any student. Many students might, for example, rarely eat lunch at the cafeteria and, therefore, have no chance of being represented in your sample. The fact that you selected *all* the students eating lunch on Tuesday makes your selection appear to be a census of a population, but that isn't true either unless all the students ate at the cafeteria on Tuesday.
  b. This is a systematic random sample because names are drawn systematically from the list of all enrolled students.
  c. This would seem to be a systematic random sample as in (b), but it suffers from the same type of defect as the cafeteria sample. Unless all students pass by the student union, using that location as a selection criterion means that some students have no chance of being selected (but you don't know which ones). Samples are often drawn this way in shopping malls by choosing a central location from which to draw the sample. It is reasonable to assume that a sufficiently representative mix of shoppers will pass by a central location during any one period.
  d. The second procedure (selecting every 10th student from the list of all enrolled students) is the best option because it uses a random sampling method.

11. a. Mean = 5.3; standard deviation = 3.27.
  b. Here are 10 means from random samples of size 3: 6.33, 5.67, 3.33, 5.00, 7.33, 2.33, 6.00, 6.33, 7.00, 3.00.

c. The mean of these 10 sample means is 5.23. The standard deviation is 1.76. The mean of the sample means is very close to the mean for the population. The standard deviation of the sample means is much less than the standard deviation for the population. The standard deviation of the means from the samples is an estimate of the standard error of the mean we would find from one random sample of size 3.

13. a. The standard error is calculated as follows:

$$\sigma_{\bar{Y}} = \frac{\sigma_Y}{\sqrt{N}} = \frac{93,500}{\sqrt{7}} = 35,339.68$$

This value represents the average standard deviation of any sample mean from the mean of means. Accordingly, it may also be referred to as the standard deviation of the sampling distribution.

b. With the exception of cases where $N = 1$, the standard error will always be less in value than the standard deviation of the population. This is expressed by the formula

$$\sigma_{\bar{Y}} = \frac{\sigma_Y}{\sqrt{N}}$$

The shape of the sampling distribution is normal; thus, even when working with a skewed distribution, we know that the sampling distribution is normal. Suggestions for reducing the sampling error include increasing the sample size.

回 CHAPTER 8

1. a. The estimate at the 90% confidence level is 16.035% to 16.365%. This means that there are 90 chances out of 100 that the confidence interval will contain the true population percentage of victims in the American population.

$$\text{Standard error} = \sqrt{\frac{(16.2)(100-16.2)}{143,120}} = 0.10$$

$$\text{Confidence interval} = 16.2 \pm 1.65(0.10)$$

$$= 16.2 \pm 0.165$$

$$= 16.035 \text{ to } 16.365$$

b.

$$\text{Confidence interval} = 16.2 \pm 2.58(0.10)$$

$$= 16.2 \pm 0.258$$

$$= 15.942 \text{ to } 16.458$$

c. If the sample size was cut in half and the percentage remained at 16.2, the confidence intervals will increase by a factor of $1/\sqrt{\frac{1}{2}}$, or about 41%.

d. Sample sizes on the order of 1,000 to 1,500 are a trade-off between precision and cost. Samples of that size yield confidence intervals for proportions with errors around ±3% at the 95% confidence level, which is sufficient for most purposes in applied social research. Doubling the sample size to 3,000 does reduce the errors but increases the cost by more. As you can see with this example, such a large sample size minimizes the standard error and thereby shortens the width of the confidence interval. Therefore, our estimates of victimization are fairly accurate no matter which confidence interval we select.

3.   a.

$$S_p = \sqrt{\frac{(0.39)(1-0.39)}{1,511}} = 0.013$$

Confidence interval $= 0.39 \pm 1.96(0.013)$

$$= 0.39 \pm 0.025$$

$$= 0.365 \text{ to } 0.415$$

b.

Confidence interval $= 0.39 \pm 2.58(0.013)$

$$= 0.39 \pm 0.034$$

$$= 0.356 \text{ to } 0.424$$

c.   There is very little difference between the 95% or 99% confidence intervals here because the sample size is reasonably large. The former interval is only one-half of a percentage point wide, the latter nearly two-thirds of a percentage point. Most large survey organizations use the 95% confidence interval routinely and that seems like the best choice here. Our conclusions about Americans' opinions about global warming will be the same in either case. The intent of this problem is to get students to recognize that they always have a choice as to what confidence interval they choose for a particular problem.

5.

$$\text{Standard error} = \sqrt{\frac{(51)(100-51)}{5,490}} = 0.67$$

Confidence interval $= 51 \pm 1.96(0.67)$

$$= 49.69\% \text{ to } 52.31\%$$

We set the interval at the 95% confidence level. However, no matter whether the 90%, 95%, or 99% confidence level is chosen, the calculated interval includes values below 50% for the vote for a Republican candidate. Therefore, you should tell your supervisors that it would not be possible to declare a Republican candidate the likely winner of the votes coming from men if there was an election today because it seems quite possible that less than a majority of male voters would support her/him.

7.

a.

$$S_p = \sqrt{\frac{(0.727)(1-0.727)}{1,500}} = 0.012$$

Confidence interval $= 0.727 \pm 1.96(0.012)$

$$= 0.727 \pm 0.024$$

$$= 0.703 \text{ to } 0.751 \text{ or } 70.3\% \text{ to } 75.1\%$$

b. Based on our answer in 7a, we know that a 90% confidence interval will be more precise than a 95% confidence interval that has a lower bound of 70.3% and an upper bound of 75.1%. Accordingly, a 90% confidence interval will have a lower bound that is greater than 70.3% and an upper bound that is less than 75.1%. Additionally, we know that a 99% confidence interval will be less precise than what we calculated in 7a. Thus, the lower bound for a 99% confidence interval will be less than 70.3% and the upper bound will be greater than 75.1%.

9.

$$S_{\bar{Y}} = \frac{S_Y}{\sqrt{N}} = \frac{1.73}{\sqrt{1,496}} = 0.045$$

$$\text{Confidence interval} = 1.97 \pm 1.65(0.045)$$

$$= 1.97 \pm 0.074$$

$$= 1.896 \text{ to } 2.044$$

11.

$$S_p = \sqrt{\frac{(21)(100-21)}{2,257}} = 0.86$$

$$\text{Confidence interval} = 21 \pm 1.96(0.86)$$

$$= 21 \pm 1.69$$

$$= 19.31\% \text{ to } 22.69\%$$

13.

a. For those who thought that homosexual relations were always wrong:

$$S_p = \sqrt{\frac{(50.2)(100-50.2)}{930}} = 1.64$$

$$\text{Confidence interval} = 50.2 \pm 1.96(1.64)$$

$$= 50.2 \pm 3.21$$

$$= 46.99\% \text{ to } 53.41\%$$

For those who thought that homosexual relations were not wrong at all:

$$S_p = \sqrt{\frac{(37.2)(100-37.2)}{930}} = 1.58$$

$$\text{Confidence interval} = 37.2 \pm 1.96(1.58)$$

$$= 37.2 \pm 3.10$$

$$= 34.10\% \text{ to } 40.30\%$$

b.

$$S_p = \sqrt{\frac{(13)(100-13)}{930}} = 1.10$$

$$\text{Confidence interval} = 13 \pm 1.96(1.10)$$

$$= 13 \pm 2.16$$

$$= 10.84\% \text{ to } 15.16\%$$

c.   Because the 95% confidence interval for those who think that homosexual relations are always wrong does include a value less than 50%, we cannot have a definite conclusion that the majority of the American public thinks that homosexual relations are always wrong.

15. a. Instructors should encourage students to think about this question and make some educated guesses.
   b.

$$S_p = \sqrt{\frac{(20)(100-20)}{459}} = 1.87$$

Confidence interval $= 20 \pm 1.65(1.87)$

$$= 20 \pm 3.09$$

$$= 16.91\% \text{ to } 23.09\%$$

   c.

$$S_p = \sqrt{\frac{(36.9)(100-36.9)}{556}} = 2.05$$

Confidence interval $= 36.9 \pm 1.65(2.05)$

$$= 36.9 \pm 3.38$$

$$= 33.52\% \text{ to } 40.28\%$$

   d. Instructors should encourage students to think about this question and make some educated guesses.

◉ CHAPTER 9

Please note that in this chapter, small differences in calculations may occur between student results and those listed below due to rounding.

1. a. H_0: $\mu_Y = 13.5$ years; H_1: $\mu_Y < 13.5$ years.
   b. The Z value obtained is -4.19. The P value for a Z of -4.19 is less than .001 for a one-tailed test. This is less than the alpha of .01, so we reject the null hypothesis and conclude that the doctors at the HMO do have less experience than the population of doctors at all HMOs.

3. a. Two-tailed test, $\mu_1 \neq \$50{,}054$; null hypothesis, $\mu_1 = \$50{,}054$
   b. One-tailed test, $\mu_1 > 3.2$; null hypothesis, $\mu_1 = 3.2$
   c. One-tailed test, $\mu_1 < \mu_2$; null hypothesis, $\mu_1 = \mu_2$
   d. Two-tailed test, $\mu_1 \neq \mu_2$; null hypothesis, $\mu_1 = \mu_2$
   e. One-tailed test, $\mu_1 > \mu_2$; null hypothesis, $\mu_1 = \mu_2$
   f. One-tailed test, $\mu_1 < \mu_2$; null hypothesis, $\mu_1 = \mu_2$

5. a. H_0: $\mu_1 = 37.2$; H_1: $\mu_1 \neq 37.2$

   b. The t-obtained is 48.32. and its P level is <.001.

$$t = \frac{49.28 - 37.2}{17.21 / \sqrt{4857}} = \frac{12.08}{.25} = 48.32$$

c. We conclude that we can reject the null hypothesis in favor of the research hypothesis. There is a difference between the mean age of the GSS sample and the mean age of all American adults. Relative to age, the GSS sample is not representative of all American adults (the GSS sample is significantly older).

7. a. The appropriate test statistic is Z for proportions.
   b. Z obtained is -5.00, $P < .0001$. Since $P(.0001) < .05$, we reject the null hypothesis. This indicates that there is a statistical difference between conservatives and liberals on their views on affirmative action. Liberals are more likely to support affirmative action policies in the workplace than conservatives.

$$S_{p_1-p2} = \sqrt{\frac{.12(1-.12)}{336} = +\frac{.27(1-.27)}{267}} = .03$$

$$Z = \frac{.12-.27}{.03} = -5.00$$

c. For a two-tailed test, we would multiple P by 2, $.0001 \times 2 = .0002$. Our decision would remain the same, we reject the null hypothesis.

9. a. "Less than" indicates a one-tailed test.
   b. $Z = -3.00$ with a significance of $.0014$. We can reject the null hypothesis and conclude that the proportion of males who support President Obama is significantly less than proportion of female voters who support the President ($.49 - .58 = .09$).
   c. The significance of -3.00 is less than $.01$ ($.0014 < .01$). The decision to reject the null hypothesis does not change.

11. a. The t obtained $= -1.17$. We fail to reject the null hypothesis. Based on 123 degrees of freedom, the t obtained is less than the t critical of 1.658.

$$S_{\bar{Y}_1-\bar{Y}_2} = 7.25(.19) = 1.377 = 1.38$$

$$t = \frac{5.71-7.32}{1.38} = -1.17$$

b. The t obtained $= 3.23$. We reject the null hypothesis. Based on 355 degrees of freedom, the t obtained is larger than the t critical of 1.960. High school graduates spend more hours per week watching television than college graduates. The difference of .84 hours ($3.25 - 2.41$) is significant.

$$S_{\bar{Y}_1-\bar{Y}_2} = 2.37(.11) = .2607 = .26$$

$$t = \frac{3.25-2.41}{.26} = 3.23$$

13. Based on the *t* obtained of −8.593 (equal variances assumed), we reject the null hypothesis. The probability of obtaining this *t* statistic is .000 (less than our alpha of .05). Respondents with a high school degree have their first child at a younger age than respondents with a bachelor's degree. The age difference between the two groups is 4.09 years (22.66 − 26.75).

▣ CHAPTER 10

1. a. The independent variable is race; the dependent variable is fear of walking alone at night.

	Race	
Fear of Walking Alone at Night	Black	White
Yes	3	4
No	5	9

b. Approximately 69% of whites (69.2%) are not afraid to walk alone in their neighborhoods at night, whereas approximately 63% of blacks (62.5%) are not afraid to walk alone. This amounts to about a 7% difference (69.2% − 62.5%) between whites and blacks who are not afraid to walk alone at night, indicating a weak relationship. Also, although we went ahead and compared percentage differences in this exercise; it is important to keep in mind that our sample size inhibits our ability to make any meaningful comparisons.

	Race	
Fear of Walking Alone at Night	Black	White
Yes	37.5%	30.8%
No	62.5%	69.2%

c. There is some difference in fears between homeowners and renters. A total of 25.0% of homeowners and 38.5% of renters are afraid to walk in their neighborhood at night. The difference between the two groups is 13.5%. Thus, there is a weak to moderate relationship between home ownership and fear of walking in one's neighborhood at night.

	Home Ownership	
Fear of Walking Alone at Night	Yes	No
Yes	2	5
Percentage	25.0%	38.5%
No	6	8
Percentage	75.0%	61.5%

3. a. Based on the student's argument the independent variable is attitude toward homosexual relations and the dependent variable is political views.

   b. 451/792 = 56.9%

   c. Those who believe that homosexuality is always wrong are more likely to be conservative (50.8%) than moderate or liberal. On the other hand, those who believe homosexuality is not wrong at all are more likely to indicate liberal political views (45.4%) than moderate or conservative.

5. In contrast with black and white male students, Hispanic male students are less likely to report being moderately or very drunk. The majority of white males and black males report being moderately or very drunk. For Hispanic males, the total percentage in these two categories is 44.5%, which is lower than the totals for the other groups (51.4% of white students and 51.7% of black students). The relationship is weak between race and getting drunk while drinking alcohol.

alchhowdrunk When you drink, how drunk do you get? * race Respondent's race (trichotomized B/W/H) Crosstabulation[a]

			race Respondent's race (trichotomized B/W/H)			
			1 BLACK:(1)	2 WHITE:(2)	3 HISPANIC: (3)	Total
alchhowdrunk When you drink, how drunk do you get?	1 NOT @ALL:(1)	Count	10	71	14	95
		% within race Respondent's race (trichotomized B/W/H)	34.5%	25.5%	25.9%	26.3%
	2 A LITTLE:(2)	Count	4	64	16	84
		% within race Respondent's race (trichotomized B/W/H)	13.8%	23.0%	29.6%	23.3%
	3 MODERATE:(3)	Count	10	108	19	137
		% within race Respondent's race (trichotomized B/W/H)	34.5%	38.8%	35.2%	38.0%
	4 VERY:(4)	Count	5	35	5	45
		% within race Respondent's race (trichotomized B/W/H)	17.2%	12.6%	9.3%	12.5%
Total		Count	29	278	54	361
		% within race Respondent's race (trichotomized B/W/H)	100.0%	100.0%	100.0%	100.0%

a. sex Respondent's sex = 1 MALE:(1)

7. Female seniors have higher educational expectations than male seniors. For example, 73.9% (32.6 + 41.3) of female students expected to complete a bachelor's degree or higher. This is higher than the combined percentage for male students – 63.3% (34.4 + 28.9).

9. Overall, the percentage of white students in private schools remains at or above 83%, higher than any of the reported percentages for public schools. Among public elementary schools, there is a 5.7% decline in the percentage of white students, from 80.9% to 75.2%. Among private elementary schools, the percentage also declines from a high of 90.7% to 83.0%. The percentage of students of color increases across all years, with greater increases among private schools.

11. The data indicate a positive relationship between students' educational expectations and parental education. The percent of students indicating a bachelor's degree or higher increases as the parents' educational level increases—from 55% of students with parents with a high school degree or less to 86.1% of students with parents who completed a graduate/professional degree.

13. In contrast with male students, female students are more likely to report being not at all or a little drunk. The data also indicate that Hispanic females (40.7%) are more likely to report being moderately or very drunk than white (38.8%) or black (25.0%) females.

alchhowdrunk When you drink, how drunk do you get? * race Respondent's race (trichotomized B/W/H) Crosstabulation[a]

| | | | race Respondent's race (trichotomized B/W/H) | | | |
			1 BLACK:(1)	2 WHITE:(2)	3 HISPANIC:(3)	Total
alchhowdrunk When you drink, how drunk do you get?	1 NOT @ALL:(1)	Count	24	82	23	129
		% within race Respondent's race (trichotomized B/W/H)	37.5%	32.8%	39.0%	34.6%
	2 A LITTLE:(2)	Count	24	71	12	107
		% within race Respondent's race (trichotomized B/W/H)	37.5%	28.4%	20.3%	28.7%
	3 MODERATE:(3)	Count	13	83	18	114
		% within race Respondent's race (trichotomized B/W/H)	20.3%	33.2%	30.5%	30.6%
	4 VERY:(4)	Count	3	14	6	23
		% within race Respondent's race (trichotomized B/W/H)	4.7%	5.6%	10.2%	6.2%
Total		Count	64	250	59	373
		% within race Respondent's race (trichotomized B/W/H)	100.0%	100.0%	100.0%	100.0%

a. sex Respondent's sex = 2 FEMALE:(2)

▣ CHAPTER 11

1. a. Degrees of freedom $= (2 - 1)(2 - 1) = 1$
    b. Chi-square $= 59.25$ (with Yates's correction is 58.22). The probability of our obtained chi-square is less than our alpha (less than 0.001). We can reject the null hypothesis and conclude that gender and fear of walking alone at night are dependent. A higher percentage of women (45.1%) than men (21.5%) report being afraid.

Sex and FEAR	f_o	f_c	$f_o - f_c$	$(f_o - f_c)^2$	$\dfrac{(f_0 - f_e)^2}{f_e}$
Men/Yes	94	150.8	−56.8	3,226.24	21.39
Men/No	343	286.2	−56.8	3,226.24	11.27
Women/Yes	242	185.2	−56.8	3,226.24	17.42
Women/No	295	351.8	−56.8	3,226.24	9.17
$\chi^2 = 59.25$					

With the Yates correction:

Sex and Fear	$\lvert f_o - f_c \rvert$	$(\lvert f_o - f_c \rvert - .50)^2$	f_c	$\dfrac{(\lvert f_0 - f_e \rvert - .5)^2}{f_e}$
Men/YES	56.8	$(56.3)^2 = 3169.69$	150.8	21.02
Men/NO	56.8	$(56.3)^2 = 3169.69$	286.2	11.08

(Continued)

(Continued)

Sex and Fear	$\mid f_o - f_e \mid$	$(\mid f_o - f_e \mid -.50)^2$	f_e	$\dfrac{(\mid f_o - f_e \mid - .5)^2}{f_e}$
Women/YES	56.8	$(56.3)^2 = 3169.69$	185.2	17.11
Women/NO	56.8	$(56.3)^2 = 3169.69$	351.8	9.01
Total				58.22

c. If α were changed to .01, we would still reject the null hypothesis. The probability of our obtained chi-square is still less than alpha.

3. a. A higher percentage of blacks, 42.8% (59/138), report being afraid to walk alone at night. Among whites, the percentage is 31.5% (219/696).

   b. Regardless of race, women are more likely than men to report being afraid to walk alone at night. The percentage of black women indicating that they are afraid is higher than white women, 57.8% versus 41.7%.

   c.

$$\text{Whites, } \chi^2 = 41.40$$

$$\text{Blacks, } \chi^2 = 23.80$$

In both cases, we would reject the null hypothesis and conclude that gender and fear of walking alone at night are dependent.

For Whites

Sex and FEAR	f_o	f_e	$f_o - f_e$	$(f_o - f_e)^2$	$\dfrac{(f_o - f_e)^2}{f_e}$
Men/Yes	59	98.2	−39.2	1,536.64	15.65
Men/No	253	213.8	39.2	1,536.64	7.19
Women/Yes	160	120.8	39.2	1,536.64	12.72
Women/No	224	263.2	−39.2	1,536.64	5.84
$\chi^2 = 41.40$					

With the Yates's correction, the chi-square is 40.35, as it is shown below:

Sex and FEAR	$\mid f_o - f_e \mid$	$(\mid f_o - f_e \mid -.50)^2$	f_e	$\dfrac{(\mid f_o - f_e \mid - .5)^2}{f_e}$
Men/Yes	39.2	1,497.69	98.2	15.25
Men/No	39.2	1,497.69	213.8	7.01

Sex and FEAR	$|f_o - f_e|$	$(|f_o - f_e|-.50)^2$	f_e	$\dfrac{(|f_o - f_e|-.5)^2}{f_e}$
Women/Yes	39.2	1,497.69	120.8	12.40
Women/No	39.2	1,497.69	263.2	5.69

For Blacks

Sex and FEAR	f_o	f_e	$f_o - f_e$	$(f_o - f_e)^2$	$\dfrac{(f_o - f_e)^2}{f_e}$
Men/Yes	7	20.5	−13.5	182.25	8.89
Men/No	41	27.5	13.5	182.25	6.63
Women/Yes	52	38.5	13.5	182.25	4.74
Women/No	38	51.5	−13.5	182.25	3.54

$\chi^2 = 23.80$

With the Yates's correction, the chi-square is 22.06:

Sex and FEAR	$|f_o - f_e|$	$(|f_o - f_e|-.50)^2$	f_e	$\dfrac{(|f_o - f_e|-.5)^2}{f_e}$
Men/Yes	13.5	169	20.5	8.24
Men/No	13.5	169	27.5	6.15
Women/Yes	13.5	169	38.5	4.39
Women/No	13.5	169	51.5	3.28

$\chi^2_c = 22.06$

5. Based on the SPSS output, we would fail to reject the null hypothesis. The obtained chi-square is 4.872, significant at .771 level. Teen residence and marijuana access are not associated.

7.

Race/First-Generation College Status	f_o	f_e	$f_o - f_e$	$(f_o - f_e)^2$	$\dfrac{(f_0 - f_e)^2}{f_e}$
White/first	1,742	1,749.6	−7.6	57.76	0.03
White/nonfirst	2,392	2,384.4	7.6	57.76	0.02
Black/first	102	93.5	8.5	72.25	0.77
Black/nonfirst	119	127.5	−8.5	72.25	0.57
Native American/first	41	36.4	4.6	21.16	0.58
Native American/nonfirst	45	49.6	−4.6	21.16	0.43
Hispanic/first	19	18.6	0.4	0.16	0.01
Hispanic/nonfirst	25	25.4	−0.4	0.16	0.01
Asian American/first	6	11.9	−5.9	34.81	2.93
Asian American/nonfirst	22	16.1	5.9	34.81	2.16
$\chi^2 = 7.51$					

Chi-square = 7.51, with 4 degrees of freedom $[(2 - 1)(5 - 1) = 4]$.

We would fail to reject the null hypothesis. The probability of our obtained chi-square lies somewhere between 0.20 and 0.10, above our alpha level.

9.

   a. Ignoring sex of the offender, we would make 1,730 errors. $E_1 = 5,940 - 4,210 = 1,730$.

   b. Considering the sex of the offender to predict sex of the victim, we would make 1,730 errors. For male offenders, we would make 1,590 errors and for the female offenders, we would make 140 errors.

   c. Lambda=(1,730-1,730)/1,730=0.0% Information about sex of the offender reduces our error in predicting the sex of the victim by (0.0×100).

   d. The lambda for Exercise 1 is stronger than the lambda for Exercise 2. Race of offender is more strongly associated with race of victim.

11.

   SPANKING and SEX: Gamma = .118. There's a very weak, positive relationship between being male and opinion of spanking.

FAVOR SPANKING TO DISCIPLINE CHILD * RESPONDENTS SEX Crosstabulation

Count

		RESPONDENTS SEX		
		MALE	FEMALE	Total
FAVOR SPANKING TO DISCIPLINE CHILD	STRONGLY AGREE	120	121	241
	AGREE	217	260	477
	DISAGREE	104	126	230
	STRONGLY DISAGREE	15	44	59
Total		456	551	1007

SPANKING and CLASS: Gamma = −.178. There's a weak, negative relationship between class and opinion of spanking.

FAVOR SPANKING TO DISCIPLINE CHILD * SUBJECTIVE CLASS IDENTIFICATION Crosstabulation

Count

| | | SUBJECTIVE CLASS IDENTIFICATION | | | | |
		LOWER CLASS	WORKING CLASS	MIDDLE CLASS	UPPER CLASS	Total
FAVOR SPANKING TO DISCIPLINE CHILD	STRONGLY AGREE	23	128	85	3	239
	AGREE	39	224	195	15	473
	DISAGREE	19	84	121	4	228
	STRONGLY DISAGREE	5	19	33	2	59
Total		86	455	434	24	999

SPANKING and MARITAL STATUS: Lambda = 0.0. There's no relationship between marital status and opinion of spanking.

FAVOR SPANKING TO DISCIPLINE CHILD * MARITAL STATUS Crosstabulation

Count

| | | MARITAL STATUS | | | | | |
		MARRIED	WIDOWED	DIVORCED	SEPARATED	NEVER MARRIED	Total
FAVOR SPANKING TO DISCIPLINE CHILD	STRONGLY AGREE	120	20	29	8	64	241
	AGREE	245	33	70	12	117	477
	DISAGREE	99	23	43	9	56	230
	STRONGLY DISAGREE	31	6	6	2	14	59
Total		495	82	148	31	251	1007

▣ CHAPTER 12

1.

$\bar{Y}_1 = 2.875$	$\bar{Y}_2 = 2.250$	$\bar{Y}_3 = 2.00$	$\bar{Y}_4 = 1.375$
$\Sigma Y_1 = 23$	$\Sigma Y_2 = 18$	$\Sigma Y_3 = 16$	$\Sigma Y_4 = 11$
$\Sigma Y_1^2 = 71$	$\Sigma Y_2^2 = 44$	$\Sigma Y_3^2 = 38$	$\Sigma Y_4^2 = 17$
$n_1 = 8$	$n_2 = 8$	$n_3 = 8$	$n_4 = 8$

$\bar{Y} = 2.125$

$N = 32$

$$SSB = 8(2.875 - 2.125)^2 + 8(2.250 - 2.125)^2 + 8(2.00 - 2.125)^2 +$$
$$8(1.375 - 2.125)^2$$
$$= 8(0.5625) + 8(.015625) + 8(.015625) + 8(.5625)$$
$$= 4.5 + .125 + .125 + 4.5$$

$$SSB = 9.25$$

$$dfb = 4 - 1$$
$$dfb = 3$$

Mean square between = 9.25/3 = 3.08

$$SSW = (71 + 44 + 38 + 17) - [(23^2/8) + (18^2/8) + (16^2/8) + (11^2/8)]$$
$$= 170 - (66.125 + 40.5 + 32 + 15.125)$$
$$= 170 - 153.75$$
$$SSW = 16.25$$
$$dfw = 32 - 4$$
$$dfw = 28$$

Mean square within = 16.25/28 = 0.58

$$F = 3.08/0.58$$
$$F = 5.31$$

Decision: If we set alpha at 0.05, *F* critical would be 2.95 ($df_1 = 3$ and $df_2 = 28$). Based on our *F* obtained of 5.31, we would reject the null hypothesis and conclude that at least one of the means is significantly different than the others. Upper-class respondents rate their health the highest (1.375), followed by middle- and working-class respondents (2.00 and 2.25, respectively) and lower-class respondents (2.875) on a scale where 1 = excellent, 4 = poor.

3.

$\bar{Y}_1 = 1.6$	$\bar{Y}_2 = 1.4$	$\bar{Y}_3 = 0.6$
$\Sigma Y_1 = 16$	$\Sigma Y_2 = 14$	$\Sigma Y_3 = 6$
$\Sigma Y_1^2 = 30$	$\Sigma Y_2^2 = 24$	$\Sigma Y_3^2 = 8$
$n_1 = 10$	$n_2 = 10$	$n_3 = 10$
$\bar{Y} = 1.2$		
$N = 30$		

$$SSB = 10(1.6 - 1.2)^2 + 10(1.4 - 1.2)^2 + 10(0.6 - 1.2)^2$$
$$= 10(0.16) + 10(0.04) + 10(0.36)$$
$$= 1.6 + 0.4 + 3.6$$

$$SSB = 5.6$$
$$dfb = 3 - 1$$
$$dfb = 2$$

Mean square between = 5.6/2 = 2.8

$$SSW = (30 + 24 + 8) - [(16^2/10) + (14^2/10) + (6^2/10)]$$
$$= 62 - (25.6 + 19.6 + 3.6)$$
$$= 62 - 48.8$$
$$SSW = \textbf{13.2}$$
$$dfw = 30 - 3$$
$$dfw = \textbf{27}$$

Mean square within $= 13.2/27 = \textbf{0.488889}$

$$F = 2.8/0.49$$
$$F = \textbf{5.71}$$

Decision: If we set alpha at 0.01, F critical would be 5.49 ($df_1 = 2$ and $df_2 = 27$). Based on our F obtained of 5.71, we would reject the null hypothesis and conclude that at least one of the means is significantly different than the others. Respondents with no degree rate their church attendance highest (1.6), followed by respondents with a secondary degree (1.4), and then respondents with a university degree (0.6).

5. The calculated F ratio is .070, significant at .991 level. We would fail to reject the null hypothesis of no difference between the group means.

7.

a.

$\overline{Y}_1 = 4.29$	$\overline{Y}_2 = 2.29$	$\overline{Y}_3 = 3.14$
$\sum Y_1 = 30$	$\sum Y_2 = 16$	$\sum Y_3 = 22$
$\sum Y_1^2 = 134$	$\sum Y_2^2 = 44$	$\sum Y_3^2 = 84$
$n_1 = 7$	$n_2 = 7$	$n_3 = 7$
$\overline{Y} = 3.24$		
$N = 21$		

$$SSB = 7(4.29 - 3.24)^2 + 7(2.29 - 3.24)^2 + 7(3.14 - 3.24)^2$$

$$= 7(1.10) + 7(0.90) + 7(0.01)$$

$$= 7.70 + 6.30 + 0.07$$

$$SSB = 14.07$$

$$df_b = 3 - 1$$

$$df_b = 2$$

Mean square between $= 14.07/2 = 7.035$

$$SSW = (134 + 44 + 84) - [(30^2/7) + (16^2/7) + (22^2/7)]$$

$$= 262 - (128.57 + 36.57 + 69.14)$$

$$= 262 - 234.28$$

$$SSW = 27.72$$

$$df_w = 21 - 3$$

$$df_w = 18$$

Mean square within $= 27.72/18 = 1.54$

$$F = 7.035/1.54$$

$$F = 4.57$$

Decision. If we set alpha at .05, F critical would be 3.55 ($df_1 = 2$ and $df_2 = 18$). Based on our F obtained of 4.57, we would reject the null hypothesis and conclude that at least one of the means is significantly different from the others. On average, white respondents have the highest number of school days missed in the past 4 weeks (4.29), followed by Hispanic respondents (3.14), and then black respondents (2.29).

b. If alpha were changed to .01, F critical would be 6.01. We would fail to reject the null hypothesis at this alpha level.

9. For each sociocultural resource we would reject the null hypothesis. For social support, the obtained F ratio is 12.17, $P < .001$. Whites report the highest level of social support (2.85) while non-Cuban Hispanics have the lowest (2.58). For religious attendance, the obtained F ratio is 56.43, $P < .001$. Church attendance is highest for African Americans and non-Cuban Hispanics in the sample (3.94 and 3.37 on the five-point scale).

回 CHAPTER 13

1. a. On the scatterplot below, the regression line has been plotted to make it easier to see the relationship between the two variables.

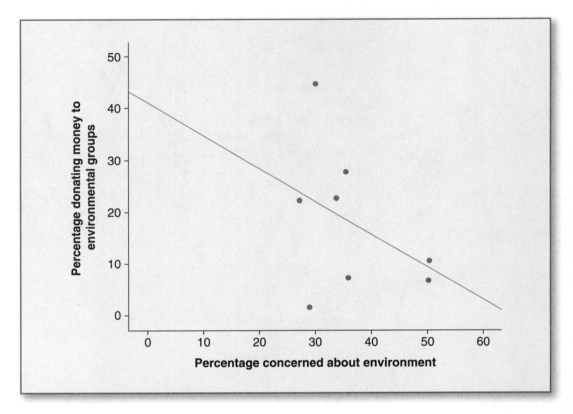

b. The scatterplot shows there is a general linear relationship between the two variables. There is not a lot of scatter about the straight line describing the relationship. As the percentage of respondents concerned about the environment increases, the percentage of respondents donating money to environmental groups decreases.

c. The Pearson correlation coefficient between the two variables is –.40. This is consistent with the scatterplot indicated a negative relationship between being concerned about the environment and actually donating money to environmental groups.

	(1)	*(2)*	*(3)*	*(4)*	*(5)*	*(6)*	*(7)*
	Percentage Concerned	*Percentage Donating*					
State	X	Y	$(X - \bar{X})$	$(X - \bar{X})^2$	$(Y - \bar{Y})$	$(Y - \bar{Y})^2$	$(X - \bar{X})(Y - \bar{Y})$
United States	33.8	22.8	−2.69	7.22	4.77	22.80	−12.83
Austria	35.5	27.8	−0.99	0.98	9.77	95.55	−9.67
Netherlands	30.1	44.8	−6.39	40.80	26.77	716.90	−171.06
Slovenia	50.3	10.7	13.81	190.79	−7.33	53.66	−101.23

(Continued)

	(1)	(2)	(3)	(4)	(5)	(6)	(7)
	Percentage Concerned	*Percentage Donating*					
State	X	Y	$(X-\bar{X})$	$(X-\bar{X})^2$	$(Y-\bar{Y})$	$(Y-\bar{Y})^2$	$(X-\bar{X})(Y-\bar{Y})$
Russia	29.0	1.6	−7.49	56.06	−16.43	269.78	123.06
Philippines	50.1	6.8	13.61	185.30	−11.23	126.00	−152.84
Spain	35.9	7.4	−0.59	0.35	−10.63	112.89	6.27
Denmark	27.2	22.3	−9.29	86.26	4.27	18.28	−39.67
	$\sum X = 291.9$	$\sum Y = 144.2$	−0.02[a]	567.76	0.04[a]	1,415.85	−357.97

$$\text{Mean } X = \bar{X} = \frac{\sum X}{N} = \frac{291.9}{8} = 36.49$$

$$\text{Mean } Y = \bar{Y} = \frac{\sum Y}{N} = \frac{144.2}{8} = 18.03$$

$$\text{Variance}(X) = S_X^2 = \frac{\Sigma(X-\bar{X})^2}{N-1} = \frac{567.8}{7} = 81.11$$

$$\text{Standard Deviation}(X) = S_X = \sqrt{81.11} = 9.01$$

$$\text{Variance}(Y) = S_Y^2 = \frac{\Sigma(Y-\bar{Y})^2}{N-1} = \frac{1,415.9}{7} = 202.3$$

$$\text{Standard Deviation}(Y) = S_Y = \sqrt{202.3} = 14.22$$

$$\text{Covariance}(X,Y) = S_{XY} = \frac{\Sigma(X-\bar{X})(Y-\bar{Y})}{N-1} = \frac{-357.97}{7} = -51.14$$

$$r = \frac{S_{XY}}{S_X S_Y} = \frac{-51.14}{(9.01)(14.22)} = -0.40^a$$

a. Answers may differ slightly due to rounding.

3. a. The correlation coefficient is −0.45.

Country State	(1) GNP per Capita X	(2) Percentage Willing to Pay Y	(3) $(X-\bar{X})$	(4) $(X-\bar{X})^2$	(5) $(Y-\bar{Y})$	(6) $(Y-\bar{Y})^2$	(7) $(X-\bar{X})(Y-\bar{Y})$
United States	29.24	44.9	2.72	7.40	−1.64	2.69	−4.46
Ireland	18.71	53.3	−7.81	61.00	6.76	45.70	−52.80
Netherlands	24.78	61.2	−1.74	3.03	14.66	214.92	−25.51
Norway	34.31	40.7	7.79	60.68	−5.84	34.11	−45.49
Sweden	25.58	32.6	−0.94	0.88	−13.94	194.32	13.10
	$\Sigma X = 132.62$	$\Sigma Y = 232.7$	−0.02[a]	132.99	0.04[a]	491.74	−115.16

$$\text{Mean } X = \bar{X} = \frac{\Sigma X}{N} = \frac{132.62}{5} = 26.52$$

$$\text{Mean } Y = \bar{Y} = \frac{\Sigma Y}{N} = \frac{232.7}{5} = 46.54$$

$$\text{Variance}(X) = S_X^2 = \frac{\Sigma(X-\bar{X})^2}{N-1} = \frac{132.99}{4} = 33.25$$

$$\text{Standard Deviation}(X) = S_X = \sqrt{33.25} = 5.77$$

$$\text{Variance}(Y) = S_Y^2 = \frac{\Sigma(Y-\bar{Y})^2}{N-1} = \frac{491.74}{4} = 122.94$$

$$\text{Standard Deviation}(Y) = S_Y = \sqrt{122.94} = 11.09$$

$$\text{Covariance}(X,Y) = S_{XY} = \frac{\Sigma(X-\bar{X})(Y-\bar{Y})}{N-1} = \frac{-115.16}{4} = -28.79$$

$$r = \frac{S_{XY}}{S_X S_Y} = \frac{-28.79}{(5.77)(11.09)} = -0.45^{[a]}$$

a. Answers may differ slightly due to rounding.

b. A correlation coefficient of −0.45 means that relatively high values of GNP are moderately negatively associated with low values of percentage of residents willing to pay higher prices to protect the environment.

5. Although somewhat difficult to visually determine, there is evidence within the scatterplot that indicates a negative relationship between education and hours/day spent watching TV. Looking to the regression equation output, this is confirmed by the negative coefficient (−.231). This means that for each year of education a person has, the number of hours they spend watching TV per day decreases by 0.231 hours. The value of the intercept (6.130) indicates that a person with 0 years of education spends 6.130 hrs/day watching television. The value for r (.268) suggests a moderate relationship between education and hours/day spent watching television. The value of r^2 is .072; thus, 7.2 percent of the variation in hours/day spent watching TV can be explained by taking into account a person's level of education.

7. The scatterplot identifies a positive relationship between respondent level of education and mother's level of education (as mother's level of education increases, so does their children's). The positive coefficient (.326) in the "Coefficients" table supports this: for each year of education a respondent's mother has, their level of education increases by .326 years (approximately 4 months). The value of the intercept (9.988) indicates that a person whose mother has 0 years of education is predicted to complete about 10 years of schooling. The value for r (.383) suggests a moderate relationship between mother's level of education and respondent level of education. The value of r^2 is .146. In other words, by only knowing mother's level of education, we can predict 14.6% of the variance in respondent level of education.

9. a. A straight line does seem to fit the data, as shown in the scatterplot.

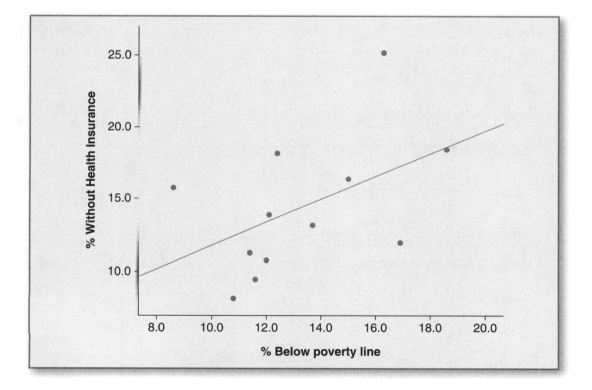

b. The equation, $\hat{Y} = 3.796 + 0.8X$, supports the assertion that a straight line best fits these data. In fact, b is 0.8, which indicates that for a 1% increase in those living below the poverty line, there is a corresponding 0.8% increase in the percentage of people without health insurance.

| | (1) | (2) | (3) | (4) | (5) | (6) | (7) |
| | % Below Poverty | % Without Health Insurance | | | | | |
State	X	Y	$(X - \bar{X})$	$(X - \bar{X})^2$	$(Y - \bar{Y})$	$(Y - \bar{Y})^2$	$(X - \bar{X})(Y - \bar{Y})$
Alabama	16.9	12.0	3.62	13.08	-2.42	5.84	-8.74
California	12.4	18.2	-0.88	0.78	3.78	14.31	-3.34
Idaho	12.1	13.9	-1.18	1.40	-0.52	0.27	0.61
Louisiana	18.6	18.5	5.32	28.27	4.08	16.67	21.71
New Jersey	8.6	15.8	-4.68	21.93	1.38	1.91	-6.48
New York	13.7	13.2	0.42	0.17	-1.22	1.48	-0.51
Pennsylvania	11.6	9.5	-1.68	2.83	-4.92	24.17	8.28
Rhode Island	12.0	10.8	-1.28	1.65	-3.62	13.08	4.64
South Carolina	15.0	16.4	1.72	2.95	1.98	3.93	3.40
Texas	16.3	25.2	3.02	9.10	10.78	116.28	32.53
Washington	11.4	11.3	-1.88	3.55	-3.12	9.71	5.87
Wisconsin	10.8	8.2	-2.48	6.17	-6.22	38.65	15.44
	$\sum X = 159.4$	$\sum Y = 173.0$	0.0^a	91.88	0.0^a	246.32	73.41

$$\text{Mean } X = \bar{X} = \frac{\sum X}{N} = \frac{159.4}{12} = 13.28$$

$$\text{Mean } Y = \bar{Y} = \frac{\sum Y}{N} = \frac{173.0}{12} = 14.42$$

$$\text{Variance}(X) = S_X^2 = \frac{\Sigma(X - \bar{X})^2}{N-1} = \frac{91.88}{11} = 8.35$$

$$\text{Standard Deviation}(X) = S_X = \sqrt{8.35} = 2.89$$

$$\text{Variance}(Y) = S_Y^2 = \frac{\Sigma(Y - \bar{Y})^2}{N-1} = \frac{246.32}{11} = 22.39$$

$$\text{Standard Deviation}(Y) = S_Y = \sqrt{22.39} = 4.73$$

$$\text{Covariance}(X,Y) = S_{XY} = \frac{\Sigma(X - \bar{X})(Y - \bar{Y})}{N-1} = \frac{73.41}{11} = 6.67$$

$$b = \frac{S_{XY}}{S_X^2} = \frac{6.67}{8.35} = 0.8$$

$$a = \bar{Y} - b\bar{X} = 14.42 - 0.8(13.28) = 3.796$$

$$\hat{Y} = 3.796 + 0.8X$$

a. Answers may differ slightly due to rounding.

c. $5 = 3.796 + 0.8X$

$X = 1.51\%$. So about 1.51% need to be living below the poverty level to have only 5% without health insurance.

d. You cannot go outside the scope of your data. That said, it is interesting to see how closely poverty and lack of health insurance are related. Although we cannot generalize statistically, this example does help us see just how closely the two are related. Thus, as we go about our research, this may be a consideration to keep in mind for future studies.

11. a. The b coefficient is $-.220$. As the duration of education increases by 1 year, the number of hours a person watches television per day decreases by 0.220 hours, holding number of children constant. The b coefficient for the number of children is .066, holding level of education constant. As the number of children in a family increases by one child, the number of hours of television viewing per day increases by .066. Yes, the relationship between education and hours of television viewing per day is as hypothesized. The relationship between the number of children a respondent has and the number of hours he or she spends watching television per day is also as hypothesized.

b. For a person with 16 years of education and 2 children, the predicted hours of television viewed per day is 2.47 hours. Using the prediction equation from Exercise 5, the predicted number of television hours viewed per day for 16 years of education is 2.43. By adding the number of children to the prediction equation, the television viewing hours per day increases by 0.04.

TV Hours per day by Eduation and Number of Children

$$\hat{Y} = 5.857 - .220(16) + .066(2) = 2.47$$

TV Hours per day by Education

$$\hat{Y} = 6.130 - .231(16) = 2.43$$

c. The r^2 in Exercise 5 using only education is .072. Error is reduced by 7.2% when using education to explain the amount of television viewed per day. When adding the second predictor variable, number of children in a family, the R^2 is .073. Error is reduced by 7.3% when using both education and number of children to explain television viewing per day. Adding number of children results in only 0.1 percentage points less error.

13. a. False. Both b and r will always have the same sign because both tell us the direction of the relationship.

b. Both a and b refer to changes in the dependent variable.

c. The coefficient of determination, r^2, is a PRE measure. PRE stands for proportional reduction of error. This means that r^2 indicates the extent to which prediction error is reduced when we take into account the independent variable in our predictions.

d. False. The regression equation serves many functions, most notably to make predictions. Whether a regression equation models a causal relationship is a matter of meeting the causal requirements as they were discussed in Chapter 1.

Regression equations are commonly used to model relationships wherein researchers look for how changes in one or more variables (referred to as the independent variables) correspond with changes in another variable (referred to as the dependent variable).

GLOSSARY

Alpha (α) The level of probability at which the null hypothesis is rejected. It is customary to set alpha at the .05, .01, or .001 level

Analysis of variance (ANOVA) An inferential statistics technique designed to test for the significant relationship between two variables in two or more samples

Asymmetrical measure of association A measure of association whose value may vary depending on which variable is considered the independent variable and which the dependent variable

Bar graph A graph showing the differences in frequencies or percentages among categories of a nominal or an ordinal variable. The categories are displayed as rectangles of equal width with their height proportional to the frequency or percentage of the category

Between-group sum of squares (SSB) The sum of squared deviations between each sample mean to the overall mean score

Bivariate analysis A statistical method designed to detect and describe the relationship between two variables

Bivariate table A table that displays the distribution of one variable across the categories of another variable

Cell The intersection of a row and a column in a bivariate table

Central limit theorem If all possible random samples of size N are drawn from a population with a mean μ_Y and a standard deviation σ_Y, then as N becomes larger, the sampling distribution of sample means becomes approximately normal, with mean $\mu_{\overline{Y}}$ and standard deviation, $\sigma_{\overline{Y}} = \sigma_Y / \sqrt{N}$

Chi-square (obtained) The test statistic that summarizes the differences between the observed (f_o) and the expected (f_e) frequencies in a bivariate table

Chi-square test An inferential statistics technique designed to test for a significant relationship between two variables organized in a bivariate table

Coefficient of determination (r^2) A PRE measure reflecting the proportional reduction of error that results from using the linear regression model. It reflects the proportion of the total variation in the dependent variable, Y, explained by the independent variable, X

Column variable A variable whose categories are the columns of a bivariate table

Conditional relationship A relationship in which the control variable's effect on the dependent variable is conditional on its interaction with the independent variable. The relationship between the independent and dependent variables will change according to the different conditions of the control variable

Confidence interval (CI) A range of values defined by the confidence level within which the population parameter is estimated to fall

Confidence level The likelihood, expressed as a percentage or a probability, that a specified interval will contain the population parameter

Control variable An additional variable considered in a bivariate relationship. The variable is controlled for when we take into account its effect on the variables in the bivariate relationship

Cross-tabulation A technique for analyzing the relationship between two variables that have been organized in a table

Cumulative frequency distribution A distribution showing the frequency at or below each category (class interval or score) of the variable

Cumulative percentage distribution A distribution showing the percentage at or below each category (class interval or score) of the variable

Data Information represented by numbers, which can be the subject of statistical analysis

Degrees of freedom (df) The number of scores that are free to vary in calculating a statistic

Dependent variable Variable to be explained (the "effect")

Descriptive statistics Procedures that help us organize and describe data collected from either a sample or a population

Deterministic (perfect) linear relationship A relationship between two interval-ratio variables in which all the observations (the dots) fall along a straight line. The line provides a predicted value of Y (the vertical axis) for any value of X (the horizontal axis)

Dichotomous variable A variable that has only two values

Direct causal relationship A bivariate relationship that cannot be accounted for by other theoretically relevant variables

Disproportionate stratified sample The size of the sample selected from each subgroup is disproportional to the size of that subgroup in the population

Elaboration A process designed to further explore a bivariate relationship; it involves the introduction of control variables

Empirical research Research based on evidence that can be verified by using our direct experience

Estimation A process whereby we select a random sample from a population and use a sample statistic to estimate a population parameter

Expected frequencies (f_e) The cell frequencies that would be expected in a bivariate table if the two variables were statistically independent

F critical F-test statistic that corresponds to the alpha level, df_w, and df_b

F obtained The F-test statistic that is calculated

F ratio or F statistic The test statistic for ANOVA, calculated by the ratio of mean square to mean square within

Frequency distribution A table reporting the number of observations falling into each category of the variable

Gamma A symmetrical measure of association suitable for use with ordinal variables or with dichotomous nominal variables. It can vary from 0.0 to ±1.0 and provides us with an indication of the strength and direction of the association between the variables

Histogram A graph showing the differences in frequencies or percentages among categories of an interval-ratio variable. The categories are displayed as contiguous bars, with width proportional to the width of the category and height proportional to the frequency or percentage of that category

Hypothesis A tentative answer to a research problem

Independent variable The variable expected to account for (the "cause" of) the dependent variable

Index of qualitative variation (IQV) A measure of variability for nominal variables. It is based on the ratio of the total number of differences in the distribution to the maximum number of possible differences within the same distribution

Inferential statistics The logic and procedures concerned with making predictions or inferences about a population from observations and analyses of a sample

Interquartile range (IQR) The width of the middle 50% of the distribution. It is defined as the difference between the lower and upper quartiles (Q_1 and Q_3)

Interval-ratio measurement Measurements for all cases are expressed in the same units

Intervening relationship A relationship in which the control variable intervenes between the independent and dependent variables

Intervening variable A control variable that follows an independent variable but precedes the dependent variable in a causal sequence abortion attitudes

Kendall's tau-b A symmetrical measure of association suitable for use with ordinal variables. Unlike gamma, it accounts for pairs tied on the independent and dependent variable. It can vary from 0.0 to ±1.0. It provides an indication of the strength and direction of the association between the variables

Lambda An asymmetrical measure of association, lambda is suitable for use with nominal variables and may range from 0.0 to 1.0. It provides us with an indication of the strength of an association between the independent and dependent variables

Least squares line (best-fitting line) A line where the residual sum of squares, or Σe^2 is at a minimum

Least squares method The technique that produces the least squares line

Left-tailed test A one-tailed test in which the sample outcome is hypothesized to be at the left tail of the sampling distribution

Linear relationship A relationship between two interval-ratio variables in which the observations displayed in a scatter diagram can be approximated with a straight line

Line graph A graph showing the differences in frequencies or percentages among categories of an interval-ratio variable. Points representing the frequencies of each category are placed above the midpoint of the category and are joined by a straight line

Marginals The row and column totals in a bivariate table

Margin of error The radius of a confidence interval

Mean A measure typically used to describe central tendency in interval-ratio variables. The arithmetic average obtained by adding up all the scores and dividing by the total number of scores

Mean square between Sum of squares between divided by its corresponding degrees of freedom

Mean squares regression An average computed by dividing the regression sum of squares (*SSR*) by its corresponding degrees of freedom

Mean squares residual An average computed by dividing the residual sum of squares (*SSE*) by its corresponding degrees of freedom

Mean square within Sum of squares within divided by its corresponding degrees of freedom

Measure of association A single summarizing number that reflects the strength of a relationship, indicates the usefulness of predicting the dependent variable from the independent variable, and often shows the direction of the relationship

Measures of central tendency Numbers that describe what is average or typical of the distribution

Measures of variability Numbers that describe diversity or variability in the distribution

Median A measure of central tendency. The score that divides the distribution into two equal parts so that half the cases are above and half below

Mode A measure of central tendency. The category or score with the highest frequency (or percentage) in the distribution of main points

Multiple coefficient of determination (R^2) Measure that reflects the proportion of the total variation in the dependent variable that is explained jointly by two or more independent variables

Multiple regression An extension of bivariate regression in which the effects of two or more independent variables on the dependent variable are examined. The general form of the multiple regression equation involving two independent variables is $\hat{Y} = a + b_1(X_1) + b_2(X_2)$

Negatively skewed distribution A distribution with a few extremely low values

Negative relationship A bivariate relationship between two variables measured at the ordinal level or higher in which the variables vary in opposite directions

Nominal measurement Numbers or other symbols are assigned to a set of categories for the purpose of naming, labeling, or classifying the observations

Normal distribution A bell-shaped and symmetrical theoretical distribution with the mean, the median, and the mode all coinciding at its peak and with the frequencies gradually decreasing at both ends of the curve

Null hypothesis (H_0) A statement of "no difference," which contradicts the research hypothesis and is always expressed in terms of population parameters

Observed frequencies (f_o) The cell frequencies actually observed in a bivariate table

One-tailed test A type of hypothesis test that involves a directional hypothesis. It specifies that the values of one group are either larger or smaller than some specified population value

One-way ANOVA Analysis of variance application with one dependent variable and one independent variable

Ordinal measurement Numbers are assigned to rank-ordered categories ranging from low to high

Parameter A measure (e.g., mean or standard deviation) used to describe the population distribution

Partial relationship The relationship between the independent and dependent variables shown in a partial table

Partial tables Bivariate tables that display the relationship between the independent and dependent variables while controlling for a third variable

Pearson's correlation coefficient (*r*) The square root of r^2; it is a measure of association for interval-ratio variables, reflecting the strength of the linear association between two interval-ratio variables. It can be positive or negative in sign

Pearson's multiple correlation coefficient (*R*) Measure of the linear relationship between the independent variable and the combined effect of two or more independent variables

Percentage A relative frequency obtained by dividing the frequency in each category by the total number of cases and multiplying by 100

Percentage distribution A table showing the percentage of observations falling into each category of the variable

Percentile A score below which a specific percentage of the distribution falls

Pie chart A graph showing the differences in frequencies or percentages among categories of a nominal or an ordinal variable. The categories are displayed as segments of a circle whose pieces add up to 100% of the total frequencies

Point estimate A sample statistic used to estimate the exact value of a population parameter

Population The total set of individuals, objects, groups, or events in which the researcher is interested

Positively skewed distribution A distribution with a few extremely high values

Positive relationship A bivariate relationship between two variables measured at the ordinal level or higher in which the variables vary in the same direction

Probability sampling A method of sampling that enables the researcher to specify for each case in the population the probability of its inclusion in the sample

Proportion A relative frequency obtained by dividing the frequency in each category by the total number of cases

Proportional reduction of error (PRE) The concept that underlies the definition and interpretation of several measures of association. PRE measures are derived by comparing the errors made in predicting the dependent variable while ignoring the independent variable with errors made when making predictions that use information about the independent variable

Proportionate stratified sample The size of the sample selected from each subgroup is proportional to the size of that subgroup in the entire population

P value The probability associated with the obtained value of *Z*

Range A measure of variation in interval-ratio variables. It is the difference between the highest (maximum) and the lowest (minimum) scores in the distribution

Rate A number obtained by dividing the number of actual occurrences in a given time period by the number of possible occurrences

Regression sum of squares (SSR) Reflects the improvement in the prediction error resulting from using the linear prediction equation, $SST - SSE$

Research hypothesis (H_1) A statement reflecting the substantive hypothesis. It is always expressed in terms of population parameters, but its specific form varies from test to test

Research process A set of activities in which social scientists engage to answer questions, examine ideas, or test theories

Residual sum of squares (SSE) Sum of squared differences between observed and predicted *Y*

Right-tailed test A one-tailed test in which the sample outcome is hypothesized to be at the right tail of the sampling distribution

Row variable A variable whose categories are the rows of a bivariate table

Sample A relatively small subset selected from a population

Sampling distribution The sampling distribution is a theoretical probability distribution of all possible sample values for the statistics in which we are interested

Sampling distribution of the difference between means A theoretical probability distribution that would be obtained by calculating all the possible mean differences $\left(\bar{Y}_1 - \bar{Y}_2\right)$ that would be obtained by drawing all the possible independent random samples of size N_1 and N_2 from two populations where N_1 and N_2 are each greater than 50

Sampling distribution of the mean A theoretical probability distribution of sample means that would be obtained by drawing from the population all possible samples of the same size

Sampling error The discrepancy between a sample estimate of a population parameter and the real population parameter

Scatter diagram (scatterplot) A visual method used to display a relationship between two interval-ratio variables

Simple random sample A sample designed in such a way as to ensure that (1) every member of the population has an equal chance of being chosen and (2) every combination of *N* members has an equal chance of being chosen

Skewed distribution A distribution with a few extreme values on one side of the distribution

Slope (*b*) The amount of change in a dependent variable per unit change in an independent variable

Spurious relationship A relationship in which both the independent and dependent variables are influenced by a causally prior-control variable, and there is no causal link between them. The relationship between the independent and dependent variables is said to be "explained away" by the control variable

Standard deviation A measure of variation for interval-ratio variables; it is equal to the square root of the variance

Standard error of the mean The standard deviation of the sampling distribution of the mean. It describes how much dispersion there is in the sampling distribution of the mean

Standard normal distribution A normal distribution represented in standard (Z) scores

Standard normal table A table showing the area (as a proportion, which can be translated into a percentage) under the standard normal curve corresponding to any Z score or its fraction

Standard (Z) score The number of standard deviations that a given raw score is above or below the mean

Statistic A measure (e.g., mean or standard deviation) used to describe the sample distribution

Statistical hypothesis testing A procedure that allows us to evaluate hypotheses about population parameters based on sample statistics

Statistical independence The absence of association between two cross-tabulated variables. The percentage distributions of the dependent variable within each category of the independent variable are identical

Statistics A set of procedures used by social scientists to organize, summarize, and communicate information

Stratified random sample A method of sampling obtained by (1) dividing the population into subgroups based on one or more variables central to our analysis and (2) then drawing a simple random sample from each of the subgroups

Symmetrical distribution The frequencies at the right and left tails of the distribution are identical; each half of the distribution is the mirror image of the other

Symmetrical measure of association A measure of association whose value will be the same when either variable is considered the independent variable or the dependent variable

Systematic random sampling A method of sampling in which every Kth member (K is a ratio obtained by dividing the population size by the desired sample size) in the total population is chosen for inclusion in the sample after the first member of the sample is selected at random from among the first ' members in the population

t distribution A family of curves, each determined by its degrees of freedom (df). It is used when the population standard deviation is unknown and the standard error is estimated from the sample standard deviation

Theory An elaborate explanation of the relationship between two or more observable attributes of individuals or groups

Time-series chart A graph displaying changes in a variable at different points in time. It shows time (measured in units such as years or months) on the horizontal axis and the frequencies (percentages or rates) of another variable on the vertical axis

Total sum of squares (SST) The total variation in scores, calculated by adding SSB and SSW

t statistic (obtained) The test statistic computed to test the null hypothesis about a population mean when the population standard deviation is unknown and is estimated using the sample standard deviation

Two-tailed test A type of hypothesis test that involves a nondirectional research hypothesis. We are equally interested in whether the values are less than or greater than one another. The sample outcome may be located at both the low and high ends of the sampling distribution

Type I error The probability associated with rejecting a null hypothesis when it is true

Type II error The probability associated with failing to reject a null hypothesis when it is false

Unit of analysis The level of social life on which social scientists focus. Examples of different levels are individuals and groups

Variable A property of people or objects that takes on two or more values

Variance A measure of variation for interval-ratio variables; it is the average of the squared deviations from the mean

Within-group sum of squares (SSW) Sum of squared deviations within each group, calculated between each individual score and the sample mean

Y-intercept (a) the point where the regression line crosses the Y-axis and where $X = 0$

Z statistic (obtained) The test statistic computed by converting a sample statistic (such as the mean) to a Z score. The formula for obtaining Z varies from test to test

NOTES

Chapter 1

1. U.S. Bureau of Labor Statistics, *Economic News Release: Usual Weekly Earnings Summary*, January 18, 2013.

2. U.S. Census Bureau, *Statistical Abstract of the United States: 2012*, Table 616.

3. Rampell, Catherine. "Women Now a Majority in American Workplaces," *The New York Times*, February 5, 2010. Retrieved from http://www.nytimes.com/2010/02/06/business/economy/06women.html.

4. Chava Frankfort-Nachmias and David Nachmias, *Research Methods in the Social Sciences* (New York: Worth Publishers, 2000), p. 56.

5. Barbara Reskin and Irene Padavic, *Women and Men at Work* (Thousand Oaks, CA: Pine Forge Press, 2002), pp. 65, 144.

6. Frankfort-Nachmias and Nachmias, 2000, p. 50.

7. Ibid., p. 52.

8. Patricia Hill Collins, "Toward a New Vision: Race, Class and Gender as Categories of Analysis and Connection" (Keynote address at Integrating Race and Gender Into the College Curriculum, a workshop sponsored by the Center for Research on Women, Memphis State University, Memphis, TN, 1989).

Chapter 2

1. Jennifer Medina, "New Suburban Dream Born of Asia and Southern California" (The *New York Times*, April 29, 2012), p. A9.

2. Gary Hytrek and Kristine Zentgraf, *America Transformed: Globalization, Inequality and Power* (New York: Oxford University Press, 2007).

3. Elizabeth Grieco, Yesenia Acosta, C. Patricia de la Cruz, Christine Gambino, Thomas Gryn, Luke Larsen, Edward Trevelyan, and Nathan Walters, *The Foreign-Born Population in the United States: 2010* (ACS-19; Washington, DC: U.S. Census Bureau, 2012). Retrieved from http://www.census.gov/prod/2012pubs/acs-19.pdf.

4. Greico et al., 2012.

5. David Knoke and George W. Bohrnstedt, *Basic Social Statistics* (New York: Peacock, 1991), p. 25.

6. Ibid., p. 41.

7. The idea of "Reading the Research Literature" sections that appear in most chapters was inspired by Joseph F. Healey's *Statistics: A Tool for Social Research*.

8. Veronica Terriquez, Melissa Dalton Radey, Robert Hummer, and Eunjeong Kim, "The Living Conditions of U.S.-Born Children of Mexican Immigrants in Unmarried Families," *Hispanic Journal of Behavioral Sciences* 28, no. 3 (2006), pp. 343–344.

Chapter 3

1. Harry Moody, *Aging: Concepts and Controversies* (Thousand Oaks, CA: SAGE, 2010), p. xxiii.

2. The U.S. Census Bureau notes that persons of Hispanic origin may be of any race.

3. U.S. Census Bureau, *Marital Status and Living Arrangements: March 1996,* Current Population Reports, P20–496, 1998, p. 5.

4. Moody, 2010, p. xxi.

5. Thomas G. Donlan, *A World of Wealth: How Capitalism Turns Profits Into Progress* (Upper Saddle River, NJ: FT Press, 2008), p. 166.

6. U.S. Census Bureau, *65+ in America,* Current Population Reports, Special Studies, P23–190, 1996, pp. 2–3.

7. Ibid., p. 6-2.

8. Edward R. Tufte, *The Visual Display of Quantitative Information* (Cheshire, CI: Graphics Press, 1983), p. 53.

Chapter 4

1. Douglas S. Massey, "The Social and Economic Origins of Immigration," *Annals, AAPSS* (July 1990), p. 510.

2. U.S. Bureau of Labor Statistics, Current Population Survey 2012, *Household Data Annual Averages*, Table 39.

3. Federal Bureau of Investigation, *Uniform Crime Report—Hate Crime Statistics 2011*, Table 11: Offense Type by Participating State, 2011.

4. This rule was adapted from David Knoke and George W. Bohrnstedt, *Basic Statistics* (New York: Peacock Publishers, 1991), pp. 56–57.

5. The rates presented in Table 4.4 are computed for aggregate units (countries) of different sizes. The mean of 13.3 is therefore called an unweighted mean. It is not the same as the gun ownership rate for the population in the combined countries.

6. Three variables, TVHOURS, SIBS, and EDUC, were taken from a GSS sample; EDUC was then recoded into another variable including only the respondents without a high school diploma.

Chapter 5

1. Johnneta B. Cole, "Commonalities and Differences," in *Race, Class, and Gender*, eds. Margaret L. Andersen and Patricia Hill Collins (Belmont, CA: Wadsworth, 1998), pp. 128–129.

2. Ibid., pp. 129–130.

3. U.S. Census Bureau, *Statistical Abstract for the United States, 2010*, Table 11.

4. Peter Dreier, John Mollenkopf, and Todd Swanstrom, *Place Matters: Metropolitics for the Twenty-First Century*, 2nd ed. (Lawrence, KS: University Press of Kansas, 2004).

5. Silvia Domínguez, *Getting Ahead: Social Mobility, Public Housing, and Immigrant Networks*, (New York: New York University Press, 2011).

6. Douglas S. Massey, *Categorically Unequal: The American Stratification System* (New York: Russell Sage Foundation, 2007).

7. Recent Census data reveal that the recession of 2008–2009 has halted this dominant migration trend.

8. The percentage increase in the population 65 years and above for each state and region was obtained by the following formula:

Percentage increase = [(2015 population – 2008 population) / 2008 population] × 100

9. The extreme values at either end are referred to as outliers. SPSS will include outliers in box plots and in the calculation of the IQR; however, SPSS extends whiskers from the box edges to 1.5 times the box width (the IQR). If there are additional values beyond 1.5 times the IQR, SPSS displays the individual cases. It is important to keep this in mind when examining the shape of a distribution from a box plot.

10. U.S. Census Bureau, *The Older Population: 2010*, p. 3.

11. $N - 1$ is used in the formula for computing variance because usually we are computing from a sample with the intention of generalizing to a larger population. $N - 1$ in the formula gives a better estimate and is also the formula used in SPSS.

12. A good discussion of the relationship between the standard deviation and the mean can be found in Stephen Gould's "The Median Isn't the Message," *Discover Magazine*, June 1985.

13. Herman J. Loether and Donald G. McTavish, *Descriptive and Inferential Statistics: An Introduction* (Boston: Allyn and Bacon, 1980), pp. 160–161.

14. Stephanie A. Bohon, Monica Kirkpatrick Johnson, and Bridget K. Gorman, "College Aspirations and Expectations among Latino Adolescents in the United States," *Social Problems* 53, no. 2 (2006): 207–225.

15. Ibid, p. 210.

16. Ibid., p. 213.

17. Ibid.

18. Depending on the settings, SPSS may or may not round off the numbers. In our example, you may get an IQR value of 13 instead of 12.50. If this is the case, activate the Descriptives table in the Output Editor by double clicking on it. Select the cell that you want to modify (in our example, select the cell where you see "13"). Then, right-click and select the option Cell Properties (or, you can go to the Format menu at the top of the Output Window and choose Cell Properties). Under the Format Value tab, you have an option to change the number of decimal places. As you change this number, you will see that in the Preview field above, the value of the cell will also change as to display the decimals. Click *Apply*, and *OK*.

Chapter 7

This discussion is based on C. Stephen Layman's *The Power of Logic* (Mountain View, CA: Mayfield, 2004).

1. This discussion has benefited from a more extensive presentation on the aims of sampling in Richard Maisel and Caroline Hodges Persell, *How Sampling Works* (Thousand Oaks, CA: Pine Forge Press, 1996).

2. This was suggested by David C. Howell in *Statistical Methods for Psychology* (Duxbury, MA: Wadsworth, 2006). Howell also notes that those who adopt a subjectivist view of probability theory tend to disagree with a hypothesis-testing orientation in general, including the use of random sampling techniques.

3. The discussion in these sections is based on Chava Frankfort-Nachmias and David Nachmias, *Research Methods in the Social Sciences* (New York: Worth Publishers, 2007), pp. 167–177.

4. We discuss more on sampling error in the next section.

5. The population of the 20 individuals presented in Table 7.3 is considered a finite population. A finite population consists of a finite (countable) number of elements (observations). Other examples of finite populations include all women in the labor force in 2008 and all public hospitals in New York City. A population is considered infinite when there is no limit to the number of elements it can include. Examples of infinite populations include all women in the labor force, in the past or the future. Most samples studied

by social scientists come from finite populations. However, it is also possible to form a sample from an infinite population.

6. Here we are using an idealized example in which the sampling distribution is actually computed. However, please bear in mind that in practice one never computes a sampling distribution because it is also infinite.

7. *TIME Magazine*, U.S. Edition, Vol. 180, No. 18, October 29, 2012.

8. *The New York Times*, May 2, 2013.

9. U.S. Census Bureau, American Fact Finder (http://www.*factfinder2.census.gov/*).

Chapter 8

1. "In U.S., Record-High Say Gay, Lesbian Relations Morally OK," Gallup Poll, May 20, 2013.

2. "Partisan Interest, Reactions to IRS and AP Controversies," Pew Research Center, May 20, 2013.

3. U.S. Department of Labor, "The Latino Labor Force at a Glance," April, 2012.

4. George J. Borjas, "The Earnings of Male Hispanic Immigrants in the United States," *Industrial and Labor Relations Review*, Vol. 35, no. 3, April 1982.

5. Marta Tienda, "The Ghetto Underclass: Social Science Perspectives," *Annals of the American Academy of Political and Social Science* 501 (January 1989): 105–119.

6. Adapted from Marta Tienda and Franklin D. Wilson, "Migration and the Earnings of Hispanic Men," *American Sociological Review* 57 (1992): 661–678.

7. Ibid.

8. Pew Hispanic Center, "Cubans in the United States," August 2006.

9. The U.S. Census 2000, IPUMS (Integrated Public Use Micro data Series).

10. The relationship between sample size and interval width when estimating means also holds true for sample proportions. When the sample size increases, the standard error of the proportion decreases, and therefore, the width of the confidence interval decreases as well.

11. "In U.S., Record-High Say Gay, Lesbian Relations Morally OK," Gallup Poll, May 20, 2013.

12. "Partisan Interest, Reactions to IRS and AP Controversies," Pew Research Center, May 20, 2013.

13. "Most Say Immigration Policy Needs Big Changes," Pew Research Center, May 9, 2013.

14. Data from "More Say There Is Solid Evidence of Global Warming," Pew Research Center, October 15, 2012.

15. Data from "'Enthusiastic' Voters Prefer GOP by 20 Points in 2010 Vote," *Gallup*, April 27, 2010.

16. Data from "22% of Americans Used Social Networking or Twitter For Politics in 2010 Campaign," Pew Research Center, January 27, 2011.

17. Data from "The Millennials: Confident. Connected. Open to Change," Pew Research Center, February 24, 2010.

Chapter 9

1. Jeff Somer, "Numbers That Sway Markets and Voters," 2012. Retrieved from http://www.nytimes.com/2012/03/04/your-money/rising-gasoline-prices-could-soon-have-economic-effects.html?pagewanted=all&_r=0.

2. Steve Hargreaves, "Gas Prices Hit Working Class," 2007. Retrieved from http://money.cnn.com/2007/11/13/news/economy/gas_burden/index.htm.

3. American Automobile Association, *Daily Fuel Gauge Report*, May 7, 2013. Retrieved from www.fuelgaugereport.com/.

4. To compute the sample variance for any particular sample, we must first compute the sample mean. Since the sum of the deviations about the mean must equal 0, only $N - 1$ of the deviation scores are free to vary with each variance estimate.

5. U.S. Census Bureau, *Statistical Abstract of the United States: 2012*, Table 232.

6. Degrees of freedom formula based on Dennis Hinkle, William Wiersma, and Stephen Jurs, *Applied Statistics for the Behavioral Sciences* (Boston: Houghton Mifflin, 1998), p. 268.

7. Lloyd D. Johnson, Patrick M. O'Malley, Jerald G. Bachman, and John E. Schulenberg, *Monitoring the Future National Results on Adolescent Drug Use: Overview of Key Findings, 2008* (Bethesda, MD: National Institute on Drug Abuse, 2009).

8. Pew Research Center, *Second-Generation Americans: A Portrait of the Adult Children of Immigrants*, February 7, 2013.

9. The sample proportions are unbiased estimates of the corresponding population proportions. Therefore, we can use the Z statistic, although our standard error is estimated from the sample proportions.

10. Paula Y. Goodwin, William D. Mosher, and Anjani Chandra, "Marriage and cohabitation in the United States: A statistical portrait based on Cycle 6 (2002) of the National Survey of Family Growth," *Vital Health Statistics* 23, no. 28 (2010): 1–45.

11. A similar discussion is presented in Joseph Healey's *Statistics: A Tool for Social Research* (Belmont, CA: Cengage, 2012).

12. Robert E. Jones and Shirley A. Rainey, "Examining Linkages Between Race, Environmental Concern, Health and Justice in a Highly Polluted Community of Color," *Journal of Black Studies* 36, no. 4 (2006): 473–496.

13. Pew Research Center, *The Gender Gap: Three Decades Old, as Wide as Ever*, March 29, 2012.

Chapter 10

1. Pew Research Center, "Immigration: Key Data Points from Pew Research," May 16, 2013. Retrieved June 24, 2013 from http://www.pewresearch.org/key-data-points/immigration-tip-sheet-on-u-s-public-opinion/.

2. *USA Today*, October 9, 1992.

3. Carmen DeNavas-Walt, Bernadette Proctor, and Jessica Smith, *Income, Poverty and Health Insurance Coverage in the United States: 2011*, Current Population Reports P60-243, 2012.

4. Full consideration of the question of detecting the presence of a bivariate relationship requires the use of inferential statistics. Inferential statistics are discussed in Chapters 9 and 11 through 13.

5. Note that this group is but a small sample taken from the GSS national sample. The relationship between home ownership and race noted here may not necessarily hold true in other (larger) samples.

6. Another way in which percentages are sometimes expressed is with the total number of cases (N) used as the base. These overall percentages express the proportion of the sample who share two properties. For example, 7 of 89 respondents (7.9%) support abortion and have job security. Overall percentages do not have as much research utility as row and column percentages and are used less frequently.

7. The same three properties are also discussed by Joseph F. Healey in *Statistics: A Tool for Social Research.* (Belmont, CA: Cengage, 2012), pp. 308–337.

8. Church attendance has been recoded into three categories.

9. For purposes of illustration, only selected categories of educational level and attendance of religious services are shown.

10. For example, see Harris Mills, "Religion, Values, and Attitudes Toward Abortion," *Journal for the Scientific Study of Religion* 24, no. 2 (1985): 119–236.

11. Mario Renzi, "Ideal Family Size as an Intervening Variable Between Religion and Attitudes Toward Abortion," *Journal for the Scientific Study of Religion* 14 (1975): 23–27.

12. Ibid.

13. Ibid.

14. Preferred family size was measured by responses to a question about the ideal number of children for a family. Those respondents who said two or fewer children were ideal were classified as preferring small families; those who answered three or more were classified as preferring large families.

15. William R. Arney and William H. Trescher, "Trends in Attitudes Toward Abortion, 1972–1975," *Family Planning Perspective* 8 (1976): 117–124.

16. William V. D'Antonio and Steven Stack, "Religion, Ideal Family Size, and Abortion: Extending Renzi's Hypothesis," *Journal for the Scientific Study of Religion* 19 (1980): 397–408.

17. Jacqueline Scott, "Conflicting Belief About Abortion: Legal Approval and Moral Doubts," *Social Psychology Quarterly* 52, no. 4 (1989): 319–326.

18. Ibid., p. 322.

19. Carol Gilligan, *In a Different Voice* (Cambridge, MA: Harvard University Press, 1982).

20. Patricia Hill Collins, "Toward a New Vision: Race, Class, and Gender as Categories of Analysis and Connection," keynote address at Integrating Race and Gender Into the College Curriculum, a workshop sponsored by the Center for Research on Women, Memphis State University, Memphis, TN, 1989.

21. Stanley Eitzen and Maxine Baca Zinn, "Structural Transformation and Systems of Inequality," in *Race, Class, and Gender*, eds. Margaret L. Andersen and Patricia Hill Collins (Belmont, CA: Wadsworth, 1998), pp. 233–237.

22. Lynn Weber Cannon, Elizabeth Higginbotham, and Marianne L. A. Leung, "Race and Class Bias in Research on Women: A Methodological Note," Research paper 5, presented at the Center for Research on Women, Memphis, TN, 1987.

23. Ibid.

24. Ibid.

25. For the purpose of this illustration, category 5 OTHER includes the following religious groups: Buddhism, Hinduism, Other Eastern Religions, Islam, Orthodox-Christian, Christian, Native American, and Inter-Nondenominational. Each of these groups will, however, be listed separately on your output.

26. Only blacks and whites are shown.

Chapter 11

1. U.S. Census Bureau, *Statistical Abstract of the United States: 2012*, Table 229.

2. Victor Saenz et al., *First in My Family: A Profile of First-Generation College Students at Four-Year Institutions Since 1971* (Los Angeles, CA: Higher Education Research Institute, 2007).

3. Because statistical independence is a symmetrical property, the distribution of the independent variable within each category of the dependent variable will also be identical. That is, if first-generation status and gender were statistically independent, we would also expect to see the distribution of first-generation status identical in each gender category.

4. Paul Mazerolle, Alex Piquero, and Robert Brame, "Violent Onset Offenders: Do Initial Experiences Shape Criminal Career Dimensions?" *International Criminal Justice Review* 20, no. 2 (2010): 132–146.

5. Ibid., p. 136.

6. Although this general formula provides a framework for all PRE measures of association, only lambda is illustrated

with this formula. Gamma, which is discussed in the next section, is calculated with a different formula. Both are interpreted as PRE measures.

7. "NSA Bugged European Union Offices, Computer Networks: Report," *Reuters*, June 29, 2013.

8. Pew Research Center/USA TODAY, June 12–16, 2013.

9. Because the two variables are nominal (not ordered), we can ignore the negative sign of gamma.

Chapter 12

1. U.S. Census Bureau, *Statistical Abstract of the United States: 2012*, Table 229.

2. Since the N in our computational example is small ($N = 21$), the assumptions of normality and homogeneity of variance are required. We've selected a small N to demonstrate the calculations for F and have proceeded with Assumptions 3 and 4. If a researcher is not comfortable with making these assumptions for a small sample, she or he can increase the size of N. In general, the F test is known to be robust with respect to moderate violations of these assumptions. A larger N increases the F test's robustness to severe departures from the normality and homogeneity of variance assumptions.

3. Elirea Bornman, "Self Image and Ethnic Identification in South Africa," *Journal of Social Psychology* 139, no. 4 (1999): 411–425. Reprinted with permission of the Helen Dwight Reid Educational Foundation. Published by Heldref Publications, 1319 Eighteenth St., NW, Washington, DC 20036-1802. Copyright © 1999.

4. Ibid., p. 412. Used with permission.

5. Ibid., p. 414.

6. M. Rosenberg, *Society and the Adolescent Self-Image* (Princeton, NJ: Princeton University Press, 1965).

7. Bornman, pp. 415–416. Bornman based the three measures of ethnic identification on responses to two scales, Phinney's (1992) Multigroup Measure of Ethnic Identity and Bornman's own 1988 ethnic identity scale.

8. Ibid., pp. 417–418.

9. Carol Musil, Camille Warner, Jaclene Zauszniewski, May Wykle, and Theresa Standing, "Grandmother Caregiving, Family Stress and Strain, and Depressive Symptoms," *Western Journal of Nursing Research* 31, no. 3 (2009): 389–408.

10. Ibid., p. 395.

11. Ibid., p. 391.

12. Sandra Hofferth, "Childbearing Decision Making and Family Well-Being: A Dynamic, Sequential Model," *American Sociological Review* 48, no. 4 (1983): 533–545.

Chapter 13

1. Refer to Paul Allison's *Multiple Regression: A Primer* (Thousand Oaks, CA: Pine Forge Press, 1999) for a complete discussion of multiple regression—statistical methods and techniques that consider the relationship between one dependent variable and one or more independent variables.

2. Center for Disease Control, "Births: Final Data for 2010," *National Vital Statistics Report*: 61(1), August 28, 2012.

3. J. M. Greene and C. L. Ringwalt, "Pregnancy Among Three National Samples of Runaway Homeless Youth," *Journal of Adolescent Health* 23 (1998): 370–377.

4. William J. Wilson, *The Truly Disadvantaged: The Inner City, the Underclass, and Public Policy* (Chicago: University of Chicago Press, 1987).

5. Stephanie Coontz, "The Welfare Discussion We Really Need," *Christian Science Monitor* (December 29, 1994): 19.

6. Preliminary analysis revealed several outliers. The scatterplots in Figures 13.12 and 13.13 depict state-level data with the outliers omitted.

7. Catherine Rampell, "U.S. Women on the Rise as Family Breadwinner," *The New York Times*, May 29, 2013.

8. Analysis is limited to women 40 years and older and those who identified working 40 hrs/week or more the week prior to taking the GSS.

9. Michael L. Benson, John Wooldredge, Amy B. Thistlethwaite, and Greer Litton Fox, "The Correlation Between Race and Domestic Violence Is Confounded With Community Context," *Social Problems* 51 no. 3 (2004): 326–342.

10. Michael L. Benson and Greer L. Fox, *Economic Distress, Community Context and Intimate Violence: An Application and Extension of Social Disorganization Theory*, U.S. Department of Justice, Document No.: 193433, 2002.

11. Ibid.

Index